CONTROLLING IMMIGRATION

A Global Perspective

Second Edition

Edited by

Wayne A. Cornelius, Takeyuki Tsuda,

Philip L. Martin, and James F. Hollifield

STANFORD UNIVERSITY PRESS, STANFORD, CALIFORNIA

Stanford University Press, Stanford, California

Printed in the United States of America

Library of Congress Cataloging-in-Publication Data

Controlling immigration : a global perspective.-- Second ed. / edited by Wayne
A. Cornelius [et al.].
    p.   cm.
  Includes index.
   ISBN 0-8047-4489-0 (cloth : alk. paper) --
   ISBN 0-8047-4490-4 (pbk. : alk. paper)
    1. Emigration and immigration--Government policy--Cross-cultural studies.
2. Immigrants--Government policy--Cross-cultural studies.   3. Human rights.
I. Cornelius, Wayne A., 1945-
JV6271.C66 2004
325'.1--dc22

                                                                    2004008719

Cover photograph © 1992 by Don Bartletti. Editorial cartoon facing page 3 used
by permission of Tom Meyer.

CONTROLLING IMMIGRATION

Published in association with the
Center for Comparative Immigration Studies
University of California, San Diego

Contents

List of Illustrations

FIGURES

TABLES

List of Acronyms

AAFI	Australians Against Further Immigration
ABS	Australian Bureau of Statistics
ACF	Australian Conservation Foundation
AESP	Australians for an Ecologically Sustainable Population
ALP	Australian Labor Party
AZC	Asielzoekerscentrum / asylum reception center
BCA	Business Council of Australia
BIMPR	Bureau of Immigration, Multicultural and Population Research
CDA	Christen Democratisch Appel / Christian Democrats
CDU	Christlich Demokratische Union/ Christian Democratic Union
CFTC	Confédération Française des Travailleurs Chrétiens / French Confederation of Christian Workers
CGIL	Confederazione Generale Italiana del Lavoro / Italian Labor Confederation
CGP	Commissariat Général du Plan / National Planning Commission
CGT	Confédération Générale du Travail / General Labor Confederation
CIC	Citizenship and Immigration Canada
CISL	Confederazione Italiana Sindicati Lavoratori / Confederation of Italian Labor Unions
CNPF	Conseil National du Patronat Français / National Businessmen's Council
CSU	Christlich Soziale Union / Christian Social Union
DACA	Departures and Arrivals Control Act
DIEA	Department for Immigration and Ethnic Affairs
DILGEA	Department of Immigration, Local Government and Ethnic Affairs
DIMA	Department of Immigration and Multicultural Affairs

DIMIA	Department of Immigration, Multicultural and Indigenous Affairs
EBSVERA	Enhanced Border Security and Visa Entry Reform Act
EC	European Community
ECC	Ethnic Communities Council
EEA	European Economic Area
EEC	European Economic Community
EMU	Economic and Monetary Union
ES	Employment Service
ESB	English-speaking-background
EU	European Union
FAIR	Federation for American Immigration Reform
FDP	Free Democratic Party
FECCA	Federation of Ethnic Communities Councils of Australia
FLN	Front National de Libération / Algerian National Liberation Front
FN	Front National / National Front
GATS	General Agreement on Trade in Services
GDP	gross domestic product
HRDC	Human Resources Development Canada
IIRIRA	Illegal Immigration Reform and Immigrant Responsibility Act
ILO	International Labour Organization
IMDB	Longitudinal Immigrant Database
INS	U.S. Immigration and Naturalization Service
IPS	International Passenger Survey
IRCA	Immigration Reform and Control Act
JCMK	Joint Committee for Migrant Workers in Korea
KFSB	Korean Federation of Small Business
KITCO	Korea International Training Cooperation Corps
LDP	Liberal Democratic Party
LFS	Labor Force Survey
LPF	Lijst Pim Fortuyn / Pim Fortuyn List
MRAP	Mouvement contre le Racisme et pour l'Amitie entre les Peuples / Movement against Racism and for Friendship among Peoples

MRCI	Ministère des Relations avec les Citoyens et de l'Immigration / Ministry of Citizenship and Immigration
MVV	Machtiging Voorlopig Verblijf / authorization for provisional residency
NAFTA	North American Free Trade Agreement
NCNP	National Congress for New Politics
NDP	New Democratic Party
NESB	non-English-speaking-background
NGO	nongovernmental organization
NKP	New Korea Party
NRC	National Research Council
NTOM	Nieuwe Toelatings en Opvang Model / New Admissions and Reception Policy
OECD	Organisation for Economic Co-operation and Development
OFPRA	Office Français pour la Protection des Refugiés et Apatrides / Office for the Protection of Refugees and Stateless Persons
OMA	Office of Multicultural Affairs
ONI	Office National d'Immigration / National Immigration Office
PAF	Police de l'Air et des Frontières / Border Police
PP	Partido Popular / Popular Party
PRWORA	Personal Responsibility and Work Opportunity Reconciliation Act
PSOE	Partido Socialista Obrero Español / Spanish Socialist Party
ROA	Rijksregeling Opvang Asielzoekers / Regulation on the Reception of Asylum Seekers
RPR	Rassemblement Pour la République / Rally for the Republic
SAC	special assistance category
SAW	Special Agricultural Worker program
SGI	Société Générale d'Immigration / Immigration Society
SHP	special humanitarian program
SMBA	Small and Medium Business Administration

SPD	Sozialdemokratische Partei Deutschlands / German Social Democratic Party
TPV	temporary protection visa
TROO	Tijdelijke Regeling Opvang Ontheemden / temporary measure for displaced persons
UDF	Union pour la Démocratie Française / Union for French Democracy
UI	unemployment insurance
UIL	Unione Italiana del Lavoro / Italian Labor Union
UMP	Union pour la Majorité Présidentielle / Union for a Presidential Majority
UNHCR	United Nations High Commissioner for Refugees
VVtV	Voorwaardelijke Vergunning tot Verblijf / conditional residence permit
WABW	Wet Arbeid Buitenlandse Werknemers / Foreign Workers Employment Act
WAV	Wet Arbeid Vreemdelingen / Foreign Workers Employment Law

Preface

This book presents the most recent research and thinking of an interdisciplinary group of immigration specialists based at institutions in the United States, Canada, and Western Europe. The group was constituted originally in 1990–1993 to carry out what was at that time a pioneering comparative study of immigration control efforts and their consequences in nine industrialized democracies. Systematic, cross-national research on immigration policy has become a much more common enterprise since the publication of the first edition of this book in late 1994. However, given the dramatic increase in international migration and refugee movements during the second half of the 1990s, and the evolution of government responses to these flows, we saw considerable merit in revisiting these labor-importing countries and expanding the range of cases to include Australia, the Netherlands, and Korea. My coeditors and I wish to thank all contributors to the first and second editions of this book for their valuable participation in what has become a vigorous, decade-long dialogue on the political economy of immigration in industrialized countries.

Our work for the second edition has benefited from the comments of the distinguished scholars who participated in a research workshop held at the Center for Comparative Immigration Studies at the University of California, San Diego in May 2002, during which first drafts of the principal papers included in this book were presented and critiqued. Seventeen of the commentaries presented at the 2002 conference have been included in this volume, and they add immeasurably to the richness of the discussion. We also thank Randall Hansen and Han Entzinger for detailed comments on the introductory chapter, and cartographer Chase Langford for the original maps included in this edition.

This project was made possible by grants to the Center for Comparative Immigration Studies by the William and Flora Hewlett Foundation and the Japan Foundation's Center for Global Partnership. The editors and other contributing authors are solely responsible for all facts and interpretations presented in this book.

Finally, we are indebted to Amanda Moran, our editor at Stanford University Press, and Sandra del Castillo, principal editor at the Center for Comparative Immigration Studies and the Center for U.S.-Mexican Studies, University of California, San Diego, for their extraordinary patience and skill in bringing this book to publication.

Wayne A. Cornelius
La Jolla, California
February 2004

Contributors

Belén Agrela is a research fellow at the Laboratory of Intercultural Studies, University of Granada. She has conducted ethnographic research in various subregions of southern Spain and is currently finishing a dissertation on the institutional construction of cultural differences, with special reference to immigration policy in Spain. Her publications include *Inmigración extranjera en la provincia de Jaén: discursos y prácticas* (coauthor, 2002) and *Mujeres de un solo mundo: globalización y multiculturalismo* (coeditor, forthcoming).

Kitty Calavita, a sociologist, is professor in the Department of Criminology, Law and Society at the University of California, Irvine. Her principal research interests are the sociology of law, state theory, and immigration policymaking historically and cross-culturally. Among her recent publications are "Immigration, Law, and Marginalization in a Global Economy: Notes from Spain," *Law and Society Review* (1998), and "The Paradoxes of Race, Class, Identity, and 'Passing': Enforcing the Chinese Exclusion Acts, 1882–1910," *Law and Social Inquiry* (2000).

Stephen Castles is principal researcher in the Centre for Migration, Policy and Society (COMPAS) at the University of Oxford. A sociologist, he has conducted research on migration and multicultural societies in Europe, Australia, and Asia for many years. His recent books include *The Age of Migration: International Population Movements in the Modern World*, 3rd ed. (coauthor, 2003) and *Ethnicity and Globalization: From Migrant Worker to Transnational Citizen* (2000).

William M. Chandler is professor of political science at the University of California, San Diego. His key research interests include the structure of conflict in advanced democracies, with particular reference to the nature and role of parties. His current research focuses on the complexities of multilevel governance within the European Union. He is coauthor of *Challenges to Federalism: Policy-making in Canada and the Federal Republic of Germany* (1989) and "Postindustrial Politics in Germany and the Origins of the Greens," *Comparative Politics* (1986).

Wayne A. Cornelius is Gildred Professor of Political Science and International Relations, and director of the Center for Comparative Immigration Studies, at the University of California, San Diego. His current research includes a comparative study of impacts of immigration control measures in the United States and Spain on migration behavior, a study of participation by Mexican migrants to the United States in home country elections, and ongoing research on determinants of mortality among migrants along the U.S.-Mexico border. His recent books include *The International Migration of the Highly Skilled* (coeditor/coauthor, 2001) and *Comparative Politics Today,* 8th ed. (coauthor, 2003).

Don J. DeVoretz is professor of economics at Simon Fraser University. His primary research interests are economic development and the economics of immigration. His recent publications include *Diminishing Returns: Economics of Canada's Immigration Policy* (1995), "Wealth Accumulation of Canadian and Foreign-born Households in Canada," *The Review of Income and Wealth* (coauthor, 1999), and "Canadian Immigration Experience: Any Lessons for Europe?" in *Migration in Europe* (2000).

Gunther Dietz is professor of social anthropology at the University of Granada, Spain. He has conducted ethnographic fieldwork on minority integration, development policies, and ethnic movements in Mexico, as well as on ethnicity and multiculturalist movements, nongovernmental organizations, and migrant communities in Spain. Recent publications include *Frontier Hybridization or Culture Clash? Transnational Migrant Communities and Subnational Identity Politics in Andalusia, Spain* (2001) and "Door to Door with Our Muslim Sisters: Intercultural and Inter-religious Conflicts in Granada, Spain," *Studi Emigrazione* (2002).

Han Entzinger is professor of migration and integration studies at Erasmus University Rotterdam in the Netherlands. He is a founder and senior member of the European Research Centre on Migration and Ethnic Relations. His research interests include international migration, integration, multiculturalism, and the welfare state. Recent publications include "The Dynamics of Integration Policies: A Multi-Dimensional Model," in *Challenging Immigration and Ethnic Relations Politics* (2000), and "The Rise and Fall of Multiculturalism: The Case of the Netherlands," in *Toward Assimilation and Citizenship: Immigration in Liberal Nation-States* (2003).

Gary P. Freeman is professor of government at the University of Texas at Austin, specializing in the politics of immigration and politics in Western democracies. He is the author of *Immigrant Labor and Racial Conflict in Industrial Societies: The French and British Experience, 1945–1975* and coeditor of *Nations of Immigrants: Australia, the United States, and International Migration.* His current research includes the impact of public opinion on European Union member state preferences for harmonized immigration and asylum policies and modeling of immigration politics in comparative contexts.

Charles P. Gomes is researcher at Casa de Rui Barbosa and professor of international relations at the Pontifica Universidade Catolica in Rio de Janeiro. He has published articles on the politics of immigration in France and the United States. Currently, he is working on a comparative study of citizenship and nationality in South America.

Randall Hansen is a tutorial fellow in politics at Merton College, University of Oxford. He is author of *Citizenship and Immigration in Post-War Britain: The Institutional Origins of a Multicultural Nation* (2000) and coeditor of *Towards a European Nationality: Citizenship, Immigration, and Nationality Law in the EU* (2001) and *Dual Nationality, Social Rights, and Federal Citizenship in the US and Europe* (2002).

Gordon H. Hanson is professor of economics in the Graduate School of International Relations and Pacific Studies and co-director of the Center for U.S.-Mexican Studies at the University of California, San Diego. His research areas include the impact of NAFTA on the U.S. and Mexican economies, and the economics of Mexican migration to the United States. He recently published "Does Border Enforcement Protect U.S. Workers from Illegal Immigration?" *Review of Economics and Statistics* (2002).

James F. Hollifield is Arnold Professor of International Political Economy at Southern Methodist University, where he also directs the John G. Tower Center for Political Studies. He has written numerous books, including *Immigrants and Markets and States* (1992), *Migration Theory, Talking across Disciplines* (coauthor, 2000), and *L'immigration et l'Etat-Nation* (1997). His most recent work looks at the rapidly evolving relationship between trade, migration, and the nation-state.

Uwe Hunger is assistant professor of political science at the University of Muenster, Germany. He has written numerous articles on immigration, party systems, and the welfare state, including: "Temporary Transnational

Labour Migration in an Integrating Europe: The Challenge to the German Welfare State," in *Immigration and Welfare: Challenging the Borders of the Welfare State* (2000), and "Party Competition and Inclusion of Immigrants in Germany," *German Policy Studies/Politikfeldanalyse* (www.spaef.com).

Christian Joppke is a member of the Sociology Department at the University of British Columbia, Vancouver. He is author of *Immigration and the Nation-State: The United States, Germany, and Great Britain* (1999) and editor of *Challenge to the Nation-State: Immigration in Western Europe and the United States* (1997). His writings have appeared in *World Politics, Theory and Society, Comparative Political Studies,* and *Comparative Studies in Society and History.*

Zig Layton-Henry is professor of politics at the University of Warwick. His main research interests are citizenship, transnational communities, and international migration. Recent publications include "Minorities, Citizens and Refugees," in *Governing Diversity* (2001), and "Patterns of Privilege: Citizenship and Nationality in Britain," in *Citizenship in a Global World* (2001).

Timothy Lim is assistant professor of political science at California State University, Los Angeles, where he is also associate director of the Center for Korean American and Korean Studies. His research focuses on the politics of transnational worker migration in Asia. He is the author of "The Fight for Equal Rights: Foreign Migrant Workers in South Korea," *Alternatives* (1999), and "Racing *from* the Bottom? The Nexus between Civil Society and Transnational Migrants in South Korea," *Asian Survey* (forthcoming).

Arend Lijphart is research professor emeritus of political science at the University of California, San Diego. His principal research interest is the comparative analysis of democratic institutions. His most recent books are *Electoral Systems and Party Systems: A Study of Twenty-Seven Democracies, 1945–1990* (1994) and *Patterns of Democracy: Government Forms and Performance in Thirty-Six Countries* (1999).

Philip L. Martin is professor of agricultural and resource economics at the University of California, Davis, chair of the University of California's Comparative Immigration and Integration Program, and editor of *Migration News* and *Rural Migration News.* His recent research has focused on the impacts of NAFTA on Mexican migration to the United States and options for dealing with unauthorized migration to Thailand. His most recent book is *Promise Unfulfilled: Unions, Immigration, and the Farm Workers* (2003).

Jeannette Money is associate professor of political science and director of the International Relations Program at the University of California, Davis. She is the author of "New Citizens: Immigrant Electoral Participation and the Host Polity," in *In Defense of the Alien* (2000), and *Fences and Neighbors: The Political Geography of Immigration Control* (1999).

Philip Muus, a human geographer, is currently associate professor of international migration at IMER, Malmö University, Sweden. His research interest is in comparative studies of international migration and asylum policies. He is coauthor of "Comparative Research on International Migration and International Migration Policy: Migration from the Maghreb and Turkey to the European Union, and from Mexico, Guatemala and El Salvador to the United States" (1998) and editor of *Exclusion and Inclusion of Refugees in Contemporary Europe* (1997).

Jeffrey G. Reitz is R.F. Harney Professor of Ethnic, Immigration and Pluralism Studies and professor of sociology at the University of Toronto. His research examines immigration, race, and ethnic relations, focusing from a comparative perspective on Canada, the United States, Britain, Australia, and Germany. He is editor of *Host Societies and the Reception of Immigrants* (2003) and coeditor of *Canadian Immigration Policy for the 21st Century* (2003).

Dong-Hoon Seol is assistant professor of sociology at Chonbuk National University, South Korea. His main research interests are economic globalization, sociology of labor markets, and international labor migration (especially foreign workers in Korea). His books include *Foreign Workers in Korean Society, 1987–1998* (1999) and *Global Capitalism and International Labor Migration* (2000).

John D. Skrentny is associate professor of sociology at the University of California, San Diego. His research has focused on policy and lawmaking for rights and opportunities for disadvantaged groups in U.S. society. Ongoing projects include a comparison of immigration, equal employment opportunity, and criminal justice law and policy in the United

States, Korea, and Japan. His work has appeared in *Theory and Society,* *Research in Political Sociology,* and *Sociological Forum.*

Daniel J. Tichenor is assistant professor of political science at Rutgers University. He is author of *Dividing Lines: The Politics of Immigration Control in America* (2002) and a forthcoming book, *A Question of Representational Bias: Organized Interests and American Political Development.* His current work focuses on American liberalism and the political integration of immigrant groups.

Harold Troper is a professor in the Theory and Policy Studies in Education Program at the University of Toronto. His research interests encompass Canadian social history, immigration, education of ethnic and minority groups, American history, and the history of education. Among his many publications is *Ethnicity, Politics, and Public Policy: Cases Studies in Canadian Diversity* (coeditor, 1999).

Takeyuki Tsuda is associate director of the Center for Comparative Immigration Studies at the University of California, San Diego. An anthropologist, his research interests include migration and ethnicity, transnationalism and globalization, and Japanese Brazilian ethnic return migrants in Japan. His current research projects examine recent countries of immigration and ethnic return migrants in comparative perspective. He is author of *Strangers in the Ethnic Homeland: Japanese Brazilian Return Migration in Transnational Perspective* (2003).

Ellie Vasta is coordinator of the Integration and Social Change Programme in the Centre on Migration, Policy and Society (COMPAS) at the University of Oxford. She is coeditor of *Australia's Italians: Culture and Community in a Changing Society* (1992) and *The Teeth are Smiling: The Persistence of Racism in Multicultural Australia* (1996), and editor of *Citizenship, Community and Democracy* (2000).

Keiko Yamanaka teaches in the Department of Ethnic Studies, University of California, Berkeley, and is a research associate with Berkeley's Institute for the Study of Social Change. Since 1994, she has been studying transnational experiences of two contrasting populations of immigrant workers in Japan: legally resident Brazilians of Japanese ancestry and undocumented Nepalese.

PART I

Introduction

1

Controlling Immigration: The Limits of Government Intervention

Wayne A. Cornelius and Takeyuki Tsuda

Since the first edition of *Controlling Immigration*, the total volume of international migration has risen impressively. In the 1990s, the estimated number of people living outside their country of birth or nationality grew from 154 million to 175 million.[1] Although this represents only about 3 percent of the world's population, there are few countries today whose economies and societies are not being profoundly reshaped by immigration or emigration.[2] Almost one out of every ten inhabitants of the world's economically developed regions is an international migrant. In the past fifteen years, even such countries as Japan and Korea, previ-

---

[1] See United Nations 2002. Migrants are defined as persons living outside their country of birth or citizenship for twelve months or more.

[2] Numerous countries are also experiencing large-scale internal migration, which can be much greater in volume than the international migration that a country experiences. For example, the number of internal migrants in China alone (130 million) is equivalent to 75 percent of the total volume of international migrants in the rest of the world ca. 2000. See Martin and Widgren 2002: 24.

ously untouched by global population movements, have become countries of immigration.

The movement of peoples across national borders has accelerated because of a robust demand for immigrant labor in advanced industrial economies, wide and growing economic and demographic disparities between First and Third World countries, and the steadily expanding web of transnational social and economic processes linking sending and receiving countries (see Hannerz 1996; Levitt and Waters 2002; Levitt, DeWind, and Vertovec 2003). In response, governments have implemented a variety of measures to reduce "unwanted" immigration and refugee flows and contain anti-immigrant public backlashes. Some receiving countries have also begun to move more proactively to accelerate immigrants' social integration and political incorporation.

This book systematically compares immigration control policies and their outcomes in eleven advanced industrial countries. The country case studies that were part of the first edition (the United States, Canada, Britain, France, Germany, Italy, Spain, and Japan) have been extensively updated or replaced with new chapters, and case studies of Australia, the Netherlands, and Korea have been added. Greater attention has been devoted in this edition to immigrant integration policies (or the lack thereof) in each country and to aspects of international migration that have become more prominent in recent years, such as organized migrant-smuggling and the nexus between immigration control and antiterrorism efforts.

We retain the two central theses used to organize the first edition. The first, which we call the "*gap hypothesis*," is that significant and persistent gaps exist between official immigration policies and actual policy outcomes. The second, the "*convergence hypothesis*," claims that there is growing similarity among labor-importing countries in terms of: (1) the policies that their governments have adopted to control immigration; (2) policies designed to integrate immigrants into host societies by providing them with social services as well as political, economic, and social rights; and (3) attitudes toward immigrants and immigration policy preferences among general publics.

THE GAP HYPOTHESIS

It is perhaps misleading to refer to the gap hypothesis as a true hypothesis since it is an empirical fact that few labor-importing countries have immigration control policies that are perfectly implemented or do not result in unintended consequences. Some scholars have argued that nation-states have retained considerable capacity to control "unwanted" flows of immigrants and refugees, while others find that most labor-importing countries are losing the battle.[3] However, most of the countries represented in this volume have experienced significant immigration control problems in the last ten years, and the gap between stated policy objectives and outcomes in these countries seems to be growing wider.[4]

Serious policy gaps have resulted not only from immigration policies that seek to "stem flows" but also those that "solicit flows" (see Guiraudon and Joppke 2001: 2; Joppke, this volume). While advanced industrial countries have had serious difficulty stemming immigration from Third World countries, when they have attempted to actively recruit certain types of immigrants they have also found it difficult to accomplish their objectives. This has been the case, for example, with West European and Japanese government programs designed to attract highly skilled and professional workers from newly industrialized countries like India and China (Cornelius, Espenshade, and Salehyan 2001). On the other hand, government attempts to recruit *low-skilled* immigrants have often been "too successful," resulting in much larger numbers of migrants than anticipated (for example, attempts by Germany and Japan to import ethnic return migrants).[5]

Most policy gaps are of two kinds: (1) those caused by the unintended consequences of policy, and (2) those caused by inadequate implementation or enforcement of policy (cf. Joppke, this volume). Given that policy gaps are empirical facts, the important questions are: how do we measure them, and how do we explain them?

---

[3] The extent to which the modern nation-state remains capable of regulating international migration and refugee flows—indeed, whether capacity to control such flows still represents an essential element of national sovereignty—is the subject of considerable scholarly debate (see, for example, Freeman 1994, 1995, 1998; Guiraudon and Lahav 2000; Guiraudon and Joppke 2001; Hollifield 1992, 2000a, 2000b; Joppke 1998; Joppke, ed. 1998; Sassen 1996; Zolberg 1999). Joppke implies that the issue itself is misplaced because nation-states have never enjoyed strong national sovereignty, even before the current era of globalization and expanded international population movements.

[4] In contrast, Freeman (1994) argues that, despite considerable variation, the general capacity of states to regulate migration is growing.

[5] Ethnic return migrants are diasporic peoples who "return" to their ancestral homeland after living outside their countries of ethnic origin for generations.

MEASURING POLICY GAPS

In cases where immigration policy is based on numerical quotas or targets, the size of the policy gap is simply the discrepancy between the officially mandated number and the actual number of immigrants who enter the country. Similarly, when governments clearly specify immigrants' maximum length of stay, gaps can be measured by how long they actually remain in the country beyond the originally stipulated period (by renewing or overstaying visas). Even if the number of immigrants to be admitted or their length of stay is not clearly specified in the country's policy, it is usually quite apparent when governments receive more immigrants than expected or they remain longer than expected. In most cases, official policies also indicate the types of immigrants the government wishes to admit (based on skill level, job classification, national origin, or ethnicity), which are often quite different from the types of immigrants that actually arrive. Policy gaps can also be quantified by statistics on unauthorized immigrants (although they are always difficult to count).

Undoubtedly, gaps are more difficult to measure when governments do not have clearly defined or coherent immigration policies. Even most Western European countries did not have explicit, officially promulgated immigration policies until the early 1970s (Hammar 1992: 256–57). In other cases, the actual goals and objectives of immigration policy are not directly specified or remain ambiguous. However, even if the officially declared immigration policy itself is quite clear, it may not be a good indication of true government intentions and objectives. As a result, the ensuing "unintended consequences" of immigration control policies may not be so unintended, or may in fact be fully intended.

The extent of negative public opinion toward immigrants is another indicator of policy gaps. The assumption here is that the wider the policy gap, the stronger the public backlash. For example, if more immigrants enter the country than officially intended, the public may feel that the government has lost control over immigration and react negatively. In Western Europe, anti-immigrant backlashes have occurred when guest-workers who were supposed to be "temporary" settled permanently, brought their dependents, and began utilizing public services conspicuously at a time of high unemployment and reductions in government services. In the 1990s, the entry of unexpectedly large numbers of asylum seekers — many of whom were suspected of being economic migrants — caused negative public reactions.

However, public opinion surveys are a problematic way to measure policy gaps, for several reasons. First, the general public frequently does not have sufficiently detailed nor accurate knowledge of the government's immigration policy and its actual consequences, especially since the public frequently misperceives the economic and social situation of immigrants in their country. Second, the public may not agree with the government's immigration policy in the first place, so it may react negatively even if the policy is being perfectly implemented. Finally, the public itself is not monolithic but consists of many disparate groups with varying interests and concerns. For instance, if the government effectively enforces a restrictive immigration policy, the average citizen may be quite satisfied, but it may cause a public "backlash" among employers and nongovernmental organizations (NGOs) concerned with immigrants' rights. In this case, certain groups among the public may actually favor a wide policy gap (see the Korean case, this volume).

EXPLAINING POLICY GAPS

Flawed Policies

One of the major reasons why governments have been unable to effectively reduce the gap between policies and outcomes is because they have continued to rely on policy instruments with inherent flaws that fail to deter unauthorized immigrants and asylum seekers but produce serious unintended consequences. In some cases, these policies could be modified to increase their efficacy, or enforcement resources could be increased—assuming the political will to do so. In other cases, the nature of the policy instrument itself (or the conditions under which it is implemented) makes it prone to failure.

One of the clearest examples of a policy instrument that has not functioned effectively as an immigration control mechanism while yielding large-scale unintended consequences is the temporary foreign worker (guestworker) program. Numerous "guestworkers" have become permanent additions to the host society's labor force, and subsequent unauthorized migration flows have been augmented by the offspring of participants in the temporary worker program. The best-documented cases are Germany's guestworker program of the 1950s and 1960s and the U.S. "Bracero" program of 1942–1964 (Freeman 1994: 25–27; Martin, Lowell, and Taylor 2000; Massey and Liang 1989). Such programs typically have multiple flaws that cause guestworkers not to return home as expected.

For example, the duration of the visa or contract is too short, so employers keep workers for longer periods than allowed; guestworkers have insufficient incentives for repatriation; limited family reunification is permitted, which promotes permanent settlement in the host country; and/or the programs limit participating workers to the lowest-wage jobs and do not allow them to switch employers, causing them to disappear into the more lucrative, illegal immigrant labor market. Moreover, temporary worker programs typically do not dry up illegal immigration from major source countries, because their existence may encourage more workers to want to migrate, the programs usually are not large enough to accommodate the majority of migrant job-seekers, and many employers prefer to hire long-term workers for jobs that are nonseasonal.

Numerous governments — most notably the United States and the countries on the borders of the European Union (EU) — invested heavily in border enforcement during the 1990s to reduce the influx of illegal immigrants (Andreas and Snyder 2000; Andreas and Biersteker 2003). This effort has included deploying large numbers of border patrol agents, increasing air and coastal patrols, and installing elaborate fences and surveillance devices. Such measures have increased the probability of apprehension, at least in the most closely patrolled areas, but they have had no discernible deterrent effect on illegal entry attempts. Highly motivated migrants driven by powerful economic incentives have found ways to circumvent tougher border controls, notably by relying to a greater extent on professional people-smugglers and by crossing in border areas not yet heavily fortified. In the case of the U.S. border with Mexico, the principal effects of a massive buildup in border enforcement resources since 1993 have been to redistribute illegal entry attempts to more remote areas, increase the financial cost and physical risk of illegal entry (people smugglers' fees and migrant fatalities have risen sharply), and induce more unauthorized migrants to extend their stays or settle permanently in the United States because of the increased difficulty of reentry (see Cornelius 2001; Reyes, Johnson, and Van Swearingen 2002). In both the United States and Western Europe, the illegal immigrant stock has continued to grow rapidly, with net increases approximating 500,000 per year since the late 1990s.[6]

---

[6] By early 2004 the stock of undocumented immigrants in the United States was estimated at 9.3 million, representing 26 percent of the foreign-born population, 5 percent of the total workforce, and 10 percent of low-wage workers in the United States (Passel, Capps, and Fix 2004).

Interior enforcement of immigration laws, especially in the workplace, should be more effective than external border enforcement because it is aimed at reducing one of the fundamental causes of international migration—the strong demand for foreign labor among employers in immigrant-receiving countries. Since the 1970s, laws penalizing employers for hiring unauthorized foreign workers have been adopted and strengthened in Western Europe, East Asia, and the United States, but they have generally failed to reduce employment opportunities for illegal migrants. The reasons are similar in each case: worksite inspections are too sporadic to constitute a realistic risk to employers who continue to hire unauthorized workers; the fines imposed are so low that they can be treated as a cost of doing business; criminal penalties are rarely enforced; fraudulent documents have proliferated among illegal immigrant job-seekers; and employers are not required to verify the documents that workers present as proof of their eligibility for employment. Current European versions of employer sanctions have fewer policy flaws and are more effective than the U.S. version (Castles and Miller 2003: 97), but there are notable exceptions (see the Spain and Italy cases, this volume).

Macro-Structural Explanations

Many labor-importing countries have had difficulty controlling immigration because the demand for foreign workers in their countries has become "structurally embedded," that is, rooted in the receiving country's economy and society in ways that are largely impervious to the business cycle as well as to government interventions (Cornelius 1998a; Tsuda 1999a). Most advanced industrial countries are now experiencing persistent shortages of labor to fill low-skilled jobs in certain industries, stemming from long-declining fertility rates and aging populations[7] (which

---

[7] Based on the medium United Nations projection of fertility rates and an assumed annual number of 500,000 immigrants, the total European Union population is expected to shrink by 50 million (11 percent) by 2050 (Demeny 2003: 11). The situation is more dire in Japan: even at the current fertility rate (which continues to decline), Japan's population is expected to shrink by 21.6 million (17 percent) by 2050 (United Nations 2000). In both Western Europe and Japan, populations would be declining even faster if it were not for children being born to immigrants. In 2003, for example, the European Union's population grew by just 0.34 percent, and about three-quarters of that increase was due to immigration (Fehr, Jokisch, and Kotlikoff 2003; Fertig and Schmidt 2003; World Economic Forum 2004). The United States and Can-

produce *absolute* shortages of young, entry-level workers) as well as rising educational levels and increasingly negative attitudes toward manual labor among the native-born population (yielding *relative* shortages). In addition, in Western Europe, generous social welfare systems (pensions, unemployment benefits, and so on) have encouraged people not to work (at least in the formal labor sector) or to retire early, creating a situation in which robust demand for immigrant labor is accompanied by persistently high "structural unemployment" rates. At the same time, powerful labor unions have made it more difficult for businesses to reduce labor costs through benefits reductions and downsizing, further increasing the demand for casual, cheap, often nonunionized immigrant labor (see Money 1999: 31).

As long as there is a strong, stable demand for foreign labor in advanced industrial economies, resourceful immigrants in pursuit of abundant and high-paying jobs (and the people smugglers and labor brokers who assist them) will always find a way to circumvent a government's immigration laws, border controls, and any other obstacle placed in their path. Indeed, the more restrictive the immigration policy, the greater the number of immigrants who will simply find ways to enter the country illegally in response to employer demand, and the larger the immigration control gap (see, for example, Morawska 2001).

Cross-national disparities and the transnational economic and social ties that span these divides play their part in reducing the efficacy of immigration control measures. Huge demographic imbalances (overpopulation in developing countries, population decline in developed countries) and differentials in wage levels and job availability between these countries propel migration across national borders, regardless of the strategies of nation-states (Massey et al. 1998; Sassen 1996, 1998). Attempts to address such structural disparities by developed countries through economic development assistance and foreign direct investment have done little to fundamentally rectify the imbalances (Ghosh 2000: 17; Lim 1992: 138). In Western Europe, regional trade liberalization, combined with large flows of development aid from richer to poorer EU member countries, halved wage disparities and transformed labor exporters like Italy and Spain into labor importers (Martin, Lowell, and Taylor 2000). But in North America, the U.S.-Mexico real wage differential *increased* by more than 10 percent during the first decade of the North

---

ada are not yet experiencing a fertility crisis, partly because immigration levels remain high in both countries and new immigrants have above-average fertility rates.

American Free Trade Agreement (NAFTA), and it remains to be seen whether free trade can make an appreciable dent in unauthorized migration, except perhaps in the long run (Cornelius 2002; Audley et al. 2003).

Transnational economic and social processes have become increasingly important in sustaining migration flows. Most importantly, such processes operate through migrant social networks that spur further migration by encouraging family reunification migration and by reducing the costs and risks of international migration for new, first-time migrants (Massey 1988; Fawcett 1989). In addition, transnational labor brokers and migrant-smuggling operations facilitate access to receiving-country labor markets. A global migration industry has developed, offering a wide array of services to migrants and their employers, including visa and travel arrangements; job, language, and cultural training; and job placement and housing in the receiving country. Some labor brokerage operations are "legitimate" businesses; others are at best semi-legal and exploit immigrants by charging exorbitant fees (Tsuda 1999b, 2003). Still others are criminal organizations that engage in coercive trafficking of women and even children for the thriving global sex industry (see Kyle and Koslowski 2001; Kyle and Liang 2001; Salt and Stein 1997). Entire flows of clandestine migrants are now organized professionally (for example, the heavy flow from Fujian province in southern China to Western Europe; see Pieke et al. 2004). By adopting more restrictive immigration policies, receiving-country governments have unwittingly increased the demand for people smugglers, whose services raise the probability of evading border controls.

Domestic and International Political Constraints

The gap between immigration control policies and outcomes is also widened by domestic political constraints that make it difficult for governments of labor-importing countries to *implement* their control measures effectively. According to the "client politics" model developed by Gary Freeman (Freeman 1995, 2002), in liberal democracies immigration policymaking is frequently "captured" by special interest groups. Lobbying by powerful employer groups, religious groups, ethnic and immigrant advocacy groups, and even labor unions[8] leads governments to adopt more

---

[8] For most of the twentieth century, U.S. labor unions were firmly in the immigration-restriction camp. In recent years, however, unions in both the United States and Western Europe have welcomed immigrants into their ranks and have joined the

expansionary immigration policies, even when the economy goes bad and general public opinion turns hostile to immigrants. Restrictive immigration legislation gets watered down before passage, and implementation of whatever legislation gets approved is half-hearted (Freeman 1995, 2002). The governments of migrant-sending countries may also try to influence the policymaking process by allying themselves with domestic interest groups (Rosenblum 2004). In Western Europe, pro-immigrant groups—sometimes mobilizing transnationally—have become active in pressuring various European Union institutions to allow the free movement of third country nationals (non-European nationals) within EU countries and to grant them other social rights (Geddes 2000: chap. 6; Hansen and Weil 2002; Kostakopoulou 2002).

The interest-group politics model tends to explain more of the variation in immigration policymaking in the "classic countries of immigration" (the United States, Canada, and Australia) than in the "reluctant" labor importers (Western Europe, Japan), where the pro-immigration lobby is much less entrenched.[9] The influence of "client politics" also depends on the country's immigration policymaking regime. Governments in which policymaking is controlled by elected representatives in legislative bodies are undoubtedly more responsive to domestic interest groups. This is especially true in countries with very active civil societies (such as the United States) or where the relationship between government and business is especially close, making it difficult for governments to defy immigrant-hungry employers. In contrast, countries such as Japan and Korea, where immigration policymaking is dominated by bureaucrats who are not publicly accountable, are less susceptible to pressures from special interest groups.[10]

---

struggle for immigrants' labor rights, "amnesty," and other pro-immigrant causes. The fundamental reason for this shift is easily discerned: unions have lost membership as manufacturing jobs have been transferred overseas; immigrants are vital to the survival and growth of unions in most labor-intensive industries. Instead of viewing immigrants as competitors who invariably depress wages and working conditions, today's union leaders increasingly recognize the collective benefit of improving conditions for all workers, domestic and foreign, regardless of legal status (see Watts 2002).

[9] See Joppke, ed. 1998: 17–18; Joppke 1998: 282; Statham 2003: 170. For some notable exceptions to this generalization, in the context of Italy and Spain, see Della Porta 2000 and the Spain chapter, this volume.

[10] However, bureaucracy-dominated immigration policymaking regimes are not always insensitive to public pressures, especially if they actively consult closely with various interest and advocacy groups before making policy (as is the case in Australia

National political culture can also contribute to policy gaps by politically (and sometimes legally) constraining the state's ability to pursue harsh immigration control measures like mass roundups and deportations. All of the labor-importing countries represented in this book are liberal democracies that have granted immigrants significant economic and social rights, and in some cases even political representation. They have active civil societies and independent judicial systems that further constrain the state's capacity to control immigration (Hollifield 1992, 2000b: 146–51). Draconian control measures are likely to be challenged and may be overturned by the courts as unconstitutional or as a violation of civil rights. Examples include government attempts to roll back immigrant rights such as Proposition 187 in California (Ono and Sloop 2002) and various measures denying social support to asylum seekers in Europe (Joppke, ed. 1998: 18–20; Statham 2003: 166).

International political pressures can also contribute to gaps between national immigration control policies and outcomes. The United Nations, the International Labour Organization, and regional organizations like the European Union have produced numerous international conventions on migrant worker rights. The most significant of these are the United Nations International Convention on the Protection of the Rights of Migrant Workers and the Members of their Families, the UN Convention on the Status of Refugees, the UN International Convention on the Elimination of All Forms of Racial Discrimination, and the (non-EU) European Convention on Human Rights.

However, there is no global enforcement mechanism that can guarantee the rights conferred upon migrant workers by international conventions; the European Union, for example, relies on individual member states to implement its policies (Geddes 2000: 31).[11] While nation-states remain the only political actors that can enforce international migrants' rights conventions, the major countries of immigration usually are not signatories to these agreements.[12] Even states that ratify such conven-

---

and to a more limited extent in Canada) or where the influence of pro-business government ministries is strong (as in Korea).

[11] Only the European Convention on the Protection of Human Rights has a supranational judicial enforcement mechanism (the European Court of Human Rights), which has had some limited impact on national immigration control policies (Guiraudon and Lahav 2000; Hammar 1992: 259).

[12] For example, by the end of 2003 only thirty out of the world's two hundred countries had ratified the United Nations convention on migrant rights, and they included none of the major countries of immigration. The small number of ratifica-

tions often exclude certain occupations dominated by immigrants, such as farmworkers and household maids. Moreover, few countries have overhauled their domestic laws to bring them into compliance with the international conventions they have ratified.

International human rights regimes sometimes have affected the ability of nation-states to control immigration through the activities of domestic NGOs, advocacy groups, and legal practitioners. These groups fight for immigrants' rights through the courts, appealing to international conventions that governments have ratified but not sufficiently enforced (Guiraudon and Lahav 2000: 171–75; Gurowitz 1999; Hansen 1999: 427–28; Sassen 1998: 51–71). In some cases, the courts have challenged, limited, and even overturned national immigration laws that are incompatible with international norms.

Ambiguous Policy Intentions

Policy gaps also occur because officially declared immigration policy is often quite different from actual intentions. In addition to turning a blind eye to immigration law violations (especially at worksites), governments sometimes enact secondary measures that tacitly undermine official policy. One does not have to subscribe to a theory of conspiratorial political elites in order to explain such contradictions. Moreover, states themselves are fragmentary and do not speak in a uniform voice. This is especially true when immigration policymaking involves a large number of government agencies with different (if not conflicting) agendas and constituencies. The extreme case is Japan, whose immigration policymaking regime consists of a grand total of seventeen ministries and agencies, but in many other labor-importing countries there is, at minimum, tension between the justice ministry (concerned with crime and security) and the economic ministries (concerned with meeting labor requirements) (see the Spain case, this volume). Additional problems result from the fact that the government agencies that make policy are frequently different from those who implement it. Those responsible for enforcing an immigration control measure may be less willing to carry out its provisions, or

---

tions is generally attributed to conflicts with national legislation. Although a much larger number of countries have ratified UN conventions prohibiting racial discrimination and on the status of refugees, few governments have seriously enforced the provisions of these conventions (see Castles and Davidson 2000:18–19; Loescher 1993; Guiraudon and Lahav 2000: 167–68).

may do so in ways that partly undermine its goals, because they do not share the same objectives as the policymakers or face different pressures and constraints.

The same holds true for the relationship between national and local governments. Although national governments make most immigration policy (often without consulting local governments), subnational agencies are responsible for implementing many of its specific provisions, especially given the increasing tendency of national governments to adopt "remote control" strategies by delegating immigration control functions to local and regional governments, officials, and employers (Guiraudon 2001). If local authorities do not share the same policy objectives and interests as the national government (or if they are not given sufficient resources), they may become lax in enforcement or simply not comply.[13]

THE CONVERGENCE HYPOTHESIS

In contrast to the indisputable reality of policy gaps, it is arguable whether true convergence is occurring across advanced industrial countries in their immigration control and immigrant integration policies. The consensus among the contributors to this volume is that the policies of the countries represented here are coming to resemble each other in important ways, to the extent that no truly deviant cases remain.[14] However, it is debatable whether these emerging similarities are examples of true policy convergence, which in the narrowest sense refers to a *group* of labor-importing countries that are moving in more or less coordinated fashion toward a single type of immigration policy.

Toward which immigration control and immigrant integration models are today's labor-importing countries converging? Although it may be useful to assess the extent to which the immigration policies of West European and Asian countries are moving toward those of the "classic countries of immigration" (the United States, Canada, and Australia), this exercise implicitly assumes an evolutionary model in which the traditional immigration countries represent the most advanced stage of policy development, which other immigration countries will eventually

---

[13] Sometimes local governments—especially in areas with large concentrations of immigrants—adopt harsher restrictive measures than national governments, because they must shoulder most of the burden of providing social services to immigrants and refugees (Money 1999: chap. 3).

[14] In some respects Canada appears to be a deviant case, as discussed below.

attain. Although this is consistent with modernization theory (from which the notion of convergence originated), we reject any unilinear theory as simplistic and empirically suspect. The immigration policies of the "classic" countries are themselves dissimilar in important ways, and even if we focus on convergence toward a single country (the United States would be the most obvious case), the policies of that country do not remain stable. U.S. immigration policy has undergone several major transformations in the post-1940 period, lurching back and forth between expansionary and restrictionist modes (Tichenor 2002; Martin, this volume).

Rather than try to assess policy convergence at the global level, it may be more useful to analyze *regional* convergences. For example, there has been substantial convergence across the fifteen EU member states in terms of refugee and asylum policy, nationality law, relaxation of border controls between EU countries, and a more skills-based immigrant admissions system (Hansen and Weil 2001; Koslowski 2000). Increasingly restrictive immigration control policies have been coupled with more liberal immigrant integration and citizenship policies, in an attempt to socially incorporate immigrants who have already become long-term residents and their offspring. Similarly, it is possible to identify general policy similarities among East Asian labor importers—for example, a reluctance to accept permanent or unskilled foreign workers, a reliance on various types of de facto guestworker programs, harsh (but ineffective) internal enforcement measures, denial of family reunification, and a general lack of social integration policies.

In general, it makes sense to analyze convergence only at the level of "*macro*" policies—general features of a country's immigration system such as the criteria for admitting legal permanent immigrants, use of temporary worker programs (or the ratio of temporary-to-permanent resident visas), and emphasis on external border control (including visa control at airports) versus internal enforcement. In contrast, "*micro*" policies are the detailed regulations, procedures, and mechanisms through which macro immigration policies are carried out. These include numerical quotas of immigrants admitted, categories of admission (such as temporary visa holders), immigrant registration procedures, procedures for verifying employment eligibility, specific rights conferred upon immigrants and asylees, strategies for border enforcement, and procedures to apprehend and deport unauthorized immigrants. Cross-national similarities in micro policies may emerge, but significant and sustained immigration policy convergence usually occurs only at the macro level. Because micro policies change frequently (sometimes on a yearly basis), only macro policies (which may change only once or twice in a generation) are stable enough to assess true convergence.[15]

Explaining Policy Convergence

Parallel path development. Immigration policies can converge simply because countries face similar domestic pressures and constraints that cause them to independently develop similar policy responses.[16] Most advanced industrial countries face the same kinds of demographic and economic challenges that shape immigration flows and policies, such as declining fertility and population aging, a structural demand for migrant labor, and economic uncertainty (which reduces public tolerance for immigration). Convergence can also be the product of similar political institutions, policymaking regimes, public opinion trends, and patterns of interest-group politics. Certain shared historical legacies (colonialism, involvement in wars of Third World countries) can also generate similar immigration pressures. In addition, similarities in the role of immigration in the nation's history — its "founding myth" — can lead to similarly inclusionary or exclusionary immigration policies. Japan/Korea, Canada/Australia, and Germany/the Netherlands provide good examples of parallel-path policy convergence.

Policy emulation. Governments frequently study the immigration policies of other countries, including their effectiveness and consequences, and decide to borrow from or reject them. Numerous governments have been impressed by Canada's apparent success at managing immigration levels; and Canadian refugee, guestworker, and multicultural immigrant integration policies have been widely adopted in modified form, most notably by Australia and Germany. The post-1993 U.S. border enforcement strategy has been imitated, albeit on a much reduced scale, by certain EU countries (see the Spain chapter, this volume). France and Germany have borrowed from the U.S. visa system used to import highly

---

[15] For instance, the current U.S. family reunification–based immigrant admissions policy has been in place since the 1960s, and there are no indications that it will change drastically in the foreseeable future (although there are constant calls to move to a somewhat more skills/labor market–based policy). Canada's current skills selection–based immigration system began in 1967, and Japan's restrictive admissions policy dates back to 1951.

[16] Hansen and Weil (2001) use this model to explain convergence in nationality law among certain groups of European countries.

skilled and professional workers. Perhaps the best example of such copy-ing is Korea, which has studied and imported several Japanese immigra-tion policies wholesale.[17]

Regional integration. Immigration policies are more likely to converge when labor-importing countries are members of a supranational, re-gional organization like the European Union. This is especially true when such organizations are not simply regional free trade blocs but agree to pursue common immigration policies and require future en-trants to adopt regional standards in this policy domain. However, even in the European Union, where regional cooperation on immigration and asylum policy is the most advanced, the "harmonization" of policies is limited not only by the reluctance of individual member states to relin-quish sovereignty over immigration control but also by a decision-making process based on unanimity, which allows dissenting member states to block the adoption of common policies (Geddes 2000: 7).

The harmonization process undoubtedly will be further complicated by the enlargement of the EU in May 2004 to include ten Central and Eastern European countries — states that lack the judicial and administra-tive mechanisms to implement EU regulations and to enforce the EU's external borders (Koslowski 2000: 169–72; Lavenex 2002; Mitsilegas 2002).[18] Despite expert forecasts that the number of new, east-to-west migrants resulting from enlargement would be relatively small (see, for example, Kupiszewski 2002), all of the fifteen current EU member states imposed restrictions on would-be migrants from the newcomer countries, ranging from exclusion from their labor markets for up to seven years (France, Germany) to making the new migrants ineligible for public benefits for several years (Britain, Spain).

Global events and geopolitics. Certain economic and political events of in-ternational scope can also promote immigration policy convergence. For example, global economic downturns can cause numerous governments

---

[17] It is important to recognize that policy learning can also lead to policy *divergence*. For instance, Japanese immigration policymakers have studied the "failures" of European immigration policy ("guestworkers" who do not go home, amnesty pro-grams that have increased illegal immigration, refugee/asylum systems that are easily abused and overburdened, public backlashes caused by permanent immi-grant settlement) and have decided to avoid adopting these policies altogether.

[18] The enlargement countries are Estonia, Latvia, Lithuania, Poland, the Czech Repub-lic, Slovakia, Hungary, Slovenia, Cyprus, and Malta.

to adopt more restrictive measures against immigrants (both those entering and those already residing in the country). The economic shock caused by the Arab oil embargo in 1973 was the catalyst for ending Western Europe's large-scale guestworker programs. The Asian economic crisis of the late 1990s caused virtually all of that region's countries of immigration (South Korea, Thailand, Malaysia, and Singapore) to significantly reduce legal immigration and attempt to expel illegal immigrants. Major geopolitical events can have similar effects. For example, in response to the September 11, 2001, terrorist attacks, the U.S. and West European governments implemented a variety of immigration control measures in the name of national security, such as increased border surveillance, tightened visa-issuance policies, and special registration and detention programs targeting immigrants from Muslim countries (Andreas and Biersteker 2003; Cole 2003: 184–233; Rudolph 2003: 615–18).

Public opinion. Governments of labor-importing countries around the world claim to be responding to mass public opinion that is increasingly hostile to expansionary immigration policies and the extension of immigrants' rights. In some cases (see the Spain chapter, this volume), it is not clear whether public opinion is driving the policy response or being led by opportunistic politicians. In Britain, immigration policymakers seem trapped between their own liberal impulses and an illiberal public (Hansen 2000: 15–16). What is unarguable is that the percentage of respondents in national public opinion surveys conducted in major labor-importing countries who cite immigration as an important issue facing the nation has risen rapidly in recent years (*Economist* 2003), and far-right, anti-immigrant political parties have emerged or gained vote share in all West European countries except Spain since the early 1990s (Boswell 2003: 15–28; Lloyd 2003). In Europe, public hostility has focused increasingly on "bogus" asylum seekers and their perceived abuse of the welfare state (Cohen, Humphries, and Mynott 2002). Governments have responded with various schemes to discourage asylum seekers, by restricting their access to social services, shortening the adjudication period and restricting appeals, detaining asylum seekers while their claims are being processed, and forcing them to apply in the first EU country that they reach (to prevent them from "shopping around" for asylum in other countries if their initial claim is denied). Similarly, the recent convergence of immigration policies in Germany, the Netherlands, and Britain toward Canada's economic needs/skills–based admissions system (cf. Favell and Hansen 2002: 592) is premised partly on the assumption that it is more palatable to the public than a U.S.-style "humanitarian" system.

In the remainder of this chapter, we review the empirical evidence from our eleven country case studies that bears on the emergence of immigration policy gaps and convergence in policymakers' choices.

CLASSIC COUNTRIES OF IMMIGRATION: THE UNITED STATES, CANADA, AND AUSTRALIA

We define as "classic countries of immigration" those that were founded, populated, and built by immigrants in modern times. As a result, immigration is a fundamental part of the founding myth, historical consciousness, and national identity of these countries, and they anticipate and welcome large numbers of immigrants. This does not mean, however, that they have always been open to immigrants, nor that immigration is not currently a source of social tension and political conflict in these countries. Indeed, during the last ten years the United States and Australia have been nearly as prone as the "reluctant" labor importers discussed below to adopt restrictive measures and indulge anti-immigrant public opinion.

The United States: Conflict and Contradictions

Of all the countries included in this study, the United States has by far the largest gap between the stated goal of controlling immigration and the actual results of policy: ever-increasing numbers of both legal and illegal immigrants. Recent efforts to reduce the influx of unauthorized migrants entering via Mexico through concentrated border enforcement operations and other control measures have not reduced the stock of such immigrants in the United States; instead, they have produced a more stable, settled population. By the beginning of the twenty-first century, 10 percent of low-wage workers in the United States were unauthorized immigrants; in agriculture, they were between 50 and 60 percent (Martin 2003: 188; Passel, Capps, and Fix 2004).

The U.S. insistence on maintaining such ineffective immigration control policies prompts Philip Martin to ask whether they are genuine efforts to reduce unauthorized immigration or primarily an attempt to manage public opinion by creating the illusion that illegal immigration is under control. Although enforcement of immigration laws in the workplace is potentially a much more effective means of immigration control, employer sanctions have also been ineffective because of the widespread availability of fraudulent documents among immigrant workers and grossly insufficient numbers of inspectors.

The political debate over immigration in the United States is fueled not only by the large numbers of unauthorized immigrants who find their way into the country but by the perceived impacts of immigration in general on the life chances of native-born workers and by the alleged failure of recent immigrants (especially Mexicans) to assimilate into U.S. society. The general public continues to assume that immigrants depress wages, compete unfairly (and effectively) for jobs that would otherwise be taken by native workers, and become a huge drain on public services. Martin notes that most empirical research does not support such assumptions.

Martin describes the debate between integrationists (assimilationists) and pluralists (multiculturalists) over the extent and pace of immigrant incorporation into U.S. society. Previous attempts to incorporate immigrants through cultural assimilation have been replaced by a greater multicultural tolerance that enables immigrants to attain socioeconomic mobility while retaining their cultural differences to a certain extent. Although the United States does not have an official immigrant integration policy, it has provided differential access to rights, benefits, and social services to immigrants depending on their legal status. Martin argues, however, that there has not been a large difference between the rights granted to citizens versus noncitizens (especially legal permanent residents), which helps to explain why fewer than half of the immigrants in the United States today have naturalized.

Martin observes that U.S. immigration policy has long followed a "zigzag" pattern, with expansionary periods followed by restrictionist ones. With the terrorist attacks of September 11, 2001, the United States clearly has entered a new restrictionist period, as immigration control has become conflated with protecting national security. Tightened border controls, much closer monitoring of foreign students, and ethnic/religious profiling of immigrants to identify and detain potential terrorists have become accepted practice in the post-9/11 era. Nevertheless, Martin notes that there has been no concerted effort to substantially reduce the number of immigrants admitted to the United States, thus demonstrating the resilience of the ideology that the United States is a nation of immigrants and the power of market forces driving contemporary immigration.

Canada: Low-Conflict Expansionism

Among the countries represented in this book, Canada seems to be the most comfortable with its immigration policy. As Jeffrey Reitz's chapter makes clear, Canada has a consensual and relatively open approach to immigration, geared more toward nation-building and national economic development than in the United States. As a result, Canada has maintained an expansionary, skills-based immigration policy that admits three times the number of immigrants per capita than the United States. Despite such high immigration levels, the public remains quite tolerant of immigrants. Reitz attributes such differences between the United States and Canada to different economic structures, cultural factors, and institutional arrangements. Canada has a fixed-target policy of admitting each year a number of immigrants equal to one percent of its population (about 300,000 immigrants per annum), regardless of short-run economic conditions. However, unlike the United States, whose immigration system is based primarily on family ties, Canada has a carefully managed points system that selects immigrants according to their education, skills, and linguistic abilities, in an effort to meet the country's long-term labor market needs. In recent years there has been more emphasis in the selection process on attracting young, skilled immigrants. Noneconomic immigrants admitted through family reunification or as refugees are kept proportionately lower, although Canada has a relatively liberal policy toward asylum seekers.

Given such clear policy objectives, it is relatively simple to measure gaps between policies and actual outcomes in the Canadian case. In terms of the number of immigrants actually admitted, Canada has consistently and significantly fallen short of its 1-percent-of-population target, which, as Reitz notes, is quite interesting since most countries receive more immigrants than desired. It is more difficult to assess whether Canadian immigration policy has been effective in providing the country with enough highly skilled and economically successful immigrants. Educational levels of immigrants were higher than native Canadians in the past, but the difference has narrowed and virtually disappears when they are compared to young native-born urban workers. Immigrant earnings are higher than in the United States, but not relative to qualifications.

The Canadian case is also distinguished by a relatively high level of public support for immigration, compared to the United States and Australia. Majorities of Canadians have consistently favored maintaining or increasing current immigration levels. The political discourse on immigration has also remained positive, with all major political parties officially supporting immigration. Reitz suggests a number of explanations for this: the positive association of immigration with nation-building and population maintenance, a small population of illegal immigrants, and simple political correctness. Another reason for high public tolerance may be Canada's policy of selecting immigrants according to skills and other qualifications to meet labor market needs, which gives the public the impression that immigrants are making a positive contribution to the economy.

Canada gives immigrants immediate access to various social services, settlement programs, and a relatively easy naturalization process. The country's official immigrant integration ideology seems to have followed a course somewhat similar to the United States: an earlier assimilationist paradigm has been replaced by a multiculturalism approach. Unlike the United States, however, Canada has an explicit and official multiculturalism policy. The greater feeling of social acceptance this policy generates among immigrants may be one reason why rates of naturalization are higher than in the United States.

Canada is something of a deviant case among the countries considered in this book because of its recent reaffirmation of expansionary immigration policies (in legislation passed at the end of 2001). The September 11 terrorist attacks on the United States did not provoke a restrictive turn in Canadian immigration policy, despite increased cooperation with the United States on border security. But Reitz suggests that the widening gaps between policy and outcomes—that is, Canada's inability to attract a sufficient number of immigrants, and the recent downward trends in immigrant job-seeking success and earnings—may erode the currently positive economic perception of immigrants. Moreover, there is growing concern about the spatial distribution of immigrants; more than 80 percent of new arrivals head for only three cities: Toronto, Montreal, and Vancouver (Beach, Green, and Reitz 2003: 3). Finally, it will become increasingly difficult for Canada to keep the proportion of family-based immigrant admissions low, given that the skills-based immigrants already living in the country eventually will want to bring in family members. Such trends may force the government to adopt policies that converge more with the United States.

Australia: Rising Ambivalence toward Immigration

The immigration histories of Australia and Canada have a number of important similarities. Both countries originated as British colonies and pursued racist immigration policies in the past, designed to keep their countries white and European, but they eventually abandoned such discriminatory policies in favor of a skills-selection system and a multicultural policy toward immigrant integration. Both still regard immigration as a means of economic development. The critical difference is that Australia is currently much more ambivalent about its immigration flow than is Canada.

According to Stephen Castles and Ellie Vasta, the Australian government has fashioned a carefully managed immigration program modeled on the Canadian system, one that admits skilled immigrants based on a qualification points test and generates a low proportion of family-based and humanitarian immigrants (refugees and asylum seekers). Australia also has a large temporary foreign worker program for highly skilled immigrants. Castles and Vasta find that the gap between immigration policies and outcomes is rather small in Australia. The points system has been relatively effective in attracting the desired type of skilled, economically successful immigrants. Indeed, the average skill level of recent immigrants is higher than that of native-born workers, and both first- and second-generation immigrants have experienced substantial occupational mobility. The illegal immigrant population is small, partly a consequence of Australia's geographical isolation from poorer, Third World countries. In terms of immigrant integration, Australia seems to have followed the American and Canadian trajectory: an earlier, assimilationist integration policy has given way to a multiculturalist stance that recognizes the nation's cultural diversity and improves immigrant access to social services and institutions. As in the United States, there is not a large difference in the rights conferred to citizens and permanent residents, and the requirements for naturalization are minimal.

The Australian government seems to have done an effective job of convincing the public that their country primarily admits skilled immigrants who contribute to its economy. However, Castles and Vasta document growing public ambivalence toward immigration, driven by rising unemployment and economic uncertainty, and the emergence of the anti-immigrant One Nation Party. Globalization and increased regional integration (which have increased the number of countries sending immigrants to Australia), together with the recent arrival of boat people (undocumented immigrants and asylum seekers), have also contributed to a sense that the country's tightly controlled immigration system is under threat. In response to the anti-immigrant backlash, government policies have taken a restrictive turn, marked by a draconian tightening of refugee and asylum policy and stronger border controls. Australia's multiculturalism program has also been downgraded and partly dismantled. However, a pro-immigrant movement is emerging, led by a conglomeration of unions and other NGOs. Although Australia has a bureaucracy-dominated immigration policymaking regime, it actively consults with various interest and advocacy groups and is responsive to public pressure. This raises the possibility that the current restrictionist period may be brief.

RELUCTANT COUNTRIES OF IMMIGRATION: FRANCE, GERMANY, THE NETHERLANDS, BRITAIN

We consider as "reluctant" countries of immigration those that have had considerable experience with immigrants but continue to deny officially that they are countries of immigration (or only recently have acknowledged this fact). Immigration has not been a fundamental part of their national identity nor their past nation-building process, and the attitudes of political elites and general publics toward immigration generally have been more negative than in the classic immigration countries. These countries have recruited most migrants temporarily (that is, as guestworkers) rather than as permanent additions to the labor force.

France: Challenges to the "Republican Consensus"

James Hollifield argues in this volume that France has been a relatively liberal immigration country because of the strength of the political ideology of republicanism—initially a form of left-wing, rights-based politics—buttressed by the labor requirements of French capitalism and the policy preferences of government economic planners in the post–World War II era. Liberal immigration and naturalization policies also derived from the early establishment, in the nineteenth century, of a pattern whereby immigrant labor was recruited privately by French industry, often with government sanction but with very little state control. The organization of foreign labor importation by the private sector largely bypassed official institutions created to manage immigration flows. The historical pattern has been for such flows to accelerate to the point where the state is compelled, for political reasons, to try to regain control. But the general ineffectiveness of France's immigration control policies has yielded a substantial gap between stated policy objectives and actual outcomes.[19]

---

[19] As in the United States, increased border enforcement ironically has promoted immigrant settlement, and attempts to reduce immigrant rights have led to surges in naturalization.

Consistent with its republican tradition, France has been willing to accept immigrants and incorporate them into the French nation under a generous naturalization policy and with no significant exclusions from the country's welfare state. However, since World War II there have been repeated efforts to curtail immigrant rights, including limiting family reunification, encouraging repatriation, restricting employment opportunities, toughening the asylum adjudication process, and expanding the powers of police to detain and deport unauthorized immigrants. Some of these measures were part of a "grand bargain" struck by liberal governments, in which tightened control over new immigration flows was accompanied by efforts to accelerate the social integration of immigrants already settled in France, through the granting of citizenship rights. In recent years, more conservative-minded governments have attempted to make France's citizenship and naturalization laws more exclusionary and seriously limit the civil and social rights of immigrants, partly in an effort to placate the anti-immigrant National Front party and win back its supporters.

Behind the increasingly negative policy stance on immigration were worsening economic conditions and higher unemployment, public anxiety about the rapidly increasing number of Muslim immigrants (about 5 million by 2003 — the largest concentration in Western Europe — including first-generation immigrants and their French-born children), and the threat of terrorism fed by Islamic fundamentalism. The most recent, right-wing government led by Jacques Chirac secured the enactment of a national ban on the wearing of Muslim head scarves and other religious symbols in public schools. While the legislation was justified as necessary to protect France's strict doctrine of the separation of church and state, it was also a clear response to public concerns about immigration in the run-up to regional elections in which the anti-immigrant National Front was again expected to do well. Part of the public backlash against Muslim immigrants is a concern that they cannot be assimilated in accordance to the republican model of the nation.

While the republican ideology has not been a primary *determinant* of French immigration policy, especially in recent years, it has clearly been a *constraint* on government actions in this area. For example, French courts have ruled repeatedly that laws seriously violating the civil liberties of immigrants were unconstitutional on the grounds that they were inconsistent with the country's republican values, derived from universal human rights. The government's anti-immigrant measures have also aroused large-scale public protests, in an active civil society. As Hollifield argues, France and other liberal democratic states have certain built-in constraints that prevent them from crossing the "invisible line" and infringing basic civil liberties in violation of their founding principles.

Germany: Coming to Terms with Immigration

The Federal Republic of Germany, formerly the "guestworker" country par excellence, now recoils from the waves of foreigners that have descended upon it since the collapse of East European Communism in 1989. The arrival in Germany of 1 million foreigners—including ethnic Germans relocating from the former Soviet Union and its satellites, relatives of immigrants already settled in Germany, applicants for political asylum, and legal and illegal foreign workers—in 1990 alone made it by far the leading recipient of immigrants among OECD nations, even while German leaders declared that their country "is not, nor shall it become, a country of immigration." It was not until summer 2002 that Germany's first comprehensive immigration policy was proposed to the parliament, and upon passage it was struck down by the supreme constitutional court on procedural grounds. A replacement law failed to gain passage in June 2003, and the issue remains in doubt.

In previous decades, as Philip Martin's chapter makes clear, Germany implemented a series of ad hoc immigration control policies, all of which went awry with major unintended consequences. In fact, the history of immigration to Germany is one of huge gaps between policies and outcomes. This is best illustrated by the country's guestworker programs, begun in the 1950s, which were intended to recruit foreign workers on a strict-rotation basis. Although no numerical quota was set nor serious limits placed on foreign worker recruitment, a much larger number of guestworkers migrated to Germany than expected, and a third of them settled there. Employers wanted them for longer periods, the workers prolonged their stays due to the high cost of living in Germany (which lengthened the time needed to accumulate savings), and many brought their dependents. Germany's asylum policy follows a similar story line. Despite its generous and open-ended commitment to provide asylum to those fleeing political persecution—a legacy of World War II—the government clearly did not expect the huge flood of asylum applicants that it received beginning in the late 1980s, nor was it ready to accommodate them. The volume of illegal immigration has also been quite large; estimates of the current stock of unauthorized workers range between 500,000 and 1.5 million.

The government's attempts to assert control over immigration have met with limited success. While it was able to shut off guestworker recruitment in the early 1970s (owing mainly to the deep recession caused by the Arab oil embargo), subsequent attempts to reduce the foreign worker population failed. Since the revision of the Basic Law in 1993, the government has been considerably more effective in reducing the flow of asylum seekers and convincing some of them to repatriate. However, attempts to control illegal immigration seem to have run into the same obstacles as in other countries: insufficient resources for border control and internal enforcement, lack of political will due to opposition from employers and pro-immigrant NGOs, and concerns that stringent controls would be economically harmful for Germany as well as immigrant-sending countries. According to Martin, Germany has been quite ambivalent in its efforts to socially integrate its unexpectedly large population of immigrants, since it simultaneously has been urging them to repatriate. Naturalization has been considerably more difficult in Germany than in other Euro-American countries, although the government recently modified its *jus sanguinis* nationality law and accepted limited dual nationality.

Such large gaps between policy and outcomes inevitably created a popular perception that the government has lost control over immigration, encouraging a public backlash led by right-wing extremists and nationalist politicians. Anti-immigrant reactions (including violent attacks on foreigners) mushroomed in the early 1990s, when the flood of asylum seekers was seen as an unacceptable economic burden in a context of high structural unemployment, especially in the former East Germany. In recent years the labor-force participation rate among immigrants has dropped sharply, and their unemployment rate is twice that of natives, further reinforcing the public perception that they are an economic burden.

The government apparently has learned from its past mistakes. Germany's new guestworker programs have been very limited, project-specific, and carefully managed. Its "green card" program, launched in 2001, is for highly skilled information technology professionals. In devising a new comprehensive immigration policy, Germany has looked to Canada (not to the United States). The government apparently feels that if it admits immigrants based on a Canadian-style skills/qualifications test and reduces noneconomic, humanitarian migration, this will reduce fiscal impacts and deflate anti-immigrant sentiment in the general public.

Although Germany has "converged" with the Canadian/Australian system, it remains to be seen whether it will be able to close the gap between policy and outcomes as effectively as those two countries have. First, Germany has been unable thus far to attract the number of skilled immigrant workers it desires, since the English-speaking, higher-paying countries of the United States, Canada, and Britain remain the favorite destinations of such workers (see Cornelius, Espenshade, and Salehyan 2001). Second, pursuing a narrowly skills-based immigration policy in a country whose economy continues to demand large numbers of unskilled workers undoubtedly will produce a large gap between policy and outcomes.

The Netherlands: A Pragmatic Approach under Fire

The Netherlands used to be a country of emigration but became a serious labor importer several decades ago. However, it is only in recent years that some government officials have begun to acknowledge that the Netherlands is, indeed, a country of immigration, and this notion remains highly controversial. As a result, the Netherlands does not have a comprehensive policy based on an overall vision of itself as a country of immigration but rather a series of ad hoc policies formulated in response to changing economic and social conditions.

Although immigration is certainly not part of Dutch national identity, Dutch society has been defined by the core values of pragmatism, tolerance, and humanism, and these national values have prevented the government from veering too far toward a restrictionist immigration policy. According to Philip Muus, Dutch policy has been a constant search for a balance between pragmatic economic interests and humanitarian concerns. Responding to the economy's need for immigrant labor, the Netherlands operated a German-style guestworker program from the early 1960s to the mid-1970s. At the same time, because of its strong tradition of humanitarianism, the Netherlands maintained a liberal asylum system, similar to Germany's pre-1993 regime.

Immigration policymaking in the Netherlands has been a story of emerging gaps between policies and outcomes, followed by attempts to close the gaps by tightening immigration controls. Virtually all of the country's ad hoc immigration policies have produced serious unintended consequences. The guestworker program of the 1960s and early 1970s brought more immigrant workers to the Netherlands than initially anticipated, and they did not repatriate as expected. After the guestworker program was officially ended, recruitment of foreign workers was allowed to continue, on a smaller scale. The generous Dutch asylum system was quickly overwhelmed as the Netherlands became one of the most attractive destinations for asylum seekers. The Dutch have been more lenient than the Germans in allowing family reunification for asylum seekers, guestworkers, and postcolonial immigrants, which gave employers "backdoor" access to foreign-born labor. Like other Euro-American countries, the Netherlands recently began to actively recruit temporary, highly skilled workers from abroad to meet the needs of its increasingly important knowledge-based industries. Muus argues that as a consequence of all this, the Dutch immigration system has become a *gedoogbeleid* (a policy that unofficially tolerates what is formally not allowed), and the most densely populated country in Europe has experienced a large influx of immigrants from Islamic countries.

As the gap between policies and outcomes grew and demographers predicted that the largest Dutch cities would have Muslim majorities within ten years, a serious public backlash developed. The initial lightning rod for anti-immigrant sentiment was Pim Fortuyn, a former Marxist academic turned populist-conservative who came close to being elected prime minister in 2002, arguing that the Netherlands was "full up" and calling Islam a "backward religion." Fortuyn's ambitions were thwarted by a fanatic protester who assassinated him a few days before the election. Fortuyn's makeshift political party has faded since then, but he succeeded in turning immigration and asylum seeking into issues that must be addressed by the "mainstream" Dutch parties.

Attempts to narrow the gaps between immigration control policies and outcomes have included repeated attempts to limit family-reunification immigration, which proved to be widely ineffective, as well as numerous measures to discourage asylum seekers, none of which changed the Netherlands' image as a welcoming destination. In February 2004 the Dutch parliament voted to round up and expel up to 26,000 failed asylum seekers who had arrived in the Netherlands before April 2001—a harsher remedy than has been applied to asylum seekers in any other EU country to date. Legalization programs and stronger controls against clandestine immigration have also been attempted, but the latter have mainly had the effect of increasing migrants' reliance on professional people-smugglers.

Meanwhile, Dutch immigrant integration policies remain generous and inclusive. Paradoxically, these policies are justified as efforts to prevent the establishment of "ethnic minorities" while allowing immigrants to maintain their cultural identities. The system has been successful in terms of housing, education, and legal rights for immigrants and has produced high rates of naturalization, but it has been less successful in promoting economic incorporation.

Britain: From "Zero-Immigration" to Controlled Immigration Country

Britain is *not* a country of immigrants, and it is emphatically not a "country of immigration." Nevertheless, despite having a supposedly "zero-immigration" policy since the 1970s, Britain has somehow managed to add between 140,000 and 170,000 people each year since 1998 through immigration. Zig Layton-Henry sees this policy outcome as a consequence of a sustained and deepening labor shortage that threatens to erode public finances, a rapidly aging population, employers lobbying for greater access to foreign-born labor, and stronger global competition for "high-end" immigrants, which has caused the government to substantially increase the issuance of work permits for skilled workers.

Thus Britain seems to have reversed a trend toward increasingly restrictive immigration policies that began in 1962, when the country started to impose stringent controls on immigration from its colonies and the British Commonwealth. In the early 1970s the government created a work permit system that generally did not allow family reunification or permanent residence. Additional restrictions, as well as a crackdown on visa overstayers, were implemented during the conservative governments of the 1970s and early 1980s. Britain further tightened its immigration system by adopting a narrower definition of British citizenship, which denied the right to immigrate to most former British subjects. And unlike other Western European countries, which have granted free movement across borders to EU nationals under the Schengen group protocols, Britain has retained strict border controls.

According to Layton-Henry, the main reason for the government's restrictive stance was a low level of public tolerance for immigration. The British public and mass media have been hostile to large-scale immigration out of concern that immigrants will threaten the country's national character and overburden the welfare system. The government assumes that large numbers of racially and culturally different immigrants will cause a strong public backlash and lead to ethnic and racial conflict. It views immigration controls as necessary not only for good race relations but also to reassure the public that immigration is being carefully managed to promote national economic interests. Even when the liberal Labour Party has been in power, it has espoused immigration policies nearly as tough as those advocated by the Conservative Party, apparently out of fear that a public perception that immigration is out of control could easily be exploited by right-wing politicians. Thus the recent move toward a more expansionary immigration policy has been accompanied by harsh measures to deter asylum seekers, although their number is far smaller per capita than in most other European countries.

While Britain has much more restrictive immigration policies than most Euro-American countries, the gap between policy and outcomes is no less prominent. Britain now has one of the largest ethnic minority populations in Western Europe. The government has had great difficulty in reducing the number of asylum seekers, prompting incessant, inflammatory media coverage. Although the illegal immigrant population (mainly visa overstayers) has been relatively small, it has also been growing recently, and highly publicized incidents involving human and labor rights violations among clandestine Chinese migrants have called attention to unauthorized immigration.

Not surprisingly, Britain's reluctance to fully accept its status as a major country of immigration has made it less willing to adopt a proactive and coherent immigrant integration policy. This has forced local governments to bear most of the burden of providing basic human services to immigrants and asylees. However, race riots beginning in the 1990s have vividly illustrated the uneven socioeconomic incorporation of immigrants, spurring the government to pay more attention to this issue.

The British government's recent turn toward more liberal admission of skilled immigrants — driven by a severe shortage of professional service workers — has been accompanied by efforts to convince the public of the economic benefits of immigration. This indicates that the future gap between policies and outcomes may be smaller, given that the government will have a policy in line with labor market needs (the unskilled labor shortage in Britain seems to be less structurally embedded). It also suggests that the government may have greater success in managing public opinion on immigration, since skilled immigrants are generally less controversial.

RECENT COUNTRIES OF IMMIGRATION: ITALY, SPAIN, JAPAN, AND KOREA

Recent countries of immigration are those that did not have notable immigration in the post–World War II era because labor demands could be successfully met by *internal* migration from poorer regions, increased utilization of previously untapped labor sources, and/or mechanization and rationalization of production. In recent decades, however, these countries have begun to import large numbers of immigrants because of negative demographic trends (which are worse than in other countries), as well as structural economic and labor market needs mainly caused by relatively recent economic growth (after the 1970s in some cases). However, the percentage of foreign-born residents remains quite low in these countries, and they generally do not officially consider themselves to be countries of immigration. This does not mean, of course, that they have never experienced large-scale immigration in the past or that immigration has never been important for their past nation-building. In addition, all of these countries have been prominent *exporters* of immigrant labor in the past, when they were less industrialized than other Euro-American countries. As a result, they have all made a transition from former countries of emigration to countries of net immigration in recent decades.

Italy: Demographic Implosion and Political Polarization

Among the latecomer immigration countries, Italy has the largest population of recently arrived, noncitizen residents, the vast majority of whom originated in northern and sub-Saharan Africa and Asia. Italy was a classic country of *emigration* for most of its history, but this trend was reversed in the early 1980s. While Italy (like Spain) was initially a way-station for immigrants attempting to get to other European countries through the "back door," it is now an important immigrant destination in its own right. In her chapter on the Italian case, Kitty Calavita shows that Italy has been experiencing the same problems as more advanced immigration countries as it attempts to negotiate a balance between strong employer demand for foreign workers and the need to maintain at least the appearance of immigration control.

The reasons why Italy became dependent on foreign workers are common to most of today's major labor-importing countries. However, the demographic implosion is more serious in Italy than in any other advanced industrial country: it has the world's lowest birthrate and the most rapidly aging population. Together with a native workforce that shuns arduous, low-wage jobs, the result has been a potentially crippling labor shortage. The strong demand for immigrant labor also reflects a largely intact social welfare state that encourages underemployment and early retirement among native workers, as well as powerful labor unions that increase the attractiveness of cheap, casual foreign labor.

Calavita argues that government interventions to control immigration to Italy eventually get overwhelmed by these powerful market forces. Italian politicians find themselves making promises to the public about controlling immigration that they cannot possibly keep: they have enacted four major new immigration control laws in the last sixteen years. Substantial gaps between policies and outcomes are virtually guaranteed by quotas that are set too low or become de facto legalization programs for unauthorized immigrants already in the country; employer sanctions that are not enforced because of legal challenges by the courts, confusion within the government over implementation responsibility, and the high percentage of illegal immigrants who work in the underground economy; and amnesty programs that fail because of the fiscal burdens that they impose on employers (a newer program based on legalization initiated by the immigrants themselves has been more successful). Meanwhile, the stock of illegal immigrants in Italy has grown robustly, to at least 300,000 today. There is growing pressure on Italy from other EU member states to improve its external border controls in order to reduce the influx of unauthorized migrants from the Balkans and North Africa.

Italy's recent record on immigrant integration is mixed. The latest immigration law affirms labor rights for immigrants and provides access to basic human services. However, some of these provisions have been obstructed by local officials fearing community backlashes. Naturalization remains very difficult. Multiculturalism has not been pursued as a social integration policy because of the widespread belief that the cultures of Third World immigrants threaten Italy's social cohesion and national identity.

Public opinion on immigration is highly polarized in Italy. Opinion surveys indicate that the Italian public is one of the most tolerant in Europe, but there is growing antagonism toward immigrants based on beliefs that they threaten public safety and take jobs from native-born workers. Right-wing political parties have made considerable headway in some parts of the country using anti-immigrant appeals. But anti-immigration political forces have been counterbalanced by a powerful coalition of pro-immigrant groups including employers, labor unions, NGOs, and religious groups that press the government for more open policies and measures to reduce the illegality and marginality of immigrant workers. Italian labor unions, well entrenched in the formal economy and thus largely insulated from immigrant-worker competition, have been particularly strong supporters of rights for foreign workers. Although the current right-of-center coalition government is considering a tough new immigration law that reverses all of the liberal provisions of previous laws, it has been restrained by strong employer lobbying and massive protests organized by immigrant advocacy groups.

Spain: Heightening the Contradictions

Like Italy, Spain's experience with immigration—especially from developing countries—is historically very limited. Only since the mid-1980s have Third World migrant workers replaced "sunbird" northern Europeans as the most numerous foreigners in Spain. The foreign-born population grew rapidly in the 1990s, to nearly 1.7 million by the end of 2003, most of them from non-EU countries. Many foreign workers continue to pass through Spain on their way to destinations in northern Europe, but Spain has become an important destination country for unauthorized migrants from Africa, Latin America, and East Asia, more than 600,000 of whom are now believed to be working in the country.

Wayne Cornelius's chapter reveals a country grappling with the issue of how to preserve legal access to the foreign labor on which major parts of the Spanish economy now depend, while not allowing illegal immigration to get out of control and thus create opportunities for political extremists of the sort now plaguing other European countries. Since 2000, however, "mainstream" politicians have come to appreciate the electoral potency of anti-immigration appeals, and Spain now seems condemned to an era of politically expedient policy experimentation, urged on by northern European countries eager to make the EU's southern perimeter less porous.

As in Italy, most illegal immigrants in Spain work in service industries, construction, and agriculture—the most dynamic, labor-short sectors of the economy. The country's vast underground economy absorbs much of this foreign labor. With one of Europe's best-performing economies since 1996, a native-born workforce no longer willing to migrate internally for employment nor to do low-wage manual jobs, and a demographic profile that virtually cries out for an expansionary immigration policy (rock-bottom fertility rates, rapid population aging), Spain is destined to be a large-scale importer of foreign workers in the twenty-first century.

Gaps between Spanish immigration control policies and their outcomes are quite large and growing. Attempts to crack down on migrant smuggling in the Strait of Gibraltar have only shunted the traffic westward to the Canary Islands. Five different legalization programs carried out since 1986 have not reduced the stock of illegal immigrants, and a dysfunctional system of interlinked work and residence permits turns once-legal foreign workers into *irregulares* with dismaying regularity. A quota system enabling employers to legally import foreign workers, mostly on short-term visas, has fallen far short of meeting the demand for such workers and is now limited to nationals of five countries with which Spain has signed bilateral migrant labor agreements. Employer sanctions enforcement is inhibited by the high percentage of illegal immigrants employed in underground-economy firms and by the closeness of government-business ties. There is no comprehensive, well-defined policy to promote the social integration of foreign workers and their dependents, even as more than half of the immigrants in principal receiving areas define themselves as long-stayers or permanent residents. The most recent revisions of the national immigration law, engineered by the government of José María Aznar, have largely shredded the labor rights and civil liberties for immigrants guaranteed by previous legislation.

Cornelius and other observers question whether the Spanish state possesses the administrative capacity needed to implement most forms of "modern" immigration control (even border enforcement seems to be failing, despite significant increases in spending). Nevertheless, the conservative government in power since 1996 has staked out a hard-line, restrictionist immigration policy, positioning itself on the vanguard of EU efforts to control unwanted flows of economic migrants and asylum seekers. Public opinion toward immigrants has hardened noticeably since the late 1990s, partly in response to anti–foreign worker riots in 2000 in a southern agricultural city, and partly to the government's scapegoating of immigrants for increases in crime. As the current wave of Third World migration to Spain proceeds, it will be increasingly difficult to sustain the contradictions between the government's harsh rhetoric on immigration and what is actually happening in the labor market and the neighborhoods.

Japan: In Denial

Although past Japanese emigration was never on the scale of Italy's or Spain's, hundreds of thousands of Japanese did emigrate to the Americas from the late nineteenth century to the mid-twentieth century, creating large communities of Japanese descendants in the United States and Brazil. The economic and demographic factors that have turned Japan into a country of immigration are similar to those operating in Italy and

Spain. However, unlike Italy and Spain, Japan has insisted on a closed-door immigration policy that prohibits the importation of any type of unskilled migrant worker and promotes only the admission of highly skilled and professional workers.

The Japanese government has maintained this restrictive stance ever since the country became a net importer of labor in the late 1980s, despite persistently strong demand for foreign workers in certain segments of the economy, because it wants to maintain the country's ethnic homogeneity and fears that large numbers of racially and culturally different immigrants will provoke social conflict and increase social welfare costs. Japan's bureaucracy-dominated immigration policy-making regime makes it relatively insensitive to lobbying by small and medium-sized employers and other pro-immigration groups. Finally, demographics are rapidly catching up with Japan's unrealistically restrictive immigration policy. The population has already ceased to grow and is projected to decline by 22 million during the next fifty years, assuming current levels of fertility and immigration. In 2001, for the first time, Japanese aged 64 years and older outnumbered those under age 15.

As a result, the gap between immigration policy and actual outcomes in Japan is substantial. Despite the blanket exclusion of unskilled foreign workers, there are probably 850,000 of them working in Japan today. Huge economic disparities exist between Japan and its neighbors in East and Southeast Asia, and with the appreciation of the Japanese yen in the 1980s, large numbers of workers in these countries began circumventing the official restrictions. Some were smuggled in clandestinely, but most entered Japan on short-term visas and overstayed them. The government has not allocated the resources nor does it have the political will to crack down on illegal immigrants in a serious and sustained way. It recognizes that numerous employers have become dependent on these workers, and it does not wish to further depress the economy, which has been in recession since 1991. Meanwhile, the government has undermined its own restrictive immigration policy by enabling large numbers of un-skilled foreign workers to be imported through various "side-door" mechanisms, as company trainees, students, entertainers, and especially ethnic-Japanese return migrants, of whom there are an estimated 330,000 now employed in Japan.

Japan's insistence on treating all foreign workers as short-term "guests" — not potential permanent settlers — has delayed the formulation of explicit, national-level policies and programs to facilitate the social integration of settled immigrants. Local governments and NGOs have scrambled to provide some basic social services and protections to foreign residents, but without the backing of the national government they have been unable to serve their clients adequately. Moreover, both unauthorized immigrants and those admitted legally through "side-door" mechanisms have suffered labor and human rights abuses because of their ambiguous status.

Thus far, the Japanese public—well known for its ethnic insularity—has shown surprising tolerance toward the immigrants arriving in the past decade, despite the long-running recession that followed the collapse of the "bubble economy" of the late 1980s. This relative tolerance is partly a function of the widely shared belief that foreign workers are alleviating Japan's labor shortage and thus contributing to the economy. Nevertheless, negative attitudes toward immigration have been on the rise recently, fed by inflammatory media coverage and statistics released at regular intervals by the National Policy Agency that identify foreigners as major contributors to crime. Responding to the public's concerns about declining security, the ruling Liberal Democratic Party included in its November 2003 election platform the goal of halving the number of illegal foreign residents in Japan within five years, but few independent observers consider such a goal realistic. Japan continues to be a nation in denial about its future as a country of immigration.

South Korea: Emulating Japan

Like Japan, Korea historically was a labor-exporting country that did not begin importing immigrants on a notable scale until the late 1980s. And as in Japan, foreign workers still constitute only a small segment of the population (roughly one percent). They are concentrated in the manufacturing and construction sectors, with a small but growing presence in service industries. Like Japan, Korea denies that it is a country of immigration, officially forbids the entry of unskilled immigrant labor, and accepts very few asylum seekers. But again like Japan, Korea has de facto "side-door" mechanisms through which significant numbers of unskilled foreign workers are admitted on a temporary basis, while little is done to reduce the stock of illegal immigrant workers.

The high degree of policy convergence between Korea and Japan is partly the result of similar domestic pressures. Like Japan, Korea traditionally has refused to recognize any ethnic diversity in its population (statistically, Korea is more ethnically homogeneous than Japan), and it emphatically declines to become a multicultural society through large-scale, permanent immigration. Nevertheless, the demand for immigrant labor in Korea has acquired a structural character because recent economic growth has been coupled with low fertility and population aging, a wealthy and highly educated native workforce that shuns unskilled jobs, and limited alternative sources of labor power. In addition, Korea has a Japanese-style, bureaucracy-dominated immigration policymaking system that has responded in similar fashion to the contradictory pressures of keeping the country immigrant-free and meeting domestic labor shortages. As a former Japanese colony, Korea inherited Japanese laws and subsequently imported many of its policies from Japan, which it has regarded as a more economically developed role model. The Korean government recently copied, wholesale, several Japanese immigration control policies and programs.

Compared with Japan, however, Korea has a much larger proportion of unskilled "trainees" and unauthorized immigrants in its foreign-born labor force. Although their presence undermines the country's official ban on unskilled foreign workers, Dong-Hoon Seol and John Skrentny argue in their contribution to this volume that there is no significant gap between policy and outcomes in Korea because no one in the government takes its official immigration policies seriously (in contrast to Japan). Instead, the primary goal of these policies is to provide the country with an inexpensive and exploitable immigrant labor force at minimal cost to the state, which they have done quite successfully.

According to Seol and Skrentny, this outcome is attributable to very strong client politics. Although immigration policymaking is dominated by the Ministry of Justice, with little active participation by political parties and immigrant advocacy groups, policymakers are influenced by highly organized small and medium-sized business owners who are the principal beneficiaries of immigrant workers. The Korean Justice Ministry has steadily expanded its "trainee" program, which has conveniently provided employers with underpaid and highly exploitable foreign workers. For similar reasons, the Justice Ministry has been even more lax than its Japanese counterpart in cracking down on illegal immigrants and the employers who hire them.

According to Seol and Skrentny, there is also not much of a gap in Korea in terms of immigrant integration policy. Although Korea insists that immigrants must be temporary and has no comprehensive social integration policy, this has been less of a problem than in Japan because, thus far, there has been virtually no permanent settlement of immigrant families. Nevertheless, the government has shown considerable sensitivity to international conventions on the rights of foreign workers, and the Korean courts have also been active in defending immigrant rights. In response to political protests and activism by foreign workers themselves, the government has implemented measures to protect the rights of trainees and undocumented immigrants, and a bill advocated by the Labor Ministry to replace the current trainee program with a less abusive work permit system was seriously considered. All this maneuvering has produced considerable fragmentation within the Korean immigration policymaking regime, but it may lead to a more expansive and responsible immigration system in the future. As long as Korean public opinion remains tolerant, the country may converge toward the more "liberal" immigration policies of Euro-American countries rather than continue to emulate Japan.

CONCLUSION: WHY DO FAILED IMMIGRATION CONTROL POLICIES PERSIST?

The cases examined in this volume provide ample evidence that today's countries of immigration (official or de facto) are now so integrated into the global labor market that few can afford to drastically reduce immigration without major, negative domestic consequences. Nevertheless, virtually all of the industrialized countries examined in this volume, with the partial exception of Canada, would prefer to classify themselves as reluctant or unwilling importers of foreign labor.

In each of these cases we can observe the interaction of four key trends: (1) high emigration from less developed countries (especially those deemed by native-born residents of receiving countries as "problem nationalities"), where economic and demographic push factors are strong and likely to remain so in the foreseeable future; (2) in the receiving countries, demographic profiles that are changing in ways that inevitably increase the demand for foreign-born labor; (3) the persistence in receiving-country economies of employer demand for low-cost, flexible labor—a *structural* demand that has become decoupled from the business cycle; and (4) the rising frequency of largely symbolic efforts by receiving-country governments to deter new immigration and discourage permanent settlement of immigrants and refugees, under pressure from an increasingly hostile public opinion. In labor-importing country after labor-importing country, this confluence of trends produces deep ambivalence about immigration in both general publics and elites. There is grudging recognition of the economic and demographic need for immigration, but it is coupled with keen sensitivity to the cultural residue being left behind by the *kind* of immigration that these countries are now experiencing. Indeed, as Cornelius notes in his analysis of the Spanish case, most advanced industrial countries are facing "a trade-off between the sociocultural costs of admitting more foreigners — many of whom will settle permanently — and the economic costs of *not* importing them."

The cases that we have examined vividly illustrate the limited effectiveness of most attempts by governments of industrial democracies to intervene in the migration process linking them to Third World labor-exporting countries, at this point in time. The record is littered with the wreckage of government interventions that appeared to work reasonably well at first but had little staying power, or that had long-term consequences exactly the opposite of the initial, intended effects. These interventions rarely dry up "unwanted" migration flows or even significantly reduce them; more often, they simply rechannel the flows and create more opportunities for people smugglers to cash in on the traffic. Yet governments continue to tinker with the control measures to which they have committed themselves, in order to improve their performance. Some have taken drastic and unprecedented steps to control immigrant and refugee flows (for example, the U.S. experiment with "concentrated border enforcement operations" since 1993), and they continue to invest in such measures, even in the face of mounting evidence that they are not efficacious.

Why do failed immigration control policies persist in today's labor-importing countries, often long past the point when it becomes apparent that they are not working? Some political parties in the labor-importing countries clearly see votes to be gained from advocating such measures, regardless of their track record; current examples include the Conservative Party in Britain, the Popular Party in Spain, and the far-right, anti-immigrant parties operating in other West European countries. Governments of widely varying ideological bent fine-tune their immigration policies and devise new ones because these measures are seen as useful in convincing the general public that they have not lost control over immigration. This political calculus has caused even liberal and moderate governments to crack down periodically on illegal immigration and "toughen" the political asylum process. In Western Europe, they lend their support to ongoing regional efforts to "harmonize" immigration and asylum policies, to restrict labor mobility within an enlarged European Union, and to forge new repatriation agreements with African and Asian sending countries. But meaningful, supralocal immigration controls remain elusive, even in Western Europe.[20] These nation-states retain a capacity to control immigration, but that capacity invariably is limited by domestic institutions and client politics. They tolerate—indeed, often create—large gaps between policies and policy outcomes in this area because the number of domestic stakeholders in an expansionary (de facto) immigration policy is very large and will continue to grow under foreseeable economic and demographic conditions. Ineffective and "symbolic" immigration control measures are thus perpetuated because they reduce the potential for a broad public backlash.

One major question, posed repeatedly but not necessarily resolved in this book, concerns the extent to which future governments in the labor-importing countries will succeed in rolling back the legal, political, and social rights of "within-country" immigrants that have made it easier for unauthorized immigrants who have entered one of these countries in recent decades to remain. Curtailing the rights of immigrants and asylum seekers is a much easier course for governments of labor-importing countries to pursue than attempting to change the basic market and demographic forces—in both sending and receiving countries—that now drive most Third World migration to these countries. This approach also avoids or mitigates most of the diplomatic costs associated with more stringent border enforcement or imposing tough new visa restrictions on the nationals of high-emigration countries. However, a large body of research indicates that it is unlikely to stem the flow of new migrants appreciably, since the availability of social services or entitlements is not a powerful magnet for would-be unauthorized entrants, as compared with other demand-pull factors.

At what point in the future will the politics of appeasing anti-immigrant public opinion collide with the national interests of the receiving countries, defined in terms of economic growth, global competitiveness, and the interest of individual citizens in maintaining lifestyles often made possible by immigrant service-providers and producers of low-cost goods? When that point is reached, the goals of national immigration policy may have to be redefined in order to reduce the large and constantly widening gap between policy goals and outcomes. Redefining the goals of their national immigration policies will also force the gov-

---

[20] For example, a newly created agency charged with reducing illegal immigration to the European Union will not have law enforcement powers in member states and will not create an EU-wide border patrol. It will begin its work in 2005 with a staff of thirty people and a budget of US$7.4 million (Black 2003).

ernments of reluctantly labor-importing industrialized countries to squarely confront rather than ignore or downplay the trade-offs between more effective immigration control and other societal goals and principles. What basic values, what civil liberties, how much in tax revenues, and how much in future economic growth are to be sacrificed in order to gain greater control over unauthorized immigration and reduce the size of the extant foreign-born population? The outcomes of ongoing debates over these questions will determine whether persistently high levels of immigration from less developed countries — in whatever form — will be tolerated in the long term. Meanwhile, market forces and demography — not government interventions — will be the most powerful determinants of international migration dynamics in the twenty-first century.

References

Andreas, Peter, and Thomas Biersteker, eds. 2003. *The Rebordering of North America: Integration and Exclusion in a New Security Context.* New York: Routledge.

Andreas, Peter, and Timothy Snyder, eds. 2000. *The Wall around the West: State Borders and Immigration Controls in North America and Europe.* Totowa, N.J.: Rowman and Littlefield.

Audley, John, Sandra Polaski, Demetrios G. Papademetriou, and Scott Vaughan. 2003. *NAFTA's Promise and Reality: Lessons from Mexico for the Hemisphere.* Washington, D.C.: Carnegie Endowment for International Peace.

Beach, Charles M., Alan G. Green, and Jeffrey G. Reitz, eds. 2003. *Canadian Immigration Policy for the 21st Century.* Montreal: John Deutsch Institute for the Study of Economic Policy/McGill-Queen's University Press.

Black, Ian. 2003. "EU Border Agency to Boost Controls," *The Guardian* (United Kingdom), November 12.

Boswell, Christina. 2003. *European Migration Policies in Flux: Changing Patterns of Inclusion and Exclusion.* London: Royal Institute of International Affairs/Blackwell.

Castles, Stephen, and Alastair Davidson. 2000. *Citizenship and Migration: Globalization and the Politics of Belonging.* New York: Routledge.

Castles, Stephen, and Mark J. Miller. 2003. *The Age of Migration: International Population Movements in the Modern World.* 3d ed. New York: Guilford.

Cohen, Steve, Beth Humphries, and Ed Mynott, eds. 2002. *From Immigration Controls to Welfare Controls.* London: Routledge.

Cole, David. 2003. *Enemy Aliens: Double Standards and Constitutional Freedoms in the War on Terrorism.* New York: New Press.

Cornelius, Wayne A. 1998. "The Structural Embeddedness of Demand for Mexican Immigrant Labor: New Evidence from California." In *Crossings: Mexican*

Immigration in Interdisciplinary Perspective, edited by Marcelo Suárez-Orozco. Cambridge, Mass.: Harvard University Press.

———. 2001. "Death at the Border: Efficacy and Unintended Consequences of U.S. Immigration Control Policy," *Population and Development Review* 27, no. 4: 661–85.

———. 2002. "Impacts of NAFTA on Mexico-to-U.S. Migration." In *NAFTA in the New Millennium*, edited by Edward J. Chambers and Peter H. Smith. La Jolla, Calif.: Center for U.S.-Mexican Studies, University of California, San Diego, and University of Alberta Press.

Cornelius, Wayne A., Thomas J. Espenshade, and Idean Salehyan, eds. 2001. *The International Migration of the Highly Skilled*. La Jolla: Center for Comparative Immigration Studies, University of California, San Diego.

Della Porta, Donatella. 2000. "Immigration and Protest: New Challenges for Italian Democracy," *Southern European Society and Politics* 5, no. 3: 108–32.

Demeny, Paul. 2003. "Population Policy Dilemmas in Europe at the Dawn of the Twenty-First Century," *Population and Development Review* 29, no. 1: 1–28.

Economist, The. 2003. "Immigration: The Natives Are Restless," October 11.

Favell, Adrian, and Randall Hansen. 2002. "Markets against Politics: Migration, EU Enlargement and the Idea of Europe," *Journal of Ethnic and Migration Studies* 28, no. 4: 581–601.

Fawcett, James T. 1989. "Networks, Linkages, and Migration Systems," *International Migration Review* 23, no. 3: 672–80.

Fehr, Hans, Sabine Jokisch, and Laurence Kotlikoff. 2003. "The Developed World's Demographic Transition: The Roles of Capital Flows, Immigration, and Policy." Working Paper No. 10096. Cambridge, Mass.: National Bureau of Economic Research.

Fertig, Michael, and Cristoph M. Schmidt. 2003. "Gerontocracy in Motion? European Cross-Country Evidence on the Labor Market Consequences of Population Ageing." IZA Discussion Paper No. 956. Bonn, Germany: Institute for the Study of Labor, December.

Freeman, Gary P. 1994. "Can Liberal States Control Unwanted Migration?" In *The Annals of the American Academy of Political and Social Science*, vol. 534, edited by Mark J. Miller. Thousand Oaks, Calif.: Sage.

———. 1995. "Modes of Immigration Politics in Liberal Democratic States," *International Migration Review* 29, no. 4: 881–913.

———. 1998. "The Decline of Sovereignty? Politics and Immigration Restriction in Liberal States." In *Challenge to the Nation-State: Immigration in Western Europe and the United States*, edited by Christian Joppke. Oxford: Oxford University Press.

———. 2002. "Winners and Losers: Politics and the Costs and Benefits of Migration." In *West European Immigration and Immigrant Policy in the New Century*, edited by Anthony M. Messina. Westport, Conn.: Praeger.

Geddes, Andrew. 2000. *Immigration and European Integration: Towards Fortress Europe?* Manchester, United Kingdom: Manchester University Press.

Ghosh, Bimal. 2000. "Towards a New International Regime for Orderly Movements of People." In *Managing Migration: Time for a New International Regime?* edited by Bimal Ghosh. Oxford: Oxford University Press.

Guiraudon, Virginie. 2001. "De-nationalizing Control: Analyzing State Responses to Constraints on Migration Control." In *Controlling a New Migration World,* edited by Virginie Guiraudon and Christian Joppke. New York: Routledge.

Guiraudon, Virginie, and Christian Joppke, eds. 2001. *Controlling a New Migration World.* New York: Routledge.

Guiraudon, Virginie, and Gallya Lahav. 2000. "A Reappraisal of the State Sovereignty Debate: The Case of Migration Control," *Comparative Political Studies* 33, no. 2: 163–95.

Gurowitz, Amy. 1999. "Mobilizing International Norms: Domestic Actors, Immigrants, and the Japanese State," *World Politics* 51, no. 3: 413–45.

Hammar, Tomas. 1992. "Laws and Policies Regulating Population Movements: A European Perspective." In *International Migration Systems: A Global Approach,* edited by Mary M. Kritz, Lin Lean Lim, and Hania Zlotnik. New York: Oxford University Press.

Hannerz, Ulf. 1996. *Transnational Connections: Culture, People, Places.* London: Routledge.

Hansen, Randall. 1999. "Migration, Citizenship and Race in Europe: Between Incorporation and Exclusion," *European Journal of Political Research* 35, no. 4: 415–44.

———. 2000. *Citizenship and Immigration in Postwar Britain.* Oxford: Oxford University Press.

Hansen, Randall, and Patrick Weil. 2001. "Introduction: Citizenship, Immigration and Nationality: Towards a Convergence in Europe?" In *Towards a European Nationality: Citizenship, Immigration and Nationality Law in the EU,* edited by Randall Hansen and Patrick Weil. New York: Palgrave.

Hansen, Randall, and Patrick Weil, eds. 2002. *Dual Nationality, Social Rights, and Federal Citizenship in the U.S. and Europe: The Reinvention of Citizenship.* New York: Berghahn.

Hollifield, James F. 1992. *Immigrants, Markets, and States: The Political Economy of Postwar Europe.* Cambridge, Mass.: Harvard University Press.

———. 2000a. "Migration and the 'New' International Order: The Missing Regime." In *Managing Migration: Time for a New International Regime?* edited by Bimal Ghosh. Oxford: Oxford University Press.

———. 2000b. "The Politics of International Migration: How Can We 'Bring the State Back In'?" In *Migration Theory: Talking across Disciplines,* edited by Caroline Brettell and James Hollifield. New York: Routledge.

Joppke, Christian. 1998. "Why Liberal States Accept Unwanted Immigration," *World Politics* 50: 266–93.

Joppke, Christian, ed. 1998. *Challenge to the Nation-State: Immigration in Western Europe and the United States.* Oxford: Oxford University Press.

Koslowski, Rey. 2000. *Migrants and Citizens: Demographic Change in the European State System*. Ithaca, N.Y.: Cornell University Press.

Kostakopoulou, Theodora. 2002. "Long-Term Resident Third-Country Nationals in the European Union: Normative Expectations and Institutional Openings," *Journal of Ethnic and Migration Studies* 28, no. 3: 443–62.

Kupiszewski, Marek. 2002. "How Trustworthy are Forecasts of International Migration between Poland and the European Union?" *Journal of Ethnic and Migration Studies* 28, no. 4: 627–45.

Kyle, David, and Rey Koslowski, eds. 2001. *Global Human Smuggling: Comparative Perspectives*. Baltimore, Md.: Johns Hopkins University Press.

Kyle, David, and Zai Liang. 2001. "Migration Merchants: Human Smuggling from Ecuador and China to the United States." In *Controlling a New Migration World*, edited by Virginie Guiraudon and Christian Joppke. London: Routledge.

Lavenex, Sandra. 2002. "EU Enlargement and the Challenge of Policy Transfer: The Case of Refugee Policy," *Journal of Ethnic and Migration Studies* 28, no. 4: 701–21.

Levitt, Peggy, Josh DeWind, and Steven Vertovec, eds. 2003. "Transnational Migration: International Perspectives," special issue, *International Migration Review* 37, no. 3: 565–892.

Levitt, Peggy, and Mary C. Waters, eds. 2002. *The Changing Face of Home: The Transnational Lives of the Second Generation*. New York: Russell Sage Foundation.

Lim, Lin Lean. 1992. "International Labour Movements: A Perspective on Economic Exchanges and Flows." In *International Migration Systems: A Global Approach*, edited by Mary M. Kritz, Lin Lean Lim, and Hania Zlotnik. New York: Oxford University Press.

Lloyd, John. 2003. "The Closing of the European Gates? The New Populist Parties of Europe." In *The Politics of Migration: Managing Opportunity, Conflict and Change*, edited by Sarah Spencer. Malden, Mass.: Blackwell.

Loescher, Gilbert. 1993. *Beyond Charity: International Cooperation and the Global Refugee Crisis*. Oxford: Oxford University Press.

Martin, Philip L. 2001. "Trade and Migration: The Mexico-U.S. Case." In *International Migration: Trends, Policies, and Economic Impact*, edited by Slobodan Djajic. London: Routledge.

———. 2003. *Promise Unfulfilled: Unions, Immigration, and the Farm Workers*. Ithaca, N.Y.: Cornell University Press.

Martin, Philip L., B. Lindsay Lowell, and Edward J. Taylor. 2000. "Migration Outcomes of Guest Worker and Free Trade Regimes: The Case of Mexico-U.S. Migration." In *Managing Migration: Time for a New International Regime?* edited by Bimal Ghosh. Oxford: Oxford University Press.

Martin, Philip L., and Jonas Widgren. 2002. "International Migration: Facing the Challenge," *Population Bulletin* 57, no. 1: 1–40.

Massey, Douglas S. 1988. "Economic Development and International Migration in Comparative Perspective," *Population and Development Review* 14: 383–413.

Massey, Douglas S., Joaquín Arango, Graeme Hugo, Ali Kouaouci, Adela Pellegrino, and J. Edward Taylor. 1998. *Worlds in Motion: Understanding International Migration at the End of the Millennium.* Oxford: Clarendon Press.

Massey, Douglas S., and Zai Liang. 1989. "The Long-Term Consequences of a Temporary Worker Program: The U.S. Bracero Experience," *Population Research and Policy Review* 8, no. 3: 199–226.

Mitsilegas, Valsamis. 2002. "The Implementation of the EU *Acquis* on Illegal Immigration by the Candidate Countries of Central and Eastern Europe: Challenges and Contradictions," *Journal of Ethnic and Migration Studies* 28, no. 4: 665–82.

Money, Jeannette. 1999. *Fences and Neighbors: The Political Geography of Immigration Control.* Ithaca, N.Y.: Cornell University Press.

Morawska, Ewa. 2001. "Gappy Immigration Controls, Resourceful Migrants, and *Pendel* Communities: East-West European Travelers." In *Controlling a New Migration World,* edited by Virginie Guiraudon and Christian Joppke. London: Routledge.

Ono, Kent A., and John M. Sloop. 2002. *Shifting Borders: Rhetoric, Immigration, and California's Proposition 187.* Philadelphia, Penn.: Temple University Press.

Passel, Jeffrey S., Randy Capps, and Michael Fix. 2004. "Undocumented Immigrants: Facts and Figures." Washington, D.C.: Immigration Studies Program, The Urban Institute, January 12.

Pieke, Frank N., Pál Nyíri, Mette Thuno, and Antonella Ceccagno. 2004. *Transnational Chinese: Fujianese Migrants in Europe.* Stanford, Calif.: Stanford University Press.

Reyes, Belinda, Hans Johnson, and Richard Van Swearingen. 2002. *Holding the Line? The Effect of the Recent Border Build-up on Unauthorized Immigration.* San Francisco: Public Policy Institute of California.

Rosenblum, Marc R. 2004. *The Transnational Politics of U.S. Immigration Policy.* La Jolla: Center for Comparative Immigration Studies, University of California, San Diego.

Rudolph, Christopher. 2003. "Security and the Political Economy of International Migration," *American Political Science Review* 97, no. 4: 603–20.

Salt, John, and Jeremy Stein. 1997. "Migration as a Business: The Case of Trafficking," *International Migration* 35, no. 4: 467–91.

Sassen, Saskia. 1996. *Losing Control? Sovereignty in an Age of Globalization.* New York: Columbia University Press.

———. 1998. "The *De Facto* Transnationalizing of Immigration Policy." In *Challenge to the Nation-State: Immigration in Western Europe and the United States,* edited by Christian Joppke. Oxford: Oxford University Press.

Statham, Paul. 2003. "Understanding Anti-Asylum Rhetoric: Restrictive Politics or Racist Publics?" In *The Politics of Migration: Managing Opportunity, Conflict and Change,* edited by Sarah Spencer. Malden, Mass.: Blackwell.

Tichenor, Daniel. 2002. *Dividing Lines: The Politics of Immigration Control in America*. Princeton, N.J.: Princeton University Press.

Tsuda, Takeyuki. 1999a. "The Permanence of 'Temporary' Migration: The 'Structural Embeddedness' of Japanese-Brazilian Migrant Workers in Japan," *Journal of Asian Studies* 58, no. 3: 687–722.

———. 1999b."The Motivation to Migrate: The Ethnic and Sociocultural Constitution of the Japanese-Brazilian Return Migration System," *Economic Development and Cultural Change* 48, no. 1: 1–31.

———. 2003. *Strangers in the Ethnic Homeland: Japanese Brazilian Return Migration in Transnational Perspective*. New York: Columbia University Press.

United Nations. 2000. *Replacement Migration: Is It a Solution to Declining and Ageing Populations?* New York: Population Division, Dept. of Economic and Social Affairs, United Nations Secretariat.

———. 2002. *International Migration, 2002*. ST/ESA/SER.A/219. New York: Population Division, Dept. of Economic and Social Affairs, United Nations Secretariat.

Watts, Julie R. 2002. *Immigration Policy and the Challenge of Globalization: Unions and Employers in Unlikely Alliance*. Ithaca, N.Y.: Cornell University Press/Institute of Labor Relations.

World Economic Forum. 2004. "Living Happily Ever After: The Economic Implications of Aging Societies." Report to the World Economic Forum Pension Readiness Initiative, Watson Wyatt Worldwide.

Zolberg, Aristide R. 1999. "Matters of State: Theorizing Immigration Policy." In *Becoming American, American Becoming*, edited by Douglas S. Massey. New York: Russell Sage Foundation.

PART II

Countries of Immigration: The United States, Canada, and Australia

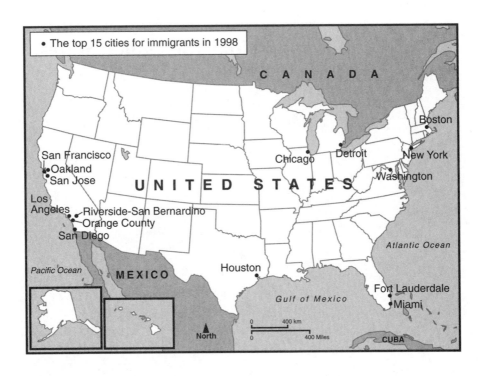

• The top 15 cities for immigrants in 1998

CANADA

UNITED STATES

MEXICO

Boston
New York
Washington
Chicago
Detroit
San Francisco
Oakland
San Jose
Los Angeles
Riverside-San Bernardino
Orange County
San Diego
Houston
Pacific Ocean
Atlantic Ocean
Fort Lauderdale
Miami
Gulf of Mexico
CUBA

North

0   400 km
0   400 Miles

2

The United States: The Continuing Immigration Debate

Philip L. Martin

The United States is a nation of immigrants. Under the motto "e pluribus unum" (from many, one), U.S. presidents frequently remind Americans that they share the experience of themselves or their forebears leaving another country to begin anew in the United States.[1] Immigration is viewed as serving the U.S. national interest; it permits immigrants to better themselves as they enrich the United States. However, there is an ever wider gap between the general U.S. goal of being an immigration country and incorporating the immigrants who arrive through legal entry channels. The major immigration debate in the United States is how to close this gap.

Since arrivals were first recorded in 1820, the United States has accepted 66 million legal immigrants, 11 percent of them from Germany and 10 percent from Mexico. However, two centuries of immigration and integration have not yielded consensus on the three major immigration

---

[1] The exceptions are American Indians, slaves, and people who became U.S. citizens when the United States acquired the territory in which they were living (Martin and Midgley 1999).

questions: How many? From where? In what status should newcomers arrive? The U.S. immigration system can be characterized as one that recognizes between 800,000 and 1 million foreigners a year as legal immigrants, admits 35 million nonimmigrant tourist and business visitors a year, and has another 300,000 to 400,000 unauthorized foreigners settle. During the 1990s there were often contentious debates over the relationship of immigrants and their children to the U.S. educational, welfare, and political systems—or, more broadly, whether the immigration and integration system served U.S. national interests and promised that immigrants and their children would integrate successfully.

U.S. immigration policy was not substantively changed by the September 11, 2001, terrorism, even though the nineteen men who hijacked the planes were foreigners who had been in the United States for periods ranging from a week to several years. However, "the most significant development in the national immigration debate [after 9/11] is what hasn't happened: No lawmaker of influence has moved to reverse the country's generous immigration policy, which for more than three decades has facilitated the largest sustained wave of immigration in U.S. history." Most Americans agreed with James W. Ziglar, commissioner of the U.S. Immigration and Naturalization Service, who stated: "These weren't immigrants. They were terrorists" (quoted in McDonnell 2002).

This chapter summarizes migration patterns, places the immigration and integration challenges facing the United States in a global context, and reviews the evolution of U.S. immigration and integration policy. Immigration is likely to continue at current levels, so that Americans will, in the words of former Census Bureau director Kenneth Prewitt, "redefine ourselves as the first country in world history which is literally made up of every part of the world" (quoted in Alvarez 2001).

U.S. IMMIGRATION PATTERNS

There are three major types of foreigners in the United States: immigrants, nonimmigrants, and unauthorized foreigners. Immigrants are foreign-born persons entitled to live and work permanently in the United States and, after five years, to become naturalized U.S. citizens. Nonimmigrants are foreigners who come to the United States for a specific time period and purpose, such as to visit, work, or study. Unauthorized foreigners, also known as undocumented workers and illegal aliens, are foreigners who enter the United States without port-of-entry inspection or who enter legally—as tourists, for example—but then violate the terms of their entry by going to work, not departing as scheduled, and so on.

Each of these categories can be further subdivided. For example, there are four major types of immigrants (see table 2.1). The largest category is relatives of U.S. residents. Of the 850,000 immigrants admitted in fiscal year 2000, 583,000 (69 percent) had family members in the United States who sponsored their admission by asking the U.S. government to admit them. There is no ceiling on the number of immediate relatives of U.S. citizens who can enter the United States, but there are ceilings on admissions of other types of immigrants, which can lead to long waiting lists for spouses and children of immigrants or adult brothers and sisters of U.S. citizens, among others.

The second-largest category of immigrants are those admitted for economic and employment reason, which in FY2000 totaled some 107,000 immigrants and their families (13 percent of all immigrants). Almost all economic-employment immigrants are in the United States when their visas become available; they simply adjust their status from temporary worker or unauthorized foreigner to immigrant.

The third group includes diversity and other immigrants, and it numbered 93,000, or 11 percent of the total, in 2000. Most diversity and other immigrants are admitted because they entered a lottery open to citizens of countries that sent fewer than 50,000 immigrants to the United States in the previous five years. Some 10 million to 15 million foreigners enter this diversity lottery each year.

The fourth group includes refugees and asylees, the 59,000 foreigners who were granted a chance to start anew in 2000 as immigrants in the United States because they faced persecution at home.[2]

Most immigrants are in the United States when their immigration visas become available; for example, in FY2000, 52 percent of immigrants were already in the country when their visas became available. This means that being admitted as an immigrant does not equate with traveling to

---

[2] Refugees are defined as persons outside their country of nationality who are unable or unwilling to return to that country because of persecution or well-founded fear of persecution on account of race, religion, nationality, membership in a particular social group, or political opinion. Asylees must meet the same criteria as refugees, but they apply for refugee status inside the United States. The president establishes an annual ceiling for refugee admissions—90,000 in FY2000 and 70,000 in FY2002. The number of asylum applications fluctuates; it was 58,688 in FY2001. The backlog was 328,820 asylum applications in September 2001, but 285,000 of these foreigners are Central Americans who will likely be allowed to stay in the United States under nonrefugee criteria.

Table 2.1. Alien Entrants to the United States, 1996–2000

	1996	1998	1999	2000	1996–2000 Average
IMMIGRANTS	915,900	654,451	646,568	849,807	766,682
Immediate relatives of U.S. citizens	300,430	283,368	258,584	347,870	297,563
Other family-sponsored immigrants	294,174	191,480	216,883	235,280	234,454
Employment-based	117,499	77,517	56,817	107,024	89,714
Refugees and aslyees	128,565	52,193	42,852	65,941	72,388
Diversity immigrants	58,790	45,499	47,571	50,945	50,701
Other immigrants	16,442	4,394	23,861	42,747	21,861
NACARA (Section 202)	0	0	11,267	23,641	8,727
Other	16,442	4,394	12,594	19,106	13,134
Estimated emigration	220,000	220,000	220,000	220,000	220,000
NONIMMIGRANTS	24,842,503	30,174,627	31,446,054	33,690,082	30,038,317
Visitors for pleasure	19,110,004	23,254,140	24,104,371	30,511,125[a]	19,395,928
Visitors for business	3,770,326	4,413,440	4,592,540		3,194,077
Foreign workers/trainees	254,427	430,714	525,700	635,229	461,518
Foreign students and dependents	459,388	598,520	603,787	699,953	590,412
ILLEGAL IMMIGRATION					
Alien apprehensions	1,649,986	1,679,439	1,714,035	1,814,729	1,714,547
Aliens deported	69,588	172,547	180,346	184,775	151,814
Alien smugglers located	13,458	13,908	15,755	14,406	14,382

Source: U.S. Immigration and Naturalization Service.

[a] Data are for visitors for pleasure and business combined; due to the temporary expiration of the Visa Waiver Program in May 2000, data are not available separately.

the United States to begin a new life, as was true in the nineteenth century. Instead, immigration in the twenty-first century means that a foreigner already in the United States adjusts her or his status to immigrant. The fact that adjustment has become more common than immigration means that the U.S. Immigration and Naturalization Service (INS)—not the U.S. Department of State—issues the majority of immigration visas. One of the core issues in U.S. immigration policy is the so-called 245(i) adjustment of status program, which allows foreigners in the United States to pay $1,000 and become immigrants without returning to their countries of origin and obtaining an immigration visa at a U.S. consulate.[3] In fall 1999 there were some 950,000 foreigners in the United States waiting for the INS to process their applications for immigration visas; most observers expect immigration to remain at more than 1 million a year between 2000 and 2010.

Mexico is the major source of immigrants to the United States, with some 174,000 immigrants (20 percent) in 2000, followed by China with 46,000, and the Philippines and India with 42,000 each. California was the most common destination for immigrants in 2000, with 218,000 (26 percent) headed there. It was followed by New York and Florida, each receiving about 12 percent of immigrants. Thus half of all immigrants in 2000 went to three states.

Between 30 and 35 million foreigners visit the United States each year as nonimmigrants.[4] Most are welcomed: the U.S. travel industry advertises to entice foreign tourists to come to the United States; businesses invite their foreign colleagues to visit; and many U.S. colleges and universities, as well as sports teams and entertainment firms, recruit foreigners as students, players, and performers. Two groups of nonimmigrants are controversial, however: foreign students, especially since the September 2001 terrorism, and foreign workers.

Before September 11, 2001, the 660,000 foreign students and their dependents in the United States were seen mostly as an economic boon for the country in both the short and the long term. U.S. educational institutions benefited by collecting full tuition from foreign students, and

---

[3] Section 245(i) was initially a three-year program (FY1995–1997) permitting illegal residents otherwise eligible for immigration visas to adjust their status without leaving the United States. This benefited foreigners in the United States given that they could have been barred from legal reentry for three or ten years if they were illegally in the United States for more than six or twelve months.

[4] INS data report admissions, not unique individuals, so a tourist who makes three visits in one year is counted three times.

the foreigners were leaving the United States with good impressions.[5] However, the fact that at least three of the September 11 hijackers were admitted as foreign students (including one who never showed up at the school that admitted him) prompted reviews of the decentralized system under which 73,000 U.S. schools may admit foreign students.[6] These individuals take their admission letter to a U.S. consulate to obtain a student visa. U.S. consular officers interview the students, primarily to ensure that they have sufficient funds to support their period of study in the United States and that they intend to return to their country of origin.

The major change since the terrorist attacks of September 11, 2001, is that U.S. schools approved to admit foreign students will now have to keep track of them, reporting their arrival on campus to the INS. Foreign students will pay a $95 fee that will be applied to developing the Student and Exchange Visitor Information System (SEVIS) through which the INS can track them and their field of study while they are in the United States.

Foreign workers were controversial long before September 11. The 635,000 foreign workers and trainees admitted to the United States in 2000 represented 30 percent of the net growth of U.S. employment, which expands by an average 2 million a year. About two-thirds of the foreign workers admitted were professionals with a bachelor's degree or higher and were filling jobs that required this level of education. They received H-1B visas, which allow them to remain and work in the United States for up to six years and to adjust to immigrant status if they find a U.S. employer to sponsor them for an immigrant visa — that is, if the U.S. employer seeks certification from the U.S. Department of Labor that no U.S. worker is available to fill the job for which the H-1B worker is re-quested. U.S. employers can hire H-1B foreign professionals fairly easily; they need only attest that they are paying the prevailing wage. However, certification is much more time-consuming, often requiring several years, and it generates considerable frustration on the part of both employers and H-1B foreigners.

---

[5] The INS reported that 660,000 foreigners held student visas in the United States in fall 2001, including more than 10,000 enrolled in flight training, trade schools, and other nonacademic programs. The U.S. Department of State issued 315,000 student visas in FY2000.

[6] The Institute of International Education reported that 425,433 foreign students were enrolled in 2,300 U.S. colleges and universities in fall 2000 and that the United States had 30 percent of the world's 1.4 million international students. The INS figure of 73,000 institutions allowed to admit foreign students means that most are not colleges and universities. Instead, they are language schools, beauty schools, driving schools, and so on.

The H-1B program illustrates the controversies that surround U.S. foreign worker programs. On one side are employers who argue that they need to scour the world to find the best and brightest workers so that they and the United States can remain globally competitive. Under this reasoning, they want few barriers between U.S. employers and foreign workers. On the other side are those who argue that there are workers available in the United States and that U.S. employers should do more to train and retrain U.S. workers to fill vacant jobs before hiring foreign workers. These critics note that foreign workers may be preferred because they will work harder than U.S. workers in hopes that their employer will sponsor them for immigrant status. Making it too easy to fill jobs with foreigners, they argue, will discourage U.S. workers from entering fields in which there are large numbers of foreigners, thus increasing employer dependence on foreign workers over time.

When U.S. employers request permission to hire foreign workers, they are asserting that the demand for labor exceeds the labor supply. But there are alternatives to admitting immigrants to reduce demand-supply gaps in the labor market. For example, labor demand can be reduced with labor-saving mechanization or trade, and labor supply can be increased with subsidized education and training or by raising labor force participation rates. Most economists recommend using policy instruments that recognize that an employer's request for foreign workers reflects that employer's decision that importing workers is cheaper than the alternatives. If policy wants to influence employer decisions about hiring foreign workers, it can do so by charging employers fees for the foreign workers they are seeking and then use the funds collected to subsidize efforts to reduce labor demand and increase supply.[7]

In 1990 the barriers between U.S. employers and foreign professionals were lowered, but the number of H-1B visas was capped at 65,000 a year. That ceiling was soon reached, due largely to three factors: the information technology sector expanded in the 1990s, employers learned that it was very easy to hire H-1Bs, and so-called body brokers were established to bring foreign workers into the United States. Employers pressed for a higher ceiling (115,000 H-1B visas), but that level also proved to be too low, and then for a still higher ceiling (195,000), which was not reached

---

[7] For example, employer-paid fees can reduce the demand for labor by subsidizing mechanization, or they can increase supply by subsidizing training. Employers had to pay $500 (later $1,000) for each H-1B worker admitted, with the funds used to subsidize training of U.S. workers and thus eventually increase the supply of U.S. professionals.

in FY2001. The ceiling is scheduled to drop back to 65,000 a year in FY2004, setting off a debate over whether the easy-entry H-1B program should be maintained in its current form.[8] Perhaps the principal lesson of a decade with the H-1B program is that professionals raise many of the same issues as do unskilled foreign workers, including what employers need do to obtain permission to have foreigners admitted to fill jobs and whether foreign workers should have an easy path to current residence.[9]

The North American Free Trade Agreement (NAFTA) includes a separate program that allows foreign professionals from Canada and Mexico to work in the United States; they enter the country by showing proof of educational qualifications or appropriate credentials and a U.S. job offer. In 2000, about 93,000 Canadian and 2,600 Mexican professionals were admitted under NAFTA, up sharply from 28,000 Canadians and 230 Mexicans in 1996.

The United States has more experience with foreign worker programs for unskilled foreign workers; until the late 1990s most foreign workers admitted to the United States had far less schooling than the average U.S. worker and were employed primarily in agriculture. The farmworker program, which issues H-2A visas, illustrates the controversy over foreign workers and the links between legal and unauthorized migration. U.S. agriculture, especially in the southwestern states, has long relied on newcomers to serve as seasonal farmworkers. Waves of newcomers — the Chinese in the 1870s and 1880s, the Japanese until World War I, Filipinos and Mexicans in the 1920s, "Okies" and "Arkies" (white Midwesterners from the U.S. Great Plains) in the 1930s, and Mexicans since World War II — have been the core seasonal farm workforce in California and other western states.

Once seasonal farmworkers learned about nonfarm jobs, they and their children got out of farmwork and were replaced by newcomers

---

[8] The United States made a commitment under the General Agreement on Trade in Services (GATS) to admit up to 65,000 H-1Bs a year. That is, the United States cannot lower the annual ceiling below 65,000.

[9] One issue not anticipated in the early 1990s was the importance of middlemen-brokers who bring H-1Bs into the United States. Many middlemen are immigrants who recruit H-1Bs in their country of origin, charge them fees, and then advertise in the United States that they have H-1B workers to send to companies for temporary assignments. In an effort to increase the regulation of these middlemen, H1-B-dependent firms (defined primarily as those with more than fifty employees, of whom at least 15 percent are H1-B workers) must attest to the U.S. Department of Labor that they did not lay off U.S. workers and that they attempted to recruit U.S. workers before receiving permission to employ H-1B workers. About half of the H-1B workers, and most of the middlemen, are from India.

without other U.S. job options; that is, for most seasonal farmworkers, economic mobility required geographic mobility. Today about 2.5 million persons work for wages on U.S. farms sometime during the year, including 1.8 million employed on crop farms. In 1987–1988, under the Immigration Reform and Control Act (IRCA) which in 1986 introduced employer sanctions to discourage illegal entries, unauthorized crop workers who were employed at least ninety days in 1985–1986 could become legal immigrants, and 1.2 million Mexican men (most of them married) changed their immigration status under the Special Agricultural Worker (SAW) program.[10] Despite their limited English skills and the high unemployment in the recession of the early 1990s, many SAWs left the farm workforce, so that a decade later only about 15 percent of farmworkers were SAWs, and the percentage of unauthorized farmworkers topped 50 percent (see figure 2.1).

With unauthorized foreigners replacing SAWs and with growing numbers of Mexicans dying in the desert in their attempts to enter the United States illegally, calls mounted for a new guestworker program that would allow Mexican workers to enter the United States legally (Cornelius 2001). President Vicente Fox of Mexico and President George Bush, both elected in 2000, agreed to devise "an orderly framework for [Mexico-U.S.] migration that ensures humane treatment [and] legal security, and dignifies labor conditions." A high-level Mexico-U.S. group was formed to consider proposals to allow at least some unauthorized foreigners in the United States to attain legal status by becoming temporary guestworkers, permanent immigrants, or both under "earned legalization."[11] However, plans for a new Mexico-U.S. migration agreement were put on hold in the aftermath of the September 11 attacks.

Illegal immigration continued to increase in the late 1990s, and more Mexican migrants who had formerly returned to Mexico each winter seem to have settled in the United States, in part because beefed-up border patrols have made reentry more difficult. The INS estimated that there were 5 million unauthorized foreigners in the United States in

---

[10] Many of these SAWs never worked in agriculture. At least half of those approved did not do the qualifying farmwork, but the SAW program assumed that the worker-applicant was truthful. Once a foreigner applied for SAW status, the burden of proof was on the government to show that the worker-applicant did not do the qualifying work claimed, and the INS was not prepared to do this (Martin 1994).

[11] Earned legalization means that unauthorized foreigners employed in the United States would get work permits that make them legal guestworkers; after several years of work they could earn full legal immigrant status.

October 1996, that about 55 percent were from Mexico and 60 percent entered without inspection, and that the number of unauthorized foreigners was increasing by 275,000 a year. Demographer Jeffrey Passel estimated that the number of unauthorized foreigners rose to about 9 million in 2000, suggesting a very rapid increase of 800,000 a year in the late 1990s despite stepped-up border patrols (see table 2.2).

Figure 2.1. Shares of Legalized and Unauthorized U.S. Crop Workers, 1989–1998

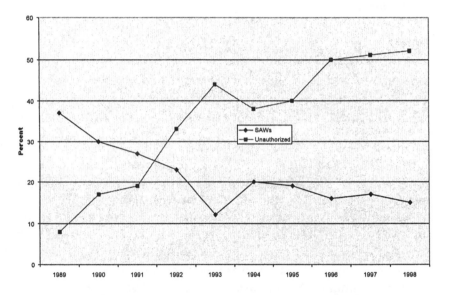

Source: National Agricultural Workers Survey, at http://222.dol.gov/dol/asp/.

Immigration is expanding and transforming the United States. In 2000 there were 28 million U.S. residents who were born abroad, 15 million native-born residents with two foreign-born parents, and 13 million residents of mixed U.S.-born and foreign-born parentage. That is, the "foreign stock" totaled 56 million, or 20 percent of all U.S. residents. Immigrants are concentrated in five U.S. cities; the metropolitan areas of New York, Los Angeles, San Francisco, Miami, and Chicago together hold 21 percent of the total U.S. population but have 50 percent of the foreign-born population.

Table 2.2. Unauthorized Foreigners in the United States, 1980–2000

Year	Millions of Unauthorized Foreigners in United States	Annual Average Change
1980	3.0	
1986	4.0	167,000
1989	2.5	−500,000
1992	3.9	467,000
1995	5.0	367,000
2000	9.0	800,000

Source: Jeffrey Passel, of the Urban Institute; personal communication.

Note: About 2.7 million unauthorized foreigners were legalized in 1987–1988.

The U.S. Census Bureau assumes a net migration of 700,000 to 900,000 a year between 2000 and 2025 (table 2.3), giving the United States a projected population of 340 million in 2025 and 404 million in 2050. The racial/ethnic composition of the U.S. population is expected to change: the non-Hispanic white share of the population is projected to decrease, the African American share to remain stable, and the Hispanic and Asian shares to double in a 35-year period (http://www.census.gov/population/www/projections/natsum.html).

Table 2.3. U.S. Population, 1990, 2000, and 2025

Millions of U.S. Population	1990 (%)	2000 (%)	2025 (%)
Non-Hispanic white	188	197	209
	(76)	(70)	(61)
African American	29	35	44
	(12)	(12)	(13)
Hispanic	22	35	61
	(9)	(12)	(18)
Asian	7	10	21
	(3)	(4)	(6)
Total[a]	249	281	340
	(100)	(100)	(100)

Source: U.S. Census Bureau 1991, 2001, n.d.

[a] Total includes 3 to 5 million American Indians.

U.S. IMMIGRATION HISTORY

Immigration to the United States occurred in waves: large influxes were followed by periods of little immigration. The first wave of immigrants to the United States came before annual arrivals began to be recorded in 1820. English immigrants, who for religious, political, and economic reasons had moved to what became the United States, represented 60 percent of the population in 1790. German sectarians sought religious freedom in Pennsylvania, Spaniards looked for Christian converts in Florida and the Southwest, and Puritans sought to establish a community in Massachusetts that would be restricted to members of their faith.

These early immigrants took big risks. Starvation, disease, and shipwreck probably killed more than one in ten of those who set sail for America. The cost of this travel was equivalent to four to six months of a laborer's wages in England. Because many immigrants could not pay for passage to America, a third of those arriving in 1776 had indentured themselves to secure passage, meaning that they were legally bound to work for up to five years for the employer who met the ship and paid the captain for their passage.[12]

The second wave of immigrants—between 1820 and 1860—fit well with American eagerness for people to help push back the frontier. Peasants displaced from agriculture in Europe and artisans made jobless by the industrial revolution were eager to depart, and steamship and railroad companies were seeking passengers. New arrivals sent what came to be called "American Letters" back to Europe, encouraging friends and relatives to join them. About 40 percent of the 5 million second-wave immigrants were from Ireland, where poverty and a famine brought on by potato blight encouraged emigration. Roman Catholics predominated in the second wave, and by 1850 the Roman Catholic Church was the largest denomination in the United States, though Protestants of various kinds outnumbered Catholics.

The third wave of immigrants began in 1880, with almost 460,000 arrivals. It ended in 1914 with 1.2 million arrivals on the eve of World War I. During the third wave, over 20 million southern and eastern Europeans came, mostly to the eastern and midwestern states, and sev-

---

[12] Lebergott (1986: 182, 185) notes that more immigrants than slaves died en route; slaves were better fed and protected, he says, because their death brought financial loss to their owners. The one-third indentured servant figure applies to immigrants arriving in 1776.

eral hundred thousand Chinese, Japanese, and other Asian laborers settled in the western states. Of those arriving in 1882, 87 percent came
from northern and western Europe, versus 13 percent from the countries
of southern and eastern Europe. By 1907 the proportions were reversed:
19 percent from northern and western Europe and 81 percent from
southern and eastern Europe, including the first large numbers of people
of Jewish and Eastern Orthodox religion.

The American frontier was closed by 1890, and most newcomers
found factory jobs in cities in the Northeast and Midwest. By 1910, immigrants comprised over half of all operatives in the steel and meatpacking industries, and foreign-born men were over half of the workforce in
cities such as New York, Chicago, and Detroit (Briggs 1992: 56–57). The
1910 census found that foreign-born residents made up 15 percent of the
U.S. population and 24 percent of the U.S. labor force.

Immigration was largely halted by World War I, but when it resumed
in the 1920s Congress enacted quotas that restricted the arrival of newcomers. Eastern Hemisphere countries had annual quotas based on the
number of persons from each country who were in the United States in
1890, a clear attempt to favor northern and western European immigrants over those from southern and eastern Europe. During the Great
Depression of the 1930s, emigration exceeded immigration. The United
States began to ease immigration restrictions after World War II, but
annual immigration stayed at about 250,000 per year through the 1950s.

Fourth-wave immigrants began arriving in the United States after
1965, when the preference system changed from privileging certain national origins to favoring would-be immigrants with family ties to the
United States or foreigners that U.S. employers wanted to hire. These
changes, coupled with prosperity in Europe, shifted the origins of most
immigrants from Europe to Latin America and Asia. During the 1970s,
the first decade that the law was in effect, Europeans represented fewer
than 20 percent of U.S. immigrants, and Mexico sent almost as many
legal immigrants as did all of Europe.

There are many similarities between immigration at the end and the
beginning of the twentieth century. The number of immigrants arriving
annually during the peak years — over 1 million — is about the same. Both
the third and fourth waves brought people from countries that had not
previously sent large numbers of immigrants, raising questions about
language, religion, and culture, and catalyzing efforts to fundamentally
change immigration policy.

U.S. IMMIGRATION POLICY

U.S. immigration policies went through three major phases: laissez-faire, qualitative restrictions, and quantitative restrictions. During its first hundred years, 1780 to 1875, the United States had a laissez-faire immigration policy that allowed states, private employers, shipping companies and railroads, and churches to promote immigration to the United States. The federal government encouraged immigration in various ways, including subsidizing railroad construction, which led to the recruitment of immigrant workers by private railroad companies. The United States also maintained high tariffs, which kept out European goods and thus created a demand for workers in U.S. factories. The federal government relied on immigrants to staff the army; immigrants were about a third of the army regulars in the 1840s and represented an even higher proportion in many state militias (Briggs 1992: 56–57).

The influx of Roman Catholics in the 1840s set off the first organized antiforeign movement, the "Know Nothing " movement embodied in the American Party. Protestant clergymen, journalists, and other opinion leaders formed the Order of the Star Spangled Banner, urging the reduction of immigration from non–Anglo-Saxon countries. Members were instructed to answer any inquiries about the Order with the words, "I know nothing about it." The Know-Nothings won seventy seats in the U.S. House of Representatives in 1854, but Congress did not enact their anti-immigrant agenda, and slavery soon replaced immigration as the major political issue of the day.

The United States began to enact qualitative restrictions on immigrants in the 1870s. In 1875, convicts and prostitutes were barred as immigrants. The Immigration Act of 1882 added paupers and "mental defectives" to the groups of undesirables who could not immigrate to the United States and for the first time barred immigration from a particular country: Chinese immigration was halted for ten years, a ban that was renewed until 1943. The importation of foreign workers coming with prearranged work contracts was banned in the 1880s.

By 1900 the major issue was how to slow the influx of immigrants from southern and eastern Europe. Restrictionists in the U.S. Congress argued that all adult newcomers should be literate in some language, and starting in 1897 Congress approved literacy tests (which were vetoed by three presidents, starting with Grover Cleveland). President Woodrow Wilson twice vetoed the literacy test, but his veto was overridden in 1917; after that date anyone over sixteen years of age who could not read in any language was refused entry.

As noted earlier, World War I virtually stopped transatlantic migration. When the influx resumed in the 1920s the numbers were large and the immigrants were still from the "wrong" part of Europe. The literacy test had not achieved the restrictionists' purpose of perpetuating the predominance of northern and western European ethnic groups in the United States. However, a study done for the U.S. House of Representatives concluded that immigrants from southern and eastern Europe had more "inborn socially inadequate qualities than northwestern Europeans" (quoted in Handlin 1952: 755), setting the stage for the use of national origin as the chief selection criterion when quantitative restrictions or quotas were introduced in the 1920s.

In 1921 Congress imposed numerical restrictions on immigration, and a 1924 immigration act set annual immigration at up to 150,000 individuals plus their accompanying spouses and children. The national origins formula prescribed that the maximum number of immigrants from any country in the Eastern Hemisphere would be "a number which bears the same ratio to 150,000 as the number of inhabitants in the United States in 1920 having that national origin bears to the number of white inhabitants of the United States" (U.S. House of Representatives 1952: 37).[13] This quota system gave preference to immigrants from northern and western Europe; during the 1930s, 1940s, and 1950s, over 80 percent of all immigrant visas went to people from countries in these regions.

Immigration fell sharply during the Great Depression despite the rise of totalitarianism in Europe. American immigration law made no special provision for refugees, and sponsorship requirements for immigration were applied in routine fashion, with the result that only an estimated 250,000 victims of Hitler's persecution of political opponents and Jews were admitted. Many of those who were turned away died in labor and death camps.

After World War II, President Harry Truman and congressional reformers sought to abolish the discriminatory national origins system that had been in place since 1924. They failed, and the McCarran-Walter Immigration and Nationality Act of 1952, passed over Truman's veto, left it intact. President John F. Kennedy took up where Truman left off, proposing thoroughgoing changes that would treat countries equally and give priority to close relatives of U.S. citizens and to people with special skills and abilities. In 1965 the Immigration and Nationality Act was finally

---

[13] Each country was guaranteed at least 100 visas, so that 154,477 visas were available annually.

amended to abolish national origins preferences and instead give priority for entry to close relatives of U.S. citizens and people with special skills and abilities.

Until the 1980s, U.S. immigration law could be described as a complex system that changed once a generation. The accelerating pace of global change late in the twentieth century affected migration patterns, and the U.S. Congress — the usual originator of changes in U.S. immigration law — responded with a flurry of legislation, including:

- The Refugee Act of 1980, under which the United States adopted the United Nations' definition of "refugee": a person with a well-founded fear of persecution because of race, religion, nationality, membership in a particular social group, or political opinion. The United States set a target of resettling 50,000 refugees a year.

- The Immigration Reform and Control Act of 1986, which aimed to reduce unauthorized immigration by imposing penalties on U.S. employers of illegal immigrants ("employer sanctions") and legalizing the status of some illegal immigrants ("amnesty").

- The Immigration Act of 1990, which raised the previous worldwide annual ceiling on immigration from 270,000 a year plus immediate relatives of U.S. citizens, to 675,000 a year including relatives plus refugees, and more than doubled the number of immigration visas granted for economic and employment reasons to 140,000 a year.

- The Anti-Terrorism and Effective Death Penalty Act of 1996, which allowed for the expedited removal of foreigners who arrive at airports without proper documents and seek asylum in the United States.

- The Personal Responsibility and Work Opportunity Reconciliation Act (PRWORA) of 1996, which made most legal immigrants arriving after August 22, 1996, ineligible for federal means-tested welfare benefits unless they are refugees, veterans of the U.S. armed services, or have worked at least ten years in the United States. When enacted, 44 percent of the projected savings were attributed to making immigrants ineligible for welfare benefits.

- The Illegal Immigration Reform and Immigrant Responsibility Act (IIRIRA) of 1996, which called for doubling of the number of U.S. Border Patrol agents but did not include an effective system to prevent unauthorized foreigners inside the United States from finding employment.

PRWORA and IIRIRA required U.S. sponsors of immigrants to prove with tax and other records that they had the resources — an income of at least 125 percent of the U.S. poverty line for the sponsor and the immigrants being sponsored taken together — to support the person(s) being sponsored for admission. Sponsors also had to sign a legally binding affidavit promising to support the immigrant. The poverty line for a family of four in 2002 was US$18,100, so a couple sponsoring two parents had to show an income of at least $22,625. If the immigrant parents arrived and then applied for and received welfare assistance, the government could sue the children to recover any benefits paid to their immigrant parents.

PRWORA has been called the third major change in U.S. immigration policy in the twentieth century. The first was the introduction of national origins quotas in the 1920s, the second was their elimination in 1965, and PRWORA, the third, set a sharp distinction between U.S. citizens and immigrants in terms of access to the social safety net. In each case, immigration legislation reflected the dominant political mood of the times — isolationism after World War I, the civil rights era of the 1960s, and the quest for a balanced budget in the 1990s.

Following the terrorism of September 2001, the U.S. Congress enacted more immigration legislation, including the Enhanced Border Security and Visa Entry Reform Act (EBSVERA) of 2001, which adds immigration inspectors and investigators, requires universities to keep better track of foreign students, and heightens scrutiny of visa applications from countries deemed sponsors of terrorism. Legislation approved in fall 2001 gave law enforcement agencies new powers to conduct surveillance, detain suspects, and attack money laundering. It is important to emphasize that, although laws enacted after September 11, 2001, restrict the rights of U.S. citizens and foreigners, immigration is not being curtailed. There is widespread support for some type of legalization program, and Congress enacted legislation that restores means-tested benefits such as food stamps to legal immigrants.

POLICY DEBATES AND RESEARCH

The immigration laws of 1996, and their softening in the following years, reflect an increasingly contentious debate over the effects that immigrants have on the U.S. economy and society, as well as uncertainty about how natives and immigrants will interact to shape twentieth-century America. Worries about immigration's short- and long-term impacts are not new. On the one hand, the United States celebrates its immigrant heritage, telling and retelling the story of renewal and rebirth brought about by newcomers. But on the other, Americans have worried since the days of the founding fathers about newcomers' economic, political, and cultural impacts.

Economic Impacts

Immigration raises the population, the labor force, and the economy. That is, countries that are open to immigrants tend to have more people, more workers, and larger economies. About 10 percent of U.S. residents were foreign-born in 2000, and 12 percent of U.S. workers were foreign-born. These foreign-born shares, while double 1970 levels, are much lower than the 15 percent foreign-born residents and 24 to 26 percent foreign-born workers in 1890 and 1910 (table 2.4).

The most recent comprehensive study of immigration and the economy was done in 1997; it focused on the United States. "The New Americans," a report sponsored by the National Research Council (NRC) in May 1997, concluded that immigrants added a net US$1 billion to $10 billion per year to the country's gross domestic product (GDP) in the mid-1990s (Smith and Edmonston 1997).[14] U.S. GDP was $8 trillion in 1996, and GDP increases by $200 billion a year when the rate of economic growth is 2.5 percent. An additional $10 billion due to immigration raises the economic growth rate from 2.5 to 2.6 percent, adding the equivalent of two weeks of "normal" U.S. economic growth. The estimate of $1 to $10 billion additional GDP due to immigration is based on a simple model of the economy. It assumes that the economic gains to "natives" — people in the United States before immigrants arrive — equal one-half of the share of U.S. GDP accruing to labor (70 percent) times the percent of the U.S. labor force that is foreign-born (10 percent) times the decline in U.S. residents' wages due to immigration (about 3 percent), or: $0.5 \times 0.7 \times 0.1 \times -0.03 = 0.001$, or one-tenth of one percent of the $8 trillion GDP, or $8 billion.

---

[14] The NRC report estimated that U.S. GDP was $200 billion a year larger because of immigration, but most of this $200 billion accrued to immigrants. The net addition to U.S. GDP for nonimmigrants was between $1 billion and $10 billion.

Table 2.4. Foreign-born Residents and Foreign-born Workers in the
United States, 1850–2000

Year	Foreign-born Population (percent)	Foreign-born Labor Force (percent)
1870	14	22
1880	13	20
1890	15	26
1900	14	23
1910	15	24
1920	13	21
1930	12	17
1940	9	12
1950	7	9
1960	5	6
1970	5	5
1980	6	7
1990	8	9
2000	10	12

Source: Kramer 2002.

When the NRC report was released, most commentators emphasized that immigration has a small and positive economic effect. However, they agreed that immigration does not make the United States rich and, further, that the important economic issues surrounding immigration are distributional: who gains and who loses as a result of immigration, and how much? The NRC estimate was based on the assumption that the U.S. economy had constant returns to scale (CRTS), which means that doubling the number of workers and the amount of capital in turn doubles output, and this assumption also means that immigration cannot raise the growth rate of wages for U.S.-born persons. Immigrants benefit the United States because the value of what they produce is more than the wages they are paid; that is, owners of capital and workers who are made more productive by the presence of immigrants gain because of the presence of immigrants.

U.S. workers who compete with immigrants may have lower wages and higher unemployment, but it has been very hard to find empirical evidence that the presence of immigrant workers reduces the wages or increases the unemployment rates of U.S. workers, such as African Americans or Hispanics, who are believed to be similar to the immigrants. Economic theory suggests that increasing the supply of labor should reduce wages or wage growth. The NRC report concluded that "immigration produces net economic gains for domestic residents," largely because it found that immigration lowered U.S. wages and prices and increased the efficiency of the U.S. economy (Smith and Edmonston 1997: S-3-4). In 1986 the President's Council of Economic Advisors reached a similar conclusion: "Although immigrant workers increase output, their addition to the supply of labor ... [causes] wage rates in the immediately affected market [to be] bid down.... Thus, native-born workers who compete with immigrants for jobs may experience reduced earnings or reduced employment" (1986: 221).

However, econometric studies that examine the interactions of immigrants and groups of workers with whom immigrants might compete in a single city, or that make comparisons between immigrants and other workers across city labor markets, find few effects of immigrants on native worker wages or employment. The starting point for such studies is the assumption that the more immigrants in a city's labor market, the lower should be wages for similar U.S. workers or the higher should be their unemployment rate. But in the 1980s few depression and displacement effects of immigrants could be found when the wages and unemployment rates of African Americans in cities with large numbers of immigrants, such as Los Angeles, were compared with their wages and unemployment rates in cities with smaller numbers of immigrants, such as Atlanta. In 1990 George Borjas summarized the literature as follows: "modern econometrics cannot detect a single shred of evidence that immigrants have a sizable adverse impact on the earnings and employment opportunities of natives in the United States" (Borjas 1990: 81). One of the most cited studies concluded that the 1980 influx of Cubans to Miami had no measurable negative effect on the wages and employment of local workers. During the four months of the Mariel boatlift, Miami's labor force increased by 7 percent, but there were no significant differences in wages and job opportunities for native-born workers in Miami and in other U.S. cities, which led to the conclusion that immigrants generated enough new economic activity to offset any negative impacts their presence might have on local workers (Card 1990).

As more data became available in the 1990s, researchers began to detect immigrants' impacts. Case studies found that immigrant worker networks dominated access to some jobs such that local workers did not learn about job vacancies, as occurred as labor contractors and other middlemen spread from farm to nonfarm labor markets (Mines and Martin 1984). But the major factor explaining why 1980s econometric studies failed to find the wage and unemployment effects predicted by economic theory is that U.S. labor markets are flexible and workers are mobile. U.S. workers who had to compete with immigrants moved away from cities with large numbers of immigrants, so that any wage depression or labor displacement impacts were quickly dispersed around the country. The 1990s literature reached the conclusion that immigrants can have the depression and displacement effects predicted by economic theory, but these effects may not be observed in econometric studies.

The other major economic issue debated in the 1990s was the public finance impact of immigrants. Do immigrants and their children pay more in taxes than they consume in tax-supported services? The National Research Council study concluded that they do; the average immigrant and his or her descendants in the United States in 1996 were expected to pay $80,000 more in taxes than they would consume in tax-supported services in 1996 dollars, based on a series of "heroic assumptions" about the future integration of the children of immigrants. The key assumption is that the children and grandchildren of immigrants will be average Americans in terms of education and income. Furthermore, the model assumed that the federal government will stabilize the ratio of debt to GDP, using a tax increase or a reduction in social spending, which increases the benefits of immigration because "the pain of higher taxes [or fewer services] is spread over a larger population" (Smith and Edmonston 1997: 338).

Studies by the National Research Council and most other public finance studies concluded that the major public finance impact of immigration was distributional: the federal government gains from immigration because the taxes paid by most immigrants exceed the cost of the federally provided services they consume, but the reverse occurs at the state and local government levels. This is important given that 75 percent of U.S. immigrants are in six states—California, New York, Texas, Florida, Illinois, and New Jersey. An examination of the state and local tax impacts of immigrants in California and New Jersey highlights the diversity of immigrants and their public finance impacts. In California, over half of immigrant households are headed by persons born in Mexico and elsewhere in Latin America, and these typically younger and less educated immigrants consumed significantly more in tax-supported public services than they paid in state and local taxes. The imbalance was especially notable for education, which is supported by about $6,000 per child per year in taxes. In 1996, households headed by Latin American immigrants in California consumed $5,000 more in state and local services, on average, than they paid in state and local taxes.

In New Jersey, by contrast, almost half of the immigrant household heads, who tended to be much older than immigrant household heads in California, were born in Europe or Canada, and the average immigrant household in New Jersey received $1,500 more in state- and local-funded services than it paid in state and local taxes in 1996. State and local "immigrant deficits" in California, New Jersey, and other states were offset by an additional $1,200 in state and local taxes paid by native-born households in California and $230 paid by native-born households in New Jersey. These studies suggest that if immigration is in the national interest but has very different federal versus state and local fiscal impacts, it makes sense to think about some form of migration adjustment assistance to head off anti-immigrant movements such as California's Proposition 187. However, except for federal reimbursement for some of the costs associated with unauthorized foreigners in state and local prisons, there has been very little federal migration adjustment assistance.

Naturalization

At its founding the United States established two important principles: all persons in the United States are to have full and equal rights, and all persons born in the United States are automatically citizens of the United States. The United States is still striving to undo the effects of the major exception to these rules — slavery — with antidiscrimination measures and preferences for minorities that cover immigrants as well as the descendants of slaves.

For most of the past two hundred years there have been few distinctions between citizens and noncitizens. Legal immigrants have been able to live where they please, seek jobs (except for government jobs) on an equal footing with U.S. citizens, and buy a house, land, or business without restriction. Both legal and unauthorized immigrants have basic constitutional rights, including the right of free speech and the free exercise of religion. Non-U.S. citizens can vote and hold office in U.S. labor unions as well as in private organizations such as churches, foundations, and fraternal groups.

To become a naturalized U.S. citizen, a legal immigrant must be at least eighteen years old, in the United States at least five years (three years for spouses of U.S. citizens), and pass a test of English and civics; typical questions are "Where is the White House located?" and "Name one right guaranteed by the First Amendment." Historically, fewer than half of immigrants to the United States have naturalized. For example, of the immigrants admitted in 1977, most became eligible to naturalize in 1982; by 1995 only about 46 percent were naturalized. Of those admitted in 1982, 42 percent were naturalized by 1995, including 71 percent of immigrants from Taiwan; 60 to 65 percent of immigrants from Vietnam, the Philippines, and the former Soviet Union; and 14 percent of Mexican immigrants. The probability that an immigrant will naturalize increases with age, education, income, and English language ability, as well as the probability that the immigrant will not return to his or her country of origin.

The number of naturalizations surged in the 1990s, surpassing 1 million in FY1996 (see table 2.5). This upsurge reflected the following:

- Approval of Proposition 187, widely regarded as a symbol of anti-immigrant attitudes, by 59 percent of California voters in November 1994.

- Rising levels of immigration and the fact that the 2.7 million unauthorized foreigners legalized in 1987–1988 became eligible to naturalize beginning in 1995.

- The Immigration and Naturalization Service's Green Card Replacement Program, launched in 1993, which required holders of legal immigrant visas to pay the INS $75 for a new counterfeit-resistant card; the cover letter noted that, for an additional $20, immigrants could become naturalized U.S. citizens.

- Enactment of the Personal Responsibility and Work Opportunity Reconciliation Act of 1996, which made some legal immigrants ineligible for federal welfare programs, creating an incentive to naturalize.

- Mexico's approval of dual nationality in 1996, which permits Mexican nationals who become citizens of another country to retain their Mexican passports and enjoy many of the rights of Mexican citizens in Mexico.

It may be decades before rising numbers of naturalized Latino and Asian voters significantly affect national election outcomes, although they already make a difference in local elections (DeSipio 1996). Latinos are still a small part of the electorate. For example, at the time of the November 1996 election in California, non-Hispanic whites were 53 percent of California's 32 million residents, but they cast 77 percent of the votes, down only slightly from 79 percent in 1992. Hispanics, in contrast, were

30 percent of the electorate but cast only 10 percent of the vote in 1992 and 11 percent in 1996. In determining whether and how a citizen will vote, income and education continue to be more reliable predictors than whether the voter is a native-born or a naturalized citizen.

Table 2.5. Foreigners Naturalized in the United States, by Fiscal Year

Fiscal Year	Persons Naturalized
1992	240,252
1993	314,681
1994	434,107
1995	488,088
1996	1,044,689
1997	598,225
1998	463,060
1999	839,944
2000 [a]	898,000
2001 [a]	613,000
Average	593,405

Source: U.S. Immigration and Naturalization Service.
[a] Data for 2000 and 2001 are preliminary.

Integration

During the nineteenth and early twentieth centuries, the leading metaphor for the incorporation of newcomers to the United States was a fusion of peoples in a "smelting pot" (Ralph Waldo Emerson), "cauldron" (Henry James), or "crucible" in which "immigrants were Americanized, liberated, and fused into a mixed race, English in neither nationality nor characteristics" (Turner 1920: 22–23). The hero of Israel Zangwill's popular play of 1908, "The Melting Pot," proclaimed: "Germans and Frenchmen, Irishmen and Englishmen, Jews and Russians — into the Crucible with you all! God is making the American!"

Reality was more complex. There is always a tension between the newcomer's desire to keep alive the culture and language of the community he or she left behind and the need and wish to adapt to new surroundings and another society. The balance between these competing forces changed over time, but there were three principles that guided what we now call integration:

- America was generally open to all kinds of immigrants. In the words of George Washington, "The bosom of America is open to receive not only the Opulent and respectable Stranger, but the oppressed and persecuted of all Nations and Religions; whom we shall welcome to a participation of all our rights and privileges."

- No ethnic group can establish a formally recognized political identity in the United States. American citizens act politically as individuals, not as members of officially defined ethnic groups.

- As to culture, laissez-faire was the rule; no group would be required to give up its character and distinctiveness, so that each immigrant group could keep some of its institutions for a time.

Two prescriptions for the accommodation of immigrants in American society were put forward over the twentieth century to reflect the ideal way for newcomers and established residents to interact: integration and pluralism. The integrationist (assimilationist) aims at eliminating ethnic boundaries, while the pluralist (multiculturalist) aims at maintaining them. For integrationists, American democracy is composed of equal individuals; for pluralists it is an equality of groups. The integrationist wants to know what the citizen believes; the pluralist wants to know who he is and where he came from.

Both positions are absurd when taken to their logical extremes, and neither has been realized in the United States. The melting pot ignores the persistence of memory and the importance of the home culture. An exclusive emphasis on integration tends to ignore the fact that ethnic affiliation persists among many Americans, even after the second and third generations, long after the language and knowledge of the "old country" have been lost.

The pluralists' insistence on group identity limits the freedom of individuals to choose their own loyalties. It assumes that ethnic boundaries remain fixed, and it overlooks the divisions within ethnic groups, allowing leaders to assert that they speak, for example, for all Mexican Americans or all Cuban Americans. This view also ignores the evidence that in an open, heterogeneous society like the United States, people work, make friends, and marry outside their ancestral communities.

The integration versus pluralism debate is played out in many venues. In college dorms, should students be placed with others of the same

race and/or ethnicity, or should they be mixed with students from un-
familiar backgrounds? Should schoolchildren be grouped for instruction
according to their home languages, or should they be brought together in
English language classes from the start? How much instruction in public
schools may be carried on in languages other than English? In the workplace, may employees converse among themselves in languages other
than English?

In 1984, historian John Higham proposed a system of "pluralistic
integration." Pluralistic integration asserts that there is a common U.S.
culture to which all individuals have access while also sustaining minorities' efforts to preserve and enhance their own integrity. In practice, this
means that public funds should not be used to promote differences between racial and ethnic groups: "No ethnic group under these terms may
have the support of the general community in strengthening its boundaries, [but] ethnic nuclei are respected as enduring centers of social action" (Higham 1988: 244).

At no time in American history has the process of accommodation
been easy or trouble-free. In the past, U.S. leaders openly expressed racial and ethnic hostility. In 1930, for example, President Herbert Hoover
rebuked Fiorella LaGuardia, congressman and former mayor of New
York, by saying that "the Italians are predominantly our murderers and
bootleggers," and he invited LaGuardia and those Italians who agreed
with him to "go back to where you belong" because, "like a lot of other
foreign spawn, you do not appreciate this country which supports you
and tolerates you" (quoted in Baltzell 1964: 30). No current public official
is likely to offer such advice to Gary Locke, the son of Chinese immigrants who was elected governor of Washington in 1996.

Integration can be regarded as a glass that is half-full or half-empty.
The "Changing Relations" study, a wide-ranging research project conducted in six cities, found that despite separation based on jobs and
housing and despite communication impeded by lack of a common language, newcomers and natives in a number of U.S. cities were cooperat-
ing to achieve local goals, such as obtaining a benefit from government
or improving their neighborhoods (Bach 1983). Yet the report is replete
with warning signals: separation rather than integration is the rule in
these cities,[15] and economic restructuring has created fears in many
communities that immigrants are a threat to natives.

---

[15] Thomas Archdeacon (1992: 548) notes that third-wave immigrants arrived in a
largely rural America: only 35 percent of the 75 million Americans in 1900 were in
urban areas. For this reason, there could be a great deal of homogeneity in the small

Numbers versus Rights

Immigration research tends to follow, rather than lead, immigration policy debates. The policy debate can be framed by extremes—with "drastically reduce or stop immigration" at one end and "eliminate border controls" at the other. The Federation for American Immigration Reform (FAIR) argues that: "With more than a million legal and illegal immigrants settling in the United States each year ... it is evident to most Americans that large-scale immigration is not serving the needs and interests of the country. FAIR advocates a temporary moratorium on all immigration except spouses and minor children of U.S. citizens and a limited number of refugees."[16] At the other extreme, the *Wall Street Journal* advocates a five-word amendment to the U.S. Constitution: "there shall be open borders."[17] High levels of immigration, this newspaper argues, mean more consumers and a larger economy with "new blood."

Daniel Tichenor (2000) notes that, despite the restrictionist elements of the 1996 legislation, the dominant tendency of U.S. immigration policy has been to be more liberal or admissionist over the past fifty years. Before PRWORA was enacted, there was a debate over numbers and rights: should the number of immigrants remain relatively high but their access to welfare benefits be restricted to help reduce federal budget deficits? Or should the number of immigrants be reduced, especially those most likely to need welfare benefits, and access to welfare benefits be the same for immigrants and U.S. citizens? The Commission on Immigration Reform recommended that U.S. immigration policy shift from full rights/more immigrants to full rights/fewer immigrants (see figure 2.2). The U.S. Congress, however, approved a move from full rights/more immigrants to more immigrants/fewer rights and then partway back toward its original stance.

The immigration and welfare debate of the 1990s suggests that U.S. policy may zigzag. Immigrants were between 10 and 15 percent of the recipients of benefits under most federally funded welfare programs in 1996. The major programs providing benefits to immigrants included Aid to Families with Dependent Children–Temporary Assistance to

---

communities where most Americans lived even though the country as a whole was becoming more diverse.

[16] FAIR's Purpose, at http://www.fairus.org/html/fair.htm.

[17] An editorial on July 3, 1986, first made this proposal, which was repeated in an editorial on July 3, 1990.

Needy Families (AFDC-TANF),[18] which provided cash assistance to poor families with children; Supplemental Security Income (SSI), which provided an average $400 a month to 800,0000 immigrants who were blind, disabled, and over age sixty-five; and the Food Stamp Program, the major food and assistance program for the poor, which served some 1 million legal immigrants.

The 1996 welfare reforms made most non-U.S. citizens ineligible for food stamps and the SSI cash assistance. For the first time, PRWORA gave states the option of making noncitizens ineligible for programs administered by states, including nonemergency Medicaid, TANF, and Title XX social services block grants. States could provide aid such as cash assistance to immigrants, but the federal government did not share the cost of such benefits.

Figure 2.2. Rights and Numbers of Immigrants in the United States

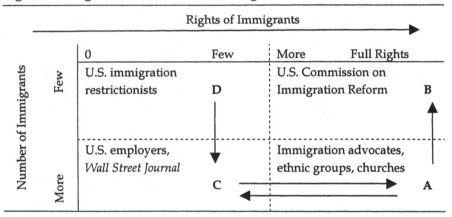

A. The United States in the mid-1990s was at "A," high and rising levels of immigration and full rights for immigrants. "A" was not stable.

B. The U.S. Commission on Immigration Reform recommended in 1995 moving toward "B," reducing immigration, preserving full rights to welfare, and so on.

C. The United States in 1996 moved toward "C," high numbers, few rights. "C" is not stable. Since 1997, about half of welfare cuts were restored.

---

[18] The Temporary Assistance to Needy Families program replaced Aid to Families with Dependent Children in 1997.

Since 1996 the eligibility of some legal immigrants to welfare benefits has been restored. The Balanced Budget Act of 1997 restored SSI and Medicaid eligibility for legal immigrants who were receiving these benefits on August 22, 1996. In 1998 immigrants who were elderly, disabled, or under age eighteen and were in the United States on August 22, 1996, had their eligibility for food stamps restored. In 2002, at the urging of President Bush, immigrants were to become eligible for food stamps after they had resided in the United States for five years; the House of Representatives voted 244 to 171 to restore food stamp benefits to immigrants in April 2002, over the objections of House leaders. In June 2002 the Senate approved giving states the option of providing Medicaid to legal immigrant children and pregnant women, with the federal government sharing the cost; the federal share is projected to total $2.2 billion over ten years. One reason why welfare benefits are being restored to immigrants is that as immigrants are spreading out to more states and more are naturalizing, more congressional representatives are hearing about immigrant concerns.

The United States is trying to manage migration between the extremes of "no borders" and "no immigrants." The result is a status quo that is criticized by both extremes and found by many others to be second best. Some 800,000 to 900,000 legal immigrants are admitted annually, and 300,000 to 400,000 unauthorized foreigners settle in the United States each year; many of the latter become legal immigrants. Despite a rapidly rising budget aimed at preventing unauthorized entries and employment, major U.S. industries are believed to have had workforces that ranged from 25 percent (meatpacking) to 50 percent (crop farms) unauthorized in 2001–2002.

Immigration research tends to follow the policy debate. During the 1980s the major policy issue was how to reduce unauthorized immigration, and the focus of much of the research was the interaction of unauthorized and legal workers in U.S. labor markets. Most studies found no significant negative impacts of unauthorized workers on U.S. workers, supporting a laissez-faire policy toward the unauthorized. During the early 1990s, when the costs of providing tax-supported services to unauthorized foreigners and their children dominated the headlines, many studies examined the taxes paid and the cost of benefits provided to immigrants, and they generally agreed that the federal government received more in taxes from immigrants than it spent to provide them services, but state and local governments often spent more on immigrants than they collected in taxes. During the late 1990s the focus shifted to the way in which immigrants and their children were integrating into the United States: were their incomes rising with time in the United States so that they were becoming Americans?

The economic impacts of immigrants and their children were addressed most comprehensively by the National Research Council in 1997, which concluded that "immigration produces net economic gains [of $1 to $10 billion] for domestic residents," largely because immigration lowers U.S. wages, and thus prices, and increases the efficiency of the U.S. economy (Smith and Edmonston 1997: S-3-4). The reactions illustrated the policy extremes. Pro-immigration groups highlighted the $10 billion figure, emphasizing the economic benefits of immigration. Restrictionist groups pointed out that, in an $10 trillion economy expanding by 3 percent a year, GDP "normally" rises by $250 billion a year, so that $10 billion represents just over one week of "normal" growth.

CONVERGENCE?

The United States is the world's major country of immigration, but Canada accepts more immigrants per capita than the United States and has a relatively generous social welfare system. Moreover, according to public opinion polls, Canadians are more satisfied with their immigration policy than are Americans. There are three key differences between the U.S. and Canadian immigration systems. First, a much higher percentage of immigrants to Canada are admitted under economic-employment criteria—over 50 percent in 2001, versus 10 percent in the United States—making it easier for the Canadian government to argue that immigrants benefit both themselves and Canadians.

Second, the Canadian immigration system is far more flexible, capable of making changes before they lead to a public backlash. For example, a film aired on Czech television in August 1997 implied that Czech Roma who reached Canada were almost sure to receive refugee status and welfare benefits. Some 1,000 Czechs flew to Canada in September 1997 (economy-class airline seats from Prague to Canada were sold out for months), and half of them applied for asylum. However, even before the independent Immigration and Refugee Board granted refugee status to the first Czech gypsies, the government imposed visa requirements on Czechs, which made it harder for Roma to get to Canada.

Third, Canadians are quick to note that their country borders the United States, not Mexico, so they have a natural buffer to absorb unauthorized migrants who may otherwise come to Canada. There are unauthorized foreigners in Canada, but estimates are that they are a far smaller percentage of residents than in the United States, where 9 million, or about 3 percent of the 281 million residents, were believed to be unauthorized in 2000.

Since the terrorism of September 11, 2001, there have been important steps toward convergence in asylum policies. About half of the foreigners applying for asylum in Canada each year enter that country from the United States, prompting a summer 2002 agreement that requires foreigners who pass through the United States intending to seek asylum in Canada to first apply for asylum in the United States. There have also been calls for a North American security perimeter, which in one version would have the United States and Canada following common visa issuance and inspection policies so that the U.S.-Canadian border remains open to trade and migration.

Convergence with Europe seems more distant. Most of the 500,000 to 600,000 foreigners who arrive in Europe each year join settled family members or seek asylum. In most European countries, newcomers are denied work permits but offered housing and food. The European system winds up channeling newcomers into welfare, not work—a sharp difference from the U.S. immigration system and one reason why Americans seem more inclined than Europeans to support immigration. Newcomers in Europe are more often seen as a drain on public finances than are newcomers in the United States.

WHITHER U.S. IMMIGRATION?

Immigration means change, often unanticipated change that is not apparent until it is far too late to reverse it. For some 250 years, residents have worried about the changes that immigration might bring and used fears of unanticipated change to argue for immigration restrictions. For example, Benjamin Franklin worried about German immigrants changing colonial Pennsylvania in the 1750s. Why, he asked, should "Pennsylvania, founded by the English, become a colony of aliens, who will shortly be so numerous as to Germanize us, instead of our Anglifying them?" (Degler 1950: 50). Franklin was right. The Germans did not become English; they became American. But the English did not remain English; they too became American, a change that Franklin did not foresee.

The world's major migration relationship is that between Mexico and the United States. There are about 109 million people alive today who were born in Mexico; by 2000, about 9 million of them had migrated to the United States, effectuating changes in Mexico as well as in the United States. Immigration and other policies in both countries will determine the eventual number of Mexico-born U.S. residents. If Mexico's economy grows as fast as hoped, the current 8:1 wage difference will be reduced, regional disparities within Mexico will narrow, and Mexico-U.S. migration should fall sharply by 2010. Reducing migration was one of the key side effects anticipated to result from the North American Free Trade Agreement, which went into effect on January 1, 1994. However, speeding up economic and job growth in Mexico required adjustments, including the displacement of workers in Mexican agriculture. Many rural Mexicans had ties to friends and relatives in the United States, and this intersection of factors prompted increased Mexico-U.S. migration in the 1990s.

This "migration hump" is at the center of U.S. immigration policy discussions today. During the 1990s the United States engaged in a costly expansion of border controls, adding agents, fences, and lights to deter the entry of unauthorized foreigners. Beginning in 1993 in El Paso, before NAFTA went into effect, the U.S. Border Patrol experimented with deterrence by massing agents on the border. Apprehensions, one measure of illegal immigration, dropped sharply; petty theft declined; and long-distance migrants who were headed elsewhere in the United States avoided entry at El Paso. The INS then implemented its new Southwest Border Strategy along the entire Mexico-U.S. border, directing most of its $1.2 billion 2001 budget and assigning 93 percent of its 9,096 agents to the Mexico-U.S. border. To "secure" this border, the INS believes it needs seven to ten more years, 3,200 to 5,500 more Border Patrol agents, and $450 million to $560 million in additional spending (U.S. GAO 2001: 7, 10).

Are INS border control efforts merely symbolic, aimed at public opinion; or are they real attempts to deter and reduce unauthorized Mexico-U.S. migration? The INS predicted that apprehensions would first rise and then fall as its Southwest Border Strategy was implemented and, further, that migrants would attempt entries at points away from urban areas. The INS developed a "border control effectiveness ratio," an estimate of the number of migrants apprehended or turned back compared to the total number who attempted entry along a particular section of the border—what the INS calls a corridor. The INS reported that between October 2000 and March 2001, effectiveness ratios ranged from 37 percent in the corridor west of Tucson to 92 percent in the corridor west of El Centro (U.S. GAO 2001: 15).

Before September 11, 2001, the U.S. immigration policy discussion seemed to be heading toward legalizing many of the unauthorized Mexicans in the United States and opening new channels for Mexicans to work in the country legally. Several factors motivated this move toward a more liberal migration policy: Mexicans and other unauthorized migrants were finding U.S. jobs during a time of very low unemployment; one migrant a day, on average, was dying in the desert trying to enter the United States; and there was a political assessment that to win reelection in 2004, President Bush would have to raise his share of the Hispanic vote from the 35 percent he received in 2000. These considerations, combined with the personal bonds between Spanish-speaking Bush and President Vicente Fox, were expected to lead to a U.S. immigration reform marked by generosity to unauthorized Mexicans and other foreigners in the United States.[19]

The September 11 terrorism halted the momentum toward a new legalization program. Instead, the U.S. government launched a major effort to locate, detain, and prosecute or deport unauthorized foreigners, especially those from Middle Eastern countries. Discussions of what to do about immigration are now shaped by concern about terrorism as well as three other factors: the economic recession that began in fall 2001 with unemployment rising from 4 to 6 percent within four months, a fall in border apprehensions from 1.6 million in FY2001 to 1.2 million in FY2002,[20] and a report by Mexico's National Population Council, Ministry of Labor, and a border studies institute that concluded: "Migration between Mexico and the United States is a permanent, structural phenomenon. It is built on real factors, ranging from geography, economic inequality and integration, and the intense relationship between the two countries, that make it inevitable" (Secretaría del Trabajo 2001).[21]

---

[19] In September 2001 President Fox said: "The time has come to give migrants and their communities their proper place in the history of our bilateral relations.... [W]e must, and we can, reach an agreement on migration before the end of this very year ... [2001, so that] there are no Mexicans who have not entered [the United States] legally, and that those Mexicans who come into the country do so with proper documents" (*Migration News* 2001).

[20] Hanson, Robertson, and Spilimbergo (1999) examined apprehension and wage data in Mexico-U.S. border areas in the 1990s and concluded that the Border Patrol was not significantly reducing illegal immigration and that "illegal immigration from Mexico has a minimal impact on wages in U.S. border areas."

[21] The report concluded that 400,000 Mexicans a year would migrate to the United States through 2030 if Mexican economic growth averaged 5 percent a year, and that 500,000 Mexicans a year would migrate if economic growth averaged 1.5 percent a year. (Legal immigration has been 125,000 to 150,000 a year.)

Recession, falling apprehensions which allow the Border Patrol to assert that it has turned the enforcement corner, and no end in sight to Mexico-U.S. migration cloud the picture for the future of Mexico-U.S. migration, as well as immigration more generally. Before September 11, legal and unauthorized immigrants were generally considered to be hardworking newcomers seeking the American dream. After September 11, it was recognized that some foreigners were intent on killing Americans and that they should be kept out of the United States. This new concern over terrorism raised two options: remain open to immigration and take steps to screen foreigners far more carefully, or try to limit immigration and thus limit the entry of terrorists. The consensus that the United States is a nation of immigrants means that the United States has kept the immigration doors open and stepped up screening, rather than close the doors to immigrants.

References

Alvarez, Lizette. 2001. "Census Director Marvels at the New Portrait of America," *New York Times*, January 1.

Archdeacon, Thomas. 1992. "Reflections on Immigration to Europe in Light of U.S. Immigration History," *International Migration Review* 26, no. 2 (Summer): 525–48.

Bach, Robert L. 1993. "Changing Relations: Newcomers and Established Residents in U.S. Communities." Report to the Ford Foundation by the National Board of the Changing Relations Project. New York: Ford Foundation.

Baltzell, E. Digby. 1964. *The Protestant Establishment: Aristocracy and Caste in America*. New York: Vintage Books.

Borjas, George. 1990. *Friends or Strangers: The Impact of Immigrants on the U.S. Economy*. New York: Basic Books.

Briggs, Vernon J. 1992. *Mass Immigration and the National Interest*. Armonk, N.Y.: M.E. Sharpe.

Card, David E. 1990. "The Impact of the Mariel Boatlift on the Miami Labor Market," *Industrial and Labor Relations Review* 43, no. 2 (January): 245–57.

Cornelius, Wayne A. 2001. "Death at the Border: Efficacy and Unintended Consequences of U.S. Immigration Control Policy," *Population and Development Review* 27, no. 4 (December): 661–85.

Degler, Carl N. 1970. *Out of Our Past: The Forces That Shaped Modern America*. 2d ed. New York: Harper and Row.

DeSipio, Louis. 1996. *Counting on the Latino Vote: Latinos as a New Electorate*. Charlottesville: University of Virginia Press.

Handlin, Oscar. 1952. "Memorandum Concerning the Origins of the National Origin Quota System." Hearings Before the President's Commission on Immigration and Naturalization, 82nd Congress, 2nd session. Washington, D.C.: U.S. Government Printing Office.

Hanson, Gordon H., Raymond Robertson, and Antonio Spilimbergo. 1999. "Does Border Enforcement Protect U.S. Workers from Illegal Immigration?" Mimeo.

Higham, John. 1988. *Strangers in the Land: Patterns of American Nativism, 1860–1925.* 2d ed. New Brunswick, N.J.: Rutgers University Press.

Kramer, Roger. 2002. "Developments in International Migration to the United States: 2002: A Midyear Report." Mimeo.

Lebergott, Stanley. 1986. *The Americans: An Economic Record.* New York: Norton.

Martin, Philip L. 1994. "Good Intentions Gone Awry: IRCA and U.S. Agriculture," *Annals of the Academy of Political and Social Science* 534 (July): 44–57.

Martin, Philip L., and Elizabeth Midgley. 1999. "Immigration to the United States." Washington D.C.: Population Reference Bureau Report, vol. 54, no. 2 (June). At http://www.prb.org.

McDonnell, Patrick J. 2002. "Wave of U.S. Immigration Likely to Survive Sept. 11," *Los Angeles Times*, January 10.

Migration News. 2001. "Fox Visits Bush," vol. 8, no. 10 (October). At http://migration.ucdavis.edu.

Mines, Richard, and Philip L. Martin. 1984. "Immigrant Workers and the California Citrus Industry," *Industrial Relations* 23, no. 1 (January): 139–49.

President's Council of Economic Advisors. 1986. *The Economic Effects of Immigration.* Washington, D.C.: Council of Economic Advisors.

Secretaría del Trabajo y Previsión Social, Consejo Nacional de Población, and Colegio de la Frontera Norte. 2001. *Encuesta sobre migración en la frontera norte de México.* Mexico City: Secretaría del Trabajo.

Smith, James P., and Barry Edmonston, eds. 1997. *The New Americans: Economic, Demographic, and Fiscal Effects of Immigration.* Washington, D.C.: National Academy Press.

Tichenor, Daniel J. 2000. "Voters, Clients, and the Policy Process: Two Faces of Expansive Immigration Politics in America." Mimeo.

Turner, Frederick Jackson. 1920. *The Frontier in American History.* New York: Henry Holt.

U.S. Census Bureau. 1991. *Census of Population and Housing, 1990.* Washington, D.C.: U.S. Census Bureau.

_____. 2001. *Census of Population and Housing, 2000.* Washington, D.C.: U.S. Census Bureau.

_____. n.d. "National Population Projections for 2025." At http://www.census.gov/population/www/projections/natsum-T5.html.

U.S. GAO (U.S. General Accounting Office). 2001. "INS' Southwest Border Strategy: Resource and Impact Issues Remain after Seven Years." GAO-01-842. Washington, D.C.: U.S. GAO, August 2.

U.S. House of Representatives. 1952. Committee on the Judiciary, House Report 1365, 82nd Congress, 2nd Session, February 14.

Commentary

Gordon H. Hanson

There is a sense among many parties that current U.S. immigration policies need fixing. High levels of illegal immigration, government inability to monitor admitted immigrants, and a generalized ineptitude in the Immigration and Naturalization Service (INS) are just a few of the problems commonly cited. While there may be widespread agreement that U.S. policy is broken, there is little agreement about what should be done to fix it. I focus my comments on some ideas for reforming U.S. immigration policy and, as an organizing device, identify three principles to guide policy reform. These principles are far from a comprehensive proposal, but they may help identify elements of a new policy on which the different sides in the immigration debate might be able to agree.

- Holding the level of immigration constant, increasing the share of immigrants who are legal would make (nearly) everyone better off.

Converting an illegal immigrant to a legal immigrant has direct and indirect effects on her behavior. Becoming legal raises an individual's incentive to acquire skills, start a small business, and make investments in and attachments to the community. Legalization also raises the individual's contribution to local, state, and federal taxes (though illegal immigrants do pay many taxes). Although legalization also increases access to public services and government benefit programs, it does not do so by as much as many might think. Illegal immigrants already have access to emergency medical care and the right to send their children to public school. Legalization, then, really only gives immigrants greater access to cash and in-kind government assistance, access that is less valuable since 1996, when the U.S. Congress excluded immigrants from many forms of government assistance. Legalization's net impact on public finances, then, is likely to be small, and perhaps positive when we factor in the increased investment incentives associated with becoming legal.

Who, then, should favor legalization (again, holding the total level of immigration constant)? Just about everyone. Illegal immigrants obviously benefit from legalization. U.S. employers would enjoy a reduction in labor turnover and in legal risk associated with hiring illegal immigrants. Employers would have to pay legal immigrants higher wages, but it is plausible that reduced labor turnover and risk would more than compensate for extra labor costs. More surprisingly, native U.S. taxpayers may also benefit. Any net fiscal cost from legalization is likely to be small (given that legalization means immigrants receive more government benefits but also pay more taxes) and borne mainly in the short run. Stronger incentives for immigrants to acquire skills and start businesses would increase their incomes over time and lessen their dependence on government benefits. And greater community stability may also lower government benefits demanded by immigrant households.

If legalization is such a good thing, why does it not enjoy more political support? One explanation is that many people fear that legalizing immigrants today will raise the incentive for greater illegal immigration tomorrow. With the weak U.S. record of enforcing borders against illegal immigration, legalization of existing illegal immigrants may be seen as an invitation for new illegal immigrants. This concern suggests that any policy that legalizes illegal aliens probably will not be terribly meaningful (or gather much support) without changes in U.S. enforcement against illegal immigration. This brings us to the second principle.

- Employer monitoring is a more efficient means to impede illegal immigration than is enforcement of the U.S. border.

In the 1990s the United States launched an experiment in combating illegal immigration. The government dramatically increased the enforcement budget of the INS and directed that the vast majority of these extra expenditures be devoted to policing the U.S.-Mexico border. There is abundant evidence that this experiment has been a failure. Despite raising the INS's enforcement budget by four times in real terms between 1985 and 2000, net illegal immigration in the United States continued at 300,000 to 400,000 individuals per year throughout the 1990s (Boeri,

Hanson, and McCormick 2002). Without a virtual militarization of the border, it seems unlikely that the United States will curtail future illegal immigration through border enforcement alone. Beyond the fiscal cost of this policy, it has exacted a large toll in human suffering by encouraging migrants to cross the border in perilous conditions (Cornelius 2000).

To date, the INS has not made a serious attempt to monitor U.S. employers, even though such monitoring is mandated by U.S. law. During the 1990s, enforcement against illegal immigration in the U.S. interior was extremely lax. Of the 1.5 million apprehensions of illegal aliens that the Border Patrol made annually in the late 1990s, fewer than 10,000 per year occurred at U.S. farms or other worksites. During the decade, the INS investigated between 5,000 and 8,000 U.S. employers per year for possible violations of U.S. laws against hiring illegal aliens. The agency fined few employers. In no year were more than twenty employers fined in excess of $20,000, and only one fine collected over the entire period exceeded $185,000 (Boeri, Hanson, and McCormick 2002).

Why might employer monitoring be superior to border enforcement in combating illegal immigration? In a given year a single INS agent can inspect dozens of firms employing thousands or tens of thousands of workers, but a single agent can apprehend relatively few illegal immigrants at the border (and even fewer illegal aliens in the country as a result of overstaying temporary entry visas). By establishing large fines for hiring illegal immigrants and by conducting random, unannounced inspections of U.S. worksites, the INS (or some other agency) could curtail the demand for illegal labor. A reduction in demand for illegal labor would in principle lead to a reduction in illegal entry, since the reduction in wages and/or loss in jobs would potentially dissuade many prospective migrants from attempting to cross the border.

Shifting from border enforcement toward employer monitoring is appealing in theory, but it faces a serious obstacle in intense and highly organized political opposition by U.S. employers. Employers themselves, however, would be hard pressed to disagree that employer monitoring is more efficient than border enforcement.

• Reducing the level of immigration or changing the composition of immigrants is likely to have smaller effects on the U.S. economy than many might think.

Perhaps the most difficult issues involved in reform of U.S. immigration policy are changing the level of immigration and shifting the composition of immigrants. There appear to be no magic solutions for resolving the current political impasse. There are, however, some observations worth making that might help tone down the debate.

In a world where the U.S. economy is linked to many other economies through international trade and capital inflows and outflows, changing the level of immigration does not have the far-reaching consequences that many might suppose. If the United States were to dramatically reduce the level of immigration, there would likely be a corresponding change in U.S. trade and investment patterns that would undo many of the effects of this change in immigration policy.

The logic behind this argument is perhaps best developed by example. Since the 1970s California has received large inflows of immigrants from Mexico, Central America, and Southeast Asia who happen to have low education levels compared to U.S. native workers. These immigrants have found jobs in labor-intensive activities, including apparel production, food processing, and harvesting fruits and vegetables. Strikingly, in the 1980s and 1990s California was one of the few U.S. states with expanding apparel employment (as most states were losing jobs overseas). One consequence of this inflow of low-skilled foreign workers has been that workers in California who were already here have faced greater competition for jobs and perhaps suffered a fall in wages.

What would have happened had these low-skilled immigrants not come to California? Rather than producing apparel, packaged food, and fruits and vegetables for itself, California would have imported these items from elsewhere in the United States and from other countries, including places like Mexico, Guatemala, and Vietnam. Would low-wage workers in California have been better off? Not necessarily. The import of these goods would still have kept their prices low in the California market. Relatively low prices for these goods, which are intensive in the use of less-skilled labor, would mean relatively low demand for the labor that produces these goods. Thus, without immigration, low-wage labor in California would still have faced competition from labor in Mexico, Central America, and Southeast Asia. It is just that it would have occurred through the import of goods rather than through the import of workers.

The key insight here is that changing trade and investment flows would be likely to undo many of the effects of changing immigration levels or changing the composition of immigrants. For reasons that probably are not worth going into, trade and investment flows would be unlikely to undo all of the effects of immigration reform. It would just mitigate them. There is one obvious and important difference between importing goods and importing workers. Immigration creates a pool of workers who have a claim on U.S. public services (and who have the obligation to pay U.S. taxes). These claims could potentially adversely affect U.S. public finances. These public finance effects may explain, in part, the opposition to immigration in parts of California.

References

Boeri, Tito, Gordon H. Hanson, and Barry McCormick. 2002. *Immigration Policy and the Welfare State*. Oxford: Oxford University Press.

Cornelius, Wayne A. 2000. "Death at the Border: The Efficacy and 'Unintended' Consequences of U.S. Immigration Control Policy, 1993–2000." Working Paper No. 27. La Jolla: Center for Comparative Immigration Studies, University of California, San Diego.

Commentary

Daniel J. Tichenor

A principal aim of this volume is to analyze what its editors describe as a marked gap between the stated goals and the actual outcomes of national immigration policy. Philip Martin's essay offers an impressive overview of U.S. immigration sources, trends, and official efforts to influence both. It does not, however, systematically address the "gap" hypothesis. I would like briefly to illuminate three significant variables that give form and substance to immigration policy gaps: the political feedbacks produced by earlier policies, the concentration or fragmentation of power among formal institutions of government, and the relative capacities of national governments to reshape migratory patterns even when there is broad official agreement on policy ends. Although I focus on how these variables affect U.S. efforts to control legal immigration, refugee admissions, and undocumented inflows, their theoretical relevance extends beyond the particular case at hand to other national contexts. Such an approach requires immigration scholars to pay closer attention to how public policies, political processes, and government structures interact over time.

Although routinely treated by social scientists as dependent variables, public policies in fact are capable of reshaping the very political order that produces them (Schattschneider 1935; Skocpol 1992; Pierson 1993). Once established, government policies often generate well-organized client groups, mass constituencies, and other positive feedbacks that reinforce early programmatic commitments. Consider the development of U.S. legal immigration policy since the 1960s. In 1965, at the heyday of Lyndon Johnson's Great Society, national policy makers dismantled racist national origins quotas in favor of a new legal immigrant admissions system that gave priority to immigrants with close relatives in the United States, with additional visas reserved for refugees and individuals with needed job skills. For White House officials and congressional reformers, the new admissions system was designed to advance Cold War foreign policy goals, a liberal civil rights agenda, and future economic growth. According to historians, they did not intend to dramatically expand the volume or composition of legal inflows (Reimers 1992). Of course, by affording visas to unprecedented numbers of Asian and Latin American newcomers in subsequent years, the new system did just that.

During the 1970s and 1980s, most ordinary U.S. citizens told pollsters of their apprehensions concerning mass Third World immigration and endorsed new official restrictions on legal admissions. By contrast, the beneficial outcomes of the new system gave employer groups, ethnic lobbies, and humanitarian organizations good reason to guard broad immigration opportunities. A clear divide now emerged between restrictive popular preferences and expansive government policies. Ultimately, "the widespread but poorly articulated opposition of the general public" was frustrated by officials and well-organized groups with strong interests in sustaining robust admissions (Freeman 1995). National business, ethnic, and civil rights organizations later successfully mobilized on behalf of the Immigration Act of 1990, which increased immigration levels by 40 percent and affirmed a visa preference system expected to facilitate record inflows from Asia, Latin America, and the Caribbean. As this example indicates, the logic of positive feedbacks suggests that the gap between policy goals and outputs may close over time, as expansive outcomes yield political forces supporting increasingly expansive policy designs.

When robust legal admissions were threatened in the mid-1990s, restrictionist initiatives were derailed by the familiar left-right coalition of employer groups, ethnic and human rights organizations, free market conservatives, and rights-oriented liberals. But new limitations on noncitizen social and civil rights were enacted in these years. In response to the "new restrictionism," record numbers of immigrants sought citizenship and access to the voting booth. Concentrated in key electoral states, these new immigrant voting blocs provided politicians with a strong incentive to endorse pro-immigration policies. During the 2000 election, candidates of both major parties openly courted these new voters by embracing expansive immigration policies and denouncing nativist traditions. Yet Philip Martin's essay appropriately raises pivotal questions about the future of U.S. immigration after September 11. Most notably, will U.S. immigration wither in the face of both elite and public alarm regarding foreign terrorist threats? If the past century of U.S. history is any indication, national security crises and wartimes have rarely been hospitable to robust immigrant admissions or rights. Still, two important political feedbacks—one rooted in the emergence of a formidable pro-immigration coalition in Washington and the other in the perceived electoral clout of new immigrant voting blocs—continue to fortify expansive policies. If one wanted to predict a major retrenchment of U.S. immigration policy, the breakdown of these positive feedbacks would be a crucial harbinger of the nation closing its doors. As I have argued, immigrant policies are more than the dependent outputs of political forces. Once adopted, they can produce political feedbacks that reinforce initial choices and that may close the gap between official intentions and outcomes (Tichenor 2002).

The distribution of power among governmental institutions of industrialized democracies also can play a crucial role in shaping immigration policy gaps. The United States, for example, affords a paradigmatic case of institutional fragmentation in which "ambition is made to counteract ambition" through a system of checks and balances, the separation of powers, federalism, and other architectural mechanisms. Because there are many authoritative and consequential policy voices in fragmented systems, government actions regulating immigration may exemplify rival policy goals. During the post–World War II decades, for instance, independent presidential orders granting generous refugee relief contradicted by design the restrictive quota laws embraced by most members of Congress. In the 1980s the Reagan and Bush administrations ignored the universal asylum language of the Refugee Act of 1980 by pursuing a consistent policy of rejecting Salvadoran asylum applicants (lest the client regime in El Salvador come under fire for human rights abuses). Fragmented systems also encourage substantial conflict and adaptation in the *enforcement* of policy decisions, yielding inevitable gaps between original designs and eventual outcomes. Consider implementation of the Immigration Reform and Control Act of 1986 (IRCA). Bureaucratic interpretations of its amnesty provisions were successfully challenged in the courts. Enforcement of its employer sanctions provisions were weakened through effective lobbying by business groups which made the most of a permeable political system. IRCA's antidiscrimination protections for aliens were simply ignored by the Reagan White House. Competing policymaking structures can spawn contradictory policy goals, and they can produce an implementation process that regularly distances policy outcomes from initial designs.

Of course, there are times when even fragmented governments speak with broad agreement on immigration policy. In these circumstances, gaps between policy aims and outcomes may nevertheless occur because of limited state capacities to control international migration. After years of what Martin calls the U.S. government's "benign neglect" of illegal immigration, today's war on terrorism has spurred broad popular and official support for better controlling porous borders and for cracking down on visa violators and unlawful entrants residing in the country. However, the capability of the United States to address these security risks is likely to be restrained in some fashion by enduring liberal-democratic hostilities toward bureaucratic intrusions and by a civil rights culture that views mass deportation campaigns like Operation Wetback of 1954 legally, politically, and morally untenable. Moreover, highly resourceful and tenacious undocumented aliens may defy even the strongest state controls due to powerful economic incentives, family connections, and other forces. The international mobility of workers and tourists today makes the task all the more daunting for industrialized democracies.

References

Freeman, Gary. 1995. "Modes of Immigration Politics in Liberal Democratic States," *International Migration Review* 29, no. 4 (Winter): 881–902.

Pierson, Paul. 1993. "When Effect Becomes Cause: 'Policy Feedback' and Political Change," *World Politics* 2: 595–628.

Reimers, David. 1992. *Still the Golden Door*. New York: Columbia University Press.

Schattschneider, E.E. 1935. *Politics, Pressures, and the Tariff*. New York: Prentice Hall.

Skocpol, Theda. 1992. *Protecting Soldiers and Mothers*. Cambridge, Mass.: Harvard University Press.

Tichenor, Daniel. 2002. *Dividing Lines*. Princeton, N.J.: Princeton University Press.

3

Canada: Immigration and Nation-Building in the Transition to a Knowledge Economy

Jeffrey G. Reitz

Many immigration issues in Canada, a "nation of immigrants," parallel their counterparts in the United States. Canada's nondiscriminatory policy admits permanent immigrants in three categories — economic, family reunification, and refugees. It allows them virtually immediate access to all major institutions of society and an easy pathway to full citizenship. Canadians, like Americans, debate whether such immigration helps or hurts the economy, whether it takes jobs from native-born workers or depletes the public treasury, and if visa access abuses exist. Canadians also debate increased cultural and racial diversity and potentials for increased inequality and conflict. They are concerned about how immigration affects relations among Canada's established cultural groups — albeit linguistic groups rather than racial groups as in the United States. And most recently, concerns have arisen about border security and society's vulnerability to terrorism.

Despite these similarities, certain features of Canadian immigration policy, and immigration's impact on the country, appear significantly

The author would like to thank Raymond Breton and Takeyuki Tsuda for very helpful comments on an earlier draft of this essay.

different from what exists in the United States. Immigration policy in Canada plays a more prominent place in overall national development strategy, and the flow of immigrants into Canada relative to the existing population is substantially larger. One could say that Canada pursues immigration as part of its continuing project of nation-building. Further, the overall impact of immigration appears more positive, at least in the court of public opinion and the arena of national politics. A relatively large proportion of Canadians approve of the country's (relatively high) immigration levels; and although immigration and related issues are popular topics for public discussion, they have not emerged as particularly divisive issues in national politics.

This essay examines the distinctiveness of Canadian immigration and the reasons for this distinctiveness. It suggests that the comparative success of Canadian immigration policy, at least over recent decades, reflects both the external environment of the society and its distinctive economic, cultural, and institutional structures.[1] Canada's high levels of immigration seem to be favored by its development strategy as a satellite nation in North America and the relatively low Canadian fertility rates that today increase immigration's demographic importance. Immigrant selection policies of successive Canadian governments have emphasized economic criteria, and the capacity to manage these policies successfully—or at least the perception of doing so—has been enhanced partly by the country's geographic isolation from all countries other than the United States and partly by the apparent "fit" between these policies and Canadian institutions. Such institutions include postsecondary education, labor market structures, and social services, which generally have differed from those in the United States by virtue of their greater emphasis on collective welfare as opposed to American individualism. These processes occur in the context of Canada's dual linguistic structure, official multiculturalism, and the new racial diversity created by immigration. Hence immigration's success in Canada is affected by constraints and opportunities created by these circumstances and by government's effectiveness in managing immigration within the social context.

This analysis implies that, for Canada, the gap between policy goals and policy outcomes has been relatively small, but it also carries implications for potential problems and difficulties. The various institutional determinants of Canadian immigration are evolving in ways that reflect both convergence and differentiation. This analysis will suggest that the *pattern* of these changes—more than either convergence or differentiation

---

[1] This analysis is based on a theoretical framework presented in Reitz 1998: chaps. 1, 3.

in itself—is creating significant actual and potential difficulties for the continued success of Canadian immigration over time. If circumstances such as a nation-building development strategy and low fertility suggest that large numbers of immigrants will be needed on a continuing basis, will other conditions that have produced public acceptance of immigration in the past prevail in the future? The answer is by no means clear. The earnings of newly arrived immigrants have been in decline for a substantial period, despite sustained efforts to address questions of appropriate selection. Although reasons for this decline are not fully known, analysis suggests the importance of basic institutional changes, such as Canada's transition to a "knowledge economy" that creates new challenges for highly skilled immigrants.

A long-term decline in immigrant economic performance threatens to strain the economy and society and threatens traditional perceptions of the economic benefits of immigration. This looming policy gap raises significant issues and dilemmas that are likely to become more salient and produce important policy changes in the future. Policy innovations to slow or reverse the decline are being advanced, but if these prove unsuccessful, Canada may need to consider altering its basic immigration strategy, making it more similar to countries such as the United States or Australia. Other issues may also affect policy change. Border controls have been a continuing concern; the 2001 terrorist attacks on New York and Washington, D.C., have heightened these concerns and affected Canada. The relative importance of such threats to successful immigration control must be assessed in terms of the factors that appear to have fostered past success.

The chapter begins by describing Canadian immigration policy and its contextual and institutional underpinnings. Although the policy lacks an explicit doctrinal justification, it appears to be guided by the theme of nation-building and employs a managerial approach to support a perception that it serves national development interests. The chapter then examines the political reception of the immigration policy, including the positions of political parties and interest groups. The analysis next turns to immigrants' economic role and impact—perceptions of which are key to the policy's success—and to the influence of Canada's distinctive social and cultural policies in incorporating immigrants. The chapter concludes with a discussion of how institutional trends are shaping the future of Canadian immigration, using illustrations from debate over the new Immigration and Refugee Protection Act 2001 (Bill C-11).

CANADIAN IMMIGRATION POLICY: A CONTINUING PROJECT OF NATION-BUILDING

From confederation in 1867 until today, nation-building has been a theme underlying Canadian immigration. Historically, immigration to Canada was sought to expand the population, boost the economy, and develop society (Reimers and Troper 1992; Green 1995). This is still true. One of the few explicit policy statements elaborating this theme was by Prime Minister W.L. Mackenzie King in 1947 when he announced Canada's resumption of a major immigration program that had been interrupted by economic depression and war. He advocated immigration "with the definite objective ... of enlarging the population of the country," citing "the danger that lies in a small population attempting to hold so great a heritage as ours" (Canada 1974: 204). This renewal of immigration was signaled by the Immigration Act of 1952. Over time, specifics of immigration policy have evolved with the Canadian economy, and efforts to harmonize immigration with the social and cultural fabric have changed along with social issues.

Major waves of immigration to Canada corresponded to economic needs (Green and Green 1996). In the nineteenth and early twentieth centuries, agricultural development was a key to exploiting Canadian economic opportunities, so immigrants were recruited primarily to settle vast territories in the West. In the 1880s, construction of the Canadian Pacific Railway produced a significant wave of immigration. The 1900s began with another economic high point, renewed agricultural development, and thirty years of substantial immigration. Following World War II, Canada resumed an expansionist immigration policy that continues today.

Two basic shifts in the specific economic objectives of Canadian immigration reflect the changing requirements of the Canadian economy over time. First, a shift from rural to urban development accompanied the broader process of industrialization. When large-scale immigration resumed in the postwar period, it consisted largely of unskilled laborers required for urban industrial employment. Up to the 1960s, much immigration to Canada's cities was by persons almost completely lacking in formal educational qualifications. These, like earlier immigrants destined for farmwork, entered the Canadian economic hierarchy at its lower levels and progressed from this starting point.

The second shift from low-skill to high-skill immigration accompanied the transition from an industrial to a postindustrial economy. Canada's points-based system for selecting so-called independent or economic immigrants, introduced in 1967 under the Immigration Act of 1952, was designed to ensure maximum employability in an economy in which skilled labor was an emerging priority. Since then, immigration selection has become a form of human resource management, upgraded and fine-tuned, with the average educational level of immigrants exceeding that of the general population.

Throughout its history, Canadian immigration policy has reflected what might be called a managerial stance. The significance of immigration for national development and the need to ensure a fit between immigration and the country's economic and social system have led to the adoption of a rather conservative management approach, particularly in the postwar period. This can be seen in the bureaucratic apparatus of immigration policy. From its earlier days as part of a Department of Manpower and Immigration, policy development today is a collaboration between Citizenship and Immigration Canada (CIC) and Human Resources Development Canada (HRDC). This includes input from in-house research units for which economic impacts and analyses are the major theme.

Management of Canadian immigration has focused on developing three policy components: the size of the program and numbers of immigrants, the evolution of "economic" immigration, and the reduction of noneconomic immigration and overall program costs.

Managing Numbers of Immigrants and Their Demographic Impact

Since World War II, the demographic impact of immigration in Canada has been greater than in the United States and most other countries of immigration. For most of the 1990s, Canada admitted between 200,000 and 250,000 immigrants per year, with a maximum of just over 250,000 in 2001 (see figure 3.1). Current government policy is to raise this to 1 percent of population per year, or about 300,000. Even at 0.7 to 0.8 percent of the population, these numbers represent about three times the per capita rate for immigration in the United States.[2] The 1996 Canadian census showed that about 17 percent of the population was foreign-born.

---

[2] Official U.S. immigration figures for most recent years varied around 700,000 to 800,000, or about 0.25 percent of population per year. Illegal immigration would boost this figure. U.S. census data, including many or most undocumented immigrants, show an immigrant population of 10 percent, suggesting that immigration plays a less significant role in demographic terms.

Figure 3.1. Immigration to Canada by Class of Entry, 1971–2001

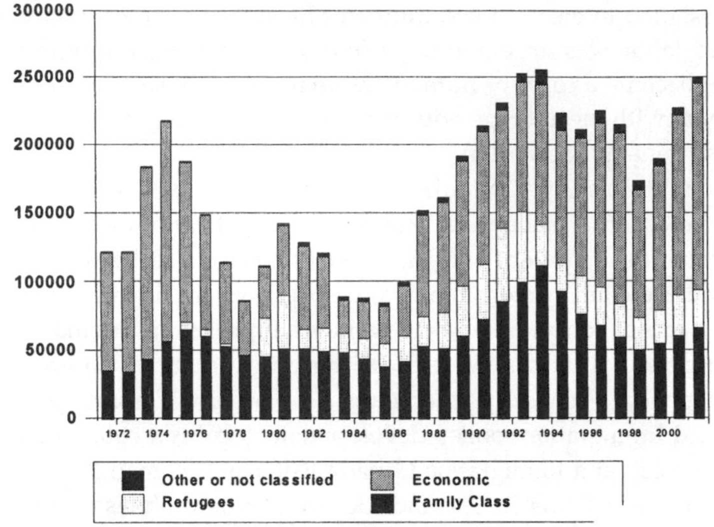

Legend:
- Other or not classified
- Refugees
- Economic
- Family Class

Source: Citizenship and Immigration Canada, *Immigration Statistics*.
Note: Categories include principal applicants and dependents. Economic class includes skilled workers, entrepreneurs, self-employed, investors, and assisted relatives. After 1980, "others" include retirees, live-in caregivers, provincial nominees, and others.

Deciding on numbers of immigrants is a key policy issue in relation to economic objectives. However, the most appropriate number of immigrants annually—the so-called absorptive capacity of the country—is one of the least analyzed aspects of immigration policy. The 1976 Immigration Act formalized immigration principles and processes and, most importantly, provided parliamentary authority for setting numbers of immigrants, previously decided through administrative regulation. The act authorized the government to set annual numerical targets for immigration in relation to its analysis of economic need and other priorities.

Realistically, the numbers are simply adjusted from year to year in response to political pressures. Before 1990, immigration levels were set in relation to labor demand and the business cycle, in what had been regarded as a prudent managerial practice. Then in the recession of the early 1990s, the Progressive Conservative government maintained higher levels than expected, based on the view that immigration stability has long-term benefits that outweigh possible short-term difficulties.[3]

---

[3] See Reitz 1998: 69–95, for a comparison of Canadian, U.S., and Australian immigration policies during this period.

Figure 3.2. Planned and Actual Numbers of Immigrants to Canada, 1980–2000

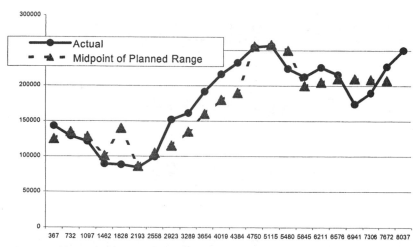

Source: Citizenship and Immigration Canada 2001: 7.

No rationale is provided for the announced target of 1 percent of population each year. (Government officials occasionally mention far higher numbers—up to 500,000 per year—as being actively considered.) The fact that actual numbers of immigrants consistently have fallen significantly short of the 1-percent-of-population target is not recognized by the government as a policy "failure." If this shortfall is considered a gap between policy goals and policy outcomes, it is opposite to other countries where numerical targets for immigration tend to be lower than the actual immigration flow. Perhaps reflecting its effort to maintain the public perception that immigration numbers are carefully managed, CIC publishes data to show a policy gap close to zero, a very close correspondence between its own year-to-year "administrative" targets and actual numbers of immigrants admitted to the country (see figure 3.2).

Most immigration department documents suggest that immigrants' origins are irrelevant to planning, so data on origins are published merely as an interesting sidelight. Of course, immigration has been a source of increasing population diversity. Up to 1970, most immigrants came from Europe, particularly Italy and other countries in southern Europe (table 3.1). After the immigration reforms of 1962 expanded immigration to include the entire world, the diversity of immigrants increased. This

Place of Origin	1961–1970 1000s	1961–1970 Percent	1971–1980 1000s	1971–1980 Percent	1981–1990 1000s	1981–1990 Percent	1991–2000 1000s	1991–2000 Percent
Africa	14.0	1.0	64.8	4.5	68.4	5.1	159.5	7.2
America, Total	246.8	17.5	401.7	27.9	280.4	21.1	294.3	13.3
Mexico	2.1	0.1	6.1	0.4	6.9	0.5	12.7	0.6
United States	161.6	11.4	178.6	12.4	75.7	5.7	60.6	2.7
Other North and Central America	6.2	0.4	2.5	0.2	40.8	3.1	43.6	2.0
Cuba			0.3	0.0	1.1	0.1	4.7	0.2
Puerto Rico			0.0	0.0	0.1	0.0	0.0	0.0
Other Caribbean	52.8	3.7	131.4	9.1	87.2	6.6	97.5	4.4
South America	24.1	1.7	82.8	5.7	68.6	5.2	75.1	3.4
Asia, Total	140.9	10.0	408.7	28.4	602.9	45.3	1313.6	59.5
Hong Kong	36.5	2.6	83.9	5.8	129.3	9.7	240.5	10.9
Taiwan			9.0	0.6	14.3	1.1	79.6	3.6
China	1.4	0.1	0.6	0.7	36.2	2.7	181.2	8.2
Macao			0.3	0.0	2.0	0.2	4.1	0.2
Vietnam/Laos/Cambodia			66.2	4.6	100.6	7.6	47.6	2.2
Philippines			54.1	3.8	65.4	4.9	131.1	5.9
Japan	0.3	0.0	6.0	0.4	4.2	0.3	9.5	0.4
South Korea			16.0	1.1	16.5	1.2	43.2	2.0
South Asia	30.4	2.2	92.1	6.4	108.6	8.2	336.1	15.2
Other Asia	72.3	5.1	70.5	4.9	125.8	9.5	240.7	10.9
Oceania and Australia, Total	33.2	2.4	31.2	2.2	17.4	1.3	22.8	1.0
Australia	26.4	1.9	14.7	1.0	5.1	0.4	8.6	0.4
New Zealand	6.8	0.5	5.2	0.4	2.4	0.2	2.3	0.1
Other			11.3	0.8	9.9	0.7	11.8	0.5
United Kingdom	341.9	24.2	216.5	15.0	92.3	6.9	57.2	2.6
Other Europe	618.9	43.8	314.8	21.9	269.2	20.2	361.1	16.3
Unidentified countries	15.8	1.1	2.7	0.2	0.3	0.0	0.9	0.0
Total	1,411.5	100.0	1,440.4	100.0	1,330.9	100.0	2,209.3	100.0

Sources: Canada, Statistics Canada, Canada Year Book (1963–64: 203; 1967: 220; 1969: 208; 1970–71: 267; 1973: 235; 1975: 188; 1976–77: 212–13; 1978–79: 186); Canada, Employment and Immigration Canada (1986: 28–30; 1992: 34–36); Citizenship and Immigration Canada Statistics (1991: 26–31; 1992: 30–35; 1993: 32–39; 1994: 32–39; 1995: 32–39; 1996: 32–39; 1997–2000). Origins in the Canadian data refer to country of last permanent residence.

change has transformed Canada from a predominantly mono-racial society into a multiracial one. In the 1960s, immigrants from the United Kingdom, other European countries, and the United States were nearly 80 percent of the 1.4 million immigrants to Canada, declining to just over 21 percent of the 2.2 million immigrants in the 1990s. By contrast, immigrants from Asia increased from 10 to 60 percent, and immigrants from Africa increased from 1 to 7 percent. Immigrants from the Caribbean and Latin America also were significant during this period, at about 15 percent during the 1970s and 1980s but less in the 1990s. Unlike the United States, Canada's Latin American population is small, and the origins of its immigrants differ in other ways as well. Canada receives more immigrants from Hong Kong and South Asia, but fewer from China and Taiwan, Korea, the Philippines, and Southeast Asia. Sources of immigration are affected not only by physical proximity but also by historical connections.

Today's immigrants are concentrated overwhelmingly in Canada's three largest urban areas. Toronto attracts 42.6 percent of the working-age immigrants; Vancouver, 18.5 percent; and Montreal, 13.2 percent— for a total of 74.3 percent. Growth in racial minorities also has occurred primarily in the major cities. Of Toronto's 2002 population of about 5 million, well over a third were of non-European origins thanks to immigration since 1970. The largest groups were Chinese (8.0 percent), South Asian (7.5 percent), and black (6.6 percent). Race is now a significant element in urban Canada's social, cultural, economic, and political life (Reitz and Lum n.d.).

Immigration has significantly boosted population growth, although the exact contribution cannot be calculated precisely because the amount of emigration is unknown. It has been estimated that of the 26.4 percent population growth between 1971 and 1991 (from 21.6 million to 27.3 million, or an added 5.7 million), the contribution of net migration was 27 percent (McVey and Kalbach 1995: 87–90).

As the Canadian birthrate has declined, immigration has become increasingly important to population growth. The 2001 census identified a milestone: over the previous five-year period, immigration had for the first time contributed more than 50 percent to population growth. Some Canadian politicians support immigration as a hedge against the aging of the population. However, this is a minor policy theme, and most analyses show little impact on the population's age distribution.[4]

---

[4] The United Nations (2000), in a cross-national projection, concluded that over the next fifty years, except for the United States, immigration will be needed to prevent

Evolution of Economic Immigration in a Knowledge Economy

The points system for selecting independent or "economic" immigrants, and the associated effort to maximize this category's representation relative to the "family class" and other noneconomic categories, has evolved into the principal policy tool for ensuring that the flow of immigrants meets the needs of the Canadian economy (with numbers of refugees being considered a separate issue). Under points-based selection, applicants are awarded points based on criteria such as education, occupational skills, and knowledge of one of Canada's official languages, English or French. The underlying assumption was that immigrants most successful in employment would make the most positive contributions to the Canadian economy and society. They would buy more goods, pay more taxes, start more businesses, create more jobs, and use fewer social services. They would not take jobs from native-born workers nor undercut their wages. Unlike the United States, where abolition of country-of-origin quotas was not expected to have a major demographic impact, Canada expected to maintain the fairly large-scale immigration under way since the end of World War II. If new immigrants from diverse origins might face uncertain prospects for integration into Canadian society, then selection criteria favoring labor force requirements might help in this regard. A positive social, cultural, and political impact also was expected.

Over time, selection standards have been raised progressively. The initial 1967 points system presented a very low hurdle in skill levels. Occupational skills, including those based on education, were taken into account, but applicants could meet the required points total based entirely on other criteria: meeting age and language requirements, a job offer, willingness to settle in an area of strong labor demand, and the discretion of the immigration officer. By 1985 the required points for economic immigrants had increased from 50 to 70 out of 100, with minimum requirements for job experience and occupation. Compared to the earlier version, the 1985 system increased the importance of occupational qualifications but reduced the importance of age and "personal suitability" requirements (see Reitz 1998: 74–79). These regulations have been

---

population decline. Furthermore, the numbers of immigrants required to maintain current dependency ratios—the ratio of the 15–64 aged population to those either older or younger—would be prohibitively large. Canada was not included in the study, but other analysts have obtained similar results for Canada. With no immigration, the median age of the Canadian population would rise from 31.6 in 1986 to 46.9 in 2036; with annual immigration of 200,000, the median age would rise to 44.7.

fine-tuned repeatedly. The version in place in December 2001 allocated 34 points for education and training, 15 for language ability, and 10 for those in the 21–44 age bracket. Although university educated professionals would be admitted most easily, applicants with only a secondary school diploma could be admitted if they satisfy other requirements.

To strengthen the economic component of immigration, "business immigrants"—including entrepreneurs, the self-employed, and investors—were added in the 1980s. The points system criteria are altered to allow the admission of persons expected to start businesses and create jobs, who will undertake self-employment in key fields such as agriculture, or who will invest a specified amount of capital (currently Can$400,000) in Canada.[5] These programs remain relatively small. In 2000, business immigrants numbered 13,645, or 6.9 percent of total immigrants; because business-class immigrants also include dependents, principal applicants in the business class totaled only about 8,000. Since rates of self-employment among immigrants are already high, at least compared to the native-born, they would not necessarily be greatly affected by business immigration.

Canada has approached its temporary foreign worker program cautiously. The temporary migration program fills a range of needs, including seasonal labor in the agricultural sector, domestic workers, management transfers in multinational businesses, and high-tech workers who may be in short supply in the domestic workforce. In 1998 about 250,000 temporary residents were authorized to live in Canada; more than one-third were Americans. The seasonal agricultural worker program is considered a success, satisfying a labor market need with minimal wage impact on the native-born workforce and with little risk of workers overstaying their term of employment.

Federal policy has attempted to increase the opportunity for individuals to obtain temporary work visas, particularly in highly skilled occupational categories. The increased admission of temporary workers with specific job offers, and their potential for conversion to permanent status, has been heralded as part of the move to a knowledge economy. To meet needs in the software sector, the federal government recently sponsored a pilot project to streamline the system for bringing workers with key skills to Canada. In this project, the job-specific validation process was replaced by a "national validation letter" stating that certain positions could not be filled by Canadian residents. One study reportedly showed that the project helped address the skills shortage while not dis-

[5] Up to 55 points are awarded for entrepreneurs and investors, 30 for the self-employed.

placing Canadian workers or affecting wage levels, and that Canadian workers learned from the temporary foreigners (Software Human Resource Council 1999).

Managing Noneconomic Immigration and Overall Program Costs

While developing the economic immigration stream, policy also has focused on reducing the noneconomic stream, along with overall program costs. There are four primary aspects: reducing the family-class proportions of total immigration, reducing budget allocations for settlement programs, imposing fees on immigrants, and addressing logistical problems of the refugee determination process.

Family-class immigrants are not the immediate dependents of principal applicants but rather more distant family members who are "sponsored" as immigrants by Canadian residents. Some of these are "assisted relatives" with family ties to Canadian residents but who also must meet certain points criteria. The long-held perception of family-class immigrants as economic liabilities has been supported by research. Published studies show that skilled workers outperform both family-class immigrants and refugees (CIC 1998). Despite the theoretical importance of family ties in promoting the social and economic integration of immigrants, data from the Longitudinal Immigration Database (IMDB) support minimizing the size of the family-class stream.

Class-of-immigration trends (figure 3.1) show the results of efforts to reduce family-class immigrants. In the early 1980s a reduction in total immigration during the recession came largely at the expense of the economic and refugee categories. Preexisting obligations to family-class applicants were maintained. As the economy recovered in the late 1980s, the numbers of economic immigrants increased dramatically. Although this increase met the overall policy objective, it seems to have resulted in an increase in family-class admissions. This coincided with recession in the early 1990s. Since then, admissions of economic applicants have been maintained or even increased, and family-class admissions have been reduced. Whether this reduction is permanent or represents only a postponement of family reunification applications remains to be seen.

Fluctuating proportions of economic-class as opposed to family-class immigrants reflect a continuing dilemma in Canadian immigration policy. Policymakers seek to choose immigrants as individuals based on human capital considerations, but immigrants come as members of families. Each economic immigrant represents a potential source of perhaps three or four subsequent family-class applicants. Under these circumstances, maintaining high proportions of economic immigrants in the short term is possible by increasing total immigration, a strategy that over the longer term generates pressures for additional family-class migration. On the other hand, policymakers may reduce or delay family-class eligibility, but they face opposing pressure from already-resident immigrants and risk reducing Canada's attractiveness as a destination. Nevertheless, in the early 1990s Canada did reduce opportunities for residents to sponsor adult married children.

Immigrant settlement programs, including counseling and language training for new arrivals, are supported by the federal immigration program and topped up by provincial governments. Settlement programs are based on local initiatives. This administrative feature helps ensure that programs meet the needs of communities, but it also militates against systematic evaluation. Hence what the government gets for the $600 million annual investment is unknown. While the federal immigration department accepts a degree of responsibility for immigrant settlement, it also aims to reduce settlement costs as much as possible. One justification for careful selection of a large economic class of immigrants is the expected reduction in settlement costs.

Immigrants can also be charged to enter Canada as a means of offsetting settlement costs. A system of fees for immigrant applicants is intended to make the program self-financing. Each principal applicant and dependent nineteen years or older is charged $500, those under nineteen are charged $100, and business applicants pay $1,000. A "right of landing" fee of $975 is also imposed on each adult. Currently, a couple with three children under age nineteen will pay $3,250 to immigrate to Canada.

Social services in general—education, health care, unemployment compensation, and social assistance—are available for immigrants, in some cases after a period of residence. Although Canada has implemented some changes to social welfare policies, legal immigrants have not been targeted in a major way. As one exception, Ontario reduced social assistance payments for sponsored immigrants by $100 per month where sponsors were not providing obligatory support.[6] That social services generally are not available for illegal immigrants, presumed to be few in number, has not been an issue in Canada.

Refugees are accepted with an acknowledgment that economic criteria are secondary. However, the potential abuse of the refugee-

---

[6] This policy is being challenged in court as a violation of the Charter of Rights and Freedoms.

determination system threatens the general perception of a well-managed immigration program. Canadian policy has extended rights protections to refugee claimants, and the system of hearings and potential for appeals may consume considerable time, during which claimants may establish themselves in Canada and acquire additional claims to residence. Large backlogs have accumulated, resulting in highly publicized cases in which years-long litigation itself became a legal basis for claims to residence rights in Canada. Average times for final determination of refugee claims are now less than one year.

PUBLIC OPINION ON IMMIGRATION AND POLITICS

The "fit" between Canadian immigration policy and Canadian society may perhaps best be judged in terms of public opinion or the political process generally. The political discourse on immigration in Canada is fairly positive, although this tone may—and almost certainly does—hide many misgivings and often outright discontent. The main questions are, what is the basis for this positive discourse, and will it continue?

Public Opinion

Seen comparatively, immigration seems to enjoy a degree of public acceptance in Canada. Gallup polls, for example, show that since 1975 the proportion of the general public wanting either to maintain or increase immigration has been at least 50 percent in every year except one (see table 3.2). In 1982, at the height of a recession, when immigrants were more likely to be seen as competitors for jobs, those favoring reduced immigration reached a high point of 55 percent. Otherwise, this figure has fluctuated between 30 and 46 percent. Even in the early 1990s, when Canada was in recession and immigration levels remained high, those wanting to lower immigration levels never reached a majority. Majorities have occasionally agreed that "overall there is too much immigration to Canada," but the proportion that *disagreed* with this statement reached a majority of 54 percent in 2000. A cross-national comparison of public opinion on immigration policy (Simon and Lynch 1999: 461) showed that opposition to immigration is lower in Canada (averaging 42.0 percent) than in the United States (49.7 percent), the United Kingdom (55.2 percent), and Australia (65.9 percent) despite the proportionally higher immigration to Canada. Although some data suggest that support is weaker in Toronto and Vancouver, where immigrant settlement is heaviest, regional differences are not large.

Table 3.2. Canadian Opinion on Immigration Levels

Responses to the question: "If it were your job to plan an immigration policy for Canada at this time, would you be inclined to increase immigration, decrease immigration, or keep the number of immigrants at about the current level?"

	Increase (%)	Decrease (%)	Keep at Current Level (%)	Don't Know (%)
National by date				
2001, July 17–23	17	33	49	1
2000, July 13–21	17	33	47	3
1999, July 13–19	17	31	50	2
1998, July 24–August 3	11	37	49	3
1997, July 22–27	9	41	44	6
1996, May 6–13	10	40	43	7
1995, May 8–12	9	44	43	4
1993, December 3–14	11	45	40	5
1992, May 6–9	13	46	37	4
1991, June 12–15	14	45	38	4
1990, September 12–15	17	32	46	5
1989, August 9–12	14	34	47	6
1998, March 2–5	14	41	42	3
1987, March 11–14	13	41	42	4
1985, October 3–5	14	42	38	6
1982	7	55	35	3
1980, September 4–6	8	42	44	7
1975, June 5–7	10	39	43	8
By region today				
Atlantic	17	31	50	3
Quebec	19	29	51	2
Ontario	15	37	47	a
Prairies	15	33	53	0
British Columbia	22	31	47	0
By education level				
Less than university	11	39	49	2
University	29	22	49	a

Source: Gallup Canada, Inc.
Note: Percentages may not add to 100 due to rounding.
a = less than 0.5 percent.

Interest Groups and Political Parties

Even minorities with misgivings about immigration can have a major political impact, yet immigration has not emerged as a high priority with voters. Public discussions of immigration in Canada remain strongly supportive, and although there are opponents, there are no prominent anti-immigrant politicians like Pat Buchanan in the United States or Pauline Hanson in Australia. With certain variations, all major political parties support immigration, as do labor unions and employer groups.

The Liberal Party governs with strong support in Quebec and Ontario, less in Atlantic Canada and the Prairies, and still less in Alberta and British Columbia. Over many decades, the Liberals have had the most pro-immigration record of any Canadian political party and fostered the commitment to raise immigration levels to 1 percent of population per year. To the left, the small labor-oriented New Democratic Party (NDP) endorses the 1 percent target while criticizing the government for failing to reach it. In keeping with its social democratic roots, the NDP advocates ending the "right of landing" fee. The labor union movement, with which the NDP is affiliated, also supports immigration but has tended to regard the emphasis on economic migration as elitist. For example, the umbrella Canadian Labour Congress has called for an end to business immigration and an increase in family-class immigration. It emphasizes the need for support services for refugees and refugee claimants, protection of immigrants from possible abuse by sponsors, and programs to combat racism. Similar policies are propounded by major unions, such as the Canadian Union of Public Employees and the Canadian Auto Workers.

Parties to the right and business interests such as the Canadian Chamber of Commerce also support immigration, but they temper their enthusiasm by not mentioning numerical targets and by including proposals to make the program more cost-effective. The lack of specific targets has been interpreted by some as a sign that these groups favor reduced immigration, although they do not say so publicly. The defeat of Brian Mulroney's Progressive Conservative government reduced the party to a very small parliamentary caucus, so their immigration policies receive scant attention. Their policy papers state no immigration targets, emphasize skill-based immigrant selection, and call for efforts to improve the use of immigrants in the labor market by promoting foreign credential assessment. The largest party on the right today is the Canadian Alliance Party (formerly the Reform Party), with enough seats to form the official opposition though it remains essentially a western-based protest party. The Alliance is sometimes described as anti-immigrant, based on statements of some party members, but its formal statements profess to support immigration. Still, the Alliance calls for stricter enforcement of sponsorship obligations for family-class immigration and immediate deportation for what it calls "bogus refugees and other illegal entrants." The party would "severely penalize those who organize abuse of the system" (Canadian Alliance 2000).

Political correctness undoubtedly plays a role in restricting anti-immigration discourse in Canada to the political margins. The difference in public opinion between Canada and other countries does not seem as great as the difference in the significance of concerns about immigration in public debate. This could mean that immigration is an issue waiting to spring forth as a major item, given some dramatic spark or precipitating events. With this in mind, we will examine the evidence on actual trends in immigrant integration in society, in economic and social perspectives.

THE ECONOMIC ROLE AND IMPACT OF IMMIGRANTS

If an expansionist immigration policy is justified primarily by economic objectives, then presumably a positive actual economic impact of immigration is a key to its political reception. However, no established criteria exist to assess this impact; in this regard the debate in Canada is as murky as elsewhere. Most public discussion has focused on the economic success of the immigrants themselves. Whatever the actual economic effects of such success, the claim of a positive effect helps offset complaints about immigrants as welfare burdens—although at the risk perhaps of inadvertently supporting an opposite complaint that immigrants take jobs from Canadians. A recent claim is that skilled immigration serves other economic needs—as a replacement population for the alleged "brain drain" to the United States or for an aging workforce. Such claims have been countered by expert opinion.[7] These issues are all apart from the question of whether immigrants actually contribute to overall economic growth or to increases in per capita income. What is the actual economic role and impact of immigrants in Canada?

A large immigrant population in highly skilled occupations—the ideal of Canadian policy—would disconfirm Sassen's (1991) celebrated

---

[7] Many skilled immigrants find that their credentials are not recognized as equivalent in Canada, and they work at lower skill levels (Reitz 2001a). DeVoretz (n.d.) has suggested that, for the most highly skilled immigrants, Canada may only be a stopping-off place where skills are upgraded before a final move to the United States.

analysis of immigration in "global cities." Her analysis focused on New York City, where the concentration of economic power in a highly affluent super-elite supposedly generated demand for immigrants to perform low-level service jobs catering to this elite. If Canada has a global city, it would be Toronto. With a population of 5 million, Toronto is the economic and commercial capital of the country, headquarters for most of Canada's corporate and financial world, a transportation hub, and the focal point for the nation's English-language media and cultural activity. However, Toronto's high level of immigration can hardly be explained entirely by elite demand for personal services. Immigrants in Toronto have not been limited to low-level service jobs. Even so-called ethnic occupations may be at high or low levels of skill.

Educational Levels of Immigrants

Unlike the low-skilled immigration of the 1950s and 1960s, immigrants arriving in Canada since 1970 possess relatively high educational levels. The earlier immigrants, particularly those from southern Europe, averaged eight years of education or less and worked in unskilled occupations. As the selection criteria have risen over time, so have immigrant educational levels. The 1996 census showed that working-age immigrants arriving in 1991–1996 averaged fourteen years of education, with nearly 30 percent having university degrees (Reitz 2001b: 610).

Educational levels of immigrants are higher in Canada than in the United States, largely because of the different origins mix and because Canada accepts few immigrants from Mexico. Apart from the Mexican cohort, immigrants in the United States are actually better educated than those in Canada (Duleep and Regets 1992; Reitz 1998) despite Canada's greater efforts to select on the basis of skill. These patterns illustrate that immigrant skill levels are not readily controlled by policymakers.

Immigrant education is meaningful primarily in relation to native-born competition. Looking at Canada and Australia, Borjas (1990) found an educational advantage for many immigrant groups in the 1970s when comparing them to the native-born. At that time, native-born Canadian and Australian educational levels were substantially lower than for the United States, enabling immigrants in both countries to earn relatively higher incomes.

However, Canada's large investments in education have changed this picture since the 1970s. Postsecondary educational participation rates have met or exceeded those in the United States, so the competitive context for newly arriving immigrants has tended to converge toward the American pattern. Immigrant educational levels in Canada still exceed those of the native-born, but the gap is now smaller.

Moreover, any immigrant skills advantage in Canada shrinks, disappears, or is reversed if immigrants are compared with their most likely native-born labor-market competitors—namely, young people in the major urban centers. For example, recent immigrants in Toronto and Vancouver are actually less educated than their native-born counterparts (this is not true in Montreal). When age is considered, the immigrant advantage appears to shrink still further (see table 3.3). An age-specific national comparison shows that recent immigrant men had the same number of years of education (about fourteen on average) as the native-born aged twenty-five to twenty-nine, though a larger proportion held university degrees (just under 30 percent). Recent immigrant women had slightly fewer years of education than native-born women (less than fourteen), and approximately the same proportion held university degrees (about 26 percent).[8]

Earnings of Immigrants

Following the introduction of points-based selection, immigrants to Canada achieved considerable economic success in relation to the native-born population, somewhat higher than their counterparts in the United States. Higher immigrant earnings in Canada in the 1970s were first shown in Borjas's (1990) comparative census analysis. The earnings of immigrants are higher in Canada partly because of the absence of any group comparable to the relatively less educated Mexican Americans. However, higher immigrant earnings in Canada also showed across most major origins groups such as Caribbean, Chinese, or other Asians. At the urban level, where most immigrants live and work, the cross-national contrast was even greater (Reitz 1998). For example, as of 1980, newly arriving black immigrants in New York and Miami averaged about half

---

[8] Education levels for immigrants overall in Ontario and British Columbia are similar (1996 census). Of working-age immigrants arriving between 1990 and 1995, those in both British Columbia and Ontario averaged about 13.5 years of education, versus provincial averages for the general population of about 13.3 years. Educational levels of immigrants in Toronto and Vancouver closely matched provincial averages. Educational levels are higher for immigrants in Quebec than in Alberta (13.7 years, compared to 13.2 years) despite the fact that the general population in Quebec has fewer years of education (12.7 percent, compared to 13.1 percent in Alberta).

Table 3.3. Education of Immigrants and Native-born in Canada, by Age and Gender, 1996

Age	Mean Years of Education				Percent with University Degrees			
	Native-born (N)	All Immigrants (N)	Recent Immigrants (past 5 years) (N)	Total (N)	Native-born (N)	All Immigrants (N)	Recent Immigrants (past 5 years) (N)	Total (N)
Men								
20–24	13.4 (17,684)	13.6 (2,164)	13.0 (565)	13.4 (19,848)	8.7 (17,684)	12.3 (2,164)	8.0 (565)	9.1 (19,848)
25–29	13.9 (19,517)	14.2 (3,926)	14.0 (1,027)	13.9 (23,443)	19.6 (19,517)	26.1 (3,926)	27.3 (1,027)	20.7 (23,443)
30–34	13.6 (24,677)	14.2 (5,240)	14.8 (1,283)	13.7 (29,917)	17.5 (24,677)	27.3 (5,240)	35.2 (1,283)	19.2 (29,917)
35–64	13.0 (87,760)	13.8 (26,718)	14.2 (2,584)	13.2 (114,478)	17.8 (87,760)	25.8 (26,718)	33.2 (2,584)	19.6 (114,478)
Total	13.2 (149,638)	13.9 (38,048)	14.2 (5,459)	13.4 (187,686)	16.9 (149,638)	25.2 (38,048)	29.9 (5,459)	18.6 (187,686)
Women								
20–24	14.2 (16,879)	14.2 (2,236)	13.4 (620)	14.2 (19,115)	15.1 (16,879)	18.3 (2,236)	10.3 (629)	15.5 (19,115)
25–29	14.4 (17,776)	14.4 (3,601)	14.3 (1,007)	14.4 (21,377)	25.9 (17,776)	28.8 (3,601)	29.7 (1,007)	26.4 (21,377)
30–34	13.9 (21,250)	14.3 (4,453)	14.5 (1,090)	14.0 (25,703)	20.1 (21,250)	27.7 (4,453)	35.0 (1,090)	21.4 (25,703)
35–64	13.1 (74,453)	13.3 (21,704)	13.4 (2,092)	13.2 (96,157)	16.3 (74,453)	20.6 (21,704)	25.1 (2,092)	17.2 (96,157)
Total	13.6 (130,358)	13.6 (31,994)	13.9 (4,809)	13.6 (162,352)	18.0 (130,358)	22.4 (31,994)	26.4 (4,809)	18.9 (162,352)

Source: 1996 Canadian Census, Public Use Microdata Files.

the earnings of native-born whites among men and about two-thirds among women; comparable figures in Toronto were 70 percent and 84 percent. Similar differences can be observed for other immigrant groups.

This does not mean that these immigrants in Canada have not encountered labor market adversity or have not experienced difficulty in securing work in occupations matching their high qualification levels. Visible concentration of immigrants in certain occupations, such as black West Indian immigrants in health occupations, often represents a downward step from pre-immigration employment. Chinese immigrants tend to concentrate in scientific and technical fields, often below their level of qualification. High rates of immigrant self-employment may reflect frustration with opportunities in the mainstream labor market.

Canadian immigrants do not earn more relative to qualifications. In fact, in Canada as well as in the United States and Australia, immigrants from certain groups, mainly non-Europeans, have performed less well relative to qualifications (see, for example, Boyd 1992). Immigrants of black and various Asian origins may therefore expect a lengthier integration into the Canadian workforce.

Immigrants' employment success can be understood in terms of its institutional context (Reitz 1998) rather than by differences in experiences within institutions. First, as Borjas (1990) pointed out, the skill selectivity of immigration policy seems to play its intended role. Second, immigrants received an important assist from the late development of Canada's educational system. In fact, after the immigration reforms of the 1960s the most important reason for higher earnings for immigrants—at least for the first cohort of non-European immigrants—was the lower educational levels of the native-born workforce (Reitz 1998: chap. 4). Thus the first cohort of non-European immigrants was able to gain relatively easy access to the Canadian middle class. The third institutional sector of relevance is labor markets. Canadian labor markets allocate relatively high wages to workers in low-skill occupations. All these institutional components may be related to Canada's greater commitment to the collective welfare versus American "individualism."

Since the 1970s, one can perceive a pervasive downward trend in the employment rates and earnings of newly arriving immigrants in most origin groups (Reitz 2001b). The decline in employment rates has the largest impact on the most recently arrived immigrants, but with continuing impact on women particularly. However, most noticeable is the decline in the earnings of those who have found employment. Whereas in 1981 immigrant men arriving in the previous five-year period earned

79.6 percent of the earnings of native-born men, by 1996 that figure had dropped to 60.0 percent. For women, the figure had fallen from 73.1 percent to 62.4 percent (DeVoretz 1995; Baker and Benjamin 1994). Citizenship and Immigration Canada IMDB data also show a negative trend that continued in the 1990s.

Of course, immigrants arriving in a period of high unemployment may be expected to encounter difficulty, similar to other new labor market entrants. This is particularly true for those lacking local connections and experience, and potentially handicapped by minority status. The recession of the early 1980s clearly created difficulties for newly arriving immigrants (D. Bloom, Grenier, and Gunderson 1995), but those arriving later in the decade experienced an expected rebound. Weak labor demand in the early 1990s undoubtedly created difficulties for newly arriving immigrants, and it was compounded by their large numbers.

However, the earnings decline also affects immigrants resident in Canada for much longer periods of time, and for them the impact of the business cycle at the time of arrival fades to insignificance. Reitz (2001b) has shown that part of the decline may be expected based on the rapid rise in education in the native-born population. Although the educational levels of immigrants in Canada have increased following upgraded selection criteria, for most of the period up to 1996 native-born educational levels have increased more rapidly. This in itself creates greater obstacles for immigrants; but given that immigrant qualifications tend to be discounted in the workforce, any increase in the emphasis on such criteria is magnified and tends to further widen the immigrant/native-born earnings gap. Moreover, the rising value of education in the native-born workforce appears not to apply to immigrants. Overall, educational change accounts for about half the decline in the earnings of immigrants (Reitz 2001b: 598–99). Clearly other factors—perhaps the generally widening earnings gaps in the labor market—are at play. The particularly poor employment situation of immigrants arriving in the early 1990s is not explained only as a temporary result of recession.

The decline in immigrant earnings in Canada has been significantly steeper than the parallel decline that Borjas (1999) reported in the United States. It is observed across most origins groups, and it appears to be based in institutional change. In effect, the convergence of the U.S. and Canadian educational systems, particularly at the postsecondary levels in the 1970s and 1980s, has produced a marked convergence in the labor market earnings of immigrants, despite divergent trends in the skills of the immigrants themselves (Reitz n.d.).

Other Economic Indicators

A trend toward lower immigrant earnings in Canada ultimately raises questions about the economic impact of immigration. Immigrants' success has been cited as evidence of the immigration program's success. The economic impact of immigration has not, however, been measured precisely, nor have implications of the trend toward declining immigrant earnings been considered.

The economic impact of immigration can be considered in terms of changes in *overall* living standards or per capita income or wealth, and in terms of changes in the *distribution* of income or wealth across the population or inequalities among population subgroups. Theories and methodologies for assessing these effects are complex, and available analyses tend to be fairly speculative.[9] More immediately observable is the impact of immigration on overall *population size*, as discussed above. Population size has many noneconomic implications, but it is certainly also an economic issue. A larger population creates a larger economy, a larger domestic market for goods and services, and greater clout for the country in dealing with other nations in matters affecting Canada's economic position. Presumably, the demographic objectives of Canada's immigration policy are partly justified in economic terms. Still, evidence from detailed empirical studies is not abundant.

Borjas's (1999: 87–89) analysis of the economic impact of immigration in the United States pointed out several ways in which immigration could contribute to economic growth. For example, immigrants increase consumer demand, and as entrepreneurs they create jobs. Borjas's analysis was based on the supposition that immigrants lower wages, thereby transferring wealth to employers and to those who use immigrant services or buy immigrants' products. He calculated this effect as significant but fairly small. What is noteworthy is that this analysis finds that the economic "benefits" of immigration are positive in the aggregate but unequally distributed. Groups who compete directly with immigrants, such as native-born African Americans, would be net losers.

Canadian research (Laryea 1998) suggests that, unlike the situation in the United States, immigrants in Canada do not compete substantially

---

[9] The Economic Council of Canada (Swan et al. 1991: 26, 36) estimated small benefits of immigration, based on a largely speculative correlation analysis of population trends across sixty-eight countries, using population size, rather than immigration itself, as the main predictor.

with native-born workers, resulting in little if any impact on inequality. By the same token, the impacts that Borjas examined would not arise in Canada. However, a downward trend in immigrant earnings might imply that the impact of immigration in Canada may be moving toward previous U.S. patterns.

Political Consequences of Immigrant Economic Performance

High earning levels for immigrants have been a key selling point for the Canadian immigration program, underscoring a presumed positive contribution to the nation's economy. To the extent that the political acceptability of immigration is owed to the economic success of immigrants, a downward trend in that success might be expected to undermine the program in political terms. As yet, little evidence of this appears in Canada. Economic problems for newly arriving groups do not quickly affect the overall tone of intergroup relations. Largely on the basis of past high income levels, simulations of the impact on public finances show positive contributions (Akbari 1995).

Still, high poverty rates are now appearing for some groups, according to recent studies based on the 1996 census (such as Ornstein 2000). There has also been increased attention to the problem of immigrants working below the skill level for which they were selected—a so-called brain waste (see, for example, M. Bloom and Grant 2001; Reitz 2001a). Skilled immigrants may often find that employers do not recognize their credentials as equivalent. Immigrant skills may be perceived as lower in quality or insufficiently relevant to Canadian conditions or to the Canadian employment situation.

Because the second generation in racial minority immigrant groups remains small, survey data with which to examine the economic success of children of immigrants are limited. Most analyses of long-term integration in the Canadian economy draw upon data from immigrants arriving much earlier—and having entered the occupational hierarchy at higher levels (see Boyd and Grieco 1998; Anisef et al. 2000).

Institutional change in Canada, including a substantial degree of convergence toward U.S. standards in postsecondary education, points to increased economic difficulties for immigrants in Canada. International relations and demographic forces point to continued reliance on large-scale immigration. The collision of these two forces may create inescapable political repercussions for Canada's immigration program in the future.

SOCIAL IMPACT: ETHNICITY, LANGUAGE, AND MULTICULTURALISM

The success of immigration policy and efforts to manage its political acceptability are shaped not only by immigrants' economic integration but also by their social and cultural integration. The two are intimately related: economic success is a prerequisite to satisfactory social participation, while lack of social acceptance inhibits economic progress.

Understanding immigrant integration in Canada requires attention to three circumstances that create both challenges and opportunities for policy management. First, immigration in Canada must be managed in relation to its linguistic balance and relations between its two founding linguistic communities. Second, the impact of Canada's "multiculturalism," heralded within the country as promoting effective integration of immigrant groups, requires assessment. And third, the racial diversity generated by recent immigration is essentially new to Canada, raising questions about the immigrant integration process and about government capacity to manage future intergroup relations.

Immigrants and French-English Relations in Canada

Immigration's impact in Canada should be placed in the context of changing relations between the founding British and French population groups. Addressing issues of English-French unity has been a major preoccupation for Canadian government and society, particularly since the 1960s. The arrival of so many newcomers obviously affects the balance; as a result, immigration policy has involved Quebec and other provincial governments.

As immigration increased the population (McVey and Kalbach 1995: 87–90), a new ethnic and cultural mix affected the traditional English-French balance. Up to the mid-1960s, two demographic processes offset one another to some extent. On the one hand, linguistic assimilation of immigrants occurred largely toward the English-speaking community in Canada. On the other, a high birthrate among French-speaking Canadians helped maintain relative population size. In 1871, 61 percent of the Canadian population was of British origin; 31 percent, French; and all others, 8 percent. By 1951 these figures were 48, 31, and 21 percent; and by 1971 they were 45, 29, and 27 percent. Historically, even in Quebec immigrants have tended to integrate into the English-speaking community. In 1971, among Quebec residents with a mother tongue other than

English or French, transfers to English outnumbered transfers to French by more than four to one (LaChapelle 1980: 33). Immigration significantly reduced the demographic weight of the French language in Quebec and in Canada generally.

Since the "Quiet Revolution" of awakening ethnic and national consciousness in Quebec beginning in the early 1960s, the Quebec government has taken a degree of control over language while attempting to address the impact of immigration. Through a series of agreements with the federal government, Quebec acquired substantial control over immigrant selection and settlement.[10] These agreements aim to ensure that, while contributing to economic development, immigration does not threaten the cultural or linguistic independence of Quebec within Canada. Administratively, all matters related to immigration and the integration of immigrants in Quebec are centralized within the provincial Ministère des Relations avec les Citoyens et de l'Immigration (MRCI). In a sense, Quebec's distinctive interest in immigration within Canada is parallel to Canada's distinctive interest in immigration within North America. Both cases show a concern with size and the need to maintain or increase economic, political, and cultural weight within the larger context.

Since 1970 Quebec has set the numbers of its immigrants as well as their main characteristics. Regarding numbers, the current agreement provides that Quebec should receive the same share of immigrants as its percentage of the Canadian population, with the right to exceed this figure by 5 percent. Further, Quebec should accept refugees in proportion to the overall percentage of immigrants it has undertaken to receive. The Quebec government has stated its desire to increase the numbers of French-speaking immigrants settling in the province. Although immigration to Quebec in recent years has been a smaller proportion of the Canadian total, Quebec's extremely low birthrate makes it more sensitive to immigration flows than previously.

---

[10] The most recent agreement, in 1991, provided for Quebec elements contained in the failed constitutional agreement. In this agreement, "an important new objective for Quebec was introduced: to preserve Quebec's demographic weight within Canada and to integrate immigrants to the province in a manner that respects the distinct society of Quebec. This objective was to be achieved primarily by Quebec's formal role in advising about the number of immigrants it wishes to receive, the attempt to ensure numbers of immigrants proportional to the population of the province, and Quebec's assumption of all integration services, with a particular emphasis on providing permanent residents with the means to learn the French language" (Young 1992).

Quebec administers its own selection system—its own points system—even though Canada retains the right to issue visas (and conduct background checks related to health and security). This system gives substantial priority to persons fluent in French, as well as to those with higher levels of education, particularly if that education was in French. A 1991 agreement (see note 10) also provides some provincial responsibilities for aspects of refugee selection and for short-term stays of temporary foreign workers. The Quebec government has expressed an interest in increasing its involvement in the temporary foreign worker program.

Canada compensates Quebec financially for its settlement programs as long as these programs correspond to those offered in the rest of the country, and as long as all permanent residents of the province, whether selected by Quebec or not, can access them.[11] Quebec has not formally evaluated how its selection scheme affects the economic impact of its immigrants, though a longitudinal study (cf. Renaud, Piché, and Gingras 1997; Piché, Renaud, and Gingras 1999) showed that immigrants arriving in 1989 have done well. The fact that so many immigrants to Quebec leave for other provinces underscores a critical weakness in provincial selection schemes, undermining Quebec's efforts to control the impact of immigration within the province. Interprovincial migration of immigrants favors the high-immigration provinces of Ontario and British Columbia; losses in Quebec are greatest in absolute numbers (CIC 2000).

Other provincial governments recently negotiated immigration agreements with the federal government, often providing for the selection of "provincial nominees." These provinces include British Columbia, Alberta, and several low-immigration provinces, but notably not Ontario. Only a very small number of provincial nominees (1,249) were admitted in 2000.

Canadian Multiculturalism

Although Canadian political leaders routinely proclaim that Canada has always been a multicultural nation, official multiculturalism originated in French-English relations and Quebec's Quiet Revolution. In fact, throughout much of its history Canadian immigration policy was quite assimilationist in that immigrants were chosen for their perceived capacity for social and cultural accommodation in the mainstream popula-

---

[11] A complex funding formula provides minimum financial guarantees, with provisions for changing circumstances. Since 1990, compensation has been the base sum of Can$90 million, increasing at the same rate as government spending generally. In 2000, the funds were approximately $103 million.

tions. Earliest preferences were for persons of British or northern European origin, and mainly market pressures occasioned the admission of others such as eastern and southern Europeans. Adoption of official multiculturalism can be traced to the French-English conflict. Thanks to pressure to protect the French language in Canada, the federal government initially adopted a policy of bilingualism *and biculturalism*. Other cultural groups, notably Ukrainians, protested. As a compromise, biculturalism was rejected in favor of multiculturalism. In effect, multiculturalism emerged from the debate over French language rights, the status of Quebec, and the political reluctance of federal Liberals under Prime Minister Pierre Trudeau to antagonize immigrant voters. Federal multiculturalism policy was officially launched in 1971, immediately embraced by all parties at all levels of government, and later entrenched in Canada's Charter of Rights and Freedoms.

Canada's brand of multiculturalism reflects a kind of live-and-let-live cultural tolerance that typifies the Canadian style. Multiculturalism is important in Canada more as a symbol than as a specific program. Only small amounts of money are available to ethnic organizations to sponsor cultural activities. However, in public discourse multiculturalism has since its adoption in 1971 become elevated to the status of a cornerstone of Canadianism and is equated with valuing cultural diversity. As a national symbol, it offers a metaphoric contrast between Canadian society as a "mosaic" versus U.S. society as a "melting pot." It is also a reflection of nationalism, as Clark (1962) pointed out. The multicultural viewpoint is most strongly expressed by those who want Canada to remain distinct from the United States (Reitz and Breton 1994).

According to Canadian mythology, immigrant integration is supposed to be assisted by multiculturalism. However, little solid evidence supports this claim. No government funds have been allocated for "program evaluation," reinforcing the impression that the policy is largely symbolic. Nevertheless, even symbols matter. Bloemraad (2002) has suggested that higher naturalization rates in Canada than in the United States may result from the symbolic feeling of acceptance that immigrants derive from multiculturalism or from the channeling of government information into ethnic organizations and communities.

Visible Minorities and Race

Historically, the racial diversity that immigration created in Canada is quite new. Because of the predominantly European population base of

Canada's nonaboriginal population up to the 1960s and the sheer size of Canada's immigration program relative to the existing population, the impact of the cultural and racial changes in the Canadian population has been profound. In 1971, racial minorities (other than aboriginal peoples) constituted less than 1 percent of the Canadian population; by 1996, as a result of immigration, they were 10 percent.

The consequence of this demographic change is that race has become an issue in Canada. It has altered the framework of intergroup relations and has raised questions about the status of official multiculturalism. Do race relations in Canada remain distinctive? Do they affect the success of immigration policy? Experience with previous European immigration and the trickle of blacks from the United States, or with issues of French-English relations and the status of aboriginal populations, may have helped prepare for the new racial diversity. But the fact that Canada has invented a new term—"visible minorities" (to avoid speaking of "race"), complete with its own legal framework—suggests important new problems. Immigration scholars in the United States ask how the impact of immigration is affected by a large native-born black population, a legacy of slavery. By the same token, one may ask how the *absence* of such a population group affects Canadian immigration.

Although most Canadians deny harboring racist views, they do express preferences regarding the racial composition of groups located in their own neighborhoods or workplaces (Reitz and Breton 1994). Polls by Environics Focus Canada show that large majorities reject the proposal that "non-whites should not be allowed to immigrate to Canada" (93 percent in 2000; Esses, Dovidio, and Hodson 2002: 72). However, a series of Focus Canada polls in 1990, 1991, and 1992 also shows that a majority—about 53 percent—agree that "Canada accepts too many immigrants from racial minority groups" (see Canadian Opinion Research Archive, Queen's University). Analysis suggests that racial bias is only one among a number of determinants of attitudes toward immigration, and that concerns about the threat to jobs and other impacts of immigration are important for reasons unrelated to racial attitudes (Palmer 1996; Esses et al. 2001).

Multiculturalism programs originally focused on the cultural identities of European minorities and not on discrimination, even though combating discrimination was one of the stated objectives of the original policy. When new groups talked about equity, access, and discrimination, it became clear that these issues did not quite fit under the rubric of multiculturalism as understood in Canada. Some multicultural programs have now shifted to include anti-racism and antidiscrimination activities, but the policy discourse around multiculturalism continues to minimize the significance of race.

Canada's policies addressing race tend to be ambiguous and ineffective. Canada's 1986 federal "employment equity" legislation offers a good example. "Visible minorities" is one of four groups designated for attention (the others being women, native peoples, and the disabled). The law covered only the small federally regulated segment of the workforce (about 5 percent) and included no effective monitoring or enforcement mechanism (Lum 1995). New employment equity legislation passed in 1995 is stronger because it authorizes the Canadian Human Rights Commission to enforce compliance through the conduct of on-site employer audits (although as an apparent trade-off, the commission's jurisdiction over systemic discrimination in employment was restricted). Despite evidence that racial discrimination is no less prevalent in Toronto or other Canadian cities than in U.S. cities, the issue is much lower on the Canadian public agenda.

Racial conflicts in Canada have not been lacking, but they have not reached anything like a crisis level. Controversies over racial bias have appeared in the media and in cultural life. Perceptions of a biased justice system in Toronto's black community have provoked both violence and reforms in policing. Huge suburban Chinese shopping malls disturbed some local officials and have caused controversy. Fears about illegal immigration and bogus refugee claims have produced complaints about an expected negative impact in Toronto. In 1995, for the first time in Ontario, race became an election issue. The newly elected Progressive Conservative government of Mike Harris unceremoniously scrapped the previous New Democratic government's equal job opportunity legislation, in a provocatively titled "Bill to Repeal Job Quotas and Restore Merit-Based Employment Practices in Ontario." Employers were ordered to destroy information collected as part of employer internal workforce surveys under the earlier legislation. In place of employment equity, the government introduced a nonlegislative and voluntary "Equal Opportunity Plan." Because of tensions surrounding these new racial issues, some fear that Toronto may be a racial time bomb, a place where the true extent of ethnic and racial conflict is now hidden but will erupt in the future.

As racial issues have grown, some racial minorities have begun to oppose multiculturalism on the grounds that it assigns minorities a marginal status (Bissoondath 1994). Others oppose it because it is said to underpin identity politics that support the rights of certain minority groups, supposedly at the expense of either majority rights or the rights of other minority groups (Kay 1998). Still others view multiculturalism as an attempt to maintain the traditional ethnic hierarchy. Multiculturalism, it is argued, socially constructs cultural identities but does little to recognize and remedy inequalities based on race. Such criticisms have prompted governments to look hard for ways to cut the already small multicultural budgets or to abandon the program entirely while still being politically correct. For example, after a 1994 federal review, funds allotted to multiculturalism were reduced by 28 percent and redirected from program to project funding. The question of whether municipal budgets should continue to fund multicultural grant programs also has been challenged regularly.

In short, while observers have credited official multiculturalism with improving intergroup relations, it is questionable whether the policy actually ever had this result. Today the growth of racial minority populations seems to be changing the role of multiculturalism, making it less a socially cohesive force but more a rallying point for demands for more potent public policy to address issues of equality and human rights.

INSTITUTIONAL CHANGE AND EMERGING POLICY ISSUES

The various institutional pressures, constraints, and possibilities that have shaped Canada's immigration policy are changing in ways that will play out in coming policy debates. The continuing importance of large-scale immigration seems dictated by Canada's perception that it requires an expansionist policy within its North American context, underscored by the country's low and declining fertility rate. The historic role of immigration in Canadian nation-building continues, while nation-building in the twenty-first century evolves rapidly. Having developed from a rural nation to an urban industrial nation, Canada today is — or aspires to be — a postindustrial society with a knowledge-based economy, confronting the challenges of globalization. For immigration policy, the challenge this juxtaposition of circumstances poses is to recruit large numbers of immigrants to fill highly skilled occupations in an emerging knowledge economy. It would be politically damaging for immigrants to a welfare state to be seen as struggling or representing a potential threat to the viability of social services. Hence an important priority is to ensure immigrants' economic success. In this respect, the relative absence of illegal immigration in Canada due to its geographic isolation is a major plus.

This analysis suggests that Canadian immigration policy and its effects will evolve in ways representing both convergence with other industrial societies *and* differentiation. Institutional convergence will not change the bases for Canada's past emphasis on a major role for immigration; its geographic isolation seems likely to ensure that meaningful immigrant selection can remain. However, the convergence of Canadian with U.S. educational institutions, and the institutional structures of a knowledge economy generally, definitely alter the circumstances that have supported past immigrant economic success.

Hence a major policy focus at present is the declining economic position of newly arriving immigrants, particularly the large numbers coming during the recession of the early 1990s. Increases in poverty rates for immigrants, particularly racial minority immigrants, could elevate controversies over the viability of immigration policy in ways not previously seen in Canada. However, the economic recovery of the late 1990s may have significantly reversed the downward trend, possibly portending a more positive future direction.

How this issue was addressed in the context of the new Immigration and Refugee Protection Act 2001 (passed in November 2001 and taking effect on June 28, 2002) was one of the most controversial features in the bill's drafting. The new act includes a number of provisions designed to facilitate economic roles for immigrants. It provides "in-Canada" application for permanent residency, including for temporary workers, spouses and partners, and students with a permanent job offer who have been studying in Canada. This option is intended to facilitate the new role planned for temporary workers in high-skill, knowledge-economy jobs. The government also has introduced a new multiyear planning process to provide greater continuity in immigration policymaking. Many or most of the key features of immigration policy—such as targets, revisions to selection criteria, and new categories such as entrepreneurs and investors—are actually enacted through "regulations" issued by Citizenship and Immigration Canada.

The key feature of the new policy is to further upgrade skill selection for permanent immigrants, with greater emphasis on education and language knowledge than previously and less emphasis on specific occupational skills. A new pass mark has been set at 75 rather than 70. Surprisingly, the government proposes achieving these increases while also increasing total immigration. The method for doing so involves the more rapid processing of a reported backlog of 500,000 applicants under the new rules. The retroactive implications of this change—many who applied and paid their fees under old rules would be considered under more stringent selection criteria—provoked much criticism. The government was forced to backtrack on retroactivity, but it holds to the long-term goal of a fairly dramatic upgrade in selection criteria. Not evident is whether the numbers of immigrants can be increased with the upgraded selection criteria after the backlog has been cleared.

Should these efforts not succeed, Canada could be forced to choose between policy alternatives as practiced by the other two traditional countries of immigration, the United States and Australia. Canada could curtail immigration significantly, as Australia has done, forgoing its developmental potential. Or Canada could opt for a more laissez-faire U.S.-style approach to immigration, allowing immigrants to assume whatever economic role they can attain. This could bring a need to address potential threats to Canada's social services environment.

The integrity of border controls and the refugee determination process present a second major issue in current Canadian immigration policy. Refugees may represent anywhere between 10 and 20 percent of all immigrants to Canada (see figure 3.1). Because refugees are admitted based on humanitarian rather than economic criteria, because of uncertainty about the integrity of the refugee determination process, and because large backlogs have compromised the capacity for effective claims adjudication, some fear that the refugee system allows abuse of Canadian generosity. Highly publicized cases such as "boat people" arriving offshore claiming refugee status have provoked much criticism.

Objective assessment of the state of Canadian border security is virtually impossible. There are no published estimates of illegal immigration in Canada. The rate of recognition of asylum applications is high compared to the United States (58 percent in 1999), and Canada grants the same rights protections to applicants as to citizens. However, many persons are in immigration detention at any one time.

In the wake of the terrorist attacks of September 11, 2001, the new immigration act contains provisions to tighten access to the refugee determination system. These include more extensive initial screening of claimants, more explicit policies regarding detention, and limitations in appeal processes and other legal opportunities in order to speed the deportation of those suspected of serious crimes. The focus on refugee determination in this connection appears to have been partly a response to criticism of Canadian policy following a much-publicized case in which a Canadian refugee claimant under deportation proceedings attempted to enter the United States for the purpose of terrorism.

Regarding the terrorist threat itself, the new immigration policy offers relatively little. Resources for border control and security matters have been increased, but cooperation with U.S. concerns about border security seem designed as much to ensure continued economic traffic as to provide increased security. A new ID card for permanent residents, a measure long overdue, has been fast tracked.

These various circumstances suggest that Canada's immigration policy faces an uncertain future. The commitment to mass immigration poses a serious challenge in the context of an overall economic strategy that emphasizes a knowledge economy, advanced education, and global competition. This situation is exacerbated by recent trends toward declining earnings for newly arriving immigrants. The existing framework of social institutions may provide sufficient support to assist in immigrant integration, or it may become a casualty of an increasingly competitive and individualistic environment. Controlling immigration and its impact may pose greater challenges for Canada in the future than in the past.

References

Akbari, Ather H. 1995. "The Impact of Immigrants on Canada's Treasury, circa 1990." In *Diminishing Returns: The Economics of Canada's Recent Immigration Policy*, edited by Don DeVoretz. Toronto: C.D. Howe Institute.

Anisef, Paul, P. Axelrod, E. Baichman-Anisef, C.E. James, and A.H. Turrittin. 2000. *Opportunity and Uncertainty: Life Course Experiences of the Class of '73*. Toronto: University of Toronto Press.

Baker, Michael, and Dwayne Benjamin. 1994. "The Performance of Immigrants in the Canadian Labor Market," *Journal of Labor Economics* 12, no. 3: 369–405.

Bissoondath, Neil. 1994. *Selling Illusions: The Cult of Multiculturalism in Canada*. Toronto: Penguin.

Bloemraad, Irene. 2002. "The North American Naturalization Gap: An Institutional Approach to Citizenship Acquisition in the United States and Canada," *International Migration Review* 36, no. 1: 193–228.

Bloom, David, Gilles Grenier, and Morley Gunderson. 1995. "The Changing Labour Market Position of Canadian Immigrants," *Canadian Journal of Economics* 28, no. 4b: 987–1005.

Bloom, Michael, and Michael Grant. 2001. *Brain Gain: The Economic Benefits of Recognizing Learning and Learning Credentials in Canada*. Ottawa: Conference Board of Canada.

Borjas, George. 1990. *Friends or Strangers: The Impact of Immigrants on the U.S. Economy*. New York: Basic Books.

———. 1999. *Heaven's Door: Immigration Policy and the American Economy*. Princeton, N.J.: Princeton University Press.

Boyd, Monica. 1992. "Gender, Visible Minority and Immigrant Earnings Inequality: Reassessing an Employment Equity Premise." In *Deconstructing a Nation: Immigration, Multiculturalism, and Racism in 1990s Canada*, edited by Vic Satzewich. Toronto: Garamond.

Boyd, Monica, and Elizabeth M. Grieco. 1998. "Triumphant Transitions: Socio-economic Achievements of the Second Generation in Canada," *International Migration Review* 32, no. 4: 853–76.

Caldwell, Gary. 1994. "English Quebec: Demographic and Cultural Reproduction," *International Journal of the Sociology of Language* 105/106: 153–79.

Canada, Department of Manpower and Immigration. 1974. *The Immigration Programme*. Canadian Immigration and Population Study, vol. 2. Ottawa: Information Canada.

Canadian Alliance. 2000. "Your Principles: Policy Declaration." Calgary: Canadian Alliance.

CIC (Citizenship and Immigration Canada). 1998. "The Economic Performance of Immigrants: Immigration Category Perspective." IMDB Profile Series. Ottawa: CIC, December.

————. 2000. *The Interprovincial Migration of Immigrants to Canada*. IMDB Profile Series. Ottawa: CIC.

————. 2001. *Pursuing Canada's Commitment to Immigration: The Immigration Plan for 2002*. Ottawa: CIC.

Clark, Samuel D. 1962. "The Canadian Community and the American Continental System." In *The Developing Canadian Community*, by S.D. Clark. Toronto: University of Toronto Press.

DeVoretz, Don J. 1995. *Diminishing Returns: The Economics of Canada's Recent Immigration Policy*. Toronto: C.D. Howe Institute.

————. n.d. "Triangular Human Capital Flows between Sending, Entrepôt and the Rest of the World Regions." In *Host Societies and the Reception of Immigrants: Institutions, Markets and Policies*, edited by Jeffrey G. Reitz. La Jolla: Center for Comparative Immigration Studies, University of California, San Diego, forthcoming.

Duleep, Harriet Orcutt, and Mark C. Regets. 1992. "Some Evidence on the Effects of Admissions Criteria on Immigrant Assimilation." In *Immigration, Language and Ethnicity: Canada and the United States*, edited by Barry Chiswick. Washington, D.C.: AEI Press.

Esses, Victoria, John Dovidio, and G. Hodson. 2002. "Public Attitudes toward Immigration in the United States and Canada in Response to the September 11, 2001, 'Attack on America,'" *Analyses of Social Issues and Public Policy*, pp. 69–85.

Esses, Victoria, John Dovidio, L. Jackson, and T. Armstrong. 2001. "The Immigration Dilemma: The Role of Perceived Group Competition, Ethnic Prejudice and National Identity," *Journal of Social Issues* 57, no. 3: 389–412.

Green, Alan. 1995. "A Comparison of Canadian and U.S. Immigration Policy in the Twentieth Century." In *Diminishing Returns: The Economics of Canada's Recent Immigration Policy*, edited by Don DeVoretz. Toronto: C.D. Howe Institute.

Green, Alan, and David Green. 1996. "The Economic Goals of Canada's Immigration Policy, Past and Present." RIIM Working Paper No. 96-04. Burnaby, B.C.: Center for Research on Immigration and Integration in the Metropolis.

Kay, J. 1998. "Explaining the Modern Backlash against Multiculturalism," *Policy Options*, May, pp. 30–34.

LaChapelle, Rejean. 1980. "Evolution of Ethnic and Linguistic Composition." In *Cultural Boundaries and the Cohesion of Canada*, by Raymond Breton, Jeffrey G. Reitz, and Victor Valentine. Montreal: Institute for Research on Public Policy.

Laryea, S. 1998. "The Impact of Foreign-born Labour on Canadian Wages: A Panel Analysis." RIIM Working Paper No. 98-06. Vancouver: Center for Research on Immigration and Integration in the Metropolis.

Lum, Janet M. 1995. "The Federal Employment Equity Act: Goals vs. Implementation," *Canadian Public Administration*, Spring, pp. 45–76.

McVey, Wayne W., Jr., and Warren E. Kalbach. 1995. *Canadian Population*. Toronto: Nelson Canada.

Ornstein, Michael. 2000. "Ethno-Racial Inequality in Toronto: Analysis of the 1996 Census." Toronto: York University Institute for Social Research.

Palmer, Douglas. 1996. "Determinants of Canadian Attitudes toward Immigration: More Than Just Racism?" *Canadian Journal of Behavioral Science* 28, no. 3: 180–92.

Piché, Victor, Jean Renaud, and L. Gingras. 1999. "Comparative Immigrant Economic Integration." In *Immigrant Canada*, edited by Shiva S. Halli and Leo Driedger. Toronto: University of Toronto Press.

Reimers, David M., and Harold Troper. 1992. "Canadian and American Immigration Policy since 1945." In *Immigration, Language, and Ethnicity: Canada and the United States*, edited by Barry R. Chiswick. Washington, D.C.: AEI Press.

Reitz, Jeffrey G. 1998. *Warmth of the Welcome: The Social Causes of Economic Success for Immigrants in Different Nations and Cities*. Boulder, Colo.: Westview.

———. 2001a. "Immigrant Skill Utilization in the Canadian Labour Market: Implications of Human Capital Research," *Journal of International Migration and Integration* 2, no. 3: 347–78.

———. 2001b. "Immigrant Success in the Knowledge Economy: Institutional Change and the Immigrant Experience in Canada, 1970–1995," *Journal of Social Issues* 57, no. 3: 579–613.

———. n.d. "Educational Expansion and the Employment Success of Immigrants in the United States and Canada, 1970–1990." In *Globalization and Society: Processes of Differentiation Examined*, edited by Raymond Breton and Jeffrey G. Reitz. New York: Greenwood Press, forthcoming.

Reitz, Jeffrey G., and Raymond Breton. 1994. *The Illusion of Difference: Realities of Ethnicity in Canada and the United States*. Toronto: C.D. Howe Institute.

Reitz, Jeffrey G., and J.M. Lum. n.d. "Immigration and Diversity in a Changing Canadian City: Social Bases of Inter-group Relations in Toronto." In *Inside the Mosaic*, edited by Eric Fong. Forthcoming.

Renaud, Jean, Victor Piché, and L. Gingras. 1997. "Immigration et insertion économique: le rôle de l'origine nationale." In *Anciennes et nouvelles minorités: démographie, culture et politique.* Paris: J. Libbey-INED.

Sassen, Saskia. 1991. *The Global City: New York, London, Tokyo.* Princeton, N.J.: Princeton University Press.

Simon, Rita J., and James P. Lynch. 1999. "A Comparative Assessment of Public Opinion toward Immigrants and Immigration Policy," *International Migration Review* 33, no. 2: 455–67.

Software Human Resource Council. 1999. "Evaluation of the Software Development Worker Pilot Project." Prepared by EKOS Research Associates Inc. Ottawa: SHRC.

Swan, N., L. Auer, D. Chénard, A. dePlaa, A. deSilva, D. Palmer, and J. Serjak. 1991. *Economic and Social Aspects of Immigration.* Ottawa: Supply and Services Canada.

United Nations. Population Division. 2000. *Replacement Migration: Is It a Solution to Declining and Ageing Population?* New York: United Nations.

Young, Margaret. 1992. "Immigration: The Canada-Quebec Accord." Ottawa: Library of Parliament, Law and Government Division.

Commentary

Don J. DeVoretz

A Canadian academic criticizing a fellow Canadian outside of Canada is always concerned about focusing on the trivial. Thus, rather than dwell on the details of Jeffrey Reitz's essay, I will present an alternative view of his systematic analysis of Canada's management and integration of its immigration flows. In fact, I will argue, unlike Reitz, that Canadian immigration and settlement policies are largely irrelevant in determining the economic outcomes of the 70 percent or less of immigrants that ultimately reside in Canada after arrival. In short, who shows up to enter Canada and who ultimately stays in Canada is largely beyond the control of immigrant authorities, and Reitz's essay ignores this key fact.

Reitz's central thesis is that Canada has an elaborate immigrant management system that, at least since 1962, has employed a points system to comb the world for skilled immigrants who, in turn, can support the subsequent admission of family members and refugees. Furthermore, Reitz argues that Canada's expansionist immigration system is a cornerstone of Canadian economic development and forms an integral part of Canada's demographic and multicultural policies.

I contest this view, arguing that Canada's main economic development strategy, at least since 1989, has been to foster free trade under the North American Free Trade Agreement (NAFTA) with the United States and Mexico, and ultimately with Chile. Moreover, I argue that this trade agreement, with its separate immigration gateway, and other worldwide competition for Canada's resident immigrants have led to the exodus of highly skilled immigrants. In this sense, Canada's inadequate immigrant settlement policies and subsequent loss of immigrants have undermined the nation's economic development. I deal with these counterarguments in detail below.

The heart of my argument is owing to John Dales, who first characterized Canada as a small entrepôt country that since the early twentieth century has faced extraordinary competition for immigrants from the United States. This competition and the fact that immigrants ultimately select their destination country together imply a limited scope for Canadian immigrant selection policy as a national development tool. Moreover, at the turn of this new century the competitive pressure from the United States, Australia, and Germany to recruit highly skilled immigrants has increased the choice of country destinations for the highly skilled. Even if a skilled immigrant does choose Canada, the competition does not end, since over 30 percent of Canada's immigrants leave via many new exit doors. For example, Canada's membership in NAFTA provides a special visa for highly skilled Canadian immigrants, after their ascension to Canadian citizenship, to enter the United States. In addition, highly skilled Chinese immigrants to Canada are now returning to Hong Kong in substantial numbers (200,000 to 300,000 in Hong Kong residence circa 2001).

Thus Canada is not managing skilled immigration flows as Reitz argues; it is simply recycling highly skilled immigrants. In fact, Canada uses next year's immigrant flow to replenish last year's Canadian emigration of the highly skilled to the rest of the world. This leads to a zero-sum game in some occupations (health care, management, academia) when the immigrant inflow merely equals or even fails to equal Canada's emigrant outflow to the United States and the rest of the world.

The combined costs of the net loss in human capital through this outflow and the associated "churning costs" of training and settling immigrants have been substantial. Some authors argue that between 1989 and 1996 this process cost Canada over Can$12.6 billion in lost human capital and productivity. Seen in this light, Canada's current immigration policies, which do not address the emigration problem, have hindered, rather than aided, Canadian economic development. In fact, Canada's inability to attract and utilize productive immigrants since 1990 is also the core of Reitz's analysis. This reduced productivity is not due, however, to discrimination or lack of skill recognition, as Reitz argues. Rather, Canada's inability to retain the best of its highly talented immigrant pool leaves Canada with a mediocre pool of immigrants.

Moreover, the most recent immigration policy changes that Reitz mentions, including raising the required points total for skilled entry, will only exacerbate the churning problem. In the future, fewer numbers of highly qualified immigrants will enter Canada, but the outflow will not subside, leaving Canada with a smaller net stock of human capital. Thus these newest policies may raise the productivity of the eventual entrants, but they will also reduce the number of entrants. In order for Canadian immigrants to fulfill their historic goal of supplementing the nation's human capital stock, Canada actually needs a more robust *emigration* policy.

Quebec has pointed the way for the rest of Canada by instituting an emigration policy of enticing back Canadian-born émigrés with tax incentives. Since 2001 Quebec has targeted erstwhile Quebec residents who are highly trained and resident abroad with the prospect of five-year tax remission if they return. If successful, this emigration policy could partially offset the powerful attractions for Quebec's émigrés to permanently settle in the United States or elsewhere in the world. We await the outcome of the Quebec experiment. More dramatic emigration policies available to Canada could also include, as in Australia, a contingency educational loan scheme. Under this scheme, highly skilled emigrants who obtained their education in Canada would have to repay their educational subsidy if they left Canada. This would deter leaving.

In sum, Canada's immigration management system does effectively control the entry gate. However, it no longer produces the desired outcome of fostering economic development while meeting its humanitarian goals by retaining large numbers of highly skilled immigrants. Only by addressing Canada's century-old emigration problem can Canada's immigration policy be judged successful, as Reitz concludes.

Commentary

Harold Troper

In 1996 several states of the former East Germany approached the Canadian Embassy in Bonn for information on what they called the Canadian immigrant integration model. The embassy responded with a four-person delegation to meet with state and local officials. As a member of that delegation, I offered an introduction to Canadian immigration, settlement, and citizenship policies and practices, minority rights, linguistic dualism, and official multiculturalism. As I finished my presentation, a municipal councilor rejoined, "I understand all you said about immigrants becoming Canadian citizens and all you said about human rights and bilingualism and multiculturalism in Canada. What is unclear to me is what you Canadians do about your foreigners."

Jeffrey Reitz's chapter reminded me of this incident and how information filters through the prism of proximate experience—in this case, the particularism of the Canadian national experiment. This is certainly true of the two major threads in Reitz's essay—the first, the interplay between immigration policy management and the Canadian economy; the second, the role of government in mediating the impact of immigration on the Canadian social context. Canada borders only the United States, and in the wake of September 11, it is under U.S. pressure to harmonize its immigration and border control procedures with its southern neighbor.

Harmonization may be the future, but as Reitz correctly notes, Canadian immigration practice is now, as it has been in the past, largely designed to further Canadian economic growth through the in-gathering of off-shore labor to the service of domestic capital. This has meant state micromanagement of immigration intake and settlement to a far greater degree than is true of the more laissez-faire and individualist U.S. model. The Ca-

nadian state not only controls and sets admission standards, sorts applicants for admissibility, and guards Canada's gates against the unwanted. It
also actively beats the bushes in pursuit of immigrants or particular subsets
of immigrants and, after arrival, oversees their settlement. And why not? If
in the past, for example, the state was heavily invested in railway construction or the startup of labor-intensive extractive industries, why not actively
protect state investment by ensuring an ample and appropriate labor force?
Of course, the Canadian economy has changed, and priorities in selecting
immigrants have changed accordingly. But as Reitz argues, an activist tradition of management remains part of the Canadian immigration process to a
degree that many Americans might find unacceptable, or have found unacceptable before September 11.

Reitz underscores the interplay between the state as a player in the Canadian economy and its role in immigration management. The same can be
said for the state's role in mediating the impact of immigration on the Canadian social context. Canadian authorities have long seen immigration
policy as a backdoor population policy. Reitz quotes Prime Minister
Mackenzie King approving the reopening of immigration as part of a strategy to enlarge population and fuel economic growth. But this is only the
first half of the prime minister's statement. He went on to say, "the people
of Canada do not wish to make a fundamental alteration in the character of
their population through mass immigration." Yet this is precisely what immigration did. In relatively short order, immigration redefined the national
demographic. During the past several decades, immigration has dramatically reshaped the nation's ethnic and racial profile. Cities that were once
outposts of Anglo conformity now reflect a pluralism of origins beyond
anything imagined or intended by Canadians less than a generation ago.

This emerging population mix challenged the identity construct that
previously legitimized a separate Canadian state in North America, a construct steeped in lore of binational compromise and linguistic duality. Suffice to say that this founding myth became increasingly dysfunctional in the
postwar period, partly as a consequence of immigration. As a result, government sensed the need for a new and positive myth, a new legitimizing
national vision. While Reitz sees official multiculturalism as something of a
political ploy, an effort at selling ethnic and immigrant voters on official
bilingualism, I think it is far more. It is part of the new national vision and,
as such, another instance of state management, designed to promote national identity consensus around values of pluralism. Has it worked? Certainly, when announced in the early 1970s, official multiculturalism was
widely embraced in urban English-speaking Canada — and even by some
elements in French-speaking Canada — as a timely articulation of the new

Canadian population reality. Of course, as Reitz notes, critics found and still find reasons to denigrate official multiculturalism. However, no matter how untested in law, questioned in practice, maligned by naysayers, and ill defined in public perception, multiculturalism continues to shape the Canadian imagination fully thirty years after it was proclaimed. The imagery of multiculturalism, of a land invested in the welcome of immigrants and their cultures, is still so dominant in the popular mind that it has the power to reduce the complex American-Canadian relationship to a simplistic formula. The United States is a melting pot; Canada is a mosaic. Whether hollow of truth or not, multiculturalism remains an article of public faith, enshrined in the Charter of Rights and Freedoms, the supreme law of the land.

What does this all mean? What does it portend for the future? And what difference does it make to immigration policy? I suggest that the still-wide acceptance of multiculturalism as an ideal, especially in urban English-speaking Canada, may help to account for the generally positive Canadian attitude toward immigration. How much it contributes is hard to say, but it certainly has served to mute criticism of immigration policy as somehow un-Canadian. It may even have consecrated the continuing intake of immigrants from nontraditional and nonwhite sources as the "Canadian way." But will official multiculturalism and its myth-making power survive an increasingly multiracial, as opposed to multiethnic, reality? Will it survive the new juncture of race and security concerns? Time will tell. As Reitz suggests, among the challenges facing Canadian immigration today is finding a management strategy for a society increasingly bifurcated by race yet committed to continuing high levels of nonwhite immigration. Stay tuned.

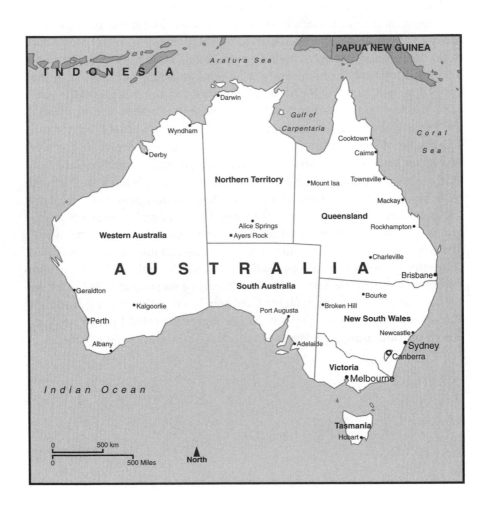

4

Australia: New Conflicts around Old Dilemmas

Stephen Castles and Ellie Vasta

Australians have mixed feelings about immigration. Since 1945, debates on immigration have been high on the public agenda. Planned mass immigration has been a key factor in transforming Australia from a small, insular society looking mainly to Britain for its values and heritage, to a larger and more diverse society that includes people from every part of the world. One Australian in four is an immigrant, and a similar proportion is the offspring of at least one immigrant parent. No other developed country except Israel can match such quotas. Since 1945, 6 million immigrants have come to Australia, 600,000 of whom were refugees or displaced persons. As a result, the population grew from 7.6 million in 1947 to 19.2 million in 2000 (DIMIA 2001a). Yet immigration and asylum remain highly controversial. The last federal election was fought and won on the issue of excluding asylum seekers, and the nation remains deeply divided on the issue.

The authors thank Caroline Alcorso (University of Sydney) for excellent research assistance in preparing this essay. We also thank Gary Freeman, Jeannette Money, and Takeyuki Tsuda for their helpful comments.

Herein lies Australia's immigration dilemma. Like the United States and Canada, it is an immigrant nation, yet many Australians see immigrants as a threat to national identity and even survival. The indigenous inhabitants of Australia were overrun and dispossessed by immigrants, namely, the British colonists who arrived in 1788. Ever since, white Australians have dreaded a similar fate. The Aboriginal and Torres Strait Islander peoples were decimated, dispossessed, and socially marginalized. Their numbers fell from an estimated 500,000 in 1788 to just 50,000 by the late nineteenth century. This near-genocide was legitimated through the racist beliefs of the time (Reynolds 1987), yet dispossession and marginalization continue to this day. The failure to deal with this historical stain and to achieve reconciliation with indigenous people is at the roots of a deep anxiety. As inhabitants of a "European outpost" on the rim of Asia, Australians have always feared that they would be colonized in turn by people from the far more populous countries of the region. Opinions and policies on immigration have always had a subtext of concern about race.

Australia was first settled as a penal colony, but free settlement was encouraged as awareness of the continent's agricultural potential and mineral wealth grew. The population expanded sharply in the 1850s following the discovery of gold. Employers called for recruitment of non-British labor to keep down wages and restrict the power of trade unions (de Lepervanche 1975). Organized labor was strongly opposed to such immigration, demanding wages "fit for white men." Racist propaganda accused the Chinese of undercutting wages, introducing crime and disease, and coveting white women. The colonial governments of Victoria, New South Wales, and South Australia introduced measures to exclude Chinese immigrants. There was a close link between racism and the emerging feeling of Australian identity and nationhood (MacQueen 1970). The White Australia policy was established by the Immigration Restriction Act, one of the first laws passed by the new federal Parliament in 1901.

European immigration remained relatively low in the early twentieth century, due to economic stagnation. However, World War II convinced policymakers that Australia needed a larger population and a stronger manufacturing sector to safeguard national sovereignty. A Department of Immigration was set up to develop a national immigration policy. The slogan used to sell this policy to a suspicious population was "populate or perish." The immigration program was designed to keep Australia white and British, and to hold the "yellow peril" of Asia at bay. However, labor demand quickly outstripped the availability of British migrants. In the late 1940s the Department of Immigration started recruiting displaced persons in European camps. Recruitment was soon extended to Italy, Greece, and Malta. Trade union opposition to non-British immigrants was overcome by promises that these workers would be tied to unskilled jobs for two years and would not displace Australian workers. The 1950s and 1960s were marked by high levels of European inmigration. Migrant workers became heavily concentrated in the expanding manufacturing industries of Melbourne, Sydney, and Adelaide (Lever-Tracey and Quinlan 1988).

The 1970s was a watershed decade in immigration history. The long economic boom was replaced by a more uncertain economic environment, and postwar full employment seemed to be at an end. The reaction of the Australian Labor Party (ALP) government of 1972-1975 was to cut immigration sharply and to emphasize the need for skilled labor. The White Australia policy was replaced by a nondiscriminatory selection system modeled on the Canadian points test. Successive governments also followed Canada in introducing a policy of multiculturalism as the basis for social policy toward immigrants. In the mid-1970s, Australia experienced the arrival of the first boat people since 1788, when Vietnamese refugees arrived on Australia's northern shores. Despite public suspicion, the Liberal-National coalition government developed a resettlement program.

From the mid-1970s to the early 1990s there was a consensus between the major political forces on a nondiscriminatory immigration policy and multicultural policies toward ethnic communities. Immigration remained relatively high, with family reunion as the largest component of entries. The ALP government's 1989 National Agenda for a Multicultural Australia emphasized the need to recognize cultural diversity as a basis for Australian social policy, citizenship, and identity. However, anti-immigration and antiminority sentiments began to grow. In 1984, historian Geoffrey Blainey warned against what he called the Asianization of Australia (Blainey 1984; see also Castles et al. 1988: 16–38). Other critics claimed that immigration would exacerbate unemployment or cause environmental degradation. In 1988, then opposition leader John Howard called for curbs on Asian immigration. In 1996, with the election of a new conservative government, Australian immigration policy was to enter a new era, shifting away from multiculturalism, cutting family reunion, and imposing draconian measures on asylum seekers.

In comparative terms, Australia is closest to Canada and the United States as a country whose founding myth is intertwined with its immigration history. It has taken over important elements of immigration and multicultural policy from Canada. It differs from the United States in the strong involvement of the state in selecting (and at times even recruiting) immigrants. Since colonial times the Australian state has also played a role in social policy and service provision for immigrants. With the emergence of multiculturalism in the 1970s, this role became even more marked, taking the new form of close collaboration with ethnic associations. Australian social policies toward immigrants have much in common with those of some European welfare states like the Netherlands and Sweden. The key feature of Australian immigration policy for many years has been the highly effective control of entries, facilitated by Australia's uniquely remote and inaccessible position. This has been challenged in recent years through trends to easier movement connected with regional and global change. The response has been an attempt to reassert control—however extreme the means. At the same time, a new skepticism about multiculturalism has paralleled trends in other immigration countries, especially those of Western Europe.

RECENT IMMIGRATION PATTERNS

Ever since Australia started its postwar immigration program in 1947, it has had a planned intake of permanent immigrants or "settlers." These immigrants have the right to work, bring in dependents, and remain permanently. Settlers are expected to become citizens; they can apply for naturalization after two years, the shortest qualifying period anywhere. Australian immigration debates focus mainly on permanent immigrants; yet it is important to realize that, with increasing regional and global integration, migratory patterns have become more complex. Australia now has large numbers of temporary foreign migrants. At the same time, growing numbers of Australians live and work abroad.

Migration Flows

Entries of permanent immigrants have been high in boom years like 1950 (185,000) and 1989 (145,000) and relatively low in recession periods like 1976 (53,000) and 1984 (69,000) (BIR 1991: 28). Ten-year averages show that immigration has been fairly constant (see table 4.1), although the average of about 90,000 a year for the 1990s represents a slight decline in numbers compared with previous decades.

Table 4.1. Permanent Immigrants to Australia, Average Annual Intakes

Years	Average Annual Intakes
1945–1960	107,000
1960–1969	130,000
1970–1979	96,000
1980–1989	110,000
1990–1999	90,000

Sources: Castles et al. 1998: 7; ABS 2002a.

Another way of measuring migration is to look at both arrivals and departures and to calculate net permanent migration. Table 4.2, which gives figures on these categories since 1992–1993,[1] shows an increase in permanent arrivals in the early 1990s and a decline followed by a new upward trend in the latter half of the decade.

In recent years, long-term temporary visitors (overseas visitors who intend to stay for twelve months or more but not permanently) have grown in number, and in 2000–2001, temporary visitors outnumbered permanent arrivals for the first time. The Temporary Residence Program is designed to help Australia recruit skilled workers (such as managers and information technology [IT] workers) from overseas. The category also includes working holiday makers, entertainers, and sports figures. In 2000–2001, a total of 160,157 temporary residence permits were granted, of which 45,669 were for skilled workers. The category of overseas student visas is also growing: 86,277 student visas were issued in 2000–2001, a rise of 16 percent over 1999–2000. Most students come from Asia, although the United States is also an important source (DIMIA 2001b).

The net long-term movement for 1999–2000 was 56,100 people. If this is added to the net permanent migration of 51,200 and adjustment is made for people who changed category (–8,200 individuals), this gives a net overseas migration figure of 99,100. This is the figure by which Australia's total population grew through immigration in 1999–2000, compared with 120,800 through natural increase. This was the highest figure

---

[1] Australian immigration figures are for financial years, which go from July to June.

since 1995–1996, indicating that downward trends in immigration in the mid-1990s have now been reversed (ABS 2001). The increased migration program for 2002–2003 (announced in May 2002 and with a target figure of 100,000 to 110,000) indicates that this upward trend will continue for the time being.

Table 4.2. Permanent Immigrants to Australia, Net Migration

Years	Number of Permanent Arrivals	Net Permanent Migration
1992–1993	76,300	48,400
1993–1994	69,800	42,500
1994–1995	87,400	60,500
1995–1996	99,100	70,500
1996–1997	85,800	55,900
1997–1998	77,300	45,300
1998–1999	84,100	49,000
1999–2000	92,272	51,000

Source: DIMIA 2001b.

However, it is important to realize that emigration by Australians is also increasing. Living abroad has become an important part of professional or personal experience, and as many as 800,000 Australian citizens currently work overseas. Many are in traditional destination countries— Britain, where one London neighborhood is popularly known as "Kangaroo Valley," and the United States—but there is an increasing trend toward employment in the fast-growing economies of Southeast and Northeast Asia.

Entry Categories

Permanent immigration has two components: the migration program, which encompasses "family stream" and "skill stream" entrants, and the humanitarian program for refugees and others admitted on humanitarian grounds. In addition, New Zealand citizens can enter and remain freely on the basis of the 1973 Trans-Tasman Travel Agreement.

As table 4.3 shows, family stream program levels have been kept fairly constant in recent years, while skill stream targets have been increased. This reflects the government's aim of focusing on economic migration while reducing family reunion. At the same time, overall migration program levels have risen and are now close to those of the early 1990s. However, it appears that many of those who enter in the skill stream are actually dependent spouses and children accompanying the primary applicant. This statistical quirk means that not all those who enter in the skill stream actually join the labor force.

Table 4.3. Australia's Migration Program Levels

Eligibility Category	1997–1998	1998–1999	1999–2000	2000–2001[a]	2001–2002[a]
Family	31,310	32,040	32,000	33,600	37,900
Skill	34,670	35,000	35,333	43,000	45,500[b]
Special eligibility[c]	1,110	890	2,850	2,400	1,600
Total	67,100	67,900	70,200	79,000	85,000

Source: DIMIA 2002.

[a] Projected.

[b] The 2001–2002 skill stream has a contingency reserve of 8,000 places, not shown in the above figures.

[c] Special eligibility applies to former citizens or residents of Australia, or dependants of New Zealand citizens resident in Australia.

About 80 percent of those accepted in the family stream are spouses or fiancé(e)s of Australian citizens or residents (who may be earlier immigrants). The next largest categories are children and parents of existing citizens or residents. It is very hard for other relatives, such as siblings, nephews, or nieces, to enter as dependents. Until 1996–1997, members of this group who entered to take up employment were counted in the family stream as "concessional family," although they were still measured against the points test, which assesses employability according to criteria of age, education, professional experience, and English language knowledge. Since 1997–1998 this group has been counted in the skill stream under the category "skilled-Australian linked/sponsored." This device reduced family entries and increased skill stream entries by 6,000 to 8,000 per year—another statistical quirk.

The skill stream is divided into a number of categories, of which the largest is "independent" (25,100 in the 2001–2002 program). This category is for applicants whose education, skill, English language ability, and ready employability (as measured by the points test) will contribute to the Australian economy. The other categories are "employer nomination," for workers nominated specifically by an employer; "business skills," for entrepreneurs who make a commitment to invest in Australia; and "distinguished talents," for people with outstanding records of achievement in a profession, the arts, or sports.

Humanitarian program targets—not shown in table 4.3—have been fairly constant at around 12,000 since the early 1990s. Australia remains one of only about ten countries in the world that have resettlement programs to select refugees in countries of first asylum in collaboration with the United Nations High Commissioner for Refugees (UNHCR). Until 1999–2000 the humanitarian program had three components: (1) refugees, as defined by the 1951 UN Refugee Convention; (2) the special humanitarian program (SHP) for people who suffer gross human rights violations but would not qualify under the 1951 convention; and (3) the special assistance category (SAC), which was established to allow people displaced by violence in such countries as the former Yugoslavia to join relatives in Australia. (The SAC was phased out in 2000–2001.) In recent years an additional non-program category has grown in importance: onshore protection visa grants, for people who claim asylum after arriving in Australia.

Actual arrivals do not correspond with program figures because some migrants granted a visa in one year may arrive in the next year, and others may not come at all. Moreover, New Zealanders are included in arrival figures but not in program figures. In addition, the government counts onshore protection visa grants toward the humanitarian program figures, even though they are not counted as permanent arrivals.

Table 4.4 shows how successful the government has been in reducing family stream arrivals relative to skill stream arrivals. In 1995–1996, the last year of the Labor government, family entrants made up 69 percent of all nonhumanitarian entrants, while skilled entrants were only 29 percent. By 2000–2001, family entrants were down to 45 percent, and skilled entrants were up to 53 percent. However, some of this apparent change may be due to the statistical quirks mentioned above. At the same time, the number of immigrant New Zealanders has grown rapidly in response to economic conditions in both the sending and receiving countries. In March 2001, it was estimated that 450,000 New Zealand citizens were present in Australia, of whom 78 percent were in the labor force (DIMIA 2001c).

Table 4.4. Permanent Arrivals to Australia, by Eligibility Category

Eligibility Category	1995–1996	1996–1997	1997–1998	1998–1999	1999–2000	2000–2001[a]
Family	46,458	36,490	21,142	21,501	19,896	21,227
Skill	20,008	19,697	25,985	27,931	32,350	35,607
Humanitarian	13,824	9,886	8,779	8,790	7,267	7,625
New Zealand	16,234	17,501	19,393	24,680	31,610	NA
Other	2,615	2,178	2,028	1,241	1,149	NA
Total	99,139	85,752	77,327	84,143	92,272	

Sources: DIMA, Immigration Update and DIMIA Immigration Update, Special Edition 2000-1.

[a] Due to changes in data collection methods, the figures for 2000-2001 are not strictly comparable to earlier ones; the apparent increase is probably slightly exaggerated.

NA = not available.

The humanitarian arrival figures in table 4.4 show an apparent decline in recent years. This is due to the increase in onshore protection visas from 1,588 in 1997–1998 to 1,834 in 1998–1999, 2,458 in 1999–2000, and 5,577 in 2000–2001. Some of these visas were granted to people who arrived by plane on a visitor visa and then claimed asylum, but increasing numbers have gone to boat people, mainly from Afghanistan, Iraq, and Iran. The number of persons arriving in Australia without permission averaged only a few hundred per year up to the late 1990s, but they rose to 920 in 1998–1999, 4,175 in 1999–2000, and 4,141 in 2000–2001 (Crock and Saul 2002: 24). Although the numbers of asylum seekers are still very low compared with other parts of the world, especially Europe, the growth is seen as undermining the tradition of strict government control of entries, which has hitherto been possible because of Australia's remote location.

IMMIGRATION AND POPULATION

Australia's immigration program has significantly changed the size and composition of the population. The 1947 census counted 7.6 million people. Of these, 90 percent had been born in Australia, and most of the overseas-born came from the United Kingdom and Ireland. By the time of the 2001 census, the population had more than doubled, to around 19 million, of whom 4 million (22 percent) were overseas-born. Table 4.5 shows how the overseas-born population has steadily increased both absolutely and as a share in total population.

Table 4.5. Australian Population, 1947–1996

Census Year	Population Born Overseas	Total Population	Overseas-born as Percent of Total Population
1947	744,187	7,579,385	9.8
1954	1,286,466	8,986,530	14.3
1961	1,778,780	10,508,186	16.9
1971	2,579,318	12,755,638	20.2
1976	2,718,318	13,548,448	20.1
1981	3,003,834	14,576,330	20.6
1986	3,247,301	15,602,163	20.8
1991	3,689,128	16,407,045	22.5
1996	3,908,213	17,892,418	21.8
2001	3,988,000	18,972,350	22.3

Sources: Australian population censuses.
Note: The 2001 overseas-born figure omits the category "other or not stated" (1,052,000 persons), which is also omitted when calculating the overseas-born percentage.

In 1971, 85 percent of Australia's immigrant population was from Europe, with half having come from the United Kingdom. By 2001 the European share had fallen to 53 percent, and those from the United Kingdom and Ireland were only 27 percent of the total immigrant population. These older groups were declining, while the share of persons born in Asia and the Middle East was up to 29 percent. New Zealand–born people made up 9 percent and were increasing fast. There were also 410,000 Aboriginals and Torres Strait Islanders (2.2 percent of the population), the only true "nonimmigrants" in Australia. However, apart from the Italians (1.2 percent of total population), no group of non-British origin makes up more than 1 percent of Australia's population. By contrast, in some European countries certain ethnic groups constitute substantial minorities, such as the 2 million Turks in Germany or the million-plus people of Algerian origin in France. The Australian people today comprises an Anglo-Australian majority and a large number of relatively small ethnic groups.

Immigration's dramatic impact on the size and composition of the Australian population is further illustrated by census data on second-generation Australians (children of immigrants). In 1996, 22 percent of the population were born overseas, while 27 percent had at least one overseas-born parent. First and second generations together made up 49 percent of the Australian population (ABS 2002a).

Demography is a political topic in Australia. In the early colonial period, governments encouraged high immigration in order to "people the empty spaces." Today, however, migration is concerned primarily with economic goals, and population growth is not generally seen as an important objective. This is somewhat curious, considering that Australia is one of the most sparsely populated countries in the world, with only about 2.5 persons per square kilometer. Australia's population is about the same as that of Tokyo, yet it is dispersed over an area almost as large as the United States. Much of Australia's interior is desert, and the overwhelming majority of people live in the coastal zones, where population density is about 50 persons per square kilometer, but this is still low compared with most developed countries.

Currently, natural increase and net migration each contribute about 0.5 percent to annual population growth. Since 1962, falling fertility has led to a decline in the rate of natural increase. Population projections by the Australian Bureau of Statistics (ABS) indicate that continued low fertility, combined with the increase in deaths from an aging population, will result in natural population increase falling below zero around 2035 (ABS 2002b). Aging and long-term population decline are beginning to be seen as problems. Australia's total fertility rate was down to 1.85 by 1994—below the reproduction rate of 2.1, but still more favorable than in Japan and most European countries. By 1996, 12 percent of the population was over sixty-five years of age, and the figure is projected to reach 23 percent in 2051 (Castles et al. 1998: 26). However, the rates of net migration needed to significantly slow this process would be very high, and there is little support for this approach.

IMMIGRANTS AND THE ECONOMY

In the early postwar years, Australia's immigration program was mainly concerned with recruiting workers for low-skill jobs in factories, construction, and services. Many of the migrants—especially those from southern Europe—were of rural, low-skilled background. Others had educational qualifications and vocational skills that were not accepted in Australia, leading to their downward mobility on arrival. The stereotype of the migrant was summed up in the pejorative "factory fodder." Construction sites or heavy industrial plants (such as the Snowy River Hydro-Electric Scheme, the mines, and the steelworks) served as entry points for successive waves of immigrants, with few workers staying on due to hard working conditions and poor industrial relations (Collins 1991; Lever-Tracey and Quinlan 1988). Labor shortages during boom years provided opportunities, and many skilled people ultimately gained recognition of their qualifications—though some never did. Others achieved promotion to skilled or supervisory positions. And still others improved their situation by setting up businesses (Collins et al. 1995).

Since the 1970s the characteristics of new immigrants have changed. Recessions and industrial restructuring have reduced the need for unskilled labor. The stress is now on attracting persons with skills that are in short supply in the domestic labor force. The average qualification level of recent immigrants is higher than that of the Australian workforce as a whole, even though entrants in the humanitarian program and the family stream often have lower skill levels. There is considerable evidence of upward occupational mobility in Australia (Wooden et al. 1994: 247–51). Many immigrants start their working life at lower levels than they occupied prior to migration, but they make up the deficit once they gain language proficiency and local knowledge. On the other hand, the returns on premigration education are often low, particularly if that education was obtained in a non–English-speaking country. Immigrants who receive education or training in Australia seem to do as well as the Australian-born population with similar qualifications.

Research also indicates substantial intergenerational mobility. Children of immigrants often do well at school and university, and gain access to professional and executive employment. Success rates vary. For example, 1991 census data showed that 18.8 percent of male Australians of Greek parentage had university degrees, compared with only 2.5 percent of their fathers. Several European immigrant groups appeared to share this pattern, although usually to a lesser degree. As for Asian immigrants, settlement is so recent that adequate data are not yet available, but mounting evidence indicates a similar picture (Birrell and Khoo 1995). However, other researchers argue that the evidence for educational success is patchy. Although there has been upward mobility in some ethnic groups, others — including those of Maltese, Dutch, German, Turkish, and Khmer parentage — have had far less positive experiences (Cahill 1996). In any case, the upward mobility of the children of postwar European immigrants was based on such favorable circumstances as full employment, increasing egalitarianism in education, and a growing tertiary sector. It is uncertain whether these conditions will exist for the children of more recent immigrants.

Some immigrants still suffer disadvantage in the labor market. Immigrant workers, both male and female, continue to be overrepresented in industrial sectors and occupations that are particularly vulnerable to job losses. Between 1986 and 1995, 32,000 manufacturing jobs disappeared, yet in the same period, Australian-born workers increased the number of jobs they held in this sector by 19,000. It appears that they were displacing immigrants who were often unable to obtain the training needed for higher skilled jobs. Many older immigrants left the workforce through early retirement or invalidity (Commissioner 1995). One consequence of such changes is that unemployment during the first three postwar recessions — 1974–1975, 1982–1983, and 1990–1991 — was much higher for non-English-speaking-background (NESB) immigrants than for English-speaking-background (ESB) immigrants or the Australian-born (Ackland and Williams 1992).[2] Economic restructuring has led to growing inequalities and polarized living standards, with increasing numbers of both wealthy and poor people. NESB immigrants and their children are disproportionately represented among those in poverty and unemployment.

Table 4.6 shows the unemployment rates of various groups in the Australian labor force in 1996. Unemployment rates for ESB immigrants were lower than for any other group. Unemployment rates for NESB immigrants were nearly twice those of ESB immigrants and considerably higher than those of the Australia-born. The heterogeneity of the NESB group is reflected in the very high unemployment rates for Vietnamese

---

[2] Australian statistics often differentiate between immigrants from English-speaking-background (ESB) countries (principally the United Kingdom, Ireland, the United States, New Zealand, Canada, and South Africa) and non-English-speaking-background (NESB) countries. These categories were highly relevant in the postwar period, but they are beginning to lose their usefulness since both include increasingly diverse groups.

and Lebanese immigrants. Aboriginal unemployment figures are also very high. Differences in unemployment rates are partly a reflection of differences in employment patterns of the various groups. Australia-born and ESB immigrants have a fairly similar distribution across industries, while NESB immigrants are more strongly concentrated in manufacturing and less strongly represented in the service sector (Foster 1996). However, such differences are themselves a reflection of other social factors. NESB immigrants may have fewer skilled jobs and work in more vulnerable types of industry because of lower levels of education, lack of vocational training, and poor English proficiency.

Table 4.6. Unemployment in Australia, by Selected Birthplace and Gender

Unemployment Rates	Females (%)	Males (%)
Australia total	7.4	7.8
Overseas-born	9.7	9.0
English-speaking countries	6.1	6.4
United Kingdom and Ireland	5.8	6.0
New Zealand	7.4	7.6
Non–English-speaking countries	12.4	10.9
Vietnam	20.4	23.2
Lebanon	30.6	24.0
Aboriginal	28.6	32.2

Source: 1996 census.

The current emphasis on skills, age, and language proficiency means that new biases have entered the immigrant selection criteria, discriminating in favor of those with good educational opportunities rather than on the basis of race or origin. Changes to immigration rules in mid-1999 aimed to make use of the qualifications gained by overseas students paying full fees in Australian universities. The new selection system allocates additional bonus points to those with Australian credentials. Whereas in the past students had to leave Australia for a two-year period before applying to migrate to Australia, they are now allowed to remain in the country as they pursue their immigration application. Many of these full-fee overseas students come from Asia and are concentrated in the business and information technology fields. Such trends are leading to a brain drain from less developed countries (for example, the health care system in the Philippines is being strained by the exodus of nurses being attracted overseas) while reducing the incentive to improve education and vocational training in Australia (Birrell 2001).

THE IMMIGRATION POLICY REGIME

The importance of immigration for Australia is reflected in institutional structures. In 1945 the ALP government set up a Department of Immigration and gave it the task of organizing the postwar immigration program. There has been an immigration minister ever since. The department soon took on the additional function of providing "post-arrival services" for immigrants, such as hostels, job-finding services, and language courses. It also became responsible for naturalization and citizenship matters. In the late 1960s the Department of Immigration was renamed the Department for Immigration and Ethnic Affairs (DIEA) in view of the growing recognition of the emergence of ethnic communities. The tasks expanded to include social and educational policy for immigrants. The 1972–1975 ALP government set up a restructured Department of Immigration and Labor. With the consolidation of multiculturalism in the late 1970s, government involvement expanded further, with the (restored) DIEA developing consultative arrangements to bring ethnic leaderships into the planning and delivery of social services. In 1987 the ALP government brought multicultural issues to the center of the federal government by setting up the Office of Multicultural Affairs (OMA) in the Department of Prime Minister and Cabinet. The responsibility for immigration policy and service delivery remained in the (renamed) Department of Immigration, Local Government and Ethnic Affairs (DILGEA).

In 1996, John Howard's Liberal-National coalition government abolished the OMA. Responsibility for multiculturalism returned to the (again renamed) Department of Immigration and Multicultural Affairs (DIMA). This represented a downgrading of multiculturalism and an upgrading of immigration policy, symbolized by the elevation of Minister Philip Ruddock to cabinet rank. By the end of the 1990s, most state governments had also abolished or downgraded their ethnic affairs units. Ruddock has pursued a policy of increasing skilled intakes, reducing family reunion, keeping humanitarian intakes constant, and introducing a harsh regime for asylum seekers, including censoring groups seeking to represent them. He was rewarded after the 2001 election by being given an even bigger portfolio in the (yet again renamed) Department of Immigration, Multicultural and Indigenous Affairs (DIMIA).

Despite all of the name changes, the main function of the department throughout this half-century has been to plan and manage the immigration program. The broad lines of policy are laid down by the prime minister and cabinet. Department officials then draw up proposals for annual admission quotas in the various categories of the migration program and the humanitarian program. This process is accompanied by consultations with interest groups. In the early part of each year, the minister and his officials travel around Australia holding open meetings on the planned program in state capitals and regional centers. These town hall meetings allow both local associations and individuals to make representations.

Program implementation is the responsibility of the Department of Immigration in Canberra and its immigration officers stationed in Australian high commissions and consulates around the world. Prospective immigrants (up to 1 million each year) apply to the nearest of these, where they may be interviewed and given medical and occupational tests. Decisions are made centrally by DIMIA, which issues visas to successful applicants. DIMIA is also "responsible for programs to combat and deter people smuggling" and for "proactive negotiations with overseas governments, international organizations and other agencies to stem unauthorized entry to Australia" (DIMIA 2002). This function of control and repression is reinforced by DIMIA's responsibility for a chain of detention centers to implement the mandatory incarceration of all persons who enter illegally (including asylum seekers). Some centers are in remote areas like Port Hedland (in northwestern Australia) and Woomera (a former rocket range in the South Australian desert). However, actual management of the camps is subcontracted to the private company Australasian Correctional Management, a subsidiary of a U.S. security corporation.

DIMIA is also responsible for issuing statistics and informing the public, and it has a small research section. Until 1996 Australia had a Bureau of Immigration, Multicultural and Population Research (BIMPR) funded by the DILGEA (as the immigration department was then named) but with considerable autonomy to carry out independent peer-reviewed research. Although this bureau was abolished by the Howard government in 1996, one aspect of immigration research was maintained within DIMA and the DIMIA: the Longitudinal Survey of Immigrants to Australia. This valuable research instrument, which began in the early

1990s and is based on regular interviews with successive cohorts of immigrants, is designed to assess the success of immigration policy by examining the employment and social outcomes of immigrants coming in different visa classes.

THE LEGAL FRAMEWORK

The main legislative basis for Australian immigration is the Migration Act of 1958. Any foreigner wishing to enter Australia must apply for a visa in advance. The only exception is a citizen of New Zealand (the 1973 Trans-Tasman Travel Agreement lays down reciprocal rights of free entry for Australians and New Zealanders). The procedure for obtaining tourist and short-stay business visas was simplified in the late 1990s, so that in most cases these can now be obtained through travel agents when purchasing tickets. Due to Australia's geographical position, immigration control is fairly easy to enforce, and there are few illegal entrants. However, in 1999 there were estimated to be 53,000 overstayers—people who entered legally but remained after the expiration of their entry visas. About three-quarters had been in Australia over one year, and many worked illegally. DIMIA seems to make little effort to detect and remove overstayers, an interesting contrast with reactions to boat people (Crock and Saul 2002: 23). This may be because many overstayers are from the United Kingdom, the United States, and other developed countries.

In the past, Australian immigration policy discriminated on the basis of race and national origin. Under the Immigration Restriction Act of 1901, non-Europeans were generally not admitted at all, while certain Europeans were seen as less desirable than others. This White Australia policy was watered down in the 1960s and finally abolished in 1972. Since then, Australia's immigration policy has been nondiscriminatory in that persons from any country, whatever their ethnic origin, sex, color, or religion, can apply to come. The only explicit discrimination is the positive one in favor of New Zealanders.

In most legal areas the differences between the rights of citizens and those of lawful permanent residents are small (Rubinstein 1995). Once accepted for entry as permanent settlers, immigrants enjoy a range of rights that are denied in many other countries of immigration. Permanent settlers have access to all employment-related, social security, and medical benefits. However, in January 1993 the ALP government decided to deny unemployment and sickness benefits to immigrants for the first six months after arrival. Fees were introduced for English language courses for adult migrants (although refugees were exempted). People sponsoring relatives as immigrants had to promise to support them if they were unemployed or in need. Since 1996 the Liberal-National Party government has made further changes. Fees for visas and compulsory English language courses for new immigrants have been sharply increased. The waiting period for most welfare benefits has been lengthened to two years for new entrants (Zappala and Castles 2000).

The centerpiece of Australia's approach to incorporating immigrants is easy access to citizenship. Historically, citizenship was closely linked to British identity. Australia has been considered an independent nation since 1901, but it did not have its own citizenship until 1949. Prior to that date, all persons born, registered, or naturalized in Australia were British subjects (Cronin 2001). The Nationality and Citizenship Act of 1948 still defined Australians as British subjects. Naturalization required five years of residence, an oath of loyalty to the British monarch, and evidence of cultural assimilation. Such conditions deterred many immigrants. As ethnic diversity increased, the pressure grew for a more inclusive notion of citizenship. By 1984 the law had been renamed the Australian Citizenship Act, the waiting period had been cut to two years, the English language requirements were relaxed, dual citizenship was permitted for immigrants seeking naturalization, and the oath of allegiance was to Australia and its people rather than to the British queen (Castles and Davidson 2000: 165–68; Davidson 1997). In recognition of the emerging global Australian diaspora, the law was further amended in 2002 to allow Australians living abroad to take another citizenship without losing their Australian one. This change in the meaning of citizenship, which may well be one of migration's most important impacts on Australian society, is closely bound up with the rise of multiculturalism.

PUBLIC DISCOURSES ON IMMIGRATION

Interest Groups

A number of groups have a special stake in immigration. Trade unions and business and industry groups have tended to form a "growth lobby" in support of immigration. In contrast, the environmental movement has opposed immigration (Warhurst 1993). Immigrant associations have lobbied for increased family reunion, and they have often made special representations for favorable policies toward specific groups (Jupp 1993). International bodies have little influence on Australia's policies, although the UNHCR does make representations on the humanitarian program.

Sending countries have had some influence when economic or financial issues are at stake. For example, when the One Nation Party unveiled an anti-Asian immigration platform, the Asian media carried numerous reports and debates that influenced potential student decisions as well as investments. We will discuss the main domestic interest groups in turn.

Trade unions have influenced immigration policy significantly over time. From the 1860s to the 1960s, unions largely supported the White Australia policy. After World War II, the unions only accepted the migration program after receiving assurances that migrants would not take jobs from Australian workers. In the 1960s and 1970s, trade union leaders also emphasized the importance of family reunion to their overseas-born members and supported the intake of refugees. Yet a certain ambivalence remained: trade unionists feared that immigration could increase unemployment, and they argued for improvements in vocational training arrangements within Australia as a substitute for skilled immigration. After the 2002 national elections, a group called Labor for Refugees was formed. It includes trade union and ALP members, and its aim is to change ALP policy regarding asylum seekers and detention centers.

Business and employer groups take an active interest in immigration policy, seeing immigration as a way to strengthen the economy and expand the domestic market. Throughout the 1990s business supported the government's emphasis on skilled migration. A leading business organization, the Business Council of Australia (BCA), has over the years supported large intakes and advocated an expansionist population policy. In its submission on the 2000–2001 migration program, the BCA strongly urged the federal government to develop a long-term population policy to guide the future of Australia's population, stating that "an economy is built on families and on children, not just by computer programmers, chefs and scientists" (BCA 1999: 5). Similarly, the Housing Industry Association, which includes both large and small construction companies, has consistently called for larger intakes of both workers and families. It stresses that more people mean a demand for more houses, which is beneficial to their industry and, they claim, to the whole economy.

Although the environmental movement is for the most part opposed to immigration, there is considerable controversy within it. A major environmental group, the Australian Conservation Foundation (ACF), adopted a policy of population stabilization in 1978 but then shifted to a more positive policy on immigration in the late 1980s. The policy had shifted to cautious opposition to large-scale immigration by the early 1990s (Warhurst 1993). Other environmental groups, such as Australians for an Ecologically Sustainable Population (AESP), seem to have been specifically set up to campaign against immigration. AESP has strong links with Australians Against Further Immigration (AAFI) and with rightwing groups like the One Nation Party. Environmentalists opposed to immigration claim that Australia has a limited carrying capacity due to lack of water and the country's thin and nutrient-poor soils. Problems of waste assimilation, loss of biodiversity, and degradation of natural resources and amenities are also put forward (Jones 2001: 50–51). There is considerable scientific dispute on all these matters. For instance, some scientists argue that Australia's carrying capacity is as high as 50 to 100 million, while others assert that the current 19 million is already unsustainable (Castles et al. 1998: chap. 4).

ETHNIC RIGHTS AND ANTI-RACISM

The late 1960s and early 1970s saw the beginning of major social transformations in Australia. This was a time when new social movements began to challenge the social and political fabric of many Western democracies. The expansion of the welfare state was linked to the emergence of nongovernmental organizations (NGOs) and community activists—often grouped together as the "community sector." They called for greater social equity and the inclusion of disadvantaged groups into the society and polity. Ethnic community groups pointed out that they were denied access to many educational and social services due to lack of information and culturally inappropriate modes of delivery. Despite formal rights to government services, they were excluded in practice.

Such demands were articulated in the language of both *rights* and *participation*. Both first- and second-generation immigrants became involved in the development and delivery of services at the community level. Immigrant associations had been initially established in response to the cultural and social concerns of specific ethnic communities. The introduction of social policies aimed specifically at immigrants, first by the ALP and then by the coalition government, put a premium on ethnic mobilization and formation of associations to speak in the name of immigrants (Vasta 1993). There was a link between the emergence of multicultural policies/services and the development of formalized ethnic lobby groups, of which the most important were (and still are, though with diminished significance) the state Ethnic Communities Councils (ECCs) and the Federation of Ethnic Communities Councils of Australia (FECCA).

The development of ethnic associations helped end assimilationism and bring in multiculturalism. This caused some observers to imply that some sinister "ethnic lobby" was having an illegitimate influence on politics as well as on family intakes (Betts 1993; Blainey 1984). In contrast, most Australian political scientists argue that there is no monolithic "ethnic vote" that can be controlled by ethnic leaders to secure specific political outcomes (McAllister 1988). Immigrants have not constituted a united political force, mainly because the differences among them in terms of social position, interests, and values are as great as those within the Anglo-Australian population. According to Jupp:

> Although its presence cannot be ignored, the ethnic lobby since 1988 has seemed peripheral to some of the major debates on immigration.... The greatest weakness of the "lobby" has probably been the absence of a sympathetic base in parliament comparable to those that exist for major ethnic groups in the USA or Canada. There are very few NESB immigrant politicians in Canberra (Jupp 1993: 220).

The period from 1972 to the early 1990s was one of political contestation on immigration and multiculturalism. Ethnic communities, community-sector associations, trade unions, and sections of the ALP called for full participation of immigrants in society, adding that it was the duty of the state to provide the conditions needed to achieve this. The concern was that political forces opposed to immigration and multiculturalism wanted to return to a racist past, epitomized by the White Australia policy and discrimination against immigrants and Aboriginal people. The period's liberal and expansionary atmosphere created a broad basis of public support for diversity and equity. However, the very success of multiculturalism led to a decline in ethnic mobilization by the early 1990s. At the same time, the concern of many Australians about the impact of globalization on their economic and social situation opened up the cultural and political space for a resurgence of anti-immigration sentiments. This was the background to the emergence of the nationalistic One Nation Party and new exclusionism of the mainstream parties in the mid-1990s (Vasta 1999).

PUBLIC OPINION ON IMMIGRATION AND REFUGEE POLICY

The first public opinion poll on immigration was taken in 1951. According to Goot (2001: 824), the most politically sensitive issues examined included the number and sources of migrants, Asian immigration, refugees, and multiculturalism. Through the 1950s and 1960s, Australia's immigration program met with considerable support. Since then, annual intake has only occasionally achieved majority support. Most polls taken in the late 1980s and early 1990s registered majority opposition, though majority support returned in 1998 and 1999. Goot suggests that perhaps attitudes to immigration do not correlate directly with the size of the migrant intake, noting that during the 1990s, when the intake had been reduced, support was low. However, lack of support may be directly related to higher levels of unemployment, which was the case in the early 1990s. Support increased as employment levels rose in the late 1990s.

During the late 1960s and much of the 1970s, polls indicated that Asian immigration was at an acceptable (low) level. From the early 1980s, as unemployment rose—and as people like Blainey (an academic historian), John Howard (then leader of the opposition), and, in the mid-1990s, Pauline Hanson (an extreme right politician) called for reductions in the Asian intake—most polls showed that respondents thought too many Asians were settling in Australia. Nevertheless, many polls reported widespread support for a nondiscriminatory policy. Goot suggests that there are two possible explanations for this contradiction. First, the respondents are hypocrites: "they may find it easy to affirm nondiscriminatory principles, but difficult to let them influence their judgment." Second, they may think that "too many Asians are coming simply because they believe that too many migrants of *any* kind are coming or they think the system of selection itself is weighted in favor of Asians" (Goot 2001: 825).

On the whole, poll figures indicate that a majority of respondents support the numbers of refugees allowed in each year. From 1978 to 1993, between 28 and 44 percent of respondents wanted to "send back" asylum seekers. Polls in the late 1970s, at the time of the first intakes of Indo-Chinese refugees, indicated that the public felt the proportion was about right or too low (Goot 2001: 825). In a recent poll, the opinion that asylum seekers should be detained in camps until their application was heard received support from 71 percent of respondents; 21 percent thought they should be allowed to live in the community pending a decision (Betts 2001: 42). One possible explanation for this is that public opinion has been influenced by the statements of political leaders and opinion makers like John Howard and Pauline Hanson. There is a stark contrast to the positive leadership of the late 1970s, which helped stimulate support for the Indo-Chinese boat people at that time.

SOCIAL POLICY: FROM ASSIMILATION TO MULTICULTURALISM

Australia's postwar immigration policy was not intended to create a multicultural society. It was driven by strategic and economic considerations. The maintenance of homogeneity, not cultural diversity, was the aim. But as it became apparent that not enough British immigrants wanted to come, recruitment was broadened to other parts of Europe, and the policy of assimilation was introduced to turn Dutch, Polish, Italian, and Greek immigrants into "New Australians." On one level this approach was a success; immigrants did find work, settle, and become citizens. On another level it was a failure; labor market segmentation and residential segregation, together with inadequate schooling and experiences of racism, were the conditions for community formation and cultural maintenance. As a policy of integration, assimilation did not work.

It was within this context that the ALP government of 1972–1975 introduced multiculturalism as a new model of integration. The aim was to redress class and ethnic minority disadvantages by improving educational facilities and social services and ensuring that immigrants could gain access to them. Recognizing cultural difference and working with ethnic community associations were vital to the reform of social policy. Successive governments continued with multicultural policies, although each one tended to emphasize different aspects to fit wider political agendas.

Australian multiculturalism has had two main aspects. The first, concerned with national identity, involves recognizing the cultural diversity resulting from recent immigration and accepting that there is no longer a single, dominant culture and set of values, although Australia's identity remains essentially white and British (Hage 1998). The second aspect, concerned with policy and social equality, involves the duty of government to ensure access and equity; in other words, government services should be accessible and provide equal standards to everyone. Migrant services include English language classes, labor market programs, and interpreter and translation services. A corollary has been the need for antidiscrimination legislation and measures to combat both attitudinal and institutional racism (Vasta 1996). A number of multicultural institutions were established, such as the Special Broadcasting Service (which provides radio and television broadcasts targeted at ethnic communities) and the federal Office of Multicultural Affairs (OMA) and similar state bodies to ensure that government services meet the needs of the various ethnic groups (Castles 2001; Castles et al. 1988).

The current Liberal-National coalition government has strong reservations about multiculturalism. During and after the March 1996 election, it declared that the needs of "ordinary Australians" (by implication, a sort of Anglo-white mainstream) should be put above minority needs. When the coalition came into office, it initially seemed that it would abandon multiculturalism and move back to the assimilationist approaches of the 1950s. However, the realities of Australia's culturally diverse society made this step impossible. The coalition government decided to water down multiculturalism and redefine it yet again. It dismantled federal government institutions such as OMA and the Bureau of Immigration, Multicultural and Population Research. Many special services that targeted immigrants and ethnic communities were also abolished or reduced. The move away from multiculturalism went even further in November 2001 with the absorption of the Department of Reconciliation and Aboriginal and Torres Straight Islander Affairs within the new Department of Immigration and Multicultural and Indigenous Affairs. Aboriginals and Torres Strait Islanders reject such a relationship because their needs are very different, and the shift also means that multicultural policies will have even less weight than before within government.

In December 1999, the Howard government launched a "New Agenda for Multicultural Australia" that largely endorses the principles of the ALP's 1989 National Agenda. However, the core values have been reworked as "civic duty, cultural respect, social equity and productive diversity." This new document argues that multiculturalism must be an inclusive concept in terms of nationhood and identity "for all Australians" and stresses the importance of the links between multiculturalism and citizenship as a set of rights and obligations by citizens toward the state. The New Agenda's attempt to support cultural respect through the notion of inclusiveness, without coming to grips with the increasing social inequality and exclusion in Australian society, is unlikely to have much effect. As Hage (2001) points out, this new version of Australian multiculturalism corresponds with John Howard's underlying belief in the essentially European nature of Australian society, as stated in a speech to the Chinese Chamber of Commerce in 1998: "We are, as all of you know, a projection of Western civilization in this part of the world. We have inherited the great European values of liberal democracy." This new version of multiculturalism is quite compatible with a return to the insular values of the 1950s — and with exclusionary immigration policies.

THE NEW IMMIGRATION PANIC

Over the past fifty years, Australia's immigration policy has been carefully planned. Due to its inaccessibility, Australia has had few problems with illegal immigrants. Immigration has always been a political issue, but conflict and political mobilization on the topic have been limited. This situation has changed dramatically since about 1996 due to two factors: the rise of the One Nation Party and the increase in arrivals of boat people on Australia's northern shores. Matters came to a head in 2001 with the "Tampa Affair" (to be discussed below) and a federal election fought largely on immigration.

During the 1996 federal election, several Liberal and National candidates criticized the provision of special services for immigrants and Aboriginal people. In one Queensland electorate, Liberal Party candidate Pauline Hanson so strongly attacked services for Aboriginal people that she was dis-endorsed as a candidate by her own party. Despite this, she won the seat as an independent, with one of the biggest antilabor swings in the country. This was widely taken as a signal that a large share of the population now viewed antiminority discourses as acceptable. Hanson quickly set up the One Nation Party to build on such feelings. In her inaugural speech in Parliament, she attacked Aboriginal people and called for a stop to immigration and the abolition of multiculturalism, warning of the "Asianization" of Australia.

Brett has suggested that such racist sentiments had grown during the ALP government, from 1983 to 1996, developing into a "politics of grievance and resentment," especially among members of the lower middle class (the self-employed and small business owners) who believed that their hard work had not been adequately rewarded and who felt insecure. They perceived minority groups such as Aborigines and migrants as failing to help themselves yet being rewarded by the state. Hanson, a small shopkeeper, became a conduit for these views. Working-class people also saw job losses and a decline in manufacturing industries, wages, and standard of living. This was the old Labor base who felt they had been betrayed (Brett 1997: 10–12). Such issues became racialized, so that immigrants (especially Asians) and Aboriginal people suffered an increase in personal abuse and attacks (Vasta 1999).

Both the Liberal-National coalition and the ALP were slow to condemn Hanson's politics. Prime Minister Howard's initial silence suggested to the nation that he condoned Hanson's views, which were consistent with his own past stance against Asian immigration.[3] It was not until October 1996 that Parliament passed a bipartisan resolution condemning racism. The resolution seemed to be motivated primarily by fear of losing Asian export orders, plus reports from universities that Asian students were failing to enroll for courses. There was no clear moral or political rejection of bigotry. The trend toward racialization of politics had an immediate impact on policy. Howard could not deliver a cut in Asian immigration because that is where many of the skilled and business migrants—and full-fee-paying Asian students—were coming from. Instead, the tightening of immigration policy was targeted at categories that were supposedly hurting national interests: family reunion and asylum seekers. The result was a much more hostile climate toward immigration and multiculturalism.

The situation was exacerbated by the increase in boat people arriving in northern Australia beginning in the mid-1990s. Chinese people were smuggled in mainly for purposes of undocumented work; and asylum seekers from the Middle East and South Asia (Iraqis, Afghans, and others) were brought in from Indonesia, usually by fishing boats chartered by people smugglers. Numbers were not high by international standards, never going much above 4,000 per year, but they sparked media campaigns and popular outrage. The government's response has been to modify Australia's refugee and asylum policy to such an extent that it has been accused of contravening the 1951 Geneva Convention and of damaging Australia's nondiscriminatory policy. Australia has long been proud of its openness to the persecuted. Refugee policy became expansionist between 1977 and 1982 in order to deal with the flow of refugees from Vietnam, Cambodia, and Laos. Although there was some disquiet, the coalition government chose a careful and considered approach of support for Vietnamese refugees, rather than fueling fears and hostilities, as the current government has done (McMaster 2001: 54).

Minister Philip Ruddock attacked the asylum seekers as "queue jumpers," claiming that they took places from "genuine" refugees who applied for resettlement through the UNHCR. He declared that arrivals of boat people were a threat to Australian sovereignty, and he announced measures to deter them and limit the rights of those who did arrive. Australia has put three main deterrents in place. First, in 1999 the government introduced the three-year temporary protection visa (TPV), which confers no right to permanent settlement or family reunion. An-

---

[3] Howard had been forced to resign as leader of the opposition in 1988, after a speech opposing Asian immigration, which was widely seen as racist.

other more dramatic deterrent has been to stop boat people from landing
and to try to send them back to Indonesia. A third deterrent is to place
them in isolated and remote detention camps, where they have been
barred from making telephone calls and from talking to lawyers, media,
and supporters. They can languish for up to three years in these camps,
where hunger strikes, riots, self-inflicted injuries, and even suicide have
become commonplace. The federal government has also introduced legal
measures to limit the right to judicial review in asylum matters (Crock
and Saul 2002: chap. 5).

Immigration came under an even stronger spotlight in August 2001
when the Norwegian freighter *MV Tampa* picked up over four hundred
asylum seekers (most from Afghanistan and Iraq) from a sinking boat off
northern Australia. The government refused the captain permission to
land the asylum seekers, and the *Tampa* anchored near the Australian
territory of Christmas Island, triggering a saga of international diplo-
macy, heated public debates in Australia, and feverish political activity
as a country previously noted for its openness to refugees rapidly
adopted draconian laws designed to exclude asylum seekers. Australia
tried to export the asylum seekers to its Pacific neighbors, Nauru and
New Guinea, and it was willing to spend vast sums of money to do so.[4]
A Labor victory had been predicted for the November election, but with
asylum now the central issue, victory went to Liberal-National Prime
Minister Howard.

The most recent border control legislation, passed in March 2002,
stipulates:

- No permanent residency for people who leave a safe country and
  attempt to enter Australia illegally by being transported to one of the
  outer islands. They will not be permitted to bring in family and cannot return if they leave for any reason.

- Refusal of refugee status for people who conceal their identity by
  destroying their documents en route.

- Minimum mandatory sentences of five years for first-time people
  smugglers and eight years for repeat offenders, with a maximum
  sentence of twenty years.

---

[4] The 2002–2003 federal budget included A$2.8 billion for border control measures—
an increase of A$1.2 billion over the previous year. A$219 was for construction of an
off-shore detention facility on Christmas Island, and A$450 was for off-shore proc-
essing on Nauru and Manus Island (Australia 2002).

Events since 1996 have tarnished Australia's reputation as an open, tolerant society and as a good international citizen. However, at the time of writing, a political movement against the new intolerance seems to be emerging. Led by churches, humanitarian groups like Amnesty International, elements of the ALP, and trade unions, it gives some hope that the pendulum will again swing to more open policies in the future. And in early 2002, Neville Roach, chairman of the government's advisory Council for Multicultural Australia, resigned his post. Roach, a prominent business leader, stated: "I think the way in which the government has handled these issues—beginning with the *Tampa*—has tended to give comfort to the prejudiced side of human nature" (BBC News 2002).

CONCLUSION

Australia has had a carefully planned and managed immigration program since 1945, with the state heavily involved in selection, admission, and integration policies. Government has consulted systematically with interest groups and the public at large and has often been sensitive to public opinion, although political leaders have also done much to shape public views on immigration and multiculturalism. In comparison with other immigration countries, Australia has been highly successful at controlling entry levels and preventing unauthorized entry. However, this success has been largely due to geographical remoteness. Australia has also been fairly successful in controlling the skills mix of immigrants, and successive governments' ambitions to import needed qualifications have been largely achieved.

Australian immigration policy has been less successful in controlling ethnic difference. The original objective of postwar immigration policy was to keep Australia white and British. Instead, mass immigration gave birth to one of the world's most diverse societies, leading to major changes in culture, national identity, and citizenship. Policymakers have also been relatively unsuccessful in limiting family reunion. Even the current government's strong emphasis on skilled migration appears to have achieved only a slight (and possibly temporary) reduction in the family share of entries. This is not surprising given the continued emphasis on immigration as a prelude to permanent settlement.

Regional and global integration are threatening Australia's ability to maintain tight control over entries. Migratory patterns are now more complex and multidirectional, in Australia and elsewhere. However, politicians and the public are finding it hard to come to terms with such changes, as the reaction to the arrivals of asylum seekers reveals. Fears of loss of sovereignty and identity have spilled over into the social policy area, leading to a questioning of multiculturalism. Here, too, Australia is following a trajectory similar to several European countries, although the result seems to be more a relabeling and redefinition of multiculturalism than its complete abolition.

The 2000 Olympic Games—the Olympics of Globalization—gave Australia the opportunity to showcase itself as a wonderful, creative, generous, warm, welcoming, and expansive twenty-first-century country. Australia became the darling of the white, multicultural, free, democratic, ex-colonial world. But there is a dark side to Australian national identity; it can be selfish, inward looking, anti-intellectual, and racist, as epitomized in the political personae of Pauline Hanson and John Howard. Despite the Olympics and the millions of dollars spent on the spectacle, in Australia there is a weak sense of consciousness about the public good; people can no longer see broader universal solutions.

Recent political responses to immigration and asylum seekers have grown largely from the rise in popularity of the right-wing and anti-minority views espoused by the One Nation Party. This became clear when the Howard government swept back into office in 2001 on a tide of anti-immigration feeling, and Pauline Hanson complained bitterly that Howard had stolen her policies—and her voters. Jupp provides an incisive summary of the current Australian situation:

> Even if the sky did not fall during 2001–2002, Australia behaved in an authoritarian manner which damaged its international reputation and revealed unhealthy xenophobia. The demise of One Nation and the revelation of the unjustified demonization of asylum seekers, has brought the situation back to normal. But the "normal situation" still includes having more than 3,000 people locked away in the Australian desert;... the abolition of effective national advocacy, monitoring and research to improve and maintain ethnic relations; an immigration policy which makes family reunion very difficult; a volatile public opinion which is potentially susceptible to racist or xenophobic attitudes; and a national political leadership which has exploited all of this (Jupp 2002: 3).

Australia today is a society that fears invasion from the north and sees difference as a threat—in effect, a return to the insularity and fear that have dominated Australian history since 1788. Perhaps the openness since 1945, and especially from 1972 to 1996, will go down in history as the exception. The emergence of new social movements from 1972 until the early 1990s created a reformist atmosphere of progressive politics concerned with social justice and equality for immigrants and refugees, indigenous Australians, women, and other disempowered groups. During this enlightened period, Australia was considered a world leader in terms of its multicultural policies for immigrants and minorities. Yet the fear of difference and change lay just below the surface.

During the recent asylum panic, the government claimed that "Afghans were really Pakistanis, that there might be terrorists aboard the *Tampa*, and that the asylum seekers were probably rich." The stated object of the hastily adopted new laws was "to prevent people smuggling, to maintain the integrity of our borders and to prevent access to our asylum system other than on our own terms" (Jupp 2002). The recurrent racism found in the Australian national identity has come to the fore over this issue. The government's rhetoric about queue jumpers, people who would pay smugglers, and people who put their children at risk when they go on hunger strikes has fueled prejudice among some of the Australian population. Typically, prejudicial sentiments appeal to the more vulnerable sectors. Furthermore, John Howard is well aware that he is exploiting a deep-rooted Australian fear—the fear of invasion by foreigners.

The Australian dilemma seems more acute than ever before. This small population of mainly European origin inhabiting a huge landmass on the rim of Asia has yet to find a secure identity. Australia's economy is highly integrated into global trade and finance. Economic links with Asia are of paramount importance. Flows of people in both directions are an essential part of these linkages. Australia's society includes people of diverse origins, cultures, and religions. A return to isolationism and monoculturalism is not an option. Yet many Australians feel threatened by this situation. They seem unable to face up to the realities of diversity and openness. Immigration remains the flashpoint for this fundamental malaise, and it is likely to be a focus of political conflict for the foreseeable future.

References

ABS (Australian Bureau of Statistics). 2001. "Migration, Australia." April 8, at http://www.abs.gov.au/austats.
———. 2002a. "Population: International Migration." February 23, at http://www.abs.gov.au/austats/abs@.nsf/.

―――. 2002b. "Population Size and Growth." February 23, at http://www.abs. gov.au/austats/abs.

Ackland, Richard, and Lynne Williams. 1992. *Immigrants and the Australian Labour Market: The Experience of Three Recessions.* Canberra: Bureau of Immigration Research.

Australia, UN Association of. 2002. "Refugee Budget Reflections," *Unity*, p. 12.

BBC News. 2002. At news.BBC.co.uk.english/world/asia-pacific: 23/1//02.

BCA (Business Council of Australia). 1999. *Submission to the 2000–2002 Migration and Humanitarian Programs and Associated Settlement Issues.*

Betts, Katherine. 1993. "Public Discourse, Immigration and the New Class." In *The Politics of Australian Immigration*, edited by James Jupp and Marie Kabala. Canberra: AGPS.

―――. 2001. "Boatpeople and Public Opinion in Australia," *People and Place* 9: 34–48.

BIR (Bureau of Immigration Research). 1991. *Australia's Population Trends and Prospects 1990.* Canberra: AGPS.

Birrell, Robert. 2001. "Immigration on the Rise: The 2001–2002 Immigration Program," *People and Place* 9: 21–28.

Birrell, Robert, and Siew Ean Khoo. 1995. *The Second Generation in Australia: Educational and Occupational Characteristics.* Statistical Report No. 14. Canberra: AGPS.

Blainey, Geoffrey. 1984. *All for Australia.* Sydney: Methuen Haynes.

Brett, Judith. 1997. "John Howard, Pauline Hanson and the Politics of Grievance." In *The Resurgence of Racism*, edited by G. Gray and C. Winter. Melbourne: Monash Papers in History.

Cahill, Desmond. 1996. *Immigration and Schooling in the 90s.* Canberra: BIMPR.

Castles, Stephen. 2001. "Multiculturalism in Australia." In *The Australian People: An Encyclopedia of the Nation, Its People and Their Origins*, edited by James Jupp. Cambridge: Cambridge University Press.

Castles, Stephen, Bill Cope, Mary Kalantzis, and Michael Morrissey. 1988. *Mistaken Identity: Multiculturalism and the Demise of Nationalism in Australia.* Sydney: Pluto.

Castles, Stephen, and Alastair Davidson. 2000. *Citizenship and Migration: Globalisation and the Politics of Belonging.* London: Macmillan.

Castles, Stephen, William Foster, Robyn Iredale, and Glenn Withers. 1998. *Immigration and Australia: Myths and Realities.* Sydney: Allen and Unwin.

Collins, Jock. 1991. *Migrant Hands in a Distant Land: Australia's Post-war Immigration.* Sydney: Pluto.

Collins, Jock, Katherine Gibson, Caroline Alcorso, Stephen Castles, and David Tait. 1995. *A Shop Full of Dreams: Ethnic Small Business in Australia.* Sydney: Pluto.

Commissioner, Federal Race Relations. 1995. *State of the Nation: A Report on People of Non-English Speaking Backgrounds.* Canberra: AGPS.

Crock, Mary, and Ben Saul. 2002. *Future Seekers: Refugees and the Law in Australia.* Sydney: Federation Press.

Cronin, Kathryn. 2001. "The Legal Status of Immigrants and Refugees." In *The Australian People: An Encyclopedia of the Nation, Its People and Their Origins*, edited by James Jupp. Cambridge: Cambridge University Press.

Davidson, Alastair. 1997. *From Subject to Citizen: Australian Citizenship in the Twentieth Century*. Cambridge: Cambridge University Press.

De Lepervanche, M. 1975. "Australian Immigrants 1788–1940: Desired and Unwanted." In *Essays in the Political Economy of Australian Capitalism*, edited by E.L. Wheelwright and K. Buckley. Sydney: Australia and New Zealand Book Co.

DIMIA (Department of Immigration and Multicultural and Indigenous Affairs). 2001a. *Over Fifty Years of Post-War Migration*. Fact Sheet 4. Canberra: DIMIA.

———. 2001b. *Key Facts in Immigration*. Fact Sheet 2. Canberra: DIMIA.

———. 2001c. *New Zealanders in Australia*. Fact Sheet 17. Canberra: DIMIA.

———. 2002. *Australian Immigration: Recent Migration Program Statistics*. Canberra: DIMIA.

Foster, Will. 1996. *Immigration and the Australian Economy*. Canberra: DIMA.

Goot, Murray. 2001. "Public Opinion on Immigration." In *The Australian People: An Encyclopedia of the Nation, Its People and Their Origins*, edited by James Jupp. Cambridge: Cambridge University Press.

Hage, Ghassan. 1998. *White Nation: Fantasies of White Supremacy in a Multicultural Society*. Sydney and New York: Pluto Press and Routledge.

———. 2001. "The Politics of Australian Fundamentalism," *Arena Magazine*, pp. 27–31.

Jones, Alan. 2001. "The Business Council of Australia's Case for Population Growth: An Ecological Critique," *People and Place* 9: 49–57.

Jupp, James. 1993. "The Ethnic Lobby and Immigration Policy." In *The Politics of Australian Immigration*, edited by James Jupp and Marie Kabala. Canberra: AGPS.

———. 2002. "Undoing the Damage and Restoring Multiculturalism." In *Beyond Tolerance: National Conference on Racism*. Sydney: Human Rights and Equal Opportunity Commission.

Lever-Tracey, Constance, and Michael Quinlan. 1988. *A Divided Working Class*. London and New York: Routledge and Kegan Paul.

MacQueen, Humphrey. 1970. *A New Britannia*. Victoria: Penguin.

McAllister, Ian. 1988. "Political Attitudes and Electoral Behaviour." In *The Australian People: An Encyclopaedia of the Nation, Its People and Their Origins*, edited by James Jupp. Sydney: Angus and Robertson.

McMaster, Don. 2001. *Asylum Seekers: Australia's Response to Refugees*. Melbourne: Melbourne University Press.

Reynolds, Henry. 1987. *Frontier*. Sydney: Allen and Unwin.

Rubinstein, Kim. 1995. "Citizenship in Australia: Unscrambling Its Meaning," *Melbourne University Law Review* 20.

Vasta, Ellie. 1993. "Immigrant Women and the Politics of Resistance," *Australian Feminist Studies* 18: 5–23.

———. 1996. "Dialectics of Domination: Racism and Multiculturalism." In *The Teeth Are Smiling: The Persistence of Racism in Multicultural Australia*, edited by Ellie Vasta and Stephen Castles. Sydney: Allen and Unwin.

————. 1999. "Multicultural Politics and Resistance: Migrants Unite?" In *The Future of Australian Multiculturalism*, edited by Ghassan Hage and Rowanne Couch. Sydney: RIHSS, Sydney University.

Warhurst, John. 1993. "The Growth Lobby and Its Opponents: Business, Unions, Environmentalists and Other Interest Groups." In *The Politics of Australian Immigration*, edited by James Jupp and Marie Kabala. Canberra: AGPS.

Wooden, Mark, Robert Holton, Graeme Hugo, and Judith Sloan. 1994. *Australian Immigration: A Survey of the Issues.* Canberra: AGPS.

Zappala, Gianni, and Stephen Castles. 2000. "Citizenship and Immigration in Australia." In *From Migrants to Citizens: Membership in a Changing World*, edited by T. Alexander Aleinikoff and Douglas Klusmeyer. Washington, D.C.: Brookings Institution Press.

Commentary

Gary P. Freeman

How can we account for the shift in Australian immigration policy in the 1990s, which put it out of sync with developments in the United States and Canada? By the late 1980s, immigration politics in all three countries closely resembled client politics (Freeman 1995). Yet the client system broke down in Australia, at least temporarily, but not in the United States and Canada (Freeman and Birrell 2001). Why?

Castles and Vasta tend to track the changes in Australia's immigration outlook from the defeat of Labor in the 1996 election, and they seem to view the preceding Labor era as a kind of Golden Age of enlightened immigration enthusiasm. However, one cannot simply attribute the change to the election of the Coalition government or to the emergence of Hansonism. The outlines of the new policies were already visible before 1996, when Labor was in government, and until the *Tampa* affair, Labor tacitly or explicitly supported most Coalition initiatives on immigration. Clearly, more long-term and fundamental factors than the party in government were at work. These factors can be grouped under three rubrics: interests, rights, and institutions.

The main interest groups that were the clients of Australian immigration policy until the 1990s were representatives of business and of the ethnic communities. These groups were eclipsed in recent years for two reasons. First, government became concerned that immigration was not sufficiently directed toward clear national economic and fiscal goals, the most pertinent indicators being high levels of unemployment among migrants and large public expenditure on migrant welfare. Second, public opinion became more restive in response to the economic and fiscal problems just mentioned, the more extensive claims being made on be-half of multiculturalism, and the rising numbers of asylum seekers. I think Castles and Vasta overplay the latent racism and fear within the Australian public. After all, Australia has, as they point out, peaceably and voluntarily settled the highest proportion of immigrants of any Western country. Nevertheless, there is clearly something to the argu-ment that Australians are uneasy about their vulnerability as an outpost of European civilization in the midst of the vast populations of the Asia Pacific, and public opinion is, therefore, easily mobilized around migra-tion issues. The consensus on immigration and multiculturalism was essentially a consensus of elites; popular opinion had never strongly embraced either policy (Betts 1996). Protest from the business sector, a strong supporter of mass immigration, was in a sense deterred by the new policy's emphasis on skill in the selection of permanent immigrants and the provision of unlimited access to temporary work visas for the highly skilled.

The plight of ethnic groups is more complicated, and the picture drawn by Castles and Vasta is inconsistent. They discount claims that ethnic groups are well organized and influential or that there is a mono-lithic ethnic vote. On the other hand, they note that multicultural policies stimulated ethnic mobilization, that ethnic associations helped to end assimilationist policies, were influential in social policy, lobbied with some success for family reunion policies, and persuaded Howard to abandon his plans to shelve multiculturalism altogether. Ethnic interest groups are most effective when public opinion on immigration is quies-cent and policy is made on a bipartisan basis, even more so when Labor is in power. The advent of the Coalition diminished ethnic influence because ethnic leaders and organizations had few ties to Coalition politi-cians and the Coalition had less to lose in terms of electoral support from the disaffection of ethnic voters.

A number of scholars contend that immigration politics is fundamen-tally shaped by a rights-based discourse (Hollifield 1992). Rights are arguably less firmly embedded in Australian institutions and culture than in other liberal democracies. The Liberal Party was not founded to protect individual rights in the European liberal tradition. It represented business but did not advocate laissez-faire. The Australian Constitution has no bill of rights, nor have the courts exercised extensive powers of judicial review. Moreover, administrative reforms in 1989 sharply lim-ited judicial oversight of immigration department decisions (Cronin 1993: 103). Little surprise, then, that Australian governments succeeded in seriously eroding the "rights" migrants had previously achieved, including family reunion privileges, access to some state-paid benefits, and retrenchment on official multiculturalism. Australia illustrates the limits of the international rights regime to affect policies of a state intent on exercising its sovereignty. The tough detention and deterrence policies with respect to asylum seekers and the steely resolve demonstrated in the *Tampa* episode, followed by Howard's definitive reelection a few months later, are stark reminders of the weakness of international institutions and norms.

Australian political institutions are also integral to an account of policy change. The central importance of the Immigration Department in laying out policy alternatives and the unusual role of Immigration Minister Ruddock, who held the portfolio throughout the decade, set Australia apart from both Canada and the United States. The party-parliamentary system also permits an Australian government with a sizable majority that so wishes, to act, even against powerful and articulate interests. If the Howard government had ideological or electoral incentives to reshape immigration policy, the department and its minister appear to have been motivated more by the bureaucracy's traditional goal of demonstrating to the public that the immigration program was being efficiently managed, that immigration was producing clear benefits to the economy and society, and that those immigrants admitted to Australia were thriving without requiring public support.

The combination of a strong proclivity to link immigration to national interests, a relatively weakly embedded liberal rights tradition, and a political system that ties governments closely to public opinion when it is mobilized goes a long way to explain Australia's divergence in the last decade. Castles and Vasta speculate that the glory days of the immigration consensus of the 1970s and 1980s may have been a temporary deviation from a more enduring restrictionist pattern. I believe it is as likely that both the previous expansionist enthusiasm and the current hard line will be replaced by a middling policy that mixes immediate family reunion, targeted skilled migration, overseas refugee selection, and modest multiculturalism in a way that commands the confidence of the general public.

References

Betts, Katharine. 1996. "Immigration and Public Opinion in Australia," *People and Place* 4, no. 3: 9–20.

Cronin, Kathryn. 1993. "A Culture of Control: An Overview of Immigration Policy-making." In *The Politics of Australian Immigration*, edited by James Jupp and Marie Kabala. Canberra: Bureau of Immigration Research.

Freeman, Gary P. 1995. "Modes of Immigration Politics in Liberal Democratic States," *International Migration Review* 29, no. 112: 881–902.

Freeman, Gary P., and Bob Birrell. 2001. "Divergent Paths of Immigration Politics in the United States and Australia," *Population and Development Review* 27, no. 3: 525–53.

Hollifield, James. 1992. *Immigrants, Markets, and States: The Political Economy of Postwar Europe*. Cambridge, Mass.: Harvard University Press.

Commentary

Jeannette Money

The "gap" hypothesis and the "convergence" hypothesis have served as useful tools for examining immigration control in advanced, industrial countries. However, scholars and policymakers would now be better served by a two-dimensional model that acknowledges the connections between immigration control and immigrant integration. If we understand a nation's immigration policy to be a function of both dimensions, we can better understand the circumstances that disturb a particular policy equilibrium. The parameters of a new immigration policy equilibrium can then be delineated by evaluating the relative political power of groups that organize to influence immigration policy.

Each nation has defined criteria for an acceptable level of (legal) immigration. Flows are not the entire picture, however. Nations offer immigrants different degrees of civil, social, political, and cultural rights. All positions appear to be viable, given an underlying political demand for flows and rights. Some states can reconcile high flows with high levels of rights because they invite migrants who are economically successful. Other states combine high flows with low levels of rights, or low flows with high levels of rights.

The two-dimensional picture of immigration policy does not predict a state's equilibrium policy. However, once we incorporate immigration control and immigrant integration into the policy equation, we can better evaluate the forces that disturb a nation's policy equilibrium. Changes in labor market needs continue to be important. Changes in a nation's demographic patterns may disturb the immigration policy equilibrium.

A nation's ability to control immigration flows also has the potential to disturb a nation's migration policy equilibrium.

Another factor that can disturb the policy equilibrium is a change in the costs associated with rights granted to immigrants, which may explain the anti-immigrant backlash now visible in Australia. Despite the tremendous influx of immigrants after World War II, Australia had not generated an anti-immigrant political party until the formation of the One Nation Party in 1997. The anti-immigrant backlash was triggered in large part by the costs that rights for a steady stream of immigrants was generating for the resident population, especially in times of high unemployment. The situation was exacerbated by the arrival of asylum-seeking boat people, an immigration control failure that upset the policy equilibrium and generated a continuing political debate.

Once immigration policy equilibrium has been disturbed, it is difficult to predict the new policy equilibrium, in part because political institutions vary across advanced industrial countries. Nonetheless, it is important to identify the groups that are likely to play a significant role in reestablishing the migration policy equilibrium: immigrant rights groups, employers, and anti-immigrant groups.

In Australia, anti-immigrant groups were strong enough to raise immigrant integration issues, and pro-immigrant employers were able to block one possible response—a reduction in flows. They forced the political debate into the integration policy arena, where anti-immigrant groups were opposed by the rights coalition, in particular by large numbers of naturalized immigrants opposed to the rollback of integration policies (Money 1999). The conservative Coalition government rolled back some rights, but Australia continues to be one of the most generous providers of immigrant rights.

As the Australian case suggests, policy responses to a particular disequilibrium may come in either the control policy arena or the integration policy arena, or both, depending on the array of political forces. Although we can anticipate the circumstances under which a policy disequilibrium will arise, the multiplicity of factors involved makes it difficult to predict the policy trajectory of any individual country.

Reference

Money, Jeannette. 1999. "Xenophobia and Xenophilia: Pauline Hanson and the Counterbalancing of Electoral Incentives in Australia," *People and Place* 7, no. 3: 7–19.

PART III

Reluctant Countries of Immigration: France, Germany, the Netherlands, and Britain

UNITED KINGDOM

BELGIUM

GERMANY

English Channel

Channel
Islands
(U.K.)

Lille •

Nord-Pas-de-Calais

LUX.

• Amiens

Haute-
Normandie

Picardie

Chalons-sur-Marne

Metz

• Caen

Rouen

Nancy

• Strasbourg

Basse-
Normandie

Versailles •

• Paris

Chanpagne-
Ardenne

Lorraine

Alencon

Île-de-France

• Troyes

Chartres

Bretagne

Rennes

• Le Mans

• Orleans

• Auxerre

Pays de la Loire

Centre

Dijon •

Franche-Comté

Besancon

Nantes

• Angers

Tours

Bourges

Bourgogne

SWITZERLAND

Chateauroux

La Roche-sur-Yon

Poitiers

Moulins

F R A N C E

Bourg-en-Bresse

• La Rochelle

Limoges

Lyon

Poitou-
Charentes

Clermont-Ferrand

Chambery

Atlantic

Limousin

Auvergne

Rhône-Alpes

Perigueux

Aurillac

Le Puy

• Valence

ITALY

Ocean

• Bordeaux

Mende

• Digne

Aquitaine

Avignon

Nice •

Bay of Biscay

Midi-Pyrénées

Nimes

Provence-Alpes-
Côte d' Azur

MONACO

Languedoc-Roussillon

Toulouse

Montpellier

Marseille

• Toulon

Gulf of Lions

Mediterranean Sea

• Perpignan

Bastia •

ANDORRA

Corse
(Corsica)

S P A I N

• Ajaccio

0   100 km

0   100 Miles

North

5

France: Republicanism and the Limits of Immigration Control

James F. Hollifield

Given the recent rise in France of the powerful anti-immigrant National Front (FN), one might conclude that immigration in France is raging out of control. Yet despite the remarkable showing of the National Front and its charismatic Jean-Marie Le Pen in the 2002 presidential election, France has remained a relatively open immigration country. Annual immigration levels have not fallen much below 100,000 since the early 1950s, every postwar government has respected the right to asylum, and France has maintained what is arguably the most liberal naturalization policy in Western Europe.

How can we explain this continuity amidst controversy and crisis over immigration? The continuity in the principles (goals) and results (outcomes) of French immigration policy is closely linked to the republican tradition and to the limits of control that are a function of rights-based politics.

IMMIGRATION AND THE REPUBLICAN TRADITION

France's long history of immigration dates from the mid-nineteenth century. France was not the only European state compelled to import labor to feed the fires of industrialization. What distinguishes France was its early willingness to accept foreigners as settlers and even as citizens. This acceptance is part and parcel of a republican tradition—egalitarian, anticlerical, and antimonarchy—stemming from the French Revolution. Republicanism stresses popular sovereignty, citizenship, and the rights of man.

Around the end of the nineteenth century, the French state began laying the legal foundations for nationality based on the birthright principle of soil (*jus soli*) rather than on blood (*jus sanguinis*). Thus the republican tradition found its expression in an open and expansive notion of citizenship, rather than a narrow, ethnocultural vision of citizenship such as that evolving in Germany of the Second Reich.

The first period of intensive immigration in France began in the 1850s, long after the Revolution of 1789. Hence immigration in France was never part of any founding myth. Even though immigration and integration are closely associated with the French republican tradition, they are not crucial to French national identity.[1] The relationship between immigration and nation building is crucial in enabling democratic states to manage immigration and finesse the gap that often exists between policy outputs and outcomes. Therefore, a key argument in this chapter is that the more closely associated immigration is with the political myths that legitimate and give life to the regime, the easier it is for the state to justify its immigration and immigrant policies and to manage the ethnic and distributional conflicts that inevitably arise as a result of immigration (Hollifield 1997).

The Demographic and Republican Nexus

Immigration in modern France is closely linked to three factors: the pattern and timing of industrialization, slow population growth, and political changes associated with the rise of republicanism. In the absence of a local labor supply, French capitalists were forced to invent a working class by recruiting foreign labor. Immigration during the early decades of the twentieth century was organized but uncontrolled, and the republican model served primarily to integrate newcomers, turning immigrant workers into French citizens, just as French peasants had been socialized into a modern, republican culture (via schools and the army) two or three generations earlier.

---

[1] The exception is French Jews, for whom the Revolution represents political and legal emancipation (Birnbaum 1995).

The state took its first halting steps to assert control over the immigrant population during World War I through the establishment of national identity cards, which marked the beginning of a French system of immigration and population control. After the war, French industry again faced dramatic labor shortages. In the early 1920s two major interest groups emerged that would influence French immigration policy — especially issues of control — well into the post–World War II period. First were employers, who created the General Immigration Society (SGI) to organize the recruitment and placement of immigrant (primarily Italian and Polish) labor. Second were the pronatalists of the National Alliance for the Growth of the French Population (Alliance Nationale Pour l'Accroissement de la Population Française), long active in Third Republic politics. Employers were interested in securing an unlimited supply of cheap foreign labor; the pronatalists were inspired by nationalist, political motives.

The pronatalists made the case for large-scale recruitment of immigrant workers and their families from Italy and Spain. Sauvy (1950) argued that such a strategy would give the French population (and the economy) a chance to catch up with more powerful European competitors, primarily Germany and Britain. By imposing a kind of national origins quota to select culturally compatible immigrants from neighboring states, France could receive a new stock of foreign population (and human capital) with minimal impact on French society and culture. Moreover, the French already had considerable experience with imported Italian labor, and Spain was viewed as a logical partner in this enterprise because of the long-standing traditions of exchange between the two Catholic countries.

In Charles de Gaulle, the pronatalists found a powerful ally in shaping postwar French immigration policy. The early Gaullist reformers felt that all necessary resources should be mobilized to modernize the economy. Recruitment policies were supported by major segments of the republican right (especially the Gaullists) oriented to big business and rapid economic growth, and by segments of the old republican left (the radicals, socialists, and eventually the communists as well).

This emerging consensus for a new immigration policy, based on expansive demographic and economic principles, was firmly anchored in universalist, republican ideals. Republicanism in postwar France included respect for the civil and human rights of foreigners, especially refugees. One of the least noticed innovations of the Tripartite Government — and one of the great accomplishments of the early Gaullist reformers — was the creation of a full-blown welfare state, built upon republican and Catholic, rather than social democratic, traditions (Ashford 1991). New immigrant workers and their families benefited from the social rights associated with the construction of the French welfare state. If we combine foreigners' civil, human, and social rights with the liberal naturalization and citizenship policies of the Fourth Republic, we can see the emergence of an expansive liberal and republican immigration policy built upon the pragmatic assessments of economic planners, the nationalist aspirations of some demographers and politicians, and the edifice of a revitalized republican synthesis (Hoffmann 1963; Weil 1991).

The Ordonnance of 1945 laid down the basic outline of immigration and naturalization policy in postwar France. The new law rejected the idea of selecting immigrants on the basis of ethnicity or national origins and placed it in the demographic and republican nexus, which helped to forge a consensus for the recruitment of foreign workers. The crises and controversies surrounding immigration control from the 1960s to the present stem largely from the turbulence of decolonization and the dismantling of the French Empire, itself a creation of nationalist and republican aspirations.

The liberal side of France's postwar immigration history cannot be told without mention of decolonization and the Algerian War, which created ethnic and racial fault lines in French society that persist to this day. A look at the size and evolution of the foreign population will help round out the historical picture (see table 5.1). By 1931 France was statistically a country of immigration, with foreigners forming 6.6 percent of the total population. The foreign population dropped slightly during World War II and early reconstruction (to 4.1 percent in 1954), rose again with successive waves of immigration in the 1950s and 1960s, reached a high of 6.8 percent in 1982, and then fell to 5.7 percent at the turn of the century (table 5.2). The first waves of postwar immigration were settlers and had a heavy labor component.

Looking at the size of the foreign population (stocks), one can argue that France has been a country of immigration since early in the twentieth century. Yet despite immigration's long and continuous history in modern France, immigration never played the role of a founding myth in any of France's various political regimes of the nineteenth or twentieth centuries. Postwar policies were designed to discourage settler immigration and encourage some nationalities, particularly North Africans, to return to their countries of origin. From the beginning of the postwar period there was a guestworker or rotation logic embedded in French immigration policy, which helps explain why governments in 1974 and 1993 could seriously contemplate a halt to all types of immigration. In order to understand the abrupt shifts from recruitment to suspension in the 1970s and to "zero immigration" in the 1990s, we must look at the origins of postwar immigration policy in the 1950s and 1960s, when immigration control was defined in the highly statist terms of economic and demographic planning.

Table 5.1. Immigrants in France by Nationality/Country of Origin, 1975, 1982, and 1990

	1975	1982	1990
Total	3,920,430	4,071,109	4,195,952
Spanish	609,605	485,764	412,785
Italians	714,650	606,972	523,080
Portuguese	659,800	644,428	605,986
Algerians	571,925	617,993	571,997
Moroccans	244,945	358,296	446,872
Tunisians	151,125	177,544	182,478
Turks	59,515	108,708	158,907
Sub-Saharan Africa	—[a]	123,392	182,479
Indochinese	—[a]	124,420	158,075

Sources: Census data from the Institut National de la Statistique et des Etudes Economiques (INSEE); Tribalat 1997: 176.

[a] Formerly under French administration.

Economic Planning and Population Policy

France's postwar system comprised two principal agencies for managing immigration and refugee flows, the National Immigration Office (ONI) and the Office for the Protection of Refugees and Stateless Persons (OFPRA), both established in 1946. The ONI was touted as a model agency for recruiting and placing foreign workers in various sectors of the French economy. Trade unions (the CGT and the CFTC), which had lobbied hard to avoid a return to the interwar system in which business organized and controlled immigration, were especially pleased to have a "neutral" state agency to oversee foreign worker and immigration policy. Business associations, such as the National Businessmen's Council (CNPF), were not yet sufficiently organized to have any formal influence on the system for regulating immigration. They offered little resistance to the new directions in immigrant worker policy except, ironically, to question the wisdom of importing large numbers of immigrant workers at a time of high unemployment as forced French laborers were returning from Germany.

The two most influential groups in setting the agenda for postwar immigration policy were economic planners and demographers, represented, respectively, by Jean Monnet, who would coordinate economic policy as head of the General Planning Commission (CGP), and Alfred Sauvy, who

Table 5.2. Immigrants in France by Category, 1946–1999 (thousands)

	1946–55	1956–67	1968–73	1974–80	1981–87	1988–92	1993–99
Workers	325.2	1,205.9	801.3	192.9	195.1	118.6	121.6
Annual rate of immigration	32.5	109.6	133.6	27.6	27.9	23.7	17.4
Percent of total immigration	49.0	44.0	39.0	14.0	17.0	20.0	21.0
Seasonal workers	247.6	1,126.9	821.9	857.3	664.2	258.5[a]	63.1[a]
Annual rate of immigration	24.8	102.4	137.0	122.5	94.9	51.7	9.0
Percent of total immigration	37.0	41.0	40.0	61.0	59.0	43.0	12.0
Family member	91.7	404.2	423.2	351.0	260.6	169.9	263.3
Annual rate of immigration	9.2	36.7	70.5	50.1	37.2	34.0	37.6
Percent of total immigration	14.0	15.0	21.0	25.0	23.0	28.0	26.0
Total	664.4	2,737.1	2,046.5	1,401.2	1,120.0	601.1[b]	687.9[b]
Rate	66.4	248.8	341.1	200.2	160.0	120.2	98.3
Percent	100.0	100.0	100.0	100.0	100.0	100.0	100.0

[a] As of 1992, the Spanish and Portuguese are no longer counted among seasonal workers.

[b] Beginning in 1988, total immigration includes other groups, such as refugees, not listed here. The annual rate for the years 1988–1995 are inflated by the inclusion of flows not counted in previous years. For a breakdown, see the annual SOPEMI reports on France (Lebon 1985–1999).

Note: The final results from the 2000 census are not yet available, but the stock of foreign population in France in 1999 was estimated to be about 3.7 million, or 5.7 percent of the population.

would become a principal adviser on economic and population issues for various Fourth Republic governments. Other academics and public figures were also influential in helping to shape French immigration policy, but *planning* was very much the spirit of the age, and immigration came to be viewed in terms of input-output tables (Tapinos 1975; Weil 1991).

Throughout the period of virtually uninterrupted economic growth from the mid-1940s to the mid-1970s, each economic plan published by the CGP contained targets for the importation of foreign labor, ranging from 430,000 workers in 1946–1947 to 325,000 in 1966–1970. These figures, while not irrelevant, had little bearing on actual immigration levels because the immigration control system during this period of rapid growth and rapid decolonization quickly slipped into private hands. The ONI became little more than a clearinghouse for employers, who went to sending countries to find the labor they needed, brought the workers to France, integrated them into the workforce, and *then* sought an adjustment of status. This bypassing of the institutions created to manage immigration flows came to be known as "immigration from within," and the legalization rate was the most important statistic for measuring the state's ability — or inability — to control immigration. By the late 1960s, almost 90 percent of new immigrants were coming to France, finding a job, and then requesting an adjustment of status (Hollifield 1992a: 45–73). Italy had given way to Spain, Portugal, and former French colonies (especially Algeria) as the principal recruiting ground for foreign workers.

It was also during this period that the ambiguous status of immigrants from North and West Africa began to pose a crucial problem of control. Following Algeria's independence in 1962, the status of these former "citizens" was unchanged. They had the right to move freely between France and their home countries. The arrival in France of hundreds of thousands of Algerians in the late 1960s led the French government to renegotiate this freedom of movement. France was reluctant unilaterally to impose restrictions on the movement of Algerian nationals, but in 1968 the government of Georges Pompidou succeeded in convincing Algerian authorities to give France greater control, provided there was no restriction on tourist visas for Algerians.

Morocco and Tunisia, which held privileged status as former colonies, became major sending countries in 1968–1973. The same was true for West African states, even though immigration from that region remained very low until the late 1980s. In effect, decolonization created a special category of protected immigrants who were quasi-citizens of France. High rates of economic growth (demand-pull), combined with an open immigration regime, made control difficult. The ambiguous status of North and West Africans has continued to play havoc with French government attempts to control immigration given that individuals in former African colonies who were born during French rule have the legal right to request "reintegration" into French nationality.

As immigration soared to over a quarter-million a year from 1956 to 1967, French governments began taking concrete steps to reassert control. Attempts to renegotiate the free movement of Algerian nationals was only one among many initiatives, most of which came not from the Foreign Ministry but from the Ministries of Labor and the Interior. A series of administrative memoranda with the force of law (*circulaires*) were drafted in the early 1970s to enforce immigration and labor laws by requiring employers to meet stringent requirements for housing and care of foreign workers before bringing them into the labor force. These administrative orders met strong resistance from sectors such as construction, mining, and manufacturing, which feared the impact that a tightening of the hiring of foreign workers might have on wages.

Because the French economy had become heavily dependent on immigrant labor by the early 1970s, employers succeeded in convincing the government to ease immigration restrictions. While the rate of adjustments of status declined slightly to around 50 percent in 1972, it rose to 60 percent the following year. Thus the French government's first real attempt to assert control over immigration (permanent workers, family members, seasonal workers, and the like) ended in failure. Even though immigration levels and the stocks of foreign labor continued to be calculated as part of the planning process, the national plans ceased to have any real importance for guiding French economic, labor, or manpower policies. The combination of high demand for labor (and for goods and services), the ambiguous status of citizens of the former colonies, and respect for foreigners' civil and human rights helped to keep the immigration valve open in France right up until the first major economic recession of the postwar period, beginning in 1973 with the Yom Kippur War and the Arab oil embargo.

STOPPING IMMIGRATION

The consensus for an open immigration regime held until 1973–1974. Stopping immigration would prove difficult, however, because the mechanisms and instruments of control had not yet been developed by the French state, and cutting ties with former African colonies would not be easy. Reestablishing control over the flows of worker immigration would take years (Hollifield 1992a).

Apart from worker immigration, French authorities struggled to deter family immigration, which remained fairly high (over 50,000 persons per year from 1974 to 1980), even after the 1974 immigration stop (see table 5.2). The justification for stopping worker immigration was clear: with the decline in economic growth and the rise in unemployment, employers should no longer be allowed to recruit foreign labor, and the denial of visas (external control) and work permits (internal control) was seen as a necessary policy response to worsening economic conditions. The new control policies were also viewed as a way to head off a rising tide of xenophobia (de Wenden 1988; Betz 1994; Thränhardt 1997). This policy shift reflected the following logic: if receiving states could stop immigration, they could solve the unemployment problem; stopping immigration creates jobs and weakens xenophobic political movements.

Responding to the growing hostility toward Algerians in France, Algeria took steps in 1973 to prevent the free emigration of its nationals to France. Yet immigration from Algeria and elsewhere continued throughout the 1970s, in large part due to increases in family reunification, which was much more difficult to control. The economic rationale for stopping worker immigration did not apply to family immigration, which was deemed humanitarian rather than economic. Still, French authorities tried to impose internal controls to slow the influx of family members by denying them work permits (a step the courts ruled illegal; Hollifield 1992a).

The French also had to cope with the continued inflow of seasonal workers, employed primarily in agriculture. From 1974 to 1987, the number of seasonal workers entering each year hovered around 60,000 (table 5.2). Some of these workers came from Spain and Portugal, and the enlargement of the European Community and the extension of the freedom of movement clause of the Rome Treaty to cover Spanish and Portuguese nationals partially resolved the issue of seasonal migration (Tapinos 1975, 1982). In the late 1970s and early 1980s, Moroccans made up the bulk of seasonal flows, to be replaced in the 1990s by East Europeans, especially Poles.

During the presidency of Valérie Giscard d'Estaing (1974–1981), there was a radical shift away from the open immigration regime. The methods used to stop immigration were heavy handed and statist, and they produced many unintended consequences (Hollifield 1992a, 1992b). The most important result was to freeze the foreign population in place. By decreeing an immigration stop, France inadvertently accelerated the processes of settlement and family reunification. Moreover, having raised expectations among the French public that the state could simply decree a halt to immigration, the government found its hands tied both by the law and by the uncontrollable effects of chain migration. The governments of Jacques

Chirac (1974–1976) and Raymond Barre (1976–1981) tried to stop family reunification by denying visas and deporting family members. The Barre government also tried to encourage return migration by paying foreigners to leave (Hollifield 1992a; Weil 1991: 107 ff).

Even as the issue of control (immigration policy) continued to be debated, the issue of integration (immigrant policy) surged onto the national agenda. The realization that millions of Muslims were settling permanently in France led to a reconsideration of existing approaches to immigration and integration. Political parties, the party system, and the electorate were increasingly polarized on both issues. The election in 1981 of a socialist president, François Mitterrand, and the first left-wing government since 1936 set the stage for important policy shifts—a kind of liberal trade-off, or what some analysts have called a "grand bargain" (Martin 1997).

The socialists opted to maintain tight control of borders and step up control of the labor market to inhibit the development of a black market for undocumented workers. Labor inspectors regulated the labor market, making snap visits to firms and imposing sanctions on employers caught using undocumented workers (Marie 1992). But at the same time the new socialist government, led by Pierre Mauroy, offered conditional amnesty to undocumented immigrants and longer (ten-year) residency and work permits for all immigrants. Anyone who had entered France prior to January 1, 1981, was eligible for a temporary residency permit, valid for three months, which would give the individual time to complete an application for an adjustment of status. By the end of the amnesty period in 1983, over 145,000 applications had been received (Weil 1991).

Strict control of entries, together with an amnesty for the undocumented, came to be seen as a good way to integrate permanent resident aliens. In addition to the amnesty, Mauroy's government (1981–1984) relaxed prohibitions against foreigners' associational and political activities, making foreigners residing in France feel more secure. Their civil liberties were protected by prohibiting the police from making arbitrary identity checks of foreign-looking individuals, but no changes were made in the nationality law or in naturalization policy, leaving this key element of the republican tradition intact. Foreigners would be welcome within strict labor market rules and regulations; they would be integrated and expected to assimilate quickly.

Having reaffirmed the previous government's commitment to strict immigration control while simultaneously taking steps to speed the integration of foreigners, the socialists seemed to be forging a new consensus on the contentious immigration issue. But the issue exploded in 1984 when the extreme-right FN won municipal elections in Dreux, an industrial town just west of Paris, on a platform calling for a complete halt to immigration and for the deportation of African immigrants. The electoral breakthrough of this neo-fascist, xenophobic, racist movement profoundly changed the politics of immigration in France and throughout Western Europe. For the first time since the end of World War II, an extremist party on the right was making itself heard and finding a new legitimacy, garnering support from large segments of the French electorate. Within a matter of years it would become "the largest working-class party in France" (Perrineau 1995). From the beginning, the National Front was a single-issue party; its leader, Jean-Marie Le Pen, called for a physical separation of the races. How did the FN's breakthrough affect French immigration policy and the republican consensus?

Crises of Control and National Identity

The rise of the National Front contributed heavily to a sense of crisis in French politics and public policy, with immigrants at the center of the maelstrom. Suddenly immigrants were seen as the cause of the French nation's economic and cultural decline, provoking a loss of confidence in the republican model, especially on the right. Immigrants were accused of taking jobs from French citizens, and Muslims were deemed to be inassimilable and hostile to republican values.

The socialist left, under President Mitterrand, and the neo-Gaullist right, led by Jacques Chirac, had very different responses to the National Front's populist appeals to economic insecurity and xenophobia. Mitterrand maneuvered to exploit the rise of the FN for political gain. From his perspective, the Front divided the right-wing electorate and, by getting working-class votes, also weakened the Communist Party, another traditional adversary of the socialists. But following the 1984 elections in Dreux, Mitterrand called for granting voting rights to immigrants in local elections, thereby forcing the mainstream parties of the right to take a stand on immigration and immigrant policy. On a more cynical note, the socialist government led by Laurent Fabius changed the electoral system from a majoritarian, single-member-district system to one based on proportional representation, just in time for the legislative elections of 1986. The immediate effect of this rule change was to allow the National Front, with roughly 10 percent of the vote, to gain thirty-two seats in the new Assembly. For the first time since Vichy, the extreme right had representation in Parliament, and a new debate over French national identity was under way.

The first step of the right-wing coalition of neo-Gaullists (Rally for the Republic, RPR) and liberals (Union for French Democracy, UDF) led by

Chirac was to change the electoral system back to the traditional dual ballot system with single member districts, under which it would have been nearly impossible for the National Front to win seats. But the damage to the right had already been done, and the task remained of recapturing FN voters. The government set about reforming immigration *and* naturalization policy, handing the entire dossier to Minister of the Interior Charles Pasqua, whose name would become synonymous with immigration reform over the next decade. Pasqua viewed immigration control primarily as a police matter, so he moved quickly to reinforce border controls by giving sweeping new powers to the border police (PAF) to detain and immediately deport anyone who did not have proper papers. He also reinforced the power of the internal police to conduct "random" identity checks of any foreign-looking or suspicious individual. A wave of terrorist bombings in Paris in 1986, which were connected to the Middle East, helped legitimize the new get-tough policy with respect to foreigners. The immediate effect of these measures was to restrict the civil liberties of foreigners, especially North Africans, thereby launching a psychological campaign against immigrants and immigration. The policies were explicitly designed to win back supporters of the National Front and to prevent any further loss of votes to the extreme right on the immigration issue. But they also heightened the sense of crisis and contributed to the growing debate over insecurity and a loss of national identity.

Yet if we look at the numbers (flows), we find considerable continuity. Immigration hovered between 100,000 and 200,000 persons annually throughout the 1980s (table 5.2). The only noticeable increase was in the number of asylum seekers, which peaked at 61,372 in 1989. With the end of the Cold War and the gradual implementation of the Schengen Agreement in the 1990s, the rate of rejection of asylum applicants rose from 57 percent in 1985 to 84 percent in 1995 (table 5.3). If flows were not raging out of control, what was the purpose of the First Pasqua Law proposed in 1986? The most controversial aspect of this reform was the attempt to weaken the birthright principle of *jus soli* by ending the practice of "automatically" attributing citizenship at age eighteen to children born in France of foreign parents. This reform, which was intended to placate right-wing nationalists and win back FN voters, was symbolic, but its effects were real. Any immigrant who had been sentenced to more than six months in prison was deemed excludable and would not be allowed to naturalize. West Africans were no longer allowed to naturalize under the streamlined procedure known as "reintegration into the French nation"; and spouses of French nationals would have to wait two years (rather than one) before they could apply for naturalization.

Table 5.3. Asylum Seekers in France, 1985–2000

Year	Asylum Seekers (N)	Rate of Rejection (%)
1985	28,809	56.8
1986	26,196	61.2
1987	27,568	67.5
1988	34,253	65.6
1989	61,372	71.9
1990	54,717	84.3
1991	47,380	80.3
1992	28,873	70.9
1993	27,564	72.1
1994	25,964	76.4
1995	20,415	83.7
1996	17,405	80.4
1997	21,416	83.0
1998	22,375	88.6
1999	30,907	80.7
2000	38,747	82.9

Source: Office Français pour la Protection des Refugiés et Apatrides (OFPRA).

The thrust of the proposed law was to require young foreigners to affirm their commitment to France by formally requesting French nationality and taking a loyalty oath.[2] What effect such a change might have on immigration flows was hazy, but the message was clear: the acquisition of French citizenship was a privilege, not a right, and it could be withheld. The First Pasqua Law provoked a firestorm of protest as civil and immigrant rights organizations mobilized against the reform, leading Pasqua and Chirac eventually to withdraw the bill from consideration.

The withdrawal of the bill was a major setback for the Chirac government, which had provided the French civil rights movement with a new rallying cry: *"Ne touche pas à mon pote!"* (Don't touch my buddy!). In addition to altering the political landscape, launching a new debate about French citizenship and national identity, and creating political opportunities for the left (Ireland 1994; Feldblum 1999), the attempted reform brought the

---

[2] The law did not affect second-generation Franco-Algerians because they were born in France of parents who were born in Algeria prior to 1962, the year of Algerian independence. Both the parents and the children were French by birth (double *jus soli*) and therefore eligible to naturalize (Weil 1991, 2002; Feldblum 1999).

power and prestige of the Council of State to bear. In ruling on the legality and constitutionality of the bill, the Council of State put the government on notice that the rights of individual foreigners and the republican tradition must be respected. This was a lesson in immigration politics and law that Minister Pasqua would not soon forget. In 1993 he held a much stronger hand, but in this round of reform the government was forced to compromise, and a special commission was appointed to hold hearings on immigration and naturalization policy reform.

After hearing expert testimony, the commission reaffirmed the importance of the republican tradition by defending the principle of *jus soli*, while at the same time stressing the importance of integrating foreigners into public and civic life (Long 1988). The whole episode of reform during the first government of cohabitation had little discernible impact on immigration flows, which remained well over 100,000 annually during the late 1980s and into the 1990s (table 5.2). The number of naturalizations remained around 50,000 (table 5.4). However, if we look at changes in the ratio of naturalizations by decree to those by declaration for the 1984–1995 period, we find an upsurge in 1985–1986 and another in 1995. This indicates that a larger number were filing for naturalization during the key years of the Pasqua reforms, while the number qualifying for "automatic" naturalization (by simple act of declaration) remained relatively constant.[3] In effect, one of the principal unintended consequences of tougher control policies in France was the revaluation of citizenship, speeding up the process of naturalization and integration of the foreign population, and inadvertently reinforcing the republican tradition.

The liberal and republican right lost its battle to eliminate the National Front and also lost the 1988 elections. Jacques Chirac was defeated in his bid to unseat Mitterrand, who won a second seven-year term; and the right also lost the legislative elections as the socialists regained control of the Assembly, albeit with the necessity of forming a minority government. Garnering 14.5 percent of the vote on the first round of the presidential election, Le Pen continued to cause problems for the right. Because his party again exceeded 10 percent of the vote on the first round of the legislative elections (but gained no seats in the Assembly), Le Pen claimed that a substantial segment of the French electorate was not being heard on the issue of immigration. In response, Charles Pasqua tried to reassure FN supporters that the RPR shared many of their "concerns and values" with respect to the

---

[3] The exception is 1994 when, with the implementation of the Second Pasqua Law, the number declaring themselves to be French shot up to 43,035, twice the average for the 1973–1992 period.

impact of immigration on French national identity. Public opinion polls at the time (1988–1989) showed that approximately a third of the electorate had sympathies for the National Front's stand on immigration.

Table 5.4. Naturalizations of Immigrants in France, 1984–2000

Year	By Decree (a)	By Declaration (b)	Total (a + b)	Ratio (a/b)
1984	20,056	15,517	35,573	1.3
1985	41,588	19,089	60,677	2.2
1986	33,402	22,566	55,968	1.5
1987	25,702	16,052	41,754	1.6
1988	26,961	27,338	54,299	1.1
1989	33,040	26,468	59,508	1.2
1990	34,899	30,077	64,976	1.2
1991	39,445	32,768	72,213	1.2
1992	39,346	32,249	71,595	1.2
1993	40,739	32,425	73,164	1.3
1994	49,449	46,633	92,484	1.1
1995	40,867	21,017	58,988	2.3
1996	58,098	21,880	79,978	2.6
1997	60,485	23,191	83,676	2.6
1998	58,123	23,789	81,912	2.4
1999	67,569	68,866	136,435	1.0
2000	77,478	63,977	150,025	1.2

Source: Lebon 1985–1999.

The new left-wing government, led by two old socialist rivals, François Mitterrand and Michel Rocard, essentially returned to the policies of the early 1980s, increasing regulation of the labor market, campaigning against illegal immigration, and taking steps to help integrate immigrants. To this end, Rocard created a High Council on Integration to study ways of speeding the integration of the foreign population, which still constituted over 6 percent of the total population (Haut Conseil 1991). The socialist governments fell back on a "grand bargain" strategy of strictly controlling inflows in order to integrate those foreigners already in the country, in hopes of depoliticizing the issue and defusing the national identity crisis.

Yet no sooner had the left returned to power than it confronted a highly symbolic controversy that struck at the heart of the republican tradition and risked splitting the Socialist Party into competing factions. The controversy arose when three schoolgirls of Moroccan descent came to a public school wearing Islamic scarves (*foulards*), in violation of the separation of church and state, one of the core principles of the republican tradition. The event immediately became a cause célèbre for the anti-immigrant right and the republican left, with more liberal elements, including Prime Minister Rocard, caught in the middle. Allowing the girls to wear the scarves would offend both the left and the right, but forcing them to remove the scarves could open a Pandora's box concerning the dividing line between the public and private spheres. Banning the scarves would raise questions about wearing other religious symbols — a crucifix or the Star of David — in the classroom. The event also heightened the sense of crisis with respect to immigration control because of widespread fear that immigrants from North Africa, especially the second generation, were prone to Islamic fundamentalism and therefore inassimilable in a secular, republican society.

Rocard and his education minister, Lionel Jospin, decided to allow the girls to wear their scarves so long as they agreed not to proselytize or in any way disrupt classes, a compromise that was ratified by the Council of State. However, the compromise did little to allay the growing fears of Islamic fundamentalism, and the "*foulards* affair" raised the specter of multiculturalism as a new threat to French unity and national identity. *Le droit à la différence* (the right to be different) became the new rallying cry of those defending multiculturalism and the rights of immigrants (Roy 1991).

Despite the almost continuous atmosphere of crisis in French politics over immigration, integration, and national identity, little had changed in terms of policy outputs (actual policies for controlling immigration) or in terms of policy outcomes (Hollifield 1992b, 1997). France continued to be open to legal immigration, with no quotas or ethnic/racial preferences, even though the left and the right did everything possible to discourage purely economic immigration. Flows continued at the level of 100,000 or more a year (table 5.2), and the liberal nationality code allowed for the relatively quick naturalization of the foreign population (table 5.4).

In terms of immigration control, perhaps the most important change came in the area of refugee policy. Under the Dublin and Schengen agreements, France committed itself to refuse entry to any asylum seeker who had passed through a "safe third country." The Schengen Agreement also engaged France in the construction of a common European territory, a Europe without internal borders, which meant a harmonization of visa and asylum policies within the Schengen group as well as increased policing of external borders. These new European initiatives in some ways challenged the republican tradition because of the limits imposed on due process and the attempt (via the Maastricht Treaty) to create a new European citizenship and grant voting rights in local elections for permanent resident aliens.

From a "Threshold of Tolerance" to "Zero Immigration"

President Mitterrand suggested in 1991 that every society has a "threshold of tolerance" for immigration, beyond which instances of xenophobia and racism are likely to increase. He did not say what that threshold might be. Charles Pasqua, soon to return to the post of minister of the interior, stated that "France has been an immigration country, but she wants to be one no longer." Pasqua claimed to be speaking on behalf of the French people, but as a powerful member of a government elected by a landslide, he made clear what the new government's immigration policy would be: "the goal we set, given the seriousness of the economic situation, is to tend toward zero immigration." This explicit linkage of immigration to the recession — which began in 1991–1992 and would push unemployment in France to postwar highs of well over 10 percent — was aimed to appeal to French voters who supported the National Front in the first round of the 1993 parliamentary elections. Immigration and integration policies were still very much at the center of French politics, and they would remain so throughout the 1990s.

Faced with a weakened, divided, and demoralized socialist opposition, and having won an overwhelming majority in Parliament, the new right-wing government headed by Edouard Balladur had a free hand to pursue draconian policies to stop all immigration, reduce the number of asylum seekers to a minimum, and reform the nationality code to block naturalization of as many resident foreigners as possible. These new policies represented a clear break from the old socialist "grand bargain." Even though Mitterrand was still president (and would be until 1995), he was a lame duck. In poor health, he was in no position to oppose what looked to be a truly dramatic shift in immigration policy. The Balladur government launched a sweeping reform of immigration and refugee policy to move France as close as possible toward zero immigration; and to discourage further settlement, the government also proposed changes to the nationality law.

What distinguishes the 1993 round of reform from earlier attempts to limit immigration (in 1974 or 1986, for example) is the clear focus on rolling back the rights of foreigners. The Second Pasqua Law directly challenged the republican model. Equal protection and due process were denied to foreigners by cutting off possibilities of appeal for asylum seekers and by giving the police greater powers to detain and deport foreigners. Social rights were to be restricted by denying foreigners access to the benefits of the social security system, especially health care.[4]

LIMITING RIGHTS TO CONTROL IMMIGRATION

What happened in the 1990s was a not-so-subtle shift in strategies and tactics for restricting immigration, away from reliance on the classic instruments of border controls and labor market regulation to a new strategy of attacking and limiting the rights of foreigners. In liberal societies, external controls are preferable to internal controls, which may infringe individuals' civil liberties. All things being equal, liberal states will opt for external control strategies. The reason for this is simple: territorial closure and sovereignty are essential to the maintenance of the social contract and the rule of law, and this cannot be questioned without questioning the authority and legitimacy of the state itself. If control cannot easily be externalized, then a series of internal control policies will come into play. The question then becomes: how far can a liberal state go in imposing such controls on individuals in (civil) society?

French politicians and the French public have been willing to accept the erosion of *negative freedom*[5] so that the state can better manage legal immigration and stop illegal immigration. The increased power of the police (both internally and at the border) to detain and deport individuals has eroded civil liberties. Limiting appeals by asylum seekers and others threatened with deportation further strengthens the state's hand in dealing with illegal immigration, but it is difficult for liberals to accept because it means more state control and less (negative) freedom.

To constrain worker and family immigration, the Second Pasqua Law (1994) required workers and foreign students to wait two years (rather than one) before bringing in family members. To inhibit permanent settlement and to control illegal immigration, the law prohibited adjustments of status for any undocumented individual who marries a French citizen, and mayors were given authority to annul any suspected marriage of convenience.

---

[4] On this point, a rift developed within the government between Minister of the Interior Pasqua and Social Affairs Minister Simone Weil, who argued for maintaining emergency health care for foreigners.

[5] Isaiah Berlin (1969) describes negative freedom as "an area within which a man can act unobstructed by others."

In this case the state inserted itself directly into the private lives of French citizens as well as foreigners. Finally, any foreigner expelled from France would be denied reentry into French territory for one year. These reforms indicate the lengths to which liberal states will go in rolling back the rights of foreigners in order to restrict immigration. A somewhat easier target is *positive freedom* revolving around the welfare state and flowing from laws designed to help the individual take advantage of opportunities afforded by negative freedom in a liberal society.[6]

The whole range of welfare benefits — from education to health care and pensions — has become a target for those wishing to control immigration by restricting foreigners' rights. Such restrictions against foreigners would seem to be less threatening to citizens depending upon the extent to which citizens are attached to social rights and determined to protect them for *all* members of society, even the most marginal and disenfranchised groups, like children, immigrants, and foreigners. France has acted to constrain the civil (equal protection and due process) and social (welfare) rights of immigrants and foreigners (Marshall 1950). If we follow this policy to its logical conclusion, then the ultimate rights that can be denied to foreigners are political (or voting) rights, which are tied to naturalization. To roll back these rights in a liberal republic requires tampering with the nationality law, and there is evidence of this in both the First and Second Pasqua laws.

However, when infringing individual and group rights or tampering with the constitution as a means of controlling immigration, governments run the risk of undermining regime legitimacy and alienating and/or endangering the citizenry. Moreover, politicians may inadvertently provoke a nationalist, xenophobic, and racist backlash, which could redound against these same politicians and undermine the rule of law (Thränhardt 1997). In states with long histories of liberal and republican governance, there are institutional and ideological checks that work to protect individuals from populist excesses. In France, the courts play a crucial role in this regard. The Council of State, which functions in part as an institutional watchdog for infringements of the rights of the individual by the state, warned the Balladur government that some aspects of the proposed reform were illegal and possibly unconstitutional. The Council of State was especially concerned with the impact of the Second Pasqua Law on the (constitutional) right of families to live together and with the provisions limiting asylum seekers' right of appeal. But the council's opinions are only advisory, even though it has great moral, political, and legal authority, and governments ignore its

---

[6] Positive freedom can be defined as having the ability (as well as the liberty) to act. See Green 1959, 1969; Rawls 1971.

views at their peril (Stirn 1991). Moreover, council decisions may presage a ruling by the Constitutional Council, which does have powers of judicial review and may stop the implementation of any law deemed unconstitutional.

This is precisely what happened in August 1993 when the Constitutional Council ruled that certain provisions of the Second Pasqua Law were unconstitutional. The judges rejected the one-year ban on reentry imposed on anyone deported from France as well as the provisions dealing with family immigration—namely, the longer waiting period for family members of foreign students and workers, and the restrictions on marriages between French citizens and foreigners. In rendering its decisions, the Constitutional Council relied specifically on the Declaration of the Rights of Man and the Citizen. Moreover, citing the Preamble to the 1946 Constitution, the Constitutional Council ruled that restrictions on the right of appeal and provisions for the automatic expulsion of refugees were unconstitutional. This ruling seemed to jeopardize France's participation in the Dublin Convention and Schengen Agreement, both of which require European states that are party to these agreements to refuse asylum to an individual who has passed through a safe third country.

The efforts of the Balladur government to move France to zero immigration did little to calm the national identity crisis. If anything, the Second Pasqua Law heightened the sense of crisis and fanned the flames of xenophobia. Nevertheless, one objective of the reforms *appears* to have been met. The average annual rate of immigration for the 1993–1999 period fell below 100,000 for the first time since the late 1940s and early 1950s (table 5.2). However, in fact, many heretofore legal flows were simply pushed underground, increasing the size of the undocumented population and raising the level of insecurity among the foreign population as a whole. The number of individuals caught trying to enter the country illegally rose steadily from 1993 onward—from 8,700 in 1993 to 10,100 in 1995 and over 12,000 in 1996.

To combat the judges and complete his reform, Interior Minister Pasqua turned one aspect of the republican tradition (popular sovereignty) against another (birthright citizenship). Claiming that the people want immigration reduced, he called for a constitutional amendment that would prepare France for entry into a border-free Europe and give the state the power to turn back asylum seekers without hearings or appeals. Ironically, later in the same year, Pasqua and the French government would block full implementation of the Schengen Agreement, claiming technical problems with the computerized system for sharing information among the Schengen countries. Clearly the French government was dragging its feet on Schengen at the European level while using Schengen as an excuse for enacting more restrictive procedures for processing asylum applications. Pasqua's amendment was approved in an extraordinary congress of Parliament in January 1994, after which Pasqua proclaimed that there would be no "government by judges" in France.

Civil Disobedience and the Limits of Control

Immigration continued to agitate French politics and society during the 1995 presidential election, the 1997 legislative elections, and the elections of 2002. The first election of Jacques Chirac as president in 1995 over left candidate Lionel Jospin did little to change French immigration policy, even though Le Pen received 15 percent of the vote on the first round of the election. The new government, led by Chirac's lieutenant, Alain Juppé, had the support of the same right-wing majority in the Assembly. But one big difference was the absence from government of Charles Pasqua, who had supported Chirac's rival, Edouard Balladur. Pasqua was replaced as minister of the interior by Jean-Louis Debré, who would soon make a name for himself by proposing further draconian steps to limit the rights of foreigners in France and to crack down on illegal immigration. The Debré Law of 1997 would test the limits of strategies for internal immigration control, leading to civil disobedience, more court rulings, new elections, and finally a resurgence of the republican left.

In the summer of 1996, the tough control policies described above were challenged by a group of Africans, most from Mali, who were either trapped by a "Catch 22" in the Second Pasqua Law (they were unable to obtain a residency permit even though they had resided in France for years, and they could not be legally deported) or whose asylum applications had been rejected. These *sans papiers* occupied a church in Paris, demanding that they be given an adjustment of status, and several launched a hunger strike. The immigrants' willingness to test the new government so openly reflected the high degree of sympathy they were able to generate among certain segments of French civil society. Over 10,000 people marched in Paris in solidarity with them, and the clergy appealed to the government not to remove the immigrants from the church by force. Nonetheless, the police were ordered to storm the church, arrest the protesters, and break up the hunger strike. The government also proudly published statistics indicating that deportations for the first six months of 1996 were up substantially over the similar period for 1995.

Apart from occasional acts of civil disobedience by the African *sans papiers*, the civil war in Algeria also had an impact on French control policy. A civil war had been raging in the former French colony since the abrupt cancellation of the 1992 elections, which Islamic fundamentalists were poised to win. The conflict pitted the Islamic radicals against the long-ruling Algerian National Liberation Front (FLN), which controls the military. The elections were canceled with the blessing of the French government, which made no attempt to hide its support for the Algerian military. French involvement in Algerian politics led to a number of terrorist attacks by Islamic militants against targets in France, which forced the government of Alain Juppé to increase security throughout the country. Security sweeps by the police and the military focused public attention on the Muslim (and African) communities in France. In October 1995 the police shot and killed one of the bombers, a young second-generation Algerian man. The press covered his life story in detail and held it up as an example of French society's failure to integrate the second-generation Maghrebi population.

As in the 1950s, French foreign policy and relations with former colonies were a driving factor in 1990s immigration and refugee policy. Various governments felt compelled to grant asylum (or temporary residence) to members of the Algerian political and intellectual elite[7] while simultaneously stepping up pressure to keep other Algerians out and maintaining a close watch on the established Algerian community in France. This atmosphere of crisis and public insecurity, together with continuing pressure from the National Front, led the Juppé government to propose a new law in late 1996 — the Debré Law — designed to resolve the ambiguous status of some *sans papiers*, particularly the French-born children of illegal immigrants and the foreign spouses of French citizens. Under the new proposal, "foreign" children under sixteen years of age would have to prove continuous residence in France for ten years, and "foreign" spouses would have to have been married for two years in order to be eligible for a one-year residence permit.

Even though the Debré Law had some liberal intent, it became the focal point of controversy and protest because of a provision added to the bill by the conservative National Assembly. The provision required all private citizens to notify local authorities whenever they received a non–European Union foreigner in their homes. Moreover, mayors were to be given authority to verify that a foreign visitor had left the private citizen's home once the visitor's visa had expired. What is most interesting about the Debré Law is not so much the effect (or lack thereof) that it had on immigration control, but the response it elicited from both groups in civil society and institutions of the liberal-republican state. Minister Debré, paraphrasing Pasqua, stated,

---

[7] From 1992 to 1997, over 400,000 upper-class and Francophone Algerians are reported to have fled the civil war, with most going to France or Canada.

"I am for zero *illegal* immigration.... The state must be given the means to deter foreigners who want to enter France without resources, papers, or jobs." Debré's focus was on those who are clearly outside the law — illegal immigrants — but public attention was concentrated on the effect that the law would have on private citizens.

Such an intrusion by the state into individuals' and families' private lives was deemed to have crossed the invisible line beyond which liberal states are not supposed to go. The Debré Law was denounced as an infringement of personal freedom and a threat to the basic civil liberties of all citizens. The European Parliament went so far as to pass a resolution condemning the law, equating it with Vichy-era regulations that required French citizens to inform on their Jewish compatriots so that the Germans could deport them to the death camps.

The Assembly approved the Debré Law (over the objections of the Council of State) but with some important modifications. Taking a step back from infringing the liberty of French citizens, the amended version required the foreigners themselves to report their movements and whereabouts to local authorities. This compromise illustrates well the limitations on the power of the liberal state to pursue strategies for internal control of immigration that cross the line between infringing the liberties of citizens and those of foreigners.

The Debré Law also seemed to violate the liberal principle that an individual is innocent until proven guilty. In order to renew their ten-year residence permits, foreigners would have to prove they were not a threat to public order and that they had maintained a regular residence in France, thus shifting the burden of proof from the state to the individual. This provision, along with another that would have given police access to asylum seekers' fingerprints, were subsequently struck down by the Constitutional Council.

The final version of the Debré Law was passed in March 1996. Provisions concerning notification of the whereabouts of foreigners were watered down. The law required African visitors to prove they had adequate accommodations and funds to live in France during their stay and to return home afterward. Throughout this policy reform, a major government concern was to devise a system for controlling entries by Africans (and other foreign visitors from developing countries) but without imposing quotas or overtly targeting specific ethnic or national groups. The resistance to quotas is born of the republican desire to maintain an egalitarian approach to the issuing of visas — where all or most applicants from developing countries would be treated equally — as well as a desire to construct a system that would not overtly discriminate against individuals coming from former

French colonies in West and North Africa. But regardless of intent, the effect of both the Pasqua and Debré laws was to severely restrict legal immigration of Africans to France.

A New "Republican Pact"

Surprisingly, Chirac decided to dissolve Parliament and call early elections in May–June 1997, largely owing to the difficulties of meeting the criteria of Economic and Monetary Union (EMU), scheduled to begin in January 1999. The Juppé government struggled to meet the stringent deflationary policies that the Maastricht Treaty on European Union forced on France, especially keeping budget deficits below 3 percent of GDP. Having been elected on a promise to heal social divisions and reduce record-high unemployment (12 to 13 percent in 1996–1997), Chirac and Juppé found themselves in a political and economic bind, unable to stimulate the economy because of their EMU commitments but unwilling to abandon French workers to their fate in a more competitive European and international economy. For this reason, Chirac decided to seek a new mandate for his government, a huge political gamble that he ultimately lost. The French socialists and their allies won control of the National Assembly, launching the third period of cohabitation government in a little over a decade, only this time the right would control the presidency and the left would control Parliament.

The change of government had major implications for immigration policy. The National Front received about 15 percent of the vote in the first round, but unlike in past elections, it refused to cooperate with other parties of the right by withdrawing its candidates from the second round of voting. This set up over seventy three-way contests in which FN candidates essentially split the right-wing vote—and helped elect a candidate of the left. Thus the National Front had a big hand in bringing down the Gaullist-liberal government and putting the left back in power.

The new government, headed by Lionel Jospin, took steps to return French immigration policy to its republican roots and to resolve the ambiguous status of the *sans papiers*. In his opening speech to Parliament in June 1997, Jospin announced that he would establish a "new republican pact" with the French people. In outlining his government's program, Jospin laid out a detailed republican vision of immigration policy:

> France, with its old republican traditions, was built in layers that
> flowed together into a melting pot, thus creating an alloy that is
> strong because of the diversity of its component parts.... Nothing

> is more alien to France than xenophobia and racism.... France
> must define a firm, dignified immigration policy without re-
> nouncing its values or compromising its social balance (*Libération*
> 1997a).

To accomplish this goal, Jospin called for (1) a new integration policy that welcomes immigrants and respects their human rights but combats illegal immigration and black labor markets, thus returning to the "grand bargain" strategies of earlier socialist governments; (2) cooperation with sending states to help control immigration at its source; and (3) a comprehensive review of immigration and nationality law, carried out by a task force chaired by immigration scholar Patrick Weil. During the campaign, Jospin promised to repeal the Pasqua-Debré laws — a promise that would come back to haunt him (see below). Finally, (4) steps were to be taken to review, case by case, the situation of all undocumented foreigners caught in the maze of regulations and contradictions surrounding the Pasqua-Debré laws. Foreigners who had waited months or years for their dossiers to be reviewed suddenly found administrative authorities willing to give them temporary residence permits.

The Weil report, published in August 1997, contained 120 propositions for modifying French immigration and nationality law. For the most part, the report steered a middle course, going back to the naturalization procedure that existed before the 1993 Pasqua Law but not creating a blanket birthright citizenship, reinforcing the rights of asylum seekers and the rights of family reunification but cracking down on illegal immigration. Finally, the report appealed to the republican tradition, linking immigration with a welcoming but secular tradition in French law and history. The report was designed to placate the right while meeting the pro-immigrant left "half way." Almost inevitably, however, the reform pleased neither the pro-immigrant left nor the anti-immigrant right.

By giving priority to immigration and nationality law reform, the Jospin government signaled its desire to confront the issue. And by appealing to French republican values as a way to resolve the immigration crisis, the government hoped to return to the earlier "republican consensus," defuse the issue, and seize the political and moral high ground. Whether the socialists and communists could reconstruct the republican consensus would depend heavily on their ability to reach out to elements of the liberal and republican right. This was the strategy adopted in the Weil report and subsequently by the government itself.

Two bills were drafted and presented to the National Assembly late in 1997. The Guigou Law (named for the justice minister) dealt with reform of the nationality code; the Chevènement Law (named for the interior minister) dealt with reform of immigration law. Both laws openly appealed to the republican tradition in an attempt to gain support from politicians on the left and the right. But the parliamentary debates demonstrated how polarized the electorate and the party system were with respect to immigration and integration. By opting to amend rather than repeal the Pasqua-Debré laws, Jospin's left-coalition government opened a breech in the ranks of the left, a breech that would prove devastating to Jospin's presidential run in 2002. The right-wing opposition of liberals and neo-Gaullists saw this as an opportunity to embarrass and weaken the government, so any chance of rebuilding the old republican consensus was lost.

The Guigou Law was narrowly approved in early December 1997. The pro-immigrant left, displeased with the government's strategy of amending rather than repealing the Pasqua-Debré laws, took a strong stand in favor of birthright citizenship, meaning an end to all restrictions on the naturalization of individuals born on French territory. The right-wing opposition denounced the reform as unnecessary and detrimental to the national interest. In effect, the Guigou Law reinstated the principle of *jus soli*, so that anyone born in France of foreign parents can acquire French nationality at the age of eighteen, so long as that individual can show continuous residence in France for at least five years after age eleven.[8] To ensure that naturalization is voluntary, the law states that any foreigner can refuse French citizenship in the six months before s/he turns eighteen or in the twelve months after his/her eighteenth birthday. To avoid having individuals fall through the cracks of the law, the Guigou Law created a "republican identity card" (note the symbolism of the name!) to be given to every minor born in France of foreign parents. Finally, the law rolls back the waiting period for foreign spouses to request naturalization, from two years to one after the marriage.

The Chevènement Law changed the Ordonnance of 1945 that governed the status of foreigners in France.[9] It eliminated the "legal entry requirement" that the Pasqua Law imposed on any foreigner seeking to adjust his or her status, though it kept "threat to public order" as grounds for exclusion. Under the law, one-year residence permits were issued to (1) all minors entering under the auspices of family reunification, (2) all foreigners who entered France before age ten and reside in France, (3) any foreigner

---

[8] Any minor born in France of foreign parents can request naturalization as early as age thirteen, if his/her parents give their consent and if s/he has resided in France for at least five years since age eight.

[9] The 1945 law has been amended no fewer that twenty-five times, including five times in the last eleven years.

who can prove they have resided in France for fifteen years, and (4) foreign spouses of French nationals and foreign parents of French children. These changes were intended to emphasize the importance and the sanctity of the family under French law. Special consideration in the issuance of residence and work permits also must be given to foreign scholars and professors invited to work in France, as well as to any foreigner who has a special personal or family situation. Foreigners who pose a threat to public order or engage in polygamy are prohibited from receiving residence permits. A special residence permit for retired people, valid for ten years and renewable, was also created.

Apart from these broad changes, the Chevènement Law eliminated a number of conditions that the Pasqua Law imposed on potential immigrants, including the requirement that parents meet certain income criteria before bringing their children to France. They need wait only one year (instead of two) after establishing their residence in France to request family reunification. The new law replaced the former "housing certification" with a statement that the foreigner has a place to stay. In a nod to the right, however, the law limited appeals by foreigners denied a residence permit. Likewise, the government would not be required to justify refusal of visas except in the case of immigration of family members. Criminal aliens are excludable, but the law requires the government to take account of the individual's personal and family situation, as required by the European Human Rights Convention.

Finally, the Chevènement Law established two new forms of asylum for individuals persecuted because of their activities "on behalf of freedom." The law created a "temporary protected status," which gives the minister of justice the power to grant "territorial asylum" to individuals in imminent, personal danger if returned to their country of origin. In another nod to the right, the length of administrative detention for irregular migrants was increased from ten to twelve days, but foreigners have additional time to appeal a deportation order.

The debate over immigration law reform in 1997 was heated. Immigrant rights organizations like Droits Devant called for demonstrations against the government, and antiracist groups like the Movement against Racism and for Friendship among Peoples (MRAP) called for vigilance against further outbursts of racism and xenophobia. Jean-Louis Debré, leader of the RPR in the Assembly and former interior minister, accused the Jospin government of waving "a red flag in front of National Front voters." Citing polls that showed a majority of French voters against increasing immigrants' rights, the opposition RPR-UDF called for a referendum on the reforms. In the midst of the political maelstrom, Interior Minister Jean-Pierre

Chevènement continued to search for the center in an effort to resurrect the grand bargain and the republican consensus, addressing the Assembly with clear republican and Gaullist overtones: "To talk of strangers is simply another way of talking about France. All of you, on both sides of the aisle, have *a certain idea* [of France], which often, thankfully, transcends partisan politics. The real issue is access to citizenship, and the French people are far more united on this subject than one might think" (*Libération* 1997b).

This "republican" strategy shifted the emphasis in immigration policy from internal controls — to limit and roll back the (civil and social) rights of resident aliens — to a "grand bargain" of relatively tough external control of borders and internal regulation of labor markets, combined with a liberal policy for integrating and naturalizing immigrants. The policy shift seems to have had a modest impact on flows, which went from 95,757 in 1996 to 139,533 in 1998 and to 119,250 in 2000 (Lebon 2001) — numbers in line with the annual averages of the 1980s and early 1990s. Over the 1997–2000 period, 76,300 individuals benefited from the review of their cases and were allowed to obtain residence permits. In this sense, France has followed the same principle of adjustment of status (and amnesty) used in other liberal democracies.

The politics of immigration control changed little following the victory of Jacques Chirac and the parties of the traditional republican right (rebaptized as the Union for a Presidential Majority [UMP]) in the elections of May–June 2002, despite the fact that Le Pen and the FN garnered 17 percent of the vote in the first round of the presidential election, eliminating Jospin and the fractured left from the second round. Le Pen carried the banner of the extreme right against Chirac and the UMP in the second round, improving his share to 18 percent but handing Chirac the largest margin of victory (82 percent) in the history of French presidential elections. In June 2002 the UMP won an overwhelming 399 out of 577 seats in the National Assembly. Thanks to the first-past-the-post dual ballot electoral system, Le Pen and the National Front won no seats, but Le Pen was successful in linking the old themes of insecurity and unemployment with illegal immigration, which helped him solidify the working-class vote.

A Harris poll conducted in March 2000 showed that 60 percent of French residents see immigration levels as too high, and Le Pen demonstrated that it is possible to tap into these anti-immigration and anti-immigrant sentiments. But the strong showing for Le Pen was not enough to bring about a radical shift in immigration policy. The new government under Prime Minister Jean-Pierre Raffarin promised to crack down on crime and increase spending on public security, but it has shown no sign of reversing policies put in place by the previous left-wing government. If anything, the government has moved in more liberal directions, taking steps (under the auspices of the United Nations High Commissioner for Refugees) to close the controversial Sangatte refugee camp near the Channel Tunnel at Calais. This move helped defuse the conflict with Britain, which had threatened to take France to the European Court of Justice for allowing illegal immigrants (stowaways) on freight trains to inhibit commerce through the tunnel between Britain and the rest of Europe.[10]

Another decision of the new government was to block an initiative by Britain and Spain that called upon the European Union (EU) to impose sanctions on sending countries that refused to cooperate in controlling illegal immigration. Joining with Sweden, the French government set itself up as the defender of African states who were threatened with the loss of EU foreign aid if they did not take harsh (illiberal) measures to crack down on illegal immigration. The EU initiative demonstrates once again that if liberal states have the capacity for extraterritorial control—as many EU member states clearly do—they will opt for further externalization of control, extending their authority to the high seas, to neighboring states, and to the territory of the sending states themselves. The Schengen and Dublin agreements, as well as the Seville initiative, seek to create buffer states, shifting many of the burdens and dilemmas of control outside the jurisdiction of the liberal state. With respect to internal control, liberal and republican states like France are constrained institutionally, ideologically, culturally, and ultimately by their civil societies. Strategies for internal control bend to these constraints.

CONCLUSION

Historically, immigration has had greater legitimacy in France than in the other major receiving countries of Western Europe. The first waves of immigration in France—the result of industrialization and a strong demand for foreign labor—were legitimized through an appeal to republican ideas and ideologies. From the very earliest days of the Republic to the various postwar governments of the Fourth and Fifth Republics, politicians have appealed to republican ideals as a way of legitimizing immigration and integrating foreigners.

Yet immigration, like republicanism, remains contested. Immigrants and immigration have come under attack in France in large part because of the

---

[10] The European Commission had ordered France to stop asylum seekers from the Sangatte camp from attempting to board trains at the Frethun rail yard, or face fines.

shift in the composition and ethnic mix of the flows, from predominantly Christian and European, to Muslim and African. This shift was the result of two developments: decolonization in the 1960s contributed to an exodus of North and West Africans to France, and European integration gradually eliminated immigration from neighboring states such as Italy, Spain, and Portugal. In the early 1970s, the justification for stopping immigration was primarily economic: to reduce unemployment. But this economic rationale, though still present, gave way in the 1980s to the arguments of Jean-Marie Le Pen and others that the French nation was being undermined by an influx of African immigrants who could never be assimilated or become good Frenchmen because of their inability to keep their private, religious views separate from their public lives. Their growing numbers were ostensibly causing a crisis of social cohesion and national identity.

Politicians began to play on these fears (Viard 1996; Thränhardt 1997; Perrineau 1995). Throughout the 1980s and 1990s, appeals to xenophobic fears led to further polarization on the issue of immigration (and contributed to the rise of the National Front). Whether these fears are rational is open to debate, but there is no doubt that they have been exploited by politicians for political gain.

By the mid-1990s, immigration control strategies in France began to change dramatically. Instead of relying exclusively on external, border controls (which were being further externalized through the Schengen and Dublin systems) or on internal regulation of labor markets, the first rightwing government of the 1990s, led by Edouard Balladur, began to roll back and limit immigrants' rights by undercutting civil rights and liberties and going after certain social rights, specifically health care. Finally, a reform of the nationality code and the erosion of the principle of birthright citizenship challenged political rights, naturalization, and citizenship.

The progression of control strategies is quite clear: the imposition of external controls (in the form of new visa regimes) in the early 1970s; the restriction on hiring foreign workers (in 1974) coupled with return policies and employer sanctions; attempts to roll back the "right" to family reunification in the late 1970s; increased labor market regulation during the socialist years of the 1980s; a return to external control strategies with the Schengen and Dublin agreements; limits on social and civil rights (the First and Second Pasqua laws and the Debré Law); and, finally, attempts to limit citizenship by changing the nationality law (the First and Second Pasqua laws).

When the state crossed the invisible line on immigration control to become a threat to civil society — and put itself at odds with the founding republican principles of the regime — institutional, ideological, and social checks came into play. As in other liberal republics, immigration control in

France is not purely a function of markets, economic interests, or national security. It is heavily dependent on the interplay of ideas, institutions, and civil society.

References

Ashford, Douglas E. 1991. "In Search of the Etat Providence." In *Searching for the New France*, edited by James F. Hollifield and G. Ross. New York: Routledge.

Berlin, Isiah. 1969. "Two Concepts of Liberty." In *Four Essays on Liberty*. Oxford: Oxford University Press.

Betz, Hans-Georg. 1994. *Radical Right-Wing Populism in Western Europe*. New York: St. Martin's.

Birnbaum, Pierre. 1995. *Destins Juifs: De la Révolution française à Carpentras*. Paris: Calmann-Lévy.

de Wenden, Catherine Wihtol. 1988. *Les immigrés et la politque*. Paris: Presses de la FNSP.

Feldblum, Miriam. 1999. *Reconstructing Citizenship: The Politics of Immigration in Contemporary France*. Albany: State University of New York Press.

Green, Thomas Hill. 1959. *Lectures on the Principles of Political Obligation*. London: Longmans.

———. 1969. *Prolegomena to Ethics*, edited by A.C. Bradley. 5th ed. New York: Kraus.

Haut Conseil à l'Intégration. 1991. *La connaissance de l'immigration et de l'intégration*. Paris: La Documentation Française.

Hoffmann, Stanley, ed. 1963. *In Search of France*. Cambridge, Mass.: Harvard University Press.

Hollifield, James F. 1992a. *Immigrants, Markets, and States*. Cambridge, Mass.: Harvard University Press.

———. 1992b. "L'Etat français et l'immigration," *Revue Française de Science Politique* 42, no. 6: 943–63.

———. 1997. *L'Immigration et l'Etat Nation: à la recherche d'un modèle national*. Paris: l'Harmattan.

Ireland, Patrick. 1994. *The Policy Challenge of Ethnic Diversity*. Cambridge, Mass.: Harvard University Press.

Lebon, André. 1985–1999. *Immigration et présence étrangère en France*. Paris: La Documentation Française.

———. 2001. "Rapport du SOPEMI." Paris: Organisation for Economic Co-operation and Development.

Libération. 1997a. "Le discours de Jospin," June 20, p. 4.

———. 1997b. "Loi sur l'immigration, Chevènement sort le grand jeu," December 5.

Long, Marceau. 1988. *Etre français aujourd'hui et demain*. Paris: La Documentation Française.

Marie, Claude Valentin. 1992. "Le travail clandestin," *Infostat Justice* 29 (September): 1–6.

Marshall, T.H. 1950. *Citizenship and Social Class and Other Essays*. Cambridge: Cambridge University Press.

Martin, Philip L. 1997. "The Impacts of Immigration on Receiving Countries." In *Immigration into Western Societies: Problems and Policies*, edited by Emek M. Uçarer and Donald J. Puchala. London: Pinter.

Perrineau, Pascal. 1995. *Le Vote de crise*. Paris: Presses de la FNSP.

Rawls, John. 1971. *A Theory of Justice*. Cambridge, Mass.: Harvard University Press.

Roy, Olivier. 1991. "Ethnicité, bandes et communautarisme," *Esprit*, February.

Sauvy, Alfred. 1950. "Besoins et possibilités de l'immigration en France," *Population* 2, no. 3: 209–34.

Stirn, Bernard. 1991. *Le Conseil d'Etat*. Paris: Hachette.

Tapinos, Georges. 1975. *L'Immigration étrangère en France*. Paris: Presses Universitaires de France.

———. 1982. "European Migration Patterns, Economic Linkages and Policy Experiences," *Studi Emigrazione*, pp. 339–57.

Thränhardt, Dietrich. 1997. "The Political Uses of Xenophobia in England, France, and Germany." In *Immigration into Western Societies: Problems and Policies*, edited by Emek Uçarer and Donald Puchala. London: Pinter.

Tribalat, Michèle. 1997. "Chronique de l'Immigration," *Population* 1.

Viard, Jean, ed. 1996. *Aux sources du populisme nationaliste*. Paris: Editions de l'Aube.

Weil, Patrick. 1991. *La France et ses étrangers*. Paris: Calmann-Levy.

———. 1997. *Mission d'étude des législations de la nationalité et de l'immigration*. Paris: La Documentation Française.

———. 2002. *Qu'est ce qu'un Français?* Paris: Grasset.

Commentary

Charles P. Gomes

The second round of France's 2002 presidential election seems to reinforce the importance of the republican model in understanding French politics. When "*le mal français*" appears on the political scene, right-wing and left-wing political parties unite to reinforce their consensus around the values that forge republican ideology. Although one of the slogans in the mass street protests against extreme right, anti-immigrant Jean Marie Le Pen was "First, second, third generation, we are all sons of immigrants," the sign that better captured the essence of the French electorate was the justification that the left offered for their vote for Jacques Chirac: "We aren't voting for the right, we are voting for the Republic." The signs and the major political discourse gravitated around the words "republic" and "democracy." The street protests illustrate clearly that it is not immigration but the republican values that still best define the French identity. France was a nation of republican citizens long before it became a country of immigrants. Therefore, the better the "republican model" functions, the more easily immigrants' ethnic or national origins are erased over time.

According to Hollifield, the republican tradition deeply frames immigration policy in France. Despite increased political will to establish more restrictive standards after 1974, this ideology remains the major factor that explains the continuity in principle and outcomes of France's postwar policies. But if we test Hollifield's main argument by supposing that the republican model covers up, more than it exposes, the different political conflicts throughout the history of French immigration policy, we can pose several critical questions regarding his analysis: Up to what extent is republicanism just part of the political discourse, with no real implications in the definition of immigration policy? Are cultural variables, like ideas and norms, as relevant as economic interests and political power in the analysis of French immigration policies? Accepting that they are fundamental variables in the explanation, have republican values, like equal protection before the law, been static since the French Revolution? Finally, how does the international environment raise causal factors that clash with the idea of French exceptionalism as a tool for political analysis?

The first critique is generally directed to all analyses that present political culture as an explanatory variable. According to more empiricist social analyses, republicanism, like Constitutionalism in the United States, should be perceived as a political tool used by political actors, and not as an analytical one. Republicanism and Constitutionalism are just speech that never becomes act, pure rhetoric to justify all sorts of political maneuvers. In the same way that U.S. politicians like to legitimize their decisions in the name of the Constitution, French politicians like to legitimize their decisions in the name of the Republic. Hollifield, however, has shown that republican ideology was not only a matter of rhetoric but also a strong factor in explaining at least part of French immigration policy. The republican model explains perfectly well the definition of French integration politics and to some extent its citizenship policies, but less well the configuration of immigration control policies. Hollifield offers a good description of how republican ideals reinforced by the Council of State and the Special Commission explain the failures of right-wing governments in changing the birthright principle of *jus soli* during the late 1980s and early 1990s. Concerning integration policy, the entire political debate around the right to wear Islamic scarves in public laic schools also shows the strength of republicanism at the expense of multiculturalism in the definition of French official policies. Regarding control policies, Hollifield is right in affirming that very little has changed in both policy outputs and policy outcomes. The role played by the courts is the main explanation for the maintenance of the level of legal immigration even during periods of economic crisis. But court decisions in favor of immigrants are not necessarily guided by republican values, even if equal protection before the law is considered to be one of the elements that compose the republican model. This point makes a connection to the second and third critiques.

The second most common criticism of political analyses that reinforce the role of norms and ideas in the understanding of specific policies is their lack of social, economic, and political micro-foundations. At times these analyses tend to hide other variables like economic interests and political power preferences by overemphasizing cognitive structures. This does not seem to be the case in Hollifield's analysis, which incorporates both elements in the description of the evolution of French immigration policy. Slow population growth and the low rural exodus during the late nineteenth century pushed "French capitalists ... to invent a working class by recruiting foreign labor." Hollifield also shows how political preferences were defined not exclusively by the force of republicanism but by other political variables that sometimes were not linked to the republican model. He points out that French colonialism was among the major political factors that explain the dynamics of immigration flows and policies. But this complexity of factors in defining the outputs and outcomes of French immigration control policies ends up reducing the scope of republicanism in the analysis.

The third point concerns the author's tendency to consider republicanism as a static ideological structure and the implication this can have on the results of the analysis. The study of the origins and the evolution of factors composing a given political culture and the impacts it can have on a given policy is a stronger method to sustain the importance of cultural explanatory variables. Only a deep analysis of the components of a more general political culture like republicanism can show how misleading the analysis based on these reified ideological structures can be. Let us take as examples two of the elements that compose the republican model: due process and equal protection before the law. Once you analyze the connection between these two elements and the politics of immigration, you realize that access to courts and equal protection before the law for all immigrants are not compact and general concepts. They do not necessarily have only one interpretation and cannot be applied to all the different areas of immigration policy. Therefore, the republican model is not a static cognitive structure; it also has its internal dynamics. The history of "equal protection before the law" for immigrants shows the conflicting nature of the concept itself. The same can be said about the access to courts accorded to immigrants. During a long period in French history, the prevailing legal doctrine in cases concerning the deportation and exclusion of immigrants accorded the government plenary discretion in these matters. This simply meant that immigrants would have no access to courts in cases concerning their deportation or exclusion. The history of these two legal norms and the growing tendency of French courts to reinforce both of them, even in cases concerning visa denial, show that these norms and their strength have less to do with French republicanism and more to do with a global legal culture that emphasizes the universalistic basis more than the nationalistic basis of the legal system.

The fourth and final critique concerns explanations that go beyond the "republican model." In fact, several international variables can be used to explain French immigration policies. In areas like immigrants' rights, France shows more convergence than exception when it comes to international rules and law. For instance, article 8 of the European Convention of Human Rights served as the legal basis for French constitutional and administrative courts to rule in favor of the "family reunification" for immigrants in the late 1970s. On the politics of control, there is a growing transfer of authority from the national toward the supranational level. Regarding the politics of citizenship, European pressures pushed France to accord the right to vote in local elections to immigrants originally from European Union countries. The acceptance of political rights for all legal immigrants is probably the next step to be taken by the incoming French government or to be ruled by the Constitutional Court in the name of equal protection before the law. This evolving process of political convergence within the European Union is eroding the idea of national cultural exceptionalism as the key element in the understanding of public policy in general and immigration policy in particular.

6

Germany: Managing Migration in the Twenty-First Century

Philip L. Martin

GERMANY AS AN IMMIGRATION COUNTRY

Germany is a country of immigration; a law giving Germany its first-ever regulated immigration system was signed in June 2002. The road from a regime of guestworkers to one of immigrants was long and twisting. On July 4, 2001, an immigration commission of political party representatives, employers, unions, and churches issued a historic report, "Organizing Immigration—Fostering Integration," which declared: "Germany is and should be a country of immigration," thus removing the *not* from the previous policy: "Germany is not a country of immigration." The commission noted that, in addition to the 75,000 foreigners who move to Germany each year to join family members,[1] some 100,000 asylum seek-

---

[1] Foreigners who have lived in Germany for one year or more and have adequate housing and a steady job are entitled to have family members join them in Germany; there are no quotas or waiting lists for family unification. However, only children under age sixteen can join their families; if they arrive after age sixteen, the argument goes, they will not get sufficient education and training to succeed in the German labor market.

ers and 100,000 ethnic Germans enter the country. The commission recommended that Germany welcome an additional 50,000 foreign professionals a year and transform its Office for the Recognition of Refugees into the Office for Migration and Refugees to manage migration.

A "green card" program launched in 2000 set the stage for the commission's recommendations. During the high-tech boom of the late 1990s, German information technology (IT) employers complained that there were at least 75,000 unfilled IT jobs and too few students graduating from German universities to fill them. As the United States tripled the number of visas available to foreign professionals and as countries from Canada to Singapore launched programs to attract foreign professionals, the German IT industry persuaded the Social Democratic Party (SPD)–Green coalition government to allow the fast track entry of foreign computer specialists. Between August 2000 and March 2002, about 14,000 five-year green cards were issued to foreign IT workers.

The green card program, in turn, arose from the failed effort of the SPD-Green government, elected in September 1998, to change German naturalization policy from one of the most restrictive to one of the most liberal in Europe. Under the new government's original plan, foreigners who became naturalized Germans could have routinely retained their original nationality. The opposition Christian Democratic Union (CDU) and Christian Social Union (CSU) opposed routine dual nationality (arguing that it would give double benefits to foreigners) and forced the SPD-Greens into a compromise law. Thus, when the IT industry asked for foreign professionals, the SPD-Green government saw a way to refocus the immigration debate on the benefits of immigration and to keep immigration out of the September 2002 national elections.

Nevertheless, immigration and unemployment were the two major domestic issues in the 2002 campaign. SPD Chancellor Gerhard Schroeder asserted that he should be reelected because he gave Germany the modern immigration law that it needed. His challenger, CSU leader Edmund Stoiber, opposed the new immigration law because of high unemployment: "with four million unemployed, we can't have more foreign workers coming to Germany."

In the early 1970s about two-thirds of the foreigners in Germany were employed wage and salary workers; the fraction had dipped to one-quarter by 2000 (table 6.1).[2] Thus a migration policy that aimed to in-

---

[2] There are more foreigners employed than suggested by wage and salary employment. About 300,000 are self-employed, and perhaps 500,000 earn less than E350 a month and thus are not enrolled in the social security system. But there is no doubt

crease the percentage of residents in the workforce wound up reducing the employment-population ratio. The gap between German government migration goals and outcomes arose from the fact that the number of guestworkers was not limited, in part because there was no expectation that they would unify their families and settle, even though laws and regulations allowed family unification and settlement. In short, Germany's migration policy gap arose from the failure to anticipate the internal dynamics of migration, including employer and guestworker interests in prolonging stays in Germany and the desire of workers to live with their families.

FROM EMIGRATION TO GUESTWORKERS: 1700–1973

Germany was primarily a country of emigration until the 1950s. Of the 66 million immigrants whose arrival was recorded in the United States between 1820 and 2000, over 7 million, or 11 percent, were from Germany. Germans were one-third of the immigrants arriving in the United States during the 1850s and 1890s and one-fourth of those arriving during the 1830s, 1840s, 1870s, 1880s, and 1950s. In the 1980 population census, some 60 million Americans, or one in four, reported German roots (Bade 1997).

In the early 1900s Germany was transformed from an agricultural into an industrial nation, and internal migration became more important than transatlantic migration. Most internal migration was east-west, from East Prussia to the central German cities of Berlin, Leipzig, and Dresden, and later to the western German Rhine and Ruhr river valleys (Bade 1987: 62). Even though "Ruhr Poles" were Prussian citizens, they differed in language and religion from local residents, and they faced integration problems. Italians were also imported to work in Ruhr-area mines and factories. Foreigners were so numerous that the 1.2 million enumerated in the 1910 and 1920 German censuses were 2 percent of the population.

Workers moving west were replaced on Prussian estates by migrants from further east. These migrant farmworkers were supposed to return home when their jobs ended, but many settled and were integrated, just as most Poles who moved west within Germany integrated successfully (Bade 2000). This early German experience with foreign workers meant

---

that Stoiber is referring to the fact that, in the minds of many Germans, foreigners have changed from being associated with work to being associated with unemployment and welfare.

Table 6.1. Foreign Residents and Employed Foreigners in Germany, 1960–2000

Year	Foreign Residents (1000s)	Foreigners Employed (1000s)	Employed Foreigners as Percentage of Foreign Residents
1960	686	279	41
1968	1,924	1,015	53
1969	2,381	1,372	58
1970	2,977	1,839	62
1971	3,439	2,169	63
1972	3,527	2,317	66
1973	3,966	2,595	65
1974	4,127	2,151	52
1975	4,090	1,933	47
1976	3,948	1,874	47
1977	3,948	1,834	46
1978	3,981	1,862	47
1979	4,147	1,966	47
1980	4,453	1,926	43
1981	4,628	1,832	40
1982	4,667	1,710	37
1983	4,535	1,641	36
1984	4,364	1,553	36
1985	4,379	1,536	35
1986	4,513	1,545	34
1987	4,241	1,557	37
1988	4,846	1,607	33
1989	4,846	1,684	35
1990	5,343	1,793	34
1991	5,882	1,909	32
1992	6,496	2,120	33
1993	6,878	2,150	31
1994	6,991	2,110	30
1995	7,174	2,094	29
1996	7,314	2,051	28
1997	7,366	1,998	27
1998	7,320	2,024	28
1999	7,344	2,015	27
2000	7,297	1,923	26

Source: http://www.bundesauslaenderbeauftragte.de/.

that "leakage into settlement" was not considered a serious consequence of migrant worker programs, but the successful integration of Ruhr Poles and Italians also did not lead to a feeling that immigrants enriched Germany.

During World War II, Germany used foreign workers from occupied nations in its factories. In August 1944, 7.5 million such workers—2 million war prisoners and 5.7 million civilian workers—were employed in German agriculture and factories, and they were about one-third of the total labor force (Herbert 1997). World War II gave German employers experience dealing with foreign workers, so that when labor shortages appeared in the 1950s, German managers were confident they could once again manage a multinational workforce.

The Federal Republic of Germany was founded in 1949 amidst massive unemployment. Currency reform, Marshall Plan aid, and a "social market economy" put Germany on the path to sustained economic growth, but unemployment remained high as West Germany absorbed millions of ethnic and East Germans.[3] There were 79,000 Italian farmworkers in Germany when the country signed a labor recruitment agreement with Italy in 1955 that permitted farmers to hire Italian workers to harvest their crops. It soon became apparent, however, that the real need for additional labor was not in the fields; it was in the German factories producing cars, machine tools, steel, and consumer durables for booming export and domestic markets.[4]

Guestworker Recruitment

In 1960 the number of job vacancies exceeded the number of registered unemployed, and German employers requested permission to recruit additional foreign workers. Hermann (1992: 7) concluded that there was "no noteworthy discussion" of alternatives to recruiting guestworkers, and analysts cite four reasons why recruiting guestworkers seemed better than exploring alternatives (Böhning 1984; Krane 1975, 1979). First,

---

[3] The former West Germany absorbed large number of Germans who moved west. Ardaugh (1987: 13) called the westward movement of 8 million Germans between 1944 and 1946 "the greatest migratory movement of modern times." Estimates of the number of Germans who moved west between the end of World War II and the construction of the Berlin Wall in 1961 range from 9 to 13 million.

[4] Thirty countries expressed an interest in sending migrants to Germany, but Germany made the decision to import only Europeans (the exception was a few hundred Koreans).

the German labor force was shrinking. A delayed baby boom limited the ability to raise female labor force participation, the greater availability of educational opportunities kept more youth in school, and better pensions prompted earlier retirements. For "family-political" reasons, alternatives to importing guestworkers were not pursued actively.

Second, leaders who had experienced postwar privation were reluctant to risk the nation's economic recovery on mechanization and rationalization alternatives to foreign workers (Lutz 1963; Kindleberger 1967). Unions did not oppose importing foreign workers in this era of full employment, especially after they secured a promise that foreigners would be treated equally and thus would not undercut German workers.

Third, Europe was unifying anyway, and Germany had agreed that Italians and other European Community (EC) nationals would have freedom of movement rights after January 1, 1968 (Böhning 1972).[5] With Italians soon able to come as they wished, recruiting guestworkers allowed Germany to regulate unilaterally the migration of EC workers.

Fourth, in the early 1960s the countries of Western Europe enjoyed a particularly advantageous international economic environment which endured longer than expected. These countries' undervalued currencies, in a world of fixed exchange rates, made them a center for export goods. Germany's Volkswagen Beetle is a symbol of this period when American multinationals sent huge sums to Germany to maximize the value of their investments by converting them to undervalued deutsche marks.

Many Germans believed that the "3 R's" — recruitment, remittances, and returns — were a form of "foreign aid" to labor emigration countries. Recruited unemployed workers would reduce joblessness in southern Europe, their remittances could supply capital for economic development and job creation, and returned workers with training and experience gained in Germany would be productive factory workers in their countries of origin — and might also favor the purchase of now familiar German equipment.

Guestworker recruitment expanded faster than anticipated. In 1960 there were 329,000 foreign workers in Germany. After the Berlin Wall closed the door from East Germany to West Germany in 1961, West Germany signed recruitment agreements with seven non–European Community recruitment countries — Greece, Morocco, Portugal, Spain,

---

[5] Freedom of movement within the EC means that a worker from any member state may enter another and remain for up to three months in search of a job. If the migrant finds employment, the host country must grant any necessary work and residence permits.

Tunisia, Turkey, and Yugoslavia.[6] The number of guestworkers employed in Germany first topped 1 million in 1964 and, after a dip during the 1966–1967 recession, climbed to a peak 2.6 million (12 percent of the wage and salary workers in Germany) in 1973. Most guestworkers were former farmers between the ages of eighteen and thirty-five, although significant numbers of semi-skilled construction workers, miners, and schoolteachers migrated to Germany to work on assembly lines.

German employers who had vacant jobs asked local Employment Service (ES) offices to refer local workers to fill them. Most ES offices made only pro forma searches for local workers before sending an employer's request for one thousand unskilled workers to the German ES office in Istanbul, for example, where Turks who had registered to work in Germany were screened for health and skills, given one-year work and residence permits, and put on trains or planes for Germany. They would be at work in Germany a day or two later. With ten Turks in line for each one recruited, Germans could be selective and they were. Some 30 to 40 percent of the Turks recruited to work in Germany were considered skilled workers at home, but most worked as manual laborers in Germany.[7]

Most migrant workers were recruited anonymously, but employers could request specific individuals. Migrants soon learned that they could jump the recruitment queue by persuading friends and relatives already employed in Germany to have employers request them by name (Martin and Miller 1980). Some migrants traveled to Germany, found a job, and then had their employers request them; between 20 and 30 percent of the Turks employed in Germany during the late 1960s and early 1970s went first as "tourists." Guestworkers soon comprised a major share of assembly line workers in major manufacturing plants, so that at GM Opel's auto assembly plant in Russelheim, the number of migrant workers increased from 2,200 in 1968 to 9,300 in 1972, or one-third of the plant's workers.

Guestworker recruitment peaked between 1968 and 1973, when the migrant workforce rose from 1 million to 2.6 million (Martin 1981). In the early 1970s, over a thousand migrants sometimes arrived in a single day.

---

[6] Greece became a member of the European Community in 1981, and Spain and Portugal became members in 1986. Greece had to wait until 1988 before its citizens got full freedom of movement rights. Spain and Portugal, scheduled to have freedom of movement rights in 1993, got mobility rights one year early, in 1992.

[7] By 1970, for example, 40 percent of Turkey's carpenters and stonemasons were employed in Germany (Martin 1980).

However, two myths discouraged planning for their settlement and integration: rotation and return. Germany's rotation policy held that, after completing one year of work (perhaps another two if a worker was especially good), the migrant would return home, put his savings to work developing his country, and be replaced by a fresh recruit. The myth of return arose because many migrants proclaimed that they wanted to return to their families and communities, languages and cultures. And most migrants did go home. Between 1960 and 1999, 70 percent of the 30 million foreigners who stayed in Germany more than ninety days left, but few Germans were prepared for the settlement of the other 30 percent. Of the 7.3 million foreigners in Germany in 2000, 40 percent had been there fifteen years or more (Beauftragte 2001: 5).

Settlement

A guestworker program aims to add workers (temporarily) to the labor force but not add settlers to the population. However, rotating guestworkers through permanent jobs was not in the interest of employers or migrants, producing a gap between goals and outcomes. Migrant workers earned high wages, but they soon learned that the instant wealth they hoped to achieve by working in Germany was rooted in the false belief that they could earn German wages while enjoying Turkish living costs. Migrants had to stay abroad longer than planned to achieve their savings goals. Given that they earned the right to unify their families in Germany after one year of work, some unified their families instead of returning home. German employers did not discourage family unification; wives of guestworkers could also work, and their presence encouraged trained and experienced migrants to remain in Germany, saving employers the cost of recruiting and training new migrants (Miller and Martin 1982; Castles 1989).

The desires of guestworkers and their German employers meant that the rotation policy was not enforced, and the number of migrants and dependents swelled to the point that guestworkers and their families outnumbered Germans in many industrial areas. The presence of migrant children in German schools made it apparent that some of the "guests" were settling in Germany, but there was no unified response; some schools taught migrant children in their parents' language to facilitate return, while others taught in German to expedite integration.

Many Germans were aware of neighboring Switzerland's unsuccessful campaigns to expel foreigners, and the slogan "Foreigners out! Germany is for Germans" became a rallying cry of fringe rightist and nationalist German politicians in the 1970s. Most of the opposition to migrants was based on guestworkers changing Germany's culture, but a few economists warned that Germany's famed industrial engine was becoming calcified because employers, with migrant labor readily available, did not aggressively develop labor-saving technologies. These Cassandras warned that the Japanese auto industry in the early 1970s had begun to experiment with robots to assemble cars after the Japanese government turned down their requests to employ migrants. German employers, meanwhile, hired Turks.

By 1973 it was clear that many guests had become permanent residents. Several events in 1973 stiffened government resolve to slow recruitment, even though employers said that more guestworkers were needed. In spring 1973, the employer-paid recruitment fee was raised from DM 300 to DM 1,000. Wildcat strikes involving migrants in summer 1973 convinced the government that it was losing control of foreign worker employment and settlement, and the October 1973 oil embargo threatened a recession that would eliminate the need for additional guestworkers. In November 1973 the government announced a recruitment stop: no more unskilled foreign workers could be recruited to Germany for jobs that lasted more than ninety days. Employers, the labor ministry, and emigration countries expected recruitment to resume in a year or two but perhaps with tougher regulation.[8]

FROM GUESTWORKERS TO MINORITIES: 1973–1989

The failure of the rotation policy was the first significant policy-outcome gap in German migration, but several subsequent gaps compounded the sense that the government could not manage guestworker migration. When the 1973 recruitment stop was announced, there were 2.6 million employed foreign workers and 4 million foreigners in Germany, and both numbers were expected to decrease as unemployment rose. The number of employed foreigners fell as expected, to between 1.8 and 1.9 million in the late 1970s, but the foreign population held steady as unemployed migrants remained for fear that they would not be permitted

[8] Foreigners Commissioner Liselotte Funke said that employers and the labor ministry preferred to continue guestworker recruitment but were willing to agree to tighter restrictions on family unification to avoid schooling and other integration issues (*Die Zeit*, February 17, 1989, p. 19).

to return to Germany if they went home. Many unified their families, so the foreign population actually rose to 4.5 million in 1980 (Bade 2000).

To discourage family unification, newly arrived spouses were not allowed to work for between one and four years, almost doubling the ratio of non-workers to workers among foreigners, from 0.7 to 1 in 1973 to 1.3 to 1 in 1980. Germany also attempted to discourage family unification by prohibiting foreigners from moving to cities that were already "overburdened" with foreigners (having 12 percent or more foreign residents). However, this measure simply reduced migrants' mobility and flexibility, two characteristics that had been their strongest advantages.[9]

The "rightist" Christian Democratic Union, Christian Social Union, and Free Democratic Party (FDP) won the 1982 election, in part because they promised to "do something" about out-of-control immigration. The CDU-CSU-FDP government's migration management policy, patterned on a 1981 French program, was to offer departure bonuses to settled foreigners who gave up their work and residence permits. A migrant family could receive a bonus of up to US$5,000, and departing workers could get their share of social security contributions refunded once they returned home. The bonus scheme reduced the foreign population from 4.7 million in 1982 to 4.4 million in 1984–1985, but the number of foreigners rebounded to 4.5 million in 1986. Most studies concluded that foreigners who took departure bonuses would have left Germany in any event, so the bonuses merely bunched up normal emigration during the two years they were available (Hönekopp 1990).

1980s: Return or Integrate, Turkey

During the 1980s German government policy was clear: "the Federal Republic of Germany is not, nor shall it become, a country of immigration." This policy failed: there were 4.6 million foreigners in Germany in 1981 and 5.8 million in 1991. German policies toward foreigners during the 1980s had three elements: promoting the integration of legally resident foreigners and their families, reducing non-EU immigration as much as possible, and encouraging the voluntary return and reintegration into their home countries of resident foreigners. There was a tension

[9] Similarly, an effort to save money on children's allowances wound up encouraging family unification. After 1975, full children's allowances were paid only to children living in Germany. This decision came as a response to newspaper stories of Turkish parents obtaining monthly allowances for up to ten real and fictitious children in Turkey.

between promoting returns and fostering integration, as reflected in Chancellor Helmut Schmidt's statement after his October 1980 reelection. Schmidt said that Germany had no choice but to integrate the guest-workers who had settled in the country after contributing to the economy during the 1960s, but he continued, "four million is enough."[10]

Turks were never more than a third of the foreigners in Germany. But because they were the last guestworkers to arrive in large numbers and the most visible, in part because they were Muslims, Turks came to mean "problem foreigners." Many Germans continue to emphasize the obstacles to the integration of Turks: their different treatment of men and women, the importance of Islam in their daily lives, and political divisions within Turkish society, as between Kurds and other Turks, that were reflected among migrants. Turkey made demands on its nationals abroad, including children born to Turkish parents in Germany. For example, upon reaching age eighteen, Turkish youths were obliged to perform eighteen months of military service in Turkey or pay DM 10,000 to have their service obligation in Turkey reduced to two months.[11]

There were about 3.5 million Turks living abroad in 2000, including 3 million in Europe, of whom 70 percent were in Germany. The Turkish government's primary goal is full membership in the European Union.[12] Many Europeans fear that EU membership for Turkey would stimulate another wave of Turkey-EU migration. During the guestworker era, about 20 percent (700,000) of Turkish men between the ages of twenty and thirty-five emigrated. A late 1980s study suggested that, given the opportunity, one-third of this age group—or 2.5 million—might emigrate, reflecting rising emigration pressure among men and a growing

---

[10] Schmidt continues to be pessimistic about integrating foreigners. In a 2002 book, *Hand on Heart*, he wrote that Germany "brought in far too many foreigners as a result of idealistic thinking that resulted from the experience of the Third Reich. We have seven million foreigners today who are not integrated, many of whom do not want to be integrated and who are also not helped to integrate. We Germans are unable to assimilate all seven million. The Germans also do not want to do this. They are to a large extent xenophobic."

[11] Those who fail to perform military service or pay cannot get their Turkish passports renewed.

[12] The Turkish government stresses that the European Union should embrace full Turkish membership because of the country's strategic position between Europe and Asia and to send a signal to other Muslim societies, such as those of North Africa, that the EU will include Muslim societies that are secular and democratic.

willingness among women to emigrate if there were a second round of guestworker recruitment (Martin 1991: 94).[13]

Integration and Unemployment

In 2000 there were about 1.9 million foreigners with wage and salary jobs in Germany, including 553,000 Turks — about the same number as in the previous five years. Many of the foreign workers had arrived as young guestworkers before 1973, and by 2000 they were between fifty and sixty years old. A large proportion were well integrated in the workplace, but some were jobless and with little prospect of finding another position.[14] The unemployment rate for foreign workers was about 16 percent in 2000, more than twice the rate for Germans.

Unemployment rates for foreign workers in Germany began to rise in the 1970s because these workers tended to be employed in manufacturing sectors that underwent economic restructuring following the hike in oil prices. Foreigners without good German language skills who were laid off often found it hard to find well-paying service jobs, in part because of their lack of German but also because of discrimination. Instead of finding other jobs, some migrants became self-employed; the number of self-employed foreigners almost doubled, from 138,000 to 263,000, between 1989 and 1999. Many self-employed foreigners serve other foreigners, operating restaurants, small shops, and travel services, so that over half of the self-employed foreigners had no employees in 1999.

One of the most difficult hurdles for advocates of more immigration is the fact that growing shares of foreigners in Germany are not in the wage and salary workforce. In industrial countries, about half of the population is in the workforce (a German population of 82 million is associated with a labor force of 41 million). In 1973 there were 2.6 million employed wage and salary workers among the 4 million foreigners in Germany (65 percent), but in 2000 there were only 1.9 million among the 7.3 million

---

[13] Turkey hopes that admission to the EU will bring assistance and foreign direct investment that creates jobs and pushes up wages, thus making migration insignificant.

[14] Foreigners have been elected to both union and independent works council posts in factories; 29 percent of those employed in 1992 were union members, and the 8,400 foreigners elected to works council posts were 4 percent of all works council members (Frey and Mammey 1996: 114). About half of all foreigners in unions are in the IG Metall union, which, with 2.8 million members, is sometimes described as the world's largest union.

foreigners (26 percent). The various explanations for the drop include higher unemployment, an increase in self-employment, and the fact that younger foreigners tend to have more children (foreigners are 9 percent of residents but account for 13 percent of births). The fact that foreigners were associated with work in the early 1970s and are associated with non-work today is one reason that many Germans oppose more immigration.

EAST GERMANS, ETHNIC GERMANS, AND ASYLUM: 1989–2000

East Germans

There was an east-west migration within Germany before and after the dissolution of the former East Germany. At the end of World War II, Germany was divided into four zones and occupied by troops from France, the United Kingdom, the United States, and the Soviet Union. Some 730,000 Germans moved from the Soviet zone to the other zones in the late 1940s, and another 3.8 million moved from East Germany to West Germany between 1949 and the building of the Berlin Wall in August 1961. Another 600,000 East Germans moved west between 1961 and 1988, including many pensioners with permission to leave.[15]

The fall of the Berlin Wall in November 1989 opened a new chapter on internal migration. Migration hastened the demise of the Communist regime in East Germany, and the fear of massive east-west migration persuaded West Germany to undertake a costly economic stabilization program to avoid "unification in the west." Some 1 million persons from the former East Germany moved into the former West Germany between 1989 and 1997, including 390,000 in 1989 and 395,000 in 1990. Internal migration from east to west continued in the 1990s at a slower but rising pace. Net migration from the former East Germany to the former West Germany was 61,000 in 2000 and 70,000 in 2001, prompting a discussion of whether Germany should continue to invest in the former East Germany to create jobs that would slow migration or simply allow East Germans to migrate west to jobs.

---

[15] In a little noted migration, some 393,000 West Germans moved east during these years.

Ethnic Germans

Ethnic Germans are mostly the descendants of Germans who migrated eastward into Romania beginning in the twelfth century and into Russia since the late eighteenth century, as well as Germans who were living in what was Germany when World War II ended, such as the western provinces of Poland. Most of the 3 million ethnic Germans who remain in Eastern Europe and the former Soviet Union no longer speak German, and many have only a few documents to prove that their ancestors were German.

Article 116 (1) of Germany's Basic Law gives those born of German parents, no matter how diluted their German heritage, the right to German citizenship if they suffered persecution after World War II because of their German heritage (those born after 1993 are not eligible for automatic German citizenship).[16] This provision was enacted in 1949, when most ethnic Germans were prohibited from emigrating. However, if they could get to Germany, the welcome mat was out for them (Bade 1994a).

Two distinct phases of migration brought about 4 million ethnic Germans to Germany between 1950 and 2000. The first, from 1950 to 1988, brought 1.4 million ethnic Germans—62 percent from Poland, 15 percent from Romania—and most spoke German. The second phase, in the late 1990s, brought about 2.6 million ethnic Germans; 99 percent were from the former Soviet Union, and few had a good knowledge of German. The number of ethnic Germans arriving peaked at 397,000 in 1989.

As the number of ethnic German immigrants rose—many prompted more by economic reasons than by affinity for Germany—the government made it more difficult for them to immigrate. After July 1, 1990, ethnic Germans had to complete a lengthy questionnaire and be approved as ethnic Germans before arriving in Germany, and winning recognition as an ethnic German required passing a test in German that between 30 and 40 percent of test takers failed.[17] Beginning in 1993, a maximum 220,000 ethnic Germans could be recognized each year, and only persons from the former Soviet Union were presumed to have been

---

[16] An individual must prove that he or she suffered persecution because of German heritage in the aftermath of World War II, but there was a blanket "proof" for East Europeans and residents of the Soviet Union until 1998. Since then, there is a blanket assumption of persecution only for residents of the Soviet Union.

[17] Applicants cannot retake the test since the test is intended to determine whether the candidate is or is not of German heritage.

discriminated against because of their German heritage.[18] The language test was made more difficult in July 1996, and the number of ethnic Germans moving to Germany annually fell from 222,000 in the mid-1990s to about 100,000 in the late 1990s.[19] Of these 100,000, about 75,000 were non–ethnic German family members.

After being accepted, ethnic German immigrants are assigned to one of Germany's sixteen states, where their claims to ethnic German heritage are verified. Once the state check is completed, the applicant receives housing and other assistance from state and local governments. Ethnic Germans have had uneven integration. They tend to be better educated than foreigners in Germany but less educated than Germans, and many do not consider themselves, nor are they perceived as, Germans. Many call themselves, and are called, Russians. Ethnic Germans from Russia have low labor force participation rates and high unemployment rates, a result of their poor German language skills and "bad attitudes." Ethnic German youth (the "Russian Mafia") are responsible for a disproportionate amount of crime.

In 1933, 525,000 German citizens were Jews, including 160,000 in Berlin. By the end of the war, there were only 15,000 Jews in Germany, and most were displaced persons from Eastern Europe. In 1990, when there were 29,000 Jews in Germany, the door was opened to Jewish immigrants from the former Soviet Union, and between 1990 and 2000 some 137,000 Jews migrated to Germany. Not all stayed; there were 85,000 registered Jews in 2000. Like ethnic Germans, "Russian Jews" are assigned to the states in proportion to the states' share of the national population.[20] The states provide housing, language training, and integration services similar to those provided to ethnic Germans, but Jewish immigrants are privileged foreigners in Germany, not German citizens.[21] For example, in Berlin, which has 12,000 Jews, the city government pro-

---

[18] Many of those recognized as ethnic Germans may not move to Germany. For example, some 250,000 ethnic Germans in Poland have German and Polish passports; they seem to regard their German passport as insurance. Currently, there is discussion of restricting the validity of permission to move to Germany to one year.

[19] Those who want to further reduce the movement of ethnic Germans to Germany note that in 1996 DM 3.1 billion was budgeted to help ethnic Germans in Germany to integrate, and DM 150 million was set aside for programs in areas where ethnic Germans now live.

[20] Because Jewish law holds that religion is assumed from the mother, many of those considered Jewish in the former Soviet Union are not considered Jewish by Jewish religious authorities in Germany.

[21] Berlin has the largest Jewish population, some 15,000 strong.

vides about US$20 million a year for the upkeep of Jewish buildings, schools, and security, far more than what is provided for the 170,000–strong Turkish community. More than 80 percent of Jewish arrivals from the former Soviet Union and their family members have been unable to find work, in part because most do not speak German.

Asylum

Germany included a liberal asylum clause (Article 16) in its 1949 Basic Law, which states: "Persons persecuted for political reasons shall enjoy the right of asylum."[22] There were relatively few asylum applications prior to 1980,[23] when a military coup in Turkey and a realization that Germany would not soon lift the 1973 recruitment stop prompted some Turks to fly to Germany (visas were not required) and apply for asylum. After being denied asylum, the Turks could appeal the decision (a process that could take years), and most asylum applicants were allowed to work while awaiting a final decision. Some Turkish newspapers reproduced Germany's asylum application form and suggested ways to complete it to maximize one's stay in Germany. Turks accounted for over half of the 110,000 asylum applicants in 1980; Germany responded by beginning to require visas of Turks and prohibiting asylum applicants from working for five years. Asylum applications dropped to fewer than 20,000 in 1983.[24]

This quick fix left Germany unprepared for the upsurge in asylum applications following the civil war in the former Yugoslavia. There were 103,000 asylum applicants in 1988, 193,000 in 1990, 256,000 in 1991, and a peak 438,000 in 1992 (an average of 1,200 a day) (see figure 6.1). As soon

---

[22] Foreigners granted asylum are entitled to live as permanent residents in Germany and to have their families join them in Germany. When individuals recognized as refugees apply to have their families join them, German authorities may insist that the papers used for family unification be checked carefully because falsified papers were often used to enter Germany. In some cases, when there is doubt about family relationships, those seeking to have family members admitted are advised to have DNA samples taken to prove the relationship.

[23] There were 1,737 asylum applications in 1967 and 10,000 in 1970.

[24] Germany dealt with other asylum surges in similar ad hoc ways. For example, Germany did not require visas of foreign children under age sixteen, so some Sri Lankan Tamils and Iranians sent their children to Germany by air to request asylum. For example, 2,500 unaccompanied minors applied for asylum in 1988. Germany imposed fines on airlines carrying minors without documents and began to require visas of unaccompanied foreign minors, and the problem was solved.

as they applied for asylum, applicants were assigned to states and cities, which were obliged to provide them with housing and food at a cost of about US$10,000 per asylum applicant per year. As unemployment rose, especially in the former East Germany, asylum housing became the focus of attacks by Germans opposed to the foreigners' presence. There were almost six hundred arson attacks on foreigners in 1992. The attackers did not distinguish asylum seekers from other foreigners in Germany, and foreign investors warned that if the government could not stop the attacks, they would stop investing in Germany.

Figure 6.1. Asylum Applications in Europe and Germany, 1983–2000

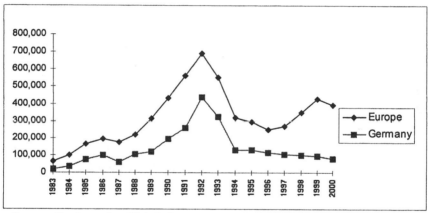

Sources: Institute for Global Communications (IGC) and United Nations High Commissioner for Refugees (UNHCR).

The CDU-CSU-FDP coalition government of the early 1990s argued that the best solution to the rising number of asylum applications, most of which were rejected, was to amend the Basic Law to eliminate the open-ended right to asylum in Germany. The Social Democratic Party and the Greens were strongly opposed to changing the Basic Law—some for historical reasons and others because they wanted to use the asylum crisis to develop an immigration system, arguing that there would be fewer asylum seekers if Germany opened legal channels for immigrants. A compromise reached in November 1992 preserved Article 16 but amended it to require foreigners seeking asylum in Germany to apply in the first "safe country" they reach. Given that Germany is surrounded by "safe countries," foreigners could no longer arrive via Poland or Hungary and request asylum, and arrivals by air could be dealt with through carrier sanctions (Bade 1994a).[25]

The 1992 compromise reduced the number of asylum applications; there were 116,000 applications in 1996 and 78,600 in 2000. Decisions were made on 105,502 applications in 2000, with asylum granted in 3,128 cases; another 8,318 applicants were granted permission to remain in Germany at least temporarily. About 60 percent of the applicants were refused asylum, and 30 percent of the applications were resolved before a decision was made.

Fighting erupted in the former Yugoslavia in 1992. By August 1995 the fighting had produced 3.5 million displaced persons and refugees, including 750,000 Bosnians, Serbs, and Croatians who fled to Germany (where a large community of Yugoslavs remained from the guestworker era), Austria, Denmark, Norway, Sweden, and Switzerland. There were about 345,000 Bosnians in Germany in 1995 when the Dayton peace accords ended the fighting; most had temporary protected status, which was renewed every three to six months and did not permit employment in Germany. The sixteen German states showed considerable ingenuity in developing carrots and sticks to persuade the Bosnians to return to Bosnia. Caring for the Bosnians cost the German states US$3 billion in 1996,[26] and German states and cities offered payments ($5,000 in some cases) to those who left voluntarily, plus money for their integration into their communities in Bosnia.[27]

---

[25] Asylum applicants evade this "safe third country" provision by claiming they were put in locked trucks in Bulgaria or Romania and do not know how they reached Germany. Germany cannot return an applicant to Poland or the Czech Republic unless it can prove that the applicant entered Germany via one of these countries.

[26] Germany has been a strong proponent of burden sharing within the European Union, arguing that countries should either care for asylum applicants and those fleeing civil wars in Europe or receive EU funds for the care of such foreigners (Hailbronner and Thiery 1997). The EU in September 2000 agreed to establish a special fund to help share out the burden of caring for asylum applicants. Germany immediately requested 30 percent of this fund, but no funds were paid out. In the case of Bosnia, for example, France and Britain told Germany that their contribution was to provide troops to keep the peace.

[27] In one remarkable case, a German city of 90,000 that hosted 800 Bosnian Muslims built 61 movable houses in Bosnia a few miles away from their Serb-controlled village. If the Bosnians are eventually permitted to return to their original village, their houses can be moved again. Each returning family also received DM 2500 (King 1998).

The asylum policy gap arose from Germany's historical experience. Article 16 emphasized that those fleeing political persecution could find haven in Germany, but it was premised on the assumption that there would be only a trickle of asylum seekers. When the numbers rose and it became clear that many were economic migrants, as with Turks in 1980, the government devised a quick fix. In 1992–1993, another quick fix reduced asylum applications by some 75 to 80 percent, but Germany still receives about 80,000 asylum applications yearly, more than any other country, and it continues to reject over 90 percent of them. In the case of asylum, reducing the number of applicants to a "tolerable" level seems to have defused the issue.

NEW GUESTWORKERS AND GREEN CARDS

In the late 1980s EC-92 measures stimulated economic and job growth in the former West Germany just as Eastern European nations eased emigration restrictions. Poles and other Eastern Europeans began to work in Germany during their summer vacations, often in agriculture. As word spread that one could earn the equivalent of a year's agricultural wages in just one month's work in Germany, hundreds of thousands of "tourists" arrived and found jobs. For foreign policy reasons, Germany was reluctant to "re-create the Berlin Wall" on its eastern borders, but it was not willing to tolerate the widespread employment of unauthorized foreigners. The compromise was to launch several foreign worker programs that, in the late 1990s, permitted some 350,000 foreigners to work temporarily in Germany (Hönekopp 1997).[28]

New Guestworkers

Guestworker programs of the 1960s were akin to shotgun blasts of workers to fill job vacancies throughout the labor market. Those of the 1990s were more like rifle shots aimed at filling vacancies in specific sectors. For example, project-tied workers' programs allow German construction firms to subcontract with foreign firms to erect the structure of a new office building, for example. The subcontracted foreign firm supplies the expertise and the workers for a particular project phase. The employer-

[28] Most of these "new guestworkers" are employed less than a full year, so they add the equivalent of about 150,000 full-time equivalent workers to the German workforce.

to-employer subcontracting agreement is checked by the German Employment Service, and the foreign workers who are admitted (for up to two years) are considered to be workers of their home countries while there are in Germany—that is, they are not enrolled in the German social security system. Project workers peaked at 95,000 in 1992 and averaged 44,000 in 2000.

The recruitment stop of 1973 applied to unskilled foreign workers coming to Germany for more than ninety days. In the 1990s Germany launched a seasonal foreign worker program that admitted workers for up to ninety days; there were 129,000 seasonal worker admissions in 1991, 226,000 in 1997, and 264,000 in 2000.[29] Most seasonal foreign workers are requested by name by German farmers, restaurateurs, or construction contractors. Their pay, housing, and travel arrangements are spelled out in bilingual contracts approved by the German Employment Service, which also ensures that local workers are not available.[30]

Three additional guestworker programs were launched in the 1990s to manage inevitable migration and to fill job vacancies in particular sectors. One program allowed workers from the Czech Republic and Poland to commute to German jobs within 50 kilometers of Germany's eastern border and to stay overnight in Germany up to two days a week. A work-and-learn program allowed 5,900 East Europeans aged eighteen to forty to live and work in Germany for up to eighteen months in 2000; 1,500 of these "new guestworkers" were from Poland.[31] Finally, Germany launched a program to admit one thousand nurses from the former Yugoslavia.

Germany's new guestworker programs of the 1990s added 2.4 million legal foreigners to the labor force, at least temporarily. Their presence is credited with overcoming some of the German labor market's immobility and rigidity; the new guestworkers were willing to move where jobs were and to accept jobs that unemployed Germans shunned, as in fruit and vegetable agriculture and in seasonal or weekend services. The new programs showed that guestworkers can be complements for employed

---

[29] The same worker sometimes returned to Germany twice in one year, so that there were 238,000 individuals involved in 2000.

[30] Both German employers and seasonal foreign workers make required payroll tax contributions that add about 35 percent to hourly wages; if workers are employed less than two months, they and their employers do not have to pay social security taxes.

[31] To obtain "new guestworkers," German employers submit work-and-learn offers to local ES offices, which transmit them to an ES office in Eastern Europe; there is no test of the German labor market.

German workers and that most of their wage-depressing effects fall on resident foreign workers (Schulz 1999).

Green Cards

None of these new programs received as much attention as the green card program. This effort by the SPD-Green government, which aimed to highlight the economic benefits of foreign professionals, was developed in response to a request for foreign workers from the computer association BITKOM. Chancellor Schroeder agreed that Germany needed more high-tech workers, and he proposed a green card program to allow non-EU foreigners paid at least $45,000 a year to live and work in Germany for up to five years. The opposition CDU based its May 2000 campaign in North Rhine-Westphalia state elections on opposition to the proposal, using the slogan "*Kinder statt Inder*" (children instead of Indians) to argue that Germans should have more children and train them for high-tech jobs instead of importing high-tech workers from India. The CDU campaign failed, and the first green cards were issued in August 2000. Of the 20,000 permits available, about 12,000 had been issued by April 2002, or fewer than 600 a month, mostly to foreigners from India (22 percent) and Eastern Europe (14 percent).[32] Although the admissions process is relatively easy for German employers (requests are to be handled within one week), few requested green card workers. Seventy percent of the cards went to foreign workers in Bavaria, Hesse, and Baden-Wuerttemberg, states that generate about a third of German gross domestic product (GDP). Most green card holders are employed in firms with fewer than five hundred workers, and 90 percent are men.

The German green card is unlike the U.S. green card and the U.S. H-1B visa program. U.S. green cards are immigrant visas that allow foreigners to live and work anywhere in the United States and to become

---

[32] There was initially some opposition within the governing SPD to the green card program. The federal minister of education and research, Edelgard Bulmahn, said: "We cannot allow companies to move abroad because of the shortage of highly skilled personnel in information technology," while Economy Minister Werner Müller highlighted the job-multiplying aspects of foreign professionals with the following example: "If you need a pianist, you cannot just hire a piano tuner. But when you employ a new pianist, you will also need additional piano tuners." Labor Minister Walter Riester at first objected to the program: "We cannot allow a general international opening of the job market. We have over four million unemployed people, among them very qualified people in the information technology field." There were 31,000 unemployed IT workers in December 1999.

naturalized citizens after five years. Most U.S. employers can have foreign professionals admitted with H-1B visas on the basis of an attestation that they are needed, and the foreigner can bring his family to the United States for up to six years. Most H-1B foreigners buy one-way tickets to the United States, hoping that their U.S. employers will "sponsor" them for immigrant visas — that is, they will advertise for U.S. workers and fail to find them, so that the U.S. Department of Labor "certifies" that a foreigner is needed to fill the vacant job. Most foreigners leave the job they were certified to fill as soon as they get their immigrant visas.

Unauthorized Foreigners

Estimates of the number of unauthorized foreign residents in Germany go from 150,000 to 1.5 million. This wide range reflects the various ways in which a foreigner can be in Germany unlawfully, including entering illegally or entering legally and then violating the terms of legal entry by working or overstaying.[33] There is agreement that the number of illegals peaks in the summer, when "working tourists" from Eastern Europe find jobs in agriculture, construction, and services, and that the number of unauthorized foreigners rose in the 1990s.

Most unauthorized foreigners in Germany are believed to enter legally, as tourists or other visitors, so border controls are a "first line of defense" against illegal migration. Interior controls, including separate residence and employment control systems, are the major checks on illegal residence and employment in Germany, as in most other European countries. Countries with long land borders and significant tourism and trade sectors find it hard to prevent entries over the "green border" and do not want to impede economically important cross-border traffic. Instead, Germany and twelve other EU member nations have developed a common external border control system, the Schengen Agreement, and a common database, the Schengen Information System, to regulate the issuance of visas and to monitor movements over a common external border.[34]

Germany's separate systems for residence and labor market registration aim to keep foreigners from living and working there illegally. The

---

[33] The problems associated with estimating the size of this population are compounded by the lack of reliable data on unauthorized foreigners.

[34] The Schengen Agreement went into effect in 1995. It includes all EU member states except Ireland and the United Kingdom.

central register of foreigners and the Aliens Authority report to the state government and the federal Ministry of the Interior,[35] while the registry of work permits and labor inspectors are the responsibility of the state governments and the federal Ministry of Labor. Computer cross-checks of data from these registers, as well as separate computer databases of workers for whom employers pay social security and health taxes, can flag suspicious individuals and employers, but the normal complaint of aliens police and labor inspectors is that they are too few to prevent illegal immigration, residence, and employment.

Foreign workers need work permits, and workers without permits, as well as their employers, can be fined or imprisoned. In 1972 Germany introduced fines for employers who hire illegal alien workers. Beginning in 1975, persons who recruited foreign workers outside lawful channels could be fined up to DM 50,000, and in 1982 punitive actions against employers included fines of DM 100,000 or three years in prison.[36] In fact, most fines are small. For example, in 1983 there were about 3,800 fines levied, and 85 percent were for less than DM 1,000. Sanctions were not politically controversial when they were introduced in 1972. Major employer and union groups endorsed sanctions on the theory that more controls were needed to assure the public that immigration was under control.[37] The few immigrant associations that existed in the early 1970s did not voice concern about discrimination; some endorsed sanctions as drawing a bright line between legal and illegal migrants and preventing anti-immigrant sentiments from growing.

---

[35] Germany has "foreigners authorities" in most cities, and these offices issue residence permits. Police in the late 1990s located between 130,000 and 140,000 foreigners a year who were suspected of being unlawfully in Germany (including visa overstayers), and they charged 10,000 a year with falsifying documents (Beauftragte 2001: 72–73).

[36] If an employer exploits foreign workers by putting them in worse conditions than similar German workers, employs five or more foreign workers without permits for thirty days or more, or employs foreign workers without permits for a second or third time, the employer can be charged with criminal violations and sentenced to three to five years in jail.

[37] The approval of sanctions was strengthened by ILO Convention 143, approved in 1975, which recommends employer sanctions, and by a draft directive issued by the European Community Commission in 1978 that also encouraged the adoption of employer sanctions. British resistance prevented its adoption Community-wide; the British objected to the draft directive because the criminal sanctions envisaged would infringe on the United Kingdom's sovereignty. Illegal foreigner employment was not a significant problem, and the British feared that employer sanctions might exacerbate employment discrimination against minorities.

Inspectors employed by the federal and state labor departments have primary responsibility for enforcing employer sanctions, but they acknowledge that the prospect of fines has not prevented between 300,000 and 500,000 unauthorized foreigners from finding jobs despite a high unemployment rate for legal foreign workers and the availability of legal channels through which migrant workers can be hired.[38] Employer sanctions became less effective at deterring unauthorized foreign worker employment in the 1990s because the government was reluctant to strictly enforce laws against Eastern Europeans; the foreign policy argument was that Germany should not endanger the transition economies of Eastern Europe with strict enforcement of employer sanctions laws.

There have been two major responses to the combination of high unemployment among German workers and the alleged labor shortages that brought large numbers of foreign workers into Germany's construction sector. One response was to blame rigidities and excesses in the German labor market for high unemployment. For example, unemployment insurance (UI) benefits and assistance can continue indefinitely at relatively high levels for jobless workers, encouraging them to shun the hard and dirty jobs that newly arrived foreigners are eager to take.[39] If minimum wages were lowered and UI benefits reduced, this argument runs, jobless German and resident foreign workers would be more likely to fill these jobs. The other response was to call for stepped-up enforcement of labor law to preserve "good jobs" in the high-wage, high-benefit German labor market. The latter response has predominated—more inspectors, more raids, and proposals that would, for example, make the

---

[38] German enforcement of employer sanctions depends largely on complaints from employers, unions, and workers and on a computer comparison of two employee lists. Employers of "dependent" employees (those who earned less than DM 4,500 monthly in the early 1990s) must register them with one of the various social insurance programs, and this list can be compared with the list of issued work permits in order to spot persons on one list but not the other. Fines are stiffer for evading social insurance taxes, which add up to 40 percent to wages, than for violations of sanctions laws. If an employer does not register employees for social insurance, the computer matching process fails to detect illegal aliens.

[39] In Germany, UI benefits are 60 to 63 percent of previous earnings for about two years, and then about 50 percent of earnings indefinitely, while in the United States benefits are typically 50 percent of previous earnings for a maximum of six months. Thus a $1200 monthly UI check is equivalent to $8.50 per hour for a 35-hour week, a fairly high wage for a 45-year-old unemployed construction worker, for example. In addition, construction workers receive a Christmas bonus equal to 77 percent of their monthly wage.

general contractor liable for all labor law and immigration violations on a worksite.[40]

MANAGING MIGRATION TO GERMANY

Germany became a reluctant land of immigration in the 1970s and 1980s in part because it pursued flawed policies that worked the first time around. The 1960s guestworker programs were based on the theory that guestworkers would rotate in and out of Germany as needed. This principle was seemingly confirmed during recession in 1966–1967, although subsequent experience showed that nothing is more permanent than temporary workers.[41] When Germany experienced a rush of asylum seekers in 1980, requiring entry visas of Turks seemed to resolve the crisis. Neither of these policies proved to be durable, but Germany did not need to seek durable policies because ad hoc changes seemed to be working, at least initially.

Germany holds a peculiar position among industrial democracies; although it is a major destination for immigrants, it has no formal policy that outlines why the arrival of foreigners is in the country's interest, that establishes priority for entry, and that lays out a clear integration path. This lack largely reflects the political power of the Christian Democratic Union and Christian Social Union, which dominated the coalition governments between 1982 and 1998 and insisted that Germany was not a country of immigration. The other major political parties—the Free Democratic Party (which was part of the CDU-CSU coalition government) and the then opposition Social Democratic Party and Greens—called for an immigration policy in the 1990s that anticipated immigrants and simplified naturalization (Hailbronner 1997a, 1997b).

For example, in 1996 the FDP proposed a quota-based immigration system under which annual admissions would be linked to economic indicators. To promote integration, "integration courses" would give graduates "integration certificates" that entitled them to unlimited work

---

[40] Liability would be joint between general contractors and subcontractors. In addition, subcontractors could be required to post a bond to cover the cost of unpaid wages and fines, which would permit the market to help determine their reliability, given that more reliable contractors could presumably get bonds more cheaply.

[41] Between 1966 and 1967, for example, the employment of guestworkers fell by 25 percent while German employment fell only 3 percent, suggesting that guestworkers could be rotated in and out of the labor market as needed.

permits.[42] The FDP proposal would have allowed foreigners born in Germany of legally resident parents to become dual nationals at age eighteen and have permitted foreigners to naturalize after eight years, down from fifteen years. The Greens proposed an immigration system in 1997 that would set 220,000 as the maximum number of immigrants admitted a year (the same as the number of ethnic German admissions) and grant German nationality to all Germany-born babies with at least one legal foreign parent. The Greens proposed that employers and governments share the cost of providing language and culture classes on a 50-50 basis. And in 1997 the Social Democrats announced "principles" for reform of immigration and integration policies.

Much of the debate up to 1998, when the CDU-CSU-FDP government was voted out of power, involved the role of naturalization and dual nationality to foster the integration of the guestworker generation and their children. About 900,000 foreigners became naturalized Germans in the 1990s. The naturalization debate reflects different answers to the question whether political participation leads or follows other forms of integration (Bade 1994b; Weber 1997). Germany has two types of naturalization: discretionary and by right. Most naturalizations are by right, and most are granted to ethnic Germans. Foreigners seeking discretionary naturalization must have lived in Germany for fifteen years, have no felony convictions, be able to support themselves, renounce their current citizenship, and, in the words of CDU leader Erwin Marschewski, "show a credible integration into our social and state order."[43] German officials can deny discretionary applications on the grounds that naturalization is not in the country's interest; it is said that denying a naturalization application involves only one official making one decision, but approving an application requires several officials and several decisions.

Germany continues to debate, often in extreme terms, whether foreigners who naturalize should retain their original citizenship. Chancellor Helmut Kohl warned: "If today we give in to demands for dual citizenship, we would soon have four, five, or six million Turks in Germany instead of three million." At the other extreme are those who assert that dual nationality would guarantee integration, even though many ethnic

---

[42] Unlimited work permits are issued without a labor market test; limited work permits are issued only after the labor department specifies that no Germans or established foreigners are available to fill the job.

[43] Since 1993, foreigners aged sixteen to twenty-three who have lived in Germany for at least eight years and have gone to school in Germany have a right to be naturalized if they apply.

Germans with German passports still consider themselves Russians. Many proponents argue that dual nationality is needed to prevent the development of a Turkish underclass, and researchers emphasize that without birthright citizenship and with continued low naturalization rates, the foreign share of the shrinking German population will rise.[44]

During the 1998 electoral campaign, all parties except the Greens issued statements in support of limiting immigration and expediting the removal of foreign criminals. One of the first acts of the new SPD-Green coalition government was to propose a reform of Germany's 1913 naturalization law that would have introduced birthright citizenship and dual nationality. As of January 1, 2000, a scaled-back plan permitted babies born to at least one foreign parent legally resident in Germany for eight or more years to be considered German citizens at birth. These children must decide whether to retain German citizenship or accept the parents' citizenship by age twenty-three; if they do not give up their parents' nationality by then, they lose German nationality.

SPD Interior Minister Otto Schily opposed a more comprehensive, quota-based immigration law in 1999 and early 2000: "There is no need for an immigration law because, if we had one, the quotas would be zero." This statement reflected public sentiment; a 2000 poll reported that 66 percent of Germans thought immigration "exceeded the limits of what is bearable," and 75 percent believed that Germany's asylum policy should reduce the maximum stay for refugees to nine months. However, a 21-member immigration commission, appointed by Schily in June 2000 to make policy recommendations, delivered a report on July 4, 2001, that laid the basis for the proposal approved by the German Parliament in March 2002.

The commission's report, "Organizing Immigration—Fostering Integration,"[45] recommended that Germany admit 50,000 more foreigners than currently arrive via family unification and as recognized asylum seekers, including 20,000 foreign professionals a year selected on the basis of a points system, another 20,000 admitted temporarily with, for example, five-year permits, and 10,000 trainees and foreign graduates of German universities who would receive two-year work visas but be allowed to adjust from temporary to permanent status. The commission's plan would open six doors for labor market immigrants. Three doors

---

[44] Since June 12, 1996, Turks who lose their Turkish nationality by becoming a citizen of another country may retain their rights to property and inheritance in Turkey.

[45] The report can be found at http://www.bmi.bund.de/dokumente/Artikel/ix 46876.htm.

would open to foreigners seeking entry on the basis of their personal qualifications: entrepreneurs who want to establish businesses in Germany, young foreigners selected through a points system, and foreign students studying in Germany. Three other doors would be opened for foreigners sought by German employers: one for corporate managers and scientists, one for foreigners sought to fill vacant jobs (shortage workers), and one for trainees to fill vacant apprenticeship slots; the shortage workers and trainees could apply for permanent residence through the points system while in Germany. In addition, foreigners with temporary protected status in Germany, such as Bosnians, would be able to apply for permanent residence status under the points system, as could rejected asylum seekers who voluntarily leave Germany and apply to immigrate from abroad (Bade and Münz 2002).

The commission recommended that the process for considering asylum applications be streamlined and that German judges document their reasons for rejecting asylum applications more fully in order to speed up appeals. The key to successful integration, according to the commission, is for foreigners to learn German. The commission proposed that more German language courses be offered to resident foreigners and that funding be doubled in order to teach 220,000 foreigners a year. The commission noted that "integration contracts," like those used in the Netherlands, could offer a quicker path to an unlimited residence or work permit to immigrants who pass a German language test and could levy penalties, such as delayed family unification, if immigrants do not learn German.

In August 2001 Interior Minister Schily included many of the commission's recommendations in an immigration bill that would establish Germany's first regulated immigration system. Under Schily's proposal, foreign professionals could obtain permanent residence permits upon arrival; students and less skilled workers would initially get temporary permits, but they could adjust to permanent status if they scored sufficiently well on a test that awarded points for being young, completing school, and knowing German.[46] EU foreigners would no longer need work and residence permits; they would simply register their presence in Germany.

Schily's bill would encourage integration by requiring foreigners who have been in Germany less than six years and do not know German to participate in German language courses or face difficulty renewing their

---

[46] Germany studied Canada's point system and, while not copying it, deemed it more relevant than the U.S. system for admitting economic employment immigrants.

residence permits. The maximum age for bringing children to live with immigrant parents in Germany would be lowered from sixteen to twelve, in an effort to ease integration into the labor market. Rules for asylum seekers would be tightened; most applicants deemed to be in need of protection would receive temporary protected status (not refugee status) for a maximum of three years and be allowed to work in Germany, but their need to remain would be continually reassessed. Rejected asylum seekers would not be allowed to apply for an immigrant work permit or residence permit unless they left Germany and applied from abroad. Finally, the new law would eliminate the "tolerated" status given, for example, to those fleeing the fighting in the former Yugoslavia. Instead, churches and humanitarian organizations would be allowed to offer a time-limited right of sanctuary to those fleeing civil wars, assuming these organizations paid the costs.

During the fall and winter of 2001–2002, the SPD-Green coalition government amended the Schilly bill and then sought a compromise with the opposition CDU-CSU, with the goal of "keeping immigration out of the 2002 election campaign." The effort to find a compromise with opposition parties failed; the CDU-CSU maintained that Germany could not increase immigration when it had four million unemployed workers. The SPD-Green bill to "steer and limit the entry of foreigners" was approved by both houses of the German Parliament in March 2002 and signed into law in June 2002. However, the manner in which the immigration law was approved in the upper house, by one disputed vote, led the constitutional court to declare the law void in December 2002; the court did not rule on the substance of the law.

Immigration became a major issue in the 2002 election campaign, with the leader of the CDU-CSU coalition, Edmund Stoiber, asserting that: "If you consider that almost half of Europe's immigrants end in Germany, it is very difficult to absorb them ... and restrictions [on immigration] are highly advisable.... We have a serious burden ... because we have too many foreign nationals who do not speak our language." A Forsa Institute poll in May 2002 found that 46 percent of Germans were against allowing in more immigrants, and 36 percent thought there were too many immigrants in the country already. On the other hand, German President Johannes Rau took the lead in promoting the integration of immigrants, saying: "Germany is a country where there was, is, and always will be immigration. And because this is so, integration is the order of the day. Those who come to us should not just be here, but also belong here. And they should know and feel that they belong."

;ION

...ry is anticipating the welcome arrival of foreign professionals who are expected to find skilled jobs and earn good incomes. Germany is not, however, admitting unskilled foreign workers as immigrants. Instead, unskilled foreigners arrive via family unification or as asylum seekers, guestworkers, or unauthorized foreigners. This raises two questions. Will Germany wind up regulating the entry of professionals, who are likely to succeed in any event, but not regulating unskilled entries? And will Germany get as many foreign professionals as it anticipates?

Germany and the United States have very different starting points on immigration and integration issues, but they now face surprisingly similar questions regarding immigrants: How many? From where? In what status? These questions are usually answered via an immigration policy that specifies which foreigners are wanted and welcomed, as well as the means by which illegal and unwanted foreigners are kept out or removed. The numbers and percentages of foreigners and foreign-born residents in both countries are the highest in a century, and both nations are grappling with fundamental questions on key integration variables such as citizenship, education, and economic status. What should integration policies aim to do? Should their goal be to blend cultures in melting pot fashion, or should it be to embrace salad bowl multiculturalism?

Germany has been debating whether to acknowledge that it is an immigration country, while the United States has been debating how many—and which—immigrants to admit. The contrast between the two countries is evident in the following statements.

- President Clinton in June 1998: "I believe new immigrants are good for America. They are revitalizing our cities. They are building our new economy. They are strengthening our ties to the global economy, just as earlier waves of immigrants settled the new frontier and powered the Industrial Revolution. They are energizing our culture and broadening our vision of the world. They are renewing our most basic values and reminding us all of what it truly means to be an American. [Americans] share a responsibility to welcome new immigrants, to ensure that they strengthen our nation, to give them their chance at the brass ring."

- Interior Minster Otto Schily in December 1998: "Germany has reached the limit, the point where we have to say we cannot bear any more. The majority of Germans agree with me. Zero immigration for now. The burden has become too great. I would not even dare publish the costs that stem from immigration. The Greens say we should take 200,000 more immigrants a year. But I say to them, show me the village, the town, the region that would take them. There are no such places."

As Germany and other industrial democracies struggle with immigration's fundamental questions, it is important to keep three things in mind. First, there are no magic bullets or quick fixes. Second, immigration and integration policies must be flexible and able to be changed quickly if their short-term consequences prove to be the opposite of the desired longer-term effects. Third, durable solutions to migration issues are more likely to be found nearer the middle than at the extremes of the options spectrum. For this reason, it is important to reinforce those seeking a middle ground between the extremes of no borders and no immigrants.

References

Ardaugh, John. 1987. *Germany and the Germans*. London: Hamish Hamilton.

Bade, Klaus J. 1994a. *Auslaender-Aussiedler-Asyl: eine Bestandsaufnahme*. Munich: C.H. Beck.

———. 1994b. *Der Manifest der 60. Deutschland und die Einwanderung*. Munich: C.H. Beck.

———. 1997. "From Emigration to Immigration: The German Experience in the 19th and 20th Century." In *Migration Past, Migration Future: Germany and the United States*, edited by Klaus J. Bade and Myron Weiner. Providence, R.I.: Berghahn.

———. 2000. *Europa in Bewegung: Migration vom späten 18. Jahrhundert bis zur Gegenwart*. Munich: C.H. Beck.

Bade, Klaus J., ed. 1987. *Population, Labour, and Migration in 19th- and 20th-Century Germany*. New York: Berg.

Bade, Klaus J., and Rainer Münz, eds. 2002. *Migrationsreport 2002: Fakten, Analysen, Perspecktiven*. Frankfurt: Campus Verlag.

Beauftragte. 1999. "Daten und Fakten zur Auslaendersituation." Bonn: Beauftragte der Bundesregierung fuer Auslaenderfragen, June.

———. 2001. "Migrationsbericht der Auslaenderbeauftragten. Efms fuer Beauftragte der Bundesregierung fuer Auslaenderfragen," November. At http://www.bundesauslaenderbeauftragte.de/.

Böhning, W.R. 1972. *The Migration of Workers in the United Kingdom and the European Community*. Oxford: Oxford University Press.

———. 1984. *Studies in International Labor Migration*. London: Macmillan.

Castles, Stephen. 1989. "Migrant Workers and the Transformation of Western Societies." Western Societies Program Paper 22. Ithaca, N.Y.: Cornell University.

Frey, Martin, and Ulrich Mammey. 1996. *Impact of Migration in Receiving Countries: Germany.* Geneva: International Organization for Migration.

Hailbronner, Kay. 1997a. "Der aufenthaltsrechtliche Status der verschiedenen Gruppen von Einwanderern in der Bundesrepublik Deutschland." In *Einwanderungsland Bundesrepublik Deutschland in der Europäischen Union,* edited by Albrecht Weber. IMIS-Schriften. Osnabrück: Universitätsverlag Rasch.

———. 1997b. "Was kann ein Einwanderungsgesetz bewirken?" *Aus Politik und Zeitgeschichte* 46: 39–46.

Hailbronner, Kay, and Claus Thiery. 1997. "Schengen II und Dubli: Der zuständige Asylstaat in Europa," *ZAR, Zeitschrift für Ausländerrecht und Ausländerpolitik* 2.

Herbert, Ulrich. 1997. *Hitler's Foreign Workers: Enforced Foreign Labor in Germany under the Third Reich.* New York: Cambridge University Press.

Hermann, Helga. 1992. "Ausländer: von Gastarbeiter zum Wirtschaftsfaktor. Köln." Der Institut der deutschen Wirtschaft. Beiträge 173.

Hönekopp, Elmar. 1997. "The New Labor Migration as an Instrument of German Foreign Policy." In *Migrants, Refugees, and Foreign Policy: U.S. and German Policies toward Countries of Origin,* edited by Rainer Münz and Myron Weiner. Providence, R.I.: Berghahn.

Kindleberger, Charles. 1967. *Europe's Postwar Growth: The Role of Labor Supply.* Cambridge, Mass.: Harvard University Press.

King, Neil. 1998. "Movable East German Mayor Finds Unusual Solution for Refugee Problem," *Wall Street Journal,* April 22.

Krane, Ronald E., ed. 1975. *Manpower Mobility across Cultural Boundaries: Social, Economic, and Legal Aspects. The Case of Turkey and West Germany.* Leiden: Brill.

———. 1979. *International Labor Migration in Europe.* New York: Praeger.

Lutz, Vera. 1963. "Foreign Workers and Domestic Wage Levels with an Illustration from the Swiss Case," *Banca Nazionale del Lavoro Quarterly Review* 16: 64–67.

Martin, Philip L. 1980. "Guestworker Programs: Lessons from Europe." Washington, D.C.: Bureau of International Labor Affairs, U.S. Department of Labor.

———. 1981. "Germany's Guestworkers," *Challenge* 3 (July 24): 34–42.

———. 1991. "The Unfinished Story: Turkish Labor Migration to Western Europe, with Special Reference to the Federal Republic of Germany." Geneva: International Labor Office.

Martin, Philip L., and Mark J. Miller. 1980. "Guestworkers: Lessons from Western Europe," *Industrial and Labor Relations Review* 33 (April).

Miller, Mark J., and Philip L. Martin. 1982. *Administering Foreign-Worker Programs: Lessons from Europe.* Lexington, Mass.: Lexington Books.

Schulz, Erika. 1999. "Zuwanderung, temporäre Arbeitsmigranten und Ausländerbeschäftigung in Deutschland," *Vierteljahrshefte zur Wirtschaftsforschung* 3.

Weber, Albrecht, ed. 1997. *Einwanderungsland Bundesrepublik Deutschland in der Europäischen Union*. IMIS-Schriften. Osnabrück: Universitätsverlag Rasch.

Commentary

William M. Chandler

Most observers would agree that Germany's historical uniqueness counts among the most basic political features of German immigration policy change. Beyond transformations in social structures, it is the legacy of warfare that has altered borders and provoked the most unusual migration patterns. The Franco-Prussian war culminated the expansion and unification of imperial Germany, including Alsace and Lorraine from France. However, the Treaty of Versailles reduced German territory by about 10 percent and increased the number of Germans living beyond the bounds of the newly formed Weimar Republic. By 1938, Hitler's threats imposed annexation of Austria and then the accession of the Sudetenland via the Munich accords. World War II temporarily expanded German territory, but unconditional surrender in 1945 opened the way for unanticipated waves of some 12 million expellees and displaced persons escaping westward before the advancing Red Army. The scale of this east to west migration, unprecedented in modern European history, occurred under conditions of economic devastation, malnutrition, and disease.

Two German states formed out of the rubble of defeat and under pressure from the occupation powers. In the western zones a conscious political redesign pursued the goal of democratization; seeking to atone for the evils of the Third Reich, the framers of the Basic Law guaranteed human rights and incorporated open liberal asylum provisions as well as the right of citizenship for Germans living beyond the nation's provisional borders.

Cold War polarization produced forty years of hostility between the two German states. Misery and oppression in the east generated a steady exodus of some 3 million easterners crossing into the Federal Republic. Construction of the Berlin Wall stemmed the outflow of East Germany's skilled labor force; the 1989 collapse of the East German regime—and the Wall—brought new immigration trends and citizenship challenges.

The Politics of Immigration

In the past, political parties generally agreed—explicitly or implicitly—not to exploit immigration and citizenship issues out of fear they might arouse anti-foreigner sentiments. After 1990, however, the quarantining of anti-foreigner politics frayed with unexpected inflows of asylum seekers and refugees, along with hundreds of thousands of ethnic Germans from the former Soviet world, placing extra burdens on the welfare system.

Tough immigration controls encouraged those seeking entry to take advantage of liberal asylum provisions. While some asylum seekers have legitimately fled war, oppression, and ethnic cleansing, others have been economic refugees taking advantage of Germany's liberal laws and social support.

Negative feelings about foreigners escalated in the early 1990s, often based on the perception that economic refugees were systematically abusing Germany's constitutional openness and generous welfare provisions. These feelings were reinforced by popular fears of increasing criminality associated with foreign sources of organized crime involved in drug trafficking, smuggling, and extortion.

At the same time that fears about the social consequences of immigration have increased, we also see partisan division displacing an inter-party elite consensus. Moreover, there seems little doubt that German voters have become more aware and more sensitive to such issues.

Europeanization

Today, economic and social policy in the European Union member states is heavily influenced by Brussels. Treaty developments in the 1990s and the removal of internal borders through the Schengen Agreement opened the way for limited convergence in how EU states deal with immigration issues.

The opening of eastern borders produced unexpected waves of refugees and asylum seekers and exposed the need for strengthening external frontiers. The increased pressure for stronger Euro-level instruments of control and a common Europe-wide policy response has been constrained by the protection of national sovereignty through a weak inter-governmental foundation. As a result, European responses to problems associated with transborder population movements, and progress to-ward common European solutions, have been painfully slow. Awareness of the need for greater EU coordination and control was evident at the Seville summit in June 2002, but the outcome of this summit also demon-strated how difficult it is to arrive at consensus within the European Union on sensitive matters like illegal immigration.

The anticipated EU expansion eastward carries with it unprecedented uncertainties and obstacles. German governmental concerns have fo-cused primarily on the expected explosion in costs of existing programs, CAP and regional structural funds, which account for 80 percent of the EU budget for which Germany has for years assumed a disproportionate burden. Enlargement also poses unknowns about the extent and charac-ter of migrations once the new member states (as many as twelve) join. Open borders, along with the goal of free movement of peoples, evoke fears of a wave of low-wage, illegal labor. Finally, as the September 11 terrorism has shown, no national system of immigration control can remain immune from international pressures.

Unresolved Problems and Policy Implications

Standing policies of restrictive citizenship and nonrecognition of Ger-many as a land of immigration left policy voids at odds with a changing world of social and ethnic diversity. The strategy of temporary work contracts, followed by workers' expected rotation back to their home-lands, was inefficient from an employer's standpoint. More importantly, over time it was incompatible with the social reality of people settling and raising families. Although this policy phase ended with an official recruitment stop in the wake of the OPEC oil crises and rising unem-ployment, it was not replaced by any positive redefinition of immigration.

The other persisting gap has a sociocultural character. As immigra-tion has changed the social and economic complexion of Germany and Europe, social integration has lagged behind. The existence of permanent foreign residents who remain disconnected from mainstream German society contradicts the multicultural character of urban Germany today. In considering the conditions of nonintegration of foreigners, we often look first at the Turkish population. Turks have lived in Germany for decades, and now have children and grandchildren born in Germany. Many are economically, if not socially, integrated, and increasing num-bers are applying for and gaining German citizenship. However, the integration question is more complex, involving many ethnicities and different legal, economic, and social circumstances. Moreover, barriers to achieving social and political integration are of growing policy concern within all European states.

The heart of the debate about how best to socially integrate immigrants has centered on the goal of assimilation as opposed to acceptance of multiculturalism. We should also not forget that unique to the German case since reunification is the fact that social integration of foreigners has overlapped with the other big problem of integration—between former East Germans and West Germans.

Policy Change: Closing the Gaps?

The more positive side of the German story is that despite some increase in politicization of immigration issues, we also observe a sea change in policy thinking and responses to these gaps. The 1998 Bundestag election should be seen as a policy watershed in several significant ways. Voters ousted the Kohl coalition and replaced it with an entirely new (and inexperienced) Red-Green majority. Although Chancellor Gerhard Schröder had waged a centrist campaign devoid of specific policy commitments, the new coalition did set forth significant innovations that bore the strong imprint of the minor partner, Alliance 90/Greens. This was particularly true with respect to the exit from nuclear energy and reform of immigration and citizenship.

One of the first actions of the new government was reform of the 1913 citizenship law, and the new law has narrowed the gap between an outdated policy and the reality of a permanent, large foreign community. A second aspect of policy change concerns the 2001 immigration law. Starting from the "green card" model, this law marks a turning point in the development of immigration as positive law on recruitment. Even if the court voids this law on procedural grounds, the principle of immigration as normal will continue to shape policy choices in the future.

Martin has appropriately focused on the current agendas and challenges of managing migration. German politics and policy in areas of immigration/citizenship have been subject to enormous transformation. No European or North American democracy has changed its immigration regime more fundamentally. In short, we observe a sea change in German immigration politics and policy that has had the effect of bringing German laws into greater convergence with those of other European Union states.

Commentary

Uwe Hunger

The perception of Germany as a "reluctant country of immigration," government officials' declarations that Germany is not a country of immigration, and the prevalence of xenophobic slogans in German electoral politics have given Germany a bad reputation with regard to friendliness toward foreigners and openness to immigration. Public discourse amplifies the stereotype of Germany as a society closed to ethnic variety. Philip Martin demonstrates, however, that Germany has been an immigration country for decades. In the 1990s, Germany was second only to the United States in terms of immigration flows, and it developed one of the most expansive immigration policies worldwide. Germany clearly is a country of immigration. But is it reluctant?

As Martin notes, German immigration policies are not the result of a loss of control. Each decision to open up the country to immigration was deliberate and driven by the intrinsic interests of the German state. This is true for the decision in favor of incorporating ethnic German refugees; the guestworker programs of the 1950s, 1960s, and 1970s; and the immigration of asylum seekers, guestworkers' family members, and Jews from the former Soviet Union in the 1980s and early 1990s. Immigration was mainly intrinsically motivated and deliberate, rather than reluctant.

Even the "generous" asylum seeker law that led to a crisis in the 1990s is the result of a deliberate political decision to demonstrate the young Federal Republic's radical break with the tradition of the Nazi regime by stressing its own openness and tolerance. Likewise, the opening of the Federal Republic to foreign workers and the suspension of the rotation principle were deliberate political decisions based on economic interests. German employers' need for a stable labor force translated into a decision for a genuine immigration policy. Furthermore, the new foreign worker programs in the 1990s and the introduction of the "green card" in early 2000 were the result of a pragmatic decision based on domestic economic needs. In sum, none of these policies was introduced hesitantly or reluctantly.

Why is it that Germany is still considered to be a "reluctant country of immigration," especially in light of the recent modernization of the citizenship law and the introduction of a new immigration law? One explanation may lie in the Janus-like character of German immigration policies and politics. Immigration policies are expansive and socially inclusive, while the symbolic politics are reserved and restrictive. In German migration research, this contrast has been characterized as functional in the sense that the rumbling and restrictive rhetoric obscures public awareness of the country's open and expansive immigration and integration policies (Bade and Bommes 2000).

From a political-economic viewpoint, one can argue that this Janus-like character of German immigration policies and politics results from the fact that the majority of immigrants in Germany have not become German citizens. In 2000, more than 4.7 million people had been living in Germany for eight years or more without having acquired German citizenship, even though the majority of them were eligible to obtain German citizenship and all the political rights that go with it. Immigrants' apparent disinclination to become German is often explained by the small benefit that naturalization confers; most immigrants already have the same social and civil rights as German citizens.

However, the importance of full citizen rights – including voting rights – should not be underestimated. As long as immigrants do not vote, political parties need not consider foreign citizens' interests and xenophobic tendencies can run rampant in election campaigns without risk (Thränhardt 1995). If increasing numbers of immigrants become German citizens, however, parties will increasingly consider their interests, and xenophobic campaigns would become less likely. This is particularly true for conservative parties, which in the history of parliamentary democracy have been the main beneficiary when voting rights were extended to new groups (for example, women).

Over the long term, increasing numbers of immigrant voters will lead to a decline in xenophobic rhetoric and symbolic reluctance to immigration. Furthermore, given the sharp decline in the German population and the positive correlation between immigration and economic growth, the public is becoming increasingly aware of immigration's benefits. This gives hope that Germany will relinquish its current symbolic politics regarding immigration, and this would bring the perception in line with the country's longtime political reality.

References

Bade, Klaus J., and Michael Bommes. 2000. "Immigration and Political Culture in a Non-Immigration Country. The German Model Revisited." Paper presented at the GAAC conference "Magnet Societies: Immigration in Postwar Germany and the United States," Loccum, June 14–18.

Thränhardt, Dietrich. 1995. "The Political Uses of Xenophobia in England, France and Germany," *Party Politics* 3: 323–45.

Provinces have the same name as
their capital unless otherwise noted.

0   40 km

0   40 Miles

North

Waddenzee

North Sea

Ijsselmeer

North Holland

• Leeuwarden

• Groningen

Friesland

• Assen

Drenthe

• Lelystad

• Zwolle

Amsterdam Flevoland

Haarlem •

Overijssel

N E T H E R L A N D S

• The
Hague   • Utrecht

South Holland

Gelderland

• Rotterdam

•Arnheim

• s Hertogenbosch

North Brabant

• Middleburg

Zeeland

Limburg

GERMANY

BELGIUM

•Maastricht

7

The Netherlands: A Pragmatic Approach to Economic Needs and Humanitarian Considerations

Philip Muus

FROM EMIGRATION COUNTRY TO COUNTRY OF HESITANT IMMIGRATION

The Netherlands is often described as a reluctant immigration country (J. Amersfoort and Surie 1987). From about 1950 to 1992, Dutch migration policy consisted of state-sponsored emigration of Dutch citizens to typical immigration countries such as Canada, Australia, and New Zealand, but also to Brazil and South Africa (Faassen 2001: 50, 53). Between 1946 and 1969, nearly half a million Dutch citizens left the Netherlands (Elich and Blauw 1981). Yet even as the Netherlands remained an emigration country in formal terms, it was experiencing major immigration inflows, both spontaneous and planned. The spontaneous movements were a direct consequence of two moments of decolonization: the massive influx of repatriates and Eurasians from the former Dutch East Indies (now Indonesia) between 1945 and 1968 (Schuster 1999: 81) and from Surinam around and after its independence in 1975.

In between these two immigrations, Dutch industries started to recruit foreign labor from countries around the Mediterranean and welcomed spontaneously arriving jobseekers from these countries as well. Although employers, the Dutch government, and the immigrants themselves saw this labor as temporary, it gradually became permanent in practice, partly as a logical outcome of continuous temporary immigration, but also as a consequence of the informal halt to further recruitment of foreign unskilled and low-skilled labor after the oil crisis of 1973.

The Netherlands' formal emigration policy was based on the belief that the country was overpopulated. Emigration of part of the labor force was supposed to contribute to Dutch industrialization efforts during post–World War II reconstruction. Emigration policy gradually lost its meaning, however, as the number of emigrants fell and the number of immigrants rose. Even though the Netherlands was described as a "de facto immigration country" in a 1983 white paper on Dutch policy on ethnic minorities, it was not until 1998 that the minister responsible for coordinating migrant integration stated that the Netherlands was indeed an immigration country. This admission came after years of high levels of in-migration (113,000 annually in the 1990s) of asylum seekers and refugees, families of settled immigrants, nationals from other European Union (EU) countries, labor migrants from outside the European Economic Area, returning Dutch citizens, and Dutch nationals born in the Netherlands Antilles and Aruba.

Nevertheless, this recognition that the Netherlands is an immigration country is not accepted by all Dutch politicians or members of the public, and whether the Netherlands can, should, may, or must be labeled as a country of immigration remains as spiritedly debated as before. Arguments circle around issues like current or future labor market needs, traditional Dutch pragmatism and tolerance for minority groups, population pressures, integration of the immigrant population, high unemployment and crime rates among some immigrant groups, the presence of "illegal" foreign residents, and the implications of returning rejected asylum seekers.

Anti-immigration sentiments have had only mild impacts on Dutch politics, but in the Islam-phobic aftermath of September 11, 2001, these sentiments strengthened and took root in a new populist party founded by Pim Fortuyn. Fortuyn's party received a third of the vote in local elections in Rotterdam in March 2002, besting the locally popular Social Democratic Party. Fortuyn and his party were soon attracting strong support (between 10 and 20 percent) in the lead-up to national parliamentary elections set for May 15, 2002. Nine days before the elections Pim Fortuyn was assassinated. The elections went forward, and the results were devastating for the ruling "purple" coalition of social democrats (Partij van de Arbeid), conservative liberals (Volkspartij voor Vrijheid en Democratie), and left-wing liberals (Democraten 66). Purple's comfortable majority of 97 seats in the 150-seat Lower Chamber of Parliament fell to a minority of 54. Fortuyn's party, the Lijst Pim Fortuyn (LPF), captured 26 seats, and the Christian Democrats (CDA), who had been in opposition for eight years, became the largest single party, with 43 seats. The winning parties—the Christian Democrats and List Pim Fortuyn—and the conservative liberals proceeded to build a new government coalition for which restricting certain aspects of immigration policy stands high on the agenda. Family reunification and family formation (migration of spouses) seem to be targeted for highly restrictive admission criteria (*Volkskrant* 2002).

One might wonder whether the gradual disappearance of the consociational aspect of Dutch democracy (Lijphart 1968) is also leading to a weakening of Dutch values, including tolerance and respect for religious and other minorities. These values helped create a stable society of firmly established religious and political communities, organized in vertical pillars (*zuilen*). Leaders of the various pillars were in contact, but most Dutch lived their lives within their own pillar. Each pillar had its own political representatives, schools, media, trade unions, employer organizations, and so on. These "pillars" of Dutch society have lost much of their importance today. Paradoxically, as Dutch society has become more culturally homogeneous and less religious (Knippenberg and de Pater 1988), immigration and immigrant policies have helped create new minorities, but this time among the immigrant and foreign-born population (Rath 1991). These new immigrant minorities would not become a new pillar in Dutch society. Instead, the structuring of the new immigrant minorities took place predominantly along horizontal lines. Membership in an ethnic group and low socioeconomic status began to overlap, and the Netherlands' post–World War II immigrant categories became the subject of discussions on a new "underclass" (Roelandt 1994).

The Netherlands has developed its immigration control policies by accepting immigration as an inevitable outcome of economic needs and humanitarian considerations. This pragmatic approach to policymaking has led to a long series of policy adjustments. Most responded to specific migration events—or fear of future migration events—making decision making on immigration policy largely ad hoc, a process that followed what was happening in practice rather than proactively shaping the conditions for immigration.

IMMIGRATION CONTROL POLICIES

Dutch immigration control policies underwent major changes in the second half of the twentieth century. These adjustments coincided with changes in the nature of immigration—from postcolonial migration to labor recruitment, family reunification and formation, asylum migration, and, finally, undocumented migration. They reflect the difficulties experienced when efforts to exert control over national borders collided with economic demands to keep borders open and with the formal lifting of external border controls within the European Union under the Schengen Agreement. These various developments redirected the focus of immigration policy toward internal controls (H. Amersfoort 1999). Finally, immigration to the Netherlands changed from immigration directly related to former Dutch interests, such as postcolonial immigration and labor recruitment from selected countries, to a flow in which immigrants' interests determine the choice of the Netherlands as a destination country. As a consequence, any country can now become a sender of migrants to the Netherlands.

Citizenship

Immigration from former colonies has been based primarily on citizenship regulations. Immigration from the former Dutch East Indies involved repatriates (mostly white Dutch nationals) and Indo-Dutch, the descendants of Dutch men and Indonesian women. Only Indo-Dutch who were officially recognized by their Dutch fathers held the status of Dutch citizen. Upon Indonesia's independence in 1949 it was agreed that all Dutch citizens there (European and Indo-Dutch) would remain Dutch citizens, and all others would automatically become Indonesian citizens. Dutch citizens living in Indonesia at independence could, within a period of two years, opt for Indonesian citizenship. Despite the Dutch government's efforts to discourage the Indo-Dutch from coming to the Netherlands (it was felt they would not be able to adapt to Dutch society),[1] they arrived in huge numbers and, paradoxically, have become the

---

[1] Dutch shipping companies were even pressured (unsuccessfully) to decrease the number of ships traveling between Indonesia and the Netherlands.

best assimilated immigrant population in recent Dutch immigration history (Schuster 1999: 81–116). In 2000, 405,000 persons in the Netherlands either had been born in Indonesia or had at least one parent born there (Muus 2000).

One important exception to the Netherlands' citizenship-based immigration was the arrival of some 12,500 Moluccans from Indonesia. Most were Moluccan military who had served in the Dutch Colonial Army and were not yet demobilized when the Republic of the South Moluccas declared independence from the new Republic of Indonesia in 1950. Faced with a precarious political situation, the Dutch government decided in 1951 to bring the Moluccan soldiers and their families to the Netherlands. Their stay was supposed to be temporary, but it became permanent when the South Moluccas' independence from Indonesia proved short lived.

Surinam's independence in 1975 opened a quite different story. Independence in Surinam was not the product of war, as in Indonesia, but of political accord. Further, Surinam's population was a fraction of that of Indonesia (fewer than 400,000 in the early 1970s). Even so, the Dutch government feared the steadily increasing in-migration of its citizens from Surinam. In fact, according to Hans van Amersfoort (1999: 143), this fear was a key reason—though not an acknowledged one—underlying the granting of Surinam's independence in 1975. Independence, which came with large sums of development aid, was supposed to halt the tide of emigration to the Netherlands. This objective was reinforced by the determination that all Surinamese born in Surinam were to become Surinamese nationals upon independence (unless they had previously opted otherwise).

Although Dutch intentions were to curb the tide of Surinamese immigration to the Netherlands, the opposite occurred in practice. One year after independence, emigration to the Netherlands exceeded 10 percent of the Surinamese population, and by the end of the year roughly a third of Surinam's population was living in the Netherlands (Penninx 1979: 51).[2] Most of the Surinamese migrants were driven by two factors: insecurity about the political future of ethnically mixed Surinam, and insecurity over the loss of Dutch citizenship. Surinamese migration to the Netherlands stayed strong until 1980, when visa requirements kicked in, and it continues today, though at lower levels. In 1982 the Surinamese population (by birth or by birthplace of at least one parent) in the Netherlands

---

[2] In the early 1980s there were an estimated 182,000 persons of Surinamese background in the Netherlands.

was estimated at 182,000; further migration and natural growth had raised that number to an estimated 303,000 by 2000 (Muus 1985, 2000).

The Netherlands Antilles and Aruba are still part of the Kingdom of the Netherlands, and the populations of these islands have full Dutch citizenship. Migration of Antillean- and Aruban-born Dutch to the Netherlands is unrestricted, and most has been a temporary migration, predominantly of students who return to the islands after completing their studies (Bovenkerk and Verschoor 1983). However, with the decline of the islands' economies in the 1990s, migration began to increase, and people from all strata of the islands' population joined the stream. In the late 1990s immigration from the Netherlands Antilles and Aruba reached annual levels of around 10,000; and in early 2000 the total estimate of the Antillean and Aruban population (by birth or by birthplace of one parent) in the Netherlands was 107,000 (Muus 2000). Return rates decreased at the same time, making the unrestricted immigration from the Antilles and Aruba a subject for public and political discussion. Formally, Dutch citizenship regulations do not allow for discrimination by birthplace in cases of (re)immigration of Dutch citizens to the Netherlands, and the immigration from overseas parts of the kingdom will remain free and uncontrolled as long as the constitutional and citizenship constructs of the Netherlands remain unchanged.

Foreign Workers and Labor Market Access

In order to regulate the migration of predominantly unskilled and low-skilled foreign labor, the Netherlands concluded a number of recruitment and social security agreements with Mediterranean countries: Italy (1960), Spain (1961), Portugal (1963), Turkey (1964), Greece (1996), Morocco (1969), the former Yugoslavia (1970), and Tunisia (1970). Even though the Dutch government never formally declared a halt to labor immigration following the 1973 oil crisis, recruitment from these countries came to a virtual standstill after 1973 due to an abundance of unemployed natives and resident foreign workers and a substantially decreased need for low-skilled workers (Muus 1985: 19–22). Prior to 1973 labor migration was predominantly male, and return rates were relatively high. The informal cessation of labor migration in 1973–1974 significantly changed this prevailing pattern. Foreign workers, though expected to go home, did not do so. Many non–European Economic Community (EEC) labor migrants decided to settle in the Netherlands (H. Amersfoort, Muus, and Penninx 1984). Family reunification policies allowed the migration to continue, and legally settled family members were sometimes allowed to enter the labor market (with restrictions).

The Foreign Workers Employment Act (WABW), which came into force in November 1979, kept open this back door to the labor market. Legally settled family members (both Netherlands-born and immigrants) of resident non-EU foreigners could ask for a declaration stating that they were exempted from the restrictive ruling of the WABW and could work. The number of declarations sought annually rose to over 10,000 for Turkish and Moroccan nationals (immigrated and Netherlands-born) in 1995 (see figure 7.1), when the WABW was replaced by the new Foreign Workers Employment Law (WAV). The WAV, like the WABW, allows the entry of new temporary foreign workers from non-EU countries only for publicly announced vacancies and when no willing Dutch or foreign resident workers or EU workers can be found. Declarations are no longer issued under the WAV; instead, alien ID cards carry a notation indicating whether the bearer is allowed to work. This administrative change has meant that one can no longer calculate the number of foreign workers in the Netherlands, because some who arrive and can work enter under an immigration title other than "foreign worker."

Backdoor immigration allowed the numbers of Turkish and Moroccan residents in the Netherlands to rise considerably in recent decades. The Turkish population grew from 53,500 (nationals) in 1974 to 308,000 (country of birth and/or birthplace of a parent) in 2000 by net migration and natural increase (see table 7.1 for the share identified by country of birth). The Moroccan population in the Netherlands increased from 29,600 (nationals) in 1974 to 262,000 (country of birth and/or birthplace of a parent) in 2000. A comparison of the Turkish populations in the Netherlands and in neighboring Germany since the informal closure of the guestworker system in 1974 reveals that the Turkish population has grown far more rapidly in the Netherlands than in Germany (Muus n.d.), primarily because of Germany's more restrictive family reunification and family formation policies, as well as Germany's success in the 1980s in financially assisting (unemployed) Turkish workers to return home.

The increase has been less impressive for workers from other "recruitment countries," and in a number of cases migrant populations in the Netherlands have decreased, not because of Dutch policies but because of improved economic possibilities back home and/or because the sending countries returned to democracy after periods of authoritarian rule and acceded to an expanded European Union (Greece, Portugal, and Spain; see H. Amersfoort, Muus, and Penninx 1984).

Figure 7.1. Net Migration of Non-Dutch to the Netherlands, by Country of Origin, 1980–1999

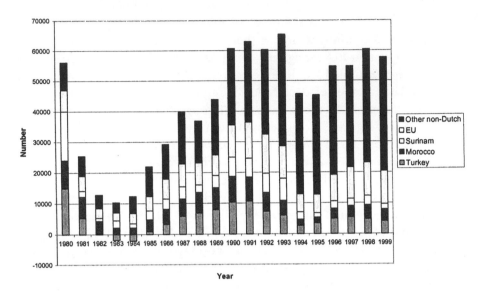

Yet migration remains a topical issue in the Netherlands. In the late 1990s the country allowed entry to a substantial number of mostly skilled non-EU temporary workers. The number of work permits issued rose from 9,500 in 1996 to 27,700 in 2000, mostly for intra-firm transferees and information technology specialists, but also for artists, trainees, and researchers from the United States, India, South Africa, Japan, and Poland. Recently work permits have also gone to persons with conditional residence permits and to asylum seekers (from Afghanistan, Iraq, Turkey, and so on); these individuals are entitled to work but only for a limited number of weeks per year.

The Dutch work permit system has proven to be quite flexible. Permits decrease in number in times of recession and increase when the economy improves. Since EU nationals are exempt from the restrictions of the work permit system, little is known about EU labor in the Netherlands. But there are strong indications in migration statistics that the immigration of EU nationals to the Netherlands recovered strongly during the economic boom of the second half of the 1990s, reaching net figures of just over 10,000 EU nationals annually at the end of the decade (figure 7.1). The Central Statistics Bureau estimates that about 5,000 EU workers from the United Kingdom, Germany, and Belgium migrated to the Netherlands each year between 1996 and 1998 (Muus 2000: 4).

In 2001 and 2002 Dutch employer organizations and multinationals with a base in the Netherlands lobbied for a faster admissions process for high-skilled non-EU labor. In April 2002 the Dutch minister of social affairs proposed that high-skilled non-EU personnel be hired under an expedited procedure if certain criteria were met, the most important being that the worker's annual salary equal at least 50,000 euros. Temporary work contracts would be of limited duration, and the worker would have to leave the Netherlands at the end of the contract period. The job vacancy would not have to be announced publicly, and the administrative process could be shortened to a few weeks.

Family Reunification and Family Formation

Family reunification and family formation, along with asylum seeking, have become important doors through which to enter the Netherlands since labor recruitment was informally halted in 1973. Dutch governments traditionally have been unwilling to impose harsh restrictions on family reunification and family formation (Muus n.d.). Workers from EU member states are free to bring their spouses (regardless of the spouse's nationality) and children under twenty-one years of age. Non-EU foreigners can bring in spouses and children aged eighteen and younger if they meet specific criteria; the non-EU worker must have a settlement permit and adequate housing and income (the specified income level has been raised over time to prevent young, low-income earners and unemployed persons from meeting the criteria too easily).

Bringing family members to the Netherlands has become somewhat more difficult of late; newcomers now must apply for visas and obtain an "authorization for provisional residency" (MVV), which can only be granted by a Dutch embassy or consular office in the country of origin. Family members who arrive without MVV authorization and apply for a stay based on family reunification or family formation must first return to their country of origin to apply for the authorization. The MVV has been strongly criticized on humanitarian grounds and was withdrawn twice. Both times, however, it was reinstated as a means to at least partially control the access that foreign workers' family members and future partners have to the Netherlands.

Table 7.1. The Foreign-born Population of the Netherlands, by Country of Birth, 1990–2000

	1990	1993	1994	1995	1996	1997	1998	1999	2000
Surinam	162,913	182,921	180,894	80,961	181,568	182,234	184,184	184,979	186,469
Turkey	149,473	165,960	165,977	167,498	169,284	172,662	175,476	178,027	181,865
Indonesia	186,063	183,651	180,426	177,668	174,762	172,134	170,327	168,011	165,781
Morocco	122,933	139,402	139,772	140,734	142,683	145,753	149,618	152,693	155,819
Germany	128,656	129,385	131,223	130,127	128,048	126,797	125,540	124,237	123,110
Other countries	467,031	574,042	589,088	610,098	637,256	669,455	708,772	748,390	802,333
Total	1,217,069	1,375,361	1,387,380	1,407,086	1,433,601	1,469,035	1,513,917	1,556,337	1,615,377
Total foreign-born population as percent of total population	8.1	9.0	9.0	9.1	9.2	9.4	9.6	9.8	10.1

Source: Statistics Netherlands.

It is not known precisely what impact these restrictions on family re-unification and family formation have had. If we consider the impressive gains in the size of immigrant communities in the Netherlands—growth patterns that continue long after the original establishment of the immigrants who arrived as foreign workers, asylum seekers, or refugees—the impact would seem very small indeed. For example, Surinamese nationals who immigrated to the Netherlands under the post-1980 visa regime could easily obtain residence permits on the basis of marriage or cohabitation with a Surinamese-born Dutch partner. Some Surinamese nationals could opt for Dutch citizenship, as was true for Surinamese immigrants who were minors at the time of independence. The strong growth of the Turkish and Moroccan populations also demonstrates that restrictive measures have had no serious impact on migration for communities as a whole, although they may cause problems for individuals in the process of migration.

Asylum seekers and refugees fall under a different migration regime. There is no way to immediately reunite an asylum seeker with family members unless they arrive simultaneously in the Netherlands. Only persons who receive refugee status can bring their partners and under-age children to the Netherlands without restriction. Individuals who receive residence permits on humanitarian grounds can only bring family members if they meet specific criteria—including the income criterion, which is difficult to satisfy until one finds stable employment.

Marriage has become a back door to settlement in the Netherlands or to formalizing an undocumented stay. The Dutch government has increased its efforts to determine whether marriages are genuine or were entered into with an eye to obtaining a residence permit. Since the early 1990s all marriages between a Dutch citizen or legally settled foreign resident and a partner living abroad are subject to verification for this purpose.

Asylum Seekers and Invited Refugees

Since the appearance of large numbers of asylum seekers in the 1980s, starting with the unexpected arrival of Tamils in 1985, Dutch asylum and refugee policy has become one of the most hotly debated areas of Dutch admissions policy. A refugee policy dating from 1977 set an annual quota of 550 for invited refugees. The quota was reduced to 250 in 1984 in response to the arrival of non-quota refugees such as Vietnamese boat people picked up by Dutch ships, family members of refugees, and spontaneous asylum seekers. The arrival of the Tamil asylum seekers in 1985 highlighted the Netherlands' lack of any system for receiving uninvited refugees, and it prompted the government to introduce government-financed boarding houses to solve at least one of the problems facing municipalities, although refugees were denied access to any further social assistance. The regulation setting up the refugee housing came to be known informally as the "Bed, Bread, and Bath Regulation."

In 1987 the government introduced the Regulation on the Reception of Asylum Seekers (ROA), which covered all asylum seekers. Asylum seekers were to be housed in so-called ROA houses and distributed in municipalities in proportion to local population size. Asylum reception centers (AZCs) were established to accommodate asylum seekers who could not immediately be accommodated in ROA houses. The ROA, described as austere but humane, had two objectives: (1) to limit the financial and social costs of accepting asylum seekers, and (2) to prevent the Netherlands from becoming an attractive receiving country (Muus 1997). It seems clear that this regulation—and all following adjustments to asylum procedure and reception policy—failed to achieve the second goal. The Netherlands has become a very important receiving country for asylum seekers, with 5,000 to 14,000 requests annually in the second half of the 1980s, 20,000 to 50,000 in the first half of the 1990s, and 23,000 to 45,000 in the second half of the 1990s (table 7.2). The growing numbers of asylum seekers strained the ROA reception system and forced changes. The asylum reception centers increased in number and size, and additional emergency centers were opened. The legal system could not handle the volume of asylum requests, and legal procedures—and the asylum seekers' stays in the reception centers—became extended.

In 1991 the Dutch government added a new status category for persons who did not qualify for residency on refugee or humanitarian grounds but who could not be extradited on policy grounds. This status, a temporary expulsion waiver (*gedoogden*), was the first serious signal of a growing problem, the inability to return to their home countries persons who were not entitled to legal status in the Netherlands. The temporary expulsion waiver provided a graduated right (over three years) to participate in and integrate into Dutch society, with permission to work after two years.

A new admission and reception policy for asylum seekers (the NTOM) followed in 1992; it was intended to streamline legal and reception procedures. All asylum seekers first went to investigation centers; those whose requests appeared to be well founded were then sent to asylum reception centers for up to six months. The state took responsibility for housing asylum seekers, while the municipalities remained responsible for housing refugees, persons with humanitarian status, and those with temporary expulsion waivers. Just as this new system was being implemented, the crisis in the former Yugoslavia sent increasing numbers of asylum seekers (mostly Bosnians) to the Netherlands. Displaced former Yugoslavs were put under a new temporary measure for displaced persons (TROO) specifically designed to relieve the pressures on the new NTOM system. Placing the Yugoslavs in temporary reception centers and denying them any process for winning the right to integrate into Dutch society was intended to discourage them from applying for asylum. However, when the crisis in the former Yugoslavia deepened, the temporary nature of the Yugoslavs' stay in the Netherlands became doubtful. The Dutch Parliament decided in March 1993 that further postponement of asylum requests from former Yugoslavs was no longer appropriate.

Table 7.2. Asylum Applications in the Netherlands, Status Granted, and Number Refused

Year	Number of Asylum Requests	Number Given Refugee Status	Number Given Humanitarian Status	Number Given Provisional Status	Number Rejected
1990	21,208	1,395	857		8,999
1991	21,615	1,364	1,920		14,544
1992	20,346	5,566	6,891		20,304
1993	35,399	10,997	4,674		15,759
1994	52,576	7,208	9,235	3,456	32,146
1995	29,258	8,585	6,203	4,318	32,297
1996	22,857	9,421	7,384	7,400	51,686
1997	34,443	6,817	5,176	5,182	28,318
1998	45,217	2,858	3,591	9,152	28,173
1999	42,729	1,518	3,471	8,512	41,367
2000	43,890	1,808	4,791	3,127	57,416

Source: Ministry of Justice, The Hague.

A new Alien Law introduced in January 1994 replaced the temporary expulsion waiver and the TROO with a new conditional residence permit (VVtV), valid for three years and carrying increasing rights to participate in Dutch society. Permit holders were allowed to work in their third year in the Netherlands, and after three years the conditional stay permit would become an unconditional stay permit if it was not feasible for the permit holder to return to his or her country of origin. The legal procedure also changed with the establishment of application centers where, within twenty-four hours, asylum seekers with well-founded cases were separated from those whose applications were deemed to be without merit. These centers were symbolically located—near the Belgian and German borders and at Schiphol airport. The emergency application centers were intended to relieve the overburdened accommodation chain by allowing only asylum seekers with seemingly well-founded requests to continue.

At this same time external control measures were stepped up with the introduction of the "safe third country" principle. It was quite obvious that all asylum seekers arriving in the Netherlands by land came via Belgium and Germany, both of which are safe third countries. Like all persons who came from declared safe countries, asylum seekers arriving via the land route were to be denied access to the Dutch procedure for asylum, although in practice it sometimes proved difficult to demonstrate that asylum seekers were always aware of the possibility, or had a real opportunity, to apply for asylum in Belgium or Germany.

Despite all the measures put in place, the Netherlands has lost little of its attractiveness for asylum seekers. The overburdening of the system, which is producing longer waiting periods, may have made the Netherlands more attractive precisely because its lengthy procedures give asylum seekers more opportunity to secure accommodation in reception centers. The majority of asylum requests are denied (see table 7.2); in the 1994–1998 period, 172,000 applications for refugee status were denied versus 32,000 approved (another 32,000 received resident status on humanitarian grounds). The number of persons who received conditional temporary status increased over these same years from 3,456 (1994) to 9,152 (1998). Even though the likelihood of receiving refugee status has decreased, not all asylum seekers whose applications are refused necessarily leave the country. The Netherlands does not expel these individuals but merely orders them to leave the country promptly, and there is no way to estimate how many former asylum seekers remain clandestinely in the country.

In one final push to regulate asylum seeking in the Netherlands, the second "purple cabinet" of social democrats, conservative liberals, and left-wing liberals developed a new Alien Law that included a partial revision of asylum procedures. This new law took effect in April 2001, and it is still too early to evaluate its effects. The 2001 Alien Law shortens to six months the period for considering asylum applications, although extensions can be made in exceptional cases. Status differences will disappear with the introduction of a single asylum residence permit, which the government devised as a means to reduce the number of appeals that applicants in the old system have filed in hopes of obtaining a "higher" status. The new Alien Law acts in conjunction with control measures put in place prior to 2001. Since February 1999, for example, undocumented asylum seekers may be rejected within twenty-four hours if they are clearly responsible for their undocumented situation (that is, if they turned their documents over to a travel agent or trafficker).[3] The burden of proof lies with the asylum seeker.

Undocumented Immigrants and Rejected Asylum Seekers

Clearly the Netherlands could improve its external controls on immigrants through more coordinated efforts at the EU level and in cooperation with its neighbor countries. This is especially true for asylum seekers, most of whom arrive in the Netherlands via Germany or Belgium, possibly after having crossed other internal EU frontiers. But a few issues cannot be easily resolved, including the presence of undocumented immigrants as illegal workers, undocumented family members of legally settled immigrants, and rejected asylum seekers who have no right to remain in the Netherlands.

Undocumented immigrants spark ongoing political and media debates in the Netherlands. Dutch politicians and the Dutch public became painfully aware of the presence of "illegal" foreigners in the Netherlands in 1992 when an airliner crashed into a high-rise apartment building in southeast Amsterdam. Although it was widely known that the building was home to many immigrants, it was less known that many of these were illegal. When the undocumented survivors of this tragedy were offered an opportunity to regularize their status, the line of applicants waiting outside government offices clearly exceeded even the highest

---

[3] This proviso was needed to deal with a growing problem. In the first months of 1997, 73 percent of all seekers of asylum in the Netherlands entered without any identity documents, 3 percent had false documents, and 21 percent held documents of questionable authenticity which required further investigation.

estimates of the number of people who had their residences in the damaged building.

However, even before the 1992 incident, there was tacit recognition of the presence of illegal workers, as confirmed by a special measure implemented in 1968 to halt the unsolicited arrival of mostly Mediterranean workers. From that date forward, all foreign workers were supposed to pass through formal recruitment channels, and any "spontaneous" labor migrant had to obtain a work and residence permit before arrival. Nonrecruited labor migrants who lacked permits were, by definition, "illegal" workers. In 1975 the Dutch government allowed all foreigners who could prove they had lived in the Netherlands with a valid passport since November 1, 1974, who had worked regularly, who had no criminal record, and who did not carry tuberculosis to regularize their status. Of the 18,000 applicants for regularization, the majority received work and stay permits. Another minor regularization of status followed in 1980, but there have been no similar efforts since that date.

Immigration control became more restrictive in the 1980s, with visa controls extended to countries like Turkey and Surinam. Nevertheless, there were no strict internal controls at workplaces or immigrant status checks on people logged into the population register or applying for the fiscal identification number required for entry in the social security and tax systems. Thus, even though undocumented foreigners were not officially allowed in the Netherlands, they were tolerated throughout the 1980s (Engbersen 1999), in line with the traditional Dutch characteristic of tolerance (*gedoogbeleid*). Workplace checks were sporadic at best, and this laxity probably reflected economic realities — serious labor shortages in agriculture, horticulture, and other low-paying, generally undesirable jobs.

The winds changed in the 1990s. There was a push in Parliament in 1995 to formalize the unofficial practice of legalizing foreign workers and their family members who had been living and working in the Netherlands for years without valid residence or employment permits. The proposal to formalize regularization of these "white illegals" went down to defeat. Instead, a one-time regularization measure in late 1997 covered all foreigners who had been in the Netherlands without valid residence permits for at least six years without interruption.

The final element of internal immigration control implemented in the 1990s was the Linkage Law (Koppelingswet), effective since July 1998. This law was fashioned to ensure that only foreigners with residence permits can obtain social security and other welfare rights. The registration files of the immigration service, census bureau, fiscal identification agency, and social services can all be cross-checked to verify the validity of foreigners' residence and work status.

Engbersen (1999) points to two developments that may have contributed to the tightening of Dutch control policies. The first is the large and increasing flow of asylum seekers since the mid-1980s. The second is an evolution in Dutch tolerance of behaviors that are not formally allowed. A failure to conform to rules and regulations became generally less acceptable, and this extended to the behavior of foreigners, especially "illegal" foreigners.

As a consequence of restrictive admission policies for immigrants in general—and especially for asylum seekers—the number of non-Dutch compelled to leave the Netherlands increased from 7,000 in 1986 to 62,000 in 1997. Some were expelled by force (14,428 in 1997, including 3,267 asylum seekers). Some received travel documents on crossing the Dutch border (25,021 in 1997, of whom 1,186 were asylum seekers). And some simply vanished after receiving legal notice to leave the country (22,555 in 1997, including 14,425 asylum seekers). These figures confirm that the policy to expel foreigners is difficult to enforce. The majority of asylum seekers whose claims are denied and who are instructed to leave the Netherlands do leave a registered address, but their real destination remains unknown. Some fraction certainly remain in the Netherlands illegally, sometimes supported by churches and other volunteer organizations.

The ineffectiveness of efforts to return rejected asylum seekers and "illegal" foreigners to their home countries has pushed this issue up the political agenda (Muus 1998). Interestingly, Dutch policy allows rejected asylum seekers to find their own way out of the country within a specified period, sometimes with financial assistance from the government. In the late 1990s about one thousand people received government assistance to leave the Netherlands and return home. The Dutch method of dealing with rejected asylum seekers is humane; it is also cost-effective when compared to the costs of forced return. It is obvious that full control cannot be achieved with this pragmatic approach. But the Dutch arrangement also recognizes the fact that even a fully enforced return, despite its high cost, is not likely to be more feasible or more effective in a liberal democracy, where open borders and humanitarian considerations are also at stake.

TOWARD EVER MORE RESTRICTIVE CONTROL

Dutch immigration controls display two general tendencies. The migration of European Community/European Union nationals is less controlled, despite the fact that growth of the European Union through the addition of new member states has meant that additional migrants and family members are entitled to free movement within the EU. Immigration control measures for non-EU nationals, and especially for countries that are not members of the Organisation for Economic Co-operation and Development, meanwhile, have become more numerous and more strict.

The number of external immigration control mechanisms has expanded to encompass visa requirements (in compliance with the Schengen Agreement); a reintroduction of the authorization for provisional residency; sanctions against carriers that, wittingly or unwittingly, deliver unauthorized immigrants to the Netherlands; assistance to authorities in so-called risk countries in checking documents of travelers headed to the Netherlands; the introduction of the "safe third country" and "safe country of origin" concepts and the addition of more nations to the list of declared safe countries of origin of asylum seekers; and negotiation of readmission agreements with peripheral countries of emigration or transmigration within the European Union. We might add the immediate rejection of applications for asylum by undocumented migrants who cannot prove that they are not responsible for their lack of documents upon entering the Netherlands. The Netherlands, like other EU countries, has also equipped special teams of police and customs agents to address the organized smuggling and trafficking of human beings.

The most important changes in immigration control have been the strengthening of internal mechanisms. Indeed, the lifting of controls at borders between Schengen countries has made the fortifying of internal controls all but inevitable. Most of these measures were implemented in the 1980s and 1990s, including workplace checks and the Linkage Law, which makes it extremely difficult to work or take advantage of any aspect of the Dutch welfare system (housing, education, health care) if one does not have a valid residence permit.

One might ask whether these increasingly restrictive immigration controls are counterproductive if, for example, they indirectly encourage migrant smuggling and the willingness of some travel agents to help would-be migrants circumvent controls (sometimes in dangerous and even life-threatening ways) in exchange for substantial sums of money. As long as there is work for undocumented immigrants in the Netherlands and as long as people face civil war and persecution around the world, they will head to countries like the Netherlands for employment or protection. Increased controls might also create a backlash against foreigners who are legally settled in the country by making them targets of internal immigration control efforts. And the immigrant or asylum seeker who arrives with the help of networks that may also be involved in criminal activities contributes to the stereotyping of immigrants and asylees as criminals.

Immigration and Integration Policies

Even though Dutch immigration policies are increasingly restrictive, Dutch integration policy is intentionally inclusive. Dutch policy to integrate immigrants began as an "ethnic minorities policy" in 1983. At least two factors help explain the birth of the ethnic minority approach. First, the Anglo-Saxon orientation of Dutch pioneers in the fields of migration and immigrant and ethnic relations may have contributed to the minorities approach (J. Amersfoort 1974; Penninx 1979). And second, "ethnic minorities policy" must be read as an attempt to prevent the development of ethnic minorities of both immigrant and non-immigrant backgrounds. Hans van Amersfoort (1999) emphasizes the Dutch welfare state ideology as contrary to the development of minorities.

Penninx (1979) analyzed the integration issue by concentrating on specific categories divided by national or cultural background (Moluccans, Surinamese, Antillean Dutch nationals, and Mediterranean workers). This selection from the wider immigrant community omitted Indo-Dutch immigrants, Germans or other Europeans, and other more or less successfully integrated immigrants (refugees) from other parts of the world. By making this selection, Penninx helped to fix the categories for future immigrant integration policies. When the white paper on ethnic minorities policy appeared in 1983, forestalling the establishment of ethnic minorities had become the basis for Dutch immigrant integration. Paradoxically, by holding to old category labels—like "refugees" and "gypsies"—the same policy that was devised to prevent the formation of ethnic minorities has helped to construct ethnic minorities in Dutch society.

The 1983 white paper aimed to realize three objectives: (1) to reduce the social and economic deprivation of members of ethnic minorities; (2) to prevent and counteract discrimination and to improve the legal position of aliens in general and targeted minority groups in particular; and (3) to create the conditions for targeted ethnic minorities to increase their

Table 7.3. Acquisition of Dutch Nationality, by Country of Former Nationality, 1990–2000

	1990	1991	1992	1993	1994	1995	1996	1997	1998
Turkey	1,950	6,110	11,520	18,000	23,870	33,060	30,700	21,190	13,480
Morocco	3,030	7,300	7,990	7,750	8,110	13,480	15,600	10,480	11,250
Suriname	1,640	4,010	5,120	4,990	5,390	3,990	4,450	3,020	2,990
Others	6,170	11,690	11,610	12,330	12,080	20,910	31,950	25,140	31,450
Total	12,790	29,110	36,240	43,070	49,450	71,440	82,700	59,830	59,170

Source: Statistics Netherlands.

Table 7.4. The Non-Dutch Population of the Netherlands, by Country of Nationality, 1990–2000

	1990	1991	1992	1993	1994	1995	1996	1997	1998
Morocco	156,900	163,697	165,138	164,567	158,653	149,800	138,700	135,700	128,600
Turkey	203,500	214,830	212,450	202,618	182,089	154,300	127,000	114,700	102,000
Germany	44,300	46,859	49,333	52,053	53,363	53,900	53,500	53,900	54,100
Other countries	287,700	307,482	330,487	360,604	363,033	367,400	360,700	373,800	377,700
Total	692,400	732,868	757,408	779,842	757,138	725,400	679,900	678,100	662,400

Source: Statistics Netherlands.

Notes: Figures reflect population numbers as of December 31 of the corresponding year.
There were 9,338 Indonesian nationals living in the Netherlands on December 31, 2000.

participation in Dutch society. A key element of the Netherlands' ethnic minorities policy was that integration should take place without the loss of cultural identity.

The ethnic minorities policies have been relatively successful in the areas of housing and education and in advancing legal rights, but far less successful in increasing minority participation in the Dutch labor market. Persistent and high unemployment among targeted groups of Dutch ethnic minorities prompted government policymakers to propose a new integration policy in 1989 based on abandoning a culture approach in order to focus on the individual immigrant. Thus Dutch policy toward ethnic minorities contained a paradox: on the one hand it sought to integrate immigrants and prevent the formation of ethnic minorities, but on the other it sought to prevent the loss of immigrants' cultural identity (Muus 1993). The ethnic integration policy proposal advanced in 1989 was not accepted in full; however, several of its component elements have found their way into Dutch politics. A Newcomers Policy was introduced in 1996 to structure the way in which "newcomers" are introduced to Dutch society. For example, all must take language classes, and an orientation course on Dutch society is recommended. Newcomers who receive social security benefits may see their benefits reduced if they fail to participate in these classes.

Thus far, Dutch policy for integrating minorities has not been able to effectively integrate all the immigrant groups that have arrived in the Netherlands in recent decades. Interestingly, naturalization rates of the non-Dutch immigrant population in the Netherlands have been high since 1992, when dual citizenship was first allowed (see table 7.3). As a consequence of these high naturalization rates, statistics show a decrease in the non-Dutch population even in years of high non-Dutch in-migration (table 7.4), and the national statistics bureau has had to change they way it requests data, moving from a nationality-based category to one determined by birth country and parents' birth country.

CONCLUSION: POLICY-OUTCOME GAPS

How best to integrate immigrants will remain a subject of intense debate among Dutch political actors and in the Dutch media. Impatience may be the best word to describe Dutch sentiment (Vermeulen and Penninx 2000). Which direction Dutch immigration and integration policies will take will depend in large measure on what the 2002 coalition government of Christian Democrats, List Pim Fortuyn, and conservative liberals proposes. The coalition seems to have a primary interest in curbing (un-wanted) immigration, but it is not yet clear whether they will put pressure on non–economically active members of the immigrant population in order to improve labor market participation.

The Netherlands is attempting to achieve a pragmatic balance in immigration control between economic interests and humanitarian considerations. Immigration control measures tend to be ad hoc reactions to fast-changing conditions, an approach that does not lend itself to a long-term vision. Economic interests have been sufficiently strong that they have been able to adapt Dutch regulations on foreign labor migration to match new economic circumstances. Problematic consequences of Dutch immigration policy have only surfaced when workers who are no longer needed have decided to remain nevertheless. The humanitarian aspects of Dutch admissions policies are by definition the least easily controlled. Generous family reunification and family formation policies have led to substantial chain migration while simultaneously opening a back door to potential labor migrants. Asylum has become one of the most difficult issues to address. The number of asylum seekers has risen steadily, some no doubt hoping to use the asylum process as a door to resident status in the Netherlands, and there is no easy solution for returning rejected asylum seekers to their countries of origin. Dutch efforts to fortify immigration controls seem also to have produced more arrivals via traffickers or human smugglers.

It is not easy to gauge the success of Dutch immigration policies given that the country has not set a numerical ceiling on annual immigration. But it is clear that the number of immigrants is sometimes far above the expectations of Dutch policymakers. Policies to restrict post-colonial immigrants have largely been unsuccessful, as in the case of Surinam. And the temporary guestworker policy of the 1960s and 1970s ultimately led to the permanent settlement of many of these labor migrants. Relatively generous family reunification policies increased the size of the guestworker communities and those of people arriving from the Netherlands' former colonies. Family reunification and family formation became accepted back doors to the Dutch labor market after the main door closed to unskilled and low-skilled migrants.

On the other hand, the Netherlands' current temporary foreign labor policy seems to be very effective, and it is becoming even more flexible for high-paid, high-skilled immigrants from outside the European Union. Policymakers now face a dilemma—how to tailor immigration to the needs of the Dutch labor market without compromising humanitarian concerns.

How should one assess Dutch asylum policy? Should one look at the number of immigrants who are recognized as refugees or given resident status on humanitarian grounds? Or should one consider the large numbers of asylum seekers whose applications are denied, leaving the country to deal with the huge problem of their return? This leads to another dilemma—how to uphold a system that protects those in need of protection but can simultaneously ensure that those with no valid claim will not be able to abuse the system. There is clearly a gap between policies and outcomes in Dutch asylum and refugee policy. The Netherlands is willing to accept bona fide refugees, but many asylum requests lack sufficient grounds for the applicants to be recognized as refugees. Changes in asylum procedures and reception policies (dating from 1987 and onward) seem to have failed in their goal of decreasing the numbers of new asylum seekers by increasing the waiting period. The 2001 Aliens Law addresses this dilemma by cutting processing time and providing for a rapid denial of applications from abusers of the asylum system. Humanitarianism and tolerance have long been key values in Dutch society, coexisting with the historical image of the Dutch nation-state as a protector of the persecuted. The essential dilemma is simple: values like humanitarianism and tolerance cannot abide setting numerical maximums on the country's intake of asylum seekers escaping their countries of origin because of factors beyond the control of the Dutch government.

The Dutch tendency to tolerate things that may be formally disallowed may itself have contributed to gaps between policy aims and outcomes in the field of immigration and asylum. By definition, this tolerance allows for greater distance between intentions and outcomes. Although there is no indication that this quintessentially Dutch trait had any real impact on immigration or approval of asylum requests, this tolerance undoubtedly underlies the less-than-rigorous status checks in the workplace in the 1980s. One may argue that it also explains the reluctance to enforce the speedy repatriation of illegal immigrants and rejected asylum seekers.

The political climate in the Netherlands has started to change, however. Zero tolerance is gaining political currency, and the failure to conform to rules and regularizations is becoming less acceptable, especially when the behaviors in question belong to foreigners—or worse, to "illegal" foreigners.

What does the future hold? Much will depend on developments in the European Union at large. The Netherlands' economic development, and also its demographic development, might lead over time to an immigration policy more attuned to the qualifications—not just the numbers—of immigrants. This aspect of immigration policy should be the easiest on which to reach consensus, while the humanitarian aspects of immigration remain the hot issues in the debate.

In many ways, the migration issues confronting the Netherlands are the same as those other European welfare states face, and they also bear similarities to recent developments in Canada and Australia. On the one hand is the recognition that borders must be kept open to highly qualified immigrants, but on the other hand are the problems of integrating humanitarian immigrants (those arriving through family reunification, family formation, and asylum categories) into the labor force and society at large. There are strong indications that the Netherlands is slowly abandoning its predominantly humanitarian approach and moving toward skill-based immigration.

Even as this shift is under way, there is still no full consensus—neither in politics nor in public discussion—that the Netherlands is, after all, an "immigration country." Recognizing this fact will be even more difficult for the governing coalition that took power in 2002, and which contains members of the List Pim Fortuyn. A portion of the Dutch population seems to be experiencing a wave of anti-immigrant sentiment, similar to those that have moved across France, Belgium, Austria, and Denmark. But interestingly, despite their shared populist approaches, the political parties behind these anti-immigrant, somewhat anti-Islam, sentiments are not easily put under one flag.

References

Amersfoort, Hans van. 1999. "Immigration Control and Minority Policy: The Case of the Netherlands." In *Mechanisms of Immigration Control. A Comparative Analysis of European Regulation Practices*, edited by Grete Brochmann and Tomas Hammar. Oxford: Berg.

Amersfoort, Hans van, Philip Muus, and Rinus Penninx. 1984. "International Migration, the Economic Crisis and the State: An Analysis of Mediterranean Migration to Western Europe," *Ethnic and Racial Studies* 7, no. 2 (April).

Amersfoort, J.M.M. van. 1974. *Immigratie en minderheidsvorming. Een analyse van de Nederlandse situatie 1945–1973*. Alphen aan de Rijn: Samson.

Amersfoort, J.M.M. van, and B. Surie. 1987. "Immigratieland tegen wil en dank. Nederland 1970–1985." In *Postmoderne Aardrijkskunde: De socio-grafische traditie voortgezet*, edited by H. v.d. Wusten. Muiderberg: Coutinho.

Bovenkerk, Frank, and Wil Verschoor. 1983. "Retourmigratie van Surinamers en Antillianen." In *Retourmigratie van Mediterranen, Surinamers en Antillianen uit Nederland*, edited by Philip Muus, Rinus Penninx, J.M.M. van Amersfoort, Frank Bovenkerk, and Wil Verschoor. The Hague: Ministerie van Sociale Zaken en Werkgelegenheid.

Elich, J.H., and P.W. Blauw. 1981. ....*En Toch Terug: Een onderzoek naar de retourmigratie van Nederlanders uit Australie, Nieuw-Zeeland en Canada*. Rottterdam: Erasmus University of Rotterdam.

Engbersen, G. 1999. "De illegale vreemdeling." In *De ongekende stad, deel I*, edited by J. Burgers and G. Engbersen. Amsterdam: Boom.

Faassen, Marijke van. 2001. "Min of meer misbaar. Naoorlogse emigranten vanuit Nederland: achtergronden en organisatie, particuliere motieven en overheidsbemoeienis, 1946–1967." In *Van Hot naar Her. Nederlandse migratie, vroeger, nu en morgen*, edited by Saskia Poldervaart, Hanneke Willemse, and Jan-Willem Schilt. Amsterdam: Stichting Beheer IISG.

Knippenberg, Hans, and Ben de Pater. 1988. *De eenwording van Nederland*. Nijmegen: SUN.

Lijphart, Arend. 1968. *Verzuiling, pacificatie en kentering in de Nederlandse politiek.* Amsterdam: De Bussy.

Muus, Philip. 1985. *Migration, Minorities and Policy in the Netherlands*. SOPEMI-Netherlands 1985. Report for the OECD. Amsterdam, University of Amsterdam.

———. 1993. *Migration, Immigrants and Policy in the Netherlands*. SOPEMI-Netherlands 1993. Report for the OECD. Amsterdam: University of Amsterdam.

———. 1997. "Shifting Borders: The Inclusion and Exclusion of Refugees and Asylum Seekers in the Netherlands." In *Exclusion and Inclusion of Refugees in Contemporary Europe*, edited by Philip Muus. Utrecht: ERCOMER, Utrecht University.

———. 1998. *Migration, Immigrants and Policy in the Netherlands*. SOPEMI-Netherlands 1998. Report for the OECD. Utrecht: ERCOMER, Utrecht University.

———. 2000. *Migration, Immigrants and Policy in the Netherlands*. SOPEMI-Netherlands 2000. Report for the OECD. Utrecht: ERCOMER, Utrecht University.

Muus, Philip. n.d. *Migration and Immigrant Policy. Immigrants from Turkey and Their Participation in the Labour Market: An International Comparison*. Forthcoming in the ERCOMER series, Ashgate.

Penninx, Rinus. 1979. "Towards an Overall Ethnic Minorities Policy? Preliminary Study." In *Ethnic Minorities*. Report 17 of the Netherlands Scientific Council for Government Policy. The Hague: WRR.

Rath, Jan. 1991. *Minorisering. De sociale constructie van 'etnische minderheden.'* Amsterdam: SUA.

Roelandt, Theo. 1994. *Verscheidenheid in ongelijkheid: Een studie naar etnische stratificatie en onderklassevorming in de Nederlandse samenleving.* Amsterdam: Thesis Publishers.

Schuster, John. 1999. *Poortwachters over immigranten. Het debat over immigratie in het na-oorlogse Groot-Brittanie en Nederland.* Amsterdam: Het Spinhuis.

Vermeulen, Hans, and Rinus Penninx, eds. 2000. *Immigrant Integration: The Dutch Case.* Amsterdam: Het Spinhuis.

Volkskrant. 2002. "Afrekenen met tamelijk ruim immigratiebeleid," May 30.

Commentary

Han Entzinger

Philip Muus is certainly right in qualifying the Netherlands as a reluctant immigration country and Dutch immigration policy as a pragmatic approach between economic and humanitarian considerations. In this respect Dutch policy does not differ dramatically from that of other European countries. Immigration policy is increasingly an affair of the European Union, and member states simply cannot afford to deviate too strongly from the common line, although certain national politicians pretend that those small margins do not apply to their own country.

The more substantial differences between the Dutch and their neighbors are not in immigration policy but in immigrant incorporation policies, where there is much more room for national traditions and specificities. More than in most European countries, public authorities in the Netherlands have been concerned with facilitating and steering processes of immigrant integration. This is possibly a characteristic of the Dutch welfare state's ambition of social engineering and its tendency to (over)regulate social processes and people's behavior. However, the objectives and the instruments of integration policies have been shifting considerably over past decades (Entzinger n.d.).

Until the late 1970s immigration to the Netherlands was seen as temporary. Consequently, all policy measures taken must be understood within the perspective of the migrants' eventual return. An exception was made for "repatriates" from Indonesia, but they were believed to have assimilated. This two-track approach made it unnecessary to reflect on modes of incorporation. Around 1980 awareness developed that many migrants would stay for good. Contrary to the situation in most other West European countries, and largely in line with Anglo-Saxon traditions, these migrants were defined primarily in terms of their shared ethnic or national origins, and therefore labeled "ethnic minorities." On this basis authorities developed an elaborate "ethnic minorities policy" aimed at promoting the migrants' participation in Dutch society without forcing them to abandon their identity as an ethnic group. Major elements of this policy were the setting up of arrangements for mother tongue teaching, the establishment of Muslim and Hindu schools, and the development of broadcasting and political consultation facilities for migrant communities, all fully financed by the state. Such forms of institutionalized multiculturalism should be understood against the backdrop of the Dutch tradition of "pillarization."

Ethnic minorities policy became more difficult to pursue as migrant communities began to expand through continuing immigration. Most communities also became more diverse internally as their length of residence increased. Besides, as a second generation came of age, it became obvious that policies of multiculturalism, no matter how respectful their intentions might have been, tended to fixate cultures rather than do justice to their dynamism. From around 1990, institutionalized multiculturalism came increasingly under fire, primarily because the migrants' socially deprived position did not improve. Unemployment rates among them continued to be extremely high, their school achievements were below expectations, and their political participation remained marginal despite relatively liberal citizenship policies and the extension of local voting rights to foreign residents. The ethnic minorities approach seemed to exclude rather than include immigrants. There was too little incentive for the mainstream institutions of Dutch society to open up to newcomers, who were assumed to create their own parallel arrangements — with public support if needed. This active public involvement in facilitating multiculturalism increased the authorities' vulnerability to anti-immigrant backlash effects.

In 1994, when the "purple" coalition government took office, "minorities policy" was rebaptized "integration policy." A stronger focus on the individual migrant replaced the communities approach, and the new policy emphasized what majority and minorities have in common over their differences. Along with this shift, integration policies also became more obliging, particularly toward migrants. The benevolent attitude of earlier years, which had made immigrants heavily dependent on public support, was replaced by one that appealed to newcomers to step up integration efforts and to familiarize themselves more quickly with the local language and social habits. The Law on Civic Integration of Newcomers of 1998 requires most newly arriving immigrants from outside the European Union to attend a free but mandatory 600-hour integration course (in which 500 hours are dedicated to learning Dutch). The concurrent shift from state to market implied that immigrants had to develop their own human capital. The considerable growth of the Dutch economy during the past decade has certainly helped many of them in doing so. Immigrants' employment situation, school achievements, and public involvement have definitely progressed.

However, there is more than just this change in appreciation of the welfare state and a balance shift from state to market. In the Netherlands and elsewhere in Europe, the liberal-egalitarian views so dominant in public policymaking since the postwar years have been losing ground to neo-conservative ideologies. Where the former tended to stress entitlements provided by the state to anyone in need, the latter brought individual responsibility and self-sufficiency to the foreground. The 2002 local and parliamentary elections in the Netherlands revealed a strong move away from liberal tolerance and cultural relativism and toward neo-conservatism with certain nationalist traits. For the first time in Dutch history, immigration and integration played a dominant role in the elections. All winning parties advocated stricter immigration policies and a stepping up of integration efforts. In their views, integration and acculturation had not advanced quickly enough.

Given the facts, this is a rather surprising view. According to virtually all traditional indicators, immigrant integration is progressing, particularly among the second generation. Our own research in Rotterdam found that Muslim youngsters generally endorse the same public values—diversity, democracy, and egalitarianism—as their Dutch counterparts. It is only in the private domain—on religion and family values, for example—that they are more conservative. This gap gets smaller, however, as their length of residence and level of schooling increase. The vast majority have friends of different ethnic origins, and only a small minority (around 5 percent) sympathize with fundamentalist movements (Phalet, Van Lotringen, and Entzinger 2000).

Thus, after some initial hesitation, the "integration machine" in the Netherlands seems to function relatively well by traditional standards commonly used in academic research. Yet most voters do not seem to acknowledge this. There is a widely shared belief that the gap is much wider than it actually is and that the pace of change is too slow. Yes, the strongly multiculturalist approach was ill-reflected. Although it was said to respect cultural diversity and to facilitate the migrants' emancipation,

292   Entzinger

in reality it perpetuated their marginalization and their dependency on public support. It also served as an excuse for not sufficiently opening up existing institutional arrangements to newcomers. Dutch multiculturalism was based on a static interpretation of culture, rather than on a dynamic one. Implicitly it served to protect traditional Dutch values from new outside impulses. Therefore, the Dutch multiculturalist approach is more conservative and nationalist than many of its proponents have believed. This leads us to the challenging conclusion that the recent shift in Dutch policy is less innovative than its advocates may think. Assimilation and institutionalized multiculturalism have more in common than might appear at first glance. Both attempt to fence off traditional Dutch society from outside changes, but both are based on the unrealistic assumption that cultures and the people who represent them do not change.

References

Entzinger, Han. n.d. "The Rise and Fall of Multiculturalism: The Case of the Netherlands." In *Towards Assimilation and Citizenship: Immigration in Liberal Nation-States*, edited by Christian Joppke and Eva Morawska. London: Palgrave, in press.
Phalet, Karen, Claudia Van Lotringen, and Han Entzinger. 2000. *Islam in de multiculturele samenleving; opvattingen van jongeren in Rotterdam*. Utrecht: ERCOMER.

Commentary

Arend Lijphart

The summer 2001 issue of the Dutch political science journal *Acta Politica* contains a debate between Rudy Andeweg and myself about the merits of consensus democracy, characterized by proportional representation, a multiparty system, and broad coalition cabinets (Andeweg 2001; Lijphart 2001). The Netherlands is a good example of consensus democracy. Andeweg, an admirer of the contrasting British-style majoritarian type of democracy, notes that the main parties in consensus democracies are too similar and too cooperative with each other. Because they do not offer clear alternatives to voters, they encourage protest voting that favors extreme right-wing and anti-immigrant parties, as in Austria, Belgium, Denmark, Norway, and Switzerland.[1] Andeweg pointed out, however, that the Netherlands did not have a significant anti-immigrant party and was therefore a striking exception to the general pattern he described, a fact he went on to explain at length. Less than a year later, his explanation would not have been necessary: the rise of populist and anti-immigrant politician Pim Fortuyn and the strong electoral support for his new party in the May 15, 2002, parliamentary election mean that the Netherlands is no longer an exceptional case.

Philip Muus's excellent analysis of Dutch immigration (and emigration) policy and practice is a tale of both continuities and changes. The sudden rise of Fortuyn's anti-immigrant party certainly appears to be

---

[1] My response, briefly, was that the same complaint can be made about two-party systems, and that the correlation between consensus democracy and anti-immigrant party strength can simply be explained in terms of the chances offered by proportional representation to *any* new and small party to get its representatives elected.

one of the major changes. However, I believe that continuity predominates in the overall picture. I would even argue that the Fortuyn phenomenon does not present as much discontinuity as appears on the surface.

In the late 1940s and early 1950s, there was a great deal of discussion in the Netherlands of the advantages and drawbacks of emigration and the relative attractiveness of Canada, the United States, South Africa, Australia, and New Zealand as potential countries in which to resettle. But the period of intensive emigration was but a brief interruption in what can be seen from a longer perspective as a strong tradition of immigration. As early as the sixteenth and seventeenth centuries, the Netherlands was already a major haven for refugees like Huguenots and Jews.

The assertion, most recently made by Pim Fortuyn, that "the Netherlands is full up" is not new. The Dutch self-image of a small country with too many people has existed at least since the beginning of the twentieth century. In the interwar years, it provided the major impetus for the ambitious reclaiming of land from the sea in an attempt to create more living space in a crowded country.

Muus points out that the Netherlands has always been a country of minorities, but the new minorities differ from the old Catholic, Calvinist, and nonreligious "pillars" in many respects. From 1917 on, the old Socialist and Liberal pillars developed a "politics of accommodation," which entailed a high degree of power sharing as well as the establishment of separate and autonomously run Catholic, Calvinist, and public nondenominational schools and other institutions (Lijphart 1968). Because early postwar emigration policy was meant for the old minorities, it followed the pattern of the old politics of accommodation. Separate agencies, one for each pillar, advised and assisted prospective emigrants; denominational compartmentalization was carefully maintained even during one's exit from the country. However, the system of separate schools, originally devised in 1917 for the old minorities, has also had an important effect on the new minorities. The law was formulated in neutral language and allowed any group to establish and run schools as long as basic educational standards were observed. Recently, quite a few non-Christian religious schools have been set up by and for the new minorities — including about thirty Muslim and six Hindu schools.

Finally, to return to the 2002 political "earthquake" caused by Fortuyn, his assassination nine days before the May 15 election, and his party's spectacular success in that election, I contend that there is much more continuity than dramatic change in these events. First of all, the incumbent cabinet, a coalition of the three main secular parties, had performed very well in many respects during its eight years in office. It was reelected in 1998 with an increased majority. It continued to have an excellent macroeconomic track record during its second term, and it also succeeded—with the Christian Democrats in opposition—in passing important new legislation on euthanasia, gay marriage, and the legalization of prostitution. Despite these achievements, however, the cabinet had become deeply unpopular. The electoral verdict was therefore first and foremost a massive vote *against* the incumbent parties, not *for* the Fortuyn party. Second, the biggest winner of votes and seats was not the Fortuyn party but the opposition Christian Democrats, who were given an opportunity to govern—an entirely normal and healthy democratic development.

Third, while it is not incorrect to include the Fortuyn party in the broad category of European anti-immigrant parties, it is probably the least objectionable of these parties. Fortuyn, who was openly gay himself, preached tolerance, and his dislike of Muslim immigrants was largely based on their discrimination against gays and women. Nor did his message carry any anti-Semitic overtones. Fourth, as a junior partner in the new coalition cabinet, the Fortuyn party had to moderate its views even more. Finally, continual dissension and quarreling among the Fortuyn party's cabinet ministers and parliamentary representatives led to the resignation of the cabinet after only three months in office—triggering new elections in January 2003, in which the party is expected to suffer heavy losses. It is therefore less likely that new Dutch immigration policies will be a dramatic break with the past than that they will continue to be policies of gradual and pragmatic adjustment.

References

Andeweg, Rudy B. 2001. "Lijphart versus Lijphart: The Cons of Consensus Democracy in Homogeneous Societies," *Acta Politica* 36, no. 2 (Summer): 117–28.
Lijphart, Arend. 1968. *The Politics of Accommodation: Pluralism and Democracy in the Netherlands*. Berkeley: University of California Press.
———. 2001. "The Pros and Cons—but Mainly Pros—of Consensus Democracy," *Acta Politica* 36, no. 2 (Summer): 129–39.

8

Britain: From Immigration Control to Migration Management

Zig Layton-Henry

British political discourse and policy practice relating to immigration have changed considerably in recent years in Britain. The buoyant economy that the Labour government inherited from the Conservatives in 1997 caused significant and sustained labor shortages for both skilled and unskilled workers. These labor shortages — and the associated problems of lost orders, unpicked crops, and failure to deliver high-quality services — prompted employers to press the government to expand the work permit system and allow more skilled immigrants to enter Britain. The major employers' organization, the Confederation of British Industry, has been increasingly willing to lobby for more immigration provided it is linked to labor and skill shortages (CBI 2002a).

Changes in political discourse and policy also reflect more favorable political circumstances. The election of a Labour government with a huge parliamentary majority in 1997, followed by its reelection with a

I am grateful to Wayne Cornelius, Gary Freeman, Randall Hansen, and Takeyuki Tsuda for their comments on an earlier version of this essay.

similar majority in 2001,[1] was a major factor creating the political space and confidence for a positive reevaluation of immigration policy. It had also become less acceptable in elite circles to exploit racism for political purposes, and the leaders of the three major parties and most candidates signed a pledge sponsored by the Commission of Racial Equality not to exploit race as an issue in the 2001 general election.[2]

The Labour government was acutely aware that its ability to manage the economy and provide good public services was crucial for its electoral success. The Conservatives' loss of reputation for economic competence, damaged in September 1992 when the English pound was forced out of the European Exchange Rate Mechanism, proved disastrous for their party's electoral chances in 1997 (Worcester and Mortimore 1999). An acute shortage of teachers, nurses, and doctors was causing considerable problems for the government, which had promised to improve standards in the schools and in health service provision, in the latter case by reducing hospital waiting lists. The skills shortage in education and health care was thus a real constraint on the success of government policy.

Two other factors also supported a more relaxed approach to immigration. The first was the successful transfer of Hong Kong to China on June 30, 1997. The subsequent stability in this new Chinese Special Autonomous Region removed fears that, following the imposition of Chinese rule, there would be a mass exodus of people, many of whom might come to the United Kingdom. British policymakers had refused to grant the 3.5 million Hong Kong Chinese, who were citizens of the British Dependent Territories, the right of access to and settlement in Britain. Only 50,000 heads of household who worked in special occupations, such as the civil service and the police, were granted the right to settle in Britain, along with their dependents. The success of the Hong Kong handover removed the possibility that Britain would confront a refugee crisis similar to the one in 1972, when Asians were expelled from Uganda.

---

[1] In the May 1997 general election the Labour Party gained a majority of 178 over all other parties. In the June 2001 general election, their overall majority was 164.

[2] Some prominent Conservative members of Parliament—Michael Portillo and John Gummer, for example—refused to sign on the grounds that the pledge pandered to political correctness. One Conservative member who did attempt to exploit racism in the general election was disciplined by William Hague, the Conservative leader, and forced to apologize for his remarks (Butler and Kavanagh 2002: 84–85).

The second factor supporting a relaxation in immigration policy was the demographics of Britain's aging population. It was widely believed that some immigration would be needed to augment the numbers of young workers, maintain economic productivity, and pay the rising cost of pensions. Although there was no clear realization of the vast amount of immigration that would be needed to make a demographic impact, concern about the aging of the population had considerable impact on the press and the general public, making it easier to argue that immigration was in the national interest.

Thus economic and political pressures in the late 1990s were favorable to a more liberal British immigration regime. Politically this was defensible as good for the economy and for public services. However, as Britain was becoming integrated into a European labor market, it was put into competition with other European states for skilled and unskilled workers. Further, the globalization of labor markets, particularly in financial services and information technology, meant that Britain was also competing with the United States and Japan for skilled professionals in some sectors. The tough immigration controls that formed the basis of British immigration policy for most of the postwar period (and had seemed fairly effective) were no longer sustainable in the face of market forces that demanded a more liberal immigration regime (Freeman 1994). And even though a major economic recession could eliminate unskilled labor shortages overnight, the skills shortages in medicine and education were long term, as was the demographic pattern of an aging population.

British politicians were aware that immigration had the potential to reemerge as a political issue (as it had in the 1970s) if government failed to reassure the electorate that a well-managed policy was in place and operating in the national interest. The tabloid press in particular regarded immigration and race relations as themes that could easily be exploited to damage the Labour Party and government. Events in Austria, Belgium, Denmark, France, and the Netherlands showed that issues relating to immigration, asylum seekers, and integration remained very potent electorally. However, in the 2001 general election, the electorate rated the subject of asylum seekers and immigration policy ninth in importance, well behind health care, education, law and order, pensions, and taxation (Butler and Kavanagh 2002: 237).

British immigration policy's shift under pressure from market forces has resulted in a substantial increase in legal immigration through expansion of the work permit system and other schemes. Illegal immigrants and asylum seekers (the latter are often condemned as "bogus" asylum seekers) are subject to political condemnation and widespread hostility in the tabloid press. The home secretary gave expression to these changes when opening the Third Reading of the Nationality, Immigration and Asylum Bill:

> It is also no longer controversial to take the view that we can welcome people legitimately into our country while being robust in developing a system that is trusted, that has the confidence of the British people, and that protects our borders and prevents clandestine entry and illegal working (Parliamentary Reports, Commons, col. 593, June 12, 2002).

One area where government complacency has been shaken is the need for more proactive policies to aid ethnic minority integration. British governments traditionally pursued policies of benign neglect over integration, leaving this as far as possible to individuals and institutions acting within broad parameters defined by government. Thus integration was interpreted as the maintenance of law and order and, in particular, controlling street crime and racist violence. As racial discrimination in public places, in advertising, and in employment and housing became issues, these were outlawed by legislation in the 1960s and 1970s. But within these broad policy objectives of maintaining law and order and eliminating racial discrimination, a pluralist multiculturalism has been allowed to flourish.

Riots by young Asians in the northern towns of Bradford, Burnley, and Oldham in summer 2001 were unexpected and dramatic. Earlier riots in London, Liverpool, and Birmingham in the 1980s had highlighted issues of policing mixed communities and the poor relationships that young people, especially African Caribbeans, had with the police. In the northern towns, inquiries drew attention to high unemployment levels among both whites and Asians on deprived estates, problems of policing, and residential segregation between white working-class estates and the inner-city Pakistani and Bangladeshi areas. Issues of relative deprivation were prominent, with poor white residents claiming that Asians had the best jobs and the best houses (*Observer*, July 7, 2002). Apart from investing funds through urban renewal budgets and the like, the government has few strategies for encouraging integration, especially of Muslim minorities, which is a key issue in towns in the north of England. Little is being done, for example, to reduce residential and educational segregation, which seems to be a marked feature of these former textile centers.

HISTORICAL BACKGROUND

British governments have managed two major immigration regimes since World War II. Until 1962 there was a very liberal regime that allowed unrestricted immigration from the colonies and the Commonwealth. There was also unrestricted immigration from Ireland, which left the Commonwealth in 1948 but was a traditional source of economic migration to Britain. The immigration of non-British subjects was controlled, but the acute postwar labor shortage meant that alien immigration was encouraged immediately following the war. Government initiatives to recruit workers included encouraging Polish former servicemen who had served under British command during the war to settle in Britain.[3] European volunteer workers were also recruited under a number of government schemes (Tannahill 1958), and there was some immigration from Italy. These migrants were all seen as valuable recruits to alleviate the severe labor shortages caused by postwar reconstruction and the recovery of the European and international trading systems. After the war, the resumption of British emigration to North America, Australia, and other Commonwealth countries encouraged the government to welcome immigration. This was the background to the large immigration from Ireland to Britain in the 1940s and 1950s, which was followed by immigration from the English-speaking Caribbean and from the Indian subcontinent (see table 8.1).

This liberal regime ended in 1962 with the implementation of the first Commonwealth Immigrants Act, which was passed as the result of a political campaign to control nonwhite immigration from the New Commonwealth (Layton-Henry 1984: 30–43). The act made Commonwealth immigrants subject to an entry voucher scheme unless they were born in the United Kingdom, held a British passport, or were included on such a passport. Other Commonwealth citizens wishing to immigrate needed a voucher from the Ministry of Labour before they could enter Britain. These vouchers were issued under three categories: Category A for migrants with a specific job to go to, Category B for those with special skills in short supply, and Category C for all other intending migrants, who would be dealt with in order of application. Those with war service were given preferential treatment.

---

[3] In May 1946 the government established the Polish Resettlement Corps, and the Polish Resettlement Act was passed in 1947. Between September 1946 and September 1948, some 114,000 Poles enrolled in the Corps (Paul 1997: 68).

Table 8.1. Estimated Net Immigration to Britain from the New
Commonwealth, 1953–1962

	West Indies	India	Pakistan	Others	Total
1953	2,000				2,000
1954	11,000				11,000
1955	27,500	5,800	1,850	7,500	42,650
1956	29,800	5,600	2,050	9,350	46,800
1957	23,000	6,600	5,200	7,600	42,400
1958	15,000	6,200	4,700	3,950	29,850
1959	16,400	2,950	850	1,400	21,600
1960	49,650	5,900	2,500	−350	57,700
1961	66,300	23,750	25,100	21,250	136,400
1962[a]	31,800	19,080	25,080	18,970	94,900

Source: Layton-Henry 1992: 13.

[a] First six months up to introduction of first controls.

In August 1965 the Labour government tightened controls by imposing a quota of 8,500 a year on the recruitment of New Commonwealth
immigrant workers and reserving 1,000 of those for applicants from
Malta. The C category vouchers were abolished because there were more
than enough Category A and Category B applicants to fill the quota. In
February 1968 the second Commonwealth Immigrants Act was passed. It
controlled the entry of British passport holders who had no close connection with the United Kingdom. This enabled a quota system to be imposed on Asians from East Africa who had retained British citizenship
when Kenya became independent and were migrating to Britain as the
result of discriminatory policies by the Kenyan government.

In 1971 a Conservative government introduced a comprehensive
immigration bill that gave government complete control over all immigration except for "patrials" — people with close connections with the
United Kingdom through birth or descent, who would remain free from
all controls. A main provision of this bill was that work permits would
replace employment vouchers, and these permits would not carry the
right of permanent residence or the right of entry for dependants. Hence-
forward, citizens of independent Commonwealth countries and British
subjects without a close connection with Britain would be treated on the
same basis as aliens for the purposes of immigration control.

The potency of immigration as a political issue did not diminish with the passage of the Immigration Act of 1971. Pressure to control nonwhite immigration intensified in 1972 due to President Idi Amin's expulsion of Asians from Uganda. The Conservative government led by Edward Heath accepted most of the Asians, a move that was viewed as a betrayal by Enoch Powell and his supporters and also by the extreme right National Front. Immigration retained salience throughout the 1970s, with the National Front exploiting a media panic over an inflow of Asians from Malawi in 1976. Although the National Front was unable to win any local government or parliamentary seats in the 1970s, its provocative marches in areas of black settlement and the modest degree of electoral support it achieved alarmed the other parties. The Conservatives in particular were pressured into adopting very stringent immigration control policies.

By the end of the 1970s both major parties were committed to a new Nationality Act. The Labour Party considered that a logical and nonracial immigration policy had to be based on a rational concept of British citizenship. They had produced proposals for reform as early as 1972 (Labour Party 1972). Leading Conservatives, including Enoch Powell, who was probably the first to urge this reform, were also convinced that the long-standing concept of "British subject" was anachronistic. Its content had been eroded by immigration control legislation, the abandonment of Britain's imperial pretensions, and the independence of almost all former British colonies. Many Commonwealth countries viewed Britain's entry into the European Community in January 1973 as the final act undermining the unity of the Commonwealth and ending the myth of common interest and allegiances between Britain and her former colonies. New citizenship legislation defining British nationality more narrowly—to those with close links to the United Kingdom by birth, settlement, or descent from a citizen—would provide a more rational and less overtly racist basis for defining who had the right of access to and abode in the territory of the United Kingdom.

The election of Margaret Thatcher as leader of the Conservative Party in 1975 marked the beginning of a strongly restrictionist period in immigration policy. Thatcher was sympathetic to Powell's views. She believed that the Labour government of 1974–1979 had allowed too much New Commonwealth immigration, that popular anxieties about it were justified, and that the Conservative Party should bring it to an end. She also felt that this would be electorally popular and would undermine the basis of support for the National Front.

The Conservative Party's election manifesto of 1979 was vague in every policy area except immigration and nationality (Conservative Party 1979). Here eight specific commitments were listed that clearly had Margaret Thatcher's wholehearted support:

- We shall introduce a new British Nationality Act to define entitlement to British citizenship and the right of abode in this country. It will not adversely affect the right of anyone now permanently settled here.

- We shall end the practice of allowing permanent settlement for those who came here for a temporary stay.

- We shall limit the entry of parents, grandparents and children over 18 to a small number of urgent compassionate cases.

- We shall end the concession introduced by the Labour government in 1974 to husbands and male fiancés.

- We shall severely restrict the issue of work permits.

- We shall introduce a register of those Commonwealth wives and children entitled to entry for settlement under the 1971 Immigration Act.

- We shall then introduce a quota system, covering everyone outside the European Community, to control entry for settlement.

- We shall take firm action against illegal immigrants and overstayers and help those immigrants who genuinely wish to leave this country — but there can be no question of compulsory repatriation.

These excessively specific election commitments led to a clash between the populist authoritarian promises of the new government and civil service pragmatism. In particular, the Conservatives were forced to drop the register of dependants and the non-EC world quota for settlement. However, they immediately set about tightening the immigration rules, in particular to deny entry to husbands and fiancés marrying or intending to marry British citizens through arranged marriages.[4] In November 1979 a white paper before Parliament proposed that husbands of women settled in Britain would need an entry certificate to be admitted to the United Kingdom and that this would be refused if the entry clear-

---

[4] In 1974 the Labour government had granted such persons the automatic right to enter for settlement, a right that had been limited by a previous Labour government in 1969.

ance officer had reason to believe that the marriage was arranged solely to gain admission to Britain, that the husband and wife did not intend living together, or that the couple had not met. An entry certificate could be issued if the wife had been born in the United Kingdom. Similar conditions would apply to applications from fiancés. Elderly dependants would be admitted only if wholly or mainly dependent economically on sons and daughters in Britain, and they must also be without relatives in their own country and have a standard of living substantially below that of their own country. These conditions were clearly designed to disqualify elderly dependants from Third World countries given that remittances from their children in Britain would be likely to raise their standard of living at home by a significant amount. The regulations governing change of category for people entering Great Britain as visitors or students were tightened in order to prevent such a change resulting in a right to settlement, and their right to seek employment was restricted.

Criticism of the rules came from an unexpected source. British wives living abroad (in Egypt or the United States, for example) who might wish to return to the United Kingdom to settle with their husbands lobbied Conservative backbenchers who, in turn, put pressure on the government. The government amended the rules so that the right of entry was extended to husbands and fiancés whose wives or fiancées had been born in, or had one parent born in, the United Kingdom, provided that the primary purpose of the marriage was not settlement. Also, elderly dependants would be allowed to enter Britain providing they were wholly maintained by their children or grandchildren. These new immigration rules were approved on March 10, 1980. The rule allowing entry to husbands and fiancés — provided the primary purpose of the marriage was not settlement in Britain — became the basis for refusing entry to many Asian spouses, mainly from the Indian subcontinent.

The major political commitment that the 1979–1983 Thatcher government fulfilled was the legislation on British nationality. The feudal and imperial concept of British subject had already been undermined; postwar immigration legislation meant that most British subjects no longer had the right to immigrate to the United Kingdom — though if resident in Britain, they could vote, stand for Parliament, work in the public service, and serve in the armed forces. The way to resolve these contradictions, it was felt, was to create a narrower and more realistic British citizenship. Because discrimination by sovereign states in favor of their own citizens was acceptable in international law, the new citizen-

ship would enable the government to cut many of its imperial obligations and at the same time make it more difficult for critics to accuse it of
operating racist immigration laws. A Conservative Party policy document published in March 1980 states: "Future immigration policies, if
they are to be sensible, realistic and fair, must be founded on a separate
citizenship of the UK and it is therefore essential that a reformed law of
nationality should for the first time make it clear who are the citizens"
(Conservative Political Centre 1980). In the longer term, the government
was also concerned about the prospect of increasing pressure to immigrate coming from Hong Kong after the British lease on most of the territory ran out in 1997.

The British Nationality Act (1981) marked a crucial break with Britain's imperial past. The three categories of citizenship that emerged—
British citizenship, citizenship of the dependant territories, and British
overseas citizenship—show how difficult the unscrambling was, though
a neater solution could easily have been achieved.[5] This landmark act
moved British nationality legislation closer to that of neighbor countries
and confirmed Britain's intention to divest itself of its imperial legacy
and obligations. The consequence was a stampede for registration and
naturalization by immigrants settled in Britain. Naturalization and registration applications rose from 38,000 in 1979 to 96,000 in 1982, despite a
substantial rise in fees.[6]

The first Thatcher government did reduce immigration through its
legislative and administrative actions, but only marginally. The government claimed, nevertheless, that it had an effective policy compared with
its Labour predecessor, that it had reduced immigration, and that it had
actively pursued illegal immigrants and overstayers. Its policies, it
claimed, were "firm but fair." They were certainly firm, but they were
fair only to those who opposed New Commonwealth immigration. They
were unfair to dependants, spouses, and refugees legally entitled to enter
Britain but who were refused admission or kept waiting for years so that
the government could claim political credit for reducing the immigration
statistics.

After 1983 the focus of immigration policy switched to refugees. Following the Tamil crisis in May 1985, the government imposed a visa
regime on Sri Lanka; this was extended under pressure from immigra-

---

[5] One result of the British Nationality Act was that male and female citizens were to
be treated equally under the immigration rules.

[6] Naturalization fees rose from £90 in 1979 to £300 in April 1982, and those for registration, from £37.50 to £70.

tion officers in 1986 to Bangladesh, Ghana, India, Nigeria, and Pakistan. In 1987 the Immigration (Carrier's Liability) Act made it an offense for airlines or shipping companies to bring people to the United Kingdom without proper documents, and it required these companies to enforce immigration laws and visa regulations or face a fine of £1,000 per passenger. This was to prove an increasingly intolerable burden on airlines, some of whose passengers used sophisticated forgeries or destroyed their documents during their flight.

In 1988 a new immigration bill was passed to keep control "in good repair." The absolute right of men who had settled in Britain before 1973 to bring their families was repealed. The European Court of Human Rights had ruled that this right discriminated against women, so by abolishing the right for men, both sexes were treated equally (badly). The right now became contingent on showing that dependants would receive adequate accommodation and financial support. Certain rights of appeal against refusal of entry and against deportation were restricted. Overstaying was made a continuing criminal offense, and the entry of second or subsequent wives in a polygamous marriage was banned, a provision that accorded well with Margaret Thatcher's known views. Douglas Hurd, the home secretary, confirmed the government's position in the debate: "Polygamy is not an acceptable social custom in this country" (Parliamentary Debates [Commons], col. 285, November 16, 1987).

THE SALMAN RUSHDIE AFFAIR

In late 1988 British Muslims became actively involved in a campaign to ban *The Satanic Verses*, by Salman Rushdie, which they regarded as a blasphemous attack on the Islamic faith. The book was published in September, and on December 2, Muslim groups turned to direct action; seven thousand demonstrators in Bolton burned a copy of the book to gain publicity, but with little success. On January 14, 1989, another copy of the book was burned at a protest meeting outside Bradford Town Hall. This time the protest was widely reported and condemned.

One month later the campaign against *The Satanic Verses* took a dramatic turn when the Ayatollah Khomeini urged Muslims throughout the world to execute Rushdie: "I inform the proud Muslim people of the world that the author of *The Satanic Verses* book, which is against Islam, the Prophet and the Koran, and all those involved in its publication who were aware of its content, are sentenced to death" (*London Evening Standard*, February 14, 1989).

Western countries immediately condemned the Ayatollah's *fatwa*, and Salman Rushdie went into hiding. Some Muslim leaders—those in Bradford, for example—supported the death sentence, but the Council of Mosques in Britain condemned the violence and urged Muslims to obey the law. On February 18, 1989, Rushdie apologized for the distress he had caused to Muslims, but the Ayatollah did not accept his apology. On February 21 the British government, with the support of the European Community, withdrew its diplomats from Tehran and sent Iran's representative home.

On February 24 Home Secretary Hurd addressed Muslims in the Central Mosque in Birmingham. He accepted that Muslims had been deeply hurt by the book, but he warned that violence or the threat of violence was wholly unacceptable and that nothing would do more damage to racial harmony than the idea that British Muslims were indifferent to the rule of law in Britain (*Independent*, February 25, 1989).

The campaign against *The Satanic Verses* raised concern about the influence of Islamic fundamentalism in Britain and Muslim groups' efforts to set up their own educational institutions, especially single-sex schools for girls. In July 1989, John Patten, minister of state at the Home Office responsible for race relations, spoke of the need for the Muslim community to integrate into British society. In a letter to the Advisory Council on Race Relations, he wrote: "One cannot be British on one's own exclusive terms or on a selective basis" (*Independent*, July 20, 1989).

Those sympathetic to the Muslim campaign—including some members of Parliament with Muslim electors—deplored the fact that the blasphemy laws applied only to Christianity, and they condemned the unwillingness of many liberals to understand the intensity of the offense to practicing Muslims. Some argued that British Muslims felt their values were being eroded in a hostile society, that only through extreme actions could they gain the attention of the media and politicians, and generally that their customs were not respected in British society.

The Rushdie affair brought the peaceful, hardworking Muslim community into considerable political prominence. Former home secretary Roy Hattersley argued forcefully that the proposition that Muslims are welcome in Britain if, and only if, they stop behaving like Muslims is incompatible with the principles of a free society, but in a free society the Muslim community can be allowed to do whatever it likes only as long as the choice it makes is not damaging to society as a whole (*Independent*, July 21, 1989). Although issues of concern to Muslims such as education, problems of adjusting to British society, and the role of the Islamic faith in a liberal secular country now receive greater attention, the campaign against *The Satanic Verses* was largely unsuccessful in achieving any concessions to Muslim demands.

Following the Rushdie affair, the immigration policy focus switched to the surging numbers of asylum seekers, and the administrations led by John Major responded by introducing the Asylum and Immigration Appeals Act 1993 and the Asylum and Immigration Act 1996. Both of these acts were intended to reduce asylum applications and expedite the asylum process.

THE SOCIAL TRANSFORMATION OF BRITAIN

Postwar immigration has dramatically transformed the ethnic composition of the British population. Official estimates put the 1953 nonwhite population at around 50,000 (Layton-Henry 1992: 10–11). By 1991 the minority ethnic population had risen to about 3.1 million, or 5.5 percent of the total population, and by 2001 it was 4 million, or 7.1 percent of the total. Between 1992–1994 and 1997–1999, the minority ethnic population increased by half a million (15 percent), while the white population increased by 450,000 (1 percent). The Indian population is the largest minority ethnic group (table 8.2), followed by Pakistanis, black Caribbeans, black Africans, and Bangladeshis (Office of National Statistics 2001).

The minority ethnic community is a very young population. While half of the white population is aged thirty-seven or less, half of the minority ethnic community is aged twenty-six or younger. Half of the minority ethnic population was born in the United Kingdom, although for children aged fourteen or less the figure is 90 percent. Fertility rates vary considerably for different groups: people of Indian origin increased by only 4 percent between 1992–1994 and 1997–1999, while the Pakistani population grew by 13 percent, Bangladeshis by 30 percent, and black Africans by 37 percent. Mixed groups also grew very rapidly; "black mixed" grew by 49 percent and "other mixed" by 28 percent.

Minority ethnic populations are geographically concentrated within the United Kingdom, with 96.8 percent living in England. Forty-nine percent live in London, where they comprise 28 percent of all residents. Other major centers of minority ethnic population are Leicester (28.5 percent), Slough (27.7 percent), Birmingham (21.5 percent), Luton (19.8 percent), Wolverhampton (18.6 percent), and Bradford (15.6 percent). The minority ethnic population is thus heavily concentrated in urban areas. London is by far the greatest source of attraction; four-fifths of all Bangladeshis and three-fifths of black Africans live there.

Table 8.2. Britain's Population by Ethnic Group, 1992–1994, 1997–1999, and 2000

	Population (1000s)			As Percent of Total Minority Ethnic Population, 2000
	1992–94	1997–99	2000	
Black Caribbean	509	508	529	13
Black African	263	362	440	11
Black other (non-mixed)	80	121	129	3
Black mixed	123	183	176	4
Indian	900	936	984	24
Pakistani	535	605	675	17
Bangladeshi	183	238	257	6
Chinese	146	154	149	4
Other Asian (non-mixed)	157	200	242	6
Other other (non-mixed)	124	158	219	5
Other mixed	184	235	239	6
All minority ethnic groups	3,204	3,700	4,039	100
White	52,563	53,010	53,004	
Total population	55,780	56,724	57,057	
All minority groups as percent of total	5.7	6.5	7.1	

Source: Office of National Statistics 2001.

INDICATORS OF INTEGRATION

Indicators of integration provide a very mixed picture. Table 8.3 presents the responses of random samples of the electorate to a question in the 1997 British Election Survey: "Are you a British citizen?"

Figures on citizenship show high levels of British citizenship among all groups apart from black Africans. If we include dual nationals, then all the major groups, apart from black Africans, had citizenship rates of

85 percent or more. The low rate among black Africans probably reflects the fact that this group includes significant numbers of students, graduate trainees, temporary residents, and asylum seekers awaiting decision on their claims.

To enhance the value of British citizenship, the government is promoting the teaching of citizenship and democracy as part of the national curriculum, arguing that "we want British citizenship positively to embrace the diversity of background, culture and faiths that is one of the hallmarks of Britain in the 21st century." The home secretary is proposing to promote British citizenship by speeding up the process of acquisition, preparing people for citizenship by language training and citizenship education, and celebrating the acquisition of citizenship through citizenship ceremonies and a modernized oath of allegiance (Home Office 2001: 29–36). Applications for naturalization rose from 38,000 in 1990 to 61,000 in 2000. However, citizenship is only one indicator of integration; access to good jobs and housing are at least equally important.

The fourth national survey of minority ethnic communities found considerable divergence between major ethnic groups in terms of employment and housing. Chinese men and women were much more likely than white men and women to be in professional, managerial, and employer positions. African Asian men were in a position of parity, although African Asian women were only three-quarters as likely to hold such a position. Pakistanis and Bangladeshis, in contrast, were found to be severely disadvantaged. They are disproportionately in manual work, especially semiskilled work. Bangladeshis are well represented in self-employment but only because of their concentration in the restaurant trade. In 1994 Bangladeshi and Pakistani men had unemployment rates of about 40 percent, the highest of all groups and two and one-half times higher than that of white men (Modood and Berthoud 1997).

Only a third as many Pakistani women and only a tenth as many Bangladeshi women are in paid work compared with other women. This is a result of these women's low levels of economic activity as well as high levels of unemployment. Modood and his colleagues found severe and widespread poverty among these groups, with over 80 percent of Pakistani and Bangladeshi households receiving an income of half the national average (Modood and Berthoud 1997). They were also the most residentially segregated minority ethnic group and the worst housed, concentrated in inner-city terraced housing. Six out of ten Bangladeshi women and nearly half of Pakistani women do not speak English or have only limited English language skills.

Table 8.3. Citizenship in Britain by Ethnic Group, 1997 (percentages)

				Ethnic Group			
	White	Indian	Pakistani	Bangladeshi	Black African	Black Caribbean	Other
Yes, British citizen	97.1	85.9	82.6	77	50.0	92.0	80.9
No, citizen of another country	2.3	13.7	14.0	14.8	42.9	5.0	18.1
Dual nationality	0.6	0.4	3.3	8.2	7.1	3.0	1.1
Total percent	100.0	100.0	100.0	100.0	100.0	100.0	100.0
Number in sample	2,481	284	121	61	70	100	94

Source: Saggar 2000: 97.

Indians and Caribbeans occupy a middle position. Indians are well represented in professional and managerial categories and other junior nonmanual positions. Surprisingly, Caribbean men earn 90 percent of white male employees' earnings, and Indians, 85 percent. Caribbean women do well in the labor market. They are much less likely than white women to be in manual work or part-time work, and most likely to be in junior nonmanual positions. Indian women are more likely to be in manual work. Caribbeans are very unlikely to be self-employed, while Indians are 50 percent more likely than whites to be self-employed. Both Indians and Caribbeans receive higher financial returns than whites from self-employment. The average Indian household has a slightly higher income than the average white household, largely because the white household average is pulled down by the large numbers of white pensioners. Caribbean households are 25 percent worse off than whites. Indians have improved their position in the housing market, with high rates of home ownership and parity with whites in owning detached and semidetached property. Caribbeans have improved their housing position but from a low base (Modood and Berthoud 1997).

THE POLICY OF THE BLAIR GOVERNMENT

Since the early 1960s the Labour Party, both in government and in opposition, has generally espoused immigration policies as tough as those of the Conservatives. This was largely for electoral reasons. Immigration appeared to cause anxiety among the electorate and hence could be exploited by right-wing politicians to the disadvantage of the Labour Party. Moreover, it was an issue that was thought to have major electoral impacts (Studlar 1978: 46–72; Miller 1980: 15–38). Labour Party leaders were determined, therefore, to neutralize immigration as an election issue as far as possible, and they maintained a firm stance on immigration controls until 2001.

However, even before Labour was returned to office in 1997, there were influential voices pressing for a reassessment of immigration and asylum policy. Inside the Labour constellation, the Institute for Public Policy Research was arguing for an approach to immigration that would stress its economic contribution to the British economy (Spencer 1994a, 1994b). In May 1996 the *Economist* urged the Conservative government to change its negative stance on immigration and asylum, arguing that the Asylum and Immigration Bill 1996 was preventing deserving asylum seekers—many of whom possessed valuable skills that would be useful to the British economy—from entering the United Kingdom. The *Econo-mist* called for an immigration policy that was in the national interest and served the needs of the domestic economy. Immigration could contribute to the skill base of the population, meet the needs of employers, and contribute to gross domestic product (*The Economist*, May 4, 1996). More recently, the London *Times* demanded an end to Britain's "absurd" im-migration policy which allows millions of pounds' worth of strawberries and cherries to rot in the fields when a buoyant labor market leaves farmers short of the fruit pickers needed for the harvest. The *Times* also criticized new rules limiting the issuing of work permits to foreign stu-dents after they complete their studies and banning asylum seekers from employment (*Times*, July 17, 2000)..

The Labour government's initial response to pressures to adopt a more positive approach to immigration was cautious. According to the party's 1997 general election manifesto,

> Every country must have firm control over immigration and
> Britain is no exception. There are, rightly, criteria for those who
> want to enter this country to join husband or wife; we will en-
> sure that these are properly enforced. We will, however, re-
> form the system in current use to remove the arbitrary and un-
> fair results that can follow from the existing "primary
> purpose" rule. There will be a streamlined system of appeals
> for visitors denied a visa (Labour Party 1997).

In July 1998, the new home secretary, Jack Straw, published a white paper (Home Office 1998) that reflected the tough stance he had taken on immigration and asylum issues while Labour was in opposition. It em-phasized the need for administrative reforms to speed up decision mak-ing on asylum applications and appeals. It promised efficient enforce-ment of immigration rules and proposed measures to deter "bogus" asylum seekers, including a reduction in cash benefits and the introduc-tion of vouchers. Straw claimed that the government was committed to giving protection to genuine refugees and supporting family reunifica-tion for those legally settled in the United Kingdom, but the emphasis of the white paper was on control and enforcement (Parliamentary Reports [Commons], July 27, 1998, cols. 35–38). Opposition spokesman Sir Norman Fowler suggested that there was a discrepancy between the home secre-tary's tough words and actions such as the abolition of the Primary Pur-pose Rule, on the one hand, and, on the other, the suggestion that he might use his discretionary powers to reduce the backlog of asylum seekers awaiting a decision on their claim by granting exceptional leave to remain to some people who had had a long wait (Parliamentary Reports [Commons], July 27, 1998, cols. 38–40).

The assumptions underlying the government's approach at this time were similar to those of previous Conservative and Labour administrations. The first assumption is that states have an absolute right to determine which noncitizens should be allowed to enter and remain within the state's territory. Immigration control is thus natural and sensible. Every state has the right to refuse entry to people without a legitimate reason for entry or who might act against the interests of the state by, for example, committing crimes or failing to support themselves (Home Office 1998: 13).

A second assumption, almost a national myth, is that Britain, a small and overcrowded island, is relatively prosperous in world terms, so it is very attractive to immigrants, particularly those from the Third World. Immigration controls are thus necessary to manage immigration in the national interest and, in particular, to prevent the rise of popular opposition to immigration due to fears of threats to the "national character" or to the hard-won benefits of the welfare state. This is a somewhat surprising assumption given that emigration from Britain has historically (though not recently) been higher than immigration and the fact that the British have considerable confidence in their ability to integrate immigrants.[7]

A third assumption underlying immigration policy is the importance and effectiveness of border controls. As an island, Britain has frontiers that are relatively easy to police. Britain—in cooperation with Ireland, with which there is a common travel area—has maintained a system of strict border checks combined with few internal controls. This contrasts with mainland European states whose long land frontiers result in a policy of relaxed border controls and stricter internal controls such as identity checks. These different approaches explain Britain's reluctance to join the Schengen Agreement and its insistence on being exempt from European Union arrangements to abolish internal frontier controls.[8]

---

[7] On occasion, though, this confidence has been challenged, as, for example, by riots in Brixton and Toxteth in 1981, in Handsworth in 1985, and in Oldham, Burnley, and Bradford in 2001.

[8] The Treaty of Amsterdam confirmed that Britain could continue to maintain its frontier controls at the borders of other European Union states.

British confidence in the policy of strict border controls has declined recently. The policy has not, for example, prevented a large rise in asylum applications. The scale of passenger and freight traffic is now so large that strict border controls are no longer possible. Strict controls would be hugely disruptive for visitors, tourists, businessmen, haulage companies, and other legitimate travelers. As it is, immigration officers are frequently criticized for refusing entry to visitors – usually visitors from Third World countries such as Zimbabwe, South Africa, India, and the Caribbean (*Independent*, February 27, 2002).

Attempts to prevent the Eurostar train and truck drivers from bringing undocumented asylum seekers to the United Kingdom from France have been controversial and only partly effective. The extension of carriers' liability legislation made haulage companies liable for fines of £2,000 for every undocumented person they brought into the country. In 2002 Eurotunnel won release from this legislation on the grounds that the numbers of people coming through the tunnel had fallen sharply. Perhaps of greater significance were Eurotunnel's losses of £132 million, which suggested that the company could not afford to pay these fines. Eurotunnel accused the British and French governments of undermining the company's business by failing to resolve the problem of asylum seekers trying to enter the tunnel to reach the United Kingdom (*Independent*, February 12 and March 13, 2002).

A fourth and frequently made assumption is that strict immigration controls are necessary for good race relations. This assumption found expression in the formula expounded by Roy Hattersley: "Integration without control is impossible, but control without integration is indefensible" (Parliamentary Reports [Commons], March 23, 1965, cols. 378–85). There was widespread support for this view in Parliament, including from opposition spokesman Sir Norman Fowler during the debate on the Immigration and Asylum bill in July 1998 (Parliamentary Reports [Commons], July 27, 1998, col. 38). In a similar vein, the government white paper announced as one of its policy principles that "the Government believes that a policy of fair, fast and firm immigration control will help to promote race equality" (Home Office 1998: 15), though there was no explanation of how this could be achieved. Presumably both government and opposition feel that the electorate needs reassurance that immigration is in the national interest and poses no threat to employment or welfare provision.

There is a difficulty with this assumption: although no government has admitted that immigration controls are largely intended to control nonwhite immigration, the history of postwar controls makes this clear (Paul 1997). Many authors have noted the inconsistency in a government policy that discriminates on racial grounds at points of entry while seeking to outlaw racial discrimination against those legally settled in the country (Spencer 1994a: 307–21). This was forcefully argued by Bernard Levin: "You cannot by promising to remove the cause of fear and resentment fail to increase both. If you talk and behave as though black men were some kind of virus that must be kept out of the body politic, then it is the shabbiest hypocrisy to preach racial harmony at the same time" (*Times*, February 14, 1978).

The transformation of public discourse and debate is thus very recent. It is being led by the Home Office and driven by labor market demand, particularly in London and the southeast of England, and by skills shortages in key areas such as health services, teaching, and information technology. Political considerations—such as easing public fears over immigration—are important as well. The Home Office is also keen to encourage integration and avoid further riots. According to the home secretary, "Migration is an inevitable reality of the modern world and it brings significant benefits. But to ensure that we sustain the positive contribution of migration to our social well-being and economic prosperity, we need to manage it properly and build firmer foundations on which integration with diversity can be achieved" (Home Office 2001).

The Home Office has sponsored research in the area of migration, in particular to measure its economic impact, so that it can publicize migration's contribution to the British economy. In 1999–2000, migrants contributed an estimated £31.2 billion in taxes and consumed £28.8 billion in benefits, resulting in a net contribution of £2.4 billion to the economy (Gott and Johnson 2002: iii). Maintaining social stability and electoral success are also key goals of government policy.

A final issue that is causing a favorable reassessment of immigration in public discourse is the aging of the British population.[9] Although the impact of aging on society and the labor market is not well understood, it is assumed that older people depend on the working population for care and support, in particular for the economic production that ensures that pensions can be paid and health care and social costs met. Young people are also seen as a force for innovation, and many commentators see increased immigration as the way for aging industrialized countries to redress the age balance of their populations (*Independent*, April 10,

---

[9] Between 2000 and 2025, the number of people in the United Kingdom over sixty years of age will rise from 12.2 million to 17.6 million.

2002). Given that immigration makes only a tiny contribution to total population, these hopes are unrealistic yet the argument is frequently raised in public discourse.

RECENT IMMIGRATION PATTERNS

Migration statistics in the United Kingdom employ widely differing concepts and definitions (Dobson et al. 2001: 39). The most widely used source is the International Passenger Survey (IPS) which defines a migrant as "a person who has resided abroad for a year or more and who states on arrival the intention to stay in the UK for a year or more." This includes returning British citizens as well as people who are not British. The Labor Force Survey (LFS) provides data on foreign-born workers as well as people born overseas who, although they were migrants, may be British or have become British though naturalization. The census also provides data on people born overseas, but it does not provide data on migration.

Estimates from the IPS show that the United Kingdom has been a net immigration country since 1983. The emigration of British citizens has been more than compensated for by the immigration of non-British nationals. Since the late 1990s, net immigration has contributed more to the British population than natural increase.

Immigration grew rapidly in the late 1980s and dramatically in the late 1990s (table 8.4). Inflows of New Commonwealth citizens were stable until the late 1980s and then steady at a higher level until 1999. European Union migration is strongly influenced by flows from Ireland, which has always been a major source of migrants to Britain. Old Commonwealth migration was fairly stable until the late 1990s, when it rose significantly. Citizens of other foreign countries generally rose throughout the period, especially during 1998–1999.

Emigration has been remarkably stable during 1981–1999, averaging 230,000 people per year (table 8.5). Generally, the emigration of British citizens is greater than that of non-British, with the exception of 1998 and 1999, when this pattern was reversed due particularly to a large rise in the emigration of all groups except New Commonwealth citizens. The outflow of European Union citizens depends very much on the strength of the Irish economy relative to that of the British. One surprising factor is the low rate of emigration of New Commonwealth citizens, which, against the general trend, shows a decline in 1998–1999.

There was a net positive immigration of non-British citizens every year between 1981 and 1999, and a net emigration of British citizens every year except for 1985, 1994, and 1998 (table 8.6). Each year since 1983, net inflows of foreign citizens exceeded 60,000, rising strongly after 1994–1995, when intakes were over 126,000, and reaching 190,000 in 1999.

The United Kingdom has the third largest foreign population in Western Europe, after Germany and France. However, the figures are very modest as a proportion of total population, averaging 3.3 percent since 1984. The corresponding figure for Germany, for example, has been between 7 and 9 percent since 1980, and for France, between 6 and 7 percent. Migrants to the United Kingdom are predominantly young people (between the ages of fifteen and twenty-four), reflecting the large numbers of overseas students and working holiday makers, a scheme developed to attract young people from Commonwealth countries such as Australia, Canada, New Zealand, and South Africa.

Immigrants to the United Kingdom are highly skilled. Two-thirds come from "high-income" countries, and some 60 percent enter professional or managerial occupations. Between 1995 and 1999, the United Kingdom gained some 100,000 professional and managerial people and 50,000 manual and clerical workers. A large and growing proportion of workers entering and leaving the United Kingdom were from European Economic Area (EEA) countries and the Old Commonwealth. Foreign workers tend to take jobs in a variety of occupations such as financial services, information technology, manufacturing, transport and communications, hotels and catering, health care, and education.

Most entry categories of people coming to the United Kingdom from outside the European Economic Area in 1995 and 2000 show a large rise over the period (table 8.7). Students are by far the largest group of entrants, with 313,000 entries, or some 52 percent of the total. There is also a large number of students from European countries who are not included in these figures. This shows the attractiveness of English language acquisition and also the strenuous efforts of the government and British universities to recruit overseas students.

The numbers of holders of work permits for more than twelve months have risen strongly. Some 104,000 new work permits were issued in 2001, a large increase over the 80,000 in 2000 (Home Office 2001). In addition, 33,000 extensions and changes of employment were granted to existing permit holders, largely to meet skills shortages in health care, education, and information technology. This category also includes internal transfers within international companies with branches in the

Table 8.4. Immigration to the United Kingdom by Citizenship, 1981–1999 (1000s)[a]

	All	British	Non-British	European Union	Old Commonwealth[a]	New Commonwealth	Other Foreign
1981	164.5	60.0	104.5	11.0	15.3	40.0	39.2
1982	215.8	98.0	117.8	18.0	16.3	43.4	41.1
1983	218.1	95.0	123.1	14.0	17.8	48.4	45.0
1984	234.7	95.4	139.3	33.8	20.6	42.8	42.0
1985	266.9	109.7	157.2	39.6	27.7	42.9	47.0
1986	287.9	120.3	167.6	54.0	22.1	42.4	49.0
1987	257.4	98.8	158.7	51.9	23.2	43.5	40.0
1988	273.4	89.2	184.2	63.2	25.5	40.9	54.5
1989	314.3	104.4	209.8	63.1	31.8	56.5	58.4
1990	340.2	105.6	234.6	61.4	36.7	59.9	77.6
1991	337.0	116.9	220.1	50.4	29.2	62.5	77.9
1992	286.6	99.5	187.1	41.3	21.1	56.5	68.2
1993	272.2	91.6	180.6	42.4	25.9	49.9	62.5
1994	321.4	117.9	203.5	48.3	23.9	58.8	72.6
1995	320.7	91.3	229.4	59.1	29.5	62.6	78.2
1996	331.4	103.7	227.8	69.5	32.1	52.4	73.8
1997	340.7	96.5	244.2	71.5	34.6	61.7	76.5
1998	401.5	111.3	290.2	77.6	59.9	52.7	99.9
1999	450.0	118.1	331.8	65.7	57.1	66.4	142.6

Sources: Dobson et al. 2001; Home Office. Figures are based on the IPS.

[a] 1984–1999 includes adjustments for asylum seekers and short-term visitors granted an extension; 1981–1983 excludes adjustments for asylum seekers.

[b] Old Commonwealth comprises Australia, New Zealand, Canada, and South Africa.

Table 8.5. Emigration from the United Kingdom by Citizenship, 1981–1999 (1000s)

	All	British	Non-British	European Union	Old Commonwealth	New Commonwealth	Other Foreign
1981	237.3	168.3	69.0	15.0	13.0	16.0	25.0
1982	263.3	191.3	72.0	11.0	13.0	19.0	28.0
1983	189.3	126.3	63.0	12.0	11.0	16.0	25.0
1984	176.9	102.5	74.3	17.9	15.0	15.3	26.2
1985	187.1	108.5	78.7	21.0	17.4	15.7	24.5
1986	229.7	132.0	97.7	24.4	21.8	12.6	39.0
1987	227.3	130.4	96.9	33.6	21.2	12.6	29.6
1988	255.5	143.2	112.4	36.9	18.2	20.8	36.4
1989	223.4	122.2	101.3	34.7	15.4	14.9	36.3
1990	251.9	135.4	116.5	45.9	20.5	13.6	36.5
1991	263.7	136.7	127.1	52.4	19.5	17.3	37.9
1992	251.5	133.4	118.1	52.4	18.1	13.7	50.2
1993	236.8	126.7	110.1	40.0	18.5	15.5	36.1
1994	212.6	108.3	104.3	38.7	16.6	16.1	32.8
1995	212.0	118.0	93.9	36.6	18.2	10.7	28.4
1996	238.4	139.2	99.2	42.7	17.7	13.5	25.2
1997	248.7	130.8	117.9	52.3	20.5	15.8	29.3
1998	223.7	111.2	112.5	47.2	20.6	10.0	34.7
1999	268.5	126.5	141.9	58.4	32.7	9.7	45.3

Sources: Dobson et al. 2001; Home Office. Figures are based on the IPS and are adjusted as for table 8.4.

Table 8.6. Net International Migration to the United Kingdom by Citizenship, 1981–1999 (1000s)

	All	British	Non-British	European Union	Old Commonwealth	New Commonwealth	Other Foreign
1981	-72.8	-108.3	35.5	-4.0	2.3	24.0	14.2
1982	-47.5	-93.3	45.8	7.0	3.3	24.4	13.1
1983	28.8	-31.3	60.1	2.0	4.3	33.8	20.0
1984	57.8	-7.1	65.0	15.9	5.6	27.5	15.8
1985	79.8	1.2	78.5	18.6	10.3	27.2	22.5
1986	58.2	-11.7	69.9	29.6	0.3	29.8	10.0
1987	30.1	-31.6	61.8	18.3	2.0	30.9	10.4
1988	17.9	-54.0	71.8	26.3	7.3	20.1	18.1
1989	90.9	-17.8	108.5	28.4	16.4	41.6	22.1
1990	88.3	-29.8	118.1	15.5	16.2	46.3	41.1
1991	73.3	-19.8	93.0	-2.0	9.7	45.2	40.0
1992	35.1	-33.9	69.0	5.2	3.0	42.8	18.0
1993	35.4	-35.1	70.5	2.4	7.4	34.4	26.4
1994	108.8	9.6	99.2	9.6	7.3	42.7	39.8
1995	108.8	-26.8	135.5	22.5	11.3	52.0	49.8
1996	93.1	-35.5	128.6	26.8	14.3	38.9	48.5
1997	92.0	-34.3	126.3	19.2	14.1	45.8	47.2
1998	177.8	0.1	177.6	30.5	39.3	42.7	65.2
1999	181.5	-8.4	189.9	7.4	28.6	56.6	97.3

Sources: Dobson et al. 2001; Home Office. Figures are based on the IPS and are adjusted as for table 8.4.

Table 8.7. Non–European Economic Area Nationals Given Entry to the United Kingdom

Purpose of Journey	Number of Journeys	
	1995	2000
Students	285,000	313,000
Work permit holders for more than 12 months	11,700	36,300
Work permit holders for less than 12 months	26,100	30,800
Agricultural workers	4,660	10,100
Working holiday makers	36,000	38,500
UK grandparent ancestry	6,620	11,000
Domestic employee	11,800	14,300
Au pair	11,700	12,900
Investors	10	50
Family reunion with other dependants	48,400	74,200
Accepted for settlement on arrival	2,400	2,290
Asylum seekers and their dependants	3,700	11,400
Others	51,200	48,000
Total	499,290	602,840

Source: Home Office 2001: 25.

United Kingdom. The Home Office has prioritized the granting of work permits to assist employers and has greatly improved turnaround times for decisions on work permit applications; 90 percent of applications are now reportedly decided within twenty-four hours (Home Office 2001).

People entering the United Kingdom by other routes are also entitled to work, so that in 2000 some 35,700 people from the European Union entered the United Kingdom to work, as did 1,180 ministers of religion. People entering for family unification or whose asylum claims are accepted are also entitled to work. Overseas students who graduate in the United Kingdom may be allowed to switch into employment, especially if they have skills that are in short supply. Also, under the working holiday maker scheme, some 40,000 young Commonwealth citizens are allowed to come for an extended two-year holiday and can take incidental employment to fund their stay. These relatively well educated visitors are regarded as a temporary, flexible workforce (Home Office 2001: 45).

The size of the foreign labor force in the United Kingdom is difficult to estimate. According to calculations by the Organisation for Economic Co-operation and Development, in 1988 the foreign labor force was 871,000, or 3.4 percent of the total British labor force; the figure rose to 1,039,000 in 1998, or 3.9 percent of the total labor force.

ILLEGAL IMMIGRATION AND EMPLOYMENT

By its very nature, illegal immigration is secretive, and it is impossible to gauge its extent. Most illegal workers probably entered the United Kingdom legally as visitors, students, working holiday makers, or asylum applicants and then violated their conditions of stay by overstaying or failing to apply for a work permit. It has generally been assumed that the numbers of illegal immigrants and workers in the United Kingdom have been relatively small. However, the buoyant demand for labor, especially in London, in the late 1990s attracted people and people smugglers. The number of persons detected trying to evade border controls rose from 3,300 in 1990 to over 47,000 in 2000. Although this may be due in part to more efficient and sophisticated methods of detection, it strongly suggests a surge in illegal immigration. The Home Office (2001: 75–81) believes 75 percent of detected cases involve organized smuggling. The desperation of would-be immigrants can be seen in the tragic deaths of fifty-eight young Chinese men who suffocated in June 2000 in the back of a container truck, trying to evade immigration controls at the port of Dover.

Illegal working is assumed to be greatest in sectors where labor demand is high but wages are low, such as catering, cleaning, and hospitality. Other frequently mentioned areas are construction and seasonal work in agriculture. These are all areas where employers are known to use subcontractors to hire workers and thus evade the obligations imposed on them by legislation.

The Asylum and Immigration Act 1996 makes it illegal for employers knowingly or negligently to employ people who do not have permission to work. A penalty of up to £5,000 can be imposed on employers for each illegal employee, if the case is proved. Employers can establish a defense by proving they were shown an approved document such as a passport or work permit that they believed to be genuine. These measures have not been effective, and successful prosecutions have been few: one in 1998, nine in 1999, and twenty-three in 2000 (Home Office 2001: 78–79).

ASYLUM SEEKERS

In the last fifteen years, the most controversial immigration issue has been asylum seekers. The daily ritual of people from the Sangatte camp near Calais, France, risking injury and death as they attempt to board freight trains entering the Channel Tunnel has received regular "crisis" coverage in the media. Politicians from the major parties vie with each other to reassure the public that the right of asylum is not a weak link in an otherwise vigorously maintained immigration regime. Modest rises in asylum applications have been met with tough responses, including the imposition of visa requirements on countries from which asylum seekers come and the imposition of carriers' liability on airlines and shippers for improperly documented persons they bring to the United Kingdom.

The tough response is also reflected in the treatment that asylum seekers receive once inside the country. Some are held in detention centers while their cases are being heard. Fast track procedures are used for manifestly inappropriate or fraudulent claims, and the government drew up a "white list" of countries from which asylum seekers were assumed not to face serious risk of persecution, so that applicants from these countries could be speedily returned. The government has also experimented with vouchers rather than cash payments to help asylum seekers cover basic costs, fingerprinting to deter multiple applications, and a dispersal policy to relieve local authorities in London and southeast England from the disproportionate costs of housing asylum seekers.

The policy of detaining asylum seekers in privately run centers or in prisons has provoked questions regarding the appropriateness of treating asylum seekers like convicted criminals. In 1998 the chief inspector of prisons, after describing government policy as a complete and utter shambles, urged government ministers to create an immigration detention service. He described conditions at the Campsfield Detention Centre near Oxford as unsafe and unsound, and he argued that a prison regime was not right for asylum seekers and detainees,[10] particularly for women and young people (*Times*, March 16, 1998; *Independent*, April 17, 1998).

Traditionally Britain has received far fewer asylum seekers than other European countries of comparable size and population, such as France or Germany. As recently as 1985–1988, applications were only 4,000 a year; they rose considerably thereafter, to 38,000 in 1990 and 93,600 in 2000.

The reaction of successive British governments to the rise in applications has been to reaffirm refugee rights to asylum while at the same time doing everything possible to prevent asylum seekers from arriving at the borders and registering a claim. In July 1998, when introducing his white paper to the House of Commons, Home Secretary Jack Straw said, "The Government are determined to maintain firm control over immigration but to do so in a way that meets our international obligations and our commitment to strengthening human rights," adding, "we will continue scrupulously to observe our international obligations to protect genuine refugees ... but many claims for asylum are made by those seeking to migrate for purely economic reasons or as a means of prolonging a stay in the United Kingdom without legitimate reason" (Parliamentary Reports [Commons], July 27, 1998, cols. 36–38).

Opposition spokesman Sir Norman Fowler agreed: "In far too many cases, applications for political asylum are a means to evade immigration control.... Three-quarters of asylum applications are refused because they do not meet the requirements of either refugee status or exceptional leave to remain. Only 6% of appeals are successful" (Parliamentary Reports [Commons], July 27, 1998, cols. 38–39).

Asylum seekers form a significant proportion of non-British immigration to the United Kingdom, comprising between a sixth and a third of the total flow (Dobson et al. 2001: 253–60). Although their claims must be dealt with individually and their potential economic contribution to the

---

10 Asylum seekers held in detention stage regular protests, including hunger strikes. In February 2002, detainees burnt down a newly built detention center at Yarl's Wood in Bedfordshire, which cost £100 million to construct (*Independent*, February 18, 2002).

country is not a criterion for granting asylum, they do have the potential to contribute to the labor market. Asylum seekers can apply for permission to work after six months, while awaiting a decision on their claim. They can also work if they gain refugee status or exceptional leave to remain.

Between 1991 and 1999, 39,265 asylum seekers and their dependants were granted refugee status; in 2000 an additional 12,135 principal applicants were granted this status. Between 1990 and 1999, 79,290 asylum seekers were granted exceptional leave to remain, as were 12,645 principal applicants in 2000. All are entitled to work. Between 1990 and 2000, 317,625 applications were refused, and 44,175 people were removed from the United Kingdom. It is not known how many of the remaining rejected asylum seekers left voluntarily. One can assume that a significant number remained and are working illegally (Dobson et al. 2001: 253–60).

There were 80,315 principal applicants for asylum in 2000. The main nationalities were Iraqi, Sri Lankan, Yugoslavian, Iranian, and Afghan. In 2001 there were substantial reductions in applications from Yugoslavians, Chinese, and Iranians but large increases in applications from Afghanistan and Somalia (Home Office 2001: 50).

The government makes every effort to reduce asylum applications and to ensure that Britain is not seen as a "soft touch" for refugees. Yet the rhetoric of politicians is not matched by results. The number of asylum seekers continues to rise, putting a strain on the budgets of some local authorities responsible for providing accommodation for them, and there have been campaigns against asylum seekers in some areas, and even some assaults and a small number of murders.[11]

In November 2001 the *Observer* conducted a survey on race relations in Britain, based on telephone interviews with 2,000 adults. The results were generally positive, but this was not true of the responses on asylum seekers, suggesting that there is little support for accepting larger numbers of asylum seekers and little opposition to the government's tough policies to deter asylum applications (see table 8.8).

---

[11] The local press in parts of Kent were so inflammatory in their reports on asylum seekers that the police warned them they might be charged with incitement to racial hatred (*Independent*, December 12, 1998). In December 2001, Scot Burrell was found guilty of the murder of Firsat Dag, a Kurdish refugee, at the High Court in Glasgow. Mr. Dag's murder was the worst event on the Sighthill estate in Glasgow, where many asylum seekers had been dispersed from the south of England.

Table 8.8. Responses to 2001 Survey on Race Relations in Britain

Questions and Response Choices	Percent in Agreement
Question: "Does Britain's immigration policy allow too many asylum seekers into the country, not enough, or about the right number?"	
Too many	61
Not enough	6
About right	33
Question: "Are asylum seekers treated very poorly, about right or very well?"	
Very poorly	20
About right	44
Very well	36
Question: "Should asylum seekers who don't agree to learn English be sent back home?"	
Agree	52
Disagree	48

Source: *Observer*, November 25, 2001.

INTEGRATION POLICY

British governments have never had a clear philosophy for integrating immigrants and settlers (Favell 1998). This is partly because Britain traditionally saw itself as a country of emigration and has only come to view itself as an immigration country since World War II. Immigration has been seen as essentially a private enterprise operation. People migrate because it is in their interest, and so it is up to them to bear the costs and adapt to their new society. Even if the state encourages immigration, its effort to attract people will succeed only if the benefits for would-be immigrants and their families outweigh the costs. The assumption of British policymakers is that immigrants will assimilate: "A systematic immigration policy could only be welcomed without reserve if the migrants were of good human stock [presumably European] and not prevented by religion or race from intermarrying with the host populations and becoming merged with it" (Royal Commission on Population 1949).

This assumption explains the preference for Irish and other European immigrants. The migration of people from the Caribbean and the Indian subcontinent raised concerns about their acceptance and possible problems of law and order—or social stability and the possibility of ethnic conflict. However, postwar governments failed to appreciate immigration's potential scale and duration, and they were reluctant to invest in schools, housing, and other facilities for immigrants. Integration policy was thus reactive and piecemeal rather than proactive and planned. The government left local authorities to cope with housing and education issues relating to immigration, and only intervened with immigration control legislation in 1962 and race relations legislation in 1965, when immigration and racial discrimination had been forced up the political agenda.

This mixture of immigration control legislation and antidiscrimination legislation was maintained in the 1960s and 1970s so that the acts controlling immigration in 1962, 1968, and 1971 were followed by antidiscrimination acts in 1965, 1968, and 1976. The political demands of opponents of immigration were met by tough immigration control policies, and the demands of liberals and the left for equal treatment and the outlawing of racism and racial discrimination were met by the antidiscrimination laws. Both sides were dissatisfied. The right's opposition to Britain becoming a multiracial, multicultural society was thwarted as high fertility rates, family reunion, and the right of asylum led to rapid expansion of the minority ethnic communities despite tough immigration controls. Liberals and socialists were dissatisfied because they felt that immigration controls discriminated against nonwhite immigrants.

Citizenship and naturalization did not become issues of debate in Britain. Commonwealth citizens were considered British subjects, with full political, social, and civic rights if resident in Britain. Although Ireland left the Commonwealth in 1948, the political rights of Irish people resident in the United Kingdom were continued under the Ireland Act 1949. Thus all the major groups of postwar immigrants had full voting rights on arrival in the United Kingdom. As immigration became a political issue, especially in the 1970s, these communities became politically mobilized and exercised their political rights, especially in support of the Labour Party.

Riots in the 1980s[12] shook the government's complacency, and substantial investment was made in urban renewal projects and reform of

---

[12] There were riots in Brixton and Toxteth in 1981 and in Handsworth in 1985.

methods for policing ethnic minority communities. The focus of concern increasingly became the contrast between formal equality/formal citizenship and the reality of substantial inequalities in terms of high levels of black children excluded from schools, high levels of ethnic minority unemployment, involvement in crime, incarceration in prison, and other issues of social exclusion. The real picture, of course, is much more complex than this stark contrast suggests. Some ethnic minority communities—such as East African Asians, Hindus, Sikhs, and Chinese—appear to be very successful in the education and labor markets, and they experience considerable upward social mobility. Other groups, such as Pakistanis and Bangladeshis, seem to be suffering high levels of poverty, unemployment, and poor housing (Modood and Berthoud 1997).

CONCLUSION: POLICY DILEMMAS

A strong economy and strong demand for labor have altered the discourse on immigration and asylum seekers in Britain. The huge demand for workers, especially skilled professionals, has forced the government to introduce a liberal immigration regime. Employers' organizations and multinational companies have welcomed this policy change. According to John Cridland, deputy director of the Confederation of British Industry, "Immigration has an important role to play in alleviating current skill and labour shortages in specific sectors" (CBI 2002b).

Surprisingly, the new approach to immigration has also been supported by Shadow Home Secretary Oliver Letwin: "The contribution of those who come seeking work, and who are entrepreneurial enough to travel, can be very large. We shouldn't cut off our noses to spite our faces" (*Independent*, April 29, 2002). These arguments, from both the private sector and the public sector, are clear. A report on the National Health Service posits that by 2022–2023 the United Kingdom could face a shortage of 25,000 doctors (Department of Health 2002). The *Independent* has reported that New Zealand refused to permit National Health Service advertisements because it is short of doctors and, further, that Nelson Mandela appealed to Britain to stop poaching South Africa's medical staff (*Independent*, October 22, 2001). Jamaica has also complained that Britain is ransacking its education system by luring away its skilled teachers (*Independent*, March 16, 2002).

Government, opposition, business, and media all realize that Britain is in a highly competitive world market for skilled workers, and this competition may well intensify in the future as advanced industrial countries attempt to meet the challenge of their demographic crises. All Western European states except Ireland have aging populations; countries such as Germany and Italy anticipate substantial population falls unless the aging trend is offset by substantial immigration.

However, this more positive environment for a more liberal immigration regime has not produced a consistently positive discourse. The home secretary in particular has made a sharp distinction between immigrants with valuable skills, recruited legally through the work permit system or through other schemes, and asylum seekers, who have been attacked as illegals seeking to evade immigration controls. To appease public concerns, government has introduced tough policies on asylum seekers, but government ministers are constrained in what they can actually do by the European Convention on Human Rights and the United Nations Convention on Refugees, which are enforced by both the British courts and the European Court. Overall, although few applicants are granted full refugee status, a large number are granted exceptional leave to remain, suggesting that the government recognizes some validity in their claims and that returning them to their home countries would put them at risk. In fact, relatively few of those whose appeals are turned down are actually deported.

There is also a gap between the formal citizenship that almost all members of ethnic minorities have and the higher levels of unemployment, policing, and poor housing that many experience. The riots in Oldham, Burnley, and Bradford in 2001 show that the construction of a multiethnic Britain is not proceeding smoothly across the country. These northern towns have high unemployment, considerable residential segregation, and substantial resentment among the local white population against Pakistani and Bangladeshi residents, whom they view as being favored while they themselves are neglected (Ouseley 2001). The British National Party has mobilized to exploit these anxieties; it won three council seats in Burnley in May 2002. Home Secretary David Blunkett recently claimed that children of asylum seekers were "swamping" some schools, suggesting that the government, despite its huge majority, still feels it must appease popular worries over immigration. Tough political rhetoric is often used to distract attention from sensible liberal policies that politicians fear will be criticized in the popular press.

Prime Minister Tony Blair has emphasized the concept of "joined-up government," but there is no consistency on immigration and asylum. Tough rhetoric goes hand in hand with practical liberal policies. Discriminatory border controls exist side by side with new laws such as the

Race Relations (Amendment) Act 2000, which extends antidiscrimination legislation to promote a multicultural society. A recent white paper, *Secure Borders, Safe Haven: Integration with Diversity in Modern Britain* (Home Office 2001), shows that the home secretary is trying to develop a more consistent and integrated policy that will include immigration, integration, and citizenship. However, even when political and economic conditions favor a more liberal immigration regime with clear positive benefits to the economy, the political management of immigration and asylum remains extremely difficult. Politicians firmly believe, despite the repeated failure of anti-immigration politics at the ballot box, that this issue has the potential to mobilize the electorate. The contemporary success of anti-immigrant parties in parts of Western Europe reinforces this fear. Thus the combination of tough political rhetoric and liberal policy practice is likely to remain a feature of British immigration politics.

References

Butler, David, and Dennis Kavanagh. 2002. *The British General Election of 2001*. New York: Palgrave.

CBI (Confederation of British Industry). 2002a. *CBI Response to the Government's White Paper on Immigration, Asylum and Nationality*, at www.cbi.org.uk, March.

——. 2002b. "CBI Says Migrants Can Help UK Economy," *CBI News Release*, April 7.

Conservative Party. 1979. *The Conservative Party Manifesto*. London: Conservative Central Office.

Conservative Political Centre. 1980. *Who Do We Think We Are?* London: Conservative Central Office

Department of Health. 2002. *Delivering the NHS Plan* (Wanless Report). London: Her Majesty's Stationery Office (HMSO).

Dobson, Janet, Khalid Koser, Gail McLaughlan, and John Salt, with the assistance of J. Clarke, C. Pinkerton, and G. Salt. 2001. *International Migration and the United Kingdom: Recent Patterns and Trends*. London: Home Office.

Favell, Adrian. 1998. *Philosophies of Integration: Immigration and the Idea of Citizenship in France and Britain*. New York: St. Martin's.

Freeman, Gary P. 1994. "Britain, the Deviant Case." In *Controlling Immigration*, edited by Wayne A. Cornelius, Philip L. Martin, and James F. Hollifield. 1st ed. Stanford, Calif.: Stanford University Press.

Gott, Ceri, and Karl Johnson. 2002. *The Migrant Population in the UK: Fiscal Effects*. Research Development and Statistics Occasional Paper No. 77. London: Home Office.

Home Office. 1998. *Fairer, Faster and Firmer: A Modern Approach to Immigration and Asylum*. CM4018, July 27.

————. 2001. *Secure Borders, Safe Haven: Integration with Diversity in Modern Britain*. CM5378.

Labour Party. 1972. *Citizenship, Immigration and Integration: A Policy for the 1970s*. London: Labour Party.

————. 1997. *Labour Party Manifesto*. London: Labour Party.

Layton-Henry, Zig. 1984. *The Politics of Race in Britain*. London: Allen and Unwin.

————. 1992. *The Politics of Immigration: Immigration, "Race," and "Race" Relations in Post-War Britain*. Oxford: Blackwell.

Miller, William Lockley. 1980. "What Was the Profit in Following the Crowd? Aspects of Conservative and Labour Strategy since 1970," *British Journal of Political Science* 10, no.1.

Modood, Tariq, and Richard Berthoud. 1997. *Ethnic Minorities in Britain: Diversity and Disadvantage*. London: Policy Studies Institute.

Office of National Statistics. 2001. *Population Trends* 105 (Autumn).

Ouseley, Herman. 2001. *Community Pride Not Prejudice: Making Diversity Work in Bradford*. Bradford Vision.

Paul, Kathleen. 1997. *Whitewashing Britain: Race and Citizenship in the Postwar Era*. Ithaca, N.Y.: Cornell University Press.

Royal Commission on Population. 1949. Cmnd 7695. London: HMSO.

Saggar, Shamit. 2000. *Race and Representation: Electoral Politics and Ethnic Pluralism in Britain*. Manchester: Manchester University Press.

Spencer, Sarah, ed. 1994a. *Strangers and Citizens: A Positive Approach to Migrants and Refugees*. London: IPPR/Rivers Oram Press.

————. 1994b. *Immigration as an Economic Asset: The German Experience*. Stoke-on-Trent: IPPR/Trentham.

Studlar, Donley T. 1978. "Policy Voting in Britain: The Colored Immigration Issue in the 1964, 1966 and 1970 General Elections," *American Political Science Review* 72.

Tannahill, John Allan. 1958. *European Volunteer Workers in Britain*. Manchester: Manchester University Press.

Worcester, Robert M., and Roger Mortimore. 1999. *Explaining Labour's Landslide*. London: Politico's.

Commentary

Gary P. Freeman

In the first edition of this book, I argued that Britain deviated from the norm of Western democracies in its aspiration to zero immigration and its relative success in deterring unwanted entries. Managing ethnic tensions was the overriding concern, and the Westminster institutional framework made politicians sensitive to popular pressure and gave government extraordinary powers to make policy. Layton-Henry's new survey emphasizes change. Are the changes sufficient to end British exceptionalism? And what explains the evolution of the British experience?

The first notable change is British officials' unprecedented willingness to recruit highly skilled migrants; the second is the rising numbers of asylum seekers and illegal immigrants. Before considering whether this marks the end of Britain's exceptionalism, we need to explain the turnabout in attitudes toward recruiting skilled migration and persistence in opposing illegal migration and asylum seeking, combined with a failure to contain these immigrants' numbers.

Layton-Henry rightly laments the tendency of government and press to conflate immigration and asylum seeking. As analysts we must avoid the same trap. Recruitment of skilled workers and deterrence of unwanted asylum seekers have almost nothing in common.

Immigration is a broad rubric. It encompasses numerous types of migration involving different decision makers, issues, interested actors, and outcomes. Migration policies can be disaggregated into four categories, producing, respectively, concentrated distributive benefits and costs (the allocation of temporary work permits is a good example), diffuse distributive benefits and costs (non-immigrant visas for tourists, for example), redistributive benefits and costs (welfare for immigrants and asylees), and regulatory costs and benefits (such as deterrent measures directed at asylum seekers) (see Freeman 2002). Although the number of temporary work permits annually may vary, it is finite so that their value to the recipient is large. Apart from the individuals receiving them, benefits go most directly to employers. Costs are concentrated on those sectors of the labor force impacted by foreign workers. The main interest groups likely to be involved, therefore, are employers and the trade unions. The general public would hardly be motivated to pay attention, especially when holders of work permits are described as filling "shortages" and otherwise helping Britain win the global competition for brainpower in a knowledge-based economy. Concentrated distributive policies can be expected, therefore, to produce client politics. The decision-making arena is bureaucratic and largely out of public view, and the outcomes are discretionary. Conflict over these matters should be modest, especially if the trade unions lend their assent (Haus 1999; Watts 2002). Given appropriate external economic conditions, policy should be expansive.

Layton-Henry nicely describes the economic context within which Britain moved toward labor recruitment. The British tendency to focus on the management of social tensions has not disappeared, but the political elite believes it is safe to pursue skilled migrants if they are packaged as essential in the new European and global economy.

While temporary labor recruitment generates a clientelist, distributive politics dominated by highly motivated private interests and bureaucrats, asylum seeking produces a mix of redistributive and regulatory politics. The asylum phenomenon ostensibly has little to do with British employers' labor market needs (although many asylum seekers are motivated by economic incentives and end up holding jobs). It is redistributive because of the costs of maintaining asylum seekers and their families while their cases are being adjudicated. It is regulatory because of the border control, policing, and other efforts undertaken to prevent asylum seekers from arriving on shore or to remove those whose cases have been found wanting. The policy arena includes national courts, the police, the foreign office, and border authorities. External actors, at both the European Union and international levels, also participate. The discourse of asylum policy is a rich mix of ideas such as fiscal burden, sponging, sovereignty, national security, queue jumping, bogus claims, people trafficking, human rights, states' obligations to outsiders, due process, and so on. Conflict is intense, often fueled by political entrepreneurs seeking to mobilize public discontent. The rhetoric of policy is likely to be restrictive, but outcomes may not reflect this.

Randall Hansen (this volume) argues that recent asylum figures represent less changes of British intentions or capacity than those of her EU neighbors, especially Germany, that have become less open to refugee claimants. Several additional factors are at work. First, British restrictiveness previously consisted of not taking action—not recruiting temporary workers, not issuing visas for permanent settlement, not meeting obligations to Asians being pushed out of former British colonies in Africa, or not accepting broad interpretations of the rules of family reunification. Except for family reunion (decisions that ran afoul of international conventions), these postures were within the government's discretion and relatively easily implemented. On-shore asylum claims and illegal immigration present a more serious challenge, and we should anticipate a greater gap between intention and outcome. Only Australia has taken a stronger stance or shown greater ability to limit asylum claims than Britain. Second, the opening of the Channel Tunnel created a new avenue for asylum seekers. Finally, the movement toward common policies in the European Union has increased rather than decreased British vulnerability, especially the institution of the border-free zone in 1993, which reduced the frontier barriers for migrants seeking to get to Britain, and the common asylum policy implemented in 1997 (the Dublin Convention) that mandates that asylum claims be heard in the country where they are first lodged. This makes it more difficult for Britain to return asylum applicants to the European Union states through which they have passed.

British policy toward legal skilled migration turned around in response to a dynamic economic environment and political pressures from employers in the private and public sectors. If retained, this removes one of the most striking peculiarities that had made Britain a deviant case. Asylum policy, in contrast, is of a piece with the highly restrictive positions of the past. What has changed is an uncharacteristic failure to approximate closely desired outcomes. Britain is now as vulnerable as its European neighbors to asylum influxes. Layton-Henry criticizes the inconsistency of promoting some sorts of migration while fiercely resisting others. To him, apparently, a migrant is a migrant whatever the circumstances of their arrival. This ignores the political reality that most voters see a major difference between orderly, planned migration and the chaotic, spontaneous migration associated with asylum seeking. Instead of an illogical contradiction, the opening to skilled migrants is precisely conditioned on the parallel attempt to eliminate uninvited and irregular entries. Inflated rhetoric directed at asylum seekers is a central element of the strategic effort to win support for economic migration. The fact that soft policy is often accompanied by tough talk is no surprise; the latter provides the cover for the former (Edelman 1964). Less deviant today than in the past, Britain, in its determination to master its borders, remains among the staunchest advocates of national immigration controls in the European Union.

References

Edelman, Murray. 1964. *The Symbolic Uses of Politics*. Urbana: University of Illinois Press.

Freeman, Gary P. 2002. "Toward a Theory of Migration Politics." Presented at the conference for Europeanists, Council for European Studies, Chicago, March 14–17.

Haus, Leah. 1999. "Labor Unions and Immigration Policy in France," *International Migration Review* 33, no. 3: 683–716.

Watts, Julie R. 2002. *Immigration Policy and the Challenge of Globalization: Unions and Employers in Unlikely Alliance*. Ithaca, N.Y.: Cornell University Press.

Commentary

Randall Hansen

In the early 1990s, Britain stood out as a country that had reduced immigration to an unavoidable core of family reunification and asylum seekers, numbering approximately 50,000 per year. The United Kingdom was Europe's (and the Western world's) closest approximation to a successful zero immigration country. Since then, both policy and policy outcomes have reversed sharply. The Labour government increased the number of work permits issued, promised to reform the Immigration Act of 1971 in order to encourage primary immigration, and "reevaluated" citizenship through the proposed incorporation of citizenship classes, language tests, and naturalization ceremonies. Most striking, asylum applications exploded, rising from 28,000 in 1993 to just under 100,000 in 2000; for the first time ever, Britain (temporarily) overtook Germany as the main European destination of asylum seekers. Fifteen years ago, immigration to the United Kingdom was limited and unwanted; today, "wanted immigration" — that is, skilled migration, is limited but encouraged, and unwanted immigration — asylum seekers — is high. Next to Germany, the United Kingdom is the most important instance in this volume of policy reversal.

The following offers the outlines of a theoretical explanation for this policy reversal. Given that Britain shares its new openness to some forms of migration with most countries of Europe, these nascent insights should apply across the continent. Where the analysis applies exclusively to the United Kingdom concerns its status as a deviant case. Did the United Kingdom really achieve a particularly effective form of immigration control, or was it rather that its "deviancy" somehow traded on the liberality of other liberal democratic states? In other words, was it that the United Kingdom never was "deviant"?

Skilled Immigration

In explaining the United Kingdom's new openness to immigration, Layton-Henry emphasizes the country's economic strength in the late 1990s, the emergence of sector-based skills shortages, and fear of international competition from the United States and the rest of Europe. This emphasis is important because it is a story about markets rather than rights. Scholarship in the 1990s emphasized the constraining effect of domestic constitutions and courts (Hansen 2000; Hollifield 1992; Joppke 1999), on the one hand, and international human rights norms and treaties (Soysal 1994), on the other, on restrictionist executives.

What is happening in the United Kingdom today is *not* a rights-based story. Rather, it is a story with three salient characteristics. First, although it is in some measure an economically determined development, it is not the sort of movement that can be accounted for by an older strain of functionalist/Marxist analysis (Castles and Kosack 1973); such arguments are, however, relevant to the case of asylum. Second, what we are seeing in the British case is the emergence of a sort of "superclass" of international migrants: highly skilled, highly paid economic jetsetters who are able to choose between a set of benefit packages offered by governments instead of companies. It is an important movement but one that is too numerically insignificant to address the demographic concerns highlighted by Layton-Henry. And third, a realistic paradigm is needed to understand this movement. It is not a matter of "losing control" (Sassen 1996), nor is it another form of the "gap" hypothesis. Rather, rationally motivated nation-states have an interest in attracting these migrants and in using regulated forms of migration control to pursue that interest.

Put another way, the two stories that dominated the 1990s — about the beneficent effects of human rights norms and/or about the sovereignty-threatening effect of globalization — get it wrong.

Unskilled Migrants: Asylum Seekers

We are talking about a very different sort of movement in the case of asylum seekers. Within several years of the United Kingdom government rejecting participation in the Schengen Agreement with reference (in part) to its particular success in controlling immigration, asylum applications tripled. Closed borders and deep water no longer suffice. There are nightly reports of asylum seekers clamoring on trains at Calais and slipping through the Channel Tunnel. Whereas the United Kingdom looked very different from other cases in the early to mid-1990s, it has now converged with, and in some measure surpassed, them as a country with a substantial gap between asylum policy (extremely restrictive) and immigration outcomes (large numbers of asylum applications). We need to ask why.

The question divides into two key parts. First, why has the United Kingdom become so attractive? And second, why has immigration control proved ineffective? There are three factors taken to explain the United Kingdom's attractiveness to asylum seekers.

- First, the English language as the world's lingua franca makes the United Kingdom more appealing to the world's migrants.

- Second, the absence of identification cards means that migrants can vanish more easily and, at the same time, acquire without difficulty the forged documents necessary to carve out an existence.

- Third, the United Kingdom's relatively buoyant economy and low unemployment serve as strong "pull" factors.

Taking these factors in reverse order, the last is unquestionably relevant. Home Office officials admit that migrants are not, as politicians and the British gutter press claim, attracted by the prospect of welfare support. A migrant interested in a life of state-supported idleness would do better to choose a country where the sun shines more and life costs less. To understand the dynamics behind economic influences, we need to attend to the continuing relevance of structural inequalities in global capitalism. Here, older functionalist/Marxist analyses are relevant. Two factors pertain: the massive inequalities in the wealth between the rich and the poor world, and the large and (especially in the United States and the United Kingdom) growing inequalities within Western societies. The former make flight attractive; the latter generate the need and possibility for a reserve army of illegal labor prepared to fulfill the mundane, precarious, and ill-paid service-sector jobs necessary to keep the economic machine functioning smoothly.

By contrast, the first two factors play no more than a secondary role for the simple but important reason that they both obtained in the early 1990s, when asylum seekers flooded en masse toward Germany and, to a lesser extent, the rest of continental Europe while simply ignoring the

United Kingdom. It was not hard to see why. At the time, migrants traveling to the United Kingdom met with lower social entitlements, much stricter immigration control, and a greater likelihood of deportation. As Freeman (1994), Joppke (1999), and others (including myself) pointed out, the United Kingdom had the world's most restrictive immigration regime. We also believed that it was the most effective. What seems now to have been the case is that its effectiveness was a function of other countries' relative liberality. That is, if it was easier to obtain access to Germany, as it manifestly was pre-1993, then rational migrants would have little interest in traveling to the United Kingdom. Since then, the waft of restrictions instituted by all European states have meant that the United Kingdom has lost its illiberal deterring effect. In other words, the success of British immigration control depended on another sort of gap: *that between its restrictiveness and others' liberality.* Now that that gap has closed, the United Kingdom looks like any other nation in terms of unwanted immigration. Put another way, the convergence of asylum policy in Europe on a highly restrictive model exposed British deviancy as a chimera.

All of this takes us back to the broader theoretical concerns motivating this volume. The "gap" hypothesis holds that there is a gap between expressed policy aims (little or no immigration) and actual policy outcomes (substantial migration). The hypothesis, or empirical observation, is of little use in the case of skilled migration. European states need skilled migration to solve labor shortages generated by the lag between the evolution of the service economy and that of national education systems. It requires that, to understand this particular form of migration, we refocus attention away from rights and institutions and (back) toward markets, but there is no policy failure requiring explanation.

Asylum, by contrast, is a case par excellence of policy failure: the British government sought to minimize asylum applications; applications went through the roof. This gap between aims and outcomes reflects, as suggested, continental European convergence on British restrictiveness. The asylum case, however, reveals yet another gap: that between asylum decisions (only 10 to 20 percent of asylum applicants are granted asylum, and another 10 percent or so are granted other humanitarian statuses) and deportation of rejected applications (between 5 and 20 percent of total year applications). Accounting for this divergence requires attending to the contradictions generated by liberal democracy itself. As Matthew Gibney and I argue elsewhere (Gibney and Hansen 2001), a series of practical and principled constraints make it extremely difficult for the liberal state to remove more than a fraction of the migrant population reaching its territory. Illiberalism outside the national territory is a function of liberalism within it.

References

Castles, Stephen, and Godula Kosack. 1973. *Immigrant Workers and Class Structure in Western Europe*. London: Oxford University Press.

Freeman, G.P. 1994. "Commentary." In *Controlling Immigration: A Global Perspective*, edited by Wayne A. Cornelius, Philip L. Martin, and James F. Hollifield. 1st ed. Stanford, Calif.: Stanford University Press.

Gibney, Matthew, and Randall Hansen. 2001. "Deportation and the Liberal State." Paper presented at the annual meeting of the International Studies Association, Chicago, February 20–24.

Hansen, Randall. 2000. *Citizenship and Immigration in Postwar Britain: The Institutional Origins of a Multicultural Nation*. Oxford: Oxford University Press.

Hollifield, James F. 1992. *Immigrants, Markets and States*. Cambridge, Mass.: Harvard University Press.

Joppke, Christian. 1999. *Immigration and the Nation-State*. Oxford: Oxford University Press.

Sassen, Saskia. 1996. *Losing Control*. New York: Columbia University Press.

Soysal, Yasemin. 1994. *Limits of Citizenship*. Chicago: University of Chicago Press.

PART IV

Latecomers to Immigration: Italy, Spain, Japan, and South Korea

9

Italy: Economic Realities, Political Fictions, and Policy Failures

Kitty Calavita

Since the republic of Italy was formed in the late 1800s, millions of Italians have emigrated, seeking economic opportunities in virtually every corner of the globe. In the three decades after World War II, over 7 million Italians left Italy, helping to form the labor force that provided the economic boom in European countries to the north (Istat 1980).[1]

In the late 1970s, Italy's migration stream began to reverse course, and by the early 1980s, for the first time, more immigrants entered Italy than left it. The 1981 census showed a net increase in population due both to return migration and to new arrivals (Macioti and Pugliese 1991: 6). Since then, the number of immigrants has increased rapidly, and Italy now has one of the fastest growing immigrant populations in Europe.

Immigration to Italy has undergone several important changes in the last decade, as has the Italian political economy. Perhaps the most important of these are the growing schism between the economies of northern and southern Italy and the correspondingly different economic roles of

---

[1] Four million of these workers returned to Italy periodically as they shuttled back and forth from jobs in northern Europe and elsewhere.

immigrants in those regions; an increase in the proportion of legal immigrants relative to the illegal population, particularly in the north; greater activism on the part of employers in demanding immigrant labor; and a new center-right coalition government that has made immigration control a centerpiece of its political platform.

The public debate over the advantages and disadvantages of immigration and the proper policy response is heated. Italy has one of the lowest birthrates in the world and a rapidly aging population. The increased standard of living over the past three decades means that fewer Italians are willing to work in low-wage jobs, and fewer still are willing to move to economically expanding regions of northern Italy for such jobs. Despite these demographic and economic trends and the role of immigrants in offsetting them, many Italians fear the emerging multiculturalism and view immigrants with suspicion. The debate intensifies with every visible landing of boatloads of immigrants and refugees, as was the case in March 2002, when the arrival in Sicily of a boatload of 928 Iraqi Kurds prompted the government to declare an immigration "state of emergency" (Martirano 2002: 9; Romano 2002: 1).

The data presented here reveal several very broad patterns. First, the new immigration to Italy is largely a labor migration, and it is perceived as such by both immigrants and policymakers, although Italians' reactions to immigrants are often based on social and cultural concerns. Second, Italian immigration policy is characterized by shifts, starts, and impasses. Finally, there is a considerable gap between the announced intention of Italian immigration policy and its outcomes. This chapter presents the latest available statistics on immigration in Italy, the integration of immigrants in Italian society, and the role of immigrants in the economy. It sketches the outlines of Italian immigration policy, and it attempts to account theoretically for its broad patterns.

AN OVERVIEW OF THE IMMIGRANT POPULATION

Italy was transformed from a country of emigration to one of large-scale immigration in part as a consequence of domestic economic growth and the increasing immigration restrictions of its northern European neighbors. The economic discrepancy between Italy and northern Europe had narrowed by the mid-1970s; its per capita income and gross domestic product (GDP) rapidly approached those of the more affluent northern European countries (Venturini 1991: 93–94). The increased employment opportunities and higher wages accompanying this "economic miracle" attracted immigrants from the developing world, much as ten or twenty years earlier southern Italians had been pulled north to industrial jobs in France, Switzerland, Germany, and even northern Italy.

This influx of immigrants occurred at precisely the moment that northern European receiving countries began closing their doors to foreign workers. To some extent, Italy became a "back door" to the rest of Europe, but it also became an alternative to northern destinations (Macioti and Pugliese 1991: 12). In a 1991 study of 1,525 legal and illegal immigrants in Italy, approximately 40 percent stated that one reason they chose Italy as a destination was its relative ease of entrance; an equal number mentioned job opportunities in Italy as a reason for their choice (CNEL 1991: 43).

Official figures on the size of the legally resident population vary according to the government agency producing the data, their sources, and the administrative purposes of the data collection. One source for the number of foreigners legally resident in Italy is the Ministry of the Interior, whose data are based on the number of residence permits issued each year. However, the Catholic service organization Caritas, which deals extensively with immigrants in the provision of services and is widely regarded as the authoritative source on information about immigrants, has argued that government data undercount foreign residents, particularly minors who do not necessarily have separate residence permits.

According to the Ministry of the Interior data, there were approximately 1,400,000 legal foreign residents in Italy as of January 1, 2001. Caritas estimates the total number of legal immigrants closer to 1,700,000 (cited in Annuario Sociale 2001: 571). The number of legal immigrants in Italy has risen almost fivefold since 1981 and has doubled in the last decade alone (figure 9.1). With a total population of 57 million, Italy still has the lowest percentage of foreign-born residents (less than 3 percent) in Europe. Immigrants are concentrated in Italy's industrial northern regions (figure 9.2), and this concentration has increased over time. Almost half of the immigrant population lives in just two regions— Lombardy (the northern region around Milan) and Lazio (the central region where Rome is located).

Although Milan, Rome, and other major cities have the largest absolute numbers of foreign-born residents, the highest per capita concentrations are found in some of the smaller towns and villages of the northeast. Altivole, in the northeast region of Veneto, has the largest ratio of immigrants to natives in Italy. In this town of 6,000 inhabitants, there are

Figure 9.1. Legal Foreign Residents in Italy, 1981, 1991, 2001 (1000s)

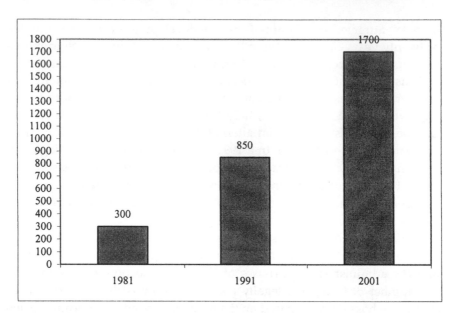

Source: Istat 2001.

Figure 9.2. Legal Foreign Residents in Italy, by Geographic Region, January 1, 1993, and January 1, 2001 (1000s)

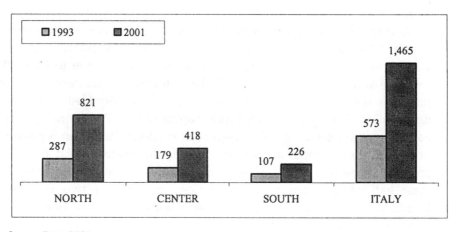

Source: Istat 2001.

approximately 900 immigrants representing twenty-five different nationalities. In Altivole, which suffers from severe labor shortages and a declining and aging local population, one of every two new hires is an immigrant (Stella 2001: 17).

It is difficult to gauge the size and distribution of the irregular or undocumented immigrant population. The Ministry of the Interior puts the number at about 250,000 (CNNItalia Online 2000). The Organisation for Economic Co-operation and Development (cited in Annuario Sociale 2001: 553) estimates that the number of illegal immigrants approaches 20 percent of the immigrant population, or about 340,000. Caritas recently estimated that there are approximately 300,000 undocumented immigrants in Italy (*Migration News* 2002a).

The majority of immigrants come from outside the European Union (EU) (table 9.1). The largest source region for non-EU immigrants is Africa. Morocco is the single largest source country, providing approximately 10 percent of the total number of legal foreign residents. If illegal residents were included, Morocco's share would be even larger. There has been a substantial increase in the share of non-EU residents since 1994, including a dramatic increase in immigration from eastern and central Europe and smaller but significant increases in the proportion of immigrants from African and Asian countries.

The proportion of female immigrants has increased slightly over time, with women now constituting approximately 45 percent of the legal immigrant stock (Ministry of the Interior 2001: 271). The distribution of female immigrants across Italy's regions roughly approximates that of the male immigrant population (Annuario Sociale 2001: 573). However, female immigrants come disproportionately from a select number of countries. While 72 percent of foreign residents from Morocco are male, females account for 66 percent of immigrants from the Philippines, 70 percent of Polish immigrants, and 68 percent of immigrants from Peru (Ministry of the Interior 2001: 278).

Not surprisingly, the degree of integration of Italy's immigrants is somewhat less than in countries of long-term immigration, where foreign residents settled decades ago and have developed deep roots. Fewer than one-quarter of foreign residents in Italy have lived there for at least five years, and only about 15 percent have lived in Italy for a decade or more, although these figures are on the rise (Caritas 2000: 170). One important indicator of integration is the rate of naturalization. The acquisition of Italian citizenship is difficult for those not born with at least one Italian parent. Because Italy is essentially a country of *jus sanguinus*, there are only two routes available to foreigners to obtain Italian citizen-ship—marrying an Italian citizen and living in Italy as a legal resident for at least ten consecutive years. In 1998, approximately 12,000 foreign citizens were granted Italian citizenship. In 1999, fewer than 11,300 achieved that status; 85 percent of these were based on marriage to an Italian, and only 15 percent were the result of long-term residency (Cari-tas 2000: 175).

Table 9.1. Legal Foreign Residents in Italy by Region and Country of Origin, 1994 and 1999

	Number of Legal Foreign Residents		Percent Increase
	1994	1999	
EUROPE	238,832	428,354	79.4
European Union	120,329	143,401	19.2
East and Central Europe	102,851	269,652	162.2
Albania	24,725	93,601	278.6
Yugoslavia	32,673	51,742	37.3
Romania	8,047	29,970	272.4
AFRICA	211,416	366,415	73.3
Morocco	78,596	147,783	88.0
Tunisia	35,693	50,647	41.9
Egypt	18,981	30,582	61.1
Senegal	19,379	31,551	62.8
Ghana	10,935	19,655	79.7
ASIA	106,286	209,230	96.9
Philippines	26,272	59,273	125.6
China	15,844	41,472	161.8
Sri Lanka	11,062	27,119	145.2

Sources: Istat 2001; ISMU-Cariplo 2001: 17.

Another way to gauge the extent to which immigrants are settling into the host society is to consider immigrants' family status and the number of immigrant children present. More than 300,000 residence permits were issued to non-EU immigrants for purposes of family unification in 2000 (table 9.2). Although the number of immigrant children in Italy is still relatively small, it is increasing rapidly. In January 2000, there were 229,851 immigrant children present, representing a 26.6 percent increase over the previous year (Istat 2000). The number of immigrant children in Italian primary and secondary schools increased from just over 6,000 in the 1983–1984 academic year to more than 85,500 in 1998–1999 (Caritas 2000: 225).

Table 9.2. Residence Permits Issued in Italy, by Purpose, 2000

Reason for Permit	Non-European Union	European Union	Total
Work	782,041	68,674	850,715
Political asylum	10,435		10,436
Family unity	323,430	31,420	354,850
Study	27,693	8,048	35,741
Tourism	7,630	868	8,498
Other	85,126	42,787	127,913
Total	1,236,355	151,798	1,388,153

Source: Annuario Sociale 2001: 572.

Although the integration of foreigners in Italy probably lags behind their integration in countries of long-standing immigration, the rate of settlement into Italian society is increasing. The incidences of binational marriage, long-term residency, naturalization, and the presence of families have all increased substantially over the last decade. As we will see in a later section, the percentage of legal immigrant workers with permanent, full-time jobs in the formal economy (in contrast to seasonal, part-time, or underground work) is higher in Italy than in any other country in Europe, suggesting that immigrants have become an integral part of the economy as well.

IMMIGRANTS OFFSET AGING AND POPULATION DECLINES

Demographers have pronounced Italy "the oldest country in the world" (Rosenblatt 2001: A17). A recent U.S. Census Bureau study shows that 18 percent of Italy's population is over age sixty-five, and by 2030 fully 28 percent of Italy's population will be sixty-five or older (Kinsella and Velkoff 2001). The president of the Banca d'Italia, citing a Eurostat study, warned that in 2025 four of the five "oldest" geographical regions in Europe will be in Italy, and this aging trend will have "profound consequences for the retirement system and for national health care expenditures." Under the headline "It Will Be Immigrants Who Save Italians' Pensions," the bank president pointed out that only a hefty infusion of young immigrants can ward off the impending crisis (*La Repubblica* 1999).

Italy vies with Spain and Japan for the dubious distinction of having the world's lowest birthrate. A recent United Nations report (United Nations Population Division 2000) found that Italy, with a birthrate of less than 1.2 per couple, has the most rapidly aging (and declining) population in the world and would have to admit over 2.2 million immigrants annually for the next thirty years in order to fill labor demand and stave off a crisis in its pension system. The *Annuario Statistico Italiano* (Istat 2001) paints a similar picture. Assuming gradual increases in immigration, Istat projects a decline in the Italian population from over 58 million in 2010 to 52 million by 2050, with a larger proportion over the age of sixty-five. This state agency also forecasts continued increases in life expectancy and an aging population. Given that pensioners already outnumber active workers in Italy, it is not hard to understand the bank president's concern and his warning, "Italy needs immigrants" (*La Repubblica* 1999).

OVERVIEW OF THE ITALIAN ECONOMY

Virtually since its unification, Italy has been divided into a thriving industrial north and a quasifeudal, agrarian south. This uneven development supplied northern industry in the post–World War II period with an almost limitless supply of cheap labor from the south. Italy's economic growth rate approached 6 percent annually from 1951 to 1971, and gross national product more than doubled. Millions of people left southern Italy between 1950 and 1975, some crossing into northern Europe but many migrating to the booming factories in northern Italy. Despite the Italian government's efforts to subsidize development in the south, the sharp economic divide persists.

In addition to this geographic split, a pronounced structural division crosscuts the Italian economy. Italy's economy includes a few very large companies with international prominence and an international market, alongside larger secondary and underground sectors comprising small, often family-run businesses. The proportion of the Italian economy corresponding to these smaller businesses has been increasing over the last twenty years. In 1981 an average company payroll was twenty workers; by 1997 the typical Italian firm had shrunk to eight workers (Ambrosini 2001a: 49).

Italy has one of the largest underground economies in the developed world. With over 28 percent of GDP delivered by this "submerged" part of the economy, which employs some 25 percent of the total workforce, this is a thriving and integral part of Italy's economic system (Eurispes 2001). Estimates suggest that the proportion of the economy that is "underground" has increased by more than 10 percent since 1994 (Eurispes 2001). Here, too, there is pronounced geographic difference, with approximately 51 percent of underground work found in Italy's southern regions (Tartaglione 2001: 3).

Unemployment historically has been high in Italy, and it remains high for much of the country. The official unemployment rate in 2001 was 9.1 percent (Istat 2001, cited in Petrini 2002: 6). There are dramatic regional variations here as well. In the north, official unemployment is only 3.9 percent (falling as low as 3 percent in some areas of the northeast); in the south it reaches 18.8 percent, affecting over half of the region's youth (Istat, cited in *Corriere della Sera* 2002a: 10; Istat 2000; Caritas 2000: 233–34).[2]

Beyond these economic and regional divisions, it is important to consider the role of state regulation and collective bargaining in the Italian economy. Union-negotiated national work contracts set wages and benefits for particular categories of work. These salary scales and benefit packages apply to virtually every sector of the formal economy (excluding very small firms). In addition, a 1970 workers' rights law places strict limitations on the conditions under which Italian workers can be laid off.[3] Taken together, these components of the formal economy render it

---

[2] With the unemployment rate so high in the south and dangerously low in the north, Italian policymakers periodically attempt to devise plans to encourage southern Italians to move north for jobs, as they did in the post–World War II period. The principal factors keeping unemployed southern Italians from taking jobs in the north are the high cost of housing in northern industrial centers relative to the modest wages of industrial employment (at approximately US$850 a month, a skilled autoworker earns little more than a supermarket clerk), and a pension and disability system that provides many households in the south with at least one source of income.

[3] The center-right government is currently pushing to revoke this protection, triggering a fierce national debate, widespread labor demonstrations, and a nationwide strike that involved close to 13 million workers (*Los Angeles Times* 2002a; Sivo 2002).

relatively inflexible from the employer's point of view, enhancing the appeal of the informal and underground sectors. The next section explores the role of immigrants in this bifurcated and segmented economy, an economy at once "inflexible" and shot through with precarious and unregulated work.

IMMIGRANTS IN THE ITALIAN ECONOMY

The vast majority of residence permits in Italy are issued for the purpose of work (table 9.2). Policymakers and employers increasingly view immigrant workers as crucial to the survival and competitive edge of the Italian economy. As immigration expert Enrico Pugliese puts it (2000: 65), "It is more and more clear that the Italian productive system needs immigrant workers, especially in the small enterprises of the north and some central regions.... We have entered a period in which immigrant workers are an integral part of the national working class and not simply part of its marginal fringe."

Immigrants' economic location varies markedly by region, by sector, and by immigrant nationality and gender, making it difficult to generalize about the role immigrants play in the Italian economy. Nonetheless, certain patterns and trends emerge as important, including the following:

- Immigrants tend to do the most arduous, undesirable work in each sector and region for the lowest pay.

- Immigrants work disproportionately in the underground economy and the secondary and tertiary sectors.

- At the same time, there has been a rapid increase in the presence of immigrants in the formal economy and in manufacturing, particularly in the northeast and in some areas of central Italy.

- Immigrants in Italy now have the highest share of full-time, regular ("legitimate") work (65 percent) in Europe (Ministry of the Interior, in CNNItalia Online 2000).

- Immigrants fill niches left by Italians in some areas and sectors, supplement scarce labor supply in others, and directly compete with local workers in some sectors and regions, particularly in the south during economic downturns.

- Immigrants are increasingly union members.

- There are dramatic differences between immigrant employment in the north and center and in the south. In the south, immigrants are most frequently farmworkers or domestic helpers; in the northeast and center they are disproportionately in manufacturing, mostly in the small and medium-size shops concentrated in those regions.

- Immigrants are more likely to be illegal and to work in the underground economy in the south versus other regions. In the north, the vast majority of immigrants are legal residents.

Immigrant workers are found in virtually every sector of the economy. They are street vendors, domestic workers, nurses, factory workers, gas station attendants, farmworkers, construction workers, garment workers, dishwashers, foundry workers, metalworkers, and office "errand boys." But they are clustered in manufacturing, agriculture, domestic service, and a variety of other services. Table 9.3 shows their distribution across these sectors in the different geographic areas of Italy. Let us briefly examine immigrants' location in these sectors.

Industry/Manufacturing

Italy has an unusually high percentage of immigrant workers in manufacturing. They are an important part of the labor force in the small and medium-size "post-Fordist" enterprises that have proliferated in the north and northeast in recent years (Pugliese, ed. 2000: 15; Caputo 2000: 91). It has been estimated that in the "industrial heartland of northern Italy," there is a 100,000 to 160,000 worker shortfall, and this number is growing (Hundley 2001: 1). Not only do immigrants offset this shrinking labor supply, but the "just-in-time" production associated with these small shops places an additional premium on the flexibility and mobility of immigrant workers.

The majority of immigrant workers in industry and manufacturing have residence permits, although many work in jobs that are "irregular" in some respect, as, for example, when social security is not paid or the employer has not complied with all government reporting requirements. According to an Italian Department of Labor estimate in 1999, in the northeast and in Lombardy, approximately 91 percent of immigrant workers were legal residents, but roughly 30 percent of them worked in jobs that were somehow "irregular" (Zincone 2001: 339).

Wages and working conditions in manufacturing and industrial services, as with all sectors, vary between the north and the south, even

Table 9.3. Non–European Union Legal Foreign Workers in Italy, by Economic Sector and Geographic Area, 1999 (percentages)

	Agriculture	Manufacturing	Construction	Domestic	Services
Northwest	9.2	26.3	11.7	30.7	22.2
Northeast	22.0	39.7	7.9	8.5	21.8
Center	15.4	33.0	9.0	22.2	20.5
South	38.3	7.6	2.8	39.7	11.6
Lombardy[a]	5.7	31.8	5.9	31.0	25.6
Lazio[b]	7.3	3.1	3.0	71.6	15.0

Source: Zincone 2001: 354.

[a] Lombardy is the region in which Milan is located.

[b] Lazio is the region in which Rome is located.

within the same categories of work (Caputo 2000: 88). What remains constant is that wages and working conditions generally are worse for immigrants than for local workers. Net wages for immigrants in metal-working can range from roughly US$600 a month in the northern regions of Piedmont and Veneto to close to $1,000 a month for a worker with seniority in north-central Emilia-Romagna. Immigrants can earn slightly more in chemical-related industries, foodstuffs, and slaughterhouses, where they perform the most grueling and precarious tasks (Caputo 2000). A few non-EU workers are in high-profile, high-skill positions, such as Brazilian engineers working for Fiat in Turin or high-tech Asian workers with Olivetti, but they are the exception.

Some low-end industrial jobs are paid by the hour or piece rate, and the proportion of illegal workers in these jobs is generally higher. For example, Rumanians, most without residence permits, often work in the underground economy in Piedmont, painting car parts for body shops and making between $30 and $35 a day. Garment workers in the south (predominantly Chinese and Bangladesh) are also paid piece rate. It is said that whole Chinese families working in the garment industry in southern Italy often earn the equivalent of $250 for a month of eight-hour to ten-hour workdays (Caputo 2000: 92). Nor are such wages confined to the south. In Altivole in Veneto, a large Chinese community works clan-destinely in garment sweatshops scattered around town. Average piece rate wages for a month of eighteen-hour days come to approximately $350. According to one report, if you work at a "phenomenal" pace, you might make $500 (Stella 2001: 17).

Construction

Unlike sectors that are more regionally specific, construction jobs are available all over the national territory, although they are somewhat more concentrated in the north. According to many observers, immi-grants' presence in low-end construction jobs is growing (table 9.3). It extends beyond what official statistics indicate, particularly in the south, where immigrants' presence in small, underground firms goes unre-ported. Indeed, the construction industry contains the greatest propor-tion of illegal immigrants working in the underground economy, in part because this sector includes many small firms beyond the pale of gov-ernment and union regulations (Caputo 2000: 90).

Immigrant construction workers are often hired as day laborers from streets and piazzas where such workers congregate. They are generally paid by the day. Wages vary from the north to the south, but they tend to be the same for legal and illegal immigrants. In some northern areas, immigrants in construction earn as much as $50 a day; and in parts of central Italy, where government regulations subsequent to the 1996 earthquake have improved wages and working conditions, they can earn $800 a month. In the south, in contrast, wages for immigrant construction workers range from about $15 to $30 a day for up to twelve hours of work (Caputo 2000).

Agriculture

Italy (like Spain) differs from the rest of Europe in the high proportion of immigrants engaged in agricultural work. Estimates suggest that approximately 38 percent of all non-EU immigrant workers in Italy are employed in agriculture (Osservatorio Ares 2001), making up roughly 10 percent of all farmworkers. In 2001 there were at least 80,000 immigrants employed in Italian agriculture, and the number has been rising approximately 15 percent annually (*Notizie Ansa* 2002a). The vast majority (88 percent) of these farmworkers are employed on a seasonal basis, with the peak season lasting from June to September. One observer has noted that new technologies, which have reduced the time required for the harvest, have meant increases in the number of immigrant workers, but they are now used for shorter periods of time (Gueye 2000: 136).

Although there are many immigrant farmworkers in the north, the heaviest concentration is in the south, where much of Italy's richest farmland is located. If irregular and undocumented workers were included in table 9.3, the disproportionate number of immigrant farmworkers in the south would be even more evident. Indeed, it is estimated that more than 73 percent of Italian agriculture (85 percent in the south) is "irregular" in some way, even when the immigrants themselves are legal (Caputo 2000: 88–89; Tartaglione 2001: 5).

Farm wages are generally paid by the day. In Campania, one of Italy's poorest regions, immigrant farmworkers work eight to ten hours a day for $10 to $15, a wage that has lost ground over the last several years. In Puglia, where immigrants pick watermelons piece rate and labor contractors take a 5 to 10 percent cut, a fast worker makes about $500 a month (Caputo 2000: 89). In the center and north, where agricultural work is generally not "irregular" and workers are more likely to be paid according to union contracts, immigrant farmworkers can earn up to $900 a month (Caputo 2000: 89). Overall, however, farmworker wages are among the lowest of any sector, and a disproportionate number of farmworkers are undocumented.

Domestic Service

Immigrant women are heavily concentrated in domestic service, including cleaning services, elder care, and childcare. They come primarily from the Philippines and South America, particularly Peru, although in recent years there has been a dramatic increase in the number of eastern European women in this sector. Almost without exception, these women's education and qualifications, and their social position prior to immigration, far exceed the menial work they find in Italy.

Because of the in-house nature of this work, one might expect it to be disproportionately irregular and clandestine. In fact, there are a significant number of immigrants in domestic service outside the reach of government regulations and social security rules. Some work under conditions that constitute a flagrant violation of established labor rights (Pugliese, ed. 2000: 18). Interestingly, however, a large percentage of immigrants in domestic service are legal and the work tends to be regular, with this sector being second only to manufacturing in numbers of workers registered with the social security system. This is related, no doubt, to the relatively generous quotas for domestic service in Italian immigration policy, to be discussed later.

Wages vary according to region and type of work. Live-in helpers in the north and center earn approximately $800 a month, while in the south they are paid no more than $500, and this, according to one observer, is true only for Philippine workers (Caputo 2000: 92). For hourly work, domestic helpers' wages range from approximately $3.50 an hour in the south (sometimes even for a married couple working together) to $8 an hour in the north. Wages can also differ depending on the worker's nationality. For example, Philippine workers are relatively highly paid, while Sri Lankans are generally not (Caputo 2000: 92). Interestingly, remuneration seems to depend less on the immigrant's legal status and more on his or her nationality and region of employment.

Immigrant Workers' Advantages and Integration

Even though manufacturing, construction, agriculture, and domestic service are the primary categories for immigrants working in Italy, immigrant workers are found in many other sectors and perform a wide range of services. They are engaged as office "errand boys," night watchmen, and dishwashers, and they are an important component of the tourism industry, particularly the hotels and restaurants on the Adriatic coast, which boom during the summer season but are virtually deserted by late August (Gueye 2000: 136). In some regions, immigrants are primarily street vendors, such as the Senegalese who sell cigarette lighters in Milan and faux designer purses in Florence, and ply the beaches of Tuscany and Sardinia in summer (Zanfrini 1996; Berti 2000: 134).

Given Italy's rapidly declining birthrates, aging population, and booming manufacturing enterprises, immigrants there—at least in northern and central Italy—not only contribute an element of flexibility and hence a post-Fordist advantage, but they also fill critical labor shortages. Underscoring immigrants' role in filling labor shortages and doing jobs most Italians shun, Venturini and Villosio (n.d.) use government data from the Italian Labor Force Survey to show that immigrant workers generally have either no effect or a complementary (positive) effect on employment opportunities for Italians. Similarly, Gavosto, Venturini, and Villosio's (1999) statistical analysis found that in most cases the effect of immigrant workers on Italians' wages was positive. Ambrosini generally concurs with this interpretation but cautions that the availability of immigrant workers may allow employers to eschew strategies that would be beneficial to local workers. For example, the presence of immigrants in the industrial north means that firms do not have to move to areas in Italy where local workers might be more readily available, nor need they raise wages or improve working conditions to attract unemployed Italians to areas of high employment (Ambrosini 2001a: 61–62).

According to Pugliese (2000: 65), "The process of stabilization is perhaps the most significant aspect of immigration in Italy in the 1990s." By this he meant that immigrants are increasingly integrated into the economy and are increasingly likely to be legal residents and have "regular" jobs. Their increased union membership is indicative of this stabilization. Although unions in Italy are experiencing changes and overall membership declines (Mottura 2000: 123), the rate at which immigrants are joining unions is increasing. According to records of the communist-affiliated Italian Labor Confederation (CGIL, one of the three largest union confederations in Italy), immigrant membership increased 22 percent from 1998 to 2000 (Mottura 2000: 124). Interestingly, immigrants working in factories in Italy's southern regions are more likely to be unionized (45 percent) than those in the post-Fordist, small enterprises of the north (30 percent). In some southern regions, union membership among immigrant factory workers is even higher than that of local workers (*Notizie Ansa* 2002b). And there are signs that immigrants might be an important component of future labor agitation. In one recent case, all sixteen immigrant workers at a slaughterhouse near Lake Como went on strike to protest violations of labor law in their plant while the nineteen Italians in the plant kept working. As one worker from Senegal said, "It was [my first strike ever], as it was for my colleagues from Morocco and from India, and we thought our Italian co-workers would join us.... Oh well, it will be for the next time" (*Notizie Ansa* 2002c: 27).

Neither the pace nor the inevitability of this stabilization process should be exaggerated. In a country where one-quarter of GDP derives from the underground economy and where immigrants are concentrated in sectors that are disproportionately irregular, undocumented immigrants and/or immigrants in irregular jobs still play a pivotal role. One recent study found that Italian employers save approximately US$13 billion annually on taxes and social security payments by using irregular immigrant workers (Osservatorio Ares 2001).

PUBLIC ATTITUDES TOWARD IMMIGRANTS

Italy's political landscape has changed substantially in the last ten years. Reforms in the aftermath of exposés of high-level official corruption in 1994 and 1995 — known colloquially as "Tangentopoli," which translates loosely as "Kickback City" — weakened the strong party system of government, and there has also been a tilt to the right among the Italian electorate. After decades of Christian Democratic and nominally Socialist governments, in 1994 industrialist and soccer magnate Silvio Berlusconi put together a coalition government made up of the Lega Nord (Northern League), Forza Italia ("Go Italy!" Berlusconi's new party), and the Alleanza Nazionale (National Alliance, the progeny of the Fascist Party of World War II). This right-wing government did not last long, but Berlusconi was reelected in 2001 and once again presides over one of the most conservative governments in Europe.

The vehemently anti-immigrant Northern League, led by Umberto Bossi, is again an important participant in Berlusconi's coalition, as is the neo-fascist National Alliance. The "Polo," as the coalition is called, emphasizes security, law and order, the fight against immigration, and regional fiscal autonomy. Local jurisdictions are increasingly governed by one or another of these rightist parties, and the presidents of the Liguria,

Lombardy, Veneto, and Piedmont regions are all Polo members. In the 2000 regional elections, the National Alliance candidate won a provincial governorship in Lazio (Rome) with his proclamations of "wild clandestine immigration" and the "social deviance" it produces (Smith 2000). According to one report, Berlusconi's advisers counseled that he "ride the tiger" of immigration (D'Avanzo 2002). With many Italians perceiving a decline in public safety and a breakdown of law and order, and with continuing high unemployment rates, Berlusconi rode this tiger successfully to carry the May 2001 elections.

The discovery in March 2002 of a boatload of nearly one thousand Kurdish refugees off the coast of Sicily and their emergency landing amid much alarmist rhetoric was called "manna from heaven" for the Berlusconi government coalition. The incident enabled the government to curtail the administrative proceedings prior to deportation as part of its declared "state of emergency." More symbolically, it has allowed the Berlusconi coalition to continue "riding the politics of fear" (D'Avanzo 2002). Umberto Bossi of the Northern League was quick to capitalize on this opportunity, exploding, "If I had my way, we would sink these smugglers' ships, blow them out of the water" (*Migration News* 2002b: 27).

The focus of much of the right's anti-immigrant rhetoric is on multiculturalism. Following a massive demonstration against the government's proposed new immigration law in January 2002, the vice president of the Italian Senate, a member of the Northern League, asserted that the pro-immigrant lobby "wants not an immigration of workers but a repopulation of the country by immigrants, which is extremely dangerous for our identity, for the social equilibrium, and for our sense of being one people" (*Notizie Ansa* 2002d: 2). Counter-demonstrators carried anti-immigrant placards, and one Northern League supporter displayed a banner proclaiming, "Yes to Polenta, No to Couscous!" Since the September 11, 2001, attacks on the United States, these anti-immigrant sentiments are mixed with concerns over terrorism and the perceived connection to Arab immigrants. Northern League supporters demonstrated outside the Islamic Cultural Center in Milan in October 2001, urging officials to "get the terrorists out of Milan" (Reuters News Service 2001).

A number of intellectual leaders have recently joined the anti-immigrant fray. Giovanni Sartori (2000) writes provocatively about the dangers of multiculturalism, focusing particular attention on the Muslim presence in Italy. Journalist Oriana Fallaci has called Arab immigration "a secret invasion," adding, "We might as well admit it. Our churches and cathedrals are more beautiful than their mosques" (Henneberger 2001).

Equally vocal on the immigration issue are a wide range of immigrant associations, employers' groups, religious groups, nongovernmental organizations (NGOs), and union confederations that advocate on behalf of immigrants and stress the benefits of both an enhanced labor supply and cultural diversity.[4] All three major union confederations in Italy—CGIL, the Italian Labor Union (UIL), and the Confederation of Italian Labor Unions (CISL)—lobby and work on behalf of immigrants. In fact, unions are second only to religious organizations as an immigrant support group. In most major Italian cities, union caucuses and advocacy groups help immigrant workers gain access to jobs, health care, housing, and coveted residence permits.

Certain traits of Italian unions help account for their support of immigrants. Italian unions have historically been influenced by progressive politics. Less narrowly focused on workplace issues than most unions in the United States, Italian unions have maintained solidarity with oppressed people in the Third World as an important part of their broader politics. Immigrant advocacy work is in some ways the domestic counterpart of this international commitment.

As immigrants increasingly enter Italy's mainstream economy, one might expect unions to view them as a competitive challenge to union workers. Quite the opposite; unions advocate for laws that enable immigrants to legalize and for their entry into the formal economy where they might be organized. This stance is at least in part the product of practical, strategic considerations (Mottura 2000). As Watts (2000) points out, union officials know that immigration flows are difficult to control and unlikely to disappear, and they have opted to welcome the new workers. At a time when unions are losing ground in all advanced capitalist countries, Italian unions see in these immigrants a vital source of their future strength (author interview with a coordinator for the CGIL Office of Immigrant Affairs).

A variety of Catholic charity associations—Caritas and Comunita' di Sant'Egidio, among others—comprise another important pro-immigrant lobby and support group. An article in *Civilta Cattolica*, a Jesuit periodical, warned that it is a "grave mistake" to perceive immigrants only as "instruments of the labor market," ignoring their "human dignity"

---

[4] For good summaries of immigrant associations in Italy and the role they serve, see Carchedi 2000.

(Simone 2002: 187). Catholic groups advocate for more liberal laws affecting immigrants and also offer crucial social services. Caritas, with a vast network of medical personnel and facilities, is the most important provider of immigrant health care in Italy. In Catholic Italy, the credibility and political impact of these service organizations working on behalf of immigrants should not be underestimated.

One highly significant recent development is the increased role that employers are playing in supporting immigration. In spring 1999, major Italian industrial organizations for the first time publicly urged the government to give them access to more immigrant workers (ISMU-Cariplo 2001: 26). Employers have kept up the heat ever since, even pressing the government for measures that would reduce the illegality and marginality of immigrant workers (Zuccolini 2002: 4). The Association of Industrialists of Udine in northeastern Italy, concerned about severe labor shortages, has formed a coalition with local neighborhood organizations to help resolve immigrants' grave housing problems and to initiate a variety of "integrative" programs (Notizie Ansa 2002e). Employers in the northeast region of Friuli-Venezia Giulia, where the unemployment rate is at an all-time low of 2.3 percent, argue that "there is no time to waste" in devising more open immigration policies (Maccaferri 2001: 1). Mirroring the diversity and breadth of immigrant advocacy groups in Italy, a mass rally was convened in Rome on January 19, 2002, following the introduction of a restrictive immigration bill in the Italian legislature (Roncone 2002: 5). There were over 100,000 participants, including people from the major unions and Catholic charities, legal and illegal immigrants from dozens of nations, students, intellectuals and artists, and leftist party officials. Against a backdrop of reggae, Peruvian, and African music, the demonstrators condemned the proposed immigration bill as "shameful" and declared themselves opposed to this project of a "xenophobic and racist society." Even the mayor of Rome was present, admonishing the government restrictionists and declaring, "Multiculturalism enriches us" (Casadio 2002).

Numerous studies have focused on ordinary Italians' attitudes toward immigration and multiculturalism. One study on tolerance of diversity found that Italians are among the most tolerant people in Europe, with only 11 percent admitting to outright intolerance, 21 percent expressing ambivalence, 54 percent "passively tolerant," and 15 percent "actively tolerant" (Il Manifesto 2001). Somewhat at odds with this portrait of Italians as relatively tolerant of diversity and consistent with the right wing's recent political successes, another study found that one-third of Italians now think immigration is their nation's worst problem (*Los Angeles Times* 2002b).

An annual survey found a slight decrease in anti-immigrant sentiment in Italy from 2000 to 2002 (Bordignon 2002). In 2002, 40 percent (compared to 46 percent in 2000) of Italians viewed immigrants as a threat to public safety; 29 percent (32 percent in 2000) felt they take jobs away from Italians; and 24 percent (27 percent in 2000) worried that immigrants threaten Italian culture and identity. Even though these figures seem high, the survey found that Italy was the only country in Western Europe where anti-immigrant sentiment was falling.

Table 9.4 presents the results of three studies that have measured Italian attitudes toward immigrants and immigrants' rights. Although the studies vary in methodology and sample characteristics, their findings are generally consistent. They suggest relatively high levels of support for immigrant voting rights while simultaneously revealing images of immigrants as potential criminals and, to a lesser extent, as contributing to unemployment.[5]

Table 9.4. Attitudes of Italians toward Immigrants as Measured in Three Studies, 1999

	Percentage of Respondents Who Agreed with Statement		
	Study 1	Study 2	Study 3
Immigrants should have the right to vote in local elections.	50.1	73.6	59.1
There is a correlation between immigrants and crime.	73.5	46.0	74.9
Immigrants increase unemployment.	38.2	33.0	28.0

Sources: Study 1, ISPO 1999; study 2, Diamanti 2000; study 3, CENSIS 2000.

---

[5] For more details on these and similar studies, see Caritas 2000: 204–09; Valtolina 2001: 143–59.

There is no question that Italians' concerns about immigration re-
volve around three primary issues: increasing multiculturalism, the notion that immigrants take jobs away from Italians, and fear that immigrants lead to crime and the decay of public order. It is more difficult to
untangle the source of these fears and to determine how much they are
based in reality. It is true that a large proportion of prison inmates in
major Italian cities are immigrants (approximately 15 percent of the Italian prison population is foreign-born), but some experts attribute this at
least in part to law enforcement biases (Melossi 2000). And as we saw
above, immigrants generally take jobs that Italians shun, so the perception that immigrants increase unemployment appears to be largely un-
substantiated. Of course, immigrants are contributing to an increasingly
multicultural society, although the degree of cultural homogeneity prior
to immigrant influxes may be exaggerated in the conventional rendering.
While perceptions of the threat that immigrants pose to Italian society
and culture may not be entirely realistic, they are nevertheless played on
and fueled by right-wing politicians and media anxious to exploit the
sensational.

It is difficult to generalize from these studies and from the wide-
ranging political expressions cited here; nevertheless, we might draw
several tentative conclusions. First, the debate over immigration in Italy
is ongoing and vigorous, with a host of political, religious, and cultural
groups taking pro-immigrant and anti-immigrant positions. Second,
anti-immigration sentiment remains high, and right-wing politicians
have capitalized on this, probably even contributed to it. Third, despite
this anti-immigrant sentiment, there is still a solid block of support for
immigration and immigrant rights. From Catholics with their concern for
the humanity of immigrants, to unions' advocacy on behalf of potential
members, to various ideologically committed advocacy groups, to employers who are alarmed at the shrinking labor supply, the pro-
immigrant force represents a powerful countercurrent to rightist nativism.

IMMIGRATION LAW AND POLICY: CONTRADICTIONS, SHIFTS, AND IMPASSE

What little immigration there was in Italy prior to the 1980s was regulated primarily by administrative decrees from various government min-

istries.[6] Together, these decrees established a system of legal immigration that was driven by the needs of individual employers who periodically requested immigrant workers to fill labor shortages. No annual ceilings or quotas were set, nor did they seem necessary.

The first indication that things were changing came in 1982, when a Ministry of Labor circular called a halt to all authorizations for foreign workers from outside the European Community. Also included in this circular was the first attempt to legalize those already present in Italy and illegally employed. This legalization program stipulated that employers had to "regularize" their illegal immigrant workers. The amnesty process required employers to pay all back taxes and social security payments, and also post a bond equal to the cost of the return ticket for the foreign workers they were sponsoring for legalization.

Not surprisingly, given the burden that this legalization program placed on employers, fewer than 16,000 immigrants were regularized. In fact, the number of irregular foreign workers in Italy increased dramatically as a consequence of this law. As Bonini (1991: 90) observed, with further legal immigration prohibited, "the condition of irregularity became a *modus vivendi*." La Terza (1987) concurs, noting that the closing down of the legal immigration channel just as more immigrants began to view Italy as a desirable destination vastly increased the number of illegal immigrants.

Italy passed its first comprehensive immigration law, Foreign Workers and the Control of Illegal Immigration, in 1986. This law was in part the product of pressure from unions and left opposition parties who contested what they saw as abuse of the rapidly growing number of illegal immigrants. However, it was also the result of substantial pressure from the European Community to close the back door to Europe now that Europe's internal borders were being dismantled. The law contained three primary components: foreign workers' rights, rules on the employment of foreigners, and another legalization program.

Speaking to the pronounced gap between the provisions of this law and its conspicuous lack of implementation, one legal scholar complained, "The chronic vice of Italian politics is an excess of legislation and a deficit of implementation" (Onorato 1989: 307). Others spoke of the law's "uncertainty" and the "bureaucratism" involved in enforcement (Minister of Labor Formica, in Sestini 1989: 331). There was considerable confusion, for example, over how to enforce the employer sanctions.

---

[6] This practice is not uncommon in Italy, where some observers have called it "government by memo" (Adinolfi 1992: 11).

Even though they contained provision for a prison term, a Ministry of Labor official stated that employer sanctions were entirely a civil matter. Labor inspectors held divergent opinions about who was responsible for enforcement. One inspector said that the Ministry of Labor was responsible and had wide discretion over the imposition of fines, while another insisted with equal certainty that labor inspectors were to notify the police when they found employers in violation (author interviews, July 1992). While there is some evidence that this latter interpretation is accurate, those responsible for immigration matters at the central police agency in Rome seemed far less interested in the early 1990s in enforcing employer sanctions than in arresting and repatriating Brazilian prostitutes (author interview, July 1992). When asked how many employer sanctions fines had been levied, a senior official from the Ministry of Labor smiled and responded, "What shall I say?" (author interview, July 1992). In addition to this bureaucratic confusion is the difficulty of regulating employers in the submerged economy, where illegal immigrants and their employees are, by definition, beyond the pale of government regulation.

The legalization program, though more widely publicized than employer sanctions, was not much more successful. When the law was passed, there were an estimated 600,000 to 1.2 million undocumented immigrants in Italy, of whom only about 107,000 applied for regularization under the 1986 law. According to Onorato (1989: 307), the most important reason for the program's failure was "the bosses' interest in not regularizing 'black labor'... in order to save on health and social security contributions and the minimum wage, and ... the general vulnerability of immigrants that led them not to seek regularization from their employers for fear of losing their jobs."

A new immigration law was passed in 1990. The "Martelli Law," named for its primary author and sponsor, then deputy prime minister Claudio Martelli, contained a blueprint for a quota worker system. Annual quotas for specific categories of foreign workers were to be arrived at in consultation with unions, employers, and other interested groups. The law also included a relatively generous legalization program. Under the Martelli Law, in contrast to previous amnesty programs, the process was to be initiated by the immigrants themselves rather than their employers, and employers did not have to pay back contributions to social security for their regularized workers. Residence permits for regularized immigrants were valid for two years and renewable for four years if the immigrants could demonstrate that they continued to work and had sufficient income. Immigrants working in the underground economy could make an "auto-certification" of income, but this required divulging the name of one's employer.

Approximately 234,000 immigrants applied for legalization under the Martelli Law, and 171,000 of these applied for renewals. The relative success of this legalization program no doubt was due to the fact that the immigrants, not their employers, initiated legalization and that employers were not required to pay back taxes. Only about 15,000 of these legalizations were based on "auto-certifications," suggesting that workers in the underground economy were reluctant to risk their jobs by, in effect, denouncing their employers.

The Martelli Law, like its predecessor, suffered from a discrepancy between the law "on the books" and the law "in action." Immigrants were even more heavily concentrated in the service sector in the underground economy in 1990, when the law was passed, than they are today, and it may be precisely this function as illegal workers in an illegal economy that limited the ability to regulate and regularize them. In other words, those characteristics that make so-called Third World immigrants attractive to certain sectors — their invisibility, marginality, and vulnerability — are the same qualities that make it difficult to control their employment (through employer sanctions) or legalize them (through regularization programs). Both employer sanctions and legalization may be destined to fail in the context of a large underground economy where immigrants' employment is partly contingent on their marginality.

Even the annual quotas for foreign workers did not work as planned. The law required a complicated process of consultation between multiple governmental agencies and interested parties before announcing the annual number of visas "for the purpose of work." In some years, no numerical quotas were fixed; when they were forthcoming, they were unrealistically low, and the consultation process "rarely conformed to the parameters of the law" (Adinolfi 1992: 70).

By 1998 Italy's experience with immigration was changing as immigrants were becoming increasingly essential to manufacturing and other sectors of the formal economy and were settling into Italian society. Law #40, passed in spring 1998, attempted to come to grips with this new reality, representing for some the first "systematic and comprehensive treatment" of the subject (McBritton and Garofalo 2000: 95). Like the 1986 immigration law, this comprehensive law responded to domestic politics and prevailing economic conditions as well as to European Community pressure to control illegal migration through the back door.

Law #40 attempted to rationalize the quota worker system, establishing a process for arriving at quotas that includes consideration of the number of foreign workers already available, employers' labor needs, unemployment rates, and so on. Once an annual quota is established, employers can send requests for workers, either by name or by number of workers needed, to the Ministry of Labor. The employer must testify that the conditions of work will equal those established under union contract and guarantee some "housing assistance." Assuming the quota has not been exhausted, the employer will receive the requested workers. These workers, even if specified by name and even if already residents of Italy, must return to their country of origin and reenter Italy with the requisite paperwork. If quota workers continue to secure work, they may renew their residence permits indefinitely without returning to their home country. In most cases, residence permits are issued for two years and are renewed if the original conditions (usually work in the formal economy) continue to be met. For the first time with this law, foreign workers (with the exception of seasonal workers) do not immediately lose their residence permits if they lose their jobs. They have up to a year to secure another job, but they must actively be seeking work.

The law also provides for an annual quota for seasonal workers. Within this quota, workers can enter Italy for periods from twenty days to six months (extendable to nine months). If they secure permanent work during this period, they must exit Italy and reenter through the permanent quota. Employers requesting seasonal workers must specify, in addition to the conditions of work and housing assistance, how they intend to ensure that the workers leave at the end of the contract period.

Law #40 also establishes a system under which any public entity may sponsor immigrants to come to Italy to work, as long as the sponsor guarantees a source of livelihood and the sponsored immigrants come within the annual quota. Besides employers' associations, entities eligible to sponsor immigrants include labor unions, immigrant advocacy groups, and other NGOs. The law also provides for family reunification, again within the quota; and relatives of legal residents, once inside Italy, can get work permits immediately.

The 1998 law also lays out the rights of foreigners in Italy. Among its major provisions are the right to equal treatment with Italian workers; access to the full range of services of the public health care system; and, for the undocumented, the right to urgent care and the right to attend public school. In addition, the law sets out an ambitious plan for a network of "reception centers" throughout Italy to provide immigrants with emergency food and shelter as well as language instruction and a range of other cultural and social services.

Finally, the law provides for a *"carta di soggiorno,"* or residence card, that for the first time creates a category of permanent legal residents. After five years of continuous legal status, if immigrants have a legitimate job and sufficient income to support themselves and their family, they and their spouses and minor children are eligible for this residence permit, which, unlike all previous residence permits, is open-ended in duration. Alongside these apparently progressive reforms, the law also signals a renewed commitment to employer sanctions, with fines of $1,000 to $3,000 for each illegal immigrant employed and a possibility of a sentence of three months to one year in prison.

Introducing an essay on the difficult implementation of this law, Fasano and Zucchini (2001: 39) muse, "Laws, like ideas, walk with men's legs. The latter can go where the law seemed to want to go, they can stand still, or they can go elsewhere altogether." Others speak more prosaically of "serious problems of application" (Marra and Pontrandolfi 1999: preface). In fact, none of the law's major components—employer sanctions, the quota worker system, reception centers, and permanent residence cards—appears "to go where the law seemed to want to go."

Employer sanctions are still rarely enforced. McBritton and Garofalo (2000: 102) explain the ineffectiveness of this provision of the law: "The lack of controls over the underground economy in general certainly limits their [the employer sanctions'] feasibility, especially vis-à-vis those employers who evade all [government regulations and reporting requirements]" and are therefore effectively outside the scope of government oversight. Because the formal economy is so highly regulated in Italy, virtually all illegal immigrants are employed in the extensive underground economy, which is by definition beyond the reach of law. Employer sanctions have also been challenged in court, with inconsistent results. Most recently, the Italian Supreme Court declared in May 2001 that it is not a crime to hire immigrants who lack *work* permits, although the same decision seems to have upheld the sanction against employers who hire immigrants without *residence* permits.

The quota worker system continues to be plagued by controversy and paralysis. The annual quota for 1998 was not announced until October and resulted in undocumented workers already in Italy taking the allotted slots. This led some observers to remark that it was a de facto "legalization rather than a foreign worker program" (Codini 2001: 26). The quota for 1999 was set in August, was not preceded by any economic analyses, and effectively consisted of a reissuing of the 1998 numbers. The quota for 2000 was arrived at relatively expeditiously in February, with 63,000 slots opened up for foreign workers. But by the spring, employers and regional officials warned of an impending shortage and requested additions, some of which were authorized (Codini 2001: 26). The following year, the initial quota of 63,000 was later increased to 83,000, with the bulk of the additions dedicated to seasonal workers (Galluzzo 2001: 18).

Along with the ad hoc and reactive quality of the quota system, the process by which workers qualify has also been subject to criticism. Referring to the requirement that temporary workers who secure a permanent job must return to their home countries to be called back in under the quota, McBritton and Garofalo (2000: 104) lament, "The regulations reproduce ... the same bureaucratic *iter*, so Kafkaesque, that the law was meant to avoid and results in a powerful incentive [for immigrant workers] to stay and become illegal, waiting for a new legalization program."

The ambitious plan to provide immigrant reception centers throughout Italy, which bears the pro-immigrant fingerprints of the leftist coalition government that spearheaded this bill, has predictably fallen short of its far-reaching goals. Most of what are euphemistically called "reception centers" are in fact detention centers for illegal immigrants. Under the heading "Is This Any Way to Welcome Them?" a journalist described conditions at one of the largest of these centers as "a maximum security prison" for illegal immigrant "guests" (Gullo 2001: 59). Caritas provides food and shelter for legal immigrants in most major cities, but space is limited and these shelters bear little resemblance to the cultural and social service enclaves envisioned in the law. The author visited one center on the outskirts of Venice; it resembled a halfway house, with residents let out during the day to work but otherwise kept under close scrutiny.[7]

The residence cards that for the first time give long-term immigrants the possibility of permanent legal status have been slow to arrive and unevenly accessible. As with much immigration policy in Italy, implementation of the residence card system is left to local authorities, in this case the provincial police. A recent study of its implementation across three provinces in Lombardy found dramatic differences in what is required to obtain this coveted document (Fasano and Zucchini 2001). In all three cases, the documents requested by local police exceeded what is required by law. In one province, the local policy was *not to release any*

---

[7] See Codini 2001: 27–28 for a summary of the critiques of these immigrant reception centers.

permanent residence cards at all, in clear violation of both the letter and spirit of the law (Fasano and Zucchini 2001). The director of immigrant affairs at the CGIL office in a large northeastern city said that local authorities were "fussy" about giving out residence cards, and the only ones he had seen were issued to immigrants married to Italian citizens (author interview, July 2002).[8]

A new immigration law is wending its way through Parliament as this is being written (*Corriere della Sera* 2002b). Consistent with the restrictionist stance of the Berlusconi/Northern League/National Alliance governing coalition, this bill would reverse most of the liberal provisions of the 1998 immigration law. It would eliminate the sponsor system, increase the focus on seasonal foreign workers, and make work contracts a prerequisite for residence permits, doing away with the one-year grace period for terminated workers to find new jobs (*Corriere della Sera* 2002c). In addition, the Berlusconi government has announced a narrowly tailored legalization program for domestic workers. This program excludes all other types of workers and requires the employers of legalizing domestic helpers to pay a heavy "tax," precipitating criticism that this legalization law is simply "for rich people," something that only the wealthy can afford (*Notizie Ansa* 2002f).

CONCLUSION

Two patterns can be discerned in Italy's immigration policy path. First, there are continuous starts, shifts, and changes of course. In less than two decades, there have been four major pieces of legislation (1986, 1990, 1998, and 2002) and innumerable amendments, decrees, and government "circulars." There were four legalization programs over twelve years (1986–1987, 1990–1991, 1996, and 1998), each accompanied by statements underscoring the extraordinary circumstances justifying this now ordinary component of Italian immigration policy.

Second, throughout this period there is a marked disjuncture between the stated purpose of a law and its effect. Whether the issue is restrictions and controls (employer sanctions, control over illegal workers,

---

[8] Antidiscrimination laws for housing have had similarly spotty effects. According to union officials and social service representatives, housing is the primary problem for immigrants in Italy (author interviews, July 2001). Despite provisions in this law that prohibit tenants from discriminating against (legal) immigrants, discrimination is widespread and largely goes unpunished (Ambrosini 2000: 140). Advertisements for rentals in newspapers often state explicitly, "No foreigners" (Smith 2000).

control over borders) or the rights accorded immigrants by law (access to permanent residence cards, reception centers, equal rights with Italian workers), the "legs" of Italian immigration law frequently do not "go where the law seemed to want to go."

Two sets of tensions may underlie both of these patterns. First, it seems probable that there is a structural inevitability both to current immigration flows and to regulatory failure at the margins of post-Fordist economies. A consistent theme throughout this volume is the difficulty of curtailing immigration from the Third World to the First World given the economic realities defining each. As Italy's standard of living approaches that of its northern neighbors and the gap with the Third World widens, the economic divide creates pressures that are difficult to reverse by legislative fiat. At the same time, European Community pressures and internal political exigencies require that immigration to Italy be controlled and that borders be secured. At a European Union summit in Seville, Spain, in May 2002, members reiterated the urgent need to secure external borders and to halt illegal migration (*Migration News* 2002c). Meanwhile, Italy's right-wing government and the highly publicized landings of illegal immigrants and refugees have fueled anti-immigrant sentiment. In this context, the search for the elusive magic bullet of immigration control yields twin results: the trial and error, ad hoc approach that accounts for the unstable terrain of Italian immigration law, and mostly—and inevitably—"error," as these efforts are doomed to fail.

The second set of tensions at play here relates to the demographic and economic reality that Italy *needs* immigrants, versus the threat of economic and cultural competition that immigrants represent for many Italians. Antipathy toward immigrants often takes the form of an aversion toward multiculturalism and/or toward the particular cultures that immigrants bring with them. In a nation that defines itself as relatively culturally homogeneous, the influx of immigrants from around the world has caused alarm. The mosque has become the symbol of multiculturalism for a range of spokespeople who object to the contamination of Italy's "pure" Christian civilization (Archbishop of Bologna, quoted in Valli 2001: 41).

Right-wing political parties have capitalized on—and fueled—these economic and cultural fears and the aversion toward immigrants they provoke. The Northern League, the National Alliance, and Berlusconi's Forza Italia have all made restricting immigration a central plank of their platforms and have reaped the benefits in local and national elections.

Even though Italy may be one of the more "tolerant" countries in Europe—and a long tradition of Catholic charity, Communist party influence, and left-wing unions shores up an important pro-immigration lobby—a hot streak of populist antagonism to immigrants is nonetheless readily available for political exploitation.

Italian sociologist Maurizio Ambrosini titled a recent book *Utili Invasori* ("Useful Invaders"), calling attention to the conflict between the utility of immigrants and the hostility toward them. The playing out of this tension has many effects. Most important, politicians who capitalize on the hostility ultimately must come to grips with the utility. The result of the conflict between what the economy needs and what politics can exploit goes beyond the grudging half-open door and the implicit message it sends to immigrants: "Wanted but not welcome" (Zolberg 1987).

It also means that politicians on the right (and the left) are likely to promise controls they cannot deliver, not only because of the difficulty of stemming the immigrant tide but also because such promises inevitably get diluted in the waters of economic reality. This is most apparent at the local level, where much of Italian immigration law is implemented. The conflict between political exigency and economic reality is embodied in regional and municipal officials from right-wing parties whose platforms are anti-immigrant but who nonetheless must respond to the need for immigrant workers. For example, the councilor in charge of immigration in Veneto, Raffaele Zanon, is a member of the anti-immigrant National Alliance. Yet faced with employers demanding immigrant workers, a tight labor market, and a growing economy, Zanon has softened his anti-immigrant stance and even taken the lead in establishing an inter-regional discussion group on the social and economic integration of immigrants (author interviews with Veneto officials, July 2001). Zanon's most recent proposal to national party officials—reported to be based on consultations with employers and the "particular needs of the region's social and economic system"—asks that regions be allowed to secure more immigrant workers (*Notizie Ansa* 2002g).

The disjuncture between the strict immigration laws and the reality of Italy's rapidly expanding legal and illegal immigrant populations parallels this conflict between the restrictionist rhetoric of the country's right-wing coalition government and the economic imperatives faced by local officials, and both derive from the same underlying logic. One journalist summed it up: "It is not easy to use an iron fist against immigration without hitting the interests of employers ... and without mortgaging the very future of the country" (D'Avanzo 2002: 15).

The tension between economic/demographic reality and antipathy toward immigrants may be responsible for the failure of apparently restrictive policies and also of liberal provisions extending equal rights to immigrants. Permanent residence cards and antidiscrimination laws for immigrant housing represent a nod to the reality and inevitability of the immigrant presence. Yet their implementation depends on the goodwill of lower-level local officials, particularly the police. In the context of widespread fear and hostility, the result is a gap between the promise of those provisions and their delivery.

Ambrosini (1999: 13) writes, "Immigration is a kind of mirror that reflects the structures, development dynamics, and unresolved questions of the host society." As we have seen, the tensions and dynamics of the Italian political economy play themselves out through immigration policy—with all its twists and turns, spotty enforcement, and inevitable failures.

References

Adinolfi, Adelina. 1992. *I Lavoratori Extracomunitari: Norme Interne e Internazionali.* Bologna: Il Mulino.

Ambrosini, Maurizio. 1999. *Utili Invasori: L'inserimento degli Immigrati nel Mercato del Lavoro.* Milan: FrancoAngeli.

———. 2000. "L'inserimento Economico degli Immigrati in Italia." In *Immigrazione e Trasformazione della Societa',* edited by Pietro Basso and Fabio Perocco. Milan: FrancoAngeli.

———. 2001a. *La Fatica di Integrarsi: Immigrati e Lavoro in Italia.* Bologna: Il Mulino.

———. 2001b. "Il Lavoro." In ISMU-Cariplo, *Sesto Rapporto sulle Migrazioni 2000.* Milan: FrancoAngeli.

Annuario Sociale. 2001. *Rapporto su Fatti, Dati, Ricerche, Statistiche, Leggi, Nomi, Cifre in Italia, in Europa, e nel Mondo.* Milan: Feltrinelli.

Berti, Fabio. 2000. *Esclusione e Integrazione: Uno Studio su Due Comunita' di Immigrati.* Milan: FrancoAngeli.

Bonini, Damiano. 1991. "L'immigrato e i Suoi Diritti," *Perspettive Sindacali* 79/80: 83–94.

Bordignon, Fabio. 2002. "Gli Immigrati Fanno Meno Paura," *La Repubblica,* March 20.

Caputo, Giustina Orientale. 2000. "Salari di Fatto dei Lavoratori Immigrati in Italia." In *Rapporto Immigrazione: Lavoro, Sindacato, Societa',* edited by Enrico Pugliese. Rome: Ediesse.

Carchedi, Francesco. 2000. "Le Associazioni degli Immigrati." In *Rapporto Immigrazione: Lavoro, Sindacato, Societa',* edited by Enrico Pugliese. Rome: Ediesse.

Caritas. 2000. *Immigrazione: Dossier Statistico 2000.* Rome: Caritas.

Casadio, Giovanna. 2002. "Immigrati, 100,000 a Roma: No alla Legge Fini-Bossi," *La Repubblica,* January 20.

CENSIS (Centro Studi Investimenti Sociali). 2000. "Le Paure degli Italiani." Working Paper. Rome: CENSIS.

CNEL (Consiglio Nazionale dell'Economia e del Lavoro). 1991. *Immigrati e Societa' Italiana.* Conferenza Nazionale dell'immigrazione. Rome: Editalia.

CNNItalia Online. 2000. "Bianco sull'Immigrazione: Ecco I Veri Numeri." At CNN-Italia.it/Italia, December 18.

Codini, Ennio. 2001. "Gli Aspetti Normativi." In *Sesto Rapporto sulle Migrazioni,* ISMU-Cariplo. Milan: FrancoAngeli.

Corriere della Sera. 2002a. "Occupazione Record, Mai Cosi' Alta dal '93," March 28.

———. 2002b. "Berlusconi: Basta Litigi nel Governo. Vicina l'intesa, Legge entro Giugno," May 17.

———. 2002c. "Che Cosa Prevede il Disegno di Legge," January 20.

D'Avanzo, Giuseppe. 2002. "Perche Bossi Cavalca la Politica della Paura," *La Repubblica,* March 19.

Diamanti, Ilvo, ed. 2000. "Immigrazione e Cittadinanza in Europa: Indagine sulla Percezione Sociale." Venice: Fondazione Nord Est.

Eurispes. 2001. *Rapporto Italia.* Rome: Ufficio Stampa Eurispes.

Fasano, Luciano, and Francesco Zucchini. 2001. "L'implementazione Locale del Testo Unico sull'Immigrazione." In ISMU-Cariplo, *Sesto Rapporto sulle Migrazioni in Italia.* Milan: FrancoAngeli.

Galluzzo, Marco. 2001. "Immigrati, Arrivano 20 Mila Regolari in Piu,'" *Corriere della Sera,* March 15.

Gavosto, Andrea, Alessandra Venturini, and Claudia Villosio. 1999. "Do Immigrants Compete with Natives?" *Labour* 13, no. 3: 603–22.

Gueye, Alioune. 2000. "Il Rafforzamento della Presenza degli Immigrati nelle Aziende e la Contrattazione Sindacale." In *Rapporto Immigrazione: Lavoro, Sindacato, Societa',* edited by Enrico Pugliese. Rome: Ediesse.

Gullo, Tano. 2001. "Se e' Questo il Modo di Acogliergli," *Supplemento, La Repubblica,* July 20.

Henneberger, Melinda. 2001. "Provocateur Is Back to 'Spit On' Detractors of U.S.," *New York Times,* October 30.

Hundley, Tom. 2001. "Cultural Attitudes Blamed for Italy's Labor Crisis," *Chicago Tribune Online,* February 23.

Il Manifesto. 2001. "Europa (In)Tollerante," March 21.

ISMU-Cariplo. 2001. *Sesto Rapporto sulle Migrazioni in Italia.* Milan: FrancoAngeli.

ISPO (Istituto per gli Studi per la Pubblica Opinione). 1999. "L'atteggiamento degli Italiani nei Confronti degli Immigrati." Research conducted for the Commissione per le Politiche di Integrazione degli Immigrati. Working Paper No. 3.

Istat (Istituto Centrale di Statistica). 1980. *Annuario Statistico Italiano.* Rome: Istituto Poligrafico dello Stato.

———. 2000. "Competitivita' del Sistema Produttivo Italiano." Rome: Istituto Poligrafico dello Stato.

———. 2001. *Annuario Statistico Italiano*. Rome: Istituto Poligrafico dello Stato.

Kinsella, Kevin, and Victoria A. Velkoff. 2001. *An Aging World: 2001*. U.S. Census Bureau, Series P95/01-1. Washington, D.C.: U.S. Government Printing Office.

La Repubblica. 1999. "Fazio: 'Saranno gli Immigrati a Salvare le Pensioni Italiane,'" July 31.

La Terza, Maura. 1987. "Innovazioni Legislative sul Lavoro degli Stranieri Extracomunitari in Italia," *Questione Giustizia* 1: 29–43.

Los Angeles Times. 2002a. "Nationwide Strike Hobbles Italy," April 17.

———. 2002b. "Rome March Supports Immigration," January 20.

Maccaferri, Alessia. 2001. "Mina Demografica sulla Crescita," *Il Sole 24 Ore*, April 30.

Macioti, Maria Immacolata, and Enrico Pugliese. 1991. *Gli Immigrati in Italia*. Bari: Laterza.

Marra, Antonio, and Fabio Pontrandolfi. 1999. *Diritti e Doveri degli Immigrati: Procedure, Documenti e Prassi*. Naples: Esselibri.

Martirano, Dino. 2002. "Clandestini, Avvistate altre Quattro Navi," *Corriere della Sera*, March 20.

McBritton, Monica, and Mario Giovanni Garofalo. 2000. "La Legge sull'immigrazione e il Lavoro." In *Rapporto Immigrazione: Lavoro, Sindacato, Societa'*, edited by Enrico Pugliese. Rome: Ediesse.

Melossi, Dario. 2000. "The Other in the New Europe: Migrations, Deviance, Social Control." In *Criminal Policy in Transition*, edited by Penny Green and Andrew Rutherford. Oxford: Hart.

Migration News. 2002a. "Southern Europe. Italy," vol. 9, no. 1 (January): 27.

———. 2002b. "Southern Europe. Italy," vol. 9, no. 4 (April): 27.

———. 2002c. "Europe. EU: Illegal Immigration, Labor," vol. 9, no. 6: 16.

Ministry of the Interior. 2001. *Rapporto del Ministro dell'Interno sullo Stato della Sicurezza in Italia*. Bologna: Il Mulino.

Mottura, Giovanni. 2000. "Immigrati e Sindacato." In *Rapporto Immigrazione: Lavoro, Sindacato, Societa'*, edited by Enrico Pugliese. Rome: Ediesse.

Notizie Ansa. 2002a. "Immigrazione: +15% Annuo Presenza Stagionali Agricultura." At www.stranierinitalia.com, February 4.

———. 2002b. "Lavoro: Extracomunitari; Poco Sindacato al Nord, Piu' al Sud in Campania 'Sindacalizzazione' Superiore alla Media Regionale." At www.stranierinitalia.com, January 12.

———. 2002c. "Lavoro: Nella 'Fabbrichetta' Scioperano Solo Extracomunitari: Un Immigrato Denuncia il Caso al Congresso CGIL Lombardia." At www.stranierinitalia.com, January 15.

———. 2002d. "Immigrazione: Calderoli, Corteo Roma Occasione per Retata Esponente Leghista, si Punta a Immigrazione da Ripopolamento." At www.stranierinitalia.com, January 19.

————. 2002e. "Immigrazione: Accordo Assindustria Udine per Case a Immigrati gli Industriali per una Sistemazione Dignitosa Extracomunitari." At www.stranierinitalia.com, February 6.

————. 2002f. "Immigrazione: Sindacati, Sanatoria Colf 'Roba' da Ricchi." At www.stranierinitalia.com, March 19.

————. 2002g. "Immigrazione: Da Regione Veneto Emendamento su Ruolo Regioni Assessore Veneto Zanon Chiede Accordi Programma Stato-Regioni." At www.stranierinitalia.com, March 4.

Onorato, Pierluigi. 1989. "Per Uno Statuo dello Straniero," *Democrazia e Diritto* 6 (November–December): 303–28.

Osservatorio Ares. 2001. "I Dati dell'Osservatorio Ares 2000." Presented at the conference "Flussi Migratori e Politiche per la Salute," Sicily, March 26.

Petrini, Roberto. 2002. "Lavoro, Boom del Posto Fisso," *La Repubblica*, March 28.

Pugliese, Enrico. 2000. "Gli Immigrati nel Mercato del Lavoro e nella Struttura dell'Occupazione." In *Rapporto Immigrazione: Lavoro, Sindacato, Societa'*, edited by Enrico Pugliese. Rome: Ediesse

Pugliese, Enrico, ed. 2000. *Rapporto Immigrazione: Lavoro, Sindacato, Societa'*. Rome: Ediesse.

Reuters News Service. 2001. "Rightists Protest in Milan, Seeking Curbs on Muslims in Italy," October 19.

Romano, Sergio. 2002. "I Satelliti Avvistano altre Quattro Navi di Clandestini," *Corriere della Sera*, March 20.

Roncone, Fabrizio. 2002. "Immigrati, Decine di Migliaia Contro le Espulsioni," *Corriere della Sera*, January 20.

Rosenblatt, Robert A. 2001. "U.S. Not as Gray as 31 Other Countries," *Los Angeles Times*, December 15.

Sartori, Giovanni. 2000. *Pluralismo, Multiculturalismo, e Estranei: Saggio sulla Societa Multietnica*. Milan: Rizzoli.

Sestini, Raffaello. 1989. "La Disciplina degli Stranieri in Europa," *Democrazia e Diritto* 6 (November–December): 329–50.

Simone, Michele. 2002. "Gli Immigrati in Italia: Un Problema?" *Civilta' Cattolica*. January 19, pp. 187–96.

Sivo, Vittoria. 2002. "Insieme allo Sciopero Generale," *La Repubblica*, March 19.

Smith, R. Jeffrey. 2000. "Europe Bids Immigrants Unwelcome," *Washington Post*, July 23.

Stella, Gian Antonio. 2001. "Altivole, Un Abitante su Sette e' Immigrato," *Corriere della Sera*, March 19.

Tartaglione, Clemente. 2001. "Riallineamento e Sommerso nel Mezzogiorno." Presented at the IRES CGIL conference "L'Emersione del Lavoro Sommerso nel Mezzogiorno," Rome, February 16.

United Nations Population Division. 2000. *Replacement Migration: Is It a Solution to Declining and Ageing Populations?* New York: United Nations Secretariat.

Valli, Bernardo. 2001. "I Musulmani che Vivono in Mezzo a Noi," *La Repubblica*, August 2.

Valtolina, Giovanni Giulio. 2001. "Atteggiamenti e Orientamenti della Societa' Italiana." In ISMU-Cariplo, *Sesto Rapporto sulle Migrazioni*. Milan: Franco-Angeli.

Venturini, Alessandra. 1991. "Italy in the Context of European Migration," *Regional Development Dialogue* 12, no. 3 (Autumn): 93–112.

Venturini, Alessandra, and Claudia Villosio. n.d. "Are Immigrants Competing with Natives in the Italian Labour Market? The Employment Effect." Forthcoming.

Watts, Julie R. 2000. *An Unconventional Brotherhood: Union Support for Liberalized Immigration in Europe*. La Jolla: Center for Comparative Immigration Studies, University of California, San Diego.

Zanfrini, Laura. 1996. "Il Lavoro degli 'Altri': Gli Immigrati nel Sistema Produttivo Bergamasco," *Quaderni ISMU* 1.

Zincone, Giovanna. 2001. *Secondo Rapporto sull'integrazione degli Immigrati in Italia*. Bologna: Il Mulino.

Zolberg, Aristide. 1987. "Wanted But Not Welcome: Alien Labor in Western Development." In *Population in an Interacting World*, edited by William A. Alonso. Cambridge, Mass.: Harvard University Press.

Zuccolini, Roberto. 2002. "Colf e Lavoratori Agricoli: Un Esercito di Irregolari," *Corriere della Sera*, January 20.

Commentary

Christian Joppke

Italy is perhaps the most complex and fascinating European "latecomer" to immigration. The core contradiction of the contemporary European immigration scene is nowhere more evident than here: against the objective (demographic and economic) need for accepting more immigrants stands a political process under the sway of populism and "security" concerns, which commands increasingly tough and exclusive stances toward newcomers. This ambivalence permeates Italy's 2002 immigration law, the so-called Bossi-Fini Law, whose tough line on immigration has been fiercely (but unsuccessfully) opposed by northern Italy's industrialists. This legislation underscores one of the two patterns of Italian immigration policy identified by Kitty Calavita: its frequent "starts, shifts, and changes of course," which in this case are associated with the turn from a technocratic center-left to a populist center-right government in 2001.

However, in its unique harshness the Bossi-Fini Law also stands apart from all previous legislation. After all, it carries the signature of two extreme right parties, Umberto Bossi's Lega Nord and Gianfranco Fini's ex-fascist Alleanza Nationale. One of its key provisions, the "*contratto di soggiorno*," makes a residence permit contingent upon a work contract. In other words, if you lose your job, you are out. This rolls the wheel back to the 1950s northern European "guestworker" era. One could even say this provision makes Italy a bit less like its European neighbors (where the permanence of most labor migrants is now a statutorily provided and constitutionally protected option) and a bit more like the new immigrant-receiving states in the Middle East or Asia, in which the migrant worker's temporariness is heavily enforced. A second harsh provision in the new law is to require digital fingerprints not just from criminal aliens or clandestines (as under the previous law), but from all legal non–European Union newcomers—including Americans, Swiss, and Japanese. The thrust of both provisions is to "securitize" and render more precarious all immigration, illegal *and* legal. This approach clearly deviates from the contemporary European mainstream, which reserves harshness for illegal immigrants and tends to welcome legal (especially high-skilled) immigrants. So firm has been Bossi's grip on shaping the new law that even a massive last-minute campaign by centrist (Catholic and entrepreneurial) forces in the Berlusconi government, which had asked for a general amnesty for illegal workers, came to nil.[1]

Calavita well depicts the domestic forces that drive (or obstruct) Italian immigration policy. However, one does not learn much about the non-domestic factors that also shape this policy, in Italy as in other European states. Foreign policy is the first of two external domains in which European states' immigration function is increasingly situated. A longstanding feature of U.S. (and other new settler states') immigration policy, this is a novelty in Europe. Particularly across southern European states (most notably Spain and Italy), there is a new convergence to tie country-specific legal migrant quotas to cooperation and readmission agreements with the most important sending states. That is, "we take your legal labor migrants if you, in turn, help us get rid of your illegal and criminal migrants—or better still, if you prevent them from transiting or leaving your country in the first place." This implies an interesting rebirth of something liberal states have in principle long discarded: selecting migrants on the basis of their national origins. Yet it comes with an entirely non-ethnic, instrumentalist thrust of combating illegal immigration and organized human smuggling. In the Italian case, the critical country is Albania, which receives significant financial payments for its cooperation in the fight against illicit boat traffic across the Adriatic Sea—if you can call it "cooperation" on the part of Albania, whose internal instability and insistence on symbolic sovereignty frustrated successive Italian governments in the 1990s. Similar wrangles and deliberate misunderstandings have marred the relationship between Spain and its major migrant-sending state, Morocco.

There is an interesting asymmetry in this respect between Europe's eastern and southern border managements: similar bilateral agreements

---

[1] As a compromise, the government promised a (nonstatutory) decree that would regularize illegal workers (on which especially small and medium-size firms in the booming northern Italian economy crucially depend) (*La Repubblica*, June 5, 2002, p. 1).

of exchanging legal quotas against cooperation in illegal migrant control are eagerly observed by east European states, simply because they all want one day to join the European Union. No such accession lever is available to discipline Morocco or Albania, which compounds the inherent instability and unreliability of these states or quasi-states (can one call the Albanian state a "state" when its local authorities are known to collaborate with the human- and drug-smuggling mafias?). However, even if Albanian authorities were more forthcoming in honoring their part of the deal, Italy still faces a unique physical handicap in controlling illegal immigration: its several thousand kilometers of unprotectable (and touristically valued) coastlines, touching on Africa to the south and the Balkans and ultimately Asia to the east. The impossibility of controlling these coastlines has made Italy an enthusiastic supporter of the recent drive toward a Europeanized, multinational border force and cross-European police cooperation.

This introduces the second external domain within which Italian immigration control is increasingly situated: the European Union. This is quite separate from the "foreign policy" domain; it is almost like a second layer of quasi-domestic constraints. One cannot discuss the immigration policy of any European Union state without considering the growing impact of European Union constraints. The Treaty of Amsterdam has even "supranationalized" this formerly "intergovernmental" policy domain, in terms of the creation of an internal "area of freedom, security, and justice" whose protection is no longer just a matter of "common interest" among member states but an "objective" of the European Union itself. Throughout southern Europe the initial push toward restrictive immigration laws and policies was a result of (northern) EU member state pressures, because — especially with the intergovernmental Schengen Agreement — Italy's and Spain's southern borders were now Europe's southern borders. The main motivation of the 1998 Turco-Napolitano Law was to introduce a stricter detention and expulsion regime because, until then, Kurdish and other (Albania-transiting or Albania-originating) boat people went free after having been given formal notice to leave Italy by a set date. And "leave" they did, though not back to Albania or Turkey but to the Netherlands or Germany to join the sizable enclaves of co-ethnics there. Although a center-left government added some immigrant-friendly niceties to this law, Italy had to pass it, first and foremost, not to be expelled from the Schengen Convention. Its key provision is to detain illegal immigrants for up to thirty days, and then to accompany them to the border. In sum, what may be Mr. Bossi's agenda today was the agenda of Italy's Schengen partners then.

External EU pressures for more restrictiveness may help explain the *second* pattern of Italian immigration policy that Calavita discerned: the marked disjunction between policy goals and effects. However, this disjunction differs from other "gaps" identified throughout this volume; it comes with a peculiarly Italian (perhaps southern European) inflection. Before Bossi and Fini, Italian political elites have all been halfhearted executioners of an unwanted European dictate, for all the reasons enumerated in Calavita's chapter: the leftist solidarity with the Third World (in what other European state could one find an interior minister who considered it his "duty to help the development of the South of the world and to welcome its populations" [Christensen 1997: 482]?); the Catholic Church and affiliated charitable organizations' interest in lost souls and clients; the unions' interest in new members; employers' interest in (informal) migrant labor; and—hovering above all that—the vague but persistent memory of Italy's "emigration" past, triggering a sense of reciprocal obligation.

This is not to deny that with Bossi and Fini a new chapter opened in Italy's young immigration history, and one that incidentally may redeem the domestic perspective suggested by Calavita. For the first time, it is not Europe and the EU but home-grown populist right-wing parties' electoral interests that function as the originator of restrictiveness. Interestingly, attesting to the many uses of "Europe" in domestic policy debates, Europe and the European Union now figure, on the opposite, as a repertory of a "decent" and "civilized" approach to immigration, which is clearly undercut and violated by the most recent legislation.

Let me close with two observations on the "gap" hypothesis. First, there is the possibility of a gap between rhetoric and practice and also between action and consequences. Politicians usually act on public mandate (though mediated by majority rule, according to which some people's or groups' preferences are temporarily ignored). This usually leads to restrictive immigration policies that conflict with constitutive precepts of liberal-constitutional states. Accordingly, one might argue that (liberal-at-heart) elites put on a restrictionist show to placate an immigrant-hostile public (that is, that they engage in "symbolic politics"), while in actual practice they let many more immigrants in to comply with the rule of law and client interests. However, this assumes organizational and attitudinal unity on the part of the state, where in reality there is a multiple division of actors, competences, and opinions. In the Italian case, Bossi and Fini, of course, really want to realize their perceived public mandate of bashing non-EU immigrants; only there are also centrist forces within the center-right coalition government that must be reckoned with (centrist forces that are delicately denounced by Bossi, otherwise the Christian knight in the battle against the Muslim invaders, as "allied with the Catholic world" [*La Repubblica*, May 16, 2002, p. 11]). Therefore, a policy gap results from the failure or incapacity of the state to act—that is, to *implement* a policy as intended.

The public contributes to the policy gap between action and consequences by becoming hostile because the state does not deliver "security" or "zero immigration" as promised, feeding the prospects of populist mavericks like Bossi. In this sense, gaps occur because of the unintended consequences of action, according to which the calamity in question ("too many immigrants") is the result of the state's own action.

Finally, and this is my second observation, the nature of the "gap" differs depending on whether we are considering policies that seek to "stem" flows (immigration control proper) and policies that seek to "solicit" flows (see Joppke 2002). In the case of "stemming," the flow already exists, and the policy moves in ex-post to contain it. In this sense, the "gap" between unwanted flow and the policy that seeks to contain it is structural; it cannot be remedied. However, this is a "presentistic" illusion, because in the long term the efficiency of the modern administrative state becomes apparent. The post–1990s toughening and increasing effectiveness of asylum regulation across Western states is a case in point.[2] In the case of "soliciting" policies, the "gap" is of an entirely different nature. As German policymakers had to experience painfully with their so-called green card scheme for highly skilled computer specialists, Germany just was not a terribly attractive destination for the "best and brightest" from mythical Bangalore. The "gap" in this case consisted of the policy's incapacity to jumpstart a wanted flow. The differing logics (and inefficiencies) of "stemming" and "soliciting" will become a hallmark of Western states' immigration policies in the twenty-first century.

References

Christensen, D. 1997. "Leaving the Back Door Open," *Georgetown Immigration Law Journal* 11, no. 3: 1.

Joppke, Christian. 2002. "European Immigration Policies at the Crossroads." In *Developments in West European Politics*, edited by P. Heywood, E. Jones, and M. Rhodes. New York: Palgrave.

---

[2] As a result of tightened asylum procedures, the annual number of asylum applicants in European Union states has dropped from 675,460 in the peak year 1992 to 384,530 in 2001 (*Financial Times*, June 11, 2002, p. 3).

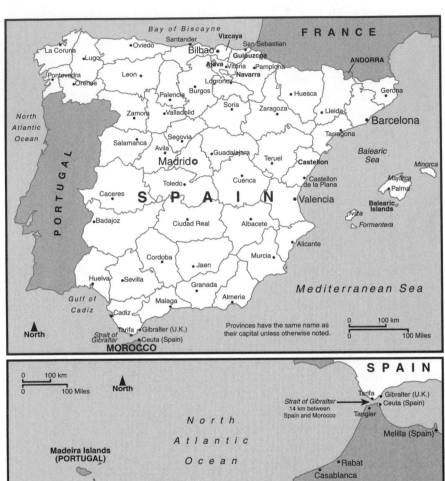

Bay of Biscayne

FRANCE

La Coruña
•Oviedo   Santander
Lugo•   Bilbao   **Vizcaya**
                                    •San Sebastian
•Pontevedra   **Guipuzcoa**
•Orense   Leon•   **Álava**•Vitoria •Pamplona   **ANDORRA**
                          Logroño•   **Navarra**
                    Burgos•
            Palencia•   •Huesca   •Gerona

North
Atlantic   Zamora• Valladolid•   Soria•   Zaragoza•   Lleida•
Ocean   •Barcelona
                    Segovia   Tarragona•
            Salamanca•   Avila•   Guadalajara•   Balearic
                    Madrid⊕   •Guadalajara   Teruel•   Sea   Minorca•
                                            Castellon   Majorca•
            Caceres•   Toledo•   •Cuenca   Castellon   •Palma
PORTUGAL   S P A I N   de la Plana
                                              •Valencia   **Balearic
            •Badajoz   Islands**
                    Ciudad Real•   Albacete•   Ibiza•
                                                      •Formentera
                                    •Alicante

            Cordoba•   •Murcia
            •Jaen
North   Huelva•   Granada•   Mediterranean Sea
        •Sevilla
        Malaga•   •Almeria
        Cadiz•
▲   Tarifa• •Gibraltar (U.K.)   Provinces have the same name as   0   100 km
North Strait of •Ceuta (Spain)   their capital unless otherwise noted.   0   100 Miles
      Gibraltar
      MOROCCO

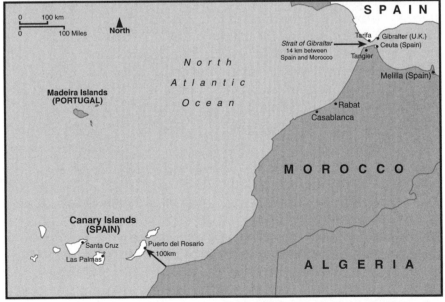

0   100 km   **S P A I N**
0   100 Miles   ▲ North

                                    Tarifa• •Gibraltar (U.K.)
                        Strait of Gibraltar   •Ceuta (Spain)
        North   14 km between
        Atlantic   Spain and Morocco   •Tangier
        Ocean
Madeira Islands   •Melilla (Spain)
(PORTUGAL)

                                              •Rabat
                                          Casablanca•

                              M O R O C C O

Canary Islands
(SPAIN)
        •Santa Cruz   •Puerto del Rosario
        Las Palmas•   ↖100km
                                          A L G E R I A

10

Spain: The Uneasy Transition from Labor Exporter to Labor Importer

Wayne A. Cornelius

THE SPANISH IMMIGRATION DILEMMA

During the 1980s Spain experienced a very rapid transition from labor-exporting to labor-importing country. Between 1973 and 1980, most of the more than one million Spanish "guestworkers" who emigrated to northern Europe (primarily France, Germany, Switzerland, and the United Kingdom) in the 1960s and early 1970s repatriated themselves.[1] By 1985–1986, Spain was experiencing substantial immigration, attracted by the beginnings of the economic boom that coincided with Spain's entry into the European Community (EC). The number of foreigners

This chapter is based in part on key informant interviews conducted in Madrid and Barcelona in 1992 and in Ceuta in 2001. I am indebted to Juan Díez Nicolás, Francisco Oda-Ángel, Lucia Fernández, Belén Agrela, Sandra Gil Araújo, and Xavier Escandell for help in obtaining data, and to Jessica Shpall for research assistance.

[1] A total of 466,394 returning migrants officially registered themselves in Spanish consulates between 1975 and 1988 (cited in Colectivo Ioé 1991). Until early 1992, the immigration office in the Ministry of Labor was anachronistically called the "Spanish Institute of Emigration."

residing legally in Spain rose sharply, from 241,971 in 1985 to 895,720 in 2000 and to 1,647,011 in 2003. Since 2000, the stock of legally registered immigrants has increased by an average of 24 percent each year. In addition, as many as 650,000 illegal immigrants are believed to be living in Spain.[2] Altogether, foreigners made up about 4.7 percent of Spain's total population in 2003.

Spain's immigrant population today is much more diverse in terms of national origins, culture, and socioeconomic status than it was two decades ago. Before the mid-1980s, foreigners in Spain were mostly relatively affluent tourists and retirees from the United Kingdom, Germany, and the Scandinavian countries who sought a warmer climate and lower living costs; they were not in the labor force. Since 1985 Spain has been receiving mostly worker-immigrants from North Africa (especially Morocco), Latin America (the Dominican Republic and the Andean countries), and Asia (mostly from China and the Philippines). By 2000, 60 percent of foreigners in Spain were from non–European Union (EU) countries (see table 10.1). By 2003 the proportion of non-EU foreigners had risen to 65 percent. While more than 334,000 originated in Morocco alone, the immigrant stock is extremely diverse in terms of national origins, with twenty countries having more than 5,000 legal immigrants in Spain (Arango 2000: 256–57). In recent years the most rapidly growing contingents have been from Eastern Europe (Romania, Bulgaria) and Latin America (Ecuador, Argentina, Colombia, Peru). There has also been a large influx of Chinese migrants, attracted by Spain's robust tourism and restaurant industries; Chinese are now the fourth largest group of non-EU immigrants in Spain (Nieto 2003; Pieke et al. 2004: 134).

The new immigrant flow contains many more young people, persons from lower-class backgrounds (although there are surprisingly large numbers of middle-class immigrants; see Díez Nicolás and Ramírez Lafita 2001a: 14), and people whose racial, religious, and other cultural attributes clearly differentiate them from the host population, such as sub-Saharan Africans and Chinese. The flow is also heavily illegal: only 17 percent of a sample of 765 African, Latin American, and Asian immigrants interviewed in 2000 in the five provinces having the largest immi-

---

[2] The nongovernmental organization SOS Racismo estimated the illegal immigrant population at 600,000 in October 2003. Immigration scholar Antonio Izquierdo Escribano, comparing the number of foreign-born people registered with municipal governments with legal residence permits issued by the Spanish government, estimated the stock at more than 650,000 in November 2003 (personal communication).

grant populations had entered Spain with a valid work permit (Díez Nicolás and Ramírez Lafita 2001a: 31).

Table 10.1. Legal Resident Foreign-born Population in Spain, by Region of Origin, 1995–2000

Region of Origin	1995	1996	1997	1998	1999	2000	Percent of Foreign Residents in 2000
Europe	255,702	274,081	289,084	330,528	353,556	361,437	40.4
Africa	95,725	98,820	142,816	179,487	213,012	261,385	29.2
Latin America	108,931	121,268	126,959	147,200	166,709	199,964	22.3
Asia	38,221	43,471	49,110	60,714	66,340	71,015	7.9
Oceania, other	1,194	1,344	1,844	1,718	1,712	1,919	0.2
TOTAL	499,773	538,984	609,813	719,647	801,329	895,720	100.0

Source: Ministerio del Interior 2002: table I.4.

Finally, since 1985 Spain has become a country of *destination* for many economic migrants from the Third World and Eastern Europe, supplementing its earlier function as a conduit for migrants heading for jobs in other European countries (especially France and Italy). Some officials estimate that more than half of those who have entered Spain illegally in recent years want to stay there; they are not in transit to any other country.[3] This change in South-North and East-West migration patterns has raised the possibility that Spain will soon be hosting a large, stable, and socially integrated foreign-born workforce—a prospect both unexpected and unsettling to most Spaniards.

---

[3] The choice of Spain as a country of destination has been made more frequently by migrants seeking short-term agricultural employment than by other segments of the immigration flow. For example, temporary agricultural jobs are plentiful in southern coastal zones like Almería; North African migrants do not need to travel farther north to gain employment. Nevertheless, as immigrant kinship networks became established in both rural and urban areas of Spain, it has become increasingly attractive as a destination country for all types of migrants. One out of five immigrants interviewed in a recent national survey reported that they had chosen Spain as a destination because they had relatives already living in the country (Díez Nicolás and Ramírez Lafita 2001a).

THE POLITICAL CONSTRUCTION OF SPAIN'S "IMMIGRATION PROBLEM"

Spanish officials describe immigration policymaking as a delicate balancing act. They feel that they must maintain enough control over illegal flows to prevent the numbers of foreigners (especially from Third World countries) from growing too rapidly and provoking a xenophobic public backlash, while simultaneously supplying a low-cost labor force that is adequate to keep the economy growing and attracting foreign investment. The balancing act has been complicated greatly by the surge of largely illegal immigration that Spain has experienced in recent years, driven by the country's robust economy. The newcomers have not yet overwhelmed social services, nor is there any evidence that they have increased unemployment appreciably by competing against native-born Spaniards for desirable, formal-sector jobs. Nevertheless, a broad consensus has emerged on the need for more effective immigration control measures and for a control system that is driven by Spain's specific labor market requirements rather than political, cultural, or diplomatic considerations.

The number of immigrants in Spain is still small by the standards of most European countries today. Spain's ratio of immigrants to total population puts it above only Finland and France. However, in absolute terms, Spain has one of the continent's largest populations of illegal immigrants, second only to France and larger than Italy's. Moreover, Spaniards are aware of, and disturbed by, the potential for massive, uncontrolled immigration fueled by huge demographic and economic imbalances between Spain and its impoverished North African neighbors. And they are increasingly willing to blame recent increases in crime (up by over 10 percent in 2001) on illegal immigration, especially from Africa.[4]

While it is still politically incorrect in Spain to mimic other Europeans who warn darkly of the continent's impending "Islamization" or "Africanization," there is growing concern and skepticism about Spain's capacity to absorb large numbers of Arab and African immigrants. In con-

---

[4] Interior Ministry officials have claimed that 40 percent of those arrested in 2001 were foreigners, while 89 percent of those detained were immigrants (Agence France Presse 2002a, 2002b). However, about 60 percent of the crimes were drug related, so the relationship between crime and immigration rates remains ambiguous. Of the 128,000 illegal immigrants who applied for regularization in 1991, fewer than 3,000 were found to have any criminal record (interview with Fernando Puig de la Bellacasa, May 1992).

trast to citizens of other industrialized countries today, Spaniards discount the notion that their country's national identity is threatened by immigration.[5] However, a multiracial, multicultural society is not seen as a desirable goal, and any immigration policy that would move Spain more quickly in this direction is to be avoided.[6] As in other West European countries, many Spaniards today are questioning whether it is possible to have a secular, non-extremist Islamic presence in their society.

Spain's preferred strategy is to avoid being cast in the role of "policeman of southern Europe," keeping the Third World hordes at bay while persuading its fellow European Union members to step up development assistance to the labor-exporting countries of North Africa. Former Prime Minister Felipe González reportedly gave each of his EU colleagues a copy of a large photograph of Morocco taken from Spain's southern coast. "This is our Rio Grande," he reminded them, pointing to the Strait of Gibraltar. "It's not far. And living standards are four, five, ten times lower on the other side" (quoted in Riding 1992).[7]

Domestically, the goal of the Spanish government for thirteen years under González and his center-left Spanish Socialist Party (PSOE) was to have a low-profile immigration policy — one that avoided arousing public passions and inflated expectations. Critics of this low-profile stance charged that it simply masked the absence of a real national immigration policy, as well as the lack of an administrative infrastructure and capacity that would be needed to implement an "active" immigration policy. To some observers, the reticence of the political class during the 1990s reflected the country's ambivalent attitudes toward the "new" immigration: many Spaniards still do not know what kind of immigration policy they really want.

---

[5] In one national public opinion survey, more than two-thirds of the respondents rejected the idea that Spain's national identity could eventually be lost through large-scale immigration (Díez Nicolás 1994).

[6] The minister of immigration in 2002 said publicly that multiculturalism is "unacceptable" for Spain. At most, he argued, Spain might become a "multi-ethnic society" (quoted in Amnesty International, "Spain: Crisis of Identity," at www.amnesty.org, April 16, 2002, p. 6).

[7] Spain's per capita income is now nine times higher than Morocco's. Fifty-five percent of Morocco's population is under 25 years of age, and labor force growth is outpacing economic growth. It has been estimated that to absorb new entrants to the labor force during the 1995–2010 period, Morocco, Algeria, and Tunisia together would have to create about ten million new jobs, equivalent to the total employed population in 1982 (Giubilaro 1997: 63).

José María Aznar and his conservative Popular Party (PP), in power since 1996, have been activists on the immigration issue. Promising it would deter illegal immigration, the Aznar government pushed through a tough new version of Spain's immigration law that, among other things, denied fundamental rights of assembly and association to illegal immigrants. Authorities have ordered several highly publicized police crackdowns on groups of illegal immigrants publicly seeking legalization.[8] The conservative government has also taken a significantly harder rhetorical line, frequently associating immigration with crime, social conflict, and imported poverty. In light of the fact that the illegal immigrant population has mushroomed and organized people-smuggling has flourished under Popular Party rule, the government may soon be dealing with a crisis of disappointed expectations.

Already, immigration has become the object of intense partisan debate, rupturing the elite political consensus on this issue that prevailed for most of the period from 1985 to the late 1990s. A serious outbreak of anti-immigrant violence in southern Spain in 2000, discussed below, polarized public opinion and contributed to the breakdown in elite consensus on immigration policy. The ruling conservatives and opposition socialists now trade recriminations, accusing each other of losing control over immigration and failing to take the steps necessary to prevent a broad public backlash against immigrants. Nevertheless, the Socialist Party has been reticent in criticizing the excesses of the conservative government on immigration. Since Prime Minister Aznar made anti-immigrant sentiment a respectable element of "mainstream" political discourse in Spain, opposition politicians risk losing vote share if they stray too far from the government's hard line.

Moreover, the recent upsurge in voting for far-right, anti-immigrant parties in nearly all West European countries except Spain has been seized upon by conservative Spanish politicians to justify more stringent immigration control measures. As one Popular Party leader warned, "Immigration is the issue that more than anything could upset Spain's harmony.... We must learn lessons from the French election [of 2002] so that in ten years' time Spain doesn't witness such a phenomenon" (quoted in Agence France Presse 2002b).

---

[8] For example, in August 2001 police evicted hundreds of illegal African immigrants from the central district of Barcelona, where they had been camping out since May. The eviction was televised nationally.

EXPLAINING THE HIGH INCIDENCE OF "IRREGULARITY" AMONG SPAIN'S IMMIGRANTS

By 1993, estimates of the illegal immigrant population ranged from 200,000 to 300,000 — this after some 110,000 foreign workers were legalized under a 1991 regularization program. By January 2002, more than 300,000 illegal immigrants were believed to be in Spain, after a sixteen-month regularization process that legalized 334,882 immigrants.[9] During 2003, 235,895 immigrants were regularized — a year in which the estimated stock of illegals rose to more than 600,000 (*El País* [Madrid], January 13, 2004).

Several factors seem to be driving the rapid increase in the "irregularity" of Spain's immigrant population. A substantial portion of the fluctuation in numbers of illegal immigrants results from Spain's complex system of short-term labor contracts, work permits, and residence permits, all mutually contingent, which causes many immigrants to move into and out of legal status continually (Calavita 1998; Calavita and Suárez-Navaz 2003).[10] This "catch-22" system has been aptly characterized by one Spanish immigration scholar as "institutionalized irregularity" (Santos 1993: 111). In addition, many regularized immigrant workers fall into illegality due to the inefficiency and ineptitude of the bureaucracy responsible for renewing work contracts (Coordinación ENAR España 2002) and because some employers prefer to keep their foreign workers in a situation of precariousness rather than convert them to permanent employees (further discussion below).

But the stock of illegal foreign workers is growing primarily because of new arrivals, attracted by economic growth and undeterred by restrictionist laws and policies. Data on participants in the 1991 legalization program suggest that most of the applicants were relatively recent arrivals, that is, since 1988 (López García 1992: 54). Thirty-six percent of a sample of non-EU immigrants interviewed in 2000 had been living in Spain for less than a year (Díez Nicolás and Ramírez Lafita 2001a: 20). One out of four interviewees admitted that they had entered Spain with no documents at all; among African immigrants, the proportion was over 40 percent (Díez Nicolás and Ramírez Lafita 2001a: figure II.2).

---

[9] Less than half (45.6 percent) of the *irregulares* who applied for legalization during this period were successful (see Bárbulo 2002a, 2002b).

[10] Arango (2000: 260) estimates that 25,000 to 30,000 illegals in 1996 were "*supervened irregulars*, that is, people who had legal status at some point in the past and then lost it" due to the rigidities of the work/residence permit system.

Nearly half of Spain's current stock of illegal immigrants originated in Africa. Especially numerous are the Moroccans (estimated to be nearly 40 percent of the illegal population), followed by Algerians, Senegalese, and Nigerians. Latin Americans comprise about one-quarter of the stock of *irregulares* (Ecuador, Colombia, Peru, and the Dominican Republic are the key sending countries). The remainder come mainly from Asia (China, Pakistan) and Eastern Europe (Romania, Poland, Ukraine, Bulgaria) (Donaldson and Essomba 2001: 54). There are striking social, economic, and demographic differences among these immigrant communities or *colectivos*, as they are known in Spain.[11] Skill and social class differences are most notable between the North Africans (who are overwhelmingly unskilled workers upon arrival in Spain) and East Europeans (skilled workers and professionals). Dominican and Peruvian immigrants are overwhelmingly female and employed in the domestic service industry, although there is a relatively high—and rising—proportion of females in all of the immigrant *colectivos* (Colectivo Ioé 2001: 249–50).[12] Chinese migrants are concentrated in the Chinese restaurant and catering sector, a burgeoning ethnic enclave that now encompasses nearly every small city and town in Spain (see Nieto 2003).

Illegal immigrants enter Spain in a variety of ways. Especially among Latin Americans, the most common mode is posing as a tourist, entering through an airport. Half of the Latin American immigrants interviewed in a 2000 survey reported that they had entered Spain in this way (Díez Nicolás and Ramírez Lafita 2001a: 24–25).[13] Those who enter on a tourist visa can easily overstay and seek employment. In 2002 alone, some 550,000 Latin Americans entered Spain as tourists, but only 86,000 left; how many stayed in Spain or moved on to another EU country is not known (Millman and Vitzthum 2003).

---

[11] For detailed ethnographic profiles of Spain's principal immigrant communities, see Giménez Romero 1993.

[12] The substantial representation of women in Spain's immigrant stock reflects more than family reunification immigration, although this type of migration is certainly occurring and will, no doubt, be accelerated by recent legalization programs. Among the Moroccan immigrant community, for example, the rising proportion of females results from a new migration of single women, originating in large cities, who seek work in domestic service and other parts of the service sector (López García 1992: 58).

[13] By contrast, 35 percent of the Asian immigrants interviewed in the same survey had entered on tourist visas, and only 18 percent of the North Africans had done so (Díez Nicolás and Ramírez Lafita 2001a: figure II.2). This exemplifies the strongly preferential treatment accorded by Spain to Latin American–origin immigrants, in the granting of visas as well as legalization (see Joppke n.d.: chap. 3).

The second most common way of becoming an illegal immigrant in Spain is to enter by sea, crossing the Strait of Gibraltar from the city of Tangier on the Moroccan coast or from Ceuta, a Spanish enclave that is completely surrounded by Moroccan territory. More than three-quarters of the 18,000 would-be illegal immigrants apprehended by Spanish authorities in 2001 were intercepted trying to enter via the Strait of Gibraltar.[14] As many as 20,000 are believed to have escaped detection in 2001, making their way from the beaches of southern Spain to jobs in the interior or in other EU countries. A second route takes undocumented immigrants from the Moroccan coast to the Canary Islands, crossing 100 kilometers of open ocean. In late 2001, a Moroccan crackdown on people smuggling across the Strait of Gibraltar shifted much of that traffic to the Canary Islands, which experienced a 500 percent increase in apprehensions of "irregulars" in the first quarter of 2002.

These perilous routes are used mainly by Moroccans and sub-Saharan Africans. The Zodiac rubber rafts in which they are transported, called *pateras*, are built to accommodate eight to ten persons but are typically loaded with forty, along with numerous open containers of gasoline. They often capsize in the rough waters of the Strait, drowning many of their passengers. The bodies of between 600 and 1,000 such victims are recovered on the beaches of southern Spain each year. In 2001, 710 bodies were recovered, making the maritime crossing to Spain more than twice as dangerous—in terms of migrant fatalities—as illegal entry into the United States at the U.S.-Mexico border (see Cornelius 2001). The actual death toll is undoubtedly much higher, since unknown numbers of migrants perish at sea, their bodies never to be recovered. Thousands of shipwrecked migrants are saved each year by Red Cross search-and-rescue teams. The migrants are treated for their injuries, in facilities provided by municipal governments in coastal areas, and turned over to immigration authorities. They are expelled within a few hours if they are of Moroccan nationality.[15]

Most clandestine entry into Spain is organized by people-smuggling rings—called *mafias* by Spanish authorities—based in Morocco. At its narrowest point, the Strait of Gibraltar is only 14 kilometers wide. The

---

[14] In 1992, only 1,717 illegal migrants attempting entry via the Strait of Gibraltar were apprehended; in 1999, only 3,569 were intercepted.

[15] Spain has a treaty with Morocco to expedite such repatriations. Morocco is the only major migrant-sending country that automatically accepts migrants expelled from Spain. In recent years, Moroccans have accounted for 94 to 97 percent of all illegal migrants expelled by Spain.

boat trip takes between two and five hours depending on weather conditions and the horsepower of the outboard motor used by the smuggler. In the fall of 2001, smugglers were charging the equivalent of about US$1,000 per head to cross the Strait of Gibraltar (compared with $550 to get to the Canary Islands).[16] Smugglers typically offer up to three trips to the Spanish mainland at no extra cost if the initial attempts are unsuccessful. Moroccan authorities periodically clamp down on these smuggling operations, usually under pressure from the Spanish government, but corruption and recurrent diplomatic conflicts between Spain and Morocco make enforcement spotty at best.[17]

Most illegal immigrants head immediately to Madrid and Barcelona because of their abundance of employment opportunities as well as kinship networks that have been established in these cities. The region of Catalonia, of which Barcelona is the capital, is also an attractive destination because of the availability of agricultural employment in the province's coastal areas. Madrid and Barcelona together accounted for 44 percent of all illegal immigrants who regularized their status in 2000.

LABOR MARKET PARTICIPATION

Both legal and illegal immigrants in Spain are employed predominantly in the service sector (see tables 10.2 and 10.3). Examples of service niches occupied disproportionately by foreign workers include domestic service, gardening, hotel and building maintenance, dishwashing in restaurants, loading and unloading of freight, and distribution of butane gas tanks to private residences. The construction industry, including public works construction, is another major source of employment for foreign workers in Spain. For example, many thousands of them were hired by

---

[16] In a sample of African, Latin American, and Asian immigrants living in Spain in 2000, most reported having paid $548 to $2,741 for their trip (Díez Nicolás and Ramírez Lafita 2001a: 28).

[17] In 2001, Spain suspended development assistance to Morocco, charging that the Moroccan government was failing to combat migrant-smuggling operations. In response, the Moroccan government claimed to have expelled more than 15,000 Africans and Asians trying to enter Spain via Morocco in the first six months of 2001 alone (El País, August 21, 2001). Morocco's crackdown on migrant smuggling in the Strait of Gibraltar in late 2001 was a direct consequence of the terrorist attacks of September 11, 2001, in the United States. The Moroccan government reportedly feared that it would be accused of flooding Europe with potential Islamic radicals (Quesada 2002).

subcontractors to build facilities for the 1992 Olympic Games, Expo '92, and the new Barcelona airport. Agriculture (especially in the south and coastal areas), mining, and small-to-midsize manufacturing enterprises (concentrated mainly in the Barcelona metropolitan area) offer additional employment opportunities.

Table 10.2. Work Permits Issued to Foreigners in Spain, by Sector, 1999

Sector	Number of Work Permits	Percent of National Total of Permits
Services	116,814	58.5
Agriculture	42,256	21.2
Construction	18,669	9.4
Manufacturing	14,809	7.4
Unclassified	7,175	3.6
TOTAL	199,753	100.0

Source: Ministerio del Interior 2002: 60. The Spanish government does not publish statistics on the stock of foreign workers in each sector of the economy, only on the flow (the number of work permits granted and renewed each year).

Table 10.3. Work Permits Delivered to Regularized Immigrants in Spain, by Sector, 1991 and 1996

Sector/Industry	Work Permits Granted to Regularized Immigrants in 1991		Work Permits Granted to Regularized Immigrants in 1996	
	Number	%	Number	%
Domestic service	23,289	21.2	2,814	21.6
Hotels	13,437	12.2	2,231	17.2
Other services	8,997	8.2	1,945	15.0
Construction	16,784	15.2	2,187	16.8
Agriculture	15,719	14.3	1,839	14.1
Retail	8,685	7.9	1,311	10.1
Manufacturing	—	—	679	5.2
Other	23,202	21.0	—	—
Unclassified	—	—	70	0.5
TOTAL	110,113	100.0	13,076	100.0

Source: OECD Secretariat 2000: table 6.

Except for the domestic service sector, there is no large-scale, organized recruitment of foreign workers by employers. Well-organized enterprises do operate in Madrid and Barcelona to place illegal female immigrants (primarily Filipinas, Dominicans, and Peruvians) in domestic service jobs. Most employers do not screen job applicants for immigration status; that is, they do not require applicants to present work permits issued by the government in order to be hired. Firms that utilize foreign workers typically have mixed workforces, including both foreigners and native-born Spaniards.

The Spanish labor markets in which immigrants participate tend to be highly segmented. In every sector of the economy, foreigners occupy the least skilled, most physically demanding, most dangerous, and most temporary jobs, with no promotion ladder, even though many of the immigrants employed in such jobs are reasonably well educated and skilled workers.[18] Because of the short-term nature of so many of the jobs held by immigrants, as well as the obstacles to obtaining long-term work permits (see below), immigrants in Spain have a higher unemployment rate than native-born workers—32 percent in one recent survey (Díez Nicolás and Ramirez Lafita 2001a: table 6.8).

In some sectors, employers seeking to hire foreigners for unskilled jobs have a preference hierarchy in hiring. In agriculture, for example, black African immigrants are the most attractive to employers because of their image as hard-working, docile, and trustworthy workers. Ecuadorians are seen as close substitutes. Magrebíes (immigrants from Morocco, Algeria, and Tunisia) are perceived as much less desirable, partly due to historically grounded prejudices against "los moros" and because they are viewed as "unproductive" and "conflictive" (Castellanos Ortega and Pedreño Cánovas 2001: 14). Discrimination in hiring against Moroccans, in particular, is institutionalized and widespread (see Solé 1995). A direct test by an ILO field research team found that one out of three job opportunities in services, construction, and manufacturing were closed to Moroccan applicants, even if they were proficient in Spanish (Colectivo Ioé 1998a). Because of the high degree of labor market segmentation and the growing stigmatization of jobs typically done by foreign workers, instances of overt labor market competition between natives and foreigners have been relatively rare in Spain. The only documented cases

[18] See Carrasco Carpio 1999; Colectivo Ioé 1998b, 1999; Mendoza 2000, 2001. A recent survey found that only 14 percent of non-EU immigrants in Spain had less than a complete primary education, and that 28 percent had at least some university-level education (Díez Nicolás and Ramírez Lafita 2001a: table 1.2).

of such competition have been in the agricultural sector. In the late 1980s, native-born citrus pickers in Valencia went on strike and growers replaced them with Moroccan immigrants. In another region, conflicts over fruit-harvesting work erupted between black Africans and poor Spaniards in 1991.

For an illegal immigrant in Spain, changing jobs is often more difficult than getting an initial toehold in the labor market. Under the Spanish immigration law (Ley de Extranjería), each time a foreign worker changes employers he must obtain a new work permit from the government. Even legal immigrants who lose their jobs and are unable to acquire a new work permit are ostensibly required to leave the country. Local branches of the national Ministry of Labor determine whether a work permit will be granted, and there is much unevenness in approvals. The bureaucratic obstacles to renewing work permits are also formidable. Foreigners seeking to renew their permits must present their Social Security cards, but only a minority of immigrants working in certain sectors (such as domestic service, for example) are able to obtain work contracts that include Social Security payments by the employer. Not surprisingly, by the end of 1995 barely one-third of Spain's immigrant workers held long-term work permits; one-quarter held permits lasting less than a year; the rest were in intermediate categories.[19]

This work permit system does not exclude immigrants from the labor market, but for many it limits their options to the underground economy or to formal-sector firms that employ them "off the books," thereby avoiding costly payments for Social Security and other employee benefits. The system has been a great boon to employers: it has helped to institutionalize a system of short-term hiring that gives them maximum flexibility to shed labor when it is not needed. The share of workers on fixed-term contracts in Spain is the highest in Western Europe. Irrespective of the worker's immigration status, the maximum duration of fixed-term employment contracts is three years, and only a small minority of

---

[19] Izquierdo Escribano 1997, cited in Arango 2000: 264. The initial work permit has a maximum duration of nine months and limits the worker to a specific employer. The first renewal is limited to one year and authorizes employment in a specific occupation, economic sector, and province. After a total of five years of legal work (two years for favored nationalities and ethnic groups), an immigrant can apply for a five-year work permit allowing free movement across economic sectors and provinces. After six years of legal work (five years for Latin Americans, Filipinos, Equatorian Guineans, and a few other groups), non-EU workers can apply for permanent resident status in Spain. See Mendoza 2001: 170 for further details.

temporary workers are converted by employers to permanent status when the legal limit is reached (Güell and Petrongolo 2003).

Foreign workers in Spain are typically paid less than natives (if native-born workers are employed in similar jobs in the same industries), irrespective of their educational credentials and prior work experience (Solé and Parella 2003). Wage discrimination is most likely to be practiced by small subcontractors and agricultural employers, whose wage and employment practices are rarely scrutinized by the government. By far the worst working and living conditions are those endured by agricultural contract workers from Africa and Eastern Europe, whose situation has been characterized as "semi-slavery."[20] In some urban sectors (such as domestic service and construction), the chronic shortage of native-born labor puts a floor under terms of employment for foreigners.

SOURCES OF SPAIN'S DEMAND FOR IMMIGRANT LABOR

With Europe's highest official unemployment rate (ranging between 15 and 23 percent during the 1990s, falling below 13 percent only in late 2001), it would seem implausible that Spain has difficulty meeting its labor requirements without substantial foreign immigration. This is, in fact, the principal rationale for Spain's restrictive immigration law: "The state regulates immigration tightly in order to protect Spanish workers from competition for scarce jobs" (Mendoza 2001: 177). Government officials routinely justify immigration control measures as necessary to meet the needs of the "1.5 million unemployed Spaniards" (Gil Araújo 2002: 89). However, it is generally conceded that official unemployment statistics are unreliable and to some extent meaningless, given the widespread practice of collecting unemployment compensation while working in the underground economy (see below).

Moreover, there is broad agreement among social scientists that Spain's current shortages of labor in certain sectors of the economy are relative rather than absolute. Recent immigrants have been channeled into certain labor market niches that have been abandoned by native-born workers (Arango 2000: 262–64; Mendoza 2000, 2001). In regions

[20] In one case investigated by Spanish police, 1,500 illegal migrant farmworkers from Bulgaria had had their passports confiscated by their ten Spanish employers and a Bulgarian labor broker. Heavy payments on a debt of (US)$1,952 per worker for job placement were being withheld from their wages (*El País*, December 14, 2001). The situation of hyper-exploited African immigrant workers in Spanish agriculture is analyzed in Hoggart and Mendoza 1999 and Mendoza 2003.

where immigrants are now a fixture of the regional economy (as in Andalucia, one of the country's poorest provinces), there are large pools of native-born labor theoretically available to fill the jobs now held by foreigners. How, then, can we explain the strong (and growing) demand for foreign-born labor? As noted above, the Spanish labor market is highly segmented, and there are strong disincentives for taking jobs in some sectors, causing a relative shortage of labor. Agriculture and domestic service are the two clearest examples of sectors in which native-born workers do not make themselves available in sufficient quantity (Altamirano Rua 1996: 117–29; Mendoza 2003).

In the case of agriculture, the temporariness of the jobs, low (but usually not illegal) wages, the remoteness of the work sites, and extremely uncomfortable working conditions (working in triple-digit heat under sheets of plastic) make it virtually impossible for employers to recruit native workers for harvesting strawberries, citrus fruits, and olives. The economic boom of the late 1970s and early 1980s enabled small and medium-sized growers to invest in greenhouses, thereby creating a new demand for hand labor.[21] At the same time, many native-born former farmworkers no longer wanted to work in agriculture. This was especially true of returned Spanish emigrants, many of whom had toiled at precisely the same kinds of jobs now "reserved" for foreigners in Spain. Those who had held better jobs abroad were even less likely to take the bad jobs held by immigrants today (Pascual de Sans and Cardelus 1990).

Domestic service used to be provided by internal Spanish migrants from impoverished provinces like Andalucia. Since the early 1980s, however, young Spanish women have not been available for such work, particularly live-in employment. They could earn considerably more and enjoy better working conditions in other types of work, such as factory employment. The gap left by the virtual disappearance of Spanish-born, live-in domestic servants has been filled by foreigners—Filipinas, Dominicans, Peruvians, Portuguese, Moroccans, even Poles (see Colectivo Ioé 2001). At the same time, rising family incomes during the economic boom period greatly increased the demand for in-house domestic service, even in middle-class homes. Finally, the aging of the Spanish population has been creating a new demand for female immigrants as care-providers for the elderly. Domestic service is not attractive to Spaniards

---

[21] Spain's zones of large-scale agriculture, in provinces like Andalucia and Sevilla, are mechanized and have much less need for harvest labor, in contrast to the small-scale, family-owned farms of regions like Meresme and Valencia, which depend heavily on foreign hand labor.

for most of the same reasons that lead them to shun agricultural labor: low (but not illegal) wages, temporariness, and poor working conditions. Spanish women now have much better options.

Employers and many public officials attribute much of the demand for foreign labor to rigidities in the labor market resulting both from restrictive labor and immigration laws and from sheer bureaucratic inefficiency. Such inefficiency has led to huge backlogs—sometimes stretching to two years—in processing employers' applications for work permits. Critics of the existing work permit system charge that it has no utility for controlling or discouraging the hiring of illegal immigrants. Quite the contrary. The 1985 immigration law requires that an employer demonstrate that no native-born worker nor citizen of a European Union member country is available to fill a job vacancy before a work permit can be issued to a non-EU foreigner. "The usual pattern," observed one legal expert, "is that no Spanish applicants come forward, and the employer just hires the foreigner illegally."[22] For example, work permits are often denied to foreigners seeking domestic service work, on the grounds that high unemployment among native-born Spaniards makes foreign labor unnecessary. "But the unemployment statistics are too highly aggregated. No Spaniards are really available for this type of work, so the employer hires an illegal. There is a real labor demand in this sector that cannot be satisfied legally."[23]

Labor legislation in Spain is more restrictive and employer compliance is more costly than in most industrialized countries today. It is easy to hire workers (except foreigners who need work permits) but very difficult to fire them, and large indemnization payments are required when workers are laid off or dismissed. Social security and other employee benefits are quite costly by international standards. The rigidities in Spain's labor market, a legacy of Francoism, have helped to increase the demand for foreign labor in two key ways. First, they make immigrants who are willing to work on short contracts or with no contracts at all (off the books) attractive as a labor source. Second, the short-term hiring system has reduced incentives for native-born Spaniards to work, at least in the formal sector of the economy. A large portion of the native-born Spanish workforce has taken advantage of the system by jumping from one short employment contract to another, interspersed with periods in which they collect unemployment compensation (*"el paro"*). Labor

---

[22] Author interview with Lidia Santos Arnau, Universidad Autónoma de Barcelona.
[23] Author interview with Magistrate Celsa Pico Lorenzo, Tribunal Superior de Justicia de Catalunya.

Ministry officials and academic experts estimate that in some provinces 60 to 70 percent of the residents are on unemployment compensation and not looking for legal employment, even while they *are* working in unregistered jobs.[24] In the heavy immigrant-using province of Andalucia, which has a special government-sponsored rural employment program, local politicians have facilitated taking advantage of the system by creating very short term or fictitious, nonremunerated public works jobs, just to qualify their holders for unemployment compensation. A controversial administrative decree issued by the Felipe González government in 1992 was aimed at curbing abuses of unemployment compensation by Spanish workers, but there is no evidence that the government forced many of them back into "immigrant jobs." The country's large underground economy still offers alternatives for those who choose to remain outside the formal sector.

Meanwhile, Spain's demographic profile continues to evolve in ways that make labor shortages more difficult to avert without substantial immigration. The country's total fertility rate has dropped to 1.2 children per woman — the lowest in the world (Italy and Japan are the other two countries vying for this distinction). In 1974, 680,000 births to Spanish parents were recorded; in 1998, there were only 364,427. The plummeting birthrate has been associated with rising educational levels among Spanish women, the end of the Franco regime, a decline in the influence of the Catholic Church, and the economic crisis of 1975–1976. When Spain's economy rebounded in the 1980s, low-fertility attitudes were already well established. It has been projected that, at the current fertility rate, Spain will lose 9,408,000 people from 1999 to 2050 — second only in Europe to Italy and the Ukraine (United Nations 2000). Only the recent influx of immigrants of childbearing age has prevented Spain from slipping into negative population growth. For example, the 20,054 children born to immigrant parents enabled Spain's population to grow by 6,477 in 1998.[25]

The Spanish population is also aging rapidly. Spain already has a higher proportion of elderly residents than either France or Germany, and life expectancy is already longer than in the United States. Assuming

---

[24] Spain devotes a larger share of social welfare spending to unemployment compensation than any other EU country (Calavita 1998).

[25] A 1999 survey found that 47 percent of Spanish women were childless, while 42 percent of Latin American immigrant women had two children and more than 30 percent of African immigrant women had three or more (Instituto Nacional de Estadística 2000).

that these demographic trends are irreversible, they will deepen the relative shortages of labor already evident in some sectors of the Spanish economy and push the country toward an absolute labor deficit in the foreseeable future (see Fernández Cordón 2001). Again, Third World immigration is the only countervailing demographic force. The median age of Spain's foreign-born population is under 35 years, compared with 45 years among native-born Spaniards (Izquierdo Escribano 1997).

THE EVOLUTION OF IMMIGRATION CONTROLS

Legislation and Labor Quota System

Before 1985, Spain had made no effort to enact a comprehensive immigration law. Its first attempt, the Ley de Extranjería (officially titled La Ley Orgánica sobre Derechos y Libertades de los Extranjeros), was approved by the Spanish Congress in April 1985 and implemented on July 1 of the same year. This highly restrictive law was almost entirely the result of external pressure associated with Spain's entry into the European Union on January 1, 1986, which required adherence to EU legislation limiting immigration from non-EU countries. Its main thrust, dubbed a "police approach" by one leading Spanish immigration scholar (Arango 2000), was to increase government powers to deal with aliens already present in the country rather than to strengthen border controls. It enabled the government to deport foreigners found to be engaged in "illicit activities," those who are in Spain without proper residence permits or legal temporary visas, those "implicated in activities contrary to the public order," and those who, "lacking legal means of earning a living, devote themselves to begging or other conduct considered socially unacceptable." Perhaps most importantly, the 1985 law restricts immigrants' access to formal-sector employment by requiring them to first obtain a work contract from an employer, then to solicit official work and residence permits separately, from two different ministries (Labor and Interior, respectively).

Accumulating evidence that the "police approach" to immigration control embodied by the 1985 law was failing to keep the stock of illegal immigrants from growing led to the creation, in 1993, of a quota system intended to channel migrant flows to specific regions and labor-short sectors of the Spanish economy. Under this system, the government each year establishes a foreign labor quota or *contingente*, supposedly reflecting provincial-level labor market trends. It also specifies which nationalities will be permitted to fill the quota. In its first year of operation, the quota system failed as a mechanism for importing new foreign workers into Spain because too few employers made job offers — an essential condition for legal entry. The lack of employer interest in 1993 has been attributed to the cost of participation (employers were required to pay for the foreign worker's return ticket) and to the easy availability of illegal immigrant labor already in Spain (Mendoza 2001: 169). The rules were soon changed to enable "irregulars" already in the country to participate, and the number of accepted applications immediately quintupled (see table 10.4).

Table 10.4. Work Permits Granted under the Spanish Labor Quota System, by Economic Sector, 1993–2002

Sector	1993	1994	1995	1997	1998	1999	2002
Agriculture	160	8,453	7,855	16,313		9,925	17,002
Construction	–	737	–	1,334		2,422	6,567
Domestic service	4,346	13,728	12,091	19,314		20,521	2,233
Other services	714	2,686	–	6,629		4,881	5,395
Unclassified	–	–	–	3,291		1,964	882
Total	5,220	25,604	19,946	46,881	28,000	39,713	32,079

Source: For 1993-1997, Mendoza 2001: table 1; for 1998-2001, Ministerio del Trabajo y Seguridad Social; for 2002, "España acogerá a 32,079 inmigrantes en 2002," *El País,* December 23, 2001.

Notes: The government set no labor quotas in 1996, 2000, and 2001, due to regularization programs occurring in those years. "Other services" refers to unskilled work in hotels and restaurants. For 1995, the "domestic service" figure includes "other services." Figures for 2002 represent the quota set by the government for that year, not work permits granted.

From the outset, the quota system has been criticized for offering too few jobs[26] in too few sectors of the economy (essentially it has functioned to provide labor only to the agricultural and domestic service industries). The number of work permits offered under the quota scheme has been relatively constant since 1994, averaging fewer than 30,000 per year, leading some to suggest that political considerations rather than labor

---

[26] For example, in 1998 there were 42,872 applications for work permits under the quota system, but the government offered only 28,000 job openings.

market dynamics were the real determinants of the labor quotas (Arango 2000: 269). Others have criticized the quota system as a disguised legalization program, drawing illegal immigrants already in Spain into the work permit system and enabling the government to meet the private sector's labor requirements while avoiding formal amnesty programs (see, for example, Moreno Fuentes 2001: 135). Responding to such criticisms, the government restricted the 2002 quota to foreign workers who are not already in Spain, to be recruited only in countries that have signed bilateral migrant labor accords with Spain (Ecuador, the Dominican Republic, Colombia, Romania, and Morocco). Finally, the quota system has been faulted for reinforcing Spain's emphasis on short-term, fixed contracts for foreign workers, which according to critics amounts to manufacturing illegality. Two-thirds of the jobs in the quota set for 2002 were short term.[27] To continue being employed in Spain under the quota system, most workers must return to their home countries and reapply for a work permit. Of course, many do not return and continue working, illegally, in Spain.

In the late 1990s, when Spain began to receive much larger numbers of Third World immigrants, concern mounted among the country's political class that neither the 1985 immigration law nor the labor quota system provided the framework for a "real" immigration policy. The Socialist Party, now in opposition, became more tolerant of illegal immigration, while the ruling Popular Party positioned itself as the bulwark against "unwanted" immigration, vowing to end the *"efecto llamado"* (pull effect) of what its leaders characterized as an excessively generous immigration law. A first attempt to revise the Ley de Extranjería, completed in April 2000 at the end of a legislative cycle in which the PSOE was still the junior partner in a coalition government, represented a significant liberalization of the 1985 law, guaranteeing immigrants' access to various public services (regardless of legal status) and emphasizing the need to promote the social integration of immigrants. The PP denounced the new law as fatally flawed and vowed to revise it extensively before it could be implemented. Having won an absolute majority in the national legislature in the March 2000 elections, the PP moved swiftly to do just that.

The harsh version of the Ley de Extranjería announced by the new conservative government in August 2000 and implemented in January 2001 rolled back all of the rights granted to immigrants in the April

---

[27] The 2,233 domestic servants to be admitted under the 2002 quota were limited to three-month visas.

amendments and shifted the emphasis from immigrant integration back to immigration control. It denied to illegal immigrants the freedoms of association, demonstration, unionization, and strike; streamlined the process for deportation; extended the time necessary for obtaining regularization; and made family reunification more difficult. It rolled back all of the rights to public services granted in the April 2000 version of the law, and barred even legal immigrants from receiving free legal aid and from participating in municipal government processes. Only access to health care and public education were preserved. In general, the situation of non-EU immigrants in Spain was worsened by the new law (Ruiz de Huidobro 2001; Vives i Ferrer 2001). Conservative President Aznar pronounced this "the most open and modern immigration law in Europe" (Aznar 2001), but opposition politicians and nongovernmental organizations (NGOs) condemned it as a serious retrogression.[28]

Border Enforcement

Only in the mid-1990s did the Spanish government initiate surveillance of "hot spots" for illegal immigration: southern coastal towns like Algeciras, the Madrid airport, and so forth. It did so under pressure from the European Union, whose northern member countries have long regarded Spain as one of the weakest points in the EU's security perimeter. The Spanish navy and Guardia Civil (which has functions analogous to the U.S. Border Patrol) have stepped up patrols along the southern coast and in the Canary Islands, but they lack the resources to maintain tight control over such a long coastline, and people smugglers quickly shift their routes in response to enforcement actions by both the Spanish and Moroccan authorities. In 2002–2003 the Spanish government deployed advanced radar surveillance equipment to detect immigrant smuggling along the southern coast, but the principal effect has been to push more of the migrant flow into the Atlantic passage to the Canary Islands.

Eight kilometers of Spain's land border with Morocco, on the Ceuta peninsula, have been fortified with watchtowers, video surveillance cameras, motion detectors, and double razor-wire fences. The cost of this high-tech security project was covered by the European Union. Hun-

---

[28] In 2003 the Aznar government secured passage of another set of restrictive amendments to the Ley de Extranjería, which gave national authorities and police access to personal data on immigrants who register with municipal governments, and required private transport companies to divulge information on their passengers.

dreds of apprehensions per night are made along this heavily fortified segment of the Spanish-Moroccan border; but just beyond the new border fence—which ends in the Strait of Gibraltar—*pateras* loaded with would-be illegal migrants leave for the mainland when night falls. Guardia Civil authorities on the ground in Ceuta and Melilla (Spain's other enclave on the North African coast) readily admit that Spain's border enforcement efforts have only symbolic import.

Interior Enforcement and Employer Sanctions

There are no internal controls on population movements in Spain, so illegal immigrants who succeed in gaining entry can move about freely by highway and train. Since 2000, under the Schengen Agreement, Spain and twelve other EU countries have dismantled most passport and customs controls on their internal borders. Illegal migrants arriving safely on a Spanish beach make their way inland, and there is nothing to stop them until they reach their preferred destination anywhere in the continental European Union. Except in central Madrid, the police and the Guardia Civil do not make routine sweeps of urban areas to detect and apprehend illegal immigrants. Turf struggles between the Ministries of Labor and Justice, the two agencies principally responsible for immigration law enforcement, have impeded a sustained, well-coordinated effort to sweep up and expel illegal immigrants already in the country.

Penalties against employers who knowingly hire illegal immigrants were included in the 1985 immigration law and were implemented beginning in 1988, but these sanctions have had no discernible deterrent effect on either employers or illegal foreign workers. The law prescribes administrative penalties and fines of 500,000 pesetas (about US$5,000) per alien but no criminal penalties. Enforcement is through comprehensive workplace inspections by the Labor Ministry that are not limited to, or even focused upon, immigration law enforcement; inspectors look for all sorts of violations, including nonpayment of legal minimum wages, avoidance of Social Security payments, health and safety violations, nonadherence to contractual agreements on working hours, vacations, and so forth. Only a small fraction of the violations detected through workplace inspections are infractions of the immigration law.[29] In prac-

---

[29] The number of such infractions detected throughout the economy in 2001 was 6,813—a 250 percent increase since 1996 but still a token level of enforcement (Izquierdo Escribano and Martínez Buján 2003: 155–56).

tice, the employers who are penalized for immigration violations are those who commit the most extreme abuses of other labor standards; they are not prosecuted simply for employing illegal immigrants. In the regions most heavily impacted by illegal immigration, like Catalonia, backlogs of uninvestigated complaints made by individual workers, labor unions, and neighbors concerning the presence of illegal immigrants have accumulated.

The Interior Ministry sometimes accuses the Labor Ministry of being too lax in enforcement of employer sanctions, but Labor Ministry and provincial government officials cite a host of obstacles to effective enforcement. There are special enforcement problems in agriculture, fishing, transportation, and construction. These are all sectors where the workforce is less stable, where there are open-air work sites where it is easier to conceal illegal immigrants, and so forth.

The huge underground economy — including domestic service, street vending, and small, unregistered firms of all sorts — presents an even more formidable challenge to immigration control via employer sanctions. As explained by one Spanish scholar: "The basic problem is that there is a high level of tolerance for the underground economy. Rapid economic growth in the 1980s and 1990s did not create enough permanent, formal-sector jobs. Therefore, a large proportion of illegal immigrants as well as native-born workers are employed in the underground economy. If it were seriously disrupted, much of the total population could be left without work."[30]

Less than aggressive enforcement of employer sanctions can also be expected because of Spain's well-entrenched *cultura del empresario* ("culture of the businessman"). The closeness of government-business ties, under both "socialist" and conservative governments, clearly limits the enforcement of employer penalties for hiring illegal immigrants as well as sanctions against "*el delito social*" — that is, failure by employers to pay Social Security and other legally mandated employee benefits. Prosecutions under the "social crime" law, which has been on the books for many years, are extremely rare. For the same reason, there is widespread skepticism that recent amendments to the immigration law that strengthen fines and criminal penalties against those who employ or transport illegal immigrants will be widely applied. Judges are likely to

---

[30] Author interview with Lidia Santos de Arnau. Most economists estimate that the underground economy accounts for at least 25 percent of Spain's gross national product (GNP).

consider the penalty disproportionate to the crime, and acquittals will be even more common than they already are.

The slowness and inefficiency of the Spanish administrative-judicial system in general pose additional obstacles to effective employer sanctions enforcement. It has been described by one magistrate as "an incredibly inefficient, time-consuming, counterproductive system, from the standpoint of immigration control."[31] One indicator of the problem is the fact that, ironically, many enforcement actions arise from employer requests for government approval of work permits for foreign-born employees. Eventually, inspectors are sent to check whether the applicant is actually working at a given firm. The employer, who has kept the foreign worker on the payroll during the lengthy adjudication period, is fined because the applicant has not yet received his legal work permit! Some employers, faced with interminable bureaucratic delays in hiring foreign workers *por la vía legal* prefer to pay a fine rather than sacrifice a large order and lose market share within their industry.

Visa Policy

Spain's second important immigration policy concession to the other members of the European Union—following the restrictive 1985 immigration law—was a tightening of visa control. Visa requirements were imposed on citizens of the Maghreb countries in 1991. Since 1992, Peruvians, Dominicans, and Cubans have been required to obtain an entry visa (Colombians and Ecuadorians were added later), but "tourists" from other Latin American nations can still enter without visas. Restricting entries from Latin America was a much more politically and diplomatically sensitive step than restricting them from the Maghreb countries. For several decades, many Latin American countries have had dual-nationality agreements with Spain, and Latin Americans are hardly perceived by Spaniards as "foreigners," given their shared linguistic and cultural attributes. "Requiring visas for Latin Americans posed great problems for the Spanish government.... It ran contrary to the policy followed by every Spanish government from Franco to the [PSOE] Socialist government," which played a leading diplomatic role in trying to forge an Iberoamerican community of nations (Díez Nicolás 1992; see also Joppke n.d.).

---

[31] Author interview with Magistrate Celsa Pico Lorenzo.

Some Spanish officials see visa restriction as potentially a more effective instrument of immigration control than either border controls or employer sanctions. Nevertheless, there are clear economic limits to this approach for a country as dependent on tourism income as Spain. Spain ranks third in the world (after the United States and France) in the number of tourists it receives—more than 50 million per year. Tourism constitutes such an important sector of the Spanish economy that authorities cannot impose draconian visa restrictions on citizens of many labor-exporting countries without risking major economic damage.

Refugee Policy

In yet another effort to achieve "harmonization" with EU immigration policies, Spain in recent years has also tightened its refugee admissions policy. The task of adjusting its refugee policy posed greater legal difficulties for Spain than passing a general immigration law in 1985. This is because Title One, Article Thirteen of the liberal, democratic constitution adopted by Spain after the demise of the Franco regime in 1978 includes the right to asylum as a fundamental, constitutionally protected human right, and states that "for humanitarian reasons," asylum petitioners "have the right to housing, public education, and social assistance"(Rives López 1989: 26). The 1985 Ley de Extranjería even prescribes that persons whose applications for refugee status have been denied will have an additional three-month period in which they can apply for work and residence permits "through the normal procedure"—that is, as economic migrants, without risk of deportation.

The number of asylum applicants grew rapidly during the second half of the 1980s and well into the 1990s. As the number of unfounded claims for refugee status mounted, the government raised the denial rate. By 1991 nearly 96 percent of asylum applications were being rejected. The turndown rate declined moderately in the following ten years; 71 percent of asylum requests were rejected in 2000. The number of asylum requests peaked in 1993 at 12,600; in 2000 there were only 7,926. Would-be asylum-seekers appear to have been discouraged by the high turndown rate, a shortening of the adjudication period (from one to two years before 1991 to an officially claimed average of about three months), and reductions in economic support. Financial assistance, provided by the government through the Red Cross and other nongovernmental organizations, is now limited to six months in most cases. The aid is also being dispensed more selectively, with asylum applicants from certain African, Latin American, and East European countries receiving nothing.

Asylum-seekers whose claims are denied are legally entitled to an additional three-month period during which they may attempt to regularize their situation by obtaining work and residence permits. However, the vast majority of rejected refugee applicants fail even to attempt this last-ditch legalization maneuver; they simply disappear into the underground economy. Most are never deported since Spain, like most labor-importing countries today, lacks an administrative/police apparatus capable of tracking rejected refugee applicants (or visa overstayers) and expelling them.

Legalization Programs

Spain has carried out five "extraordinary" legalization programs since it became a country of immigration: in 1986, 1991, 1996, 2000, and 2001. Moreover, there is an ongoing process of regularization that benefits foreigners who marry Spanish citizens, who obtain work permits, and who can prove that they have been living in Spain for more than five years. None of this seems to have made a significant dent in the country's stock of illegal immigrants.

The earliest regularization program—attempted at a time of great fear and confusion within the immigrant population, caused by the recent enactment of the Ley de Extranjería—was poorly planned and publicized. It had little credibility in the eyes of distrustful illegal immigrants, and only 38,181 foreigners legalized their work and/or residence situation (Colectivo Ioé 1992). Forty-one percent of the 18,729 regularized immigrants who received work permits got them for just three months or less of work (Izquierdo Escribano 1992).

The 1991 legalization program was preceded by a government survey that found that the vast majority of illegal immigrants already residing in Spain intended to stay and, eventually, bring their families. These results are believed to have contributed to the government's decision to undertake a more extensive regularization program. The 1991 program was also a product of domestic politics: major newspapers had published inflated estimates of the numbers of illegal immigrants, alarming public opinion; labor unions, along with immigrants rights and church groups, were pressing for a broad amnesty. The government presented the regularization to the Spanish public as the "lid" to unwanted immigration—a program that would help those illegals already settled in the country while limiting access to Spain for potential newcomers (Hibbs 1994: 63). The program was implemented despite objections from other European Community nations, which opposed any sort of regularization program in Spain on the grounds that it would only encourage more illegal immigration from non-EC countries.

The main legalization program of 1991 was much more successful than its predecessors in getting people to apply.[32] To increase the credibility of the program, information and application materials were widely disseminated through NGOs, labor unions, and immigrant associations. Enforcement of employer sanctions through workplace inspections was temporarily suspended. Applicants were required to demonstrate that they had been living in Spain prior to May 15, 1991; that they had work contracts from employers; and that they had *arraigo* ("roots") in their local community, which could be demonstrated with children's school enrollment records, long-term housing rental contracts, membership in voluntary associations, and other means. A total of 110,113 illegal immigrants were regularized under this program and a much less successful follow-up effort to legalize family members of the primary applicants.[33] Moroccans were the principal beneficiaries of the 1991 regularization, accounting for more than 40 percent of the 128,127 applicants.

Despite its large intake of illegal immigrants, the 1991 program is often characterized as unsuccessful because a large portion of the initial beneficiaries dropped back into *la clandestinidad*. Only 64 percent of the immigrants who applied for legalization in 1991 were still in legal status two years later (Izquierdo Escribano 1997: 150–51). This outcome was virtually predetermined by the employment instability inherent in Spain's short-term hiring practices, coupled with the legal requirement that immigrants must renew their work permits frequently during their first five years of residence in Spain. Labor unions and NGOs have estimated that by 1995 at least one-half of those who regularized themselves in the 1991–1992 legalization process had been denied renewal of their initial one-year work permit or did not seek renewal (Mendoza 2001: 171).

The government estimated that as many as 200,000 illegal immigrants did not apply for regularization in 1991. Until the late 1990s, top immigration officials were adamant that the legalization program would not

---

[32] The best description of the program's structure and procedures can be found in Sagarra Trias et al. 1991.

[33] Only about 6,500 dependents applied, reportedly because of distrust generated by long delays in delivery of legalization papers to the primary applicants.

be repeated, arguing that much of the new illegal immigration experienced by Spain since 1991 had been encouraged by the regularization program.[34] Nevertheless, in 1996 yet another legalization process was carried out. This regularization was ostensibly the corollary of a February 1996 change in the rules concerning work permits, extending their duration and giving immigrants easier access to indefinite permits (Arango 2000: 271). Eligibility was limited to immigrants whose work permits had lapsed and their dependents. Only 13,076 workers benefited from the 1996 regularization (OECD 2000: 61).

Ironically, what was to become the largest in Spain's series of rolling legalizations was carried out in 2000–2001, during a period of significant hardening in the country's immigration policy and in public opinion toward immigrants. The catalyst was, in fact, the conservative government's new version of the Ley de Extranjería, which legally opened the door to deportations of illegal immigrants en masse. The spike in deportations in the months immediately following implementation of the new law incited widespread protests by pro-immigrant groups as well as highly publicized hunger strikes and sit-ins in churches by groups of "irregulars." The government soon found it necessary to launch another regularization, aimed especially at masses of immigrants who had applied for and been denied work and residence permits and who would otherwise have been vulnerable to deportation (Zeghondi 2001: 57). Some 229,874 immigrants were able to legalize themselves by December 2000 (Ministerio del Interior 2002: table VII.4). Latin American immigrants were particularly successful, with residence permit approval rates ranging from 77 percent (Colombians, Ecuadorians) to 89 percent (Brazilians).

As protests over impending deportations of those left out of the 2000 regularization process continued in various parts of the country, the government was forced to continue the process. It announced that all "irregulars" who had arrived in Spain before January 23, 2001, could apply for legalization on humanitarian and "rootedness" (arraigo) grounds. In addition, an extraordinary regularization program tailored

---

[34] According to these officials, some of the post-1991 arrivals were deceived by professional people-smugglers into thinking that they could still benefit from the 1991 amnesty; others simply hoped that they could participate in some future regularization program (author interviews with Fernando Puig de la Bellacasa and Raimundo Aragón Bombín, Ministerio de Trabajo, Madrid, 1992). Among the illegal immigrants who applied for regularization in 2000, 30 percent told interviewers that their decision to migrate to Spain had been influenced significantly by the regularization program (Encuesta de Regularización 2000).

for the estimated 150,000 illegal Ecuadorian immigrants in Spain was carried out in 2001.[35] The precipitating event for this special amnesty was an accident near the city of Lorca in southern Spain, in which twelve illegal Ecuadorian immigrants were killed when the overcrowded van transporting them to work crashed into a train. Protest demonstrations over the plight of the hitherto largely invisible Ecuadorian immigrant community led the government to take action. At first, Ecuadorian irregulars were told to voluntarily return to their home country, apply for a visa there, and return to Spain with the promise of a legal employment contract and with travel costs covered by the Spanish government. When some 25,000 Ecuadorians unexpectedly applied, the government aborted this costly "circular regularization," opting to regularize the illegal Ecuadorians in Spain. Including those who benefited from "Operación Ecuador," a total of 334,882 illegal immigrants were regularized during the sixteen-month process that ended on January 14, 2002 (Bárbulo 2002a). Independent analysts dismiss as unrealistic the notion, insisted upon by the Aznar government, that 2001 brought Spain's last regularization.

Bilateral Migration Agreements

In recent years the Spanish government has negotiated bilateral migration agreements (*convenios*) with six of the most important source countries for immigration to Spain: Morocco, Colombia, the Dominican Republic, Ecuador, Nigeria, and Romania. Although Spain views these accords explicitly as an immigration control mechanism, they ostensibly serve other objectives as well, including combating employer exploitation of foreign workers, enabling prompt repatriation of apprehended illegal migrants (including minor children), training of migrants who can be "agents of development" in their home countries after repatriation, and channeling labor from the signatory countries into labor-short sectors of the Spanish economy (see Gil Araújo and Dahiri 2003: 99–116).

The terms of Spain's agreements with high-emigration countries are not uniform (for example, the Nigerian agreement presently covers only repatriation), but their consistent logic is "to exchange privileged access

---

[35] The Ecuadorian community mushroomed in the late 1990s, becoming the largest immigrant group in Madrid and one of the largest in Spain, as a severe economic crisis in Ecuador stimulated mass migration to both the United States and Europe (see Jokisch and Pribilsky 2002).

to Spain's annual labor quota [for] these countries' readmission of their illegal immigrants expelled from Spain" (Joppke n.d.: chap. 3). In 2002 the Aznar government limited recruitment of workers to fill the annual labor quota to the countries with which Spain has signed migration accords.

THE SOCIAL INTEGRATION OF IMMIGRANTS

Spain has yet to develop a comprehensive, well-defined policy to promote the social integration of foreign workers and their dependents. A "Plan for the Social Integration of Immigrants" was adopted in late 1994, but it was essentially a laundry list of general goals (combating discrimination, reducing barriers to immigrant integration, and so on), rather than a blueprint for concrete actions (Arango 2000: 270). Its successor, the Programa GRECO (Programa Global de Regulación y Coordinación de la Extranjería y la Inmigración en España), in operation since 2000, limits integration services to immigrants who are paying Social Security and income taxes, thereby excluding irregulars as well as legal immigrants working in the underground economy (Gil Araújo 2002: 87–89).

The Spanish government has not attempted to limit access to public schools or health care facilities for immigrants and their children based on legal status. All immigrant children are encouraged to enroll in schools, and the vast majority are matriculated. The National Health Service offers free care and covers 100 percent of the population, including immigrants. The Red Cross, Caritas, SOS Racismo, and other non-governmental agencies provide a variety of social services to immigrants, irrespective of legal status. These services, often dispensed through *centros de acogida* (social service centers) operated by the NGOs, are funded primarily by the government (often at levels inadequate to meet the demand for services) and the Catholic Church. They include child care for working mothers, Spanish language instruction, and legal aid. Utilization of tax-supported services by foreigners has not yet become a front-burner public issue in Spain, partly because most provincial and municipal governments have avoided creating earmarked social service programs for immigrants (see Ulmer 1997).

Spain's treatment of the "second generation" — the children born in Spain to illegal-immigrant parents — is much more problematic. These offspring have practically no legal rights nor assured access to basic human services. For example, the 1985 immigration law guarantees public education only to the children of *legal* immigrants. While the public schools usually do not discriminate against the children of illegals in terms of enrollment, such children are not eligible for scholarships for post-elementary study, nor do they have access to vocational training at public institutions. Because of their irregular status, children of illegal immigrants finishing elementary school do not receive a *certificado de escolaridad* (diploma), and they are not eligible for work permits when they enter the labor force. Therefore it is exceptional for the native-born child of an illegal immigrant to gain legal entry into the formal labor market; most are limited to employment in the underground economy.

In Spain, the nationality of children is determined by their parents' nationality (*jus sanguinis*), regardless of their place of birth. Foreigners can acquire Spanish citizenship through residence in the country, but it must be legal and continuous residence. Naturalizations are few (11,999 in 2000, for example). Moroccans, many of them residents of Spain since the early 1970s, have accounted for a plurality of recent naturalizations, followed by Peruvians and Dominicans (Ministerio del Interior 2002: table VI.1).

Limited access to housing is a problem for many immigrants in Spain, irrespective of legal status. A great deal of antiforeigner discrimination is practiced by landlords, who claim to be concerned about potential drug traffic and other crime problems. As a result, severe overcrowding problems have developed in immigrant communities, with twenty persons (four to ten families) sometimes occupying a single apartment. In Madrid, Third World–style squatter settlements populated entirely by foreign workers and their families have emerged, often occupying undeveloped plots of land sandwiched between middle- and upper-class residential areas. The city council of Madrid has recognized the existence of several of these settlements, affixing numbered metal plaques to each *chabola* (shack), which is typically constructed of discarded construction materials and sheets of plastic. Most of these irregular settlements do not have urban services except for electricity, which is "borrowed" from lines in adjacent neighborhoods.

Overcoming housing discrimination and residential segregation is often cited as the acid test of the Spanish government's effort to promote immigrant assimilation. Unfortunately, little progress can be identified in this area. More generally, officials, as well as nongovernmental observers, concede that not much social integration has occurred thus far among first-generation immigrants, especially those from Third World countries. The most integrated are Latin American immigrants (especially Peruvians and Dominicans), who have the advantages of shared language and cultural traits, followed by sub-Saharan Africans, North Africans, and Asians (Aparicio and Tornos 2001: 115–18; cf. Díez Nicolás and Ramírez Lafita 2001a: 200). The Spain-born children of immigrants, regardless of nationality, seem to be integrating well, at least linguistically, through the public school system; the vast majority of such children are bilingual. However, if their parents are illegal immigrants, they face the formidable post-school barriers to economic mobility described above.

The challenges of social integration will certainly become more acute as family reunification migration proceeds and as more permanent settlement occurs. By 2000, more than half of the immigrants interviewed in high immigrant-receiving zones indicated a preference for long stays or permanent settlement in Spain (Díez Nicolás and Ramírez Lafita 2001a: 201). While the complex work permit system works against employment stability, it does not seem to be preventing the post-1985 wave of immigrants from putting down roots.

THE PUBLIC RESPONSE TO IMMIGRATION

Until recently, Spanish leaders have pointed with pride to their country as Europe's principal deviant case in terms of public and governmental tolerance for immigration. Partly, this condition can be explained by the relatively small immigrant presence (and hence the low salience of the immigration issue among the Spanish public) except in the largest metropolitan areas. It is true that Spain has largely managed to avoid the overt social tensions, recurrent violence, and right-wing extremist parties that have been provoked elsewhere by recent South-North migrations.[36]

However, violent attacks on foreigners have become more frequent in Spain in recent years. The brutal murder of a female Dominican immigrant by a "skinhead" in November 1992 sparked widespread concern about the growth of xenophobic tendencies in Spain. In 1999, violence flared between Magrebí immigrants and their Spanish neighbors in the town of Terrasa, Catalonia. And the potential for a serious anti-immigrant backlash in Spain was dramatically demonstrated in February 2000 by four days of anti-immigrant rioting in El Ejido, a city in the southern province of Almería. In response to a Moroccan immigrant's

---

[36] Spain has one very small but growing far-right party, called Democracia Nacional, which agitates against the "immigrant invasion." There are also small anti-immigrant parties that contest elections only at the local and regional levels.

murder of a young Spanish woman in a public marketplace, scores of immigrant homes were destroyed and fifty-eight people were injured (Federación Estatal de Asociaciones de SOS Racismo 2001). The government's response to this rampage was lethargic at best. The incident was exploited by conservative politicians, including some affiliated with the Popular Party, in their 2000 electoral campaigns (Calvo Buezas 2000a: 54–55).[37] Scattered anti-immigrant violence has continued, including a May 2002 arson attack on a church attended by Romanian immigrants in a town 50 kilometers from Madrid.

On the surface, Spaniards have been remarkably tolerant of the influx of "new immigrants" that has occurred since the mid-1980s, especially by comparison with their counterparts elsewhere in Western Europe. Sample surveys done in the 1990s repeatedly found that their attitudes toward immigrants are benign and even, in some respects, sympathetic. Even when asked specifically about immigration from Muslim countries, Spaniards are tied with Italians as the most tolerant among the general publics in fifteen European countries (see table 10.5 and Calvo Buezas 2000a: 140–44). Most Spaniards accept the need for controls on immigration from less developed countries (56 percent in one national survey done in 2000), but only one-quarter believe that Third World immigrants should be forced to return to their country of origin (Diéz Nicolás and Ramírez Lafita 2001b: tables 5.1 and 5.3), and less than 25 percent feel that too many foreign workers are being admitted by the government under the labor quota system (Díez Nicolás 1999: table 3.16).

This high level of acceptance is all the more remarkable given the fact that Spaniards seem willing to blame foreigners for exacerbating a variety of social and economic problems in their country. In one recent national survey, 59 percent agreed that immigrants from less developed countries have caused more crime in Spain, and 43 percent believed that Third World immigration increases unemployment among Spaniards (Diéz Nicolás and Ramírez Lafita 2001b: tables 5.15 and 5.20). In this and

---

[37] The El Ejido incident touched off a national debate—which continues to reverberate—about the conditions that gave rise to such intense anti-immigrant violence. Some NGOs and academic analysts have stressed the latent racism of the native-born population (Calvo Buezas 2000b; Federación Estatal de Asociaciones de SOS Racismo 2001; Goytisolo and Naïr 2000). Others emphasize the brutal economic inequalities generated by the modern Spanish agricultural economy, which subjects both immigrants and the native-born poor in places like El Ejido to substandard working and living conditions, inevitably generating inter-group tensions (Castellanos Ortega and Pedreño Cánovas 2001; Azurmendi 2001). The mass media uniformly denounced the events in El Ejido as racist and xenophobic.

earlier opinion surveys, hostility toward foreigners was found to be greater among lower-class Spaniards (presumably because they are more likely to view immigrants as potential competitors for jobs), the less educated, and residents of the largest metropolitan areas (where crime, overcrowding, and other "big city" problems are more likely to be blamed on immigrants). However, more recent analyses suggest that Spain's middle class is becoming a bastion of anti-immigrant sentiment (Escandell 2004).

Table 10.5. Attitudes toward Muslim Immigration in EU Countries, 2000

Question: "If people from Muslim countries wish to work here in the European Union, do you think that they should (1) be accepted without restrictions; (2) be accepted but with restriction; (3) not be accepted; or (4) don't know."

	Be Accepted without Restrictions	Be Accepted with Restrictions	Not be Accepted	Don't Know
Belgium	11.78	53.67	30.43	4.11
Denmark	27.37	60.52	8.12	3.99
Germany	7.55	57.53	28.8	6.11
Greece	9.61	67.72	19.49	3.18
Italy	29.53	55.13	9.62	5.72
Spain	29.51	57.7	5.18	7.61
France	13.87	61.35	20.73	4.05
Ireland	15.56	59.17	11.71	13.56
Luxembourg	9.04	61.15	26.32	3.5
Netherlands	10.62	68.11	16.17	5.11
Portugal	18.17	50.53	18.42	12.87
Great Britain	15.81	55.83	17.55	10.81
Finland	21.36	63.77	11.42	3.45
Sweden	35.4	51.25	7.66	5.69
Austria	12.61	59.15	11.52	16.72

Source: Eurobarometer Survey No. 53, April–May 2000. Data compiled by Alan Kessler, University of Texas at Austin.

The results of several national and regional survey studies show a clear hierarchy of acceptance or preference regarding the integration of various nationalities into Spanish society, with Latin Americans at the top, followed by East Europeans, sub-Saharan Africans, and North Africans. Much of the Spaniards' hostility toward North Africans is rooted in a centuries-old fear of "*los moros*," who are today associated with Islamic fundamentalism as well as a high propensity to commit crimes. Large-scale immigration from countries like Morocco is seen as undoing the Christian reconquest of Spain in 1492, after seven hundred years of Muslim rule. Anti-Moroccan attitudes also reflect the strong bias of many Spaniards against anyone of lower social-class background.

Although most observers recognize the persistent liberal impulse in the Spanish public's overall response to immigration, some warn that high levels of tolerance for immigration—particularly from the Third World—may be a thing of the past. In fact, the survey evidence indicates a hardening of Spanish public opinion toward Third World immigration in the late 1990s (see table 10.6). This change probably reflects the growing size, visibility, and stability of the non-EU immigrant population in Spain, as well as a sharp increase in media coverage of immigration events (such as the almost daily reports of people smugglers landing their cargo on Spanish beaches or drowning them). The shift toward intolerance may have accelerated since 2000, in response to events like the El Ejido violence and the harder line being taken in government rhetoric and policy. On the other hand, surveys of the Spanish school-age population in the 1990s reveal that, while the proportion of students with "hard" xenophobic attitudes increased slightly between 1993 and 1997, the percentage of students who are strongly pro-immigrant also grew (Calvo Buezas 2000a: table 14.14).

Table 10.6. Preference for Limiting Third World Immigration to Spain
(national survey data, in percentages)

Survey item: "Spain should limit the entry of immigrants from less developed countries."

Response	Year of Survey									
	1992	1993	1994	1995a	1995b	1996	1997	1998	1999	2000
Strongly agree	6	6	6	6	9	8	5	6	8	10
Agree	49	43	48	50	47	53	47	46	49	56
Disagree	30	34	32	31	29	23	29	33	27	23
Strongly disagree	7	6	5	5	7	6	6	6	5	4
Don't know/no response	9	11	10	9	8	11	14	10	11	7

Source: Díez Nicolás and Ramírez Lafita 2001b: table 5.1.

Pointing to such mixed evidence, some knowledgeable observers insist that a broadly based anti-immigrant backlash in Spain is not inevitable, especially if strong labor market segmentation persists. They argue that as long as foreigners do not compete for the kinds of jobs held by native Spaniards, the economic benefits of their presence will override cultural-racial objections, and ambivalent attitudes toward immigration are likely to continue (Díez Nicolás n.d.). In fact, national opinion surveys have repeatedly found that large majorities of Spaniards *believe* that Third World immigrants are filling jobs that native-born workers do not want (see Vallés, Cea, and Izquierdo 1999: table 3.4).[38]

THE GROWING CONTRADICTIONS OF SPANISH IMMIGRATION POLICY

Like other modern industrial countries today, Spain faces a trade-off between the sociocultural costs of admitting more foreigners—many of whom will settle permanently—and the economic costs of *not* importing them. Government, business, and most members of the general public want access to cheap, flexible, disposable immigrant labor for industries like agriculture, construction, tourism, and domestic service. With the country facing demographic implosion due to fertility rates ranked among the world's lowest for two decades, and with Spaniards even in the least prosperous regions no longer willing to migrate internally to take manual jobs, the supply of native-born workers available to fill many key niches in the economy is demonstrably inadequate. While somewhat curtailed in recent years, the Spanish welfare state continues to provide generous benefits that reward native-born Spaniards for not working, at least in the formal economy.

Since 1996, Spain has had one of the most rapidly growing economies in Europe. The unemployment rate has been halved, and the government has been running budget surpluses. This impressive economic boom has been fueled to a large extent by the influx of immigrant labor. Indeed, the most robust sectors of the Spanish economy—tourism, agriculture, construction—all rely heavily on foreign workers. It is also widely recognized that the vitality of Spain's very large and diversified underground economy, which supplies and otherwise supports many firms in the mainstream economy, depends on continued access to immigrant

---

[38] Eighty percent of Spaniards expressed this belief in a 2000 survey by the Centro de Investigaciones Sociológicas (Barómetro del CIS, February 2000).

labor. The darkest cloud on the economic horizon seems to be a consequence of population aging: the rapidly increasing "dependency ratio"
of economically inactive transfer payment recipients to taxpayers, which
will put severe pressure on government budgets for pensions and health
care (see Abío et al. 2003).

Nevertheless, an overtly expansionary national immigration policy is
unlikely. The Aznar government proved that taking a hard line on immigration pays significant electoral dividends, and this has not been lost
on opposition politicians. Social issues like crime remain potent, and
immigrants are convenient scapegoats. And with anti-immigrant sentiment on the rise throughout Europe, Spanish officials anticipate continuing pressure from other members of the European Union to tighten
Spain's immigration controls. Indeed, EU pressure provides useful political "cover" for Spanish officials already bent on a restrictionist immigration policy, and EU resources can be used to finance the construction
of a technologically state-of-the-art Maginot line on Spain's southern and
eastern coasts. None of this involves altering domestic economic and
institutional arrangements that favor the increasing use of immigrant
labor.[39]

By the early 1990s, a consensus had formed in Spanish officialdom
around the need to design a system that would legally admit the number
of foreign workers that Spain needs economically and is capable of integrating socioculturally. The basic idea of the quota system implemented
in the second half of the decade is that the government will work with
employers to ensure that their labor requirements are met, while convey-
ing to the general public the sense that the policymakers are "in control"
and "doing something" about unwanted immigration. But the "*sistema de
cupos*" has not functioned efficiently as a mechanism for controlled importation of foreign labor. The system generates far too few job offers
from businesses, while illegal migrants continue to flood into the labor
market. The basic problem may be that employers who use foreign labor
are comfortable with well-established, informal recruitment mechanisms
and want to avoid further entanglement in government bureaucracy.

Critics doubt that the Spanish state has the administrative capacity to
implement a labor market–driven quota system, nor, indeed, other forms
of "modern" immigration control. Land and maritime borders remain
remarkably porous despite sharp increases in spending on border enforcement. Workplace enforcement is of only symbolic import. Regular-

[39] Spain has used EU resources to similar advantage in the area of environmental
policy. See Luaces 2002.

ized immigrants fall into illegality and fail to gain permanent legal resident status because a dysfunctional bureaucracy makes it impossible for them to string together enough periods of (legal) temporary employment. Apprehended illegal immigrants under deportation orders reach the legal limit of forty days of confinement and are released to the streets, without possibility of legal employment.[40] Disappointed asylum seekers also remain mostly at large, because there is no administrative capacity (nor will) to round them up and expel them. Meanwhile, the supply of foreign-born labor expands by 20 percent or more per annum and the economy booms.

As Spain becomes an increasingly attractive destination for racially and culturally distinct Third World migrants, the contradictions between the government's hard-line rhetoric on immigration and what is actually happening in the labor market and the neighborhoods will become more difficult to sustain. Spain harbors a latent current of racist, xenophobic sentiment that could eventually be mobilized by an extremist, "Le Pen"–style party or movement. In a deep, prolonged economic recession (even one caused by exogenous factors), public tolerance for immigration could diminish rapidly. And more events like the El Ejido riots could catalyze a generalized anti-immigrant backlash. In the foreseeable future, however, this scenario of draconian anti-immigration measures enacted under intense public pressure is one that probably can be avoided, if only because the number of Spanish stakeholders in an expansionary (de facto) immigration policy will continue to be very large. However reluctantly, these stakeholders would concur with the assessment of the Labor Ministry's former senior immigration policymaker: "For Spain, there is simply no alternative to immigration."[41]

References

Abío, Gemma, Eduard Berenguer, Holger Bonin, Joan Gil, and Concepció Patxot. 2003. "Is the Deficit Under Control? A Generational Accounting Perspective on Fiscal Policy and Labour Market Trends in Spain," *Investigaciones Económicas* 27, no. 2: 309–41.

Agence France Press. 2002a. "Growth in Spanish Crime Rate Linked to Illegal Immigration," February 12.

———. 2002b. "Spain Tackles Immigration to Stem Rise of Far Right," April 26.

---

[40] For case material, see Coordinación ENAR España 2002.

[41] Interview with Raimundo Aragón Bombín, May 1992.

Altamirano Rua, Teófilo. 1996. *Migración: el fenómeno del siglo. Peruanos en Europa, Japón, y Australia.* Lima: Pontificia Universidad Católica del Perú.

Aparicio, Rosa, and Andrés Tornos. 2001. *Estrategias y dificultades características en la integración social de los distintos colectivos de inmigrantes llegados a España.* Madrid: Instituto de Migraciones y Servicios Sociales, Ministerio de Trabajo y Asuntos Sociales.

Arango, Joaquín. 2000. "Becoming a Country of Immigration at the End of the Twentieth Century: The Case of Spain." In *Eldorado or Fortress? Migration in Southern Europe,* edited by Russell King, Gabriella Lazaridis, and Charalambos Tsardanidis. London: Macmillan.

Aznar, José María. 2001. "Estamos cumpliendo el mandato de los ciudadanos, que es gobernar," Junta Directiva del PP en Génova, March 12. At http://www.pp.es.

Azurmendi, Mikel. 2001. *Estampas de El Ejido: un reportaje sobre la integración del inmigrante.* Madrid: Taurus.

Bárbulo, Tomás. 2002a. "Interior afirma que ha regularizado a 334,882 inmigrantes, la mitad de los que lo solicitaron," *El País* (Madrid), January 18.

———. 2002b. "El fin de las regularizaciones ordenado el 14 de enero por el Gobierno deja a 250,000 inmigrantes en la clandestinidad," *El País* (Madrid), February 6.

Calavita, Kitty. 1998. "Immigration, Law, and Marginalization in a Global Economy: Notes from Spain," *Law and Society Review* 32, no. 3: 529–66.

Calavita, Kitty, and Liliana Suárez-Navaz. 2003. "Spanish Immigration Law and the Construction of Difference: Citizens and 'Illegals' on Europe's Southern Border." In *Globalization under Construction: Governmentality, Law, and Identity,* edited by Richard W. Perry and Bill Maurer. Minneapolis: University of Minnesota Press.

Calvo Buezas, Tomás. 2000a. *Inmigración y racismo: así sienten los jóvenes del Siglo XXI.* Madrid: Cauce.

———. 2000b. "El conflicto structural en El Ejido: 'A la caza del Moro,'" *Sociedad y Utopía: Revista de Ciencias Sociales* (Universidad Pontificia de Salamanca, Campus de Madrid) 16: 23–37.

Carrasco Carpio, Concepción. 1999. *Mercados de trabajo: los inmigrantes económicos.* Madrid: Instituto de Migraciones y Servicios Sociales, Ministerio de Trabajo y Asuntos Sociales.

Castellanos Ortega, Mari Luz, and Andrés Pedreño Cánovas. 2001. "Desde El Ejido al accidente de Lorca," *Sociología del Trabajo* (Madrid), nueva época 42 (Spring): 3–31.

Colectivo Ioé. 1991. "Inmigrantes indocumentados en España," *L'Evenement Europeenne* (Paris) 11: 135–54.

———. 1992. "Los trabajadores extranjeros en España: informe para el Instituto Sindical de Estudios." Madrid: Colectivo Ioé. Unpublished.

———. 1998a. "The Occurrence of Discrimination in Spain." In *Documenting Discrimination against Migrant Workers in the Labour Market: A Comparative*

Study of Four European Countries, edited by Roger Zegers de Beijl. Geneva: International Labour Organization.

———. 1998b. *Inmigración y trabajo: trabajadores inmigrantes en el sector de la construcción*. Madrid: Instituto de Migraciones y Servicios Sociales, Ministerio de Trabajo y Asuntos Sociales.

———. 1999. *Inmigración y trabajo en España: trabajadores inmigrantes en el sector de la hostelería*. Madrid: Instituto de Migraciones y Servicios Sociales, Ministerio de Trabajo y Asuntos Sociales.

———. 2001. *Mujer, inmigración, y trabajo*. Madrid: Instituto de Migraciones y Servicios Sociales, Ministerio de Trabajo y Asuntos Sociales.

Coordinación ENAR España. 2002. *Informe sobre la situación real del racismo y xenophobia en el Estado español*. Madrid: Coordinación ENAR España.

Cornelius, Wayne. 2001. "Death at the Border: Efficacy and Unintended Consequences of U.S. Immigration Control Policy," *Population and Development Review* 27, no. 4: 661–85.

Díez Nicolás, Juan. 1992. "Cultural and Economic Factors That Shape Spanish Attitudes toward Immigrants." Paper presented at the Center for U.S.-Mexican Studies, University of California, San Diego, November.

———. 1994. *Actitudes hacia los inmigrantes*. Madrid: Observatorio Permanente de la Inmigración, Instituto de Migraciones y Servicios Sociales, Ministerio de Trabajo y Asuntos Sociales.

———. 1999. *Los españoles y la inmigración*. Madrid: Observatorio Permanente de la Inmigración, Instituto de Migraciones y Servicios Sociales, Ministerio de Trabajo y Asuntos Sociales.

———. n.d. *Las dos caras de la inmigración*. Madrid: Observatorio Permanente de la Inmigración, Instituto de Migraciones y Servicios Sociales, Ministerio de Trabajo y Asuntos Sociales. Forthcoming.

Díez Nicolás, Juan, and María José Ramírez Lafita. 2001a. *La voz de los inmigrantes*. Madrid: Instituto de Migraciones y Servicios Sociales, Ministerio de Trabajo y Asuntos Sociales.

———. 2001b. *La inmigración en España: una década de investigaciones*. Madrid: Instituto de Migraciones y Servicios Sociales, Ministerio de Trabajo y Asuntos Sociales.

Donaldson, Michael, and Miquel Ángel Essomba, eds. 2001. *Informe anual 2001 sobre el racismo en el Estado español*. Barcelona: Donaldson and Essomba/Icaria.

Encuesta de Regularización 2000. "Encuesta de Regularización 2000." Madrid: Ministerio del Interior / Universidad de Coruña.

Escandell, Xavier. 2004. "General Public Attitudes toward Immigration: Regional Differences in Southern Europe." PhD dissertation, University of Illinois, Champaign-Urbana.

Federación Estatal de Asociaciones de SOS Racismo. 2001. "El Ejido: racismo y explotación laboral." In *Informe anual 2001 sobre el racismo en el Estado español*, edited by Michael Donaldson and Miquel Ángel Essomba. Barcelona: Donaldson and Essomba/Icaria.

Fernández Cordón, Juan Antonio. 2001. "El futuro demográfico y la oferta de trabajo en España," *Migraciones* (Instituto Universitario de Estudios sobre Migraciones, Universidad Pontificia Comillas, Madrid) 9: 69–103.

Gil Araújo, Sandra. 2002. *Inmigración y gestión de la diversidad en el contexto europeo: informe sobre las políticas migratorias en los países bajos y el estado español.* Madrid: Instituto de Estudios sobre Conflictos y Acción Humanitaria, Instituto de Estudios Transnacionales.

Gil Araújo, Sandra, and Mohammed Dahiri, eds. 2003. *Movimientos migratorios en el Mediterráneo Occidental: ¿un fenómeno o un problema?* Córdoba, Spain: Ayuntamiento de Córdoba, Instituto de Estudios Transnacionales/Instituto de Estudios sobre Conflictos y Acción Humanitaria.

Giménez Romero, Carlos, ed. 1993. *Inmigrantes extranjeros en Madrid.* 2 vols. Madrid: Consejería de la Integración Social, Comunidad de Madrid.

Giubilaro, Donatella. 1997. "Migration from the Maghreb and Migration Pressures: Current Situation and Future Prospects." International Migration Papers, no. 15. Geneva: Employment and Training Department, International Labour Office.

Goytisolo, Juan, and Sami Naïr. 2000. *El peaje de la vida: integración o rechazo en la emigración en España.* Madrid: Aguilar.

Güell, Maia, and Barbara Petrongolo. 2003. "How Binding Are Legal Limits? Transitions from Temporary to Permanent Work in Spain." Discussion Paper No. 782. Bonn, Germany: Institute for the Study of Labor (IZA), May.

Hibbs, C.R. 1994. "Immigration Policy and the Quotidian Hassles of Being: Foreign Workers in Madrid and San Diego." Master's thesis, University of California, San Diego.

Hoggart, Keith, and Cristóbal Mendoza. 1999. "African Immigrant Workers in Spanish Agriculture," *Sociologia Ruralis* (European Society for Rural Sociology) 39, no. 4: 538–62.

Instituto Nacional de Estadística. 2000. *Encuesta de Fecundidad 1999.* Madrid: INE.

Izquierdo Escribano, Antonio. 1992. *La inmigración en España, 1980–1990.* Madrid: Ministerio de Trabajo y Seguridad Social.

———. 1997. *La inmigración inesperada.* Madrid: Trotta.

Izquierdo Escribano, Antonio, and Raquel Martínez Buján. 2003. "La inmigración en España en 2001." In *Inmigración: mercado de trabajo y protección social en España,* edited by Antonio Izquierdo Escribano. Madrid: Consejo Económico y Social.

Jokisch, Brad, and Jason Pribilsky. 2002. "The Panic to Leave: Economic Crisis and the 'New Emigration' from Ecuador," *International Migration* 40, no. 4: 75–99.

Joppke, Christian. n.d. "Europe's Two Postcolonial Constellations: North-Western and South-Western." Forthcoming.

López García, Bernabé. 1992. "Las migraciones magrebíes y España," *Alfoz* (Madrid) 91–92: 78–86.

428   Cornelius

Luaces, Pilar. 2002. "Circumventing Adaptation Pressure? Implementing EU Environmental Policy in Spain," *South European Politics and Society* 7, no. 3: 81–108.

Mendoza, Cristóbal. 2000. "African Employment in Iberian Construction: A Cross-Border Analysis," *Journal of Ethnic and Migration Studies* 26, no. 4: 609–34.

———. 2001. "The Role of the State in Influencing African Labour Outcomes in Spain and Portugal," *Geoforum* 32: 167–80.

———. 2003. *Labour Immigration in Southern Europe: African Employment in Iberian Labour Markets.* Burlington, Vt.: Ashgate.

Millman, Joel, and Carlta Vitzthum. 2003. "Europe Becomes New Destination for Latinos Searching for Work," *Wall Street Journal*, September 12.

Ministerio del Interior, Delegación del Gobierno para la Estranjería y la Inmigración. 2002. *Anuario estadístico de extranjería, año 2000.* Madrid: Comisión Interministerial de Extranjería.

Moreno Fuentes, Francisco Javier. 2001. "Migration and Spanish Nationality Law." In *Towards a European Nationality: Citizenship, Immigration, and Nationality Law in the EU*, edited by Randall Hansen and Patrick Weil. New York: Palgrave.

Nieto, Gladys. 2003. "The Chinese in Spain," *International Migration* 41, no. 3: 217–34.

OECD Secretariat. 2000. "Some Lessons from Recent Regularisation Programmes." In *Combating the Illegal Employment of Foreign Workers.* Paris: OECD.

Pascual de Sans, Angels, and Jordi Cardelus. 1990. *Migració i historia personal: investigació sobre la mobilitat des de la perspectiva del retorn.* Barcelona: Bellaterra.

Pieke, Frank N., Pál Nyíri, Mette Thuno, and Antonella Ceccagno. 2004. *Transnational Chinese: Fujianese Migrants in Europe.* Stanford, Calif.: Stanford University Press.

Quesada, Begona. 2002. "Spanish Outpost Illustrates Immigration Quandary," *Reuters News Service*, April 23.

Riding, Alan. 1992. "For González, 10 Years in Power, One More Race," *New York Times*, October 26.

Rives López, Isabel. 1989. *La Ley de Extranjería.* Madrid: Decálogo.

Ruiz de Huidobro, José María. 2001. "El régimen legal de la inmigración en España: el continuo cambio," *Migraciones* (Instituto Universitario de Estudios sobre Migraciones, Universidad Pontificia Comillas, Madrid) 9: 69–103.

Sagarra Trias, Eduard, et al. 1991. *El trabajador extranjero y la regularización de 1991.* ITINERA Cuadros, no. 1. Barcelona: Fundación Paulino Torras Domènech.

Santos, Lidia. 1993. "Elementos jurídicos de la integración de los extranjeros." In *Inmigración e integración en Europa*, edited by Georges Tapinos. Barcelona: Itinera.

Solé, Carlota. 1995. *Discriminación racial en el mercado de trabajo.* Madrid: Consejo Económico y Social.

Solé, Carlota, and Sonia Parella. 2003. "The Labour Market and Racial Discrimination in Spain," *Journal of Ethnic and Migration Studies* 29, no. 1: 121–40.

Ulmer, Eva C. 1997. "Spain and the Challenge of Immigration: Political and Social Responses to a Novel Phenomenon, 1985–1995." PhD thesis, Trinity College, University of Oxford.

United Nations. 2000. *Replacement Migration: Is It a Solution to Declining and Ageing Populations?* ESA/P/WP.160. New York: Population Division, Dept. of Economic and Social Affairs, United Nations Secretariat, March 21.

Vallés, Miguel S., María Ángeles Cea, and Antonio Izquierdo. 1999. *Las encuestas sobre inmigración en España y Europa.* Madrid: Observatorio Permanente de la Inmigración, Instituto de Migraciones y Servicios Sociales, Ministerio de Trabajo y Asuntos Sociales.

Vives i Ferrer, Núria. 2001. "Las modificaciones de la Ley de Extranjería: historia de una odisea parlamentaria." In *Informe anual 2001 sobre el racismo en el Estado español,* edited by Michael Donaldson and Miquel Ángel Essomba. Barcelona: Donaldson and Essomba/Icaria.

Zeghondi, Ghassan Saliba. 2001. "Proceso de regularización 2000–2001." In *Informe anual 2001 sobre el racismo en el Estado español,* edited by Michael Donaldson and Miquel Ángel Essomba. Barcelona: Donaldson and Essomba/Icaria.

Commentary

Gunther Dietz and Belén Agrela

In the past two decades, Spain has evolved rapidly from a classic country of emigration to a new "pole of attraction" for immigration into the European Union (EU). Far from being a "one-way process" of substitute migration, however, this "uneasy transition" reflects a highly heterogeneous migration pattern, comprising at least four crosscutting processes.

- Second- and even third-generation Spanish emigrants are not abandoning their ties to their country of origin. They travel frequently to Spain and maintain kinship and/or communal ties to their villages. This new generation of "Spanish Germans," "Spanish French," or "Spanish Swiss" cultivates an identity characterized by a diasporic longing for their ancestors' Mediterranean roots.

- Spaniards who migrated as guestworkers to western and northern Europe but did not succeed in integrating into their host society tend to return home when they retire. Some are accompanied by their children, whose limited knowledge of Spain comes from brief holiday visits; their integration into the Spanish school system and labor market is increasingly problematic.

- Retirement migration also drives intra-European migration toward Spain. Although rarely seen as part of the overall migration phenomenon, European "trans-migrants," many of whom spend half the year in their home country and half on the Canary or Balearic Islands or the southern Spanish Mediterranean shore, account for nearly half of the migrants residing in Spain.

- Finally, as a result of Spain's entry into the European Union and its participation in the Schengen Agreement, non-European immigrants are increasingly choosing Spain as a destination and as a transit point to all countries covered by the Schengen accord.

Policy reactions to the new diversity in migrant flows have been somewhat heterogeneous. In general, they tend to establish an ethnicized hierarchy of migrants and of the "problems" related to immigration (Agrela 2002). The large segment of intra–European Union migrants is made statistically and politically invisible by virtue of its being excluded from official immigration data, from the discourse on migration, and from governmental integration measures. Spanish émigré communities, as well as return migrants and their families, are also marginalized from migration policy as the institutions that formerly dealt with their concerns are either dissolved or redirected toward non-EU immigrants.

Thus immigration is officially—and artificially—perceived and treated as a south-north phenomenon. The formal and legal classifications of migrants—refugees or asylum seekers, settled or temporary immigrant workers, undocumented immigrants, and so on—are combined with ethnocultural and symbolic labels that reflect an implicit ethno-religious hierarchy of "others." In this hierarchy, the lowest position is ascribed to the Spanish Roma community, followed by Muslims and/or Arabs. A comparison of public attitudes toward "others" in Spain's "high-immigration" versus "low-immigration" regions shows that this bias against Muslims and Arabs has a long history (ASEP 1998), but since the attacks of September 11, 2001, this historically rooted fear has been channeled discursively through the overlapping of external security, internal security and criminality, and migration control.

In contemporary Spain, political and institutional reactions to increasingly heterogeneous migration patterns seem to evolve around three different but interrelated policymaking axes, which combine and redistribute traditional jurisdictions in migration control and immigrant integration policies: the centralism-federalism axis, the statism-privatization axis, and the universalism-multiculturalism axis.

The Centralism-Federalism Axis

Spain first had to address immigration and immigrant integration issues at about the same time that it was dealing with democracy and multilevel governance as part of the European Union. Since Franco's death in 1975 and throughout the subsequent drafting of a democratic constitution, Spain's nationalist-centralist legacy has been gradually but thoroughly transformed, and a slow process of administrative decentralization had ended up federalizing the state as a whole.

Nevertheless, this federalization is not uniform, nor does it include interregional compensation or exchange mechanisms. Instead, the Constitution distinguishes two kinds of regions: (1) those shaped by "historical nationalisms" and their distinctive cultural and linguistic features, and (2) regions lacking their own cultural and/or ethno-nationalist identities. The result was an asymmetrical, ethnically biased process of devolution from Madrid to the regions during the 1970s and early 1980s. The official distinction between "fast track" and "slow track" regions has "ethnicized" subnational conflicts and negotiations on devolution and the appropriate allocation of governing responsibilities among the various levels of government.

In this context in which subnational regions were made to compete with one another, immigration quickly becomes a major concern for both anti-immigrant ethnic regional nationalisms and anti-centralist multiculturalist regionalisms. Catalonia, the Basque Country, and Andalusia began in the mid-1990s to develop their own "migration policies," legally limited to migrant integration services but in fact attempting to influence national immigration policy as well in center-region confrontations over "contingent" distribution negotiations, "regularization campaigns" for undocumented immigrant workers, and the recent establishment of quota systems for temporary agricultural laborers.

Paradoxically, these subnational challenges to the Spanish state's monopoly on migration issues are limited, rather than reinforced, by harmonization "pressure" from the supranational European Union. Because the coordination and harmonization of immigration within the EU still falls to central governments — not the EU Commission or European Parliament — national executives can cite "EU pressure" or "Brussels" to justify implementing restrictive migration control and border enforcement policies, on the one hand, and retaining or regaining central authority over migration policy, on the other.

This is evident in two recent shifts in Spanish migration policy — away from allowing undocumented migrants to disappear quietly into the booming shadow economy, and away from employing temporarily legalized, mostly Moroccan immigrant workers already in Spain, in favor of temporarily "imported," mostly Eastern Europeans for seasonal contract work in agriculture. In both cases, the central government claims that EU pressures influenced its tightening of policy measures.

Thus multilateral and supranational measures such as the Schengen Agreement end up restricting the federalization of migration policy in Spain, where immigration policy interests contrast sharply between the central and regional governments. Despite official restrictions, some regional governments are developing their own de facto migration policies, focusing on immigrant integration into Spain's regionally and sectorally segmented labor markets. This is seen as highly appropriate given that regional and local governments bear the core financial and infrastructural burdens of the central state's migration control measures at the same time that they are denied a voice in policymaking. Local governments operate programs for temporary and longer-term housing, schooling, and health care for both legal and undocumented immigrants. As a result, local and regional actors have outstripped national agencies' expertise on integration measures.

The growing gap between the central government's migration control, policing, and gatekeeping functions inside "Fortress Europe" and regional proficiency regarding migrant integration measures became evident in Melilla, an immigration control outpost and one of Spain's two remaining enclaves in northern Morocco. Spain's central government had devolved authority over social services and integration policy to Melilla in the 1990s. In early 2002 the municipal government—overwhelmed by the huge and costly task of controlling, housing, and training an increasing population of "unaccompanied Moroccan minors" from the eastern Berber region—threatened to "de-devolve" responsibility for migration-related issues. The "de-devolution," which would have proved profoundly embarrassing to Spain's central government and the country's regionalist movements as well, was averted through an emergency grant to Melilla, but the gap between national/supranational immigration control and regional/local migrant integration measures has yet to be bridged.

The Statism-Privatization Axis

The conflict between the various levels of government regarding authority and responsibility for immigration-related issues is crosscut by the involvement of powerful nongovernmental organizations (NGOs); Church and faith-based immigrant support groups, neighborhood associations, community organizations, and trade unions have emerged as knowledgeable interlocutors in the debate. In the course of the last decade, these actors' skill and experience in delivering social services, health care, and legal assistance have made them better prepared than their governmental counterparts (Domingo, Kaplan, and Gómez Gil 2000), to the point that regional governments sometimes pattern their programs on the pioneering efforts of NGOs. One example is an Andalusian NGO network for primary health care provision via an unofficial "social security card" for undocumented migrants, a system that is being incorporated into the national-level GRECO program.

The "nongovernmentalization" of Spanish migration policy reflects the central government's tendency to subcontract and privatize public administration, making migration policy a test case for "lean government." In the course of this shift toward outsourcing and subcontracting immigrant integration, the governmental agencies dealing with migrant populations at the national, regional, or local level differentiate sharply between "friends" and "foes" — between NGOs that deliver assistance and claims-making support movements, which are not eligible for state funding (Dietz 2000).

However, official attempts to "privatize" and "depoliticize" NGOs are doomed to fail; nongovernmental actors only succeed in their mediation functions toward their (often undocumented) immigrant constituencies if they offer alternative channels for claims-making and participation. Consequently, NGOs cannot be reduced to private, market-driven forces. They are becoming strategic, sometimes "monopolistic" pillars of the immigration policies of the central state, regions, and municipalities. They deliver services in such diverse domains as housing (acting as landlords, informal mediators, and legal guarantors), health care (through their own network of volunteer physicians and nurses, as well as the above-mentioned health card), legal assistance (lawyer volunteers), and schooling (literacy and language courses, as well as pioneering intercultural education projects implemented in "magnet" schools). Sometimes, however, NGOs end up performing tasks in which immigrant integration and migration control functions overlap, if, for example, a government-funded initiative requires an NGO that is servicing a migrant clientele to incorporate some surveillance and policing tasks. The result is often to divide the migrant support organizations, hence weakening their advocacy efforts.

The Universalism-Multiculturalism Axis

The combination of the centralism/federalism and statism/privatization axes in Spanish migration policy has promoted a third trend: a gradual shift away from universalist and generalist approaches in integration policy. The uneven devolution of responsibilities to regions and the prolonged periods during which central and regional agencies with similar mandates coexist create parallel structures for vocational training and labor market issues. This situation has been exacerbated by the emergence of NGOs with special expertise in relatively circumscribed service domains that are narrowed further as they are adapted to meet the needs of a particular clientele.

Thus ethnic, religious, legal, and gender subgroups have emerged as defining features of increasingly subdivided measures. Some NGOs work with a particular national or ethnic group; others focus on specific domains, such as the secondary labor market, professional training, regularization, linguistic and/or religious instruction, and health issues. From the perspective of NGOs and many of their constituent organizations (such as Moroccan trade unions, Senegalese trade associations, Muslim women's associations), this fractionalization is justifiable as an empowerment strategy that aims at integration through the recognition of difference. Government institutions, through outsourcing and subcontracting immigrant services, actively promote this trend toward the "multiculturalization" of integration measures, something they view as a question not of empowerment but of efficiency.

Paradoxically, this shift from universalist to multiculturalist service provision risks replicating the hierarchy of "others" (Zapata-Barrero 2001). Migrants' access to citizenship rights and political participation in Spain is heavily segmented, not only in legal terms imposed "from above" by national and EU legislation, but also—and increasingly— "from below" through national, ethnic, religious, and gender-based distinctions. The consequences of this confluence of distinctions and hierarchies become evident when analyzing the images of "migrant others" in Spanish media and opinion polls. Clearly, a discourse is emerging in which only some migrant groups are identified with insecurity, criminality, and—since September 11, 2001—the "threat of terrorism" (Gil Araujo 2002).

The constant mixing of images of undocumented seasonal workers, shadow economic activities, petty criminality, and large-scale drug trafficking has created a xenophobic short circuit that runs directly from immigration to informality to illegality to insecurity. Political uses—and abuses—of such short circuits will determinate which of Cornelius's three alternative scenarios will prevail in Spanish migration policy. However, as Cornelius notes, these alternatives are not mutually exclusive. A "nativist backlash" will most directly affect Spanish policymakers' sometimes benevolent, often negligent attitude toward immigrants.

This backlash may coexist with a quota system of temporary work permits limited by region, season, and sector according to labor market needs and entrepreneurial interests. This quota system could also coexist with tightened immigration restrictions as specified by the European Union, restrictions that will be billed as the price Spain has to pay to "become European." Through its role as a pan-European gatekeeper, "Spain, a country of the South, must entrench itself against the South" (Goytisolo and Naïr 2000: 132).

References

Agrela, Belén. 2002. "La política de inmigración en España: reflexiones sobre la emergencia del discurso cultural," *Migraciones Internacionales* 1, no. 2.

ASEP (Análisis Sociológicos, Económicos y Políticos, S.A.). 1998. "Actitudes hacia los inmigrantes." Madrid: Ministerio de Trabajo y Asuntos Sociales, Observatorio Permanente de la Inmigración.

Dietz, Gunther. 2000. "El desafío de la interculturalidad: el voluntariado y las organizaciones no-gubernamentales ante el reto de la inmigración." Granada/Barcelona: Laboratorio de Estudios Interculturales/Fundació "la Caixa."

Domingo, Andreu, Adriana Kaplan, and Carlos Gómez Gil. 2000. "Chivos expiatorios fáciles: inmigrantes sin papeles en Europa, informe sobre España." Barcelona/Alicante: Centre d'Estudis Demogràfics/Alicante Acoge.

Gil Araujo, Sandra. 2002. "Extranjeros bajo sospecha: lucha contra el terrorismo y política migratoria en EEUU y la Unión Europea." In *De Nueva York a Kabul: Anuario CIP 2002*, edited by M. Aguirre and M. González. Madrid/Barcelona: Centro de Investigación para la Paz/Icaria.

Goytisolo, Juan, and Sami Naïr. 2000. *El peaje de la vida: integración o rechazo de la emigración en España*. Madrid: Aguilar.

Zapata-Barrero, Ricard. 2001. *Ciudadanía, democracia y pluralismo cultural: hacia un nuevo contrato social*. Barcelona: Anthropos.

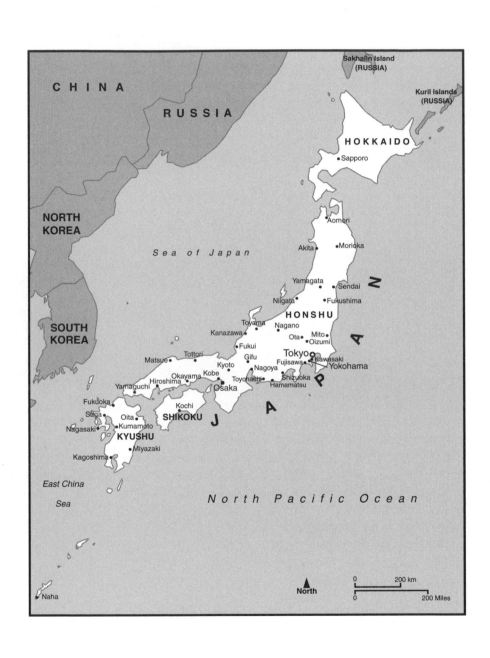

CHINA

RUSSIA

Sakhalin Island
(RUSSIA)

Kuril Islands
(RUSSIA)

HOKKAIDO

•Sapporo

NORTH
KOREA

Sea of Japan

Aomori

Akita •Morioka

Yamagata

SOUTH
KOREA

Niigata

Sendai
•Fukushima

HONSHU

Toyama

Nagano

Kanazawa

Ota Mito
•Oizumi

Matsue

Tottori

Fukui

Gifu

Kyoto

Nagoya

Tokyo

Kawasaki
Fujisawa
Yokohama

Yamaguchi

Hiroshima

Okayama Kobe

Osaka

Toyohashi
Hamamatsu

Shizuoka

Fukuoka
Saga •Oita
Nagasaki Kumamoto

Kochi

SHIKOKU

JAPAN

KYUSHU

•Miyazaki

Kagoshima

East China

Sea

North Pacific Ocean

Naha

North

0   200 km

0   200 Miles

11

Japan: Government Policy, Immigrant Reality

Takeyuki Tsuda and Wayne A. Cornelius

IMMIGRATION TO JAPAN: MYTHS AND REALITIES

Japan represents one of the most intriguing laboratories in the world today for observing the interplay among labor market forces, public tolerance for immigration, and government attempts to regulate it. Until the late 1980s, Japan was the only major advanced industrial country in the world that did not rely on unskilled foreign labor. Although the country experienced labor shortages in the late 1960s and early 1970s, it was able to meet its labor requirements through increases in labor productivity and greater use of "untapped" sources of labor—females, the elderly, and rural workers (Mori 1997: 37–42). Regardless of whether this was the result of a deliberate government effort to keep the country "immigrant-free,"[1] Japan was frequently cited by U.S. social scientists as proof that an

This chapter is based in part on fieldwork conducted by the authors in July and November 1992 and during 1994–1995 in the cities of Tokyo, Yokohama, Kawasaki, Fujisawa, Oizumi, and Ota. Interviews were conducted with national and local government officials, employers, labor brokers, representatives of nongovernmental and labor organizations, journalists, academics, and local residents.

advanced industrial society can have a prosperous, growing economy without immigrant labor (Muller 1993; Reubens 1982). At the end of the 1980s, however, Japan lost its unique status among First World countries and finally succumbed to the pressures of global migration. Because of severe domestic labor shortages, the country suddenly found itself with a rapidly expanding stock of migrant workers from various Pacific Rim countries.

Although it may seem that Japan made a transition from a former country of emigration to a country of immigration in this manner (Douglass and Roberts 2000: 7; Watanabe 1994), the notion that Japan was not an immigration country until recent decades is a myth. From 1910 to 1945, when significant numbers of Japanese left the country to colonize Asia and then fight in World War II, 2.1 million Koreans immigrated to Japan—some as forced laborers—to work in Japanese factories (see Weiner 1994). Although a good number of them repatriated after the war, many remained in Japan, creating a Korean Japanese minority of well over 1.5 million that continues to suffer from ethnic discrimination and economic marginalization. Thus the post-1985 influx of foreign workers is just the latest chapter in Japan's immigration history.

Because Japan has developed into a country of immigration under very different domestic, regional, and historical contexts, its immigration policies and modes of immigrant incorporation are quite distinct from the Euro-American countries considered in this book. However, like these countries, a rather substantial gap has already emerged between Japanese immigration policy and its outcomes, leading to a number of serious negative consequences.

PROFILE OF FOREIGN WORKERS IN JAPAN

For a country that currently prides itself on its ethnic and racial homogeneity, Japan has a very diverse immigrant population, with a significant number of migrants from East and Southeast Asia, Latin America, and even the Middle East (see tables 11.1 and 11.2). Although the number of legally registered foreigners reached 1,686,444 in 2000, this figure includes hundreds of thousands of Korean Japanese who were born in Japan but have not naturalized. The total population of foreign workers

---

[1] The government had discussions about introducing foreign workers to Japan in 1967, 1973, and 1976 but decided against it (Sellek 2001: 23; cf. Bartram 2000: 25).

can be better estimated by examining the various visa categories under which they are admitted to Japan. In addition to the approximately 100,000 visas issued to skilled and professional workers in 2000, unskilled foreign workers entered Japan under three visa categories: "trainees" (36,199 in 2000), pre-college "students" (37,781), and "entertainers" (53,847). In addition, there are well over 330,000 Latin American *nikkeijin* (Japanese descendants born and raised outside of Japan) registered as foreigners in Japan. When these numbers are combined with those who are in Japan illegally, the total number of foreign workers is probably close to 950,000, approximately 850,000 of whom are unskilled or semi-skilled. Although this is still just 0.75 percent of Japan's total population of 127 million, it represents a sharp increase from the pre-1985 era.

While a plurality of Japan's foreign workers are clustered in the Tokyo-Yokohama, Osaka, and Nagoya metropolitan areas, smaller concentrations can be found in almost all parts of Japan. Many foreign workers (especially the ethnic Japanese from Latin America) are clustered in smaller industrial towns in Gunma, Shizuoka, and Aichi Prefectures. Foreign workers employed in the service sector tend to cluster in the inner cities of large metropolitan areas. Since the Japanese recession started in the early 1990s, the general trend has been toward greater geographic dispersion as foreign workers, faced with a tighter job market, have moved to more remote regions of Japan in pursuit of jobs (Sellek 2001: 98).

Most migrant workers in Japan are employed by small and medium-sized subcontractors in the manufacturing and construction sectors. By comparison with other industrialized countries, foreign workers are significantly underrepresented in Japan's service sector, except for the "entertainment" industry. According to one estimate, 52 percent of foreign workers are in the manufacturing sector, 22 percent in the construction sector, 16 percent in "entertainment," and only 10 percent in other parts of the service sector.[2] However, the greatest potential growth in unskilled foreign worker employment in Japan is in the service sector, and there has already been a notable shift toward service-sector jobs among illegal foreign workers in Japan in response to a decline in jobs in manufacturing and construction (Komai 2001: 40–43).

---

[2] Statistics compiled from Komai 1995: chap. 2.

Table 11.1. Legally Registered Aliens in Japan, by Nationality, 1991–2000

Nationality	1991	1992	1993	1994	1995	1996	1997	1998	1999	2000
Korean	693,050	688,144	682,276	676,793	666,376	657,159	645,373	638,828	636,548	635,269
Chinese	171,071	195,334	210,138	218,585	222,991	234,264	252,164	272,230	294,201	335,575
Brazilian	119,333	147,803	154,650	159,619	176,440	201,795	233,254	222,217	224,299	254,394
Filipino	61,837	62,218	73,057	85,968	74,297	84,509	93,265	105,308	115,685	144,871
Peruvian	26,281	31,051	33,169	35,382	36,269	37,099	40,394	41,317	42,773	46,171
U.S.	42,498	42,482	42,639	43,320	43,198	44,168	43,690	42,774	42,802	44,856
Other	104,821	114,612	124,819	134,344	142,800	156,142	174,567	189,442	199,805	225,308
TOTAL	1,218,891	1,281,644	1,320,748	1,354,011	1,362,371	1,415,136	1,482,707	1,512,116	1,556,113	1,686,444

Table 11.2. Estimated Visa Overstayers in Japan, by Nationality, 1991–2000

Nationality	1991	1992	1993	1994	1995	1996	1997	1998	1999	2000
Korean	25,848	35,687	39,455	43,369	47,544	51,580	52,387	52,123	62,577	60,693
Filipino	27,228	31,974	35,392	37,544	39,763	41,997	42,547	42,608	40,420	36,379
Chinese	17,535	25,737	33,312	39,738	39,511	39,140	38,296	37,590	34,800	32,896
Thai	19,093	44,354	55,383	49,992	44,794	41,280	39,513	37,046	30,065	23,503
Malaysian	14,413	38,529	30,840	20,313	14,511	11,525	10,390	10,141	9,989	9,701
Taiwanese	5,241	6,729	7,457	7,871	7,974	8,502	9,409	9,430	9,437	9,243
Peruvian	487	2,783	9,038	12,918	15,301	13,836	12,942	11,606	10,320	9,158
Iranian	10,915	40,001	28,437	20,757	16,252	13,241	11,303	9,186	7,304	5,824
Myanmarese	2,061	4,704	6,019	6,391	6,189	5,885	5,900	5,829	5,487	4,986
Indonesian	582	1,995	2,969	3,198	3,205	3,481	3,758	4,692	4,930	4,947
Bangladeshi	7,498	8,103	8,069	7,565	7,084	6,500	6,197	5,581	4,936	4,263
Pakistani	7,864	8,001	7,733	6,921	6,100	5,478	5,157	4,688	4,307	3,414
TOTAL	159,828	278,892	298,646	293,800	286,704	284,500	282,986	276,810	271,048	251,697

CAUSES OF RECENT IMMIGRATION TO JAPAN

Changes in Labor Demand and Supply

Japan has recently faced various demographic, labor market, and global pressures similar to many Euro-American countries that have forced it to import large numbers of unskilled immigrant workers. The rapid expansion of the Japanese economy in the 1980s (which increased total employment by some 4.4 million workers from 1986 to 1991 alone) created a rising demand for low-skilled labor. In addition, there has been an increasing need for more temporary, casual workers among Japanese companies in order to cut production costs in the face of competition from developing countries with cheaper labor.

However, by the late 1980s the domestic labor supply became unable to meet the demand for unskilled and flexible labor, threatening to cripple the booming Japanese economy, especially among small and midsize firms in the manufacturing and construction sectors. This labor shortage has occurred because of a combination of several demographic, economic, and social trends:

- *The rapid shrinking and aging of the Japanese populace.* Japan's total fertility rate has fallen by almost one-third since 1965, to about 1.3 children per woman—tied with Italy for the world's lowest fertility rate—and it continues to decline. Even at the current fertility rate, Japan's population is expected to peak in 2006 at 127.8 million and will shrink by 21.6 million (17 percent) from 2000 to 2050 (United Nations 2000) (see figure 11.1). As a result, the total workforce is expected to contract by as much as 13.8 percent by 2025 (Mori 1997: 90).

- *A better-educated and socially mobile Japanese populace.* Japanese youth are increasingly well educated and affluent and have come to actively shun unskilled "3K" factory jobs characterized as *kiken* (dangerous), *kitanai* (dirty), and *kitsui* (physically difficult).

- *Depletion of previously underutilized sources of labor power* (see Mori 1997: 57–59, 65–68). Japan's female labor force participation rate has risen considerably in the postwar era to become one of the highest among industrialized countries, making further significant increases unlikely. Similarly, a substantial expansion in the number of elderly workers in Japan is equally unlikely, despite rapid population aging, because the labor force participation rate for those over age 60 is also quite high and has been stable for decades.

- *The limitations of mechanization and off-shore production.* Mechanization, as a labor-saving technique, began to show its limits in the late 1980s, partly because Japan's factories were already much more mechanized than those in other industrialized countries. Relocation of production abroad to take advantage of overseas labor supplies has already been pursued aggressively for decades and is reaching its limits. Also, small and medium-sized firms, where the labor shortage is most acute, generally do not have the know-how and capital required to relocate part of their production overseas (cf. Sellek 2001: 42). And companies in the construction and service sectors that produce for Japanese domestic consumers and clients generally cannot move abroad.

Since the demand for foreign workers in Japan is being driven by demographic and socioeconomic changes that are of long duration and not easily reversible, it has become relatively insensitive to cyclical economic fluctuations (Douglass and Roberts 2000: 19–20; Mori 1997: 65). Although Japan has been in a prolonged and serious economic recession since the bursting of the bubble economy in 1991, the downturn's impact on foreign worker employment has been relatively mild because the labor shortage has persisted among smaller, subsidiary companies (Mori 1997: 74). According to a 1995 Tokyo Metropolitan Institute for Labor survey (cited in Komai 2001: 34–35), very few foreign workers were fired during the recession. Similarly, a 1996 survey of employers in the city of Hamamatsu found that more than 40 percent of firms had added new foreign workers to their payrolls during the recession of the 1990s (Cornelius and Kuwahara 1998). Although many foreign workers have seen their salaries and overtime reduced, and others have had greater difficulty finding jobs, there has been no mass unemployment nor an exodus of migrant workers from Japan in response to the recession (Sellek 2001: 10–11, 96–97).

In fact, according to Ministry of Labor estimates, the total foreign worker population (including illegals, excluding permanent residents) has been growing steadily during the recession (cf. Watanabe 1998).[3] And the number of illegal foreign workers has not declined significantly either, remaining in the 270,000–300,000 range during most of the ten-year recession. According to one Justice Ministry official, visa overstayers have *prolonged* their stays in Japan in response to the recession because it

---

[3] The foreign worker population grew by close to 10 percent from 1995 to 1998 (OECD 2000: 215).

Figure 11.1. Projected Population of Japan

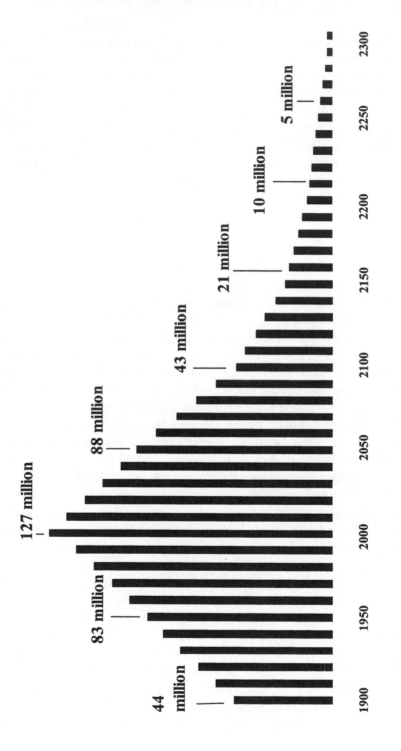

Source: United Nations 2000.
Note: Assumes a fertility rate of 1.34 children per woman and no change in current level of migration.

is taking them longer to achieve their financial goals (*Daily Yomiuri*, November 15, 2001), a trend documented among legal immigrant workers as well (Tsuda 1999a). In this manner, demand for foreign labor in Japan has become structurally embedded.

Once the Japanese economy recovers and enters another period of sustained growth, the demand for foreign-born labor is likely to become much more robust. According to various forecasts based on an annual economic growth rate of 3 to 4 percent and annual increases in labor productivity of 0.0 to 3.5 percent, Japan will experience labor shortages ranging from 130,000 to 559,000 workers per year (Mori 1997: 90–91). A recent United Nations report estimates that, because of population aging and low fertility, Japan would have to import over 640,000 immigrants per year just to maintain its present workforce, or face a 6.7 annual drop in GDP (United Nations 2000).

Transnational Linkages and Migration Systems

Japan has become very attractive as a migration destination because of the huge wage differentials between it and many Third World countries, partly resulting from the rapid appreciation of the yen following the Plaza Agreement of 1985. However, migration never consists of an indiscriminate flood of peoples from any country with lower income and employment opportunities. Nor are migration flows dictated by some logic of geographical proximity. Although immigrants from nearby East and Southeast Asian countries are heavily represented in Japan, the country's largest contingent of foreign workers is from distant South America.

The "migration system" that consists of Japan and the migrant-sending countries of Asia and Latin America is a product of various transnational economic, sociopolitical, and ethnocultural linkages that have developed between them and channels immigrants to Japan in response to economic incentives. It is no coincidence that the East and Southeast Asian countries that send the largest number of immigrants to Japan (Korea, China, the Philippines, and Thailand) are the ones that receive the most Japanese foreign direct investment and trade. The flow of Japanese capital across national borders and the relocation of production facilities to various Asian countries by Japanese multinational firms create employment opportunities for local native workers, giving them access to the resources and connections necessary to migrate to Japan (Sassen 1991: 32–33). In addition, these Asian countries were colonized by Japan before World War II, which created various historical, economic, and sociocultural linkages that have channeled migrants to Japan. For instance, the relocation of large numbers of laborers during colonization created large Korean and Chinese minority communities in Japan. Some of the newcomers from Korea and China in the late 1980s and early 1990s were able to migrate because of their ties to these "oldcomer" communities in Japan (Mori 1997: 148). In the case of South America, migration was fueled by ethnic ties (see Tsuda 1999b). From about 1900 to 1960, several hundred thousand Japanese emigrated to South America, creating large ethnic communities, especially in Brazil. It is now the second- and third-generation descendants of these original emigrants (the nikkeijin) who are "return migrating" to Japan.

Further, extensive transnational migrant labor brokerage and smuggling networks have developed between Japan and the principal source countries. The most prominent and extensive labor broker systems for legal migrants are those than bring nikkeijin workers to Japan. For example, numerous labor broker offices (usually posing as travel agencies) in various South American cities recruit nikkeijin and send them to Japan, at which point they are turned over to a Japanese labor broker firm, which technically hires the nikkeijin and places them in Japanese companies needing their labor. Not only do these transnational migrant labor brokers give the nikkeijin direct access to a wide range of jobs in various Japanese companies, they also handle the paperwork needed to acquire a visa, finance all travel expenses, and provide housing, transportation, insurance, and an array of other employment and social services in Japan.

In addition, there is a vast array of international labor brokers who smuggle illegal migrant workers into Japan for exorbitant fees (Herbert 1992: 111; Komai 1995: 29–30; Sellek 2001: 37). They usually take one of three forms: (1) those that masquerade as "language schools" in Japan, accepting "students" from abroad with false documentation and Japanese guarantors for visas (Komai 1993: 75–76, 1995: 56; Sellek 2001: 88); (2) Chinese "snakehead" networks that relay migrants through several operatives on various routes and smuggle them into Japan using fake passports or by boat to remote sites where they are picked up by relatives, friends, or brokers; and (3) operations that recruit mainly women in Thailand and the Philippines, promising them jobs as receptionists, waitresses, or models in Japan but actually selling them to Japanese brokers who in turn sell them to employers in the country's thriving sex industry. A good number of migrant workers utilize such networks and would not have been able to migrate to Japan nor would have chosen the country as a migrant destination had it not been for the aggressive recruitment efforts and assistance of such labor broker and smuggling operations.

CURRENT POLICY AND POLICYMAKING ON FOREIGN WORKERS

The immigrant profile and composition of any country is not simply the product of economic incentives that motivate migration and the transnational networks that channel it. Immigration is also affected by the policies that governments adopt to regulate and control migrant flows. The Japanese government, which operates on the myth that it is an ethnically homogeneous nation and is not and never was a country of immigration, has one of the most highly restrictive immigration policies among advanced industrialized countries. It is based on three fundamental principles:

- *No unskilled foreign workers will be admitted.* Even when confronted by a crippling labor shortage in the late 1980s, the Japanese government refused to officially open its doors to unskilled migrant workers. The revised Immigration Control and Refugee Recognition Act (implemented in 1990) maintained Japan's long-standing ban on unskilled foreign workers and imposed tough penalties on those employers and labor brokers who knowingly recruit and hire illegal aliens. Subsequent revisions to the immigration law (in 1998 and 1999) have introduced penalties against immigrant smugglers and on the illegal immigrants themselves.

- *The government should facilitate the admission of only highly skilled and professional foreign workers.* While forbidding the acceptance of unskilled immigrants, the revised Immigration Control and Refugee Recognition Act expanded the number of legal residence statuses (mainly skilled and professional visa categories) from eighteen to twenty-seven and simplified immigration procedures in order to meet the increasing demand for foreign managerial and technical staff (including experts on international business law and accounting) as well as foreign language instructors as a result of the globalization of Japanese business and corporations (Mori 1997: 103–105). This caused a sharp increase in the number of foreign professional workers in Japan, which continues to grow during the recession (Fuess 2003: 249–50). Although North America and Europe supplied most of these skilled foreign workers in the past, a greater number of them now come from Asia (Fuess 2003: 251). Concerns that Japan is falling behind in information technology (especially the Internet) has recently caused the government to further loosen restrictions on skilled labor migration in the near future by making it easier for information technology (IT) professionals from several Asian nations (including China, India, and Korea) to work in Japan.

- *All foreigners should be admitted on a temporary basis only.* All foreign workers in Japan are granted only temporary visas (although some can be renewed an indefinite number of times), and none are admitted as permanent immigrants. Nor does the government permit the immigration of family members of foreign workers residing in Japan (except for the Japanese-descent nikkeijin) since this would encourage foreigners to settle in Japan. This official insistence on temporariness has made the presence of foreign workers more acceptable to the Japanese public and has relieved the national government of the burden of providing expensive social services to immigrant settlers.

During the fourteen years since the revised Immigration Control Act was implemented, there has been no discernable shift in the Japanese government's official immigration policy. In fact, a 1999 report dealing with immigration policy issued by the Economic Planning Agency recommended that the government maintain its policy of not accepting unskilled foreign workers and simply reiterated the above principles (OECD 2000: 214; cf. Sellek 2001: 106–107). In 2000, the Ministry of Justice released a new basic immigration control plan that mainly reiterates current policy directions—despite acknowledging the long-term settlement of immigrant workers in Japan and the need for a more stable residential status for refugees.

Such highly restrictive immigration policies are quite surprising, given the country's considerable economic need and demand for unskilled foreign workers discussed above. Why is there such a large discrepancy in Japan between official immigration policy and economic reality? Of course, immigration policymaking is never simply a direct response to economic needs because it involves different government bodies with varying amounts of political power responding to different pressures, only some of which are economic.

The Japanese immigration policymaking regime has been quite insensitive to economic pressures because it is dominated by the bureaucracy, with little active participation by the democratically elected Diet, beyond rubber-stamping legislation handed down by the bureaucrats after proforma policy debates. Since government bureaucrats are not publicly elected or accountable, they have been relatively unresponsive to public lobbying by employers and business owners. Labor-deficient Japanese company managers who have directly contacted or even visited the Ministries of Labor and Justice to demand more liberal immigration policies report that they have either been met with blank stares or were simply given the official government party line (that they should mechanize and rationalize production and increase employment of women and the elderly instead of relying on foreign workers).

There are also other reasons why the economic demand for immigrant labor has not been effectively translated into commensurate political pressure. Labor-deficient small and medium-sized businesses in Japan have not been an effective political force despite their efforts because they are far less powerful than the larger corporations and do not control the politically influential big business organizations (cf. Bartram 2000: 25). Since larger corporations have not suffered from serious labor shortages nor need as much flexible and casual migrant labor, they have not supported the smaller businesses and their demands for a more open immigration policy. In fact, when the government was revising the immigration law in the late 1980s, the big business organizations (including the Nikkeiren and Keizai Doyukai) were unwilling to advocate the importation of unskilled foreign laborers.

This does not, of course, mean that the Japanese bureaucracy has been completely unresponsive to economic needs nor that they speak in one monolithic voice. During the immigration policy debate of the late 1980s, a grand total of seventeen government ministries and agencies were involved in immigration policymaking, each responding to different pressures and possessing different, if not conflicting, viewpoints and agendas, including those that strongly advocated more open immigration policies. On the liberal end of the policy spectrum were those ministries most responsive to the demands of labor-deficient Japanese industries, most notably the Ministries of Construction, Agriculture, Transportation, and Forest and Fisheries, all of which generally advocated the legal admission of foreign workers. The Ministry of Foreign Affairs, which is most concerned with Japan's international responsibilities and bears the brunt of foreign criticism over Japan's exclusionary immigration policies, also took a liberal stance.

However, there is relatively poor coordination and cooperation between the ministries, which rarely produce policies based on a balanced discussion and compromise between a diversity of represented opinions and positions. Instead, Japan's ministries constantly compete for power, and conflicts over jurisdiction and territorial infringements are frequent, resulting in defensive rivalries, jealousies, and animosities. As a result, policymaking often resembles a tug-of-war between competitive segments of the bureaucracy, with certain ministries (and their policy positions) prevailing over others through hierarchical power struggles.

In terms of immigration policymaking, the ministries that took the most conservative stance (Labor and Justice) dominated. The Ministry of Labor, which is concerned with domestic labor standards, claimed that unskilled foreign laborers would lower wages and working conditions, cause labor market segmentation, delay the development of labor-saving technologies, create social conflict, and result in tremendous social welfare costs. Nonetheless, the Ministry was concerned with facilitating employer access to legal foreign labor and was willing to promote a new program to accept technical trainees from abroad. However, the Ministry of Justice (which outranks all the others and is in charge of immigration control) wrested complete control over immigration policymaking from other ministries and agencies. Unfortunately, the Ministry of Justice has taken the hardest line, resisting all expansionary immigration policies and insisting on sanctions against employers who hire illegal foreign workers. Former Justice Ministry insiders (retired bureaucrats) report that the Ministry is one of the most conservative, closed-minded institutions in Japanese society and is still dominated by domestic security and ideological concerns to maintain the nation's ethnic homogeneity and cultural purity. Because the Ministry of Justice emerged on top of the bureaucratic hierarchy in terms of immigration policymaking, its restrictive position was directly reflected in Japan's 1990 revised immigration law.[4]

SIDE-DOOR MECHANISMS FOR IMPORTING UNSKILLED FOREIGN LABOR

Of course, official immigration policy is one thing, actual outcomes quite another. Despite Japan's apparent ban on unskilled foreign workers, over 850,000 of them are actually working in Japan, as noted earlier. It is no surprise that Japan has such a large gap between policy and outcomes given that it has an immigration policy that accepts only skilled professionals from abroad but a labor market that needs unskilled immigrant workers.

---

[4] In contrast to some other types of Japanese policymaking, neither the Prime Minister's Office nor the dominant Liberal Democratic Party has provided much leadership.

This wide discrepancy in Japan is partly the result of economic pressures and the structural embeddedness of immigrant labor in advanced industrialized nations. Regardless of how restrictive government policies are, it can be argued that Japan's labor shortage and the demand for flexible migrant labor (as well as the income and employment disparities between Japan and Third World countries) are so great that highly motivated and resourceful migrants (as well as the extensive migrant-labor broker networks on which they rely) will always find a way to circumvent the government's official policies, immigration control mechanisms, and any other barriers it throws in their way. In this manner, the economic pressures and the transnational networks that drive migration can overwhelm government attempts to control it, making migrant flows relatively insensitive to immigration policies. There is no doubt that when Japan recovers from its current prolonged recession and the economy again begins to expand, this gap between policy and outcomes will grow much wider.

At the same time, governments themselves also actively undermine their own immigration policies by literally saying one thing and doing another. Official immigration policy (driven by political ideologies) is not always a good reflection of actual government intentions, which are frequently driven by different, practical considerations. This can sometimes cause governments to deliberately create a gap between stated policies and actual practices.

Although the Japanese government has officially prohibited the importation of unskilled foreign labor, it has not lost touch with economic reality, nor has it been as unresponsive to economic pressures and demand for foreign workers as it appears on the official surface. As concessions to labor-deficient Japanese employers, the Ministry of Justice has created various "side-door" mechanisms that enable the legal importation of large numbers of unskilled foreign workers under visa categories officially intended for other purposes. The most significant of these side-door policies are the admission of the nikkeijin and the expansion of the "trainee" program. In addition, although many unskilled immigrant workers enter Japan as pre-college "students" and "entertainers," the Ministry of Justice has either looked the other way or made only half-hearted attempts to crack down on the widespread abuse of these visa categories.[5] With the front door officially closed to all but skilled and

[5] In both cases, the Ministry of Justice has issued "ordinances" and by-laws in order to reduce these abuses through better regulation and strict new standards. Although this led to temporary declines in the number of those entering Japan as students and

professional workers, over half of the estimated 850,000 unskilled immigrant workers in Japan have entered through the side door.

Corporate Trainee Programs

The Japanese company trainee program is one important means through which migrant labor is imported through the side door. Since the early 1990s, Japan has been admitting anywhere from 40,000 to 55,000 trainees per year (54,049 in 2000). In 2000, 36,199 trainees (22,163 of them from mainland China) were residing in Japan. Shortly after the revised immigration law was implemented, the Ministry of Justice modified by decree the traditional trainee program (formerly restricted to official agencies and large multinational corporations) to enable small and midsize companies suffering from labor shortages to accept trainees from abroad (see Komai 1995: 41).

As a result, although the program is officially justified as a form of overseas development assistance that enables trainees from developing countries to acquire technical skills at Japanese companies, it is being widely abused as a source of inexpensive, unskilled foreign labor (see, for example, Komai 1992; Miyajima 1993: chap. 5; Oishi 1995). Not only do the "trainees" perform jobs that require minimal or no training, most of the companies that participate in the program are too small to have the resources to provide any substantial on-the-job training or classroom instruction (Oishi 1995: 35). In addition, Japanese employers have to pay these trainees only a "trainee allowance" since they are not classified as workers entitled to real wages. According to one survey of employers participating in the trainee program, 72 percent of them were using their trainees simply as cheap, unskilled laborers (Komai 1992: 46). Not surprisingly, a number of trainees disappear into the underground (and more profitable) immigrant labor market, and some are overstaying their visas as well (3,055 at the beginning of 2000).

In 1993 the Ministry of Justice (in another decree) implemented a new Technical Intern Training program. The length of stay of trainees in Japan was extended to two years (and then to three years in 1997) from the previous one-year duration. The new system requires that the first nine months be devoted to both on-the-job skills training and off-the-job class-

---

entertainers, the new rules were not effectively enforced and the abuse of these visa categories is still rampant. Indeed, the number of foreigners overstaying these visa types remained stable or increased after these ordinances were issued (Sellek 2001: 89, 91, 110–17).

room instruction (including study of the Japanese language). If trainees pass a skills evaluation after nine months of skills training and classroom instruction, they are allowed to change their residence status to "technical interns," who then become official employees receiving full wages and protections guaranteed under Japan's labor laws. Since the new program allows trainees to become full-blown workers for a full fifteen months, it moves closer to an officially acknowledged (front-door) guest-worker program when compared to the old trainee system.

Importing "Ethnic Japanese" from Latin America

Numerically the most important of Japan's immigration side-door mechanisms has been the policy of allowing descendants of Japanese emigrants in Latin America to "return" to Japan. There are currently well over 330,000 South American nikkeijin immigrants in Japan, mainly from Brazil but also from Peru, Bolivia, and Argentina. As long as they can prove their Japanese descent, the nikkeijin (up to the third generation) are legally accepted under "Spouse of Japanese" or "Long-Term Settler" visas, which have no activity restrictions and can be renewed an indefinite number of times, making their holders de facto permanent residents.

Although the nikkeijin work exclusively as unskilled migrant laborers in small and medium-sized Japanese factories (and were tacitly admitted for this purpose) (cf. Kajita 1994: 172), the government officially justifies the policy as an opportunity for the nikkeijin to learn the Japanese language and culture, meet their Japanese relatives, travel the country, and thus explore their ethnic heritage. Therefore, by appealing to ideologies of ethnic ancestry and homeland, the Japanese government was able to acquire a much-needed, large migrant labor force without contradicting, at least at the level of official appearances, the fundamental principle of Japanese immigration policy that no unskilled foreign workers will be accepted. In addition, because of their common racial descent, government officials assumed that the nikkeijin would be culturally similar to the Japanese and would assimilate smoothly to Japanese society, in contrast to other foreigners, thus avoiding the social disruption and ethnic conflict associated with culturally and racially different foreigners (Miyajima 1993: 59; Tsuda 1999b). However, since most of the nikkeijin immigrants are of the second and third generations and were born and raised in South America, most speak Japanese poorly and have become culturally Latin American. As a result, they are ethnically marginalized and socially segregated in Japan as foreigners and have become Japan's newest ethnic minority (see Tsuda 2003).

The nikkeijin are considered highly desirable as migrant laborers because they are the most ethnically preferred of all foreigners and are virtually the only source of legal and legitimate foreign labor. As a result, they command the highest wages among all unskilled foreign workers in Japan (see Tsuda, Valdez, and Cornelius 2003; Yamanaka 2003a). Japanese employers generally praise them for their work ethic and willingness to do overtime, and they claim that they are better than Japanese part-time or temporary workers. Given the limited size of the Japanese-descent populations in South America, the nikkeijin cannot possibly supply Japan with the number of foreign workers that its economy will demand in the future.

Importing Part-time "Student" Labor and "Entertainers"

The admission of foreigners on pre-college "student" visas (*shugakusei*) represents yet another of Japan's current "side-door" immigration policies. This was a new visa category created by the revised Immigration Control Act in 1990 in order to encourage more foreign students to study in Japan. In 2000, there were 37,781 pre-college shugakusei registered in Japan, a vast majority of whom (26,542) had come from China. Although they are in Japan ostensibly to learn the Japanese language or to participate in vocational training programs, they were initially permitted to work part-time for twenty hours a week to support themselves. In 1998 the government increased the number of hours these "students" can work per week from twenty to twenty-eight during the academic school year and forty during summer and winter vacations. However, most work illegally for longer hours,[6] and many of them are becoming full-time, unskilled foreign workers, most notably in the service sector (see Komai 1995: 119). There are also indications that this side-door policy is beginning to resemble a *backdoor* mechanism to import illegal foreign workers. Not only are many of these "students" overstaying their visas (11,359 in 2000), a number of them are now entering Japan on false documentation, and the "language schools" that accept them are sometimes nothing more than immigrant-smuggling firms.

---

[6] According to a Tokyo Metropolitan Government survey (cited in Komai 2001: 58–59), 65.1 percent of pre-college students surveyed were working an average of 35.4 hours per week.

A final side-door mechanism for bringing unskilled workers to Japan involves those who enter as "entertainers" (53,847 in 2000). Like the "trainees" and "students," they are legally admitted to Japan under a professional visa category, but most (90 percent, according to Ishihara 1992: 176) actually work as bar hostesses in sleazy nightclubs or as prostitutes. A vast majority of them are from the Philippines, but smaller numbers also come from other Asian countries.

Again, this side-door supply of "entertainers" has a backdoor, illegal component as well. In addition to the large number of those who over-stay their visas (12,552 in 2000), many of them are undocumented female migrants (mainly from the Philippines and Thailand) who are deceived and exploited by labor brokers (often with ties to criminal syndicates) and forced to work as bar hostesses or prostitutes (see Oka 1994: 58–59; Sellek 2001: chap. 6). Called *Japayuki-san* (literally Ms. Going-to-Japan), they are held hostage by their labor brokers and employers, who confiscate their passports and force them to repay huge debts they have incurred for being smuggled into Japan. Others are not paid wages, work under conditions of sexual slavery and forced confinement, and are threatened with physical violence or punishment. Despite efforts by the Philippine government to reduce the number of Filipina migrant women channeled into the global sex industry and the Japanese government's attempt to regulate bars and nightclubs that employ foreign "entertainers"—and despite criticism from international human rights groups—little has been done to combat this illicit trafficking of women.

THE BACK DOOR: THE LIMITS OF IMMIGRATION CONTROL

The huge gap between Japan's closed-door immigration policies and the presence of large numbers of unskilled foreign workers is also the result of ineffective policy mechanisms for controlling immigration. As a result, the country has a large number of illegal immigrants, mainly from East and Southeast Asia.

Porous Borders and Unauthorized Immigration to Japan

In the late 1980s and early 1990s, the government attempted to reduce the flow of illegal immigrants from certain countries by revoking previous visa-exemption agreements, beginning with Bangladesh and Pakistan in 1989. After stringent tourist visa requirements were imposed, the

flow of new immigrants from these two countries was significantly reduced, only to be replaced by a flood of illegal Iranian workers. This
produced a strong negative public reaction partly because the new immigrants congregated in two of Tokyo's largest public parks to socialize
and engage in petty commerce, causing the government to impose visa
requirements on Iranians, which, in turn, reduced the flow of new immigrants from that country. The government took similar action against
Malaysians and Peruvians in 1992. Despite the short-term effectiveness
of this visa issuance policy, it has been ineffective in keeping out illegal
foreign workers in the long term, since most of them have simply entered
on tourist visas (as well as student, trainee, and entertainment visas) and
overstayed. In fact, four of the five countries that had their visa exemp-
tion status revoked are among the top twelve countries that send visa
overstayers to Japan (see table 11.2).

In 2000, the government counted 251,697 visa overstayers, over 90
percent of whom are assumed to be in the workforce. However, the total
number of illegal immigrant workers in Japan considerably exceeds this
number because the count of overstayers does not include people who
work illegally in violation of their visa activity restrictions or who enter
Japan with false documentation. The use of forged visas has become
quite prominent, especially among Thai immigrants (Sellek 2001: 109).
However, the most sensational cases have been the "fake nikkeijin" —
mainly Peruvians who purchase false documentation of Japanese ancestry (frequently from Peruvian nikkeijin) and even have their facial features altered in an attempt to enter Japan as "ethnic Japanese" (see
Fuchigami 1995: chap. 1).

In addition, there are immigrants who have entered Japan clandestinely by various means, and their true numbers cannot be accurately
estimated. Most immigrants enter the country through one of the international airports, apparently making them easy to detect. Yet those who are
denied entry into Japan are very few compared to the stock of unauthorized immigrants residing in the country, and their numbers have been
declining in recent years.[7] In addition, Japan simply cannot patrol thousands of miles of coastline in order to interdict immigrants attempting to
enter illegally by boat. In 1999, 9,337 foreigners were apprehended while
attempting to enter Japan illegally (3,056 of these were by boat), which is
estimated to be only 10 percent of the total number of immigrants smuggled illegally into Japan (Friman 2001: 298). When these different types of

---

[7] The number of foreigners denied entry into Japan in recent years has declined steadily from 27,137 in 1991 to 8,273 in 2000.

unauthorized immigration are considered, the illegal immigrant population is probably over 400,000.

Ineffective Internal Enforcement

Like other countries of immigration, not only has Japan had trouble controlling its borders, it has also been ineffective in enforcing its restrictive immigration laws within the country. There has been no large-scale, systematic roundup and deportation campaign to reduce the population of illegal foreign workers in Japan, and only a relatively small portion of the total unauthorized immigrant population is actually apprehended by the government each year (in the range of 50,000 to 55,000 since 1995). Although this may appear somewhat substantial, a majority of the unauthorized immigrants who are "apprehended" actually turn themselves in, usually right before they plan to return to their home countries (cf. *Agence France Presse*, August 2, 1996; Sellek 2001: 31). According to one official at the Immigration Bureau, "We mainly rely on rumors, threats, and propaganda efforts to get the illegals to turn themselves in." Appropriately enough, next to him hung a Justice Ministry anti–illegal immigration poster that read: "Let's obey the immigration law. Your cooperation is appreciated." Undocumented migrant workers have also surrendered en masse in the past in response to misleading rumors about the harshness of new penalties to be implemented by the government against illegal immigrants and their employers.[8]

In terms of the internal enforcement of immigration laws at the workplace, Japan opted for employer sanctions (modeled after those in the United States and Europe) after a well-publicized power struggle between the Ministries of Justice and Labor in the late 1980s. The Ministry of Labor proposed creating a work permit system (which would give it control over the employment of foreigners), but the Ministry of Justice vehemently objected, preferring an employer sanctions law that would make the employment of illegal foreign workers a criminal issue, over

---

[8] When the government passed the employer sanctions provisions in 1989 as part of the revised Immigration Control Act, thousands of visa overstayers (mistakenly believing that *they* and not their employers would be penalized) rushed to turn themselves in to immigration authorities before the law was implemented in 1990. This false rumor was the product of misleading articles in English-language newspapers in Japan (Komai 1995: 6). A similar reaction occurred (to a lesser extent) in response to the 1999 revision of the Immigration Control Act, which finally *did* introduce penalties against illegal immigrants.

which it could retain control. Eventually the Ministry of Justice (which outranks the Ministry of Labor) won the battle and passed an employer sanctions law as part of the revised Immigration Control Act, imposing fines of up to 2 million yen (equivalent to about US$15,600 in mid-2002) and criminal penalties of up to three years in prison for both employers who knowingly hire illegal aliens and the labor brokers who recruit them.

Not only is Japan's employer sanctions law similar to those of the United States and Europe, it is equally flawed and unenforceable. In fact, only a minuscule portion of the thousands of employers and labor brokers who hire unauthorized foreign workers have been penalized for violations (for example, 351 in 1992 and 692 in 1993). Since Japanese employers are not obligated to verify employment eligibility, many do not check the papers of their foreign employees (Kuwahara 1998: 377), making it difficult to prosecute them for knowingly hiring illegal immigrants.

In addition, there seems to be little political will within the Ministry of Justice to effectively enforce the employer sanctions law because of the essential role now played by foreign workers in certain sectors of the Japanese economy (cf. Yamanaka 2003a). Indeed, according to one Ministry bureaucrat responsible for immigration policy, when the Japanese Diet passed the revised immigration law in 1989, there was an implicit agreement with the Ministry of Justice that it would not aggressively enforce the new employer sanctions law, in apparent deference to the large numbers of Japanese companies that need illegal immigrant workers to survive.[9] Again, official policy is one thing but actual intention is quite another, producing a notable gap between policies and outcomes.

Even if the Ministry of Justice were willing to enforce immigration laws (both employer sanctions and the ban on unskilled immigration), it is seriously hampered by a lack of resources at the Immigration Bureau (Spencer 1992: 763). The Bureau has a total of 2,500 officers (up only several hundred in ten years), of which a mere 1,000 are responsible for inspecting thousands of private businesses for immigration law violations and for apprehending, detaining, and deporting the hundreds of thousands of immigrants working illegally in Japan. As a result, apprehensions of illegal immigrants and their employers are usually restricted to sporadic and token efforts (cf. Shipper 2002a: 50–51; Yamanaka 2003a).

---

[9] In fact, the law has a supplementary provision that exempts companies that were employing or subsequently hired undocumented foreign workers who were already in Japan when the law was implemented (Komai 1995: 6).

The Japanese police, with a force of 220,000 officers and on-the-ground community policing, is much better positioned to catch illegal immigrants. Even high-ranking police officials in Ota City, which has one of the highest concentrations of unauthorized foreign workers in the country, stated that, if ordered to do so, they would probably be able to round up all of the illegal immigrants in the area with the help of a vigilant public. However, although police officials do state that they deal with all criminal violations, including those of immigration law, they do not actively search for and apprehend unauthorized immigrants. The police tend to view the issue of illegal immigrants as mainly a Ministry of Justice problem that should be dealt with by the Immigration Bureau, and they themselves do not direct precious time and resources to the effort.

In response to the ineffectiveness of its previous immigration control mechanisms, Japan has recently introduced a host of new ones. In 1998 the government began penalizing various types of immigrant smugglers (and those who assist them) with fines of up to 10 million yen (about US$78,000 in mid-2002) and prison sentences of up to ten years. Starting in February 2000, new penalties against visa overstayers were also implemented (fines of up to 300,000 yen, or about US$2,300, and three years imprisonment). The government has also attempted to reduce the level of nikkeijin migration in response to the increase in "fake nikkeijin," it has proposed increasing the number of immigration officials by 1,100 in five years, and it will expand a pilot program designed to introduce machine-readable visas at Japanese embassies abroad in order to combat the proliferation of fake visas (*Kyodo News Service*, August 29, 2001; Sellek 2001: 109). Although it is still too early to assess the effectiveness of these new measures, past experience suggests that they will be ineffective.

Not only has the government been unwilling to narrow the gap between policy and outcomes by serious internal enforcement of laws against illegal immigrants and their employers, it has also been unwilling to reduce the population of undocumented foreign workers through a legalization program. Government officials seem strongly opposed to a large-scale amnesty for undocumented workers, fearing that it would encourage more illegal immigration (see Komai 2001: 110). However, the Ministry of Justice has been granting special residency permits to a growing number of visa overstayers who have married Japanese nationals, are raising children born with a Japanese partner, or have developed other ties with Japan (such as having children enrolled in Japanese schools who would find it difficult to return home). The number who have been granted amnesty tripled over five years to reach a record 7,750 in 2002.

Nonetheless, because the Ministry has not publicly released the criteria it uses for legalization, the outcome for overstayers requesting amnesty remains quite uncertain, especially in light of local immigration officials' considerable discretion in such cases.

Gaps and Consequences

There is no doubt that large gaps between official immigration policies and actual outcomes have serious negative repercussions. The Japanese government's disingenuous importation of unskilled foreign workers through the side door and back door has led to serious human rights abuses against, for example, "entertainers" who are forced to become sex workers and against "trainees" who are exploited as cheap unskilled laborers. Even the legally accepted and ethnically privileged nikkeijin are sometimes deceived by labor brokers who promise easier jobs and higher pay than are actually available. Unauthorized immigrants in Japan are sometimes forced to toil under poor working conditions, receive low wages, lack standard worker rights and protections, and do not have access to adequate medical care and insurance. Those who are apprehended are detained, sometimes for more than two years if they lack proper documents, in facilities that do not meet international standards (*Daily Yomiuri*, April 25, 2002).

Japan remains distinctive among the Euro-American countries discussed in this book for its exclusionary and restrictive immigration policies. Not only is this policy stance a result of the country's myth of ethnic homogeneity, amnesia about its immigrant past, and a close-minded immigration policymaking regime. It is also a product of policy learning. Japanese immigration policymakers have carefully studied the gaps and failures of U.S. and European immigrant policy, including "guest workers" who do not go home, amnesty programs that have increased illegal immigration, refugee/asylum systems that are easily abused and overburdened, and the racial conflicts and backlashes that socioeconomically marginalized, permanent immigrant populations have supposedly created. As a result, Japan's policymakers have decided that the best way to avoid such negative outcomes is simply to *not* become a country of immigration.

However, the more exclusionary a country's immigration policies, the greater the gaps between policy and outcomes and the more severe the negative human rights consequences. Because of unfavorable long-term demographic trends, structural demand for immigrant workers, entrenched migrant labor recruitment networks, and a long-awaited economic recovery, it is quite apparent that immigration to Japan will increase dramatically in the future regardless of the restrictive nature of the country's immigration policy, subjecting more people to exploitation and abuse. Closed-door immigration policies that produce human rights abuses are basically equivalent to condoning such abuses. Worse, there are signs that Japan's immigration policies are being adopted by other East Asian countries, which in the past looked to Japan as a distinctive Asian model of industrialization and economic success. Despite the huge policy gaps in Japan's immigration system, Korea has already copied a number of Japanese policies, partly because they make foreign workers easier to exploit as a flexible and inexpensive workforce (see the following chapter on South Korea).

The most effective way to avoid such policy gaps and their negative consequences is not to increase enforcement of current immigration laws but to liberalize them. The Japanese government must begin to openly admit unskilled immigrants under new visa categories that will guarantee them basic workers rights and protections. As part of an ongoing review of immigration policy, for example, the Ministry of Justice is considering a proposal for a visa category for elderly care-givers and nurses in response to the rapid aging of Japan's populace and a projected need for close to a million nursing-care workers by 2005 (*Daily Yomiuri*, April 26, 2000; Kondo 2002: 431).

But change will not come easily in Japan's bureaucracy-dominated policymaking regime, in which power over immigration is concentrated in the conservative Ministry of Justice. One cannot expect more open immigration policies from a ministry responsible for criminal prosecution and enforcement, federal litigation, legal registration and protection, and immigration and naturalization control. Fortunately, the Japanese bureaucracy is being restructured and downsized to reduce its disproportionate power and make the country's political system more responsive to the democratic process. Unfortunately, the Ministry of Justice has not been a direct target of the current reforms.

Immigrant Settlement, Social Integration, and Human Rights

Because the government officially continues its closed-door stance on immigration, it is creating another serious gap—between a policy that regards foreign workers as strictly temporary and a reality in which immigrants are beginning to settle for the long term, if not permanently, in

Japanese society (see Okuda 2000; Sellek 2001: 104–106; Tajima 2000: 361). Immigrant settlement has become prevalent among the nikkeijin, many of whom have brought their families to Japan and have been living in the country for many years (Tsuda 1999a).[10] Even among other foreign workers, the average stay in Japan already exceeded five years by 1996, and over half of the immigrants from the Philippines, China, and Thailand stated that they wished to settle in Japan (1996 survey, cited in Komai 2001: 66–67). Even among visa overstayers, nearly half have been in Japan for at least three years (Komai 2001: 70–71). Highly visible immigrant communities have sprouted in parts of Tokyo as well as in outlying Japanese industrial cities and towns in Gunma and Aichi Prefectures, supported by a vast array of ethnic businesses, churches, employment agencies, and ethnic media (see Okuda 2000; Okuda and Tajima 1992, 1993; Tajima 2000: 361; Tsuda 2003).

Again, the gap between policy and outcomes has led to negative consequences. The Japanese government has done almost nothing to provide immigrant settlers with basic social services or to facilitate their social integration, viewing them strictly as labor power to be regulated and not as people with needs and rights. In fact, recent policy changes have focused on further tightening immigration control mechanisms in an effort to increase domestic security in response to concerns over international terrorism (including recent Al Qaeda terrorist threats connected to Japan's decision to send Self-Defense Forces to Iraq) and concerns about Japan's rising crime rate (partly attributed to foreigners). These measures include stepped-up inspections at airports and seaports, increased screening of visa applicants and airline passengers, tightened visa requirements for foreign students, and biometric scanning to prevent illegal entry by foreigners. Given the current political environment, it will be a long time before immigrant social integration and human rights will make it onto the government's policymaking agenda.

Because the national government has been oblivious to the immigrants' social needs, local governments have had to deal with the foreign residents and their dependents who are already living in their neighborhoods and communities. Municipal governments in cities with large immigrant populations have generally been receptive, supporting foreign workers with health insurance, counseling, public housing, informa-

---

10 The Japanese government allows the immigration of family members only for the Latin American nikkeijin, who are permitted to bring their spouses to Japan on the same visas even if they are not of Japanese descent. The right of family reunification has been denied to all other foreign workers.

tive handbooks and pamphlets, ethnic festivals, language classes, assistance with alien registration, and even limited political representation (see Miyajima and Kajita 1996; Pak 2000). In addition, immigrants with families in Japan have been strongly encouraged to enroll their children in Japanese schools, and schools with large numbers of foreign students have created "Japanese classes" with specially trained teachers and personal tutors. Local municipal governments have not provided such services and support only by default. They have done so proactively, because they hold themselves responsible for the welfare of all local residents (including foreigners) and they benefit from immigrants, who support the local economy as workers, consumers, and taxpayers. Local governments also strive to avoid conflicts between Japanese and foreign residents (Pak 2000: 251).

Thus a de facto division of labor has emerged in which the national government is concerned only with *immigration* policy (the regulation of immigration flows and border control) and local governments take care of *immigrant* policy (provision of basic services and rights that facilitate the immigrants' social integration). Although a type of "local citizenship" for immigrants is emerging (Pak 2000), it is an uneven, haphazard, and uncoordinated conferral of rights without firm governmental guarantees. In fact, most Japanese cities have *not* been active in welcoming and assisting their foreign residents (Komai 2001: 120; Machimura 2000: 191), either because the number of immigrants is very small or because the immigrants' employers have little political clout (Machimura 2000: 184–85; cf. Pak 2000: 268–69). Even the more supportive municipal governments are hampered by a lack of resources. In addition, undocumented foreign workers are generally not included in the social incorporation programs of local governments (Pak 2000: 250) and must frequently rely on their own ethnic community networks or the assistance of nongovernmental organizations (NGOs) (Roberts 2000; Shipper 2002b).

Therefore, the national government will have to become engaged in immigrant integration policy. The current patchwork of disparate local immigrant policies needs to be replaced by a coherent, national policy directed by the Japanese government and backed by federal resources.[11] Even if the national government does not create a formal "immigrant

---

[11] Some academics and immigrant NGOs have proposed the creation of an Integration Bureau within the federal government that would formulate a comprehensive immigrant integration policy and coordinate efforts by various ministries to provide social services and rights to immigrants. However, the government is opposed to this idea and is unwilling to reform the immigration policymaking system (Kondo 2002: 433).

integration policy," it must at least provide increased access to social services and basic social rights to immigrants. For instance, in 1996 the Ministry of Health and Welfare finally began compensating hospitals for part of the unpaid medical charges for foreign workers who had no health insurance, thus relieving local governments of this cost. There have also been moves toward a national education policy for immigrant children. In the early 1990s the Ministry of Education began a program to increase the number of Japanese-language teachers for foreign students, set aside hours for special Japanese language classes, and issued a language textbook and teaching guide.

Beyond such tokens gestures, it is unlikely that the Japanese government will confer even limited sociopolitical rights on immigrant foreigners any time soon. A bill recently submitted to the Diet to grant voting rights in local elections to permanent residents (most of whom are Korean Japanese born and raised in Japan but still not granted Japanese citizenship) has been indefinitely shelved because of strong opposition from members of the dominant Liberal Democratic Party (LDP). The bill was introduced and backed by the Komeito Party (one of three parties of the ruling coalition) which is popular with Korean Japanese; if passed, the bill would have given the party a half-million new voters in local elections. However, hard-liners from the LDP (which would be politically weakened in certain districts if these new voters were added to the rolls) argued that the legislation will harm Japan's national interest and might be unconstitutional. The Liberal Democrats suggest that Korean Japanese should naturalize if they want voting rights.[12]

In the face of such governmental resistance, it is clear that immigrants themselves must demand their social and political rights through collective mobilization or through the courts. So far, public protest by immigrants in Japan has been limited, nor have they become active participants in Japanese labor unions. In recent years, however, the Japanese courts seem to have become more active in defending the rights of immigrants, especially visa overstayers. In September and October of 2003, the Tokyo District Court repealed deportation orders against the families of two unauthorized immigrants who had been living in Japan with their families for a long time, and ordered immigration authorities to grant

---

[12] As a compromise, the LDP secretary general floated a proposal that would offer local voting rights only to "special" permanent residents (mainly from Korea and Taiwan) who came to Japan during the country's colonial rule in East Asia. This proposal pleased neither the opponents nor the proponents of the bill (the latter claiming that it would create discriminatory inequality among Japan's permanent residents).

them special residency permits (the government is appealing the decision). In a case that has more significant repercussions, the Japanese Supreme Court ruled in January 2004 that it is illegal for authorities to bar all undocumented immigrants from the national health insurance program.

Perhaps the most notable immigrant rights court case was that of Ana Bortz, a Brazilian journalist who was ejected from a jewelry store in Hamamatsu by the storeowner, who had banned all foreign customers because of his concern over rising foreigner crime. Bortz took the storeowner to court for racial discrimination, claiming a violation of the United Nation's International Convention on the Elimination of All Forms of Racial Discrimination, which Japan had ratified in 1995. The judge ruled in her favor and awarded US$12,500 in damages, stating that the international convention was effective as domestic law on racial discrimination against foreigners in the absence of any specific and unequivocal law in Japan (including in the Constitution). Although this case seems to have had limited social impact among Japanese residents in Hamamatsu (Yamanaka 2003b), it could well set a precedent for other foreign residents to fight for civil rights, whether or not they appeal to international human rights conventions (cf. Gurowitz 1999). Japan's minority groups (the Korean Japanese immigrant minority and also the Burakumin and Ainu) have been successful in the past in getting a number of discriminatory laws revised or overturned through the courts.

Refugee Policy

On the subject of human rights, Japan will also have to loosen its highly restrictive policy on refugee admissions. Although it ratified (under international pressure) the United Nations Convention and Protocol Relating to the Status of Refugees in 1981, Japan has no real refugee program, with the exception of the 10,500 Indo-Chinese refugees it admitted from 1979 to 1999 on temporary visas (only 3,400 have remained in the country). In 2000, there were only 3,800 refugees and asylum seekers living in Japan. In addition, Japan accepts very few applications for asylum. From 1989 to 2000, it accepted a mere 68 of 1,365 applications for refugee recognition (a 5 percent acceptance rate). In contrast, the United States approved 89,499 of 395,558 adjudicated asylum cases from 1989 to 1999 (22.6 percent).[13] Even Britain, which has highly restrictive immigration

---

[13] During this same period, the United States approved 1,019,474 of 1,511,055 applications for refugee status (67 percent).

and refugee laws, granted asylum to 51,400 of 552,705 applicants between 1991 and 2000 (9 percent).

In Japan, even those whose asylum applications are accepted are not formally conferred refugee status but are given Long-Term Settler visas that must be renewed periodically and that leave their holders subject to deportation. Only persons who have resided in Japan for a lengthy period (usually ten years) are eligible for permanent residence. Germany's contemporary "refugee horror story" is all the justification most Japanese immigration policymakers need for avoiding a more liberal refugee and asylum policy. However, Japan is coming under increasing criticism from NGOs and international human rights organizations (including the United Nations High Commissioner for Refugees) for its restrictive refugee and asylum policies and for its inhumane detention of unsuccessful asylum seekers who are awaiting deportation.

In a high-profile incident in May 2002, Chinese police forcibly removed five North Korean asylum seekers from the Japanese consulate in Shenyang, China. The Chinese government claimed that Japanese embassy officials had asked them to remove the asylum seekers, but the Japanese government insisted that no such request was made and that the Chinese police had infringed on Japan's territorial sovereignty over its overseas consulates. Despite Japan's hard-line stance toward all asylum seekers, the government was suddenly insisting on a "humanitarian solution" for the North Korean asylees (who were eventually given safe passage to South Korea). This incident has forced the Japanese government to review its ambiguous and restrictive policies toward refugees and asylum seekers. As a result, the Ministry of Justice submitted a bill to revise the country's refugee policy, which is currently being deliberated by the Diet and is believed likely to pass. Although it abolishes the sixty-day deadline for applicants to file for refugee status and grants temporary residential status for asylum-seekers without visas or with expired visas, it imposes new conditions that subject them to deportation even if they are recognized as refugees.

THE PUBLIC OPINION CONSTRAINT: CAN JAPAN BECOME A MULTIETHNIC SOCIETY?

Undoubtedly, the type of immigration and immigrant policies Japan adopts in the future will have much to do with the type of immigration country Japan will become. Will the country be able to make a smooth transition to a tolerant, multiethnic immigrant society?

Even in the late 1980s, when immigration was a highly contentious issue, the Japanese public was surprisingly tolerant toward foreign workers. For example, in a nationwide survey conducted in 1990, a very high proportion of respondents (71.4 percent) declared themselves in favor of allowing the admission of unskilled foreign laborers—although a majority (56.5 percent) felt that unskilled foreign workers should be accepted only under certain conditions, most notably by placing limits on their length of stay in Japan (Prime Minister's Office 1991). In fact, only 14.1 percent of the poll respondents endorsed the government's stance of denying entry to all unskilled foreign workers. Polling data, however, reveal a marked generational divide in public opinion, with young people considerably more tolerant than older Japanese.[14]

Looking beneath the surface of general public opinion, however, one finds considerable ambivalence among the Japanese public. As a general proposition, immigration is fine so long as it meets certain conditions (such as temporariness). When the public is asked whether they would be willing to live next door to foreign workers, their responses are much more cautious. In fact, a survey conducted by the Tokyo city government found that 64 percent of Tokyo residents disliked having foreigners in their neighborhoods, and only 28 percent welcomed outsiders (*Wall Street Journal* 1994). A survey by the Institute of Public Policy found that 56.6 percent of respondents felt anxiety toward foreign workers and that this anxiety increased in proportion to their residential proximity to foreigners (cited in Komai 2001: 132).

It seems that those Japanese who complain about foreign workers in their midst do so not primarily on ethnic or racial grounds but because of "practical" difficulties. For example, local residents frequently complain that foreigners do not sort their garbage correctly, are too noisy in their apartments, and do not obey Japanese community rules. In contrast to Japanese immigration policymakers, who are concerned about maintaining Japan's perceived ethnic homogeneity, only 6.7 percent of the respondents in a national survey mentioned "the threat to Japan's unique culture" as a reason for opposing the employment of unskilled foreign laborers (Prime Minister's Office 1991). Far more respondents were concerned about possible crime and rising unemployment among foreign workers, as well as conflicts in local communities. However, it should be

---

[14] For instance, a 1989 Asahi Shimbun poll found that 70 percent of those in their 20s and 30s favored the admission of unskilled foreign workers under certain conditions, compared to only 56 percent of the general public.

noted that such negative consequences are frequently associated with the disruption of ethnic and cultural homogeneity in Japan.

Regardless of the reasons, public opinion toward unskilled foreign workers (especially overstayers) has become more intolerant recently, possibly indicating future convergence with the ambivalent public attitudes toward immigrants prevalent in the United States and Europe. According to the Prime Minister's Office's polling data from 2000, the proportion of the Japanese public willing to accept unskilled foreign workers has remained quite high (67.7 percent), but those who are against their admission has risen substantially, from 14.1 percent in 1990 to 21.2 percent in 2000. Such trends are not surprising given that anti-immigrant hostility generally rises during economic recessions. Nevertheless, this hardening of public attitudes is notable because the "foreign worker problem" has ceased to be a contentious social issue (as the immigrant population has stabilized) and has almost disappeared from public and media discourse. In addition, the recession has caused foreign workers to disperse to various parts of the country in search of jobs, giving Japanese residents in areas with high immigrant concentrations the illusion that the foreign population has declined during the recession.

The Japanese media has continued to publish prominent articles about alleged increases in foreigner crime even though crime and arrest rates among migrant foreigners (which are inflated for numerous reasons) have actually been lower than those of the Japanese population as a whole (Herbert 1992: 111–14; Kohei 1994; cf. Friman 2001: 300–303). This type of exaggerated and biased reporting has fueled public fears that immigration (especially illegal immigration) is leading to a deterioration in public safety (cf. Herbert 1992: 111–12, 115).[15] In fact, 49.2 percent of the Japanese public already feel that illegal immigrants have had a bad impact on Japanese society, and close to 50 percent want the government to deport illegal immigrants (up significantly from 32.1 percent and 33.6 percent, respectively, ten years ago) (Prime Minister's Office 2000).

In response to such public concern over rising foreigner crime, the Japanese government has decided to halve the number of illegal immigrants by mobilizing immigration officers and police as part of a plan (backed by the prime minister and the Cabinet) to reduce the rising crime rate and keep Japan one of the safest countries in the world. This effort

---

[15] Politicians have also made inflammatory remarks in this regard. For example, Tokyo's unapologetically nationalist governor, Shintaro Ishihara, publicly warned that foreigners have often committed atrocious crimes and could be expected to riot in the event of a severe earthquake (*New York Times*, April 11, 2000).

has been accompanied by an increase in funding and in the number of immigration officers; it will be focused on Tokyo, where an estimated half of Japan's visa overstayers reside. Never before has there been such a concerted, nationwide effort to crack down on illegal immigrants. This is also the first time the police have been mobilized to cooperate with immigration authorities in apprehending unauthorized foreigners.

Looking toward the future, it is troubling that many Japanese living in areas with high immigrant concentrations fear nativist backlashes, public protests, and even violence against foreigners (à la Germany and other European countries) if the immigrant population expands considerably.[16] Many of them feel that the ethnically homogeneous and restrictive nature of Japanese society makes it difficult to incorporate large numbers of foreigners. Such pessimistic attitudes about Japan's ability to tolerate foreigners are also reflected in public opinion surveys. In a 1991 survey by *Asahi Shimbun*, fully half of the respondents agreed with the statement that "Japan is a country with strong racial discrimination."[17]

The likelihood of a backlash depends heavily on the rate at which foreigners are brought into the country and how successfully they are incorporated into Japanese society. For a country with exclusionary ethnic tendencies, a sudden and massive influx of alien, unassimilable foreigners is likely to produce a serious backlash. Indeed, there have already been some ominous signs. Serious public incidents, bordering on violence, have occurred between local Japanese residents and immigrants (Komai 2001: 133; Tsuzuki 2000). In the early 1990s, when Japan was immersed in a contentious public debate over immigration, Japanese right-wing groups demonstrated against immigrants and distributed neo-Nazi flyers urging Japan to expel immigrant foreigners (*Asahi Shimbun*, April 7, 1993; *Japan Times*, October 16, 1989). This is especially worrisome because the immigrant population in Japan is still miniscule compared to those of the United States and Europe. However, Japan has always had vocal and prominent right-wing extremist groups that sometimes resort to violence to promote their ends. As in the case of Germany, even if the general public remains restrained, violent reactions from a small minority of extremists could engender a general social crisis.

---

[16] There has been violence directed against immigrants in Japan's past. In an extreme case, during the Kanto earthquake of 1923 thousands of Korean residents were attacked and killed based on false rumors that they were rioting and killing Japanese.

[17] In a more recent survey of Tokyo residents, 57 percent said that the Japanese discriminate against foreigners (*Wall Street Journal* 1994).

However, one potentially crucial difference between public attitudes toward immigrants in Japan and Germany is that the Japanese are more likely to see foreign workers as playing a positive economic role. This perception is reflected in public opinion surveys in which respondents who favor the acceptance of foreign workers believe that they are helping to alleviate the country's labor shortage and are a source of cheap labor. There has been little fear of direct job competition with foreigners; a majority of survey respondents express the belief that foreign workers are primarily employed in jobs shunned by native-born Japanese (see, for example, Prime Minister's Office 1991). Most Japanese (70.3 percent) feel that if labor shortages return in the future,[18] Japan will have little choice but to accept foreign workers (Prime Minister's Office 2000). This contrasts with the past experiences of countries like the United States and Germany, when immigration based on family reunification and refugee/asylum admissions caused the public to feel that too many foreigners were feeding off the economy and the welfare system by taking advantage of humanitarian immigration policies.

As Japan comes to terms with its current status as a country of immigration and engages in public and policy debates about the proper course of action, it is perhaps useful to once again consider the country's history of immigration. Despite the current Japanese assumption (among government officials, citizens, and even some academics) that Japan has never been a country of immigration (cf. Douglass and Roberts 2000: 10–11), migration has always been essential for the formation of the Japanese nation-state. Of course, the Japanese themselves originated on the Asian continent in prehistoric times and migrated to Japan in successive waves. In early Japanese history a significant number of Koreans and Chinese migrated to Japan and brought Chinese learning and knowledge, which were essential to the development of Japanese culture. During the Meiji period (1868–1912) and afterward, many Westerners (and Chinese) came to live in Japan as merchants or to provide expertise for Japanese modernization. As noted earlier, millions of Koreans and some Chinese migrated to Japan in the pre–World War II period to man its factories, thus providing crucial assistance to Japan's colonization and war effort. Indeed, it is only in the postwar period that the notion developed of Japan as a country that has prospered because of its unique racial homogeneity (see, for example, Komai 2001: 14; Lie 2001; Oguma 1995), indicating that

---

[18] Sixty-eight percent of the public anticipates labor shortages in the future.

it is a rather recent and arbitrary ideological construct.[19] As was the case numerous times in the past, the ethnic diversity currently being introduced to Japan by the migration of unskilled foreign workers will again prove crucial for the continued prosperity of the country.

Of course, it is unlikely that the Japanese government will suddenly discard its ideology of ethnic homogeneity and instead promote an image of Japan as benefiting from its past ethnic diversity. However, whether under the guise of "internationalization" or in the name of continued economic prosperity, the government will have to prepare the public for the future as Japan again becomes a major country of immigration. One hopes that its future attempts to control public opinion will be more successful than its current attempts to control immigration.

References

Bartram, David. 2000. "Japan and Labor Migration: Theoretical and Methodological Implications of Negative Cases," *International Migration Review* 34, no. 1: 5–32.

Cornelius, Wayne A., and Yasuo Kuwahara. 1998. *The Role of Immigrant Labor in the U.S. and Japanese Economies: A Comparative Study of San Diego and Hamamatsu, Japan.* La Jolla: Center for U.S.-Mexican Studies, University of California, San Diego.

Douglass, Mike, and Glenda S. Roberts. 2000. "Japan in a Global Age of Migration." In *Japan and Global Migration: Foreign Workers and the Advent of a Multicultural Society*, edited by Mike Douglass and Glenda S. Roberts. London: Routledge.

Friman, H. Richard. 2001. "Immigrants, Smuggling, and Threats to Social Order in Japan." In *Global Human Smuggling: Comparative Perspectives*, edited by David Kyle and Rey Koslowski. Baltimore, Md.: Johns Hopkins University Press.

---

[19] In the prewar period, when Japan was colonizing Asia and attempting to build the "East Asia Co-Prosperity Sphere," the dominant ideological discourse claimed that the Japanese shared a common racial and cultural heritage with Koreans and Chinese (especially vis-à-vis the West). Yet, as is the case with all ideologies that justify colonialism, it was a contradictory discourse in which the Japanese nation (conflated with race) was also seen as superior to other Asian countries, which obligated Japan to lead subordinate and inferior Asian peoples and raise them to a level commensurate with their "natural" abilities (Weiner 1994: 22–32, 1997: 13). During the Meiji period, before Japanese colonization, however, the government promoted an ideology of the Japanese nation as one large family (with the emperor as head) in order to build and consolidate the nation-state. Thus the myth of racial homogeneity may have had its roots in this period (see Oguma 1995; cf. Gluck 1985).

Fuchigami,, Eiji. 1995. *Nikkejin Shomei* (Proof of Nikkejin Status). Tokyo: Shinhyoron.

Fuess, Scott M. 2003. "Immigration Policy and Highly Skilled Workers: The Case of Japan," *Contemporary Economic Policy* 21, no. 2: 243–57.

Gluck, Carol. 1985. *Japan's Modern Myths: Ideology in the Late Meiji Period.* Princeton, N.J.: Princeton University Press.

Gurowitz, Amy. 1999. "Mobilizing International Norms: Domestic Actors, Immigrants, and the Japanese State," *World Politics* 51, no. 3: 413–45.

Herbert, Wolfgang. 1992. "Conjuring Up a Crime Wave: The 'Rapid Growth in the Crime Rate among Foreign Migrant Workers in Japan' Critically Examined," *Japan Forum* 4, no. 1: 109–19.

Ishihara, Takumi. 1992. *Gaikokujin Koyo no Honne to Tatemae: Rodoryoku Sakoku no Ura de Nani ga Okite Iru Ka* (Real and Professed Intentions in the Employment of Foreigners: What's Really Going on Behind-the-Scenes in This Closed-Door Country?). Tokyo: Shodensha.

Kajita, Takamichi. 1994. *Gaikokujin Rodosha to Nihon* (Foreign Laborers and Japan). Tokyo: NHK Books.

Kohei, Hashomoto. 1994. "Zainichi Imin Rodosha no Hanzai to Sono Suii" (Trends in Crime by Immigrant Workers in Japan). Kenkyu Ripoto (Research Report) 8. Tokyo: PHP Research Institute.

Komai, Hiroshi. 1992. "Are Foreign Trainees in Japan Disguised Cheap Laborers?" *Migration World* 20: 13–17.

———. 1993. *Gaikokujin Rodosha Teijyu eno Michi* (The Road to Settlement of Foreign Workers). Tokyo: Akashi Shoten.

———. 1995. *Migrant Workers in Japan*, translated by Jens Wilkinson. London: Kegan Paul International.

———. 2001. *Foreign Migrants in Contemporary Japan*, translated by Jens Wilkinson. Melbourne, Australia: Trans Pacific Press.

Kondo, Atsushi. 2002. "The Development of Immigration Policy in Japan," *Asian and Pacific Migration Journal* 11, no. 4: 415–36.

Kuwahara, Yasuo. 1998. "Japan's Dilemma: Can International Migration Be Controlled?" In *Temporary Workers or Future Citizens? Japanese and U.S. Migration Policies*, edited by Myron Weiner and Tadashi Hanami. New York: New York University Press.

Lie, John. 2001. *Multiethnic Japan.* Cambridge, Mass.: Harvard University Press.

Machimura, Takashi. 2000. "Local Settlement Patterns of Foreign Workers in Greater Tokyo: Growing Diversity and Its Consequences." In *Japan and Global Migration: Foreign Workers and the Advent of a Multicultural Society*, edited by Mike Douglass and Glenda S. Roberts. London: Routledge.

Miyajima, Takashi. 1993. *Gaikokujin Rodosha to Nihon Shakai* (Foreign Workers and Japanese Society). Tokyo: Akaishi Shoten.

Miyajima, Takashi, and Takamichi Kajita, eds. 1996. *Gaijkokujin Rodosha kara Shimin e* (From Foreign Worker to Citizen). Tokyo: Yuhikaku.

Mori, Hiromi. 1997. *Immigration Policy and Foreign Workers in Japan*. New York: St. Martin's.

Muller, Thomas. 1993. *Immigrants and the American City*. New York: New York University Press.

OECD (Organisation for Economic Co-operation and Development). 2000. *Trends in International Migration: Annual Report 2000 Edition*. Paris: OECD.

Oguma, Eiji. 1995. *Tanitsu Minzoku Shinwa no Kigen* (The Origin of the Myth of Ethnic Homogeneity). Tokyo: Shinyosha.

Oishi, Nana. 1995. "Training or Employment? Japanese Immigration Policy in Dilemma," *Asian and Pacific Migration Journal*, 4, nos. 2–3: 367–85.

Oka, Takashi. 1994. "Prying Open the Door: Foreign Workers in Japan." Contemporary Issues Paper No. 2. Washington, D.C.: Carnegie Endowment for International Peace.

Okuda, Michihiro, and Junko Tajima, eds. 1992. *Ikebukuro no Ajiakei Gaikokujin: Shakaigakuteki Jittai Hokoku* (Ikebukuro's Asian Foreigners: A Sociological Report). Tokyo: Mekon.

———. 1993. *Shinjuku no Ajiakei Gaikokujin: Shakaigakuteki Jittai Hokoku* (Shinjuku's Asian Foreigners: A Sociological Report). Tokyo: Mekon.

———. 2000. "Asian Newcomers in Shinjuku and Ikebukuro Areas, 1988–1998: Reflections on a Decade of Research," *Asian and Pacific Migration Journal* 9, no. 3: 343–48.

Pak, Katherine Tegtmeyer. 2000. "Foreigners Are Local Citizens Too: Local Governments Respond to International Migration in Japan." In *Japan and Global Migration: Foreign Workers and the Advent of a Multicultural Society*, edited by Mike Douglass and Glenda S. Roberts. London: Routledge.

Prime Minister's Office. 1991. "Public Opinion Survey on Foreign Workers: Summary." Tokyo, March.

———. 2000. *Gaikokujin Rodosha Mondai ni Kansuru Seron Chosa* (Public Opinion Survey about the Foreign Worker Problem). Tokyo.

Reubens, E. 1982. "Low-Level Work in Japan without Foreign Workers," *International Migration Review* 15, no. 4: 749–51.

Roberts, Glenda S. 2000. "NGO Support for Migrant Labor in Japan." In *Japan and Global Migration: Foreign Workers and the Advent of a Multicultural Society*, edited by Mike Douglass and Glenda S. Roberts. London: Routledge.

Sassen, Saskia. 1991. *The Global City: New York, London, Tokyo*. Princeton, N.J.: Princeton University Press.

Sellek, Yoko. 2001. *Migrant Labour in Japan*. New York: Palgrave.

Shipper, Apichai W. 2002a. "The Political Construction of Foreign Workers in Japan," *Critical Asian Studies* 34, no. 1: 41–68.

———. 2002b. *Pragmatism in Activism: Organizing Support for Illegal Foreign Workers in Japan*. Cambridge, Mass.: Program on U.S.-Japan Relations, Harvard University.

Spencer, Steven A. 1992. "Illegal Migrant Laborers in Japan," *International Migration Review* 26, no. 3: 754–86.

Tajima, Junko. 2000. "A Study of Asian Immigrants in Global City Tokyo," *Asian and Pacific Migration Journal* 9, no. 3: 349–64.

Tsuda, Takeyuki. 1999a. "The Permanence of 'Temporary' Migration: The 'Structural Embeddedness' of Japanese-Brazilian Migrant Workers in Japan," *Journal of Asian Studies* 58, no. 3: 687–722.

———. 1999b. "The Motivation to Migrate: The Ethnic and Sociocultural Constitution of the Japanese-Brazilian Return Migration System," *Economic Development and Cultural Change* 48, no. 1: 1–31.

———. 2003. *Strangers in the Ethnic Homeland: Japanese Brazilian Return Migration in Transnational Perspective*. New York: Columbia University Press.

Tsuda, Takeyuki, Zulema Valdez, and Wayne A. Cornelius. 2003. "Human Capital versus Social Capital: Immigrant Wages and Labor Market Incorporation in Japan and the United States." In *Host Societies and the Reception of Immigrants*, edited by Jeffrey Reitz. La Jolla: Center for Comparative Immigration Studies, University of California, San Diego.

Tsuzuki, Kurumi. 2000. "*Nikkei* Brazilians and Local Residents: A Study of the H Housing Complex in Toyota City," *Asian and Pacific Migration Journal* 9, no. 3: 327–42.

United Nations. 2000. *Replacement Migration: Is It a Solution to Declining and Ageing Populations?* New York: Population Division, Dept. of Economic and Social Affairs, United Nations Secretariat.

Wall Street Journal. 1994. "World Wire," June 6.

Watanabe, Susumu. 1994. "The Lewisian Turning Point and International Migration: The Case of Japan," *Asian and Pacific Migration Journal* 3, no. 1: 119–47.

———. 1998. "The Economic Crisis and Migrant Workers in Japan," *Asian and Pacific Migration Journal* 7, nos. 2–3: 235–54.

Weiner, Michael. 1994. *Race and Migration in Imperial Japan*. New York: Routledge.

———. 1997. "The Invention of Identity: 'Self' and 'Other' in Pre-War Japan." In *Japan's Minorities: The Illusion of Homogeneity*, edited by Michael Weiner. New York: Routledge.

Yamanaka, Keiko. 2003a. "Feminization of Japanese-Brazilian Labor Migration to Japan." In *Searching for Home Abroad: Japanese-Brazilians and the Transnational Moment*, edited by Jeffrey Lesser. Durham, N.C.: Duke University Press.

———. 2003b. "A Breakthrough for Ethnic Minority Rights in Japan: Ana Bortz's Courageous Challenge." In *Gender and Migration: Crossing Borders and Shifting Boundaries*, edited by Mirjana Morokvasic-Muller, Umut Erel, and Kyoko Shinozaki. International Women's University Series, vol. 1. Opladen, Germany: Verlag Leske+Budrich.

Commentary

Keiko Yamanaka

Tsuda and Cornelius reveal the glaring inadequacy of Japan's immigration policy and public services for receiving increasing numbers of immigrant residents and their families. Official policy that permits only the immigration of skilled labor grossly ignores the economic and social realities of a growing immigrant population throughout the country. As a result, Japan lacks a social integration policy to address the issues of equality, human rights, and cultural tolerance, a lack that has caused confusion and generated inconsistent responses from local officials, employers, and citizens in the treatment of foreign residents. The authors describe the various causes of the gap that has opened between immigration policy and economic reality since the late 1980s, when the first wave of migrants arrived in Japan, but they only briefly describe the historical origins and political processes that produced Japan's contemporary immigration policies and problems.

Japan has dealt with non-Japanese residents on its territory since 1859. During its colonization of Asia in the early twentieth century, Japan attempted to control the large numbers of diverse ethnic minorities within its imperial territories through assimilation. During the American occupation after World War II, Japan's Ministry of Justice passed a series of restrictive decrees and laws about immigration, nationality, and residence that were intended to control the 600,000 former colonial citizens from Korea who remained in the country after the war. Many governmental officials in immigration bureaus had been agents of the former Special Police Forces responsible for surveillance of Korean immigrants and dissidents, and they continued to regard them as threats to public security after the war. Nonetheless, from 1952 to 1985, when Japan experienced little immigration, the government ratified a number of international human rights conventions that would subsequently lead to changes in domestic laws about the treatment of immigrants and ethnic minorities.

History demonstrates that Japanese immigration policy has been influenced more by external forces than by internal forces. Since the late 1980s, the government has retained obsolete policies that are out of sync with the country's rapidly changing labor market. As Tsuda and Cornelius document, many side-door and backdoor mechanisms have developed through which more than half a million immigrants have entered Japan. This has led to the development of robust grassroots activism by Japanese citizens to defend the rights of foreign workers. This may result in a type of "transnationalism from below," where citizens of various nationalities, ethnicities, and classes exercise power by transcending national boundaries in order to criticize and challenge governmental authoritarianism and to deal with the complexities of Japan's new multiculturalism.

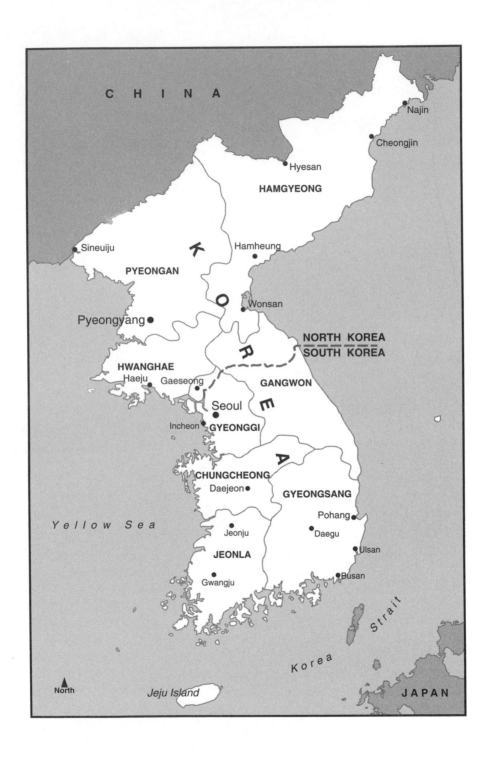

12

South Korea: Importing Undocumented Workers

Dong-Hoon Seol and John D. Skrentny

Is there a gap between immigration policy and outcomes in South Korea?
Is South Korea failing to control immigration? In support of both propositions is the fact that South Korea (henceforth Korea) may be the only
industrialized nation in which undocumented workers outnumber foreign workers who are in the country legally. Almost 80 percent of immigrants are illegal. This certainly suggests a failure to control immigration,
and it is hard to imagine a policy that aims for such an outcome. Korea
denies it is a country of immigration yet allows entry to hundreds of
thousands of foreign workers. It would appear that the "gap hypothesis"
at the heart of this volume is amply confirmed by the Korean case.

The situation is not, however, so simple. One cannot assume that
Korea's policy goal is to prevent undocumented workers. A full understanding of Korea's immigration situation requires envisioning the Korean state not a monolithic, unitary actor but as a fragmented state over-
seeing a patchwork of immigration programs and laws that sometimes
work at cross-purposes. The large numbers of illegal workers in Korea
reflect more a failure of will than a failure of policy. The strongest state
actors want to ensure an inexpensive, compliant workforce for jobs that

South Koreans no longer want to do and to provide this workforce at minimal cost to the state and minimal disruption to society. In sum, Korea wants cheap labor but no foreign settlement and no multicultural society. Judged in terms of this goal, Korean policy is a success, there is no gap, and immigration is controlled to the desired degree.

Korea has a structurally embedded demand for foreign labor, which is compounded by an aging population. Its policies can best be understood as the result of a fragmented state in which each institution pursues its own interests (Skrentny 2002), along with the client politics that characterize some parts of this fragmented state (Freeman 1995). Korean immigration policies are mostly the result of the Justice Ministry's solicitude toward small businesses, which are the primary employers of migrant workers, as well as the fact that opponents to this immigrant influx (namely, the Labor Ministry and the administration of Kim Dae-Jung) have not been able to mobilize the political strength to oppose the powerful business/Justice Ministry combination. Undergirding the policy discussion is Korean political culture, including the axiom that Korea must not become a multicultural society and therefore must avoid hosting a large immigrant settler population. Indeed, the Korean word for immigrant is best translated as "sojourner," a usage that emphasizes the short-term nature of all foreign visitors. Because immigrant settlement has been avoided, the more pressing migration issue in Korea is the widespread human rights violations suffered by both documented and undocumented migrant workers.

FROM EMIGRATION TO IMMIGRATION

Korea denies that it is a country of immigration, and its population is about 99 percent ethnic Korean. In fact, Korea has a long tradition of exporting workers. During the late-nineteenth-century decline of the Chosun dynasty and Japan's colonization of Korea early in the twentieth century, some 2.5 million Koreans fled to China and central Asia (C.W. Lee 2001). Those who fled to China are called *joseonjok*, and those who went to Russia or central Asia are the *goryeoin*. Another 400,000 Koreans emigrated to Japan between 1910 and 1938, after Japan's confiscation of businesses and farms destroyed their livelihoods. Japan forced about a million Koreans into labor in Japan during World War II, and approximately half, with nothing left in Korea, remained in Japan after the war, despite encountering severe discrimination (Cornelius 1994; Fukuoka 1996).

Other emigrations followed. Korea sent 10,226 nurses and 6,546 miners to West Germany between 1960 and 1976, and 19,587 service and construction workers to Vietnam between 1966 and 1973, in conjunction with U.S. armed forces' activities there. Middle Eastern oil-producing states received 1,112,611 South Korean construction workers from 1974 to 1995. Out-migration to countries such as Saudi Arabia, Iran, Iraq, Kuwait, and Bahrain peaked in 1982, but levels fell thereafter with the drop in oil prices and the slowdown in construction in the Middle East. The numbers fell further in 1990 because of the Gulf War, and few Koreans remain in the Middle East today (Seol 1999: 92; Seok 1986).

Approximately 2 million Koreans, most highly educated and skilled, have gone to the United States and another 140,000 to Canada since 1965 (Choson Ilbo Sa 2001: 101). However, these numbers have also declined markedly in recent years; over 30,000 Koreans emigrated in 1978 and 1979, but just over 12,000 emigrated in 1999, 2000, and 2001, about half to the United States and half to Canada.[1]

Korea transitioned to a country of labor importation around 1987, when there were nearly 6,500 migrant workers in Korea, all undocumented. Their numbers increased rapidly, such that there were 45,000 undocumented workers in Korea in 1991 (table 12.1; Seol 2000a). By 1991, out-migration from Korea was mostly limited to a small group of high-skilled and professional workers and their family members (J. Lee 2002; Shin and Chang 1988).

Foreign labor soon became a political issue in Korea, although it was still far from mainstream politics. The issue first hit the public consciousness in January 1995 when thirteen Nepalese workers held a sit-in at Myeongdong Cathedral in Seoul, a traditional site of labor and democracy movement demonstrations. The demonstrators, who were in Korea legally as "trainees," had three simple demands: "do not hit us, pay us our wages, return our passports; we are not animals" (Park, Lee, and Seol 1995).

Migrant workers still constitute a small but growing presence in Korea. In late 2001 there were 329,555 foreign workers in Korea, the majority

---

[1] Cornelius and Tsuda (this volume) report that there are 60,000 Korean visa overstayers in Japan, including women "entertainers" and (male) construction workers and longshoremen. Very few are in the manufacturing sector. However, the Korean government does not consider Japan to be a destination for Korean emigrants; rather, these individuals are viewed as short-term visitors to Japan, and they do not appear in Korean emigration statistics.

Table 12.1. Numbers of Migrant Workers in Korea, 1987–2001[a]

| | | Registered Migrant Workers | | | |
	Total	Professionals	Post-Training Workers[b]	Industrial Trainees	Undocumented
1987	6,409	2,192	0	0	4,217
1988	7,410	2,403	0	0	5,007
1989	14,610	2,474	0	0	12,136
1990	21,235	2,833	0	0	18,402
1991	45,449	2,973	0	599	41,877
1992	73,868	3,395	0	4,945	65,528
1993	66,919	3,767	0	8,644	54,508
1994	81,824	5,265	0	28,328	48,231
1995	128,906	8,228	0	38,812	81,866
1996	210,494	13,420	0	68,020	129,054
1997	245,399	15,900	0	81,451	148,048
1998	157,689	11,143	0	47,009	99,537
1999	217,384	12,592	0	69,454	135,338
2000	285,506	17,000	2,063	77,448	188,995
2001	329,555	19,549	8,065	46,735	255,206

Source: Seol 2000b: 190; calculated from the Statistical Yearbook of Departures and Arrivals Control, released by the Justice Ministry.

a Number of migrants calculated as of December 31 of each year except 1992, when the tally was made on July 31.

b The Work-After-Training Program, introduced in April 1998, allows foreign trainees who pass certain skill tests after two years of training to spend the next year as "workers." In January 2002, the program changed to one year of training followed by two of work.

Table 12.2. Original Visa Status of Illegal Sojourners in Korea[a]

Country of Origin	Total	Short-Term Visitors (C-3)	Short-Term Business (C-2)	Industrial Trainees (D-3)	Visa Waiver (B-1)	Smuggled	Other Visa Categories
China	151,313	61,134	47,055	24,092		10,293	8,739
(Korean Chinese)	(91,736)	(36,098)	(24,930)	(14,788)		(9,812)	(6,108)
Bangladesh	17,087	226	240	5,427	10,279	1	914
Philippines	16,078	6,902	735	5,412	9	1	3,019
Mongolia	13,952	10,301	1,295	275	510	2	1,569
Vietnam	10,608	1,270	641	7,563	33	19	1,082
Other (91 countries)	46,940	11,688	5,641	9,688	14,377	183	5,386
Total	255,978	91,521	55,607	52,457	25,208	10,476	20,709
	(100%)	(36%)	(22%)	(20%)	(10%)	(4%)	(8%)

Source: Office for Government Policy Coordination 2002.

[a] Illegal sojourners' self-reporting data, March 25–May 25, 2002.

illegal (table 12.1). There were also 95,473 legal aliens in Korea who were not classified as workers or trainees,[2] for a total foreign population in 2001 of 420,041, or about 0.9 percent of Korea's total population. Foreign workers made up 1.5 percent of the employed population (including self-employed) and 2.5 percent of all workers.

The vast majority of legal migrant workers in Korea enter through a visa category for industrial trainees which, despite its name, is for un-skilled workers. About 50,000 of Korea's undocumented workers are former trainees who either fled their sponsoring workplace or overstayed their visa.

Korea offers various visas for skilled workers, based on occupational type, such as education professionals or entertainers. The largest cate-gory is the E-2 visa, which is reserved for teachers of foreign languages, mostly English. There were 6,414 E-2 visa holders in Korea in 2000, a relatively large number but one that is not likely to increase substantially in the future and hence will have little impact on Korean society. The "entertainers" category includes primarily women involved in sex work; there were 3,916 of these E-6 visa holders in Korea in 2000, 82.3 percent of whom were women. In 2000 Korea's Ministry of Commerce, Industry, and Energy launched a special "gold card system" aimed at establishing a new, easy-access E-7 visa for software programmers, mostly from In-dia.

There are 147,128 overstayers in Korea who arrived on various kinds of short-term visas. They overstay to work in manufacturing, construc-tion, restaurants, or as domestics.[3] An unknown number also enter ille-gally. Smugglers have brought some Chinese, mostly joseonjok, in through Korea's 2,400 kilometers of coastline. A government survey of undocumented workers in early 2002 found that nearly 10,500 had been smuggled into Korea (table 12.2), and authorities have captured 5,023 smuggled would-be immigrants over the past seven years.

Korea accepts almost no refugees. About ten refugees from North Korea were admitted annually in the mid-1990s. That number has since

---

[2] The legal nonworkers include visa holders in the E, F, G, and H categories in the Korean system—culture/art visitors, students, religious workers, investors, intra-company transferees, and dependents of skilled workers.

[3] A government survey of illegal sojourners in May 2002 found that 34.8 percent were working in manufacturing, 21.8 percent in construction, 13.7 percent in restaurants, 3.7 percent in household services, 3.4 percent in personal services, and 22.6 percent in other industries (Office for Government Policy Coordination 2002).

risen—to 148 in 1999, 312 in 2000, and 583 in 2001.[4] In its entire history, Korea has received only one refugee from a country other than North Korea.

Immigration to Korea comes mostly from other Asian nations. The largest sending state by far is China. Slightly more than half of Chinese immigrants to Korea are joseonjok. Other sending countries include the Philippines, Vietnam, Bangladesh, and Indonesia (tables 12.3 and 12.4).

Not surprisingly, almost a third of immigrant workers reside in Seoul, Korea's economic and demographic center. Other areas with large populations of migrant workers are Incheon, a port on Korea's west coast; Busan, Korea's second largest city; and Daegu, an industrial city in the interior. Each of these cities accounts for about 5 percent of the total immigrant population, with the remainder widely dispersed throughout the country.

Migrant workers in Korea are mostly found in small and medium-sized firms. Others work in the sex industry. An unknown number, all tourist visa overstayers, work as domestics. In contrast with the situation in Western nations, migrant workers in Korea do not have a significant presence in agriculture, and they are only beginning to work in restaurants and other services.

WHY IMMIGRATION TO KOREA?

The reasons why Korea transitioned from a country of emigration to one of immigration largely parallel those given for other countries discussed in this volume. The specific timing of Korea's emergence as a receiving country can be explained in part by a relaxation of requirements for tourist visas prior to the Asian Games in 1986 and the Olympics in 1988 (Seol 2000b). But the key driver is a labor shortage in certain industries and occupations. Korea has experienced stunningly rapid economic development (Amsden 1989; Haggard 1990; Vogel 1993; Lie 1998). According to World Bank statistics, in 1960 Korea's gross national product (GNP) of US$1.9 billion clearly identified it as a Third World country. By 1980, GNP reached $61 billion, and by 2000 it was $455 billion. Per capita GNP

---

[4] There is obviously more room for growth. Almost all North Korean refugees come to South Korea via China. The Korean government announced that about 30,000 refugees from North Korea were residing outside South Korea (mostly in China) in 1999. NGOs estimate the number to be between 140,000 and 200,000 (C.W. Lee 2001: 23).

Table 12.3. Numbers of Registered Legal Aliens in Korea, by Nationality, 1985–2001

	Total	Taiwan	United States	Japan	Philip-pines	China (joseonjok)	Vietnam	Indonesia	Bangla-desh	Pakistan	Other
1985	40,920	25,008	7,750	2,472	251	2 (NA)	0	19	11	27	5,380
1986	41,603	24,822	8,369	3,018	183	1 (NA)	0	21	17	20	5,152
1987	42,810	24,512	9,440	3,531	276	0 (NA)	0	24	13	27	4,987
1988	45,102	24,088	11,147	4,164	303	4 (NA)	0	31	15	30	5,320
1989	47,205	23,828	12,738	4,926	338	42 (NA)	0	51	7	40	5,235
1990	49,506	23,582	14,019	5,323	578	147 (NA)	0	78	11	27	5,741
1991	51,021	23,464	14,922	5,725	630	192 (125)	0	128	11	57	5,892
1992	55,832	23,479	16,806	6,031	1,051	935 (419)	0	511	77	57	6,885
1993	66,688	23,461	18,921	8,169	2,396	4,804 (2,143)	370	582	149	73	7,763
1994	84,905	23,259	19,611	8,436	5,704	11,264 (4,667)	2,660	1,553	1,272	433	10,713
1995	95,145	22,365	20,769	9,103	6,101	14,264 (4,357)	4,513	3,308	2,161	517	12,044
1996	123,870	22,766	25,158	12,082	6,447	18,170 (4,487)	7,004	8,994	4,207	547	18,495
1997	143,900	22,844	26,887	13,458	7,479	24,063 (6,048)	8,593	12,560	4,663	1,024	22,329
1998	122,613	22,678	25,352	12,801	5,076	20,003 (6,157)	5,335	8,899	2,346	801	19,322
1999	139,730	22,796	25,205	12,984	7,971	26,685 (10,575)	6,598	12,687	2,452	1,196	21,156
2000	170,446	22,654	22,139	13,765	12,276	39,784 (19,556)	10,312	14,970	2,919	2,472	29,155
2001	164,835	22,363	21,383	14,501	9,827	46,695 (25,688)	6,542	9,414	2,964	1,309	29,837

Source: Justice Ministry of Korea, Statistical Yearbook of Departures and Arrivals Control, various years.

Table 12.4. Numbers of Migrant Workers in Korea, by Visa Status and Home Country

| Country of Origin | Documented Residents[a] | | | | Undocumented |
| | Registered Workers | | Industrial Trainees[b] | | |
	Professionals[c]	Post-Training Workers	KFSB, etc.	Overseas Korean Firms	
China (Korean Chinese)	902 (268)	519 (196)	21,503 (13,234)	20,232 (6,733)	95,625 (57,348)
Philippines	2,227	255	8,507	1,427	12,890
Vietnam	41	415	13,914	902	7,786
Bangladesh	18	173	7,168	308	14,475
Indonesia	113	390	14,247	1,716	3,191
Thailand	31	39	2,473	128	12,449
Mongolia	29	33	410	5	13,088
Uzbekistan	348	34	2,726	439	4,933
Pakistan	29	18	2,331	18	6,054
Sri Lanka	3	31	1,930	517	1,744
Russia (Korean Russians)	1,878 (17)	0 (0)	0 (0)	3 (0)	1,299 (30)
India	216	0	1	132	2,449
Nepal	29	89	1,706	21	908
Kazakhstan	43	11	1,198	37	1,125
Myanmar	7	61	573	51	1,470
Iran	6	0	54	1	1,985
Total	15,634	2,068	78,744	26,103	188,995

Source: Justice Ministry of Korea, *Statistical Yearbook of Departures and Arrivals Control,* 2001.

a The statistics on documented residents reflect entry visa status, not current status, so they include overstayers and runaways.
b There are two kinds of industrial trainees in Korea: those recruited by the private employers' associations (the KFSB, Construction Association of Korea, National Federation of Fisheries Cooperatives, and Korea Shipping Association since 1994), and those brought by overseas Korean firms to work in the head companies in Korea since 1991.
c There are seven visa categories for professionals: professors, foreign language teachers, researchers, technology instructors, specialty occupations, arts and entertainment visitors, and other specialized occupations.

increased from US$67 to $1,597 to $9,628 over this same period. The Korean economy is now comparable in size to Australia, the Netherlands, Spain, and Mexico; per capita wealth still falls far below that of Australia and the Netherlands, though it is well above that in Mexico and about the same as Spain's (World Bank 2001).

Although Korea is not as rich as neighboring Japan, which in 2000 had a per capita GNP of $37,500, Korea nevertheless obviously enjoys significant wage differentials with its poorer neighbors. In 2000 per capita GNP was $2,045 in Thailand, $1,046 in the Philippines, $805 in China, $728 in Indonesia, and $400 in Vietnam (World Bank 2001).

In short, the standard "push" factors are operating to bring immigrants to Korea, and the "pull" factors are there as well. As in other industrialized nations with wealthy, well-educated populations, there is a shortage of labor in certain occupations and at certain wage levels. In 1987, for example, when foreign workers began to come to Korea, the Labor Ministry reported a shortage of 103,804 manual workers. In 2001 the number of foreign workers had climbed to more than 300,000, but there were still 44,225 manual labor positions to be filled (figure 12.1).

Figure 12.1. Foreign Manual Workers and Manual Labor Shortages in Korea, 1987–2001

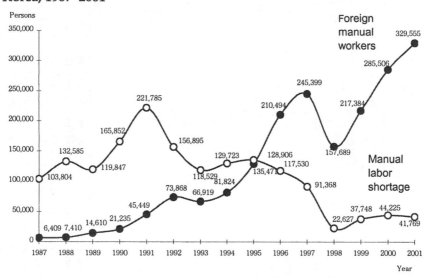

Sources: Labor and Justice ministries, various years; Labor Ministry, *Labor Demand Survey*.

Because they work in niches that Koreans avoid, immigrants do not compete with Korean workers, and none of the recent shifts in the Korean labor market can be traced to the presence of foreign workers. These shifts resulted from the economic restructuring implemented in response to the Asian financial crisis. Korea was caught in the 1997–1998 collapse of the Asian economies. Like Thailand and Indonesia, Korea had heavily leveraged foreign debt. When the (mostly Western) investors took their money out of Korea, the won collapsed and Korea was unable to service its debt. In exchange for a billion-dollar IMF bailout of its economy, Korea had to reform inefficient industries, opaque accounting practices, and inflexible labor markets. Korea's largest industrial conglomerates had formerly provided what amounted to lifetime employment. The IMF pressured Korea to change this practice, and business leaders, government, and labor unions reached an agreement that gave unions more organizational rights in return for the employers' right to lay off workers during economic downturns and allowed nonstandard workers (Moon and Mo 1999, 2000).

Increased flexibility in the Korean labor market did not greatly affect foreign workers because they rarely worked in industries with secure employment in the first place. However, they did take jobs that the newly unemployed Koreans might want, so the government encouraged immigrants to leave by offering to waive the fines that are usually imposed on departing illegals. About a third of all foreign workers in Korea (some 87,000) left in a mass exodus. But the numbers quickly returned to pre-crisis levels (table 12.1), probably because of the "structural embeddedness" of the demand for foreign labor in Korea (Cornelius 1998).

The aging of the Korean population is reinforcing the economic demand for migrant workers. Although the demographic situation is not as dire in Korea as in Japan, Korea's fertility rate fell from 6.0 in 1960 to 2.7 in 1980. The 2000 rate of 1.5, one of the lowest in the world, is below replacement level. According to a United Nations report, Korea would need to import 1.5 million immigrants (100,000 per year) over the 2035–2050 period in order to sustain its 1995 dependency ratio (*Chosun Ilbo*, March 23, 2000). The report does not consider economic growth factors (including productivity growth), but it remains highly likely that demographic shifts will increase the demand for foreign labor.

Could another domestic labor source be found? The obvious choices are women and the elderly, who might mitigate labor shortages in some areas. However, there is no reason to assume that women and the elderly would be willing to take the jobs that male workers now shun. Moreover, the female economic participation rate is already quite high. In 1999, 47.4

percent of Korean women worked (*Korea Statistical Yearbook*, 2001, p. 137).[5] Although efforts are under way to increase the percentage of elderly in the workforce (*Chosun Ilbo*, February 3, 2002), there are few in Korea who see this group as a significant substitute for foreign labor.

Another solution might be to reduce demand for immigrants by mechanizing or moving jobs to the countries where the immigrants reside. However, the firms that hire immigrants make low-end products and are not wealthy enough to mechanize, and they also lack the resources to establish international connections for an offshore move (Seol 1999). Hence "pull" factors are likely to become even more powerful in the future.

In addition to economic pushes and pulls, networks and economic ties between nations also help explain the origins of immigration to Korea, in a pattern typical in international migration generally (Massey 1999; Sassen 1988). Much of Korean immigration can be understood in terms of ethnic ties and trading or investment ties. The joseonjok and goryeoin émigrés are now two, three, or even four generations removed from Korea, but their Korean relatives may still serve as information resources or job contacts. The worker trainee system, described below, privileges countries with economic ties to Korea and thus facilitated immigration ties.

Korea joined the ranks of destination countries partly through these networks but also through media and tourism. A 1994 survey found that the largest percentage of foreign migrant workers got information about Korea through news media (34.0 percent). Others learned about Korea from neighbors who had gone there (19.8 percent) and through events such as the 1988 Olympics and the 1986 Asian Games (18.3 percent). Industrial trainees received most information through the media, sports events, and advertisements in their home countries (Seol 1999: 229–31).

The trainee system set up a network of official migration recruiters and brokers to bring immigrants from various parts of South and Southeast Asia, a network that has its parallel in a web of brokers involved in illegal migrant recruiting.[6] Brokers play a role in channeling immigrants

---

[5] Other evidence points to low female participation in the paid economy, especially for married women (M. Lee 1998). Even so, it is rare to find anyone promoting an increase in the number of economically active women as a way to avoid importing migrant labor.

[6] Brokers are usually co-nationals with connections to Korean brokers stationed in Korea.

to Korea rather than to the more wealthy Japan. There may be a larger wage gap between Bangladesh and Japan, for example, than between Bangladesh and Korea, but the broker fee facilitating the move to Korea is lower. Although the broker fee to Korea is lower than those for Japan and Hong Kong, it is still quite high, ranging between US$4,000 and $9,000, including travel. There is some randomness to the process; one worker from the Philippines noted that a person might end up in Korea simply because he met a broker from Korea who promised a safe and cheap passage to go there (author interview). An immigrant's destination, then, may actually be determined by which broker he or she happens to meet and which broker fee he or she can pay.

GOVERNMENT POLICYMAKING ON IMMIGRATION

Korean immigration policy traditionally has been based on the principle that foreign workers should complement the Korean economy. In practice, this has meant a preference for professionals and technical workers and a ban on unskilled workers. The basic immigration law, the Departures and Arrivals Control Act, or DACA, is strongly oriented toward bringing skilled workers to Korea and preventing foreigners' permanent settlement. Any legal foreigner who wants to work must obtain "sojourner status," and it is illegal for employers to hire foreign workers who do not have this status (J.H. Lee 2002).

The emphasis of Korean law, however, falls most fully on preventing foreign settlement. The Justice Ministry, which includes the Immigration Office and which enforces DACA, does not offer any long-term visa that does not take an applicant's skill level into account. However, closing Korea's "front door" to low-skilled and unskilled workers only created a need for a "side door" for importing foreign workers. In the late 1980s the Korean Federation of Small Business (KFSB) began to lobby for access to foreign labor. In 1991 Korea's Justice Ministry—following Japan—created the Industrial Technical Training Program (ITTP) to meet this need.[7]

Like the Japanese industrial trainee program, the ITTP was ostensibly for teaching and transferring skills to less developed countries. It was

---

[7] The Labor Ministry, the prime minister's Committee for Industrial Training, and the Small and Medium Business Administration (SMBA) were also involved in instituting this program, but the major actor was clearly the Justice Ministry. For more on the history of ITTP, see Seol 2000a.

originally limited to Korean companies with investments or partnerships with firms in these nations. It also limited trainees to fifty per company or 10 percent of the company's workforce. Only 10,000 trainees were originally admitted for six months of training, with a possible six-month extension.

Nevertheless, domestic small and medium-sized manufacturing employers were still having difficulty filling low-wage, menial jobs, and many were forced, despite the threat of fines, to hire undocumented workers who had overstayed their tourist or short-term visas. The shortage of workers for low-end jobs was exacerbated in 1992 when the government deported 10,000 illegal workers. Under increasing pressure from the KFSB, the Justice Ministry expanded the ITTP program to allow companies without foreign affiliates to get Justice Ministry approval to import trainees through private recruiting agencies.

The more recent history of ITTP is one of continual expansion in the number of trainees admitted (most to fill low-wage jobs at domestic companies) and their length of stay, along with delayed deportations of illegal workers. The Justice Ministry continues to underestimate the need for foreign labor, necessitating these repeated expansions of the trainee program which tend to follow strong lobbying efforts by the KFSB. There has been comparatively little organized resistance to this typical case of "client politics."

In June 1993 the Justice Ministry extended the ITTP training period to two years, and in November 1993 the number of trainees admitted was increased by an additional 20,000. The ITTP program was operated through a new Korea International Training Cooperation Corps (KITCO), similar to Japan's JITCO. However, whereas JITCO is composed of business, labor, and government interests, KITCO is totally dominated by business in the form of the KFSB. After the Justice Ministry gives permission to Korean firms without foreign affiliates to hire trainees, KITCO has exclusive rights to import and distribute trainees to these companies. The original system of companies with foreign affiliates continues to function outside of KITCO.

Another program expansion occurred in September 1994, when the Justice Ministry allowed another 10,000 trainees to come to work in Korea's footwear sector, which was facing stiff competition from other Asian countries. In January 1996, trainees were allowed to work outside of the manufacturing sector for the first time; the Justice Ministry allowed 1,000 trainees to enter the fishing industry, demonstrating clearly that there was no technical training going on in the ITTP. In 1996, the trainee pool was expanded by another 30,000, and the training period was extended to three years. In 1997 the Korea Construction Federation oversaw another expansion, allowing trainees to work in the construction industry.

This system set the stage for Korea's current labor migration problems. "Trainees" under the ITTP program are not in most cases being trained for anything and are only filling menial jobs that Koreans refuse to take. Since trainees are not classified as workers, their pay was considerably below that of even undocumented workers (trainee wages were 59 percent of undocumented workers' wages in 1994 [Seol 1999]), and trainees were not guaranteed worker rights such as the right to unionize and to bargain collectively. Moreover, trainees are behind from the start because of the fees (between US$2,000 and $3,000) they pay agencies in their home countries to obtain placement in Korea.

This exploitative system encouraged tens of thousands of trainees to run away from their jobs and join the ranks of the undocumented. In 1994, undocumented workers' demands for compensation for work-related injuries drew public attention and convinced the administration of President Kim Young-Sam to acknowledge undocumented workers' basic labor rights and to include them under the industrial accident compensation insurance. The administration also ordered the Labor Ministry to monitor labor law violations, including unpaid wages, a mission that sometimes brought the Labor Ministry into conflict with the Justice Ministry. Then, following the 1995 protest by Nepalese trainees at Myeong-dong Cathedral, the Labor Ministry, asserting its authority with regard to the treatment of workers already in the country, announced the Measure for the Protection and Control of Foreign and Industrial and Technical Trainees. This ruling required that trainees be paid the government-set minimum wage or more, that they be paid directly by employers, and that they need not surrender their passports to their employers.

In 1997 the ruling New Korea Party (NKP) and the opposition National Congress for New Politics (NCNP) submitted reform bills to the National Assembly to eliminate the exploitative trainee program and replace it with a work permit system. The bills had the support of migrant workers and nongovernmental organizations (NGOs) working for migrants. They were opposed, however, by the KFSB, which staged a rally in front of the federal government complex and claimed that a new law was unnecessary. They noted that even Japan had no such system for migrants. The KFSB carried the day, and the work permit system remains the Holy Grail of reformers in NGOs, academia, and the Labor Ministry.

The Justice Ministry has revised the trainee program in response to criticisms, but it refuses to abandon it completely. In 1998 it eased the exploitative aspects of the program by creating the Work-After-Training Program for Foreigners, which allows trainees who pass a skills test to obtain a visa that allows them to spend their third year of training as workers fully covered by Korean labor law, and the ministry later revised this to allow two years as "worker" after one year as "trainee."

The ITTP program remains overwhelmingly oriented toward manufacturing; in early 2001 the ITTP included 98,000 trainees in manufacturing, compared to only 1,000 each in fishing and construction, even though there is strong labor demand in non-manufacturing sectors. Nearly 56,000 of an estimated 255,000 undocumented foreigners in Korea were working in the construction sector in 2001.

In July 2002 the Justice Ministry initiated several new measures in its constantly changing migrant worker policy. It expanded the overall quota of trainees to 145,500 and increased sector quotas in response to specific labor shortages, raising the construction quota to 7,500 and the fishing and livestock quota to 5,000. The ministry, in collaboration with the Small and Medium Business Administration (SMBA), also created the first labor-importing mechanism not linked to training and reinforced ethnic preferences in the labor migration policy system.[8] Overseas Koreans over the age of forty and with family (cousins or closer relatives) in Korea would receive special two-year visas to work in the labor-starved service industry—supplying cheap labor to restaurants, cleaning companies, and nursing facilities but excluding bars and sex-based "room salons" and karaoke hostess bars. Employers can now hire up to ten overseas Koreans provided they show they cannot find workers domestically. The government expects between 40,000 and 50,000 overseas Koreans to take advantage of the new program (*Joongangilbo*, July 18, 2002; *Korea Herald*, July 18, 2002; *Chosun Ilbo*, July 18, 2002).

The Korean system had national origin (mostly intra-Asian) preferences long before the implementation of the 2002 measures. The trainee system is based on official relationships with Korea's major trading partners, and that rationale fits with the program's original limitation to Korean companies with overseas affiliates. The program began with eleven nations, and more were added in 1994.

---

[8] Joseonjok were given a separate (and large) quota in the ITTP and, along with Filipinos, were paid higher wages in the beginning of the program, but this wage preference was soon eliminated.

The inside story is different, however. Country choices were made by officials closely linked to the small companies that employed migrants. The first sending states were chosen based mostly on research done by a KFSB official who examined the national origins of Korea's undocumented foreign workers in the late 1980s and early 1990s. If economic ties or migrant labor pools led to the choice of the first ten countries in the program, it was politics—mostly based on Korea's drive to get Third World support for its 1991 admission to the United Nations—that decided the next four. Even though KFSB leaders continued to influence the process and had formal decision-making power, they were under pressure from immigration brokers who oversaw the trainee system from inside particular countries, and especially from the Ministry of Foreign Affairs and various overseas Korean embassies. When President Kim Young-Sam visited Uzbekistan and Kazakhstan in 1994, he offered quotas for migrant workers as gifts. Mongolia received a worker quota in 1996 after its president visited Seoul. The administration of Kim Young-Sam was able to add Indonesia, an old South Korea ally, to the list after that country's labor minister visited Korea and lobbied for a worker quota.

There are no explicit gender preferences in the trainee system, but individual companies can request male or female trainees from KITCO (C.W. Lee 2001). Chinese, Filipinos, Indonesians, and Vietnamese workers are split evenly between men and women. In contrast, Pakistanis and Bangladeshis are almost all male. The work that male and female migrants do is gender segregated, and there are some ethnic concentrations. Undocumented joseonjok and Filipina women dominate in domestic service. Three-fourths of entertainer visas go to women, mostly Filipinas and Russians. Many more illegal sex workers enter Korea from Russia; the network of illegal prostitutes is facilitated by illegal organizations in Russia, but overseas Koreans are also very active in arranging for this trafficking in women.

Because there is no settlement in Korea, there are no government policies for settlement or incorporation. Whatever incorporation efforts do exist come not from government but from private organizations, especially NGOs. Approximately 150 groups—most of them religious, predominately Protestant and Catholic groups—work in this area, providing consulting services, educating migrants on their rights and legal protections, and helping to fashion a migrant worker health insurance program. Illegal workers also rely on their own networks of friends for help in finding jobs and housing. To this end, foreigners have set up meeting places in Seoul and other major cities where information can be exchanged and new friends added to the networks.[9]

Regarding Korea's closed door to refugees other than North Koreans, it is difficult to find any discussion of this as "policy." The closed door may be the result of a fear that North Korean refugees will one day overrun South Korea, or that South Korea's economic development is still vulnerable. The country's desire to maintain ethnic homogeneity is perhaps the strongest factor here, trumping humanitarian concerns about the world's growing refugee populations.

THE POLICYMAKING REGIME

Korean policymaking on immigration is a complex, even messy process, involving many players with widely varying degrees of power, interest, and/or involvement. Immigration policymaking serves to highlight the fragmented nature of the Korean state more generally, and it is impossible to understand immigration policy without taking this fragmentation into account.

The fact that the trainee system has been continuously revised but not discarded demonstrates the relative power of the Justice Ministry, the Small and Medium Business Administration, and the SMBA's client, the KFSB. The SMBA is a relatively distant player, weighing in periodically in support of KFSB interests. The Justice Ministry runs the Immigration Office, implements the DACA immigration law, and issues most rulings and policy revisions with considerable discretionary authority.

It is not difficult to see why the KFSB wants to maintain the trainee system, which supplies its member businesses with cheap labor.[10] Why the Justice Ministry is so eager to please the KFSB is harder to understand. The ties are rooted in the fact that the KFSB runs KITCO, the labor recruiting body. All KITCO chairmen since 1994 are officials retired from

---

9. In Itaewon, Seoul's foreign district (established primarily for U.S. servicemen and their families), there are restaurants serving *halal* food to the Islamic foreign worker population.

10 The negative aspects for an employer of trainees is that if a trainee runs away, the company loses the right to bring others, and the KFSB cannot return the employer's deposit. The KFSB, however, loses nothing if a trainee runs away, and the companies that hire runaways benefit from the system. Illegal immigrants work hard, are flexible, and require few benefits. Runaways generally leave one low-paying job for another, so the same kinds of companies benefit whether they are employing trainees or illegal workers.

the Immigration Office. As the middleman in the labor-importing process, KITCO has made its officials' jobs very lucrative through corruption. Several KITCO officials have been arrested for bribery, including KITCO's chairman in 1995, its director and manager in 1996, and its subdirector and various staff members in 1997. In 2002 the former vice president of KFSB and the head of KFSB's international cooperation team were arrested for taking bribes, mainly from labor recruiters in sending states (*Daehan Maeil*, April 5, 2002). Other groups that benefit from the current system are the twenty agencies that provide "consulting services" to industrial trainees (though their actual purpose is to prevent runaways). These agencies charge a monthly fee for each trainee they oversee.

Korean immigration policymaking, then, is dominated by business interests. The KFSB created the trainee system with help from Justice Ministry officials, and now the KFSB, the ministry, the SMBA, and various groups that make money from it all work to retain it.

There are some interesting twists, however, in what looks like a rather straightforward situation. The Justice Ministry is sometimes at cross-purposes with itself. Its enforcement of immigration law and its own interests in helping maintain Korea's ethnic and racial homogeneity require it to try to stem the same tide of illegals that its own policy encourages. Hence the Justice Ministry periodically announces expansions of the trainee system (which encourages undocumented workers through runaways) at the same time that it pursues efforts to control undocumented workers.

Moreover, Justice is generally opposed by the Labor Ministry, which oversees trainees and workers once they are in Korea. The Labor Ministry, which has been tasked with monitoring human rights violations, is sensitive to Korea's international image (Seol and Skrentny 2001). It has long supported the worker permit system favored by NGOs. At the instruction of President Kim Dae-Jung, Labor, Justice, and the KFSB work together in developing policy, but the Labor Ministry obviously has conflicts with the other two. According to Choi Tai-Ho, deputy director of the Employment Policy Division at the Labor Ministry, "The Labor Ministry holds the position that migrant workers should have legal worker status for a specified period, and also that an objective assessment is needed to determine the overall number of migrant workers needed in the labor market.... The Justice Ministry and KFSB, on the other hand, feel that the current trainee system should be maintained" (*Report on the First Multi-Party Informal Meeting on Migrant Workers*, 2002).

When the courts have weighed in on immigration, the cases have generally involved the rights of trainees and undocumented workers. The courts have usually sided with the foreign workers. The Korean courts' ruling that undocumented workers are entitled to compensation for job-related injuries encouraged the Labor Ministry to issue regulations in 1994 that placed undocumented workers under the Industrial Accident Compensation Insurance Act and the Labor Standards Act. A 1995 case also ruled that trainees were considered to be workers under the Labor Standards Act under certain conditions (C.W. Lee 2001).

Although national presidents tend to be less closely involved in immigration policymaking, Kim Dae-Jung and his predecessor, Kim Young-Sam, have both pushed for reform. Although Korean presidents are strong and Kim Dae-Jung has pushed through some controversial policies,[11] he has refrained from expending his political capital on migrant workers. His administration favors abolishing the work-after-training system and replacing it with a work permit system, but Kim's efforts at reform, which began in earnest in fall 2000, stopped short when Korea's economy slid into recession. Immigration reform quickly fell to the bottom of the government's agenda.

Unlike the situation in many nations in Europe, where socialist parties have worked for immigrant rights (Jacobson 1996), Korean political parties generally have not taken the lead in immigration. All parties in Korea are basically conservative, and no left-wing groups enjoy seats in the National Assembly.

Unlike Japan, where obvious policy conflicts exist between local governments that have to cope with immigration and the national government, which generally denies that an immigration situation exists, there are no conflicts between various levels of government in Korea. This is so largely because the numbers of immigrants are still relatively small.

Korean NGOs are active on immigration issues, but they are still very young and relatively weak. The lead group on immigrant issues is the Joint Committee for Migrant Workers in Korea, or JCMK, which formed in 1995 from smaller NGOs and church groups, in cooperation with the Korean Federation of Trade Unions. A second trade union, the Federation of Korean Trade Unions, also supports equal treatment for foreign workers, but neither union group makes this issue a priority (C.W. Lee 2001).

---

[11] Perhaps the best example is the reform of the medical system in August 2000. The reform so angered doctors that many went on strike (*Korea Herald*, August 9, 2000).

The print media give the plight of foreign workers front-page treatment, and television coverage frequently includes disturbing videos on these workers' conditions. Editorials strongly criticize the trainee system because it exploits foreign workers, allows—if not encourages—their abuse, and leads to massive numbers of undocumented workers. The main exceptions to media criticism of the ITTP are the business papers, which refrain from criticism but do not offer a defense of the current system.

What does the Korean public want? Koreans generally oppose the importation of foreign labor, but they are most tolerant of joseonjok migrants. While 34 percent favor and 40 percent oppose joseonjok entering Korea to work, the comparable numbers for other foreigners coming to Korea are 13 percent in favor and 64 percent opposed (Seol 1999). Perhaps because of their inexperience with foreigners, Koreans are largely undecided on a number of migrant worker issues. When asked for their views on foreigners moving into their neighborhood, about 20 percent of Koreans said they disliked or strongly disliked this prospect, 22 percent welcomed it, and 57 percent were undecided. Responses were similar when Koreans were asked about the prospect of foreigners in their workplace. There was stronger opposition to a question about Koreans marrying foreigners, with 61 percent strongly opposed, 30 percent undecided, and only 9 percent in favor (Seol 1999).[12]

CONTROLLING ILLEGAL IMMIGRATION

If the Korean government really wants to limit the influx of illegal foreign workers, then the country's effort at immigration control is a failure. However, to assume that this is really the government's goal is problematic. At minimum, there are different opinions on migration between different ministries—and sometimes within a single ministry, as we saw in the case of the Justice Ministry, which both promotes the trainee program and supports measures to control illegal immigration.

The immigration "problem" in Korea, as noted above, is mainly due to trainees who escape their assigned employers or others who come legally and then overstay their short-term visas. Although Korean law

---

[12] Koreans hold to a double standard on these and related issues. Only 11 percent dislike having Koreans working in foreign countries, but 63.8 percent are opposed to foreigners working in Korea; 43 percent dislike having foreign companies operate in Korea, but only 7 percent dislike the idea of Korean companies operating abroad (Seol 1999).

imposes sanctions on undocumented workers and the employers of undocumented workers, in practice the Korean government mostly ignores the illegal hiring of foreign workers and usually does nothing to find or deport them. The law imposes a hefty fine (up to 10 million won) on employers of undocumented workers, but few employers pay any fine at all. Fines against illegal workers (about 100,000 won for each month spent in Korea) are frequently suspended temporarily in the hope the illegals will take advantage of this window of opportunity to return home.[13]

Thus the large numbers of illegal workers and the failure of sanctions to deter the hiring of illegal workers should not be understood as a failure to control immigration. In fact, immigration is subject to the exact degree of control that the Justice Ministry and KFSB desire. Kim Dae-Jung apparently can tolerate this situation, and Korean society loses little from the presence of undocumented foreigners. Because there is no family unification immigration, legal or illegal, virtually all migrants are employed. There are no migrants on public welfare and no migrant dependents using schools or other government services. Moreover, the Korean government appears able to expel foreigners when it wants to do so. The government forcibly deported 10,000 illegal workers in 1992, and in July 2002 the Justice Ministry announced it would deport 256,000 illegal workers who had not left the country by May 2003, creating a special body to carry out the task (*Joongangilbo*, July 18, 2002; *Korea Herald*, July 18, 2002; *Chosun Ilbo*, July 18, 2002).

THE FUTURE OF KOREAN IMMIGRATION POLICY

There is every indication that the demand for foreign labor will continue and increase in Korea, just as in other industrialized countries. A wealthier, better educated, and shrinking population all but guarantees it. The more interesting questions are: How will they brought in? Will they stay?

In the short term at least, Korea will likely expand the ITTP program by bringing in more trainees and lengthening the duration of their stay,

---

[13] In the absence of an effective policy, trainees' employers become enforcers of the law, which explains why they have taken drastic measures — such as the (now illegal) confiscation of trainees' passports — to keep their trainees from joining the ranks of the undocumented. Another approach at trainee retention is that used by the KFSB, which withholds a portion of a trainee's pay until the trainee's term is over. In some cases, employers have beat or imprisoned runaway workers who were caught (Moon 2000).

as it announced in July 2002. However, in light of the incremental reforms made in recent years, such as the creation of the work-after-training visas and new service visas for joseonjok, it appears that the ITTP will eventually be phased out. The combined might of the Labor Ministry, migrant worker NGOs, labor unions, and much of the news media has failed to force reform in the past. But if the next president makes migration reform a priority issue, or if political parties can exert more pressure in the National Assembly than they did in 1997, the momentum could be built to bury the ITTP.

What would take its place? The reform favored by nearly all anti-ITTP forces is a work permit system, similar to that now in place in Taiwan. The work permit system would eliminate the key condition that makes the ITTP so exploitative: in a work permit system, there is not a single day that the foreign worker is not covered by Korea's labor laws regarding pay, collective bargaining, accident insurance, and the like. Workers would still be treated differently from Korean citizens, however, in that they would not be able to change jobs without permission from the Labor Ministry.[14]

In the meantime, reformers are pressing for foreign workers' human rights. Even though KFSB representatives highlight the fact that trainees in Korea receive better treatment than many illegal immigrants in the United States (trainees are housed in dormitories, for example; Seol and Skrentny 2001), there are numerous cases—highlighted by the Korean press—of human rights abuses. For example, there are reports of rapes of female trainees. Housing is sometimes substandard. A Chinese trainee was severely beaten when he protested after being threatened with deportation. Another from Bangladesh was beaten on the head with a stick and required stitches. There are numerous cases of wages not being paid. In fact, one might argue that the Korean system institutionalizes and legalizes the "coyote" system that brings Mexican undocumented immigrants to the United States. In Korea, the brokers who facilitate the migration of trainees make false promises of high wages, charge exorbitant fees, and trap workers in cycles of debt (*Korea Herald*, May 1, 2000; *Korea Times*, May 25, 2000). Even though undocumented workers and industrial trainees are covered by most provisions of Korea's Labor Standards

[14] One NGO—the far-left Seoul Gyeonggi Incheon Region Equality Trade Union Migrants' Branch—is a lonely dissenter on the work permit system. This NGO claims that the work permit would not allow foreign workers to change jobs freely. This NGO is also alone in making workers' right to family reunification a priority.

Act, their marginal legal status makes it difficult for them to benefit fully from this legal protection. NGOs struggle constantly to ensure that labor law is enforced to the fullest extent with regard to foreign workers.

Besides a work permit system, there is a second option that could take the place of the ITTP: an ethnic preference based on expansion of the new short-term service visas for joseonjok. Although global norms are turning away from ethnic preferences systems — at least in the West — it appears these norms might not matter in Korea. When asked about the likelihood that Southeast Asian nations would criticize Korea's ethnic preferences program, a government official stated simply that, "Visa laws are a matter of national sovereignty. No one can interfere with them" (*Korea Times,* July 18, 2002). There is a large supply of joseonjok workers to be tapped (more than 2 million), and importing ethnic Koreans would obviously entail less disruption of Korea's ethnically homogenous society. To be sure, employers are not demanding joseonjok workers. Indeed, surveys show that Korean employers have strong preferences for Indonesian, Filipino, and Chinese workers, and the weakest preference for joseonjok, whom they say change jobs frequently and are insufficiently respectful at the job site (*Chosun Ilbo,* January 9, 1995; Seol 1999).[15] On the other hand, the public prefers joseonjok to other workers.

There are few indications today that Korea is close to admitting any low-skilled immigrants on a permanent basis. The aversion to foreigner settlement extends even to the joseonjok; there are no renewals for trainees or trainee-workers. It is telling that the "amnesties" the Korean government offers to undocumented workers are so far removed from the understanding of "amnesty" in the West, where amnesty programs allow undocumented workers to become legal immigrants or even permanent residents. In Korea, "amnesty" merely means a breathing space during which an illegal worker can leave the country and the government will waive the fine the person would normally be required to pay. Though a few leftist NGOs or unions may pose family unification as the next agenda item for discussions of immigration policy in Korea, their voices are marginal indeed.

The antipathy toward settlement seems to go both ways. In contrast to the situation in many receiving nations, there is almost no evidence that migrants want to settle in Korea. To be sure, there is a rapidly growing

---

[15] Despite employers' apparent bias against joseonjok, these workers earn somewhat higher wages than other migrants, even controlling for employment sector (Seol 1999).

group of visa overstayers (63,000 in 2001) who have been in Korea for more than two years, and about 10,000 foreigners have married Koreans (Chosun Ilbo Sa 2001: 97).[16] But Korea makes it very hard for foreigners to marry Koreans. It denies them long-term residence visas, forcing them to make expensive trips abroad to renew their short-terms visas (C.W. Lee 2001).[17] And though visa overstayers can, in theory, bring in their family members to overstay their tourist or short-term visas in turn, there are still no discernible signs of migrant settlement in Korea. When economic times got rough in 1998, out-of-work migrants did not become homeless, beg on the streets, demonstrate for welfare assistance, or turn to crime. They packed up and went home. It was easy to do so because they had not brought their spouses or children. Their ties to Korean society are few. Because there is no settlement, there is no settlement policy, at either the national or the local level, and there is none on the horizon.

The wild card in Korea's future immigration policy is the stability of North Korea, a national anachronism if there ever was one. Since the decline of its supporter states in the Soviet bloc, North Korea's Stalinist hereditary dictatorship has been teetering on the brink of collapse, with large parts of the rural population facing starvation and malnutrition. Refugees from North Korea are the exception in Korea's non-settlement of foreigners. They have received generous job training, financial aid, housing, and other assistance. But their numbers are very small; only 900 came from 1980 to 2000 (*Korea Herald*, April 24, 2000). Though rarely mentioned, lurking in the background of discussions of migrant workers in South Korea is the possibility of the labor market being flooded with low-skilled, difficult-to-place North Korean laborers who were never paid according to performance and likely do not even understand the meaning of the word "profit." Though all Koreans look forward to the day of reunification, those who examine the situation without the roman-

---

[16] Nearly all 22,000 F2 "long-term resident" visas are held by ethnic Chinese who have resided in Korea for decades (basically all of Korea's post–World War II history). These visas originated in a 1882 agreement that allowed Chinese to own and lease land in Korea (C.W. Lee 2001).

[17] Before 1997, Korean law granted citizenship to any foreign woman who married a Korean man. Now, foreign men and women can both apply for naturalization, but it is very difficult to obtain. "Foreign spouses of Korean nationals may apply for naturalization if they have been domiciled in Korea continuously for two years.... Yet the applicant has to meet additional conditions, which give the government wide room for discretion.... The financial threshold is high.... Also required are recommendations from two or more high-ranking people.... Few migrant workers can overcome these hurdles" (C.W. Lee 2001).

tic visions of ethnic nationalism see a task far more daunting than Germany's reunification, and possibly disastrously debilitating for the South Korean economy. If serious cracks start to show in the North Korean regime, it is likely that all migrant labor to South Korea will cease.

CONCLUSION: A GLOBAL PATTERN IN IMMIGRATION POLICIES?

It is difficult to apply the gap hypothesis to the Korean case. A policy gap exists, but only trivially. The formal policy of "no unskilled immigration" is window dressing; no one in Korea takes it seriously. Korean businesses and most parts of the Korean state want unskilled migrants, and they get them. What *is* taken seriously as an overall policy is "no unskilled *settler* immigration" or, to put it another way, "no multicultural society." And on this issue, it cannot now be shown that there is a policy gap. Immigration to Korea is as controlled as Korea wants it to be.

One could maintain, of course, that the Korean case does indeed confirm the gap hypothesis. Interpreting the facts presented in this chapter differently, one could say that Korean policymakers *wanted* a gap between policies and outcomes. That is, policymakers in the Justice Ministry intentionally undermine the official "no unskilled immigrants" policy by creating policies that bring in unskilled immigrants (as trainees) and letting in the undocumented. It seems, however, that this and our interpretation rest on what is considered to be the "official policy" of Korea. There is no reason to consider the ban on unskilled immigrants as "The Policy" and privileged in some absolute sense. Koreans do not go to the lengths that the Japanese do to deny there is any immigration going on. They realize there are many immigration policies. The ITTP scheme for bringing in unskilled workers, for example, amends the DACA immigration law to allow this importation of labor. The use of the label "trainee" meant lower wages, fewer rights, more government control, and considerably less chance of foreigner settlement. The decision not to deport or heavily fine visa overstayers is also a policy to the extent that it is a conscious decision. And it is bringing about the intended results: cheap workers for Korea. The only immigration ban that is treated seriously in Korea is the ban on settlement, and no Korean policies undermine it.

Not surprisingly, some of the most important theories to explain failure to control immigration simply do not apply to the Korean case. The problem of immigration in the West is that immigrants come but then do not leave, even when they are unemployed, causing a drag on (especially

European but also North American) welfare states and leading to demands for accommodation of cultural differences in schools and other areas (Soysal 1994). Many theories to explain this situation emphasize the role of *rights* leading to proliferating numbers of foreign settlers. These are rights to family reunification and rights against arbitrary or mass deportations.

Consider, for example, the "liberal state" approach associated with Hollifield (1992) and Joppke (1998). A major factor in the increase in immigration and the failure of control that they describe has been family reunification rights which, according to Joppke, were the creation of the courts. In Korea there are no family reunification rights. Unlike in Europe, where guestworkers stayed and brought families (Jacobson 1996), in Korea thus far there is no myth of return. Most foreign workers do go back home, and almost none bring their families. Even the undocumented do not bring in their spouses or children.

Moreover, the Korean state has deported migrants en masse when policymakers believed they had to, and it promises to deport 250,000 in 2003 if it must. Some newspapers have called this bad policy and suggested that the government will not go through with the promised deportations (*Korea Herald,* July 22, 2002). Some migrant workers and NGOs held a sit-in at Myeongdong Cathedral in protest (*Korea Herald,* July 23, 2002). But the main reasons the media oppose the deportation is that it would leave the market starved for cheap labor—not that it would be a violation of migrant worker rights.

A possible explanation for Korea's divergence from the rights model is that it simply does not qualify as a liberal state. If we follow Joppke and consider a liberal state as one that has independent courts and a consistent rule of law, however, then Korea would qualify. It has made two democratic transitions of presidential power, and its Supreme Court is not averse to striking down laws that violate the Constitution or to overturn government policies.

Theories of the impact of international human rights regimes are similarly inapplicable to the Korean case. If Korea recognizes no constitutionally grounded rights to family reunification or against arbitrary deportation, neither does it recognize international rights in these areas. To be sure, human rights certainly play a role in Korea. Domestic NGOs on a variety of issues use human rights norms and United Nations conventions or covenants to advance their causes (similar to those in Japan; Gurowitz 1999). Korean dictators in the 1970s and 1980s ratified, or at least paid attention to, some human rights norms (while violating others). Kim Dae-Jung strove for and attained the Nobel Peace Prize; clearly international human rights matter. But they do not matter equally to all branches of the government. And to some branches and on some issues they do not matter at all. Thus, though the Labor Ministry appears very aware of global norms on migrant worker rights in areas like worker payment and injury compensation—and pursues reforms to bring Korea into alignment with them (Seol and Skrentny 2001)—other parts of government, including the SMBA and the Justice Ministry, show little concern.

Korean policy has its origins in a fragmented state and the Justice Ministry's client politics. Both the trainee system and the huge proportion of illegal workers wonderfully serve the interests of the small and medium-size companies represented by the KFSB. Other parts of the state, meanwhile, push for reforms, and the Labor Ministry and the courts issue regulations and rulings that somewhat mitigate the harsh policies of the Justice Ministry.

This leaves open the question of why there is such demand for immigrant labor in Korea. The answer is unequivocal; Korea has followed the same path as many other nations that through economic development and wage increases created a situation in which certain industries remained in the country even though there were not enough citizens to fill the jobs (Cornelius 1998).

A final issue remains to be addressed. Does the examination of the Korean case, the most recently industrialized country of the cases considered in this volume, reveal a general convergence of the world's immigration policies? Korea shares with the world a policy of sanctions against employers who hire undocumented workers and fines for workers who do not have their papers in order. And just as in those other countries, these penalties are weakly enforced.

After these similarities, however, Korea mostly parts company with the West. It resembles Japan (as described by Cornelius and Tsuda in this volume) in several respects, but usually with its own variations. First, both countries have formal, official policies of banning all low-skilled or unskilled foreign workers, though in Korea pronouncements to this effect are rare and as a policy it is not taken seriously.

Second, both Korea and Japan have trainee programs, and indeed Korea's was essentially copied from Japan's, right down to the name of the agency that overseas foreign labor recruitment (KITCO versus JITCO). However, Korea's policy has differences. It is totally dominated by small business interests, and the KFSB literally runs KITCO as a private organization, without interference from labor unions or other organized interests. The Korean policy, with its alarming rate of runaways, is more obviously a failure than the Japanese one, a fact that somehow does not dissuade the KFSB or the Justice Ministry from continuing to support it.

Third, both countries have large ethnic return migrant populations, and they show preferences for these workers in the more intimate services such as maids, nurses, and other domestic help. However, whereas the Japanese *nikkeijin* are given what amounts to permanent settlement in Japan, Korea's joseonjok and goryeoin are not allowed to settle. They are given no preferences in the trainee program's limit of three years total in Korea, and the new service visas are limited to only two years.

Fourth, both countries import workers for their sex industries with "entertainment" visas. The difference here is that the Korean entertainer visas go relatively unused. Japan's population is 2.5 times greater than Korea's, but there are almost 14 times more migrants on entertainment visas in Japan than in Korea (54,000, compared to 3,900).[18] Korea also does not have the "student" visas for language or vocational schools that function as a way to bring unskilled labor to Japan. Because Korea lacks these other mechanisms for importing foreign workers, the trainee system is of much more importance there than in Japan.

Fifth, both countries have largely avoided the responsibilities assumed by Western nations in settling refugee/asylee populations. Korea, however, now faces the growing and potentially massive problem of North Koreans at its doorstep, and it has made some moves to settle those that find their way to Korea (usually through China).

Korea's convergence with Japan is rooted in several factors. Most important among them is the fact that Korea is a former colony of Japan. Much of Korean law came from Japan, and the country's modern political and economic institutions had their start during the period of colonization. Explaining the similarities with Japan is not difficult. Korea's development model of a strong state and reliance on large business groups (*chaebol* in Korea and *zaibatsu* in Japan, though the Chinese character used to symbolize them is the same) was copied from Japan (Myers and Peattie 1984; Haggard and Moon 1993; Eckert 1993; Vogel 1993; Hamilton and Biggart 1988).

The policymaking regimes in the two countries are also somewhat similar, with much autonomy for the ministries, lesser roles played by

---

[18] The illegal trafficking of Thai or Filipina women who are promised office, restaurant, or modeling jobs in Japan but are instead forced into prostitution has a counterpart in Korea. The primary difference is that in Korea the women are from Russia and Uzbekistan.

political parties in the legislative bodies, and a strong hard-line position played by the Justice Ministry, though business groups exert more influence on immigration policy in Korea. It is not surprising that Korea looked to a more developed peer nation when creating its labor importation policy, especially given that Korean policymakers had a pattern of looking to Japan.[19] Japan's trainee system had just what Korean policymakers were looking for: a scheme to bring in cheap, compliant labor that would not settle. (Today's reformers look to Taiwan's work permit system as a model that provides rights but similarly avoids settlement.)

Korea shares with Japan problems of economic and demographic pressures that create the need for migrant workers. Furthermore, both countries are (or claim to be) nearly homogenous as regards the ethnic background of the populace. Though such claims are branded as reactionary and/or racist in the West, in both Japan and Korea this ethnic homogeneity is said to be precious, valuable, delicate, and something that should be preserved.

For all these reasons, it is not surprising that Korean policy resembles, at least in it broad outlines, that of Japan. Yet if Korea is like Japan, both countries are different from the West. The key difference is the steadfast refusal to allow family reunification of unskilled migrant workers. It must be emphasized that Western nations' position on this question is the key to the whole immigration "problem" as it exists in the West. Family reunification allows immigrant numbers to get out of control, and it allows the admission of economically inactive persons. In fact, the admission of nonworking children and husbands or wives can be economically detrimental to the host society (Jacobson 1996). Yet Western societies allow these family immigrants because of rights or for humanitarian reasons.

To a remarkable degree, however, policy in Korea and Japan treats migrant workers as machines (or as the Nepalese protesters put it, as "animals"), not as humans. They are there to do the work Koreans will not do. They serve no other function, and they are not seen as part of the

---

[19] A survey of the Korean civil administration found that 43 percent of bureaucrats listed "foreign examples" as the source of new policy; 21.9 percent cited "past precedents," and 11.4 percent credited "original ideas." When asked which two countries have a policy environment most similar to Korea's, the responses were: Japan, 87.7 percent; the United States, 42.1 percent; Taiwan, 28.1 percent; and the former West Germany, 5.2 percent. When asked which two countries most often serve as referents for policymaking in Korea, the results were: Japan, 93.9 percent; the United States, 77.2 percent; Taiwan, 6.1 percent; West Germany, 5.2 percent; and Singapore, 2.6 percent (Woo-Cumings 1995: 154).

nation-building project other than in the labor they (temporarily) provide. They are not expected to have human needs, and the Korean government has been reluctant to provide even the most basic access to housing and health care.[20] Moreover, if a migrant seeks to attend to the very human desire of an intimate partner, Korea makes it difficult by not allowing permanent residence even to those migrants married to nationals. For these reasons, we believe it cannot now be said that the world is showing a common pattern of losing control of immigration.

References

Amsden, Alice. 1989. *Asia's Next Giant: Late Industrialization in Korea*. New York: Oxford University Press.

Chosun Ilbo Sa. 2001. *The Chosun Almanac*. Seoul: Chosun Ilbo Daily.

Cornelius, Wayne. 1994. "Japan: The Illusion of Immigration Control." In *Controlling Immigration*, edited by Wayne A. Cornelius, Philip L. Martin, and James Hollifield. 1st ed. Stanford, Calif.: Stanford University Press.

———. 1998. "The Structural Embeddedness of Demand for Mexican Immigrant Labor: New Evidence from California." In *Crossings: Mexican Immigration in Interdisciplinary Perspectives*, edited by Marcelo M. Suárez-Orozco. Cambridge, Mass.: David Rockefeller Center for Latin American Studies, Harvard University.

Eckert, Carter. 1993. "The South Korean Bourgeoisie: A Class in Search of Hegemony." In *State and Society in Contemporary Korea*, edited by Hagen Koo. Ithaca, N.Y.: Cornell University Press.

Freeman, Gary P. 1995. "Modes of Immigration Politics in Liberal Democratic States," *International Migration Review* 24, no. 4.

Fukuoka, Yasunori. 1996. "Koreans in Japan: Past and Present," *Saitama University Review* 31, no. 1: 1–15.

Gurowitz, Amy. 1999. "Mobilizing International Norms: Domestic Actors, Immigrants and the Japanese State," *World Politics* 51, no. 3: 413–45.

Haggard, Stephen. 1990. *Pathways from the Periphery: The Politics of Growth in the Newly Industrializing Countries*. Ithaca, N.Y.: Cornell University Press.

Haggard, Stephen, and Chung-in Moon. 1993. "The State, Politics, and Economic Development in Postwar South Korea." In *State and Society in Contemporary Korea*, edited by Hagen Koo. Ithaca, N.Y.: Cornell University Press.

Hamilton, Gary G., and Nicole W. Biggart. 1988. "Market, Culture and Authority: A Comparative Analysis of Management and Organization in the Far East," *American Journal of Sociology*. 94: 52–94.

---

[20] Korean policy on these points resembles U.S. policy toward Chinese and Japanese immigrants in the late nineteenth century (C. Lee 2002).

Hollifield, James F. 1992. *Immigrants, Markets and States*. Cambridge, Mass.: Harvard University Press.

Jacobson, David. 1996. *Rights across Borders*. Baltimore, Md.: Johns Hopkins University Press.

Joppke, Christian. 1998. "Why Liberal States Accept Unwanted Immigration," *World Politics* 50: 266–93.

Lee, Catherine. 2002. "Race, Gender and the Political Economy of Nation-Building: Chinese and Japanese Immigration to the U.S., 1870–1920." Ph.D. dissertation, University of California, Los Angeles.

Lee, Chul-Woo. 2001. "'Us' and the 'Them' in Korean Law: The Creation, Accommodation and Exclusion of Outsiders in South Korea." Presented at the Hiroshi Wagatsuma Memorial Conference on Rule of Law and Group Identities Embedded in Asian Traditions and Cultures, University of California, Los Angeles.

Lee, Jae-Hyup. 2002. "Controlling Foreign Migrant Workers in Korea." Presented at the Law and Society Annual Conference, Vancouver, May 30–June 1.

Lee, Jennifer. 2002. *Civility in the City: Blacks, Jews, and Koreans in Urban America*. Cambridge, Mass.: Harvard University Press.

Lee, Mijeong. 1998. *Women's Education, Work and Marriage in Korea*. Seoul: Seoul National University Press.

Lie, John. 1998. *Han Unbound: The Political Economy of South Korea*. Stanford, Calif.: Stanford University Press.

Massey, Douglas. 1999. "Engines of Immigration: Stocks of Human and Social Capital in Mexico," *Social Science Quarterly* 81: 33–48.

Moon, Chung-In, and Jongryn Mo, eds. 1999. *Democratization and Globalization in Korea: Assessments and Prospects*. Seoul: Yonsei University Press.

———. 2000. *Economic Crisis and Structural Reforms in South Korea: Assessments and Implications*. Washington, D.C.: Economic Strategy Institute.

Moon, Katherine H.S. 2000. "Strangers in the Midst of Globalization: Migrant Workers and Korean Nationalism." In *Korea's Globalization*, edited by Samuel S. Kim. New York: Cambridge University Press.

Myers, Ramon H., and Mark Peattie, eds. 1984. *The Japanese Colonial Empire, 1895–1945*. Princeton, N.J.: Princeton University Press.

Office for Government Policy Coordination. 2002. "Reform Plan of Foreign Workers Program." Unpublished, July.

Park, Seok-Woon, Chongkoo Lee, and Dong-Hoon Seol. 1995. "Survey of Foreign Workers in Korea, 1995." In *Policies and Protective Measures Concerning Foreign Migrant Workers*, edited by Korea Research Institute for Workers' Human Rights and Justice. Seoul: Friedrich-Ebert-Stiftung.

Sassen, Saskia. 1988. *The Mobility of Labor and Capital*. New York: Cambridge University Press.

Seok, Hyunho. 1986. "Republic of Korea." In *Migration of Asian Workers to the Arab World*, edited by Godfrey Gunatilleke. Tokyo: United Nations University.

Seol, Dong-Hoon. 1999. *Oegukin nodongja wa hanguk sahoe*. Seoul: Seoul National University Press.

———. 2000a. "Past and Present of Foreign Workers in Korea, 1987–2000," *Asia Solidarity Quarterly* 2: 6–31.

———. 2000b. *Nodongryeok eui gukje idong*. Seoul: Seoul National University Press.

Seol, Dong-Hoon, and John D. Skrentny. 2001. "How Do International Norms Affect Domestic Politics? A Comparison of Migrant Workers and Women's Rights in South Korea." Presented at the meeting of the American Sociological Association, Anaheim, Calif.

Shin, Eui Hang, and Kyung-Sup Chang. 1988. "Peripherization of Immigrant Professionals: Korean Physicians in the United States," *International Migration Review* 22, no. 4: 609–26.

Skrentny, John D. 2002. *The Minority Rights Revolution*. Cambridge, Mass.: Belknap Press, Harvard University Press.

Soysal, Yasmin. 1994. *The Limits of Citizenship*. Chicago: University of Chicago Press.

Vogel, Ezra. 1993. *Four Little Dragons: The Spread of Industrialization in East Asia*. Cambridge, Mass.: Harvard University Press.

Woo-Cumings, Meredith. 1995. "The Korean Bureaucratic State: Historical Legacies and Comparative Perspectives." In *Politics and Policy in the New Korean State*, edited by James W. Cotton. New York: St. Martin's.

World Bank. 2001. *World Development Indicators 2001*. Washington, D.C.: World Bank.

Commentary

Timothy C. Lim

South Korea presents a particularly interesting immigration case, if only because it is the most recent country to experience relatively large-scale (albeit still limited) immigration. As a latecomer to immigration, South Korea may tell us a great deal about the changes, if any, in the general dynamics and/or nature of the immigration process. South Korea's fledgling experience with immigration may offer further support of the convergence hypothesis, which posits a growing similarity among industrialized, labor-importing countries in terms of policy instruments, efficacy of control measures, social integration, and general-public reactions to immigration flows. Does South Korea represent an anomalous case — a new Asian model of immigration control? Or does it represent, at most, a minor variation on an otherwise monotonous theme of convergence?

Dong-Hoon Seol and John Skrentny suggest that Korea does differ in important ways from most other labor-importing countries, including the fact that more of its immigrants are illegal than legal. Indeed, estimates from June 2002 put the number of undocumented workers in South Korea at 77 percent of all foreign workers in the country. And this figure may be an *under*estimation, because it is based on the number of overstayers and does not include people smuggled into the country. Yet this is not Korea's only important difference from other labor-importing countries.

According to Seol and Skrentny, a much more significant difference relates to why there are so many illegal workers in the first place — because there has been no serious effort made to control illegal immigration. Why is this the case? The explanation is complicated, but it primarily reflects the nature of client politics in Korea. Significantly, in emphasizing the centrality of client politics, the authors take issue with another aspect of the convergence hypothesis. Specifically, they challenge the notion that, unlike other labor-importing countries, Korea's immigration policy — or rather the gap between the *goals* and *outcomes* of its immigration policy — can be explained by the growth of rights-based liberalism.

In South Korea, the most significant gains made by foreign immigrants — especially by illegal workers — are likely a product of a rights-based process. The Korean courts, in particular, have played an important role in extending basic labor rights to foreign workers, against the will of immigration officials. And although Seol and Skrentny give rather short shrift to international human rights norms and standards, it can be argued that important gains for immigrants ultimately are (or will be) a product of these norms and standards. To be sure, the authors note that the Ministries of Labor and Foreign Affairs are aware of global norms on migrant worker rights and pursue reforms to bring Korea into alignment with them, but they conclude that this awareness is outweighed by the dynamics of client politics.

Seol and Skrentny are certainly right for the short run. In the longer run, however, the picture is less clear. My research on this issue indicates that human rights matter a great deal, although the impact on policy is gradual and incremental. Consider the progress that immigrants have made. Undocumented workers now have the same basic labor rights as domestic workers; they are entitled to compensation for industrial accidents, severance pay, and other basic protections. More importantly, the push toward a work permit system, which would "legalize" the work most immigrants now do, *is* likely to achieve success in the near future despite the intense opposition of the Korean Federation of Small Business. Such progress — *any* progress — likely would not have occurred in the absence of a rights-based framework.

None of this is to imply that a rights-based approach can explain everything. It cannot. But neither should it be dismissed as irrelevant. In this sense, then, the question is not whether "rights matter" but *how much* they matter. And this requires us to adopt a longer-term perspective. Indeed, in looking at the Korean case generally, it is crucial to keep in mind that immigration to South Korea is a very recent phenomenon. Thus it would be wise to avoid making hasty conclusions or placing too much emphasis on present-day conditions. On this point, it is important to recognize that even the Korean case's one clear-cut difference can literally change overnight. If the government were to implement a new work permit system, the distorted proportion of undocumented to documented workers would immediately disappear as formerly illegal workers were given official permission to live and work in Korea. Were this to happen, Korea would suddenly become much the same as most other labor-importing countries.

Does this mean that the convergence hypothesis is correct? To a significant extent, the answer would have to be yes. Korea's mode of immigration control certainly has distinctive characteristics, but the same could be said for all labor-importing countries. More important is the manner in which the effort to control or manage immigration is shaped by common pressures and constraints. And in this regard, Korea is clearly *not* unique. At the same time, one could argue that latecomers to immigration warrant special attention. In the case of Korea, the *pace* of change is significant. So, too, are the *agents* of change. For change has not merely been imposed upon or granted to immigrants; to an important extent, it has been shaped by the immigrants themselves. Their refusal, for example, to abide by the conditions of the trainee program led directly to reforms in the system.

The immigrants did not, however, act alone. Another crucial agent of change in Korea is the network of civil and religious organizations. Not only have these nongovernmental groups put unremitting pressure on the government, but they have also served a vital quasi-governmental role in protecting and promoting the basic rights of immigrants. Any analysis of the immigration process in Korea—and, perhaps, other latecomers to immigration—must take into account the agency of immigrants and NGOs. In this sense, Korea may indeed represent a new model of immigration—but one premised on activism rather than state management.

Index